Index Emblematicus

The English Emblem Tradition

1

Jan van der Noot
A Theatre for Worldlings

Paolo Giovio
The Worthy Tract of Paulus Jovius

Lodovico Domenichi
Certain Noble Devises both Militarie and Amorous

Geffrey Whitney
A Choice of Emblemes

EDITED BY PETER M. DALY
WITH LESLIE T. DUER AND ANTHONY RASPA
CO-EDITOR FOR CLASSICS: PAOLA VALERI-TOMASZUK
ASSISTED BY RÜDIGER MEYER AND MARY V. SILCOX

UNIVERSITY OF TORONTO PRESS
Toronto Buffalo London

© University of Toronto Press 1988
Toronto   Buffalo   London
Printed in Canada
ISBN 0-8020-5748-9

Canadian Cataloguing in Publication Data

Main entry under title:
The English emblem tradition
(Index emblematicus)
Includes bibliographies and indexes.
Partial contents: V. 1. A theatre for worldings / Jan
van der Noot. The worthy tract of Paulus Jovius /
Paolo Giovio. Certain noble devises both militarie
and amorous / Lodovico Domenichi. A choice of
emblemes / Geffrey Whitney.
ISBN 0-8020-5748-9 (v. 1).
1. Emblem books, English—History. 2. Emblems—
History and criticism. 3. Emblem books, English—
Indexes. I. Daly, Peter M., 1936-   . II. Duer,
Leslie T. III. Raspa, Anthony. IV. Series.
PN6351.E63 1988   828.3   C88-093687-8

The research costs of the Index Emblematicus have been supported by generous
grants from the Social Sciences and Humanities Research Council of Canada.

Publication of this volume is made possible by a grant from the Canadian
Federation for the Humanities using funds provided by the Social Sciences and
Humanities Research Council of Canada

CONTENTS

PREFACE

This volume is the first in a sub-series of the *Index Emblematicus* dedicated to the English Emblem Tradition. It applies the same principles to English works that were applied to the various editions and translations of Alciato's emblems. However, discussions with colleagues, users, and reviewers of the Alciato volumes have resulted in the introduction of certain improvements, particularly in the creation of indexes. These improvements were facilitated by advances in micro-computing technology.

We should like to record here a special debt of thanks to our programmer, Mr Bryan Haley, who created the new computer programmes which have enabled us to subject English emblems and imprese to the electronic scrutiny necessary for the creation of indexes and concordances. Alciato's emblems were processed on a main-frame computer, with all the well-known costs, complications, and frustrations. However, the revolution in micro-computers has made it possible to do the same work in the office or study, where it is not only cheaper, but where one is master in one's own house.

Even when micro-computers are used, research of this kind is still highly labour-intensive. The project could not have been carried out without the generous support of the Social Sciences and Humanities Research Council of Canada, which provided research grants.

The emblems of Jan van der Noot are reproduced by permission of the Huntington Library, and those of Geffrey Whitney by permission of the University of Illinois at Urbana-Champaign.

INTRODUCTION

THE EMBLEM

There is a veritable renaissance of interest in emblematics, and not merely as an ancillary to the study of the history of art and literature, but also for its own sake. The scope of emblem study is broad indeed, embracing printed books - over 1,000 were published in over 2,000 editions and printings, and no one even knows how many manuscript collections still exist - literary and theatrical analogues in all European vernacular languages and Neo-Latin, as well as the whole field of 'applied emblematics,' which can take the form of wall and ceiling decoration, painting and portraiture, tapestry, embroidery, glass, and jewellery. The emblem in all its manifestations must be regarded as both an art form and a symbolic mode of communication.

Formerly a no-man's land, an unclaimed territory bordering literature and the fine arts, the emblem is currently being re-mapped bibliographically. Scholarly reprints and indexes, the Henkel/Schöne *Emblemata*[1] and the *Index Emblematicus* being two examples, are making accessible tracts of this lost terrain. Articles and books are providing descriptions of certain features of the topography of the emblem landscape.

This resurgent interest also manifests itself in the many conferences and symposia dedicated in whole or part to emblems; in the increased number of articles and books published; and the emergence of a new journal *Emblematica* and a new monographic series 'Studies in the Emblem,' both published by AMS Press. There are several large-scale, computerized bibliographic projects underway, which promise to place the whole subject of emblems on a firmer basis. The use of micro-computers will not only make the results more accessible to more scholars, but also facilitate new approaches to the interpretation of this cultural phenomenon.

This is, in short, an exciting time of re-discovery and re-evaluation. Modern perspectives deriving from communications theory, semiotics, and the sociology of production and reception are being applied to the emblem in an attempt to arrive at a better understanding of the role of the emblem in its society, and of the interaction between emblems proper and other cultural forms. But, as I have argued elsewhere,[2] this systematic investigation of the emblem is still in its infancy, although the theoretical groundwork in terms of genre theory has largely been done.[3]

A NOTE ON DEFINITIONS AND THE SELECTION OF TITLES

There have been many attempts to define the emblem genre over the years, and this has influenced bibliography. Mario Praz[4] had a broad understanding of what constitutes an emblem, and his selection of titles is consequently generous. Rosemary Freeman,[5] on the other hand, had a narrower conception, restricting the use of the term to the three-part combination of motto, picture, and epigram as found in Alciato. Consequently her bibliography of English emblem books up to 1700 lists only twenty-four books in some forty-six printings, omitting more works than it includes. Huston Diehl's recently published *Index of Icons in English Emblem Books, 1500-1700* (Norman and London: University of Oklahoma Press, 1986) is based on Freeman's bibliography and therefore fails to fulfil the claim of 'including every icon in every English emblem book ... printed in the sixteenth and seventeenth centuries' (p 4).

Since the emblem is a mixed form, a hybrid combining graphics and texts, it is inevitable that there will be borderline cases where works have only a loose connection with the emblem tradition. However, if we regard the emblem as both an art form and a mode of symbolic thought - recognizing the interdependence of emblem and imprese - then it is important that bibliographies and indexes be generous and catholic in what they contain.

In order to reflect more accurately the pervasive influence of emblematic forms and modes in English publications during the sixteenth and seventeenth centuries, we have embraced a broader conception of the emblem than Rosemary Freeman and Huston Diehl. The *Index Emblematicus* will include not only emblem books with the three-part form popularised by Andrea Alciato, but also *emblemata nuda*, collections of imprese, iconologia, works on emblem and impresa, and finally collections of prose or poetry in which emblematic plates form an integral part. Manuscript emblems have been excluded.

Most emblematic and impresa literature can be divided into four main groups:

1   emblem books in the strict sense, that is, the tight three-part form as introduced by Alciato;
2   expanded forms, for example, Van der Noot, who adds a book-length prose commentary to his collection of emblems, or Hawkins, who employs a complex nine-part structure;
3   emblematically illustrated works such as meditations, where the plate becomes an integral if minor part, for example, Drexel;
4   theoretical discussions of emblem and impresa, which provide many examples of actual imprese, for example, Giovio and Estienne.

For purposes of bibliography and indexing we would include all such works under the generic heading of emblem books, without differentiating books with emblems from emblem books.

THE ENGLISH EMBLEM TRADITION

By comparison with the production of emblematic works on the Continent, England's contribution is extremely modest. Small though it may be, it is none the less more significant than Freeman's pioneering study and Diehl's *Index* suggest. According to our bibliographic research, which forms the basis of the *Index Emblematicus*, over fifty titles in at least 135 printings and editions were published up to 1700. The number grows as new titles and further editions are discovered.[6]

It is now forty years since Freeman's influential study first appeared. For two generations of English readers it has been the first and last word on the subject of emblems. But in several important respects the work is dated. Its generic assumptions have had a negative effect on bibliography. Freeman's notion of the disjunction of word and image in the emblem, and her normative and evaluative judgements, have in some respects been an obstacle to better appreciation. We are not suggesting that Whitney will fare better today than yesterday when compared with Donne, Herbert, or Shakespeare. But we would no longer consider it appropriate to compare Blake's symbolic poem on the marigold with Wither's emblem epigram on the same subject to the disparagement of the emblem. Literary scholars like Freeman often appear to forget that the emblem depends on the interaction of word and image, and that the *pictura* must be accorded equal importance in the process of semantic and semiotic communication. Furthermore, they also make the tacit assumption, which is usually false or at least unprovable, that the author of the emblem texts was in some way also responsible for the *picturae*.

THE PURPOSE OF THE INDEX EMBLEMATICUS

Although literary scholars show an increasing awareness of the emblem as a symbolic mode of communication, the emblem books themselves still remain largely terra incognita. But that is hardly suprising, given the fact that over a thousand emblem books in all European languages have survived, but only a handful have been reprinted. The dearth of scholarly editions, as distinct from reprints, and the paucity of reliable critical studies largely accounts for this ignorance. In a review article 'Recent Studies in the English Emblem,' Jerome Dees observes that criticism has proceeded largely in a vacuum, and he concludes that English studies of the emblem 'are in the curious position of being more advanced in assessing their influence than understanding what they are ....'[7]

The nineteenth century paid virtually no critical attention to emblems. The basic groundwork without which modern Shakespeare studies would be unthinkable has never been done for the emblem.

The *Index Emblematicus* volumes dedicated to the English Emblem Tradition will attempt to remedy the situation by providing a uniform and systematic set of indexes to all emblematic works published in English up to 1700. The volumes will render the material accessible by providing:

1   an introductory and bibliographic note on each emblematic work, followed by a facsimile reproduction of title-page and all preliminary matter;
2   facsimiles of the emblems, where necessary slightly reduced in size and re-assembled, if the original was printed over two or more pages;
3   descriptions of pictures, translations of mottoes in foreign languages, a list of key words from the epigram and information on dedicatee, bearer (of an impresa), and references;
4   all key words clearly flagged;

5   concordances and indexes to the various fields of information which
     make up the emblem or impresa as a whole.

         It is the intention to proceed chronologically, rather than alphabetically
or thematically.   Thus Volume One contains the first four books of emblems
and imprese to have appeared in English.

DESCRIPTION OF PICTURES

Just how much picture description to provide is a vexed question, and one
upon which complete agreement can hardly be expected. Some art historians
might argue for greater detail and for the inclusion of information on composition and style. The amount of description is, however, determined by the
purpose of the *Index Emblematicus*, which is to render accessible the key
motifs in the pictures. Consequently, we have concentrated on the symbolically
relevant motifs, paying less attention to background, foreground, and other
illustrative material, unless such material demonstrably adds to the significance
of the central motif or motif cluster. The purpose of the brief description of
the picture is then to provide the necessary minimum information upon which
the Index is based.
         The pictures are not read in isolation from the texts; rather, information
from mottoes and epigrams is used to help identify motifs in the pictures.
Thus, classical figures are named wherever possible. Phrixus riding the golden
ram is identified as 'Phrixus' rather than merely as a 'man riding a sheep'
(Peacham, p 214). Similarly, allegorical figures are named according to the
personifications they represent, as for instance 'Truth' rather than 'woman.'
Birds, trees, creatures, and all other objects are likewise identified with the
assistance of the text. Thus, instead of describing the picture in Van der Noot's
emblem C vii^v as 'A bird rises to heaven in the smoke of a log fire' the bird
is identified as an eagle and the logs as cedar, using information from the
epigram.
         Since our picture descriptions are essentially identifications of motifs,
we employ the technical vocabulary of heraldry when describing heraldic
motifs. The use of such technical terms provides for greater clarity and differ-
entiation of information. In the language of heraldry, adjectives and noun
modifiers usually follow their nouns, for example, 'lion rampant,' 'martlet
argent' and 'shield quartered.' In the indexes these heraldic groupings appear
at the end of the appropriate entry, forming sub-groupings complete in themselves. Thus 'lion->couchant->affronté' (Whitney, p 120) will come at the end
of the entries under 'lion,' while the technical terms 'couchant' and 'affronté'
will appear at the appropriate place in the alphabetical index.
         Reference to left and right in our descriptions of the pictures is largely
governed by the practices of art historians. Thus, left and right normally
describe the positioning of objects and figures from the point of view of the
reader as he looks at the emblem. However, when a figure is described as
holding an object in the right hand, it is the right hand of the figure to
which this refers. Furthermore, when groupings of motifs or scenes have a
symbolic relevance for the figure depicted in the picture, these are also denoted
as left or right from the vantage point of the figure in the emblem.

TREATMENT OF KEY WORDS IN INDEXES

The indexes are based on key words, which are specially flagged in the editions of the individual works. As in the *Index* volumes devoted to the emblems of Andrea Alciato, the key words in foreign languages are indexed separately, as well as in English translation. All key words are modernized and lemmatized so as to circumvent the problems of morphology, inflectional endings, and conjugated forms, as well as the vagaries in spelling, which are encountered everywhere in the vernacular languages of the sixteenth and seventeenth centuries.

Before the key words were sorted into indexes, a certain amount of pre-editing was required. All modern languages are rich in inflected and conjugated word forms, which pose problems for those creating indexes and concordances. This was overcome by a process of lemmatization, which reduced each key word to its basic form. In the case of nouns the nominative singular is used unless the noun only exists in the plural form. Verbs are cited in the infinitive in all European languages with the exception of Latin where convention requires the use of the first-person singular of the present tense. Adjectives, irrespective of the gender of accompanying nominal forms, are reduced to nominative masculine singular. Adverbs are reduced to adjectival forms wherever possible. In this way we created larger groupings of words that belong together semantically as variations of the same root, but which otherwise would have been scattered throughout the alphabetical index.

Capitalization can on occasion raise problems of interpretation. Some abstract nouns can refer either to a concept or to a personification of that concept, for example, fame and Fame, victory and Victory, virtue and Virtue. Usually the presence of the allegorical figure in the emblem picture is sufficient grounds for capitalizing the noun in question. However, there are borderline cases where abstract mottoes, with nouns in lower case, are illustrated by personifications. For instance, the motto to Whitney's emblem on love and death (p 132) reads: 'De °morte, et de °amore: °Iocosum,' which we translate as 'A °joke about °Death and °Love.' The picture shows Cupid and Death equipped with bows and arrows. It was decided to capitalize the four relevant nouns in the index in order to alert users to the presence of personifications of love and death. Whitney's use of lower-case nouns is preserved in the quoted motto which accompanies the standardized and capitalized key words in the Motto Index. Whitney's epigram names both Cupid and Mors, which noun is regarded as an English proper name for the purposes of indexing. 'Mors' therefore appears in the English epigram index rather than the Latin index.

Another complication is presented by the homograph. For instance, the word 'arms' can denote weapons, but it can also refer to the heraldic coat-of-arms. Such homographs are differentiated by adding a number to the end of the word: thus arms in the sense of weapons appears as 'arms,' and the coat-of-arms as 'arms1.' These number suffixes are retained in the edition, indexes, and listings to indicate homographs.

Obsolete words are given special attention. The original obsolete form is accompanied by its modern equivalent in brackets, for example, heben [= ebony]. Both forms will appear in the appropriate indexes: heben [= ebony] and ebony [= heben]. Recognizable words which in the context have a special meaning are treated in the same way. Noot's epigram to emblem Biii^v speaks of 'fire' but refers to 'lightning,' the 'tree' and 'leaf' in Noot's epigram Ciii^v refer to 'oak,' and the 'fowl' of Noot Ciiii^v is a 'Phoenix.' The indexes contain both van der Noot's actual words and their references, which would otherwise have been lost to the searcher.

All mottoes in foreign languages are reproduced in their original orthography, but key words deriving from them are standardized and lemmatized for the purpose of indexing. This means that in the case of Latin consonantal 'i' and 'u' are replaced by 'j' and 'v,' and capitalization is regularized.

Mottoes in foreign languages are translated into English. This requires consistency in the use of language, which, at its simplest, means selecting the same English word where several words are available for one and the same notion. Although synonyms often reveal stylistic or syntactical differences, we are more concerned with semantic distinctions than with style, level, and tone. The dual origins of English have given us both 'to weep' and 'to cry,' 'naked' and 'nude.' From the semantic view point these pairs of words convey the same meaning, and to save the reader from unnecessary searching, we have consistently used 'to weep,' and 'naked.' At times other considerations determined the choice. We chose 'to weep' in order to avoid a possible homograph in 'to cry,' which can mean both 'to weep' and 'to shout.'

THE CONCORDANCES AND INDEXES

The concordances and indexes that make up the *Index Emblematicus* provide systematic access to a large and diffuse body of information. The purpose is identification rather than interpretation. The motifs in the pictures, for example, are identified and described neutrally, and not interpreted. Thus, Brutus falling upon his sword (Whitney p 170) is described as the suicide of Brutus, but the meaning of the action is not interpreted as bad conscience or the triumph of fortune over virtue. Like his source Alciato, Whitney indicates in the motto that the meaning of Brutus' suicide is the victory of Fortune over Virtue, and the Motto Index therefore cites 'fortuna' and 'virtus.'

Whereas, strictly speaking, an index lists single words with no context whatsoever, a concordance cites the key words in their natural contexts, no matter how delimited. The disadvantage of listing single words is that the user is forced to return to the original text in order to determine whether the term listed is the one he is seeking. Concordances that cite the natural context frequently enable the user to determine immediately whether or not this is the usage that he is interested in. However, the shorter the natural context, the less valuable it is.

In the *Index Emblematicus* we employ both indexes and concordances. However, for indexes proper we use a procedure that takes into account the advantages of computer-sorting: we string together key words that belong together, linking each word to the next by means of an arrow, which indicates to the user that the terms are related to each other contextually. These contextual strings of key words - words reduced to their most basic forms and linked by means of an arrow - place the indexes of the *Index Emblematicus* somewhere between the traditional index and the traditional concordance.

Each emblem book is accompanied by its own set of concordances and indexes, and the final volume of the series will contain cumulative indexes to all the individual works.

There are individual concordances and indexes for each part of the emblem: the motto, picture, epigram, commentary, references, bearer, and dedication.

The Picture Index lists the symbolically relevant motifs in the *picturae*. It provides lemmatized key words accompanied by a portion of the picture description sufficient for the immediate understanding of the word or motif in question. It would have been prohibitively expensive, although much easier, simply to cite the complete picture description as a context for the key word. However, that is in fact seldom necessary. We have, therefore, shortened the descriptions printed in the edition so as to obtain a self-explanatory context.

The Motto Index is composed of lemmatized key words followed by the complete motto. We have included an English index containing the English translations of the key words that appear in mottoes in different languages. An alphabetical list of all mottoes, accompanied where appropriate by English translations, is also provided.

The Epigram Index contains the key words from the various epigrams.

Some writers identify sources for their emblem texts or pictures, or simply refer to other writers. This can be valuable information. Such names are listed in a Reference Index, but only when the emblem writer himself provides them.

Especially in the case of imprese the names of bearers can be useful information to the historian. The Bearer Index simply lists the names of all bearers alphabetically according to the surname.

The Dedication Index contains an alphabetical list of the names of persons to whom emblems were dedicated.

Each Index includes a special list of proper nouns. The Proper Noun List will contain not only names of persons such as Aeneas, gods such as Jupiter, and places such as Rome, but also personifications such as Death and Love.

HOW TO USE THE INDEXES

The Indexes are alphabetical listings, not classified groupings as is the case with the Icon Class. In order to obtain the maximum information available in any concordance or index, the user must always be prepared to make a list of synonyms, and also of related words. Whereas there may in fact only be one word for the precious stone known as diamond, or the bird called eagle, the user must look under 'pig,' 'piglet,' 'sow,' and 'swine' for verbal references to the pig. The user should also remember that abstract nouns may also be used as personifications; these appear in upper case in the Proper Noun Indexes to the various fields.

When compiling word fields, especially for abstract concepts, the user would be well advised to think negatively as well as positively and look, for instance, under 'injustice,' 'dishonour,' and 'godless.'

NOTES

1 Arthur Henkel and Albrecht Schöne, *Emblemata. Handbuch zur Sinnbildkunst des XVI. und XVII. Jahrhunderts* (Stuttgart: Metzler, 1967; 2nd ed, 1976).

2 Peter M. Daly, 'Directions in Emblem Research - Past and Present,' *Emblematic*a 1 (1986), 167.

3   Albrecht Schöne, *Emblematik und Drama im Zeitalter des Barock* (Stuttgart: Beck, 1964; 2nd ed, 1967); Dietrich Walter Jöns, *Das 'Sinnen-Bild.' Studien zur allegorischen Bildlichkeit bei Andreas Gryphius* (Stuttgart: Metzler, 1966).

4   Mario Praz, *Studies in Seventeenth-Century Imagery* (London: Warburg Institute, 1939; 2nd ed, Rome: Edizioni di Storia et Letteratura, 1964).

5   Rosemary Freeman, *English Emblem Books* (London: Chatto & Windus, 1948; rpt 1967).

6   Alan R. Young draws attention to two hitherto unknown collections of English emblem prints in his essay 'Wenceslaus Hollar and Two Unidentified English Emblem Books' in *The English Emblem and the Continental Tradition*, ed. Peter M. Daly (New York: AMS Press [forthcoming], pp 147-198. I have argued that there exists an edition of Thomas Combe's *Theater of Fine Devices* that pre-dates the unique copy of the 1614 edition in the Huntington Library: 'The Case for the 1593 Edition of Thomas Combe's *Theater of Fine Devices*,' *JWCI* 49 (1986), 255-7.

7   Jerome Dees, 'Recent Studies in the English Emblem,' *ELR* 16 (1986), 391-420.

JAN VAN DER NOOT

A THEATRE FOR WORLDLINGS

(LONDON: HENRY BYNNEMAN, 1569)

edited by

Peter M. Daly

Jan van der Noot, 1539-1590

A Theatre for Worldlings,

London: Henry Bynemann, 1569,

8°: A-R8 S2

20 emblems unpaginated; 'Declaration' paginated by leaf 1-107, 91-115 misnumbered 83-107 [= 230 pp]

translated from the French by Theodore Roest, [Edmund Spenser]

20 plates, copied from Dutch edition, 1568, accompanied by epigrams and sonnets, followed by a 230 page 'Declaration' of the author (verso unpaginated).

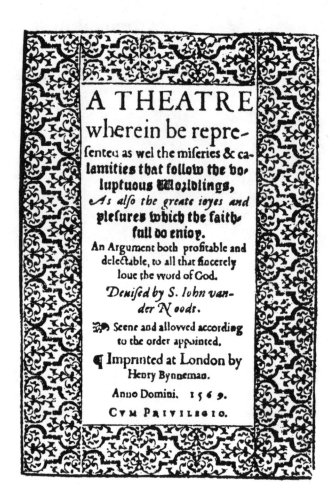

STUDIES

Bender, John B. *Spenser and Literary Pictorialism*. Princeton: University Press, 1972, pp 149-157.

Bondanella, Julia M.C. 'Petrarch's Canzone 323 and Its Renaissance Analogues.' Diss. University of Oregon, 1973.

Brachin, Pierre. *Un disciple de Ronsard: Jan van der Noot, patrice d'Anvers*. Paris: Archives des Lettres Modernes, #24, 1959.

Chew, Samuel C. *The Pilgrimage of Life*. New Haven & London: Yale University Press, 1962, p 285.

Davis, Charles R. 'Petrarch's *Rime* 323 and Its Tradition Through Spenser.' Diss. Princeton University, 1973, pp 106-59.

Fletcher, Jefferson B. 'Spenser's Earliest Translations,' *JEGP*, 13 (1914), 305-8.

Forster, Leonard. *Janus Gruter's English Years: Studies in the Continuity of Dutch Literature in Exile in Elizabethan England*. Leiden: University Press; London: Oxford University Press, 1967.

_____. 'The Translator of the "Theatre for Worldlings",' *ES*, 48 (1967), 27-34.

Freeman, Rosemary. *English Emblem Books*. 1948; rpt. London: Chatto & Windus, 1967, pp 51-2 and 239.

Friedland, Louis S. 'The Illustrations in *The Theatre for Worldlings*,' *HLQ*, 19 (1956), 107-20.

_____. 'Introduction' to *Theatre for Worldlings*. New York: Scholars' Facsimiles & Reprints, 1939.

_____. 'Spenser's Earliest Translations,' *JEGP*, 12 (1913), 449-70.

Galland, René. 'Un poète errant de la Renaissance: Jean Van Der Noot et l'Angleterre," *Revue de littérature comparée*, 2 (1922), 337-50.

Harper, Anthony J. 'On the Development of a Poetic Language in Northern Europe: Jan Van der Noot's Apocalyptic Sonnets and their English and German Translations," *Strathclyde Modern Language Studies*, 1 (1981), 47-60.

Hodnett, Edward. *Aesop in England: a Concordance of the Motifs in Seventeenth-Century Illustrations of Aesop's Fables*. Charlottesville, Virginia: University Press, 1979.

Hyde, Thomas. 'Vision, Poetry, and Authority in Spenser,' *ELR*, 13 (1983), 127-45.

Johnson, Francis R. *A Critical Bibliography of the Works of Edmund Spenser Printed Before 1700*. Baltimore: Johns Hopkins Press, 1933.

Jones, H.S.V. *A Spenser Handbook*. New York: Appleton-Century-Crofts, 1930, pp 120-5.

Köppel, Emil. 'Über die Echtheit der Edmund Spenser zugeschriebenen "Visions of Petrarch" und "Visions of Bellay",' *Englische Studien*, 15 (1891), 53-81 and 27 (1900), 100-11.

Pienaar, W.J.B. 'Edmund Spenser and Jonker Jan van der Noot,' *ES*, 8 (1926), 33-44 and 67-76.

Pollard, A.W. and G.R. Redgrave. *A Short-Title Catalogue of Books Printed in England, Scotland, and Ireland and of English Books Printed Abroad 1475-1640*. London: Bibliographical Society, 1926. Revised 2nd ed., W.A. Jackson, F.S. Ferguson, Katharine F. Pantzer (2 of 3 vols. available - 1 A-H, 2 I-Z), 1976, 1986. #18602.

Praz, Mario. *Studies in Seventeenth-Century Imagery*, 2nd edition. Rome: Edizioni di Storia e Letteratura, 1964, pp 213-14, 437.

Rasmussen, Carl J. '"Quietnesse of Minde": *A Theatre for Worldlings* as a Protestant Poetics,' *Spenser Studies*, 1 (1980), 3-27.

Righetti, Angelo. 'Le due versioni spenseriane della canzone cccxxiii de Petrarca,' *Annali di Ca'Foscari*, 5 (1966), 115-22.

Russell, Daniel. 'Du Bellay's Emblematic Vision of Rome,' *Yale French Studies*, 47 (1972), 98-109.

Satterthwaite, Alfred W. 'A Re-examination of Spenser's Translations of the "Sonets" from *A Theatre for Worldlings*,' *PQ*, 38 (1959), 509-15.

————. *Spenser, Ronsard, and Du Bellay*. Princeton: University Press, 1960, pp 25-36, 255-63.

Smart, George K. 'English Non-dramatic Blank Verse in the Sixteenth Century,' *Anglia*, 61 (1937), 370-97.

Smit, W.A.P. and W. Vermeer. 'Introduction' and 'Notes,' *Het Bosken en Het Theatre*. Amsterdam and Antwerp: Wereldbibliotheek 'Onze oud Lettern,' 1953. Reprint of Van der Noot's Flemish edition.

Smith, Constance. 'A Seventeenth-Century Manuscript of "A Vision" Attributed to Thomas More,' *Moreana*, 37 (1973), 5-14.

Stein, Harold. *Studies in Spenser's Complaints*. New York: Oxford University Press, 1934, pp 109-51, 67-70.

Van Dorsten, J.A. *The Radical Arts: First Decade of an Elizabethan Renaissance.* Leiden: University Press, 1970, pp 75-85.

Vermeylen, August. *Leven en Werken van Jonker Jan Van Der Noot.* Antwerp, 1899.

Witstein, S.F. *De Verzencommentaar in 'Het Theatre' van Jan Van Der Noot.* Utrecht: Instituut voor Vergelijkend Literatuuronderzoek, 1965.

Zaalberg, C.A. 'Introduction' and 'Notes' to the facsimile ed. of Jan van der Noot's *Lofsang van Braband (Hymne de Braband).* Zwolle: Tjeenk Willink, 1958.

INTRODUCTORY NOTE

A Theatre for Worldlings, published in 1569 by Henry Bynneman, is a translation of a Flemish emblem book by Jan van der Noot, *Het Theatre oft Toon-neel*. Van der Noot (1539 or 1540-1595) was an outspoken Reformed Protestant, possibly a Calvinist, and was thus forced to flee from the Spanish authorities in Antwerp. He arrived in London in 1567, joining thousands of other Protestant refugees from the Netherlands. Considered a notable Flemish poet, indeed the first poet of the Renaissance in the Netherlands, Van der Noot's other works include *Het Bosken* (c. 1567), *Poetische Werken* (1572), *Das Buch Extasis* (1576), and *Cort Begripp dere XII Boecken Olympiados* (1579).

In 1568, while Van der Noot was living in London, first *Het Theatre* and then a French edition, *Le Theatre*, were published by John Day.[1] The English translation appeared the next year, and a German translation by Balthasar Froe was published in Cologne in 1572. The Flemish edition is dedicated to Roger Martens, the Lord Mayor of London and himself a Fleming, while the French and English editions are dedicated to Queen Elizabeth.

This is arguably the first English emblem book ever printed, pre-dated only by Thomas Palmer's manuscript collection *Two hundred poosees* (British Library Sloane MS. 3794). However, that claim depends, as always, on a theory of the emblem genre. Freeman and those who cling to a narrow, literary conception of the emblem will only accept as emblems those combinations of text and image that have the three-part structure introduced under Alciato's name. However, many scholars today doubt that Alciato regarded the three parts as constituting the emblem genre, which in any case did not exist prior to the 1531 printing in Augsburg of the *Emblematum liber*. As Miedema[2], Russell[3] and Scholz[4] have shown conclusively, it took decades for the three parts to establish themselves as the necessary constituents of the emblem form. There are several early unillustrated editions of Alciato, and some editions of La Perrière's *Theatre des bons engins* (Paris, 1539) appeared without mottoes and yet others without pictures. The absence of mottoes is thus no reason to refuse to regard Van der Noot's *Theatre* as an emblem book.

The twenty etched copperplate engravings of *Het Theatre* are unsigned. The same engravings appear in the French edition, but the English and later the German editions contain anonymous woodcut copies of the engravings, most reversed. Michael Bath has recently discovered marked resemblances between the watercolour illustrations for a manuscript copy of Marot's 'Des Visions de

Petrarque' and the woodcuts to *A Theatre for Worldlings*. He argues that the woodcuts are copies of the paintings and, further, that the engravings are copies of the woodcuts.[5] Neither the woodcuts nor the engravings are artistically remarkable. For many years it was believed that Marcus Gheerhaerts the Elder was responsible for the engravings. Louis Friedland has examined the claim, however, and suggests that the artist is not Gheerhaerts, but possibly Lucas de Heere, who was in London at the time and who wrote commendatory verses for the Flemish and French editions of *Theatre*.[6]

Het Theatre and its translations contain three groups of emblems and a long prose commentary - in Friedland's facsimile edition of *A Theatre* this commentary runs to 230 pages, when the misnumbering of the original leaves is taken into account. The first group of poems, 'Epigrams,' is a translation of Clément Marot's translation of Petrarch's *Rime* 323, entitled 'Des Visions de Petrarque.' It is a sequence of six allegorical visions concerning the death of Laura. The second group, 'Sonets,' is a translation of eleven visions of the fall of Rome from Joachim Du Bellay's *Songe*, a sonnet sequence appended to his *Les Antiquitez de Rome*. Van der Noot omitted four of Du Bellay's poems from *Songe*, nos. 6, 8, 13, 14. The third group, the last four 'Sonets,' was written by Van der Noot himself and is based on St. John's visions in the Book of Revelation. The prose commentary was borrowed largely from Dutch translations of the works of two Protestant reformers, John Bale's *The Image of bothe Churches* and Heinrich Bullinger's *In Apocalypsin conciones centum*.[7] It has usually been seen as a stock expression of medieval world-contempt and anti-papal propaganda, but recently attempts have been made at a closer, more complex reading of *A Theatre*, particularly its neglected commentary.[8]

Theodore Roest tells us that he translated the prose commentary from the Flemish, but according to textual collations by several critics, the English translation of the verse was made from the French edition, with perhaps an occasional glance at the Flemish. In the French *Theatre*, of course, only the commentary is translated from the Flemish. The 'Epigrams' are reprinted from Marot, the 'Sonets' from Du Bellay, and the Apocalypse sonnets were rewritten in French by Van der Noot.

The English translator of the prose commentary names himself as Theodore Roest. The name is Dutch and his translation is accurate; no more is known of him.[9] The translator of the verse has long been believed to be Edmund Spenser. Around the turn of the century this identification was called into question, especially by Köppel. Without denigrating Köppel's work, one can justly say that the value of his study lies not in itself but in its agency as a spur to more careful consideration of *A Theatre for Worldlings*. Until recently, most English studies have in fact dwelt almost exclusively on proving the English verse translations to be Spenser's. Since the translator is not named in *A Theatre*, the evidence centres on the appearance of its sonnets and epigrams as 'The Visions of Bellay' and 'The Visions of Petrarch, formerly translated' in Spenser's *Complaints, containing sundrie small poems of the Worlds Vanitie* issued by William Ponsonby in 1591. These are skilled revisions of the verse in *A Theatre* (omitting Van der Noot's four Apocalyptic sonnets and replacing them with the four sonnets from Du Bellay that Van der Noot left out of the *Theatre*). The epigrams from Petrarch are left much the same, but the sonnets from Bellay are quite extensively revised. The arguments, both against and overwhelmingly for Spenser as the verse translator of *A Theatre* have been usefully summed up by

Harold Stein.[10] Spenser's responsibility for the translation is so generally accepted that the verse portion of *A Theatre* appears in anthologies of his work.

One can only conjecture as to how Spenser, who would have been 16 or 17 years old at the time, came to translate for Van der Noot. He was still at Merchant Taylors' School, where the headmaster Richard Mulcaster encouraged his students' interest in modern languages. Forster has shown (p 33) that Mulcaster had connections with the Dutch community in London, and it is possible that he suggested Spenser for the task. The uneven quality of *A Theatre* both as translation and as verse can thus be attributed partly to Spenser's youth, but also to the haste in which the translation was evidently prepared (see Stein, pp 126-135).

NOTES

1　*Het Theatre* does not name a publisher, but Harold Stein established that Day, the publisher of the French edition, was also the publisher of the Flemish edition (*Studies in Spenser's Complaints*. N.Y.: Oxford University Press, 1934, p 111).

2　Hessel Miedema, 'The Term "Emblema" in Alciati,' *JWCI*, 31 (1968), 234-250.

3　Daniel S. Russell, 'The Term "Emblème" in Sixteenth-Century France,' *Neophil*, 69 (1975), 337-351.

4　Bernhard Scholz, '"Libellum composui epigrammaton, cui titulum feci Emblemata": Alciatus's Use of the Expression *Emblema* Once Again,' *Emblematica* 1 (1987), 213-26.

5　The manuscript is in the Stirling Maxwell Collection of Glasgow University (Ms. SMM2). Michael Bath, 'Verse Form and Pictorial Space in *A Theatre for Worldlings*,' forthcoming.

6　Louis S. Friedland, 'The Illustrations in *The Theatre for Worldlings*,' *HLQ*, 2 (1956), 107-20.

7　S.F. Witstein, *De verzencommentaar in 'Het Theatre' van Jan Van Der Noot* (Utrecht: Instituut voor Vergelijkend Literatuuronderzoek, 1965).

8　See, for example, J. A. Van Dorsten, *The Radical Arts* (London: Oxford, 1970), pp 75-85; and Carl J. Rasmussen, '"Quietnesse of Minde": *A Theatre for Worldlings* as a Protestant Poetics,' *Spenser Studies*, 1 (1980), 3-27.

9　Leonard Forster uncovered some information on a Roest in the London Dutch community, but unfortunately there is nothing to link him to *A Theatre for Worldlings* ('The Translator of the "Theatre for Worldlings",' *ES*, 48 [1967], 27-34).

10　Stein, pp 114-25. Alfred W. Satterthwaite stands alone in suggesting that Spenser did not translate the four Apocalypse sonnets, in *Spenser, Ronsard, and Du Bellay* (Princeton: University Press, 1960), pp 255f.

A Note on Reduction and Montage

In the original printing epigram and illustration are on facing pages; these have been brought together on one page in this edition. The reproductions appear in the original size.

Picture

In the foreground, a °hind is chased by °two °dogs. In the upper right background, the hind, collapsed against a °rock, has its hindquarters torn by the dogs.

Epigram

gentle   hind   pursue   two   dog   black white   force   cruel   race   rock   die death   vanquish   noble   beauty   wail destiny

Epigrams.

BEing one day at my window all alone,

    So many strange things hapned me to see,

As much it grieueth me to thinke thereon.

At my right hande, a Hinde appearde to me,

So faire as mought the greatest God delite :

Two egre Dogs dyd hir pursue in chace,

Of whiche the one was black, the other white.

With deadly force, so in their cruell race

They pinchte the haunches of this gentle beast,

That at the last, and in shorte time, I spied,

Vnder a rocke, where she (alas) opprest,

Fell to the grounde, and there vntimely dide.

Cruell death vanquishing so noble beautie,

Oft makes me waile so harde a destinie.

Van der Noot *Theatre* London 1569 Bii^v

Picture
In the foreground a two masted sailing °ship, with billowing °sails, runs before the °wind. At the right, the ship is °wrecked on a °rock.

Epigram
sea ship heben [= ebony] white ivory sail gold silk tackle wind sky treasure freight storm rock water misfortune grief lose drown rich

Epigrams.

AFter at Sea a tall Ship dyd appere,
   Made all of Heben and White Iuorie,
The failes of Golde, of Silke the tackle were:
Milde was the winde, calme feemed the fea to be:
The Skie eche where did fhew full bright and faire.
With riche treafures this gay fhip fraighted was.
But fodaine ftorme did fo turmoyle the aire,
And tombled vp the fea, that fhe, alas,
Strake on a rocke that vnder water lay.
O great misfortune, O great griefe, I fay,
Thus in one moment to fee loft and drownde
So great riches, as lyke can not be founde.

Picture
At the left, a °laurel-tree, with °birds on its branches and flocking to them, grows in a °circular enclosure; birds are perched on the °fence and on the ground. At the right the laurel-tree and the fence have been broken by a °storm. °Rain falls from dark clouds.

Epigram

branch	laurel-tree	green	wood1
paradise	noble	plant	bird	shade
melody	spirit	ravish	sky	dark	welkin
heaven	fire [= lightning]	royal	tree
root			

Epigrams.

*T*Hen heauenly branches did I see arise,

    Out of a fresh and lusty Laurell tree

*A*midde the yong grene wood. Of Paradise

Some noble plant I thought my selfe to see,

Suche store of birdes therein yshrouded were,

Chaunting in shade their sundry melodie.

*M*y sprites were rauisht with these pleasures there.

While on this Laurell fixed was mine eye,

The Skie gan euery where to ouercast,

*A*nd darkned was the welkin all aboute,

When sodaine flash of heauens fire outbrast,

*A*nd rent this royall tree quite by the roote.

Which makes me much and euer to complaine,

For no such shadow shal be had againe.

Picture
°Four bare breasted °nymphs, °Naiads, sit under leafy trees. Three are huddled over an °open °book. A °spring1 gushes from the ground.

Epigram
wood1   rock   spring1   water   shepherd clown   Muse   nymph   accord   tune   voice heart   rejoice   delight   earth   devour spring   grieve

Epigrams.

Within this wood, out of the rocke did rise

    A Spring of water mildely remblyng downe,

Whereto approched not in any wise

The homely Shepherde, nor the ruder cloune,

But many Muses, and the Nymphes withall,

That sweetely in accorde did tune their voice

Unto the gentle sounding of the waters fall.

The sight wherof dyd make my heart reioyce.

But while I toke herein my chiefe delight,

I sawe (alas) the gaping earth deuoure

The Spring, the place, and all cleane out of sight.

Whiche yet agreues my heart euen to this houre.

Picture
At the left, a °crested °phoenix stands on a mound, on which leafy plants grow. At the right, the phoenix, with °wings displayed, pecks its °breast so that the °blood gushes onto the ground. It stands besides a °dead °tree. Presumably there is a °dead °spring1.

Epigram
phoenix wood1 purple wing gold crest break tree spring1 devour water dry phoenix smite die pity love heart burn pain

Epigrams.

I Saw a Phœnix in the wood alone,

  With purple wings and crest of golden hew,

Straunge birde he was, wherby I thought anone,

That of some heauenly wight I had the vew :

Untill he came vnto the broken tree

And to the spring that late deuoured was.

What say I more ? Eche thing at length we see

Doth passe away : the Phœnix there, alas,

Spying the tree destroyde, the water dride,

Himselfe smote with his beake, as in disdaint,

And so forthwith in great despite he dide.

For pitie and loue my heart yet burnes in paine.

Van der Noot   *Theatre*   London 1569 Bvi^v

Picture
A bare breasted °woman, with her °right hand to her breasts and eyes downcast, walks on a mound covered with °herbs and °flowers. At the left the same woman, looking over her °left shoulder, walks with raised hands, her head surrounded by a dark °cloud. A °snake bites her °left °heel.

Epigram
lady   herb   flower   love   proudly foresake   white   robe   snow   gold   waist cloud   shroud   serpent   heel   languish joy   earth   bitter   grief   heart

Epigrams.

AT laſt ſo faire a Ladie did I ſpie,

   That in thinking on hir I burne and quake,

On herbes and floures ſhe walked penſiuely.

Milde, but yet loue ſhe proudely did forſake.

White ſeemed hir robes, yet wouen ſo they were,

As ſnowe and golde together had bene wrought.

Aboue the waſte a darke cloude ſhrouded hir,

A ſtinging Serpent by the heele hir caught,

Wherewith ſhe languiſht as the gathered floure :

And well aſſurde ſhe mounted vp to ioy.

Alas in earth ſo nothing doth endure

But bitter grieſ that dothe our hearts anoy.

Picture

A °Roman °building on a stepped base with °Doric °columns supporting its roof. The °metopes seem to be charged with °bulls' heads alternating with °discs. There is a °pediment on the front, with the inscription °"SPQR" flanked by two female figures. A balustrade crowns the building. An °earthquake brings °fire and °destruction to the building. There is a circular °temple on a hill at the top right.

Epigram

hill   hundred   pillar   diamond   Doric
brick   marble   wall   crystal   thousand
ray   gold   step   parget   ceiling   floor
lapis-lazuli   emerald   world   vanity
earthquake   shake   building   stone

Sonets.

O*N hill, a frame an hundred cubites hie*
    I sawe, an hundred pillers eke about,
All of fine Diamant decking the front,
And fashiond were they all in Dorike wise.
Of bricke, ne yet of marble was the wall,
But shining Christall, which from top to base
Out of deepe vaute threw forth a thousand rayes
Upon an hundred steps of purest golde.
Golde was the parget : and the sielyng eke
Did shine all scaly with fine golden plates.
The floore was Iaspis, and of Emeraude.
O worldes vainenesse. A sodein earthquake loe,
Shaking the hill euen from the bottome deepe,
Threwe downe this building to the lowest stone.

Picture
At the left, a four sided °obelisk covered with °hieroglyphs, supported by °four °lions °sejant on a °pedestal, supports an °urn. At the right the obelisk lies °broken on the ground under °rain and °clouds. There is a sea with ships at the right rear.

Epigram
spire diamond archer pot gold vessel ash emperor four lion worthy tomb corpse world grief endure tempest stick heaven noble monument

Sonets.

*T*Hen did appeare to me a sharped spire

Of diamant, ten feete eche way in square,

Iustly proportionde vp vnto his height,

So hie as mought an Archer reache with sight.

Vpon the top therof was set a pot

Made of the mettall that we honour most.

And in this golden vessell couched were

The ashes of a mightie Emperour.

Vpon foure corners of the base there lay

To beare the frame, foure great Lions of golde.

A worthie tombe for such a worthie corps.

Alas, nought in this worlde but griefe endures.

A sodaine tempest from the heauen, I saw,

With flushe stroke downe this noble monument.

Sonets.

I *Saw raisde vp on pillers of Iuorie,*
  Whereof the bases were of richest golde,
The chapters Alabaster, Christall frises,
The double front of a triumphall arke.
On eche side portraide was a victorie.
With golden wings in habite of a Nymph.
And set on hie vpon triumphing chaire,
The auncient glorie of the Romane lordes.
The worke did shewe it selfe not wrought by man,
But rather made by his owne skilfull hande
That forgeth thunder dartes for Ioue his fire.
Let me no more see faire thing vnder heauen,
Sith I haue seene so faire a thing as this,
With sodaine falling broken all to dust.

Van der Noot   *Theatre*   London 1569 Cii[v]

Picture
°Statue of °charioteer, in °Roman °armour, with a raised left hand and a °palm °branch in his °right hand stands in a °chariot pulled by °three °horses. This sculpture group stands on the top of a °triumphal °arch, which has two tiers, each with columns at the corners. The front is decorated with °two °Victories flanking the top of the arch. The end bears a plaque with the inscription °"CIV[ITAS] AVGV[STO] CAES[ARI] SEMP[ER] CONS[VLI]" [THE CITY TO AUGUSTUS CAESAR FOREVER CONSUL]. At the right the triumphal arch has collapsed.

Epigram
pillar ivory base gold chapter alabaster frieze crystal triumph arch Victory golden wing nymph chair [= chariot] glory Rome lord dart Jupiter fire heaven dust sudden fall

Van der Noot *Theatre* London 1569 Ciii^v

Picture
At the right a °palm-tree grows on top of °seven °hills [= °Rome] by a °river [= °Tiber]. In the rear, on the far shore, °four °men °destroy a palm-tree by uprooting it. °Two other °palms grow beside it.

Epigram
Dodona tree [= oak]   seven   hill   shade   conqueror   leaf [= oak]   Italy   stream   ancient   trophy   spoill   sign   race1   Trojan   blood   barbarous   villain   outrage   honour   noble   bough   trunk   root disdain twin tree

Sonets.

*T*Hen I behelde the faire Dodonian tree,

    Upon seuen hilles throw forth his gladsome shade,

And Conquerers bedecked with his leaues

Along the bankes of the Italian streame.

There many auncient Trophees were erect,

Many a spoile, and many goodly signes,

To shewe the greatnesse of the stately race,

That erst descended from the Troian bloud.

Rauisht I was to see so rare a thing,

When barbarous villaines in disordred heape,

Outraged the honour of these noble bowes.

I hearde the tronke to grone vnder the wedge.

And since I saw the roote in hie disdaine

Sende forth againe a twinne of forked trees.

Picture
At the top left, an °eagle flies from a cliff towards the °sun.   At the right, the eagle falls through °clouds emitting °flames to the ground.   On the ground, the eagle or °phoenix(?) sits in the midst of a °fire.

Epigram
bird [= eagle(?)]   sun   heaven   trust wing   dam1   cloud   temple   god   fire body   dust   fowl   light   ash   worm [= phoenix(?)]

Sonets.

I Saw the birde that dares beholde the Sunne,

With feeble flight venture to mount to heauen,

By more and more she gan to trust hir wings,

Still folowing th'example of hir damme:

I saw hir rise, and with a larger flight

Surmount the toppes euen of the hiest hilles,

And pierce the cloudes, and with hir wings to reache

The place where is the temple of the Gods,

There was she lost, and sodenly I saw

Where tombling through the aire in lompe of fire,

All flaming downe she fell vpon the plaine.

I saw hir bodie turned all to dust,

And saw the foule that shunnes the cherefull light

Out of hir ashes as a worme arise.

Van der Noot *Theatre* London 1569 Cv[v]

Picture
In the right foreground a °river °god reclines against a °pot. He wears a °laurel °garland. He holds a °palm branch in his °right hand and a °olive branch in his °left hand. °Water flows from his pot into the °river [= °Tiber]. At his feet a °wolf suckles °two °babies [= °Romulus and °Remus].

Epigram
ghost [= rivergod Tiber] beard Saturn
pot water stream Trojan duke
[= Aeneas] Turnus fight bitch wolf
suck two baby [= Romulus and Remus]
tree [= olive] peace conquer palm
laurel olive fall green laurel die

Sonets.

THen all aftonned with this nightly ghoſt,
I ſaw an hideous body big and ſtrong,
Long was his beard, and ſide did hang his hair,
A griſly forched and Saturnelike face.
Leaning againſt the belly of a pot
He ſhed a water, whoſe outguſhing ſtreame
Ran flowing all along the creckie ſhoare
Where once the Troyan Duke with Turnus foughs.
And at his feete a bitch Wolfe did giue ſucke
To two yong babes. In his right hand he bare
The tree of peace, in left the conquering Palme,
His head was garniſht with the Laurel bow.
Then ſodenly the Palme and Oliue fell,
And faire greene Laurel witherd vp and dide.

Picture
A °Naiad, naked save for a cloak, is seated on a °river [= °Tiber] bank and °laments. A town with some trees is on the opposite shore.

Epigram
river [= Tiber] wail nymph gold hair Rome honour glory praise god worship booty Hydra Hercules seven head crime Nero Caligula rule

Sonets.

Ard by a riuers side, a wailing Nimphe,
  Folding hir armes with thousand sighs to heaue
Did tune hir plaint to falling riuers sound,
Renting hir faire visage and golden haire,
Where is (quod she) this whilome honored face?
Where is thy glory and the auncient praise,
Where all worldes hap was reposed,
When erst of Gods and man I worshipt was?
Alas, suffisde it not that ciuile bate
Made me the spoile and bootie of the world,
But this new Hydra mete to be assailde
Euen by an hundred such as Hercules,
With seuen springing heds of monstrous crimes,
So many Neroes and Caligulaes
Must still bring forth to rule this croked shore.

Van der Noot   *Theatre*   London 1569 Cvii^v

Picture
An °eagle rises to °heaven in the °smoke of a °fire fuelled by °cedar logs. From the right, dark °clouds, pouring out °rain, approach the fire. Various buildings are in the hilly background.

Epigram

hill	flame	triple	heaven	incense
cedar	balm	odour	perfume	white bird
wing	fly	throne	god	sing melody
smoke	fire	ray	gold	shower grief
change	scent	sulphur	corrupt	smell

Sonets.

Vpon a hill I saw a kindled flame,

Mounting like waues with triple point to heauen,

Which of incense of precious Ceder tree

With Balmelike odor did perfume the aire.

A bird all white, well fetherd on hir winges

Hereout did flie vp to the throne of Gods,

And singing with most plesant melodie

She climbed vp to heauen in the smoke.

Of this faire fire the faire dispersed rayes

Threw forth abrode a thousand shining leames,

When sodain dropping of a golden shoure

Gan quench the glystering flame. O greuous chaunge!

That which erstwhile so pleasaunt scent did yelde,

Of Sulphure now did breathe corrupted smel.

Picture
°Eight °Naiads, some bare breasted, flee the attack of °three °satyrs. Two Naiads have been caught. There is a °spring1 in the left foreground. A °horn, a °lute, and a °musical score °book lie at the right.

Epigram
spring1 rock crystal sun yellow gold Pactolus plain art nature pleasure eye sleep accord mermaid song ivory hundred nymph hill naked Faun foot water foul

Sonets.

I Saw a fresh spring rise out of a rocke,
Clere as Christall against the Sunny beames,
The bottome yellow like the shining land,
That golden Pactol driues vpon the plaine.
It seemed that arte and nature striued to ioyne
There in one place all pleasures of the eye.
There was to heare a noise alluring slepe
Of many accordes more swete than Mermaids song,
The seates and benches shone as Iuorie,
An hundred Nymphes sate side by side about,
When from nie hilles a naked rout of Faunes
With hideous cry assembled on the place,
Which with their feete vncleane the water fouled,
Threw down the seats, & droue the Nimphs to flight.

Van der Noot   *Theatre*   London 1569 Di^v

Picture
°Echidna, wearing °armour and a plumed °helmet, stands with a °globe in her raised °left hand and supports a °standard of °trophies with her °right hand; the trophies are °shields, °arrows, and a °cuirass.   Behind her are huddled the bound figures of °naked but °crowned °kings.

Epigram
Morpheus   inconstancy   heaven   Typhoeus sister   morion   majesty   god   stream shore   trophy   world   hundred   vanquish king   foot   arms   shame   fear   war thunder   wonder

Sonets.

AT length. euen at the time when *Morpheus*
  Most truely doth appeare vnto our eyes,
Wearie to see th'inconstance of the heauens :
I saw the great. Typhæus sister come,
Hir head full brauely with a morian armed,
In maiestie she seemde so matche the Gods.
And on the shore, harde by a violent streame,
She raisde a Trophee ouer all the worlde.
An hundred vanquisht kings gronde at hir feete,
Their armes in shamefull wise bounde at their backe
While I was with so dreadfull sight afrayde,
I saw the heauens warre against hir tho,
And seing hir striken fall with clap of thunder.
With so great noyse I start in sodaine wonder.

Sonets.

I Saw an vgly beast come from the sea,

   That seuen heads,ten crounes,ten hornes did beare,

Hauing theron the vile blaspheming name.

The cruell Leopard she resembled much :

Feete of a beare, a Lions throte she had.

The mightie Dragon gaue to hir his power.

One of hir heads yet there I did espie.

Still freshly bleeding of a grieuous wounde.

One cride aloude. What one is like (quod he)

This honoured Dragon,or may him withstande ?

And then came from the sea a sauage beast,

With Dragons speche, and shewde his force by fire,

With wondrous signes to make all wights adore

The beast, in setting of hir image vp.

Picture

The scene comprises several episodes from revelations.   At the top right, the °winged and °crowned °apocalyptic °woman, in the °orans position, stands on a °crescent °moon.   Her head is encircled by °stars. She is surrounded by a °mandorla [Rev. 12.1; 12.14].   To her left, °God, as a °bearded °old-man lifts up her °child by the hands [Rev. 12.5].   To the left of God, the °archangel °Michael, °staff in hand, flies over a °seven °headed °beast, which is casting floods of °water from its mouth [Rev. 12.3-15]. At the top left, °flames issue from °clouds.   Below the flames a °beast with the °horns of a °lamb [= °ram] peers over a °mound at the scene below [Rev. 13.11]. At the bottom right stands the °beast from the °sea with °seven °heads and °ten °horns, and upon his horns °ten °crowns. The beast is like a °leopard with the feet of a   °bear and the mouth of a °lion [Rev. 13.1-3].   To the left of the beast, five men kneel in worship; one is dressed in °papal °regalia [Rev. 13.4].

Epigram

beast sea seven head ten crown horn
blasphemy   cruel   leopard   foot   bear
lion throat dragon power blood wound
honour force fire adore beast image

Van der Noot *Theatre* London 1569 Diii^v

Picture

°Five men in °armour, one a °king wearing a °crown, kneel before the crowned °Whore of °Babylon who sits on a °seven °headed °beast. The heads of the beast are °crowned. The whore holds aloft a covered °cup in her °right hand [Rev. 17.3].

Epigram

woman [= Whore of Babylon] beast orange hair blasphemy pride beast seven head ten horn glory scarlet pearl gold heart wine whoredom cup mystery blood martyr angel heaven Babylon fall

Sonets.

I Saw a Woman sitting on a beast

Before mine eyes, of Orenge colour hew :

Horrour and dreadfull name of blasphemie

Filde hir with pride. And seuen heads I saw,

Ten hornes also the stately beast did beare.

She seemde with glorie of the scarlet faire,

And with fine perle and golde puft vp in heart.

The wine of hooredome in a cup she bare.

The name of Mysterie writ in hir face.

The bloud of Martyrs dere were hir delite.

Most fierce and fell this woman seemde to me.

An Angell then descending downe from Heauen,

With thondring voice cride out aloude, and sayd.

Now for a truth great Babylon is fallen.

Picture
At the top left, a °man with many °crowns rides on a rearing °horse, the word of God, a °sword issuing from the man's °mouth. He is followed by three of his men. In the centre top, an °angel flies in front of the °sun and sends forth °birds after the routed °soldiers at the right. The fleeing men and the °seven °headed °beast with °crowns are falling into a °pit of °fire.

Epigram
white horse man faith flame countenance word God noble name robe blood heaven army angel bird war king eat flesh beast flee pit fire

Sonets.

THen might I see vpon a white horse set

The faithfull man with flaming countenaunce,

His head did shine with crounes set therupon.

The worde of God made him a noble name.

His precious robe I saw embrued with bloud.

Then saw I from the heauen on horses white,

A puissant armie come the selfe same way.

Then cried a shining Angell as me thought,

That birdes from aire descending downe on earth

Should warre vpon the kings, and eate their flesh.

Then did I see the beast and Kings also

Ioinyng their force to slea the faithfull man.

But this fierce hatefull beast and all hir traine,

Is pitilesse throwne downe in pit of fire.

Van der Noot *Theatre* London 1569 Dvᵛ

Picture
On a °cliff at the left one of the °angels of the °plagues stands holding a °staff in its °right hand and points upwards with his °left hand. Beside him is the °kneeling and °praying figure of °St John. In the valley in the background is the heavenly city of °Jerusalem.

Epigram
earth   heaven   Saint John   sea   holy
city   Lord   spouse   abode   God   man   tear
square   city   twelve   gate   pearl   house
gold   pavement   stone1   stream   crystal
triumph   seat   life   fruit   Church

Sonets.

I Saw new Earth, new Heauen, sayde Saint Iohn.
And loe, the sea (quod he) is now no more.
The holy Citie of the Lorde, from hye
Descendeth garnisht as a loued spouse.
A voice then sayde, beholde the bright abode
Of God and men. For he shall be their God.
And all their teares he shall wipe cleane away.
Hir brightnesse greater was than can be founde.
Square was this Citie, and twelue gates it had.
Eche gate was of an orient perfest pearle,
The houses golde, the pauement precious stone.
A liuely streame, more cleere than Christall is,
Ranne through the mid, sprong from triumphant seat.
There growes lifes fruite vnto the Churches good.

PAOLO GIOVIO

THE WORTHY TRACT OF PAULUS JOVIUS

(LONDON: SIMON WATERSON, 1585)

edited by

Leslie T. Duer

Paolo Giovio

The Worthy Tract of Paulus Jovius,

London: Simon Waterson, 1585

8°: *8 A–H2
72 unnumbered leaves

Translated by Samuel Daniel
(1562?–1619)

135 unillustrated imprese

with Samuel Daniel's collection
of *Certaine notable devises
both militarie and amorous*

THE
Worthy tract of

Paulus Iouius, contayning a
Difcourfe of rare inuentions, both
Militarie and Amorous
called Imprefe

VVhereunto is added a Preface contay-
ning the Arte of compofing them, with
many other notable deuifes.

By Samuell Daniell late Student
in Oxenforde.

At London,
Printed for Simon Waterfon.
1585.

STUDIES

Duncan-Jones, Katherine. 'Two Elizabethan Versions of Giovio's Treatise on *Imprese*,' *ES*, 52 (1971), 118-23.

Farmer, Norman K., Jr. 'Introduction' to *The Worthy Tract of Paulus Jovius (1585): Translated by Samuel Daniel; together with Giovio's 'Dialogo dell' Imprese Militari et Amorose'*. Delmar, N.Y.: Scholars' Facsimiles & Reprints, 1976.

Freeman, Rosemary. *English Emblem Books*. 1948; rpt. London: Chatto & Windus, 1967, pp 47-8.

Goldman, Lloyd. 'Samuel Daniel's *Delia* and the Emblem Tradition,' *JEGP*, 67 (1968), 49-63.

Kau, Joseph. 'Daniel's *Delia* and the *Imprese* of Bishop Paolo Giovio: Some Iconological Influences,' *JWCI*, 33 (1970), 325-28.

_____. 'Daniel's Influence on an Image in *Pericles* and Sonnet 73: An *Impresa* of Destruction,' *SQ*, 26 (1975), 51-53.

_____. 'Samuel Daniel and the Renaissance *Impresa*-makers: Sources for the First English Collection of *Imprese*,' *Harvard Library Bulletin*, 18 (1970), 183-204.

Koppenfels, Werner von. 'Two Notes on *Imprese* in Elizabethan Literature: Daniel's Additions to *The Worthy Tract of Paulus Iovius*: Sidney's *Arcadia* and the Tournament Scene in *The Unfortunate Traveller*,' *RenQ*, 24 (1971), 13-25.

Maurer, Margaret. 'Samuel Daniel's Poetical Epistles, Especially Those to Sir Thomas Egerton and Lucy, Countess of Bedford,' *SP*, 74 (1977), 418-44.

Pollard, A.W. and G.R. Redgrave. *A Short-Title Catalogue of Books Printed in England, Scotland, and Ireland and of English Books Printed Abroad 1475-1640*. London: Bibliographical Society, 1926. Revised 2nd ed., W.A. Jackson, F.S. Ferguson, Katharine F. Pantzer (2 of 3 vols available - 1 A-H, 2 I-Z), 1976, 1986. #11900. STC rev. adds 11900.5.

Praz, Mario. *Studies in Seventeenth-Century Imagery*, 2nd edition. Rome: Edizioni di Storia e Letteratura, 1964, pp 352-4.

Redgrave, G.R. 'Daniel and the Emblem Literature,' *Transactions of the Bibliographical Society*, 11 (1910), 39-58.

Rees, Joan. *Samuel Daniel*. Liverpool: University Press, 1964.

Sayle, Charles E. *Early English Printed Books in the University Library Cambridge*, 4 vols. Cambridge: University Press, 1900-1907. #2108.

Scott, Mary Augusta. *Elizabethan Translations from the Italian*. 1916; rpt. Boston & New York: Burt Franklin, 1969.

Spriet, Pierre. *Samuel Daniel (1563-1619): sa vie - son oeuvre*. Bordeaux: Didier, 1968.

INTRODUCTORY NOTE

The main body of Samuel Daniel's *The Worthy Tract of Paulus Jovius* (1585) is an acknowledged translation of Giovio's *Dialogo dell'Imprese Militari et Amorose*. Until recently, Daniel's additional material, his 'To the Frendly Reader,' discussing and defining *imprese,* and his appended chapter 'certaine notable devises both militarie and amorous, Collected by Samuell Daniell' were considered to be his own composition.[1]

Within the space of four years, however, four independent studies were published which overturn this assumption. In 1968 Pierre Spriet established that Daniel's 'To the Frendly Reader' was translated from Girolamo Ruscelli's *Discorso* and the bulk of his 'certaine notable devises' from Lodovico Domenichi's *Ragionamento*.[2] Through a detailed comparison published in 1970, Joseph Kau concluded that the 'notable devises' were taken, with the exception of possibly one paragraph (XXVI), from Domenichi's work and from Gabriel Simeoni's *Le Imprese Heroiche et Morali*.[3] Further, he identifies the editions that Daniel worked from as the French editions of Domenichi and Simeoni rather than the Italian originals. Kau also suggests that Daniel may have used a French translation of Giovio as well, though he was unable to verify this.[4] In a brief note published in 1971, Werner von Koppenfels points out that the 'notable devises' are derived from Domenichi and Simeoni, with only the last device being Daniel's own contribution. He too concludes that Daniel depended on the French text (Lyons: Roville, 1561), and in a note claims that 'Daniel followed Ruscelli's edition [of Giovio] through about two-fifths of the treatise (the caesura occurring around p. dv of the *Worthy Tract*), and then turned to Domenichi's French text for the rest of his task.'[5] Katherine Duncan-Jones's 1971 article also points out Daniel's debt to Ruscelli, Domenichi, and Simeoni. She describes Daniel's translation of Giovio as a 'close and readable version of the work' and of Ruscelli as 'a skilful piece of joinery,' but suggests that the many 'errors and misprints' of the appended 'notable devises' are a result of hasty compilation.[6] This last judgement may result from her unawareness that Daniel used a French edition of Domenichi and Simeoni.

Duncan-Jones accuses Daniel of deliberately misleading the reader into believing these works to be his own. 'His friend "N.W." [the author of the commendatory epistle] appears to be himself misled, or a party to the deception, since he says that Daniel seems "to have beene very familiarly acquainted" with Domenichi and Alciati, as well as with Contile and Ruscelli' (p 122). If one looks at N.W.'s actual words in the epistle, however, the deception is reduced. There N.W. says, 'But you present us an order to frame *Devises*, in shew glorious, in forme plain, in title strange: the which is so much the more to bee esteemed, being derived from the most pure springs *Lucas Contile*, and *Ruscelli*.'[7] This sentence seems to acknowledge openly that the introductory essay's discussion of *imprese* relies on Ruscelli.

NOTES

1   Joan Rees, *Samuel Daniel* (Liverpool: Liverpool University Press, 1964), p 5.

2   Pierre Spriet, *Samuel Daniel (1563-1619): sa vie - son oeuvre* (Bordeaux: Didier, 1968), pp 41-4.

3   These works by Ruscelli, Domenichi, and Simeoni were all appended to their various editions of Giovio's *Dialogo*. For a detailed look at the complex publishing history of the *Dialogo* see Mario Praz, *Studies in Seventeenth-Century Imagery* (Rome: Edizioni di Storia e Letteratura, 1964), pp 352-4.

4   Joseph Kau, 'Samuel Daniel and the Renaissance *Impresa*-makers: Sources for the First English Collection of *Imprese*,' *Harvard Library Bulletin*, 18 (1970), 183-204.

5   Werner von Koppenfels, 'Two Notes on *Imprese* in Elizabethan Literature: Daniel's Additions to *The Worthy Tract of Paulus Iovius*; Sidney's *Arcadia* and the Tournament Scene in *The Unfortunate Traveller*,' *RenQ*, 24 (1971), 13.

6   Katherine Duncan-Jones, 'Two Elizabethan Versions of Giovio's Treatise on Imprese,' *ES*, 52 (1971), 123.

7   In Samuel Daniel's *The Worthy Tract of Paulus Jovius* (London, 1585), sig *5.

Giovio *Imprese* London 1585 Biiii^r

Motto
Aut °Caesar aut nihil.

°Caesar or nothing.

Bearer
Caesar °Borgia

Giovio *Imprese* London 1585 Biiii^r

Picture
A °winged °hart.

Bearer
Charles de °Bourbon, Constable of France

Giovio *Imprese* London 1585 Biiii^r

Motto
°Feriunt summos °fulmina °montes.

°Lightning °strikes the °mountain tops.

Picture
The °mountain °Chimera or °Acroceraunia struck by °lightning.

Bearer
Francesco °Borgia, Duke of °Candia

Reference
°Horace

Giovio *Imprese* London 1585 Biiii^v

Motto
°Cursum intendimus °alis.
[ironic attribution]

We °wing our °way.

Picture
A °winged °hart.

Bearer
Charles de °Bourbon, Constable of France

Commentary
ironic motto bestowed upon Charles de Bourbon by Motta Augruing(?) after the Battle of Pavia, 1525.

Giovio *Imprese* London 1585 Biiii^v	Giovio *Imprese* London 1585 Bv^v

Picture
°Gold °candleflyes [= °moths] dispersed.

Bearer
Ippolita °Fioramonda, Marquise of Scaldasole

Motto
Ita et °virtus.

Thus also °virtue.

Picture
A °laurel-tree between °two °lions.

Bearer
Lorenzo de' °Medici

Giovio *Imprese* London 1585 Bv^r	Giovio *Imprese* London 1585 Bvi^r

Motto
°Virtuti °fortuna °comes.

°Fortune, °companion of °virtue.

Bearer
Giasone del °Maino

Motto
Hoc °opus.

This is my work.

Picture
The °stern of a °ship.

Bearer
Cardinal Rafael °Riario

Giovio *Imprese* London 1585 Bvi[v]

Motto
°Margherita Te suola di cuor' °amo.
[understood]

°Margherita, I °love thee solely.

Picture
The letter °"T" and a °pearl in the middle
of a °shoe °sole, worn on a hat [pun on
Latin "margarita" = pearl, or Italian
"margherita" = pearl or flower; pun on
"suola" = sole (of shoe) and "suola,"
archaic form of "sola" = sole, alone]

Bearer
Sebastiano del °Mancino

Giovio *Imprese* London 1585 Bvi[v]

Motto
°Margherita te °adoro.
[understood]

°Margherita, I °adore thee.

Picture
The letter °"T" and a °pearl set in a
°gold °plate, worn on a hat [pun on Latin
"margarita" = pearl]

Bearer
°Panmolena

Giovio *Imprese* London 1585 Bvi[v]

Picture
A °white wax °candle, worn in a cap.

Bearer
Agostino °Porco

Giovio *Imprese* London 1585 Bvii[r]

Motto
I °repent me the °cost of my °lady.
[understood; pun on Pentecost depicted in
picture]

Picture
The °descent of the °Holy °Ghost upon the
°twelve °apostles in an °agate.

Bearer
Cavaliere °Casio

Giovio *Imprese* London 1585 Bvii[v]

Motto
Egli e como °dio °vuole.

He is as °God °wills.

Bearer
°Castruccio, Lord of Lucca

Giovio *Imprese* London 1585 Bvii[v]

Motto
Porto le °corna ch'ogni Huomo le °vede, e qualch' Altro le porta che nol °crede.

I bear °horns that everyone can °see. Someone else bears them too, but does not °believe it.

Bearer
Prince of °Salerno

Giovio *Imprese* London 1585 Bvii[v]

Motto
E sara quel che °dio °vorra.

It shall be as °God °wills.

Bearer
°Castruccio, Lord of Lucca

Giovio *Imprese* London 1585 Bviii[r]

Motto
Plus ultra.

Further.

Picture
The °Pillars of °Hercules.

Bearer
Emperor °Charles V

Giovio *Imprese* London 1585 Bviii^r

Picture
A °tinderbox.

Bearer
°Charles, Duke of °Burgundy

Giovio *Imprese* London 1585 Cii^r

Motto
°Comminus et °eminus.

°Near and °far.

Picture
A °hedgehog °crowned.

Bearer
°Archers of the Guard of °Louis XII [King of France]

Giovio *Imprese* London 1585 Ci^v

Motto
°Honni soit qui °mal y °pense.

Let him be °dishonoured who °thinks °evil of it.

Picture
°St. George on °horseback within a °white °shield, parted with a °red °cross.

Bearer
Knights of the °Garter

Giovio *Imprese* London 1585 Cii^r

Motto
Mi °nutrisco.

I °nourish myself on it.

Picture
A °salamander in a °fire.

Bearer
°Francis I, King of France

Giovio *Imprese* London 1585 Cii^v | Giovio *Imprese* London 1585 Ciii^r

Motto
Donec totum impleat °orbem.

Until it fills the whole °world.

Picture
The °crescent °moon.

Bearer
°Henry II, as Dauphin of France

Motto
Tanto °monta.

So much does he °excel.

Picture
The °Gordian °knot.

Bearer
King of °Spain

Giovio *Imprese* London 1585 Cii^v | Giovio *Imprese* London 1585 Ciii^v

Motto
Cum °plena est, sit °emula °Solis.

When °full, she may °rival the °sun.

Picture
A °full °moon.

Bearer
°Henry II, King of France

Motto
°Anna di no.
[understood]

°Anna say no.

Picture
A °duck.
[pun on Spanish "annadino" = duck].

Bearer
unnamed knight of the house of °Porres.

Giovio *Imprese* London 1585 Ciii^{v}

Motto
°Mal va. [understood]

It goes °ill.

Picture
A bush of °green °mallows.
[pun on Spanish "malva" = mallow, and "malvada" = rogue]

Bearer
Diego de °Guzman

Giovio *Imprese* London 1585 Ciiii^{r}

Motto
Sic vos non vobis.

Thus you [°fight] not for yourselves.

Bearer
Antonio de °Leiva

Giovio *Imprese* London 1585 Ciiii^{r}

Motto
Los °llenos de °dolor y, Los °vazios de °speranza.

Those that are °full contain °sorrow, those that are °empty, °hope.

Picture
A °wheel with °buckets for drawing °water.

Bearer
Diego de °Mendoza

Giovio *Imprese* London 1585 Ciiii^{v}

Picture
An °opened °book.

Bearer
°Alfonso I, King of Naples

Giovio *Imprese* London 1585 Cv^r

Motto
Malo °mori quam °foedari.

I prefer to °die than to be °dishonoured.

Picture
An °armelin, or °ermine surrounded by a °ring of °dung.

Bearer
°Ferrante, son of Alfonso I, King of Naples

Giovio *Imprese* London 1585 Cv^v

Motto
°Naturae non °artis °opus.

A °work of °nature, not of °art.

Picture
A °mountain of °diamonds.

Bearer
°Ferrantino, son of Alphonso II, King of Naples

Giovio *Imprese* London 1585 Cv^v

Motto
°Dia de mas °valer.
[understood; pun on "diadem"]

A °day of more °worth.

Picture
°Three °saints' °diadems linked, with the word °"valer" in the middle [pun on "dia de mas" of motto].

Bearer
°Alphonse II, King of Naples

Giovio *Imprese* London 1585 Cv^v

Motto
°Recedant °vetera.

Let °old [°offences] be °forgiven.

Picture
A °closed °account °book with leather strings and buckles, and with °flames rising from the margins, inscribed °"1485".

Bearer
°Frederick I, King of Naples

Giovio *Imprese* London 1585 Cvi^r	Giovio *Imprese* London 1585 Cvi^v

Motto
°Quietum nemo °impune °lacesset.

Though I am °peaceful, no one will °attack me with °impunity.

Picture
A °mastiff or °greyhound crouching on hind legs with front up, under °pine °tree.

Bearer
Francesco °Sforza, Duke of Milan

Picture
A °mulberry-tree.

Bearer
Lodovico °Sforza, Duke of Milan

Picture
A °helmeted °lion sitting on a great °fire.

Bearer
Galeazzo °Sforza, Duke of Milan

Motto
°Suave.

°Gentle.

Picture
A °yoke.

Bearer
Giovanni de' °Medici; later °Pope °Leo X

Reference
°B Matt 10.20

Giovio *Imprese* London 1585 Cvii^v

Picture
°Florence sitting on a °chair, a °yoke under her feet.

Bearer
Cosimo de' °Medici

Reference
°Cicero: "Roma patrem patriae Ciceronem libera dixit." [Rome, freed, called Cicero father of his country.]

Giovio *Imprese* London 1585 Cviii^r

Motto
Semper.

For ever.

Picture
A °diamond between °three °feathers, respectively °green, °white, and °red.

Bearer
Lorenzo de' °Medici and his successors, including °Pope °Leo X

Giovio *Imprese* London 1585 Cviii^r

Picture
°Three °diamonds.

Bearer
Cosimo de' °Medici

Giovio *Imprese* London 1585 Cviii^r

Motto
Semper

Forever.

Picture
A °falcon grasping °diamonds in its °talons.

Bearer
Piero de' °Medici, son of Cosimo

Giovio *Imprese* London 1585 Cviii^v

Motto
In °viridi teneras °exurit °flamma °medullas.

In the °green, the °flame °consumes their tender °marrows.

Picture
°Billets of °green °wood stacked; °smoke and °flame issuing from within.

Bearer
Piero de' °Medici, son of Lorenzo

Reference
Agnolo °Poliziano

Giovio *Imprese* London 1585 Di^r

Motto
°Candor °illesus.

°Purity °unharmed.

Picture
The °sun with °beams shining through a °crystal °lens, producing °flames, all set in a °white °hood.

Bearer
Giulio de' °Medici as °Pope °Clement VII

Giovio *Imprese* London 1585 Cviii^v

Picture
The word °"GLOVIS" set within the perimeter of a °triangular °shield.

Bearer
Giuliano de' °Medici, son of Lorenzo, when Duke of °Nemours

Giovio *Imprese* London 1585 Dii^r

Motto
Inter omnes.

Among all.

Picture
A °comet.

Bearer
Ippolito de' °Medici

Reference
°Horace: "Micat inter omnes Julium sidus velut inter ignes luna minores." [As the moon among lesser lights, so shines the Julian constellation amid all (others.)]

Giovio *Imprese* London 1585 Dii^v

Motto
Hinc aliquando °eluctabor.

Sometime I shall °struggle out of here.

Picture
The °moon, °eclipsed.

Bearer
Ippolito de' °Medici

Giovio *Imprese* London 1585 Diii^v

Motto
°Fidem °fati °virtute °sequemur.

With my own °virtue I shall °strive to achieve the °promise given to me by °destiny.

Picture
A °capricorn.

Bearer
Cosimo de' °Medici

Giovio *Imprese* London 1585 Diii^r

Motto
°Rhinoceros nunquam °victus ab °hoste cedit.

The °rhinoceros never turns away °defeated from the enemy.

Picture
A °rhinoceros.

Bearer
Alessandro' °Medici, Duke of Florence

Giovio *Imprese* London 1585 Diiii^r

Motto
°Jupiter °merentibus °offert.

°Jupiter °rewards the °deserving.

Picture
An °eagle holding a °crown in its °beak.

Bearer
Cosimo de' °Medici

Giovio *Imprese* London 1585 Diiii^r

Motto
Uno avulso non deficit alter.

When one is torn away, a second does not fail.

Picture
A °golden °bough.

Bearer
Cosimo de' °Medici

Reference
°Virgil

Giovio *Imprese* London 1585 Dv^v

Motto
°Sauciat et °defendit.

It °wounds and °defends.

Picture
An °iron °dog's °collar with sharp °spikes.

Bearer
Nicolo °Orsini, Count of Pitigliano

Commentary
Collar worn by shepherd's mastiffs to ward off wolves.

Giovio *Imprese* London 1585 Dv^v

Motto
Il me °plait le °trouble.

°Trouble °pleases me.

Picture
A °camel disturbing the °water of a °river.

Bearer
Virginio °Orsini

Giovio *Imprese* London 1585 Dv^v

Motto
Prius °mori quam °fidem °fallere.

°Die rather than °betray °trust.

Picture
A spiked °iron °collar grasped by °two °hands which are pierced by the °spikes; in the middle of the collar, a °rose.

Bearer
house of °Orsini

Commentary
Collar worn by shepherd's mastiffs to ward off wolves

Giovio *Imprese* London 1585 Dvi^r	Giovio *Imprese* London 1585 Dvi^v

Motto
°Ingenio °experior °funera digna meo.

I °suffer °ruin worthy of my own °invention.

Picture
The °brazen °bull of °Perillus.

Bearer
Prospero °Colonna

Motto
°Fides hoc uno, °virtusque °probantur.

°Virtue and °faith are °tested by this alone.

Picture
A °touchstone.

Bearer
Fabrizio °Colonna

Giovio *Imprese* London 1585 Dvi^v	Giovio *Imprese* London 1585 Dvi^v

Motto
°Samnitico non °capitur °auro.

He is not °corrupted by °Samnitic °gold.

Picture
A °vessel [°urn?] "made after the ancient form."

Bearer
Fabrizio °Colonna

Reference
G. °Fabricius [Luscinus, mentioned by Cicero]

Motto
Erit altera °merces.

The one or the other will be my °reward.

Picture
A bough of °palm wreathed with bough of °cypress.

Bearer
Marcantonio °Colonna

Giovio *Imprese* London 1585 Dvii^r	Giovio *Imprese* London 1585 Dvii^v

Motto
°Natura dictante °feror.

I °fly where °nature bids me.

Picture
A °heron with the °sun above and °clouds below; °marsh and °sedge below the clouds; possibly °rain and °hail falling.

Bearer
Marcantonio °Colonna

Motto
°Fortia facere et °pati °Romanum est.

To do °brave °deeds and to °suffer is °Roman.

Picture
A °hand burning in the °fire upon an °altar.

Bearer
Muzio °Colonna

Giovio *Imprese* London 1585 Dvii^v	Giovio *Imprese* London 1585 Dviii^r

Motto
Semper °pertinax.

Always °pertinacious.

Picture
A °vesture [= °garment] in the midst of a °fire.

Bearer
Marcantonio °Colonna

Reference
°Pliny the Elder: "that lint of India, called albestin ..."

Motto
°Flectimur non °frangimur °undis.

We are °bent but not °broken by °waves.

Picture
°Bullrushes in a °river.

Bearer
house of °Colonna

Giovio *Imprese* London 1585 Dviii^v

Motto
°Venena °pello.

I °banish °poisons.

Picture
A °fountain surrounded by °toads and °snakes, with a °unicorn putting his °horn in the °water.

Bearer
Bartolomeo °Alviano

Giovio *Imprese* London 1585 Ei^v

Motto
°Probasti me °Domine, et °cognovisti.

You °tested me, O °Lord, and °knew me.

Picture
°Gold in a °furnace °fire.

Bearer
Francesco °Gonzago, Marquis of Mantua

Giovio *Imprese* London 1585 Ei^r

Motto
°Obstrepuit inter °olores.

It °clamored among the °swans.

Picture
A °gander among °swans.

Bearer
Bartolomeo °Alviano, as proposed by Cotta of Verona, his poet, but refused.

Giovio *Imprese* London 1585 Eii^r

Motto
Non °cedit °umbra °soli.

°Shade does not °yield to the °sun.

Picture
A °marble °block [°quadret] with an iron °stile set in the middle, opposite to the °sun.

Bearer
Giacomo °Trivulzio

Giovio *Imprese* London 1585 Eii^r

Motto
°Loco et °tempore.
[later changed to: A °lieu et °temps.]

In °place and °time.

Picture
A °metal °globe containing °flames issuing through °apertures.

Bearer
Alfonso d' °Este, Duke of Ferrara

Reference
°Ariosto

Giovio *Imprese* London 1585 Eii^v

Motto
°Inclinata resurgit.

When °pressed down, it °raises itself again.

Picture
A °palm-tree weighted down with a °marble °block tied to the top.

Bearer
Duke of °Urbino

Reference
°Pliny, the Elder

Giovio *Imprese* London 1585 Eiii^v

Motto
Hoc per se °nihil est, sed si °minimum addideris °maximum fiet [= fieret].

This by itself is °nothing, but if you should add even the °least to it, it would become the °greatest.

Picture
Many °black °numbers scattered in a °field1 or °border.

Bearer
Ottaviano °Fregoso, °Doge of Genoa.

Giovio *Imprese* London 1585 Eiiii^r

Motto
°Expiabit aut °obruet.

It will °purge or cause °ruin.

Picture
°Jupiter's °lightning.

Bearer
Hierosin °Adorno

Giovio *Imprese* London 1585 Eiiii^v

Motto
Non vos °alabereis.

You shall not °boast.

Picture
An °elephant attacked by a °dragon.

Bearer
Sinibaldo and Ottobuono °Fieschi

Giovio *Imprese* London 1585 Ev^v

Motto
Aspicit °unam.

It sees °one only.

Picture
A clear °azure °sky with °stars above a °compass °needle and compass, set upon a °sea °card [= °chart].

Bearer
Sinibaldo °Fieschi

Giovio *Imprese* London 1585 Ev^r

Motto
Nous °scavons bien le °temps.

We °know well the °time.

Picture
A clear °sky, a calm °sea; upon the sea a °nest with the necks of birds looking over the upturned end of the nest; the °halcyons are coloured °azure, °red, °white, °green, °yellow.

Bearer
house of °Fieschi

Reference
°Pliny the Elder

Giovio *Imprese* London 1585 Evi^r

Motto
°Unguibus et °rostro, atque °alis °armatus in °hostem.

°Armed with °nails, °beak, and °wings against the °enemy.

Picture
A °griffin °argent in a °field1 °gueles.

Bearer
Gianpaolo °Baglioni

Giovio *Imprese* London 1585 Evi^v

Motto
°Spiritus °durissima °coquit.

A °noble °mind °digests even the most painful °injuries.

Picture
An °ostrich devouring a °horseshoe °nail.

Bearer
Girolamo °Mattei

Giovio *Imprese* London 1585 Eviii^r

Motto
Diversa ab illis °virtute °valemus.

We are °strong because our °skill differs from theirs.

Picture
A male and female °ostrich looking at their eggs; the °rays from their °eyes °hatch the °eggs.

Bearer
Pietro °Navarro

Giovio *Imprese* London 1585 Evii^r

Motto
Si °sursum non efferor °alis, saltem °cursu praetervehor omnes.

Though I do not °soar high on my °wings, I outstrip all in °running.

Picture
An °ostrich °cursant.

Bearer
Marquis of °Vasto

Giovio *Imprese* London 1585 Eviii^r

Motto
Aut cum hoc aut in hoc.

Either with this or on this.

Picture
A °Spartan °shield.

Bearer
Marquis of °Pescara

Giovio *Imprese* London 1585 Eviii^v	Giovio *Imprese* London 1585 Fi^v
Motto Sans point °sortir hors de l'°orniére. Without °straying from the °path. **Picture** A °wheel. **Bearer** Louis de La °Tremoille	**Motto** °Mitem °animum °agresti sub °tegmine servo. I have a °soft °soul beneath a °rough °appearance. **Picture** A °wild °man with a °club in one hand. **Bearer** Charles d' °Amboise
Giovio *Imprese* London 1585 Fi^r	Giovio *Imprese* London 1585 Fi^v
Motto °Obstantia °nubila °solvet. It will °dissolve °confronting °clouds. **Picture** The °sun, °or, surrounded by thick °clouds in a °field1, °azure. **Bearer** Louis de °Luxembourg	**Motto** Pour °dompter °folie. To °tame °folly. **Picture** A °harness used by °farrier when °shoeing wild °horses. **Bearer** Francesco °Sanseverino, Count of Caiazzo

Giovio *Imprese* London 1585 Fi^v

Motto
°Distantia °iungit.

It holds °distant things °united.

Picture
A °lion °rampant in a °field1 °argent, all
sown with °buckles.

Bearer
Edward °Stuart, Lord of °Albany, cousin of
James IV

Giovio *Imprese* London 1585 Fiii^r

Motto
°Fortibus non °deerunt.

The °brave will not °lack them.

Picture
A °bundle of °javelins.

Bearer
Andrea di °Capua, Duke of Tremoli

Giovio *Imprese* London 1585 Fiii^r

Motto
°Officium °natura °docet.

°Nature °teaches one's °duty.

Picture
A °crane holding up the °left °claw in
which is grasped a °stone.

Bearer
Duke of °Amalfi

Reference
°Pliny

Giovio *Imprese* London 1585 Fiii^v

Motto
Hoc fac et °vives.

Do this and you shall °live.

Picture
A °balance or °scales.

Bearer
Count of °Metalone

Giovio *Imprese* London 1585 Fiiii^r

Motto
°Natura °maiora facit.

°Nature does °greater things.

Picture
The slopes of the erupting °volcano, °Mount °Aetna, are covered from the top down with °snow, °burnt and consumed °stones, and °fertile °field1s.

Bearer
Gian Battista °Castaldo

Giovio *Imprese* London 1585 Fv^r

Motto
°Servari et servare meum est.

My °duty is to °guard myself and others.

Picture
°Two °bundles of °ripe °millet.

Bearer
Maria d' °Aragon, Marquise of Vasto

Giovio *Imprese* London 1585 Fiiiiv

Motto
Conantia °frangere frangunt.

They °break those which are trying to break them.

Picture
°Rocks in a °turbulent °sea.

Bearer
Vittoria °Colonna, Marquise of Pescara.

Giovio *Imprese* London 1585 Fv^v

Motto
Dov'é gran °fuoco é gran °fumo.

Where there is great °fire, there is great °smoke.

Picture
A large °chimney with a large °fire within.

Bearer
Odet de °Foi, Viscomte de Lautrec

Giovio *Imprese* London 1585 Fv^r	Giovio *Imprese* London 1585 Fvi^v

Picture
°Five °ears of °corn [= °wheat].

Bearer
Teodoro °Trivulzio.

Motto
Discretis sua °virtus inest.

When separated, each has its own °virtue.

Picture
The °spheres of the °four °elements, separated.

Bearer
Marquis of °Vasto

Motto
Finiunt pariter °renovantque °labores.

They finish at the same time and °renew their °labour.

Picture
°Two °sheaves of °ripe °corn [= °wheat].

Bearer
Marquis of °Vasto

Motto
°Iunoni °Lucinae °dicatum.

°Dedicated to °Juno °Lucina.

Picture
The °temple of °Juno °Lucina and within, an °altar with a °fire.

Bearer
Marquis of °Vasto

Giovio *Imprese* London 1585 Fvii^r

Motto
Qui °vivens °laedit °morte °medetur.

He who °hurts in °life, °heals in °death.

Picture
A °scorpion.

Bearer
Lodovico °Gonzaga

Giovio *Imprese* London 1585 Fviii^r

Motto
Cum °crepitat, °sonora °silent.

When it °rattles, loud °words °subside.

Picture
A °rattle.

Bearer
Marquis of °Vasto

Giovio *Imprese* London 1585 Fvii^v

Motto
Alterutra clarescere °fama. Sive °bonum, sive °malum, fama est.

To become °famous in one way or the other, whether it be °good or °bad, it is fame.

Picture
The °temple of °Diana at °Ephesus.

Bearer
Lodovico °Gonzaga

Giovio *Imprese* London 1585 Fviii^r

Motto
°Fragrantia durant °Herculea collecta °manu.

When gathered by °Hercules' °hand, they keep their °fragrance.

Picture
°Quinces, °or, scattered over a °field1, °gueles.

Bearer
Count of °Santa Fiora

Giovio *Imprese* London 1585 Gi^r

Motto
°Servus °curru °portatur eodem.

The °slave °rides in the same °chariot.

Picture
A °triumphal °chariot, drawn by °five °white °horses, °emperor within, a °slave behind him holding °laurel °garland.

Giovio *Imprese* London 1585 Gi^r

Motto
Fal con °tempo.
[understood: pun on picture]

Do it in °time.

Picture
A °falcon holding in her °talons the °counterweight of a °clock.

Bearer
Ippolito d' °Este

Reference
A figure on the park gate of the baths ("stews") of °Diocletian.

Giovio *Imprese* London 1585 Gi^v

Motto
Totum adimit quo °ingrata °refulget.

The °ungrateful takes away all with which she °shines.

Picture
The °sun, °eclipsed by the °moon.

Bearer
Ascanio °Sforza

Giovio *Imprese* London 1585 Gi^v

Motto
Non °suefro mas de lo que puedo.

I °suffer no more than I am able.

Picture
A °kneeling °camel.

Bearer
Ippolito d'°Este

Giovio *Imprese* London 1585 Gii[r]	Giovio *Imprese* London 1585 Gii[r]
Motto Melior °fortuna °notabit. Better °fortune will °write on it. **Picture** A °white °tablet. **Bearer** Lodovico of °Aragon	**Motto** °Ball' ontos. [Gk] °Aim true. **Picture** An °arrow hitting the °white1 of a °target. **Bearer** Alessandro °Farnese
Giovio *Imprese* London 1585 Gii[r]	Giovio *Imprese* London 1585 Gii[v]
Motto °Crocodili °lachrymae. °Tears of the °crocodile. **Picture** A °crocodile. **Bearer** Sigismondo °Gonzaga	**Motto** °Votis subscribunt °fata secundis. °Destiny makes °wishes come true. **Picture** A °scroll of °white °paper. **Bearer** Alessandro °Farnese

Giovio *Imprese* London 1585 Gii^v

Motto
Hoc uno °Iupiter °ultor.

With this alone °Jupiter °punishes.

Picture
°Jupiter's °triple forked °lightning.

Bearer
Alessandro °Farnese

Giovio *Imprese* London 1585 Giii^v

Motto
°Sufficit °unum in °tenebris.

°One °suffices in °darkness.

Picture
A °triangular °candlestick.

Bearer
Isabella °Gonzaga, Marquise of Mantua

Giovio *Imprese* London 1585 Giii^r

Motto
°Sustinet nec °fatiscit.

He °holds up and does not °weary.

Picture
Kneeling °Atlas bearing up the °heavens, which contain the °zodiac and °signs.

Bearer
Andrea °Gritti

Giovio *Imprese* London 1585 Giiiir

Motto
°Triumphali e °stipite °surgens °alta petit.

°Rising from °triumphal °stock it seeks the °heights.

Picture
A °laurel-tree with some large °branches cut off, and one °twig growing straight upward to a great height.

Bearer
son and heir of the Marquis of °Vasto

Giovio *Imprese* London 1585 Giiii^r

Motto
°Probasti me °domine.

You °tested me, O °Lord.

Picture
A °furnace °testing °gold.

Bearer
Francesco °Gonzaga II, Marquis of Mantua, also borne as part of the impresa of Andrea Gonzaga, his grandson.

Giovio *Imprese* London 1585 Giiii^r

Motto
°Fortibus non °deerunt.

The °brave will not °lack them.

Picture
A °bundle of °darts.

Bearer
Andrea °Capua, Duke of Thermopylae, also borne as part of the imprese of Andrea Gonzaga, his grandson.

Giovio *Imprese* London 1585 Giiii^r

Picture
°Mount °Olympus with the °altar of °faith.

Bearer
Frederico °Gonzaga II, Duke of Mantua, also borne as part of the impresa of Andrea °Gonzaga, his nephew.

Giovio *Imprese* London 1585 Giiii^r

Motto
Nec °spe, nec °metu.

Without °hope or °fear.

Picture
"°Cattle ... without °body."

Bearer
Ferrante °Gonzaga, also borne as part of the impresa of Andrea °Gonzaga, his son.

Giovio *Imprese* London 1585 Giiii[r]

Motto
°Virtutis °trophaea novae non °degener addet.

In keeping with °family tradition, he will add new °trophies of °valour.

Picture
A °round °shield, °fringed; °four °circles, one at each side, bound by a °laurel °wreath. In each circle an °impresa.

Bearer
Andrea °Gonzaga

Giovio *Imprese* London 1585 Gv[r]

Motto
Ingentia °marmora findit °caprificus.

The °fig-tree splits huge blocks of °marble.

Picture
A block of °marble split by a °fig-tree.

Bearer
°Cola, Count of Campobasso

Reference
°Martial

Giovio *Imprese* London 1585 Giiiiv

Picture
A °firebrand and °bucket of °water.

Bearer
Galeazzo °Visconti

Giovio *Imprese* London 1585 Gv[v]

Picture
A °raven.
[pun on bearer's name Corvinus]

Bearer
Mathias °Corvinus, King of Hungary

Giovio *Imprese* London 1585 Gv^v

Motto
°Sina alienaque °pignora °nutrit.

Her °breasts °nourish also an °offspring not her own.

Picture
A °wolf with distended °udder.

Bearer
John °Szapolya, King of Hungary.

Giovio *Imprese* London 1585 Gvi^r

Motto
°Contemnit °tuta °procellas.

°Secure, she °despises °storms.

Picture
A °Siren.

Bearer
Stefano °Colonna

Reference
From the arms of the house of °Colonna.

Giovio *Imprese* London 1585 Gv^v

Motto
Non deest °generoso in °pectore °virtus.

There is no lack of °courage in a °noble °heart.

Picture
A °lion °rampant in a °field1 °gueles holding a °sword in his °paw.

Bearer
Francesco Maria della °Rovere, Duke of Urbino

Giovio *Imprese* London 1585 Gvi^r

Motto
Cum °pudore laeta °foecunditas.

Happy °fecundity accompanied by °modesty.

Picture
A °peahen sheltering under her °wings °six of her °young1, three under each wing.

Bearer
Duchess of °Florence

Giovio *Imprese* London 1585 Gvi^v

Motto
Aequabit °nigras °candida una °dies.

One single °bright °day will °equal the °black ones.

Picture
A °pot full of little °black °stones with °one °white °stone among them.

Bearer
Iacopo °Sannazzaro

Giovio *Imprese* London 1585 Gvii^r

Motto
Vel °Iovi °cedere nescit.

He does not °yield, even to °Jupiter.

Picture
The °god °Terminus.

Bearer
°Erasmus

Reference
°Varro

Giovio *Imprese* London 1585 Gvii^r

Motto
Pro °bono °malum.

°Evil for °good.

Picture
A °hive of °bees with °honey.

Bearer
Lodovico °Ariosto

Giovio *Imprese* London 1585 Gvii^r

Motto
Nulla °dies sine °linea.
[understood]

Not a °day without a °line.

Picture
°Apelles °painting.

Bearer
°Erasmus, proposed by St. Thomas More

Giovio *Imprese* London 1585 Gvii^v

Picture
The °caduceus of °Mercury with the °cornucopia.

Bearer
Andrea °Alciato

Giovio *Imprese* London 1585 Gvii^r

Motto
°Incerta °animi decreta °resolvet.

She will °dispel the °uncertainties of the °mind.

Picture
The °Sphinx.

Bearer
Camillo °Giordano

Giovio *Imprese* London 1585 Gvii^v

Picture
A °beaver.

Bearer
Paolo °Giovio

Reference
°Juvenal

Giovio *Imprese* London 1585 Gviii^r

Motto
Wan °Got °will.

When °God °wills.

Picture
A °tree with °grafts.

Bearer
Giulio °Giovio

Giovio *Imprese* London 1585 Gviii[v]

Motto
°Translata °proficit °arbos.

A °tree makes °progress when °transplanted.

Picture
A °peach-tree laden with °fruit.

Bearer
Lodovico °Domenichi

Giovio *Imprese* London 1585 Hi[v]

Motto
Simul °astu et °dentibus utor.

I use my °cunning and my °teeth simultaneously.

Picture
A °fox with bared °teeth.

Bearer
della °Volpe, knight

Giovio *Imprese* London 1585 Gviii[v]

Motto
Longo °splendescit in °usu.

With long °use it °shines.

Picture
A °plowshare.

Bearer
Lodovico °Domenichi

Giovio *Imprese* London 1585 Hii[r]

Motto
°Pavent °oves, °Timent °canes, °intrepidus maneo.

The °sheep are °frightened, the °dogs °fear, I stand °intrepid.

Picture
A °wolf with °bloody °lamb between legs, looking back at °two °mastiffs, one mastiff looking back toward the other.

Bearer
Giovanni °Chiuchiera

LODOVICO DOMENICHI

CERTAIN NOTABLE DEVISES BOTH MILITARIE AND AMOROUS

[LONDON: SIMON WATERSON, 1585]

edited by

Leslie T. Duer

Lodovico Domenichi

Certaine notable devises both militarie and amorous,

28 unillustrated imprese

appended to Daniel's translation of Giovio, *The Worthy Tract of Paulus Jovius,* (London: Simon Waterson, 1585)

8°: H2ᵛ–H8

HERE FOLLOVV,
TOVCHING THE FOR-
mer subiect, certaine notable de-
uises both militarie and
amorous,
Collected by Samuell Daniell.

Certaine gentleman of Italie named *Hermet Stampo*, a Prelate,
bare for his deuise a *Laurell* tree
menaced with lightning, with
this briefe : *Nec forte, nec fato*, to
signifie that his vertue could not be endama-
ged or anoyed by any fatale chaunce, for
lightning (as writeth *Plinie*) hath no powre to
hurt the *Laurell*.

The same *S. Stampo*, being created Marquise of *Somonio*, and hauing married a wife,
leauing his Ecclesiasticall habite: represented
this deuise: two *Palme* trees, the male and female, which neuer bring foorth fruite, vnles
they are one planted by the other, adioyning
thereunto this mot : *Mutua fœcunditas.*

His brother the Earle *Maximian*, being a-
morous of a Lady named *Anna Morenna*, who
afterward was his wife, had for his *Impresa* a
silk worme, which only liueth with the leaues
of

STUDIES

Duncan-Jones, Katherine. 'Two Elizabethan Versions of Giovio's Treatise on *Imprese*,' *ES* 52 (1971), 118-123.

Farmer, Norman K., Jr. 'Introduction' to *The Worthy Tract of Paulus Jovius (1585): Translated by Samuel Daniel; together with Giovio's 'Dialogo dell' Imprese Militari et Amorose'.* Delmar, N.Y.: Scholars' Facsimiles & Reprints, 1976.

Freeman, Rosemary. *English Emblem Books.* 1948; rpt. London: Chatto & Windus, 1967, pp 47-8.

Goldman, Lloyd. 'Samuel Daniel's *Delia* and the Emblem Tradition,' *JEGP*, 67 (1968), 49-63.

Kau, Joseph. 'Samuel Daniel and the Renaissance *Impresa*-makers: Sources for the First English Collection of *Imprese*,' *Harvard Library Bulletin*, 18 (1970), 183-204.

Koppenfels, Werner von. 'Two Notes on *Imprese* in Elizabethan Literature: Daniel's Additions to *The Worthy Tract of Paulus Giovio*: Sidney's *Arcadia* and the Tournament Scene in *The Unfortunate Traveller*,' *RenQ*, 24 (1971), 13-25.

Maurer, Margaret. 'Samuel Daniel's Poetical Epistles, Especially Those to Sir Thomas Egerton and Lucy, Countess of Bedford,' *SP*, 74 (1977), 418-44.

Pollard, A.W. and G.R. Redgrave. *A Short-Title Catalogue of Books Printed in England, Scotland, and Ireland and of English Books Printed Abroad 1475-1640.* London: Bibliographical Society, 1926. Revised 2nd ed., W.A. Jackson, F.S. Ferguson, Katharine F. Pantzer (2 of 3 vols. available - 1 A-H, 2 I-Z), 1976, 1986. #11900. STC rev. adds 11900.5.

Praz, Mario. *Studies in Seventeenth-Century Imagery*, 2nd edition. Rome: Edizioni di Storia e Letteratura, 1964, pp 352-4.

Redgrave, G.R. 'Daniel and the Emblem Literature,' *Transactions of the Bibliographical Society*, 11 (1910), 39-58.

Rees, Joan. *Samuel Daniel.* Liverpool: University Press, 1964.

Sayle, Charles E. *Early English Printed Books in the University Library Cambridge*, 4 vols. Cambridge: University Press, 1900-1907. #2108.

Scott, Mary Augusta. *Elizabethan Translations from the Italian.* 1916; rpt. Boston & New York: Burt Franklin, 1969.

Spriet, Pierre. *Samuel Daniel (1563-1619): sa vie - son oeuvre.* Bordeaux: Didier, 1968.

INTRODUCTORY NOTE

See Introductory Note to Giovio

Domenichi *Devises* London 1585 Hii^v

Motto
Nec °sorte, nec °fato.

Not by °chance nor by °fate.

Picture
A °laurel-tree threatened by °lightning.

Bearer
Hermet °Stampo

Reference
°Pliny

Domenichi *Devises* London 1585 Hiii^r

Motto
Suol di cilo °vivo.

Only of this do I °live.

Picture
A °silk-worm.

Commentary
The °mulberry in Lombardy is called °mora [punning allusion to name of the lady Anna °Moronna].

Bearer
Count Massimiliano °Stampo

Domenichi *Devises* London 1585 Hii^v

Motto
°Mutua °foecunditas.

°Mutual °fecundity.

Picture
°Two °palm-trees, °male and °female.

Bearer
Hermet °Stampo, Marquis of Sonomo(?)

Domenichi *Devises* London 1585 Hiii

Motto
In utraque °fortuna.

I °prosper either way.

Picture
A °caltrap.

Bearer
Count Battista di °Lodron

Domenichi *Devises* London 1585 Hiii^r	Domenichi *Devises* London 1585 Hiii^v

Motto
In °aeternum.

°Forever.

Picture
A °stockdove [= wild °pigeon] with a °diamond held in its °bill. [pun on lady's name "Diamante"]

Bearer
Gasparo de °Maino

Motto
Trovommi °amor del tutto °disarmato.

°Love found me completely °disarmed.

Picture
A °snail, its °head out of its °shell, °wounded with an °arrow.

Bearer
Count Maurizio °Pietra

Reference
°Petrarch

Domenichi *Devises* London 1585 Hiii^v	Domenichi *Devises* London 1585 Hiii^v

Motto
Quod huic deest me °torquet.

What this creature lacks °torments me.

Picture
A °lizard.

Commentary
The °lizard, unlike other creatures, does not °love.

Bearer
Frederico °Gonzaga, Duke of Mantua

Motto
°Perculsus °elevor.

Though °struck I am °raised.

Picture
A °ball hit high by a strong °arm.

Bearer
Carlo °Ursino

Domenichi *Devises* London 1585 Hiiii^v

Motto
°Lamazabatani. [Hebrew]

Why have you °forsaken me?

Picture
A °gold °ring set with °false °diamond.

Bearer
anonymous young gallant of °Salerno

Reference
°B Matt 17.46

Domenichi *Devises* London 1585 Hv^r

Motto
°Lasciai di me la meglior parte a dietro.
I °left the better part of me behind.

Picture
An °elephant, without °tusks.

Bearer
Count Clemente °Pietro

Reference
°Pliny
°Petrarch

Domenichi *Devises* London 1585 Hiiii^v

Motto
Di °amante °falso.
[understood pun on "false diamond"]

Say, °false °lover.

Picture
A °gold °ring set with °false °diamond.

Bearer
anonymous young gallant of °Salerno.

Domenichi *Devises* London 1585 Hv^r

Motto
Hinc sola °salus.

This is my only °salvation.

Picture
A °raven °fighting a °chameleon.

Bearer
Count Clemente °Pietro

Domenichi *Devises* London 1585 Hvʳ

Motto
°Aude aliquid °dignum.

°Dare something °worthy.

Picture
An °eagle °flying near °sun, °burning its
°feathers.

Bearer
Count Clemente °Pietro

Domenichi *Devises* London 1585 Hvᵛ

Motto
Sic °frustra.

Thus in °vain1.

Picture
A °remora holding fast a °ship under
°sail.

Bearer
Giovanni Battista °Bottigella

Reference
°Pliny

Domenichi *Devises* London 1585 Hvʳ

Motto
Ex hoc in hoc.

For this reason.

Picture
A °sword.

Bearer
Count Clemente °Pietro

Domenichi *Devises* London 1585 Hvᵛ

Motto
His °ducibus.

With these as °guides.

Picture
A decorated °sword entwined by a °serpent
holding in its mouth a °garland of
°laurel.

Bearer
Ippolito °Girami

Domenichi *Devises* London 1585 Hv^v

Motto
°Flectimur °obsequio non °viribus.

We °bend out of °compliance and not because of °force.

Picture
A °palm-tree.

Domenichi *Devises* London 1585 Hvi^r

Motto
°Frustra °vigilant.

They stand °guard in °vain1.

Picture
°Argus guarding °Io in the form of a °cow.

Domenichi *Devises* London 1585 Hvir

Motto
°Vertitur ad °solem.

It turns towards the °sun.

Picture
A °marigold turning towards °sun.

Bearer
Livia °Tormiella

Domenichi *Devises* London 1585 Hvi^v

Motto
Est mihi °sorte datum.

It is given to me by °chance.

Picture
An °eagle, possibly carrying °Jupiter's °lightning °bolts in his °talons.

Bearer
Girolamo °Pallavicino

Domenichi *Devises* London 1585 Hvi[v]

Motto
°Proprio alitur °succo.

It °nourishes itself from its own °moisture.

Picture
A °snail in its °shell.

Domenichi *Devises* London 1585 Hvii[r]

Motto
°Ingenium °superat °vires.

°Talent °overcomes °strength.

Picture
A °cross-bow °bent with a °rack.

Bearer
Consalvo °Fernando

Domenichi *Devises* London 1585 Hvii[r]

Motto
°Lasciviae °penitentia.

°Penitence for °lasciviousness.

Picture
A °buck °lying in a °ditch.

Bearer
unnamed °Dutch gentleman living in °Naples.

Domenichi *Devises* London 1585 Hvii[r]

Motto
Esto tiene su °remedio y non yo.

This creature has his °remedy, but I do not.

Picture
An °hart °wounded by an °arrow, with the °herb °dictamnum in its °mouth.

Reference
Phoebus' complaint to Daphne cited in °Ovid: "Hei mihi quod nullis amor est medicabilis herbis". [Alas for me, love can be cured by no herbs].

Domenichi *Devises* London 1585 Hvii[v]

Motto
Soli °Caesari.

To °Caesar alone.

Picture
Julius °Caesar's °horse with °human °forefeet.

Bearer
Pyrho di °Stipiciana

Reference
°Pliny

Domenichi *Devises* London 1585 Hviii[r]

Motto
°Pistos soi °parameno [Gk].

I shall °remain °faithfully with you.

Picture
A °sword.

Bearer
A "noble minded gentleman"

Domenichi *Devises* London 1585 Hvii[v]

Motto
Quod me °alit me °extinguit.

That which °nourishes me °extinguishes me.

Picture
A °burning °torch, °inverted, the °flames being °extinguished by °melting °wax.

Bearer
unnamed amorous gentleman of °Milan.

GEFFREY WHITNEY

A CHOICE OF EMBLEMES AND OTHER DEVISES

(LEYDEN: PLANTIN, 1586)

edited by

Peter M. Daly and Anthony Raspa

Geffrey Whitney, 1548–1601

A Choice of Emblemes and other Devises,

Leyden: Plantin, 1586

4°: *4 **4 ***2 A–Z4 a–f4
[20] 230 pp [2]

250 emblems

A CHOICE
OF EMBLEMES,
AND OTHER DEVISES,

For the moſte parte gathered out of ſundrie writers,
Engliſhed and Moralized.
AND DIVERS NEWLY DEVISED,
by Geffrey Whitney.

A worke adorned with varietie of matter, both pleaſant and profitable: whe-
rein thoſe that pleaſe, maye finde to fit their fancies: Bicauſe herein, by the
office of the eie, and the eare, the minde maye reape dooble delighte throu-
ghe holſome preceptes, ſhadowed with pleaſant deuiſes: both fit for the
vertuous, to their incoraging: and for the wicked, for their admoniſhing
and amendment.

To the Reader.
Peruſe with heede, then frendlie iudge, and blaming raſhe refraine:
So maiſt thou reade vnto thy good, and ſhalt requite my paine.

Imprinted at LEYDEN,
In the houſe of Chriſtopher Plantyn,
by Francis Raphelengius.
M. D. LXXXVI.

STUDIES

Bath, Michael. 'Whitney's Concluding Emblem and the Legend of the Oldest Animals,' *RES*, NS 33 (1982), 295-96.

Chew, Samuel C. *The Pilgrimage of Life*. New Haven & London: Yale University Press, 1962, p 286.

Fieler, Frank B. 'Introduction' to *A Choice of Emblemes*. N.Y.: Benjamin Blom, 1967, pp ix-xvii.

Freeman, Rosemary. *English Emblem Books*. 1948; rpt. London: Chatto & Windus, 1967, pp 56-61, 233.

Gordon, Donald. '"Veritas Filia Temporis": Hadrianus Junius and Geoffrey Whitney,' *JWCI*, 3 (1940), 228-40.

Green, Henry. 'Introductory Dissertation' and 'Essays Literary and Bibliographical,' in *A Choice of Emblemes*. London: Lovell Reeves, 1866; rpt. New York: Benjamin Blom, 1967.

Horden, John. 'Note' to *A Choice of Emblemes (1586)*. Menston: Scolar, 1969.

Hunter, G.K. 'Madrigal Verses from Whitney's *Choice of Emblems*,' *N&Q*, 7 (1960), 215-16.

Hunter, Kathryn. 'Geoffrey Whitney's "To Richard Cotton, Esq.": An Early English Country-House Poem,' *RES*, ns 28 (1977), 438-41.

Klein, Joan Larsen. '*Hamlet*, IV.ii.12-21 and Whitney's *A Choice of Emblemes*,' *N&Q*, 23 (1976), 158-69.

Leisher, John Franklin. 'Geoffrey Whitney's *Choice of Emblemes* and Its Relation to the Emblematic Vogue in Tudor England.' Diss. Harvard University, 1952.
New York: Garland, 1987.

Madelaine, R.E.R. '*The Duchess of Malfi* and Two Emblems in Whitney and Peacham,' *N&Q*, 29 (1982), 146-7.

Manning, John. 'Unpublished and Unedited Emblems by Geffrey Whitney: Further Evidence of the English Adaptation of Continental Traditions,' *The English Emblem and the Continental Tradition*. Ed. Peter M. Daly. New York: AMS Press, 1988, in press.

Nolde, Sister M. Simon. 'Whitney's *A Choice of Emblemes* & Three Commonplace Collections of Erasmus.' Diss. St. Louis, 1964.

Pollard, A.W. and G.R. Redgrave. *A Short-Title Catalogue of Books Printed in England, Scotland, and Ireland and of English Books Printed Abroad 1475-1640*. London: Bibliographical Society, 1926. Revised 2nd ed. W.A. Jackson, F.S.

Ferguson, Katharine F. Pantzer (2 of 3 vols. available - 1 A-H, 2 I-Z), 1976, 1986. #25438.

Praz, Mario. *Studies in Seventeenth-Century Imagery*, 2nd edition. Rome: Edizioni di Storia e Letteratura, 1964, pp 205-6, 219-22, 228, 535.

Richards, Bernard. 'Whitney's Influence on Shakespeare's Sonnets 111 and 112, and on Donne's Third Satire,' *N&Q*, 27 (1980), 160-61.

Rusche, H.G. 'Two Proverbial Images in Whitney's *A Choice of Emblemes* and Marlowe's *The Jew of Malta*,' *N&Q*, 11 (1964), 261.

Sayle, Charles E. *Early English Printed Books in the University Library Cambridge*, 4 vols. Cambridge: University Press, 1900-1907, no 6496.

Scott, Mary Augusta. *Elizabethan Translations from the Italian*. 1916; rpt. Boston & New York: Burt Franklin, 1969.

Stroup, Thomas B. 'Dido, the Phoenix, and Milton's Sonnet XVIII,' *Milton Quarterly*, 4 (1970), 60.

Thron, E. Michael. 'Jaques: Emblems and Morals,' *SQ*, 30 (1979), 84-9.

Tramer, Irma. 'Studien zu den Anfängen der puritanischen Emblemliteratur in England: Andrew Willet - George Whitney.' Diss. Berlin, 1934.

Tung, Mason. 'Emblematic Inventions of Alciati and Whitney," *EM*, 24 (1973-74), 9-17.

_____. 'Whitney's *A Choice of Emblemes* Revisited: A Comparative Study of the Manuscript and the Printed Versions," *SB*, 29 (1976), 32-101.

Wilson, Gayle Edward. 'Dryden and the Emblem of Fortuna-Occasion,' *PLL*, 11 (1975), 199-203.

_____. 'Emblems in *Paradise Regained*,' *Milton Quarterly*, 6(1972), 77-81.

INTRODUCTORY NOTE

Geffrey Whitney's *A Choice of Emblemes* was published in 1586 by the Plantin press in Leyden (opened in 1583 and operated from 1585 by Plantin's son-in-law Francis Raphelengius). There was only one printed edition, but we are fortunate in also having the manuscript version (Harvard MS. Typ 14) which was presented to Robert Dudley, Earl of Leicester on, according to the printed 'Epistle Dedicatorie,' 28 November 1585.[1]

The manuscript is bound in sixteenth-century vellum and contains 98 folios. It consists of 197 emblematic drawings in pen-and-ink, sepia, and blue watercolour, with the text of mottoes, poems, and some marginalia (a fraction of that in the printed *Choice*) written in a clear Italic hand.[2] The existence of this copy affords us an unusual and fruitful opportunity to study the changes in emblem iconography when a work moves from a private to a public forum. John Manning has examined the manuscript, particularly the emblems dropped from the printed version, and declares: 'These suppressed emblems express the nature of the original, more intimate and private communication between poet and patron, and through them we gain some insight into the poet's expectations of his patron's moral and political views, and of his literary taste.'[3] Whitney evidently felt some changes were called for when he prepared his work for publication. Although the larger part of *Choice* remains the same, a few emblems were omitted, others added, some verses altered to suit their new pictures, the marginalia increased, dedications added, and so on.

Leicester left England for the Low Countries on December 8, 1585 (just ten days after being presented with the manuscript), as the Queen's Lord Lieutenant and Captain General of the English forces aiding the Dutch in their struggle against Spain. Whitney followed as a supernumerary in the train of Janus Dousa, rector of the University of Leyden and an ambassador sent by the Dutch States General to ask for Queen Elizabeth's aid. Leicester was in Leyden during January 1586, and Whitney seems to have been present when he was entertained as the honoured guest at the University on January 11.

It is possibly at this time that Whitney was persuaded to publish his emblem book. After he had presented his collection of emblems to Leicester, as he tells us in 'To the Reader,' he was 'earnestlie required by somme that perused the same, to have it imprinted: whose requeste, when I had well considered, althoughe I did perceive the charge was verie heavie for mee .... Yet knowinge their favours to bee such unto mee, as in dewtie I mighte not denie them any thinge I can: I did rather choose to undergoe any burthen, and almoste fainte in forwardnes to satisfie them, then to shewe anie wante of good will, in denyinge their continuall desires.' Whitney took rooms close to the University and the Plantin printing shop and matriculated from the University of Leyden on March 1, 1586. Fieler goes so far as to suggest that the printing of Choice may have been politically motivated as part of the campaign to glorify Leicester in preparation for his assuming sovereign power in the Low Countries.[4]

The printed *Choice* was completed 4 May 1586, the date of 'To the Reader.' Whitney thus had a very short time - three to four months - to revise his manuscript and choose woodcuts for it from the enormous Plantin stock. The speed of revision and printing shows in the many punctuation and spelling errors, and in the discrepancies between picture and verse in emblems 33, 82, 94, 100, and 169. In the manuscript it had been possible to alter the drawn picture from its original to suit Whitney's verse. When these drawings were replaced with the already existing woodblocks, Whitney evidently did not always have time to alter his verse to conform with the pictures. Another sign of the hasty preparation for publication is the order of the emblems in *Choice*. In the manuscript the emblems are ordered so that no more than three are together from each source. This pattern is disrupted in the printed version, and the only rationale behind the change seems to be a need to place the emblems that would take longer to ready for printing in the later stages of the book. We therefore find all but one of Whitney's newly devised emblems and all those emblems with woodcuts copied from emblem books not published by Plantin in the second part of *Choice*.

On his title-page Whitney describes *Choice* as 'For the moste parte gathered out of sundrie writers, Englished and Moralized. And Divers Newly Devised.' An attractive book, its printing was made possible by the large number of woodcut blocks the Plantin press possessed from its printings of earlier Continental emblem books. Compared to 197 emblems in the manuscript, the printed Choice has 247 woodcuts (with one naked emblem, p 61) – 113 emblems in Part 1 and 135 in Part 2. Of these woodcuts, 207 are identical with their sources, being printed from the same woodblocks, 25 are copied from their sources (the original books having not been printed by Plantin), and 15 'newly devised.' Mason Tung lists the following as the sources for the woodcuts,[5] with Montenay, Aneau, and La Perrière being copied, the others printed from the same woodblocks:

Alciato, *Emblemata* 1577 – 87
Sambucus, *Emblemata* 1564 & 1576 – 51
Paradin, *Symbola Heroica* 1567 – 32
Junius, *Emblemata* 1585 – 21
Faerno, *Fabula Centum* 1573 – 16
Montenay, *Emblèmes* 1571 – 9
Aneau, *Picta Poesis* 1552 – 8
La Perrière, *Le Theatre* 1545 – 8

Whitney also borrowed most of his mottoes from his sources. According to Tung, 'only 79 mottoes differ from their source emblems. Of these 11 are of minor changes' (p 43).

On the whole, Whitney treats the sources for his verses with great freedom. Approximately half the verses are close to their originals, but the rest are widely altered, particularly through Whitney's expansion of the moral and its applications. A variety of verse and stanza forms appear in *Choice*, such as poulter's measure, or four or ten lines of iambic pentameter. The most common is the sextet, a verse of iambic pentameter rhyming ababcc, well suited to Whitney's style of exposition of the woodcut and moral application.

Marginal annotations had been added to emblem books for many years. Alciato's *Emblemata*, for example, was annotated from 1549 onward, and Claude Mignault's extensive commentaries began to appear in Plantin editions of *Emblemata* in 1573. Whitney has his own reasons for adding marginalia, which he explains in his 'To the Reader': 'I have now in diverse places, quoted in the margent some sentences in Latin, & such verses as I thoughte did beste fit the severall matters I wratte of .... First I noted the same in Latin, to helpe

... some of my acquaintaunce wheare this booke was imprinted, who havinge no taste in the Englishe tonge, yet weare earnestly addicted to the understandinge hereof: and also, wheare I founde any verse, of sayinge agreable with the matter, I did gather the same of purpose for my owne memorie, not doubtinge but the same may bee also frutefull to others.' Ovid is the most frequently cited author by far, followed by Horace, the Bible, Reusner, Virgil, Alciato, Propertius, Aelian, Pliny, Claudius, and Seneca. Renaissance authors such as Aeneas Silvius (Pope Pius II), Angelo Poliziano Ambrogini (Politianus), Coelius Augustinus Curio, Joachim du Bellay, Antonio de Guevara, William Lily, Sir Thomas More, Erasmus, and Georgius Sabinus are also to be found.[6] In his title page, half title page and epistle to Leicester, Whitney takes great pains to emphasize his 'newly devised' emblems - 15 in number (95, 112, 114, 129, 131, 145, 161, 167, 168a, 184, 185, 198, 203, 225, 230). This list of emblems not traced to other sources may diminish with more research, as Green predicted in his time (p 237), and as Tung currently points out (p 75), though it is unlikely that any new emblematic sources will be found.

NOTES

1   Another manuscript version of some of the mottoes and poems of *Choice* does exist (Bodleian MS Rawlinson poetry 56). It is now generally agreed, however, that it is a copy of part of the printed book made by an unknown admirer for Mistress Elizabeth Parrott. See Rosemary Freeman, *English Emblem Books* (London: Chatto & Windus, 1967), p 237; John F. Leisher, 'Geoffrey Whitney's *Choice of Emblemes* and Its Relation to the Emblematic Vogue in Tudor England,' Diss. Harvard University, 1952, (New York: Garland, 1987), p 404; Frank B. Fieler, 'Introduction' to *A Choice of Emblemes* (New York: Benjamin Blom, 1967), pp x-xi.

2   For a more complete description of the manuscript *Choice* see Mason Tung, 'Whitney's *A Choice of Emblemes* Revisited: A Comparative Study of the Manuscript and the Printed Versions,' *SB*, 29 (1976), 35ff; and Fieler, p xi.

3   John Manning, 'Unpublished and Unedited Emblems by Geffrey Whitney: Further Evidence of the English Adaptation of Continental Traditions,' *The English Emblem and the Continental Tradition*, edited by Peter M. Daly (New York: AMS Press, 1988), in press.

4   Fieler, p xiii.

5   Mason Tung's article supersedes and corrects the early work done by Henry Green on the sources of *Choice*, published in his facsimile edition of *Choice* (1866), reprinted by Blom, 1967.

6   Tung, p 63.

A Note on Reduction and Montage

Reproductions are reduced to 93%, and where the text runs over to the following page in the original, it has been gathered onto the same page in this edition. Whitney's marginalia, which appeared to the left of his emblems, have been moved to the right to allow for larger reproductions. Because of the poor quality of the original and the level of reduction these marginalia are frequently difficult to read, and the reader is advised to consult the original size facsimile reprints by Scholar Press or Benjamin Blom.

REFERENCES AND ABBREVIATIONS

Whitney quoted all proper names in Latin since his marginalia are in Latin throughout, e.g. Anulus rather than Aneau, Morus for Sir Thomas More. However, most modern users of this volume will expect vernacular forms, and so to facilitate searches, we have cited all names in their usual vernacular forms, the exception being names of classical writers. An author's name is accompanied by an abbreviated reference to one of his works, unless Whitney, as is often the case, failed to mention the title.

In order to make it easier to follow up Whitney's references, we have retained his choice of titles, where necessary indicating in brackets the proper title. For instance, Whitney refers in a shoulder note to a work by Eutropius, which he entitles *Rerum Romanarum Libri*, the proper title of which is *Breviarium ab urbe condita*. The column showing Whitney's citation of title also contains Whitney's Latinized spelling of the author's name, which is important in cases where the identity of the writer is a matter of conjecture.

We have not attempted to verify the accuracy of Whitney's references. Elizabethans were somewhat lax in their citations, which have more the function of rhetorical evidence by *testimonia* than they are scholarship in the modern sense.

Abbreviation	Whitney's Citation of Name and Title
Aelian, V H	Aelianus, *Varia Historia*
Aelian, N A	Aelianus, *De natura animalium*
Aeneas Sylvius, R G A	Aeneas Sylvius [Piccolomini Pope Pius II], *Commentarium de rebus gestis Alphonsi*
Alciato	Andreas Alciatus
Alciato, Emblem	Andreas Alciatus, *Emblemata*, [Padua: Tozzi, 1621]
Ambrose	Ambrosius
Anacreon	Anacreon
Aneau, Pict poes	Anulus, *Picta poesis*
Anselm	Anselmus
Apollinaris, Ep	Sidonius Apollinaris, *Epistulae*
Appianus, Hann	Appianus, *Hannibal*
Appianus, Mithr	Appianus, *De bellis Mithridaticis*
Appianus, B. Civ. 1	*Appianus, De bellis civilibus*
Augustine, Ep	Augustinus, *Epistulae*
Augustine, Psa	Augustinus, *Enarrationes in Psalmos*
Aurelius Victor	Sextus Aurelius Victor
Ausonius, Ed	Ausonius, *Edyllia*
Ausonius, Epigr	Ausonius, *Epigrammata*
B Acts	Bible, Acts of the Apostles
B Cor	Bible, Corinthians

B Eccl	Bible, Ecclesiastes
B Ep	Bible, Epistles
B Eph	Bible, Ephesians
B Esd	Bible, Esdras
B Gen	Bible, Genesis
B Isa	Bible, Isaiah
B Jdg	Bible, Judges
B Jud	Bible, Jude
B Ki	Bible, Kings
B 1Macc	Bible, Maccabees
B Mk	Bible, Mark
B Pet	Bible, Peter
B Rom	Bible, Romans
B Tim	Bible, Timothy
Bellay, Joachim du	Belleius
Bernard, Ep	Bernardus, *Epistulae*
Bias	Bias
Bourgogne(?)	Antoine de Borbonius [= Borgonius?]
Cato, Num P 2 R R	Cato, *Origines* (Numa Pompilius 2 Romanus Rex)
Cato, R R	Cato, *De re rustica*
Chrysostom, Hom	Chrysostomus, *Homiliarium*
Cicero, Coel	Cicero, *Pro Coelio*
Cicero, Off	Cicero, *De officiis*
Cicero, Or	Cicero, *De oratore*
Cicero, Phil	Cicero, *Philippicae*
Cicero, Tusc	Cicero, *Tusculanae disputationes*
Claudian, Ad Hon	Claudianus, *Ad Honorium*
Claudian, IV Cons Hon	Claudianus, *De quarto consulatu Honorii*
Claudian, Sen ver	Claudianus, *De sene Veronensi*
Claudian, Stil	Claudianus, *De consulatu Stilichonis*
Claudian, Nupt Hon	Claudianus, *De nuptiis Honorii et Mariae*
Claudius, In Ruf	Claudianus, *In Rufinium*
Crates Thebanus	Crates Thebanus
Curio, Coelius	Coelius Curio
Demetrius Phalereus	Demetrius Phalereus, *De elocutione*
Demosthenes, Arg I	Demosthenes, *Aristogiton*, I
Diodorus Sic	Diodorus Siculus
Erasmus, Adag	Erasmus, *Adagia*
Erasmus, Chil	Erasmus, *Chiliades* [= *Adagia*]
Erasmus, Ep	Erasmus, *Epistolae*
Eutropius, Pun	Eutropius, *De Bello punico*
Eutropius, R Rom	Eutropius, *Rerum Romanarum libri* [= *Breviarium ab urbe condita*]
Faerno, Fab	Faernus, *Fabulae centum*
Cornelius Gallus	Cornelius Gallus
Gellius, N A	Aulus Gellius, *De Laide* [= *Noctes Atticae*]
Gellius, N A	Aulus Gellius, *De laude silentii* [= *Noctes Atticae*]
Gellius, N A	Aulus Gellius, *De vaniloquio* [= *Noctes Atticae*]
Giraldi, Battista	Baptista Gyraldus

Gregory, Mor	Gregorius, *Moralia*
Gregory, Hom	Gregorius, *Homiliarium*
Guevara, Ep	Antonio de Guevara, *Epistulae*
Herodotus	Herodotus
Horace, A P	Horatius, *Ars poetica*
Horace, C	Horatius, *Carmina* [= *Odes*]
Horace, Ep	Horatius, *Epistulae*
Horace, Sat	Horatius, *Saturae*
Horace, Ser	Horatius, *Sermones* [= *Saturae et epistulae*]
Isidore, Etym	Isidorus, *Etymologiae*
Isidore, Sent	Isidorus, *Sententiarum libri tres*
Isidore, Sol	Isidorus, *Soliloquium*
Jerome, Ep	Hieronymus, *Epistulae*
Junius, Emblem	Hadrianus Junius, *Emblemata*
Juvenal, Sat	Juvenalis, *Saturae*
Lucan	Lucanus, *Pharsalia*
Lucretius	Lucretius, *De rerum natura*
Maffei, Raffaele, Pol	Volaterranus, *Politica Praecepta*
Martial, Sat	Martialis, *De falce ex ense* [= *Saturae*]
Martial, Sat	Martialis, *Ad Regulum* [= *Saturae*]
Maximianus	Maximianus
Mignault, Claude	Minois [= Minos]
Moecenas	*In Maecenatis obitum* [post-Virgilian text included in a IX C. Virgilian MS]
More, Epig	Morus, *Epigrammata*
Nemesianus, Ecl	Nemesianus, *Eclogae*
Nepos, Cornelius	Cornelius Nepos
Ovid, A A	Ovidius, *Ars amatoria*
Ovid, Am	Ovidius, *Amores*
Ovid, Ep	Ovidius, *Heroides* [= *Epistulae*]
Ovid, F	Ovidius, *Fasti*
Ovid, Med Fac	Ovidius, *Medicamina faciei*
Ovid, Rem Am	Ovidius, *Remedia Amoris*
Ovid, Met	Ovidius, *Metamorphoses*
Ovid, Pont	Ovidius, *Epistulae ex Ponto*
Ovid, Trist	Ovidius, *Tristia*
Paulinus Nolanus, Ep	Paulinus Nolanus, *Epistulae*
Palladius Soranus	Palladius Soranus [= ?Palladius Rutilius Taurus Aemilianus, *Opus agriculturae*]
Persius	Persius, *Saturae*
Petronius Arb	Petronius Arbiter, *Cena Trimalchionis* [= in *Satyricon*]
Petrarch, Rem	Petrarch, *De remediis utriusque fortunae*
Pindar	Pindarus
Platina(?), Bartolomeo D P	Plat., *De prosperitate* [= Seneca, *De Providentia*]
Plautus, Amph	Plautus, *Amphitruo*
Plautus, Aul	Plautus, *Aulularia*
Plautus, Capt	Plautus, *Captivi*
Plautus, Poen	Plautus, *Poenulus*
Plautus, Rud	Plautus, *Rudens*

Pliny, H N	Plinius, *Historia naturalis*
Plutarch, Ama	Plutarchus, *Amatorius*
Plutarch, L E	Plutarchus, *De liberis educandis*
Plutarch, Mor	Plutarchus, *Moralia*
Plutarch, Vit Marc	Plutarchus, *Vita Marcelli*
Plutarch, Is et Os	Plutarchus, *De Iside et Osiride*
Plutarch, Serm	Plutarchus, *Sermones*
Poliziano, Angelo	Politianus, Angelus
Propertius	Propertius, *Elegiae*
Reusner, Parad poet	Reusnerus, *Paradisus poeticus*
Ricci, Pietro, P L	Petrus Crinitus, *De poetis latinis*
Ricci, Pietro, H D	Petrus Crinitus, *De honesta disciplina*
Roville(?), Guillaume	Guillaume Lill' [= Guillaume Roville de Lille]
Sabellicus	Sabellicus
Sabine, George	Georgius Sabinus
Sambucus	Joannes Sambucus, *Emblemata*
Seneca, Agam	Seneca, *Agamemnon*
Seneca, Herc Fur	Seneca, *Hercules Furens*
Seneca, Hipp	Seneca, *Hippolitus* [= *Phaedra*]
Seneca, Oct	Seneca, *Octavia*
Seneca, Oed	Seneca, *Oedipus*
Seneca, Tranq	Seneca, *De tranquillitate animi*
Seneca, Troad	Seneca, *Troades*
Servius	Servius, Commentary on Virgil Aen. VI. De littera y
Silvius	see Aeneas Sylvius
Silius, Pun	Silius Italicus, *Punica*
Stobaeus	Stobaeus
Suetonius, Ner	Suetonius, *Nero*
Terence, Adelph	Terentius, *Adelphi*
Terence, And	Terentius, *Andria*
Tertullian	Tertullianus, *Apologia*
Theocritus	Theocritus, *Edyllia*
Tibullus	Tibullus, *Elegiae*
Tremellius	Tremellius [translator of the Bible]
Valerius Maximus	Valerius Maximus
Virgil, Aetna	Virgilius, *Aetna*
Virgil, Aen	Virgilius, *Aeneis*
Virgil, Ecl	Virgilius, *Eclogae*
Virgil, Geor	Virgilius, *Georgicon*
Vegetius	Renatus Vegetius

Whitney *Emblemes* Leyden 1586 p.001

Te ſtante, virebo.

Motto

Te °stante, °virebo

With you °standing, I shall °flourish.

Picture

A °spire or pointed °obelisk, set on a °plinth, entwined with °ivy.

Epigram

spire ivy bloom pillar princess [= Elizabeth] branch church storm tyrant fire sword persecution free foe queen [= Elizabeth]

A MIGHTIE Spyre, whoſe toppe dothe pierce the ſkie,
  An iuie greene imbraceth rounde about,
And while it ſtandes, the ſame dotĥ bloome on highe,
But when it ſhrinkes, the iuie ſtandes in dowt:
    The Piller great, our gratious Princes is:
    The braunche, the Churche: whoe ſpeakes vnto hir this.

I, that of late with ſtormes was almoſte ſpent,
And bruſed ſore with Tirants bluddie bloes,
Whome fire, and ſworde, with perſecution rent,
Am nowe ſett free, and ouerlooke my foes,
    And whiles thow raignſt, oh moſt renowmed Queene
    By thie ſupporte my bloſſome ſhall bee greene.

Whitney   *Emblemes*   London   1586   p.002

Qua dij vocant, eundum.

Motto
Qua °dij °vocant, °eundum.

Where the °gods °call, we must °go.

Picture
Seated beside a roadway, wearing a °winged °helmet and holding a °caduceus, °Mercury points to the °path at his feet. In the right background a °traveller with a °staff walks away from a standing fig-ure with outstretched arms.

Epigram
travel   Mercury   path   journey   Lord
guide   stumble   fall   God

THE trauaylinge man, vncertaine where to goe,
　When diuers wayes before his face did lie,
Mercurius then, the perfect pathe did showe,
Which when he tooke, hee neuer went awrie,
　　But to his wifhe, his iorneys ende did gaine
　　In happie howre, by his direction plaine.

This trauailinge man : doth tell our wandringe ftate,
Before whofe face, and eeke on euerye fide,
Bypathes, and wayes, appeare amidd our gate,
That if the Lorde bee not our onlie guide:
　　We ftumble, fall, and dailie goe aftraye,
　　Then happie thofe, whome God doth fhew the waye.

Whitney *Emblemes* London 1586 p.003

°Prouidentia.

Svche prouidence hathe nature secret wroughte
In creatures wilde, and eeke such knowledge straunge,
That man, by them in somme thinges maie be taughte,
As some foretell, when weather faire will chaunge,
Of heate, of raine, of winde, and tempests rage,
Some showe by signes, and with their songs presage.

But leauing theise, which almost all doe knowe,
The Crocodile, by whome th'Ægyptians watche,
Howe farre that yeare shall mightie Nilus flowe,
For theire shee likes to laie her egges, and hatche,
Suche skill deuine, and science to foretell,
Hath Nature lente vnto this Serpent fell.

Which showes, They should with due regarde foresee,
When anie one doth take in hande a cause,
The drifte, and ende, of that they doe decree,
And longe thereon to ponder, and to pause,
For after witts, are like a shower of rayne
Which moistes the soile, when withered is the graine.

Motto
°Providentia.

°Foresight.

Picture
A °crocodile, presumably laying her °eggs, on the bank of a °river (°Nile).

Epigram
Providence nature creature knowledge teach foretell crocodile Egyptian Nile egg hatch science serpent

Reference
Nicholas °Reusner

Nic. Reusnerus.
Quò sacer excurret Nilus in arua
Præscius: adunte libera ponit
Oua: monens merito nos Crocodilus
Quæ fata immineant, ante videre.

Veritas temporis filia.

Whitney *Emblemes* London 1586 p.004

THREE furies fell, which turne the worlde to ruthe,
Both Enuie, Strife, and Slaunder, heare appeare,
In dungeon darke they longe inclofed truthe,
But Time at lengthe, did loofe his daughter deare,
And fetts alofte, that facred ladie brighte,
Whoe things longe hidd, reueales, and bringes to lighte.

Thoughe ftrife make fier, thoughe Enuie eate hir harte,
The innocent though Slaunder rente, and fpoile:
Yet Time will comme, and take this ladies parte,
And breake her bandes, and bring her foes to foile.
Difpaire not then, thoughe truthe be hidden ofte,
Bycaufe at lengthe, fhee fhall bee fett alofte.

Motto

°Veritas °temporis °filia.

°Truth, the °daughter of °Time.

Picture

On the right, °winged °Time, holding a a °scythe liberates a kneeling figure of °Truth from a cave. On the left °snake-haired °Envy eats her °heart; °Strife stands on a °bellows with her foot and holds an °inverted °torch to the ground. °Slander, holding an upright °torch, has her hand on the brow of a kneeling figure whose °hands are clasped in °supplication.

Epigram

three Furies Envy Strife Slander dungeon Truth Time daughter fire heart band foe

Diſſidia inter æquales, peſſima.

Motto
°Dissidia inter °aequales, °pessima.

°Dissensions among °equals are the °worst.

Picture
In the top left, a °swallow with a °grasshopper in its °beak returns to its °nest situated among the °ruins of a °palace.

Epigram
swallow nest grasshopper danger love time friend tyrant God gift grace name envy virtue foe

T H E Swallowe ſwifte, dothe beare vnto her neſte
The Graſshopper, that did no daunger feare,
For that ſhee thought, they louide togeather beſte,
Bycauſe they both, obſerude one time of yeare,
    And bothe, did ioye theire iarringe notes to ſounde,
    And neare the houſe they bothe, theire dwellings founde.

Yet time, and tune, and neighbourhood forgotte,
For perfect frende, a tyrant ſhee became,
Which taxeth thoſe, whome God dothe heare allotte
Like gifts of grace, to winne a laſting name,
    Yet Enuie ſoe theire vertues doth deface,
    It makes them foes, to them theie ſhould imbrace.

Alciatus.
Stridula ſtridentem, vernam
verna, hoſpita ladu
Hoſpitam, & aligeram pen-
niger ales auera?

      Formica grata eſt formica, Cicada cicada
      Et doctis doctus gaudet Apollo choris.

Nic.Reuſnerus.

Reference
Andrea °Alciato
Nicholas °Reusner

Whitney *Emblemes* London 1586 p.006

Temeritas.

Motto
°Temeritas.

°Rashness.

Picture
A °charioteer, with a °whip in one hand, tries to °rein in, with his other hand, the °two galloping °horses pulling his °chariot.

Epigram
wagoner   rein   horse   fierce   tame   order
havoc   man   affection   soul   untamed
reason   bridle   will   guide

THE waggoner, behoulde, is hedlonge throwen,
And all in vaine doth take the raine in hande,
If he be dwrawen by horſes fierce vnknowen,
Whoſe ſtomacks ſtowte, no taming vnderſtande,
    They praunce, and yerke, and out of order flinge,
    Till all they breake, and vnto hauocke bringe.

That man, whoe hath affections fowle vntamde,
And forwarde runnes neglecting reaſons race;
Deſerues by right, of all men to bee blamde,
And headlonge falles at lengthe to his deface,
    Then bridle will, and reaſon make thy guide,
    So maiſte thow ſtande, when others downe doe ſlide.

Intestinæ simultates.

Whitney *Emblemes* London 1586 p.007

WHEN ciuill sworde is drawen out of the sheathe,
  And bluddie broiles, at home are set a broache,
Then furious Mars with sworde doth rage beneathe,
And to the Toppe, deuowring flames incroache,
  None helpes to quenche, but rather blowes the flame,
  And oile doe adde, and powder to the same.

Inteſtine ſtrife, is fearefull moſte of all,
This, makes the Sonne, to cut his fathers throate,
This, parteth frendes, this, brothers makes to bralle,
This, robbes the good, and ſetts the theeues a floate,
  This, Rome did feele, this, Germanie did taſte,
  And often times, this noble Lande did waſte.

Motto
°Intestinae °simultates.

°Internal °dissensions.

Picture
At the right an °arsonist sets °fire to a °house; at the left, a second man, carrying a °bucket of °oil, scales a °ladder placed against the wall of the burning house. At the foot of the ladder, a third man °stabs another man, still resisting, who has been forced to the ground.

Epigram
civil sword bloody home Mars rage flame oil powder intestine strife son cut father throat rob brother thief friend Rome Germany land [= England]

Whitney *Emblemes* London 1586 p.008

Non tibi, sed Religioni.

THE paftors good, that doe gladd tidinges preache,
  The godlie forte, with reuerence do imbrace:
Though they be men, yet fince Godds worde they teache,
Wee honor them, and giue them higheste place,
    Imbaffadors of princes of the earthe,
    Haue royall Seates, thoughe bafe they are by birthe.

Yet, if throwghe pride they doe them felues forgett,
And make accompte that honor, to be theires:
And doe not marke with in whofe place they fett,
Let them behowlde the affe, that I S I S beares,
    Whoe thowghte the men to honor him, did kneele,
    And ftaied therfore, till he the ftaffe did feele.

For, as he paff'd with I S I S throughe the ftreete,
And bare on backe, his holie rites about,
Th'Ægyptians downe fell proftrate at his feete,
Whereat, the Affe, grewe arrogante and ftowte,
    Then faide the guide: oh foole not vnto thee,
    Theife people bowe, but vnto that they fee?

Motto
Non °tibi, sed °Religioni.

Not for °you, but for °religion.

Picture
°Worshippers kneel in °reverence before an °ass bearing a °statue of °Isis; the °driver is about to °beat the °ass with a °stick.

Epigram
pastors preach godly reverence God word teach royal seat pride honour ass Isis kneel staff Egyptian prostrate arrogant guide bow

Experientia docet.

Whitney   *Emblemes*   London   1586   p.009

A YOVTHEFVLL Prince, in prime of luftie yeares,
Woulde vnderftande what weather fhoulde betide,
For that hee thoughte, with manie noble Peares
To paffe the time, on huntinge forth to ride :
　　Th'Aftronomer, did wifhe hym ftaie at courte,
　　For prefent raine, fhould hinder all their fporte.

Which ftaied the Prince, but raine did none difcende,
Then, wente hee forth with manie Gallantes braue,
But when he thought the clowdes, did droppes portend,
Hee roade afide, a plowghmans fkill to craue,
　　Whoe, looking ftraighte vppon the varijng fkie:
　　Saide, twentie daies I thinke it will bee drie.

Proceedinge.then, his iudgement true was founde,
Then, (quoth the Prince) weare thou the doctours Roabe,
And geeue to him, thy Harrowe on the grownde,
And in exchaunge, take thou his Spheare, and Gloabe :
　　And further faied, henceforthe wee will allowe,
　　That learninge fhall vnto Experience bowe.

Motto
°Experientia °docet.

°Experience °teaches.

Picture
A °king with °crown and °sceptre on a rearing °horse watches as a °ploughman gives his °harrow to an °astronomer, in exchange for a °sphere(?) or °astrolobe and presumably the °doctor's °robe.

Epigram
youthful　prince　weather　hunting astronomer　court　rain　sport　gallant cloud　ploughman　sky　twenty　day　dry judgement　doctor　robe　harrow　ground sphere　globe　learning　experience

Sirenes.

Motto
°Sirenes.

°Sirens.

Picture
°Three °mermaids, one playing a °lyre and another a °woodwind instrument, watch from the left as a rowing °galley, with °Ulysses tied to the mast, moves away to the right. A °wrecked °hull lies in the distance.

WITHE pleaſaunte tunes, the SYRENES did allure
Vliſſes wiſe, to liſten theire ſonge :
But nothinge could his manlie harte procure,
Hee ſailde awaie , and ſcap'd their charming ſtronge,
    The face, he lik'de : the nether parte, did loathe :
    For womans ſhape, and fiſhes had they bothe.

Which ſhewes to vs, when Bewtie ſeekes to ſnare
The careleſſe man, whoe dothe no daunger dreede,
That he ſhoulde flie , and ſhoulde in time beware,
And not on lookes, his fickle fancie feede :
    Suche Mairemaides liue, that promiſe onelie ioyes
    But hee that yeldes, at lengthe him ſelfe diſtroies

Virg. Aeneid.
lib. 5. & Oui-
dius lib. 5.
Metamorph.

Nic. Reuſnerus.
Illectos nautas
dulci modulamio
ne voci,
Merchant
auide fluctibus
Iorsus.

    Haec Venus ad muſas : Venerem exhorreſcite Nimpha,
    In vos armatus aut amor inſiliet.
    Cui contra muſæ, verba hæc age dicito marti :
    Altger huc ad nos non volat ille puer.

Laertij retra-
sticon hence
Claud Mi-
noem conuci-
ſum.

Epigram
siren   Ulysses   tune   listen   song   heart
charm   face   like   nether   part   loath
woman   fish   beauty   snore   careless
danger   fly   beware   fickle   fancy
mermaid   promise   joy   destroy

Reference
°Ovid, Met 5
°Virgil, Aen 5
Nicholas °Reusner
Claude °Mignault

Res humanæ in summo declinant.

THE gallante Shipp, that cutts the azure surge,
  And hathe both tide, and wisshed windes, at will:
Her tackle sure, with shotte her foes to vrge,
With Captaines boulde, and marriners of skill,
    With streamers, flagges, topgallantes, pendantes braue,
    When Seas do rage, is swallowed in the waue.

The snowe, that falles vppon the mountaines greate,
Though on the Alpes, which seeme the clowdes to reache.
Can not indure the force of Phœbus heate,
But wastes awaie, Experience doth vs teache:
    Which warneth all, on Fortunes wheele that clime
    To beare in minde how they haue but a time.

      Paßibus ambiguis fortuna volubilis errat,
        Et manet in nullo certa, tenaxq̧ loco.
      Sed modò læta manet, vultus modò sumit acerbos
      Et tantùm constans in leuitate sua est.

Periand. pet
A sson.
*Si fortuna iuuat
cauelo tolli,
Si fortuna tonat
caueto mergi.*

Ouidius 4.
pont. 3.
*Tu quoque fac
timeas, & quæ
tibi læta videtur
  Dum loqueris
fiers tristia posse
puta.*

Ouidius 5.
Tust. 9.

Whitney *Emblemes* London 1586 p.011

Motto
Res °humanae in °summo °declinant.

At their °summit, °human °affairs °decline.

Picture
A sailing ship °flounders in the waves off a °sea °shore on the left, while the °sun's rays melt °snow on °mountains in the foreground.

Epigram
ship azure surge tide wind tackle shot foe captain mariner skill streamer flag top-gallant pendant sea rage wave snow mountain Alps cloud Phoebus heat experience teach fortune wheel climb time

Reference
°Ausonius
°Ovid, Pont 4, 3
°Ovid, Trist 5 [8]

Fruſtra.

Whitney *Emblemes* London 1586 p.012

Motto
°Frustra.

In °vain1.

Picture
A °barrel punched by many small °holes °discharges °water on all sides.

Epigram
poet Danaus daughter tun toil water run reprehend three wretch ingrate covet blab secret suffice

THE Poettes faine, that DANAVS daughters deare,
Inioyned are to fill the fatall tonne:
Where, thowghe they toile, yet are they not the neare.
But as they powre, the water forthe dothe runne.
No paine will serue, to fill it to the toppe,
For, still at holes the same doth runne, and droppe.

Which reprehendes, three sortes of wretches vaine,
The blabbe, th'ingrate, and thoſe that couet still,
As firſt the blabbe, no secretts can retaine.
Th'ingrate, not knowes to vſe his frendes good will.
The couetous man, thowghe he abounde with ſtore
Is not ſuffiſde, but couetts more and more.

Whitney *Emblemes* London 1586 p.013

Superbiæ vltio.

O F NIOBE, behoulde the ruthefull plighte,
Bicaufe fhee did difpife the powers deuine:
Her children all, weare flaine within her fighte,
And, while her felfe with tricklinge teares did pine,
Shee was transformide, into a marble ftone,
Which, yet with teares, dothe feeme to waile, and mone.

This tragedie, thoughe Poëtts firft did frame,
Yet maie it bee, to euerie one applide:
That mortall men, fhoulde thinke from whence they came,
And not prefume, nor puffe them vp with pride,
Leſte that the Lorde, whoe haughty hartes doth hate, [ftate.
Doth throwe them downe, when fure they thinke theyr

Efte procul leti, cernant mea funera triſtes;
Non fimilis toto mæror in orbe fuit.
Bis feptem natos peperi, bis pignora feptem:
Me miferam! Diuûm fuftulit ira mihi.

Dirigui demûm lacrymis, & marmora manant.
Sic mihi mors dolor eſt, fic mihi vita, dolor.
Difcite, mortales, quid fit turgefcere faſtu,
Et quid fit magnos poſthabuiſſe Deos.

Fabula Niobes
Ouid. 6. Me-
tamorph.

De numero fi-
liorum, vide
Aul. Gellium
lib. 10. cap. 6.

Rapt. Gyral-
dus.

Motto
°Superbiae °ultio.

°Vengeance on °pride.

Picture
°Apollo and °Diana kill °Niobe's °child-
ren with °arrows shot from above. On a
mountain in the middle right, °Niobe,
bent over under a wind, is being turned
to °stone.

Epigram

Niobe	despise	power	divine	child
slain	tear	pine1	transform	marble
wail	moan	tragedy	poet	mortal
presume	pride	Lord	haughty	heart
hate				

Reference
°Ovid, Met 6
°Gellius, 20, 6
Baptista °Gyraldus [= Battista Giraldus]

In vitam humanam.

Whitney *Emblemes* London 1586 p.014

Motto
In °vitam °humanam.

On °human °life.

Picture
The °laughing °Democritus and the °weeping °Heraclitus sit facing each other in a landscape. Democritus has his hands raised and spread; Heraclitus, holding his hands to his face, has two °books; one on his lap, the other near his feet.

Epigram
wicked world false crime Heraclitus weep joy folly Democritus laughter age sin fool stage sight decay bad Satan fury

De his, Seneca lib. De Tranquillitate vitæ.

THE wicked worlde, fo falfe and full of crime,
Did alwaies mooue HERACLITVS to weepe,
The fadinge ioyes, and follies of that time,
DEMOCRITVS did driue to laughter deepe,
    Thus heynous finne, and follie did procure
    Theife famous men, fuche paffions to indure.

What if they liude, and fhoulde behoulde this age
Which ouerflowes, with fwellinge feas of finne:
Where fooles, by fwarmes, doe preffe vppon the ftage,
With hellifhe Impes, that like haue neuer binne:
    I thinke this fighte, fhoulde haften their decaye
    Then helpe vs God, and Sathans furie ftaie.

        Damnofa quid non imminuit dies?
        Ætas parentum peior auis tulit
        Nos nequiores, mox daturos
        Progeniem vitiofiorem.

Horatius.

Reference
°Seneca, Tranq
°Horace

Voluptas ærumnosa.

Whitney *Emblemes* London 1586 p.015

Motto
°Voluptas °aerumnosa.

°Sorrowful °pleasure.

Picture
°Diana, with a °laurel °wreath, a °falcon, and a °staff, °watches as a fallen °stag-headed °Actaeon is attacked by °three of his °hounds.

Epigram
Actaeon well Diana greedy bold stag transform hound prey fancy unlawful beast affection base devour deed deface

Actæon heare, vnhappie man behoulde,
When in the well, hee sawe Diana brighte,
With greedie lookes, hee waxed ouer boulde,
That to a stagge hee was transformed righte,
    Whereat amasde, hee thought to runne awaie,
    But straighte his howndes did rente hym, for their praie.

Ouid. lib: 3.
Metamorph.

By which is ment, That those whoe do pursue
Theire fancies fonde, and thinges vnlawfull craue,
Like brutishe beastes appeare vnto the vewe,
And shall at lenghte, Actæons guerdon haue:
    And as his houndes, soe theire affections base,
    Shall them deuowre, and all their deedes deface.

Horatius r.
Epist. 11.
Sperne voluptaTes, nocet empta dolore voluptas.

    Cornibus in Ceruum mutatum Actæona sumptis,
      Membratim propry diripuere canes.

    Ita diu placitum, voluptati vt mœror comes consequatur.

Anulus, in picta poeli.

Plautus in Amphit.

Reference
°Ovid, Met 3
°Horace, Ep 1, 12
°Aneau, Pict poes
°Plautus, Amph

Quod potes, tenta.

Motto
Quod potes, tenta.

Try what you can.

Picture
A troop of °armed °Pygmies is about to °attack °Hercules, who, °club in hand, sleeps against an embankment.

Epigram
Hecules club lion skin sleep pigmy kill foolish dwarf force strength work shame power weakling strive mighty sot learned defame

WHILE, HERCVLES, with mightie clubbe in hande.
In Lyons skinne did sleepe, and take his ease:
About him straighte approch'de the Pigmeis bande,
And for to kill this conquerour assaies,
  But foolishe dwarffes? theire force was all to smalle,
  For when he wak'de, like gnattes hee crush'd them all.

This warneth vs, that nothinge paste our strengthe
Wee shoulde attempte: nor anie worke pretende,
Aboue our power: lest that with shame at lengthe
Wee weakelinges prooue, and fainte before the ende.
  The pore, that striue with mightie, this doth blame:
  And sottes, that seeke the learned to defame.

  Turpe est quod nequeas capiti submittere pondus,
  Et pressum inflexo mox dare terga genu.

Hi homun-
ciones extre-
mas Ægypti
partes inhabi-
tant agricola-
tioni dediti,
Subinde cum
gruibus bel-
lum gerunt.
Plinius lib. 7.
cap. 1. &
Aul. Gellius
lib 9 cap. 4.

Propertius.

Reference
°Gellius, 9 4
°Pliny, 7,2
°Propertius

Ludus , luctus , luxus.

Whitney   *Emblemes*   London   1586   p.017

BEHOVLDE the fruites of dronkenneſſe, and plaie :
Here corage, brawles with Cutthroate for a caſte,
And ofte in fine , if that they lacke to paie,
They ſweare it out , or blade it at the laſte:
   This, frendſhippe breakes this, makes vs laugh d to ſcorne,
   And beggerie giues , to thoſe that riche are borne.

The Lapithans, by drinke weare ouerthrowne,
The wiſeſt men , with follie this inflames:
What ſhoulde I ſpeake, of father N O A H aloane,
Or bring in L O T T , or H O L O F E R N E S names:
   This S I M O N, and his ſonnes, did ouerthrowe,
   And B E N E D A B, made flee before his foe.

And he that lik'd to ſpende his time at dice,
This lawe in Rome, S E V E R V S did prouide:
That euerie man, ſhoulde deeme him as a vice,
And of his Landes, an other ſhoulde bee guide:
   Like Lawes beſide , did diuers more deuiſe,
   And wiſedome ſtill, againſte ſuche vnthriftes cries.

Tunc ſumus incauti, ſtudioq́ aperimur ab ipſo,   *Iurgiaq́, & rixæ, ſollicitusq́ dolor,*
  Nudaq́ per luſus pectora noſtra patent.   *Crimina dicuntur, reſonat clamoribus æther,*
Ira ſubit deforme malum, lucriq́ Cupido   *Inuocat iratos & ſibi quiſque deos.*

Propertius.
Vino forma perit, ...
no corrumpitur ætas.
Horat. 1 Epiſt. 19
Ludus enim genuit tre-
pidum certamen, &
iram :
Ira truces inimicitias,
& funebre bellum.

Virgilius.

Geneſ. 9.

Geneſ. 19.
Iudic. 13.
1 Machab. 15.

3 Regum 2.

Ouidius

Motto
°Ludus, °luctus, °luxus.

°Gaming, °grief, °gluttony.

Picture
Four °men sit at a table in a bower under a tree. One °drinks from a °mug. A second, who also holds a wing, watches the remaining two as they argue over a move made in a °game of °backgammon. Two other men °wrestle on the ground at the right.

Epigram
drunkenness   play   courage   brawl
cutthroat   pay   swear   blade   friendship
break   laugh   scorn   beggars   richly
Lapithan   drink   overthrow   Noah   Lot
Holofernes   Simon   Benhadad   flee   foe
dice   time   Rome   Severus   vice   land
guide   law   wisdom   unthrift

Reference
°Propertius   °Horace, Ep 1, 19
°Virgil   °B Gen 9, 19   °B Jdg 13
°B Macc 1, 15   °B Ki 3, 20   °Ovid

In auaros.

Motto
In °auaros.

On °misers.

Picture
An °ass, laden with °foodstuffs: °jugs, a °cask(?), bags filled with °bread(?), a spitted °fowl, and a °rabbit, °eats °thistles.

SEPTITIVS ritche, a miſer moſte of all,
Whoſe liuinges large, and treaſure did exceede:
Yet to his goodes, he was ſo much in thrall,
That ſtill he vſd on beetes, and rapes to feede:
    So of his ſtoare, the ſweete he neuer knewe,
    And longe did robbe, his bellie of his due.

This Caitiffe wretche, with pined corpes ſo heare,
Compared right vnto the fooliſhe aſſe,
Whoſe backe is fraighte with cates, and daintie cheare,
But to his ſhare commes neither corne, nor graſſe,
    Yet beares he that, which ſettes his teeth on edge:
    And pines him ſelfe, with thiſtle and with ſedge.

Nic. Reuſnerus.
*Frigoris impatiens: pa-
tiens: operumque, fa-
misque:*
*Ecce rudes Aſinus dat
rudis ore ſonos.*

Perditiſſimus ego ſum omnium in terra,
Nam quid mihi opus vita eſt, qui tantum auri
Perdidi, quod cuſtodiui ſedulò? egomet me fraudaui
Animumque, meum geniumque, meum, &c.

At nunc deſertis ceſſant ſacraria lucis,
    Aurum omnes victa iam pietate, colunt.
Auro pulſa fides, auro venalia iura,
    Aurum lex ſequitur, mox ſine lege pudor.

Plautus in Aulol.

Propertius 3. 13.

Epigram
Septitius   rich   miser   treasure   goods
thrall   beet   feed   sweet   rob   belly
caitiff   wretch   ass   back   dainty   corn
[= wheat]   grass   thistle   sedge

Reference
Nicholas °Reusner
°Plautus, Aul
°Propertius 3, 13

Nec verbo, nec facto, quenquam lædendum.

Whitney *Emblemes* London 1586 p.019

Motto

Nec °verbo, nec °facto, quenquam °laedendum.

Neither in °word nor in °deed should anyone be °injured.

Picture

°Nemesis holds a °bit and °bridle as she walks through a landscape.

Epigram

Nemesis goddess just arm measure way rein bit lewd harm wicked speech offend square deed right1 imp race

Reference

Angelo °Poliziano

HEARE, NEMESIS the Goddeſſe iuſte dothe ſtande,
With bended arme, to meaſure all our waies;
A raine ſhee houldes, with in the other hande,
With biting bitte, where with the lewde ſhee ſtaies:
And pulles them backe, when harme they doe intende,
Or when they take in wicked ſpeeche delite,
And biddes them ſtill beware for to offende,
And ſquare theire deedes, in all thinges vnto righte:
    But wicked Impes, that lewdlie runne their race,
    Shee hales them backe, at lengthe to theire deface.

Eſt dea: quæ vacuo ſublimis in aere pendens.
It nimbo ſuccincta latus: ſed candida palam:
Sed radiata comam: ac ſtridentibus inſonat alis.
Hæc ſpes immodicas premit: hæc infeſta ſuperbis
Imminet: huic celſas hominum contundere mentes,
Succeſſusq́, datum: & nimios turbare paratus.
Quam veteres NEMESIM &c.
            & pauló pòſt:
Improba vota domans: ac ſummis ima reuoluens
Miſcet: & alterna noſtros vicê temperat actus, &c.

Politianus ele-
ganter NEME-
SIM deſcribit
in Manto ſuo
ſic incipiens.

Whitney *Emblemes* London 1586 p.020

Minuit præfentia famam.

Motto

°Minuit °praesentia °famam.

°Presence °diminishes °fame.

Picture

A man with a °staff climbs the °snow-covered slopes of a °mountain. A °goat stands at the edge of a meadow on the top of the mountain. The °sun has apparently °melted the snow from the peak.

Epigram

report snow hill valley doubt heart coward fear truth sun ground simple truth

Reference

°Virgil, Aen 4
°Ovid, Met 12

R EPORTE, did ringe the fnowe did hide the hilles,
And valleys lowe, there with alofte did rife:
Which newes, with dowte the hartes of manie filles,
And Cowardes made, for feare at home to friefe:
　But thofe that went, the truthe hereof to knowe,
　When that they came, might fafelie paffe the fnowe.

For whie, the Sonne did make the fame to wafte,
And all about, difcouered had the grounde:
So, thoughe ofte times the fimple bee agafte,
When that reportes, of this, or that, doe founde,
　Yet if they firfte, woulde feeke the truthe to knowe,
　They ofte fhoulde finde, the matter nothing foe.

Mobilitate viget, viresq̃ acquirit eundo,
Parua metu primo, mox fefe attollit in auras, &c.

Nocte dieq̃ patet: tota eft ex ære fonanti,
Tota fremit, vocesq̃ refert, iterátque quod audit, &c.

Virg. lib. 4.
Æneid. in de-
fcrip. famæ.
Et Ouid. Me-
tam. lib. 11.
De domo fa-
næ fic,

Turpibus exitium.

Motto
°Turpibus °exitium.

°Destruction to the °shameless.

Picture
A °scarab or °dung-beetle in the centre of a large °rose.

Epigram
scarabee scent rose beautiful filthy smell die house dung worm neighbour meat mansion vile delight sick hear counsel reprobate

Reference
°Propertius 3, 17

Whitney   *Emblemes*   London   1586   p.021

THE Scarabee, cannot indure the sente
Of fragant rose, moste bewtifull to see :
But filthie smelles, hee alwaies doth frequent,
And roses sweete, doe make him pine and die:
   His howse, is donge : and wormes his neighbours are,
   And for his meate, his mansion is his fare.

With theise hee liues, and doth reioice for aie,
And buzzeth freshe, when night doth take her place,
From theise, he dies, and languisseth awaie:
So, whose delites are filthie, vile , and base,
   Is sicke to heare, when counsaile sweete we giue,
   And rather likes, with reprobates to liue.

Vos vbi contempti rupistis frena pudoris,   Fluminaq; ad fontis sint reditura caput, &c.   Propers. 3, 17.
  Nescitis capta mentis habere modum.   Quàm possit vestros quisquam reprehendere cursus,
Flamma per incensas citius sedetur aristas,   Et rapidæ stimulos frangere nequitia.

Nullus dolus contra Casum.

BEHOWLDE the craftie foxe,
Vppon Danubius plaies,
What time throwgh frofte, both man, and beafte,
Thereon did make their waies.

At lengthe, with PHOEBVS beames,
The frofte began to flake:
So that the yce with fwelling ftreame,
To fundrie peeces brake.

Where, on a peece the foxe,
Doth to his tackling ftande:
And in the fighte of Regenfpurge,
Came driuing by the Lande.

At which, the townefmen laugh'de,
And faied, this foxe, on Ice:
Doth fhewe, no fubtill crafte will ferue,
When Chaunce doth throwe the dice.

Regitur fatis mortale genus:
Nec fibi quifquam fpondere poteft
Firmum, & ftabile: perq, cafus
Voluitur varios femper nobis
Metuenda dies, &c.

Seneca in Oed.

Whitney *Emblemes* London 1586 p.022

Motto
Nullus °dolus contra °Casum.

No °cunning against °chance.

Picture
Townspeople watch as a °fox on an °ice-flow floats down a °river (°Danube) past a °town (°Regensburg).

Epigram
fox Danube play frost man beast Phoebus beam ice stream Regensburg townsman laugh subtle craft chance dice

Reference
°Seneca, Oedip

Whitney *Emblemes* London 1586 p.023

Mibi pondera, luxus.

WHEN autumne ripes, the frutefull fieldes of graine,
 And CERES doth in all her pompe appeare,
The heauie care, doth breake the stalke in twaine,
Wherebie wee see, this by experience cleare:
  Hir owne excesse, did cause her proper spoile,
  And made her corne, to rotte vppon the soile.

Soe worldlie wealthe, and great aboundaunce, marres:
The sharpenes of our sences, and our wittes,
And oftentimes, our vnderstanding barres,
And dulles the same, with manie carefull fittes:
  Then since Excesse procures our spoile and paine,
  The meane preferre, before immoderate gaine.

———— *nec te iucunda fronte fefellit*
Luxuries pradulce malum, qua dedita semper
Corporis arbitriis, hebetat caligine sensus
Membraq; Circais effeminat actius herbis.

Motto
Mihi °pondera, °luxus.

°Excess is a °burden to me.

Picture
A °sheaf of °grain (°wheat). Many of the individual stalks are broken.

Epigram
autumn ripe field grain Ceres ear break stalk excess spoil corn [=wheat] soil wealth abundance mar sense wit understanding excess pain mean1 gain immoderate

Reference
°Claudian 1

Claud.

Latet anguis in herba.

OF flattringe ſpeeche, with ſugred wordes beware,
Suſpect the harte, whoſe face doth fawne, and ſmile,
With truſting theiſe, the worlde is clog'de with care,
And fewe there bee can ſcape theiſe vipers vile:
With pleaſinge ſpeeche they promiſe, and proteſt,
When hatefull hartes lie hidd within their breſt.

The faithfull wight, dothe neede no collours braue,
But thoſe that truſte, in time his truthe ſhall trie,
Where fawning mates, can not theire credit ſaue,
Without a cloake, to flatter, faine, and lye:
No foe ſo fell, nor yet ſoe harde to ſcape,
As is the foe, that fawnes with freindlie ſhape.

Tuta, frequensq; via eſt, per amici fallere nomen. Ouid. 1. Art.

Sic iterum, ſic ſæpe cadunt, vbi vincere aperte Idem 2. Faſt.
Non datur: inſidias, armaq; tecta parant.

Whitney *Emblemes* London 1586 p.024

Motto
°Latet °anguis in °herba.

The °snake °hides in the °grass.

Picture
A °snake °coils up the stem of a pair of °strawberry plants.

Epigram
flatter speech sugar word heart face fawn1 smile care escape viper promise hateful breast faithful colour trust truth cloak feign lie foe friendly

Reference
°Ovid, A A 1
°Ovid, Fast 2

Curis tabescimus omnes.

I F griping greifes, haue harbour in thie breste,
   And pininge cares, laie seige vnto the same,
Or straunge conceiptes, doe reaue thee of thie rest,
And daie, and nighte, do bringe thee out of frame:
      Then choose a freinde, and doe his counsaile craue,
      Leaft secret sighes, doe bringe vntimelie graue.

Continuall care, did P L I N I E S harte possesse,
To knowe what caufde V E S E V V S hill to flame,
And ceased not, now this, nowe that, to gesse:
Yet, when hee coulde not comprehende the same,
      Suche was his fate, pursuing his desier,
      He headlonge fell into the flaming fier.

Non opibus mentes homini, curaq́, leuantur, &c.

O Curas hominum, ô quantum est in rebus inane.

Motto
°Curis °tabescimus omnes.

We are all °consumed by °cares.

Picture
A °winged °figure °reclines at the foot of the °volcano °Vesuvius. At the top a man clutches his breast; a second man, °Pliny, is °falling into the mouth of the volcano.

Epigram
grief   harbour   breast   care   siege
conceit   rest   friend   counsel   secret
sigh   untimely   grave   Pliny   know
Vesuvius   hill   flame   fate   desire   fall
fire

Reference
°Virgil, Geor 1
°Tibullus, 3, 3
°Persius 1

Vesuus, secundum Seruium Virgil. lib. Georg. 1. mons est Liguriæ sub Alpibus.

Tibul lib. 3. cap. 3.
Persf. 1.

Otium sortem exspectat.

Whitney *Emblemes* London 1586 p.026

Motto
°Otium °sortem °exspectat.

°Idleness awaits its °destiny.

Picture
A °miller lies asleep at the base of a °windmill waiting for a °wind to move the sails. A man with a sack stands on the steps of the mill, watching for wind.

A Windmill faire, that all thinges had to grinde,
Which man coulde make, the father lefte his sonne:
The corne was broughte, there nothing lack'd, but winde,
And Cuſtomers, did freſhlie to it ronne:
    The ſonne repoaſ'de his truſte vppon the mill,
    And dailie dreamide on plentie at his will.

Thus he ſecure, a while his daies did paſſe,
And did not ſeeke, for other ſtaie at all:
And thoughe hee founde, howe coulde the profit was,
And that ſoe ſmall, vnto his ſhare did fall:
    Yet ſtill he hoap'de, for better lucke at laſte,
    And put his truſte, in eache vncertaine blaſte.

Vnto this foole, they maie compared bee,
Which idlie liue, and vainlie hoape for happe:
For while they hope, with wante they pine, wee ſee:
And verie fewe, are luſ'de on fortunes lappe:
    While graſſe doth growe, the courſer faire doth ſterue,
    And fortune field, the wiſhers turne doth ſerue.

Epigram

windmill	grind	father	left1 [= wheat]	son	corn
wind	customer	trust	dream		
plenty	secure	profit	share	small	
hope	luck	fool	idle	vainly	hope
fortune	grass	courser [= horse]	starve		

Ovid. 1. Pont. 6.
Cernis ut ignauum cor-
rumpant otia corpus?
Vt capiant vitium
ni moueantur aqua.

Plaut. Rud.
... vigilare decet ho-
minem.
Qui vult ſua tempori
conficere officia.
Nam qui dormiunt li-
benter, ſine lucro, &
cum malo quieſcunt.

Reference
°Ovid, Pont 1, 6
°Plautus, Rud

Dolus in suos.

Whitney *Emblemes* London 1586 p.027

Motto
°Dolus in suos.

°Treachery towards one's own.

Picture
°Two °fowlers watch from behind a tree as °four °birds, °ducks, are °lured into their °net by a live °decoy.

Epigram
net fowl tame duck fly flight doubt traiterous heart fall betray kindred innocent prey subtle friendship overthrow

Reference
Andrea °Alciato [Emblemata 50]

WHILE nettes were sette, the simple fowles to take,
  Whoe kepte theire courſe alofte, and woulde not lighte,
A tamed ducke, her hoame did ſtraighte forſake,
And flewe alofte, with other duckes in flighte,
  They dowtinge not, her traiterous harte at all,
  Did flie with her, and downe with her did fall.

By this is mente, all ſuche as doe betraie,
Theire kindred neare, that doe on them depende,
And ofte doe make, the innocent a praie,
By ſubtill ſleighte, to them that ſeeke theire ende
  Yea vnto thoſe, they ſhoulde moſte frendſhip ſhowe,
  They lie in waite, to worke theire ouerthrowe.

    Perfida cognato ſe ſanguine polluit ales,
      Officioſa aliis, exitioſa ſuis.

And. Alciat.
De Anate.

In Astrologos.

Whitney *Emblemes* London 1586 p.028

HEARE, ICARVS with mountinge vp alofte,
Came headlonge downe, and fell into the Sea:
His waxed winges, the fonne did make fo fofte,
They melted ftraighte, and feathers fell awaie:
   So, whilfte he flewe, and of no dowbte did care,
   He mooude his armes, but loe, the fame were bare.

Let fuche beware, which pafte theire reache doe mounte,
Whoe feeke the thinges, to mortall men deny'de,
And fearche the Heauens, and all the ftarres accoumpte,
And tell therebie, what after fhall betyde:
   With blufhinge nowe, theire weakeneffe rightlie weye,
   Leaft as they clime, they fall to theire decaye.

    Illud quod medium eft, atque inter vtrumque, probamus.
    Dum petit infirmis nimium fublimia pennis
      Icarus, Icariis nomina fecit aquis.
    Vitaret cælum Phaëton, fi viueret, & quos
      Optauit ftultè tangere, nollet equos.

Motto
In °Astrologos.

Against °astrologers.

Picture
°Icarus °falls into the °sea after the °sun has melted the wax used to bind the °feathers of his °wings.

Epigram
Icarus fall sea wax wing sun melt feather fly seek mortal man search heavy star betide weakness weigh climb fall

Reference
°Martial 1
°Ovid, Trist 1

Martial. 1.

Ouid. Trift. 1.

Amor in filios.

Whitney *Emblemes* London 1586 p.029

Motto
°Amor in °filios.

°Love for °offspring.

Picture
A °ringdove broods on a °nest in the crotch of a °leafless °tree.

Epigram
Boreas   bush   tree   spring   ring   dove
make   nest   young1   plume   brook
preserve dame   starve [= die]   Medea
Procne   shame   cruel   infant   blame
mother   tyrant   serpent seed   bird
savage   brute   condemn

WHEN Boreas coulde, dothe bare both buſſhe, and tree,
   Before the Springe, the Ringdoue makes her neſte:
And that her yonge both ſofte, and warme, mighte bee,
Shee pulles her plumes, bothe from her backe, and breſte:
      And while ſhee ſtryues, her broode for to preſerue,
      Ofte times for coulde, the tender damme doth ſterue.

MEDEA nowe, and PROGNE, bluſſhe for ſhame:
By whome, are ment yow dames of cruell kinde
Whoſe infantes yonge, vnto your endleſſe blame,
For mothers deare, do tyrauntes of yow finde:
      Oh ſerpentes ſeede, each birde, and ſauage brute,
      Will thoſe condempne, that tender not theire frute.

In victoriam dolo partam.

Whitney *Emblemes* London 1586 p.030

Motto
In °victoriam °dolo partam.

On °victory gained by °guile.

Picture
A female, °bare °breasted figure, °Prowess, °tears out her °hair in great bunches as she sits on the °tomb of °Ajax. The tomb bears the inscription °"D AIACIS."

Epigram
doleful   dame   despair   Prowess   mourn
Ajax   tomb   golden   hair   wrong   sentence
Agamemnon   doom   Ulysses   tongue   judge
dead   Achilles   grave   valiant   heart
Ajax   win   arms   subtle   speech   knight
impatient   lose   wits   wrought   end1
grief

WHAT dolefull dame is this in greate difpaire?
  This prowes is, whoe mournes on AIAX toombe:
What is the caufe, fhee rentes her goulden haire?
Wronge fentence pafte by AGAMEMNONS doombe:
    But howe? declare, VLISSES filed tonge,
    Allur'de the Iudge, to giue a Iudgement wronge.

For when, that dead ACHYLLIS was in graue,
For valiante harte, did AIAX winne the fame:
Whereby, he claimde ACHYLLIS armes to haue,
VLISSES yet, was honored with the fame:
    His futtle fpeeche, the iudges did preferre,
    And AIAX wrong'de, the onelie man of warre.

Wherefore, the Knighte impatient of the fame,
Did loofe his wittes, and after wroughte his ende:
Loe, heare the caufe that mooude this facred dame,
On AIAX toombe, with griefe her time too fpende:
    Which warneth vs, and thofe that after liue,
    To beare them righte, when iudgement they do giue.

Caecum odium.

Whitney *Emblemes* London 1586 p.031

Motto
°Caecum °odium.

°Blind °hatred.

Picture
An °envious man covers his °eyes and pulls along his companion as they walk away from a °burning °house. A third man battles the °fire that threatens to consume what is presumably his house.

Epigram
envious neighbour house flame harm
shut eye despite wealth abound
repent God know heart reward desert

Reference
°Ovid, Met 2
°Horace, Ep 1, 2

Th'Enuious man, when neighboures howse dothe flame,
　Whose chiefe delighte, is in an others harme,
Doth shutte his eies, and will nott see the same,
But pulles awaie, his fellowe by the arme :
　　And sayeth, departe, wee care not for this ill,
　　It is not ours, let others care that will.

Too manie liue, that euery wheare are founde
Whoe daye and nighte doe languishe in dispite,
When that they see, an others wealthe abounde :
But, those herein that moste of all delighte,
　　Let them repente, for God whoe knowes theire harts,
　　Will them rewarde, accordinge to deserts.

Vixq̃, tenet lacrymas quia nil lacrymabile cernit, &c.

Inuidus alterius rebus macrescit opimis.

Inuidia Siculi non inuenere tyranni

Maius tormentum.   ———

Ouid. Meta-
morph D. iu-
uidia sic.
Horatius l.
epist. 2.

In pœnam sectatur & umbra.

THE wicked wretche, that mischiefe late hath wroughte,
  By murther, thefte, or other heynous crimes,
With troubled minde, hee dowtes hee shalbe caughte,
And leaues the waie, and ouer hedges climes:
    And standes in feare, of euerie busshe, and brake,
    Yea oftentimes, his shaddowe makes him quake.

A conscience cleare, is like a wall of brasse,
That dothe not shake, with euerie shotte that hittes:
Eauen soe there by, our liues wee quiet passe,
When guiltie mindes, are rack'de with fearfull fittes:
    Then keepe thee pure, and soile thee not with sinne,
    For after guilte, thine inwarde greifes beginne.

Conscius ipse sibi de se putat omnia dici.

Conscia mens vt cuique sua est, ita concipit intra
  Pectora, pro facto spemq̃, metumq̃ suo.

Whitney *Emblemes* London 1586 p.032

Motto
In °poenam °sectatur et °umbra.

For °punishment even a °shadow is °pursued.

Picture
A man with an °upraised °sword takes fright at his °shadow. °Jupiter sits astride an °eagle in a shining bank of clouds at the upper left.

Epigram
wicked wretch mischief murder theft crime trouble mind doubt catch fear shadow quake conscience clear wall brass shot guilty mind fearful pure soil sin guilt grief

Reference
°Cato
°Ovid, Fast 1

Cato.
Ouid. Fast.

Ei, qu: semel sua prodegerit, aliena credi non oportere.

MEDEA loe with infante in her arme,
Whoe kil'de her babes, shee shoulde haue loued beste:
The swallowe yet, whoe did suspect no harme,
Hir Image likes, and hatch'd vppon her breste:
    And lefte her younge, vnto this tirauntes guide,
    Whoe, peecemeale did her proper fruicte deuide.

Oh foolishe birde, think'ste thow, shee will haue care,
Vppon thy yonge? Whoe hathe her owne destroy'de,
And maie it bee, that shee thic birdes should spare?
Whoe sluc her owne, in whome shee shoulde haue ioy'd
    Thow arte deceaude, and arte a warninge good,
    To put no truste, in them that hate theire blood.

        MEDEÆ *statua est: natos cui credit Hirundo?*
        Fer alid: viden' hac mallet vt ipsa suos?

Whitney *Emblemes* London 1586 p.033

Motto
Ei, qui semel sua °prodegerit, aliena °credi non °oportere.

He who has once °squandered his own, ought not to be °trusted with another's.

Picture
A °swallow approaches its °nest built in the niche sheltering a °statue group of °Medea °killing her °child with a °sword.

Ouid. lib.7.
Metamorf

Epigram
Medea infant kill babe love swallow suspect harm image hatch breast young1 tyrant fruit divide [= kill] foolish bird care young1 destroy bird slay deceive warning good trust hate blood [= offspring]

Bourbon.is

Reference
°Ovid, Met 7
Antoine de °Bourgogne(?)

In momentaneam felicitatem.

Motto
In °momentaneam °felicitatem.

On °momentary °happiness.

Picture
A leafy °vine laden with °gourds entwines and climbs the trunk of a °pine tree.

Epigram

fruitful	gourd	pine	fruit	leaf
divide	experience	wise	peacock	lose
plume	despise	fool	presume	cold	heat
frost	bloom	root	rot	fade	fortune
wheel	boast	worldly	pride	slide	fame

THE fruictfull gourde, was neighboure to the Pine,
And lowe at firfte, abowt her roote did fpread,
But yet, with dewes, and filuer droppes in fine,
It mounted vp, and almofte towch'de the head:
  And with her fruicte, and leaues on euerie fide,
  Imbrafde the tree, and did the fame deride.

To whome, the Pine with longe Experience wife,
And ofte had feene, fuche peacockes loofe theire plumes,
Thus aunfwere made, thow owght'ft not to defpife,
My ftocke at all, oh foole, thow much prefumes:
  In coulde, and heate, here longe hath bene my happe,
  Yet am I founde, and full of liuelie fappe.

But, when the frofte, and coulde, fhall thee affaie,
Thowghe nowe alofte, thow bragge, and frefhlie bloome,
Yet, then thie roote, fhall rotte, and fade awaie,
And fhortlie, none fhall knowe where was thy roome
  Thy fruicte, and leaues, that nowe fo highe afpire
  The paffers by, fhall treade within the mire.

Let them that ftande, alofte on fortunes wheele,
And bragge, and boafte, with puffe of worldlie pride
Still beare in minde, howe foone the fame maie recle,
And alwayes looke, for feare theire footinge flide:
  And let not will, houlde vp theire heades for fame,
  When inwarde wantes, maie not fupporte the fame.

Petrus Crinitus de honefta difciplina lib.1.cap.14.

Nic. Reufnerus, Cærulcus cucumis, tumidiq. cucurbita vetre, Cruda ieuet, ftomatho permitfa, fitim.

Reference
Pietro °Ricci(?,) Hon disc 2 14
Nicholas °Reusner

Ære quandoque falutem redimendam.

Whitney *Emblemes* London 1586 p.035

Motto
°Aere quandoque °salutem °redimendam.

°Safety must sometimes be °bought with °money.

Picture
A °beaver pauses to tear off his °testicles as he is °pursued by a °hunter and °two °hounds.

THE Beauer flowe, that prefent daunger feares,
  And fees a farre, the eager howndes to hafte,
With grindinge teethe, his ftoanes awaie he teares,
And throwes them downe, to thofe that haue him chafte:
    Which beinge founde, the hunter dothe retire,
    For that he hath, the fruicte of his defire.

Theife, foueraigne are difeafes for to heale,
And for mannes healthe, from countries farre are broughte,
And if herein, the writers doe not faile,
This beafte doth knowe, that he therefore is foughte:
    And afterwarde, if anie doe him coarfe,
    He fhewes his wante, to mooue them to remorfe.

Thus, to his paine he doth his life preferue:
Which teacheth vs, if foes doe vs purfue,
Wee fhowlde not care, if goodes for life maie ferue,
Althoughe we giue, our treafure to a iewe:
    No ritches, maie with life of man compare,
    They are but droffe, and fortunes brittle ware.

Then life redeeme, althoughe with all thow hafte,
Thoughe thow arte pore, yet feeke, and thow fhalte finde,
Thofe ritches pure, that euermore fhall lafte,
Which are the goodes, and treafures, of the minde:
    Noe man fo pore, but god can bleffe his daies,
    Whoe patient IOB, did from the dunghill raife.

Vt corpus redimas, ferrum patieris & ignes,   Vt valeas animo, quicquam tolerare negabis?
  Arida nec fitiens ora lauabis aqua.   At pretium pars hæc corpore maius habet.

Nic. Keufnerus.
Mordicus pe ici. ma-
difeata ptribs toter
        Infidias cafur oan
effugit artis fiuer.

Epigram
beaver danger hound teeth stone
[= testicle] hunter desire disease
heal health beast know remorse pain
life preserve foe pursue goods give
treasure Jew riches dross fortune
life redeem poor pure treasure mind
God bless patient Job dunghill

Crates Theba-
nus cum the-
faurum fpon-
te perderet,
Hinc abite ait,
mala diuitiæ:
latius enim eft
a me vos de
merg: quam
ego a vobis
ipfe.

Ouid. lib. 1.
De Remed.
amoris.

Reference
Nicholas °Reusner
°Crates Thebanus
°Ovid, Rem Am 1

Durum telum necessitas.

Whitney *Emblemes* London 1586 p.036

Necessitie doth vrge, the Popiniaye to prate,
And birdes, to drawe their bucketts vp, and picke theire meate
    through, grate:
Which warneth them, whoe needes muſt eyther ſerue, or pine:
With willing harte, no paines to ſhunne, and freedome to reſigne.

    Placet tibi factum Mitio? M ɪ. *non ſi queam*   Terent. in
    Mutare : nunc, cum nequeo, aquo animo fero.   Adel. 4.7.

Motto
°Durum °telum °necessitas.

°Necessity is a °hard °weapon.

Picture
A child and a man observe a °parrot in a °cage.

Epigram
necessity   popinjay   prate   bird   meat
serve   pine1   pain   shun   freedom   resign

Reference
°Terence, Adelph 4,7

Inimicorum dona, infausta.

Whitney *Emblemes* London 1586 p.037

Motto
°Inimicorum °dona, °infausta.

°Gifts of °enemies are °unlucky.

Picture
°Ajax and °Hector °exchange a °sword and °girdle.

Epigram
foe gift fear fate life reave [= bereave] power Lynceus eye blind Ajax sword Hector girdle mortal foe truce

Reference
°Virgil Aen 2
Andrea °Alciato [Emblem 168]

I F of thy foe, thow doeft a gifte receaue,
Efteeme it not, for feare the fates doe lower,
And with the gifte, ofte tyme thie life doe reaue,
Yea, giftes wee reade, haue fuche a fecret power,
    That oftentimes, they L Y N C E V S eies doe blinde,
    And he that giues, the taker fafte doth binde.

To A I A X heare, a fworde did H E C T O R fende,
A girdle ftronge, to him did A I A X yeelde,
With H E C T O R S gifte, did A I A X woorke his ende,
And A I A X gifte, hal'de H E C T O R throughe the fielde:
    Of mortall foes, then fee noe gifte thow take,
    Althoughe a while, a truce with them thow make.

————   ————aut vlla putatis
Dona carere dolis Danaum, &c.

Sic titulo obfequij, quà mittunt hoftibus hoftes
    Munera, venturi præfcia fata ferunt.

Lacoon apud
Virgilium lib.
Æneid 2. de
equo, inecator
Troianis.
Alciat.

Non locus virum, sed vir locum ornat.

To the Honorable Sir PHILLIP SIDNEY Knight, Gouernour
of the Garrison and towne of Vlißing.

THE trampinge steede, that champes the burnish'd bitte,
  Is mannag'd braue, with ryders for the nones:
But, when the foole vppon his backe doth sette,
He throwes him downe, and ofte doth bruse his bones:
  His corage feirce, dothe craue a better guide,
  And eke such horse, the foole shoulde not bestride.

By which is ment, that men of iudgement graue,
Of learning, witte, and eeke of conscience cleare,
In highe estate, are fitte theire seates to haue,
And to be stall'd, in sacred iustice cheare:
  Wherein they rule, vnto theire endlesse fame,
  But fooles are foil'd, and throwne out of the same.

——magnum hoc ego duco,
Quòd placuit tibi, qui turpi secernis honestum.

Claud. 4. Honor.
Tu ciuem, patrimque
geras, in consule conftu.
Nos tibi, hos tua re-
meant & i publica
vota

Horat. 1. Ser.6.

Whitney *Emblemes* London 1586 p.038

Motto
Non °locus °virum, sed °vir °locum °ornat.

Not the °place the °man, but the °man °adorns the °place.

Picture
A °horseman, mounted on a °rearing °horse.

Epigram
steed bit rider fool throw courage guide horse judgement learning wit conscience high estate1 justice rule endless fame

Reference
°Claudian, IV Hon
°Horace, Sat 1, 6

Dedicatee
Sir Philip °Sidney

Mediocribus vtere partis.

Whitney *Emblemes* London 1586 p.039

Motto
°Mediocribus °utere °partis.

°Accept °moderate °possessions.

Picture
A °dog with his °muzzle and front °paws in a °stream searches for his °bone.

Epigram
fortune mean estate1 suffice hope fate content calling despise vainly climb fall land credit report Tagus seek Ganges golden sand empty purse court greedy dog moan brook deceive shadow bone

Reference
°Horace, C 2, 16
°Ovid, A A 2
°Horace, Ep 1, 10

WHOME fortune heare allottes a meane eſtate,
    Yet giues enowghe, eache wante for to ſuffiſe:
That waueringe wighte, that hopes for better fate,
And not content, his cawlinge doth deſpiſe,
    Maie vainlie clime, but likelie ſtill to fall,
    And liue at lengthe, with loſſe of maine, and all.

And he that poaſtes, to make awaie his landes,
And creditttes all, that wandringe heades reporte:
Maye Tagus ſeeke, and Ganges goulden ſandes,
Yet come at lengthe, with emptie purſe to courte:
    Let ſuche behoulde, the greedie dogge to moane,
    By brooke deceau'd, with ſhaddow of his boane.

Non minor eſt virtus, quàm quærere parta tueri,
    Caſus ineſt illis, hîc erit artis opus.

Seruiet æternùm, quia paruo neſciat vti,
Cui non conuenitet ſua res, vt calceus olim,
Si pede maior erit, ſubuertet: ſi minor, vrget.
Lætus ſorte tua viues, ſapienter Ariſti.

Hor. 2. Car. 16.
Vtatur paruo heni, mei
    paternum
Splendet in menſâ tenui
    ſalinum:
Nec leues ſomnos ti-
    mor, aut Cupido
        Sordidus auſert.

Ouid. lib. 2.
Art.

Horatius 1.
Epiſt. 10.

Biuium virtutis & vitij.

Whitney *Emblemes* London 1586 p.040

Motto
°Bivium °virtutis et °vitii.

The °crossroads of °virtue and °vice.

Picture
°Hercules stands between °Virtue, i.e. °Athena with °helmet, °shield and °spear and °Vice, i.e. °Venus accompanied by °Eros.

WHEN HERCVLES, was dowtfull of his waie
Inclofed rounde, with vertue, and with vice:
With reafons firfte, did vertue him affaie,
The other, did with pleafures him entice:
    They longe did ftriue, before he coulde be wonne,
    Till at the lengthe, ALCIDES thus begonne

Oh pleafure, thoughe thie waie bee fmoothe, and faire,
And fweete delightes in all thy courtes abounde:
Yet can I heare, of none that haue bene there,
That after life, with fame haue bene renoumde:
    For honor hates, with pleafure to remaine,
    Then houlde thy peace, thow waftes thie winde in vaine.

But heare, I yeelde oh vertue to thie will,
And vowe my felfe, all labour to indure,
For to afcende the fteepe, and craggie hill,
The toppe whereof, whoe fo attaines, is fure
    For his rewarde, to haue a crowne of fame
    Thus HERCVLES, obey'd this facred dame

Virgil. in Fragm.
de littera y.
*Quifquis enim duros
cafus virtutis amore
Vicerit, ille fibi lau-
deinque decufque pa-
rabit.
At qui defidiä luxûm-
que fequetur inertem,
Dum fugit oppofitos in-
cauta mente labores,
Turpis, inópfque fimul,
miferabile tranfiget
auom.*

Epigram

Hercules	way	virtue	vice	reason
pleasure	entice	strive	win	Alcides
pleasure	smooth	sweet	fame	renown
honour	hate yield	will	labour	endure
ascend	steep	craggy	hill	reward
crown	fame			

Reference
°Servius

Pœna sequens.

Whitney *Emblemes*   London   1586   p.041

Motto
°Poena °sequens.

°Punishment °following.

Picture
A °thief, leaning backwards over a seat in °sleep, is °strangled by the °sack of °stolen °meats about his °neck.

Epigram
night   sceptre   day   thief   rob   greedy shop   sack   flesh   neck   alehouse   sleep offend   escape   just   punishment   plague pike   justice

Reference
°Juvenal 13
°Seneca, Troad

WHEN silent nighte, did scepter take in hande,
   And dim'de the daie, with shade of mantle blacke,
What time the theeues, in priuie corners stande,
And haue noe doute, to robbe for what they lacke:
   A greedie theefe, in shambles broke a shoppe,
   And fil'de a sacke, with fleshe vp to the toppe.

Which done, with speede he lifted vp the sacke,
And bothe the endes, abowt his necke he knittes,
And ranne awaie, with burden on his backe
Till afterwardes, as hee at alehowse sittes:
   The heauie loade, did weye so harde behinde,
   That whiles he slept, the weighte did stoppe his winde.

Which truelie showes, to them that doe offende,
Althowghe a while, they scape theire iust desertes,
Yet punishment, dothe at theire backes attende,
And plagues them hoame, when they haue meriest hartes:
   And thoughe longe time, they doe escape the pikes,
   Yet soone, or late, the Lorde in iustice strikes.

Iuuenalis 1 ; de
malis sic ait.
His sunt qui trepidant,
& ad omnia fulgura
pallent,
Cùm tonat : exanimes
primo quoque mur-
mure cœli.
Senec. Troad.
Qui non ... da priuata,
... passus, nares.

Venter, pluma, Venus, laudem fugiunt.

W H Y flieſt thow hence? and turn'ſte awaie thie face:
    Thow glorie brighte, that men with fame doeſt crowne:
G L O. Bycauſe, I haue noe likinge of that place,
Where ſlothfull men, doe ſleepe in beddes of downe:
    And fleſhlie luſte, doth dwell with fowle exceſſe,
    This is no howſe, for glorie to poſſeſſe.

But, if thow wilte my preſence neuer lacke,
S A R D A N A P A L, and all his pleaſures hate,
Driue V E N V S hence, let B A C C H V S further packe,
If not, behowlde I flie out of thie gate:
    Yet, if from theiſe, thow turne thie face awaie,
    I will returne, and dwell with thee for aie.

Magnum iter aſcendo, ſed dat mibi gloria vires:
Non iuuat ex facili lecta corona iugo.

Cernis vt ignauum corrumpant otia corpus?
Vt capiant vitium, ni moueantur aquæ?

Propert. 4. 11.

Ouid. 1. Pont. 6.

Motto
°Venter, °pluma, °Venus, °laudem °fugiunt.

The °stomach, °feather °bed and °Venus °run away from °praise.

Picture
°Glory, a woman, °flees through a °doorway from the presence of a °naked °couple lying on a °bed; beside the bed stands a °table laden with °food and °drink.

Epigram
fly glory fame crown slothful sleep bed fleshly lust excess Sardanapal pleasure hate Venus Bacchus

Reference
°Propertius, 4, 11
°Ovid, Pont 1, 6

Mens immota manet.

To Sir ROBERT IERMYN *Knight.*

Whitney *Emblemes* London 1586 p.043

By vertue hidde, behoulde, the Iron harde,
The loadeftone drawes, to poynte vnto the ftarre:
Whereby, wee knowe the Seaman keepes his carde,
And rightlie fhapes, his courfe to countries farre:
    And on the pole, dothe euer keepe his eie,
    And withe the fame, his compaffe makes agree.

Which fhewes to vs, our inward vertues fhoulde,
Still drawe our hartes, althoughe the iron weare:
The hauenlie ftarre, at all times to behoulde,
To fhape our courfe, fo right while wee bee heare:
    That Scylla, and Charybdis, wee maie miffe,
    And winne at lengthe, the porte of endleffe bliffe.

Confcia mens recti famæ mendacia ridet.

Sufficit & lòrgum probitas perdurat in æuum,
Perq́ fuos annos hinc bene pendet amor.

Motto
°Mens °immota °manet.

The °mind °unmoved °remains.

Picture
A man °kneeling before a °chart on the ledge of a low wall holds a °compass up to the °stars; below a °stag °drinks from a °stream.

Pfalm. 41.
Quemadmodum
defiderat Ceruus
ad fontes aquarû:
Ita defiderat ani-
ma mea ad te
Deus, &c.

Epigram
virtue	hide	iron	loadstone	star
seaman	card [= chart]	course	compass	
heart	heavenly	star	Scylla	Charybdis
win	port	bliss	virtue	

Virg. in Ætna.
Eft merito pi tae no-
mini tutiffuma virtus.

Ouid. 4. Faft.

Ouid. de medic.
faciei.

Reference
°B Ps 41
°Virgil, Aetna
°Ovid, Fast 4
°Ovid, Med Fac

Dedicatee
Sir Robert °Jermyn

Whitney *Emblemes* London 1586 p.044

Defiderium ſpe vacuum.

Motto
°Desiderium °spe °vacuum.

°Desire °void of °hope.

Picture
A °lion °devours its °prey °as it is observed by an °envious °dog. °Animals in the background.

Epigram
lion prey dog hope vain1 son hope greedy friend death aged sire end1 young old heir looking-glass

Reference
°Ovid, Met 1

THE Lyon fierce, behoulde doth rente his praie,
  The dogge lookes backe, in hope to haue a ſhare,
And lick'd his lippes, and longe therefore did ſtaie.
But all in vaine, the Lion none coulde ſpare:
    And yet the fighte, with hope the dogge did feede,
    As if he had, ſomme parte there of in deede.

This reprehendes, the ſonnes, or greedie frendes,
That longe do hope, for deathe of aged Sires:
And on theire goodes, doe feede before theire endes,
For deathe ofte times, doth fruſtrate theire deſires.
    And takes awaie, the yonge before the oulde,
    Let greedie heires, this looking glaſſe behoulde.

  Filius ante diem patrios inquirit in annos:
  Victa iacet pietas, &c.

  Ouid. 1. Me-
  tamurph.

Furor & rabies.

Whitney *Emblemes* London 1586 p.045

Motto
°Furor et °rabies.

°Fury and °madness.

Picture
°Agamemnon, wearing a °crown, holds aloft his °sword as he supports his °shield bearing the inscription °"Agamemnon" and a °lion1 °rampant. In the background an encampment opposite °Troy in °flames.

THE crewell kinges, that are inflam'de with ire:
With fier, and sworde, theire furious mindes suffise:
And ofte to showe, what chiefelie they desire,
Within theire sheildes, they dreadefull shapes deuise.
   Some Griphins feirce, some ramping Lions beare,
   Some Tygers fell, or Dragons like to weare.

All which bewraye, theire inwarde bloodie thoughte,
Suche one, beholde, kinge AGAMEMNON was.
Who had in shielde, a ramping Lion wroughte
And eke this verse, was grauen in the brasse:
   Mannes terror this, to feare them that beholde:
   Which shielde is borne, by AGAMEMNON *boul'ie.*

Dum furor in cursu est, currenti cede furori:
Difficiles aditus impetus omnis habet.

Ovid. 1. Remed.

Epigram
cruel   king   ire   fire   sword   furious
mind   shield   dreadful   griffin   lion
bear   tiger   dragon   bewray [= betray]
bloody   thought   Agamemnon   shield   verse
brass   terror   fear

Reference
Claude °Mignault
°Ovid, Rem Am 1

Varij hominum senſus.

To Sir HENRY WOODHOWSE *Knight.*

Whitney *Emblemes* London 1586 p.046

Aɴ aged dame, in reuerence of the dead,
With care did place, the ſculles of men ſhee founde,
Vppon an hill, as in a ſacred bed,
But as ſhee toil'de, ſhee ſtumbled to the grounde:
Whereat, downe fell the heades within her lappe,
And here, and there, they ranne abovt the hill:
With that, quoth ſhee, no maruaile is this happe,
Since men aliue, in myndes do differ ſtill:
    And like as theiſe, in ſunder downe do fall,
    So varried they, in their opinions all.

Mille hominum ſpecies, & rerum diſcolor vſus.
Velle ſuum cuique eſt, nec voto viuitur vno.
Mercibus hic Italis, mutat ſub ſole recenti
Rugoſum piper, & pallentis grana cumini:
Hic ſatur irriguo mauult turgeſcere ſomno:
Hic campo indulget, hunc alea decoquit: &c.

Motto
°Varii °hominum °sensus.

°Various are the °opinions of °men.

Picture
A kneeling °woman collects into her °apron several °skulls scattered on the ground with the help of another woman; in the background, a °horse is °trotting on a hill; °skulls piled beside a °chapel.

Epigram
aged dame reverence dead care place skull men hill toil fall head alive mind differ vary opinion

Reference
°Persius 5

Dedicatee
Sir Henry °Woodhouse

Perſius ſ

Marte et arte.
To Sir WILLIAM STANDLEY Knight.

Whitney *Emblemes* London 1586 p.047

WHERE courage great, and confaile good doe goe,
With laftinge fame, the victorie is wonne:
But feperate theife, then feare the ouerthrowe,
And ftrengthe alone, dothe vnto ruine ronne:
    Then Captaines good, muft ioyne theife two, in one:
    And not prefume with this, or that, alone.

As valiant hartes, and corage highe befeeme,
The Captaines boulde, that enterprife for fame:
Soe mufte they ftill, of pollicie efteeme,
And wifedomes rules, to bringe to paffe the fame:
    While Cæfar great, fubdùde the countries farre:
    In gowne at home, did TVLLIE helpe to warre.

VLISSES wife, and DIOMEDES forme,
Are heare fet downe, for valiant wightes to viewe:
The one deuifde, the other did performe,
Whereby, they did the Troiane force fubdue:
    The one, his foes with witte, and counfaile harm'de,
    The other, ftill him felfe againfte them armde.

Motto
°Marte et °arte.

By °Mars and by °art.

Picture
A °scholar dressed in a °philosopher's °cap, (°Diomedes or °Cicero) with a °tablet under his arm converses with a °soldier in a plumed °helmet with °sword, °shield and °spear (°Ulysses or °Caesar).

Epigram

courage	counsel	fame	victory
overthrow	strength	ruin	captain
presume	valiant	heart	policy	wisdom
Caesar	country	subdue	gown	home
Tully	war	Ulysses	wise	Diomedes
Trojan	force	foe	wit	harm

Andr. Alciat.
*Viribus hic præftat,
hic pollet acumine mètis
Nec tamen alterius,
non eget alter ope.*

Hor. 1. Carm 10.
*Rebus anguftis anime-
fus, atque
Fortu appare: fapien-
ter idem
contrahes vento ni-
mium fecundo,
    Turgida vela.*

Reference
Andrea °Alciato [Emblem 41]
°Horace, C 2, 10

Dedicatee
Sir William °Stanley

Labor irritus.

Whitney   *Emblemes*   London   1586   p.048

Motto
°Labor °irritus.

°Labour in °vain1.

Picture
°Ocnus and another °ropemaker are making a °rope from °grasses. An °ass in the foreground eats a newly made coil of rope.

Epigram
Ocnus   rope   rush   grass   toil   work   ass spoil   spin   wicked   wasteful   wife spend   lewdly

Reference
°Juvenal 6

HEARF, Ocnus ftill the roape doth turne and winde,
Which he did make, of rufhes and of graffe:
And when with toile,his worke was to his minde
He rol'de it vp, and lefte it to the affe:
　Whoe quickelie fpoil'd, that longe with paine was fponne,
　Which being kept, it might fome good haue donne.

This Ocnus fhewes, a man that workes and toiles,
The Affe declares, a wicked waftfull wife:
Whoe if fhee maie, fhee quicklie fpendes and fpoiles
That he with care, was getting all his life,
　And likewife thofe, that lewdely doo beftowe
　Suche thinges, as fhoulde vnto good vfes goe.

　　　Prodiga non fentit pereuntem femina fenfum:
　　　At, velut exhaufta rediuiuus pullulet arca
　　　Nummus, & è pleno femper tollatur aceruo,
　　　Non vnquam reputant quanti fua gaudia confient.

Iuuenalis 6.

In eum qui sibi ipsi damnum apparat.

THE rauening wolfe, by kinde my mortall foe,
  Yet lo, inforſde, I foſter vp her whelpe:
Who afterwarde, as it did ſtronger growe,
Thoughe as my owne, I longe the ſame did helpe:
  Yet, coulde I not contente it with my teate,
  But that my ſelfe, hee rent to be his meate.

No willinge minde, to pleaſe him might ſuffiſe,
No dilligence, to geue the tyraunte ſucke,
Though whelpiſhe daies, his nature did diſguiſe,
Yet time at lengthe vnto my euell lucke,
  Bewray'de his harte, a warninge good to thoſe,
  Whoe in theire howſe, doe foſter vp theire foes.

For, thoughe throughe neede they frendlie ſeeme a while,
Or childiſhe yeares, do cloke their cancker'd minde,
Althoughe ſome doe, releeue them in exile,
And ſpend theire goodes, in hope to alter kinde:
  Yet all theire ioue, and care to doe them good,
  Suche will forgett, and ſeeke to ſpill theire blood.

Whitney *Emblemes* London 1586 p.049

Motto
In eum qui sibi ipsi °damnum apparat.

On him who prepares °loss for himself.

Picture
A °goat °suckles a °wolf °cub.

Epigram
wolf mortal foe foster whelp teat meat tyrant suck evil luck betray warning friendly childish cloak canker mind exile love care forget spill blood

Nic. Reuſnerus.
Inipa. tus ſtabulis ſ...
impus: vbere raptos
Dilaniatque foroe mi-
jerm cum matribus
agnos.

Claudius Minois è Græco.
Nutricus per me, tan-
dem fera ſauset in me.
Vertere naturam
gratia nulla poteſt.

And. Alciat.
Improbitas nulla justi-
tur obſeque.

Reference
Nicholas °Reusner
Claude °Mignault
Andrea °Alciato [Emblem 64]

Garrulitas.

Whitney *Emblemes* London 1586 p.050a

BETIME when sleepe is sweete, the chattringe swallowe cries,
And doth awake the wearied wighte, before he would arise:
Which carpes the pratinge crewe, whoe like of bablinge beste:
Whose tounges doe make him almoste deafe, that faine would take
    his rest.

Ecclesiaſt. 20.
Qui multis vti-
tur verbis, lædet
nimam suam.

Paradisus poëticus.
Hei non vna dies, non
vna reducit hirundo:
multiplici vigilans pru-
dentia surgit ab vsu.

Horat. 1. Epiſt. 8.
ſed tacitus paſci ſi poſ-
ſet coruus; haberet
plus dapis, et rixæ mul-
to minus, inuidiæque.

Motto
°Garrulitas.

°Garrulousness.

Picture
A °sleeping man is °awakened by a °swallow chattering in its °nest in the eaves.

Epigram
sleep swallow awake weary wight prate tongue deaf rest

Reference
°B Eccl 20
°Reusner, Parad poet
°Horace, Ep 1, 8

Quære adolescens, vtere senex.

WHILST youthe doth laste, with liuelie sappe, and strengthe,
With sweate of browe, see that for age thou toyle:
And when the same, arresteth thee at lengthe,
Then take thy rest, let younglinges worke, and moyle:
    And vse thy goodes, which thou in yowthe haste wonne,
    To cheare thy harte, whil'st that thy glasse shal ronne.

Ouid. 2. Art.,
n ...es anni que si-
ui colenda labores,
... .
senecta pede.

Whitney *Emblemes* London 1586 p.050b

Motto
°Quaere °adolescens, °utere °senex.

°Youth °seek, the °old man °use.

Picture
An °old man °sits at a dining °table while, outside a °young man °labours in the °field.

Epigram
youth strength sweat age toil rest goods win youth heart glass [= hourglass] run

Reference
°Ovid, A A 2

Vitæ, aut morti.

WITHIN one flower, two contraries remaine,
For proofe behoulde, the spider, and the bee,
One poison suckes, the bee doth honie draine:
The Scripture foe, hath two effectes we see:
Vnto the bad, it is a sworde that slaies,
Vnto the good, a shielde in ghostlie fraies.

De littera & spiritu.
S. Paulus Cor. 1.
cap. 3.
Paradisus poeticus.
Visus abest manui su-
cens pede flamine texo,
Altius lanigera fer-
tilitate nates.
Non dubium e quouis
api ingenii liquerent
Flue, sed recte ger-
mine, uelin syn.

Whitney *Emblemes* London 1586 p.051a

Motto
°Vitae, aut °morti.

For °life, or for °death.

Picture
A °flower gives °honey to a °bee and °poison to a °spider.

Epigram
one flower spider bee poison honey
Scripture bad sword good shield

Reference
°B Cor 1, 3
°Reusner, Parad poet

Nil penna, fed vfus.

To. Pr.   Dr.

Whitney   *Emblemes*   London   1586   p.051b

T H E Hippocrites, that make fo great a fhowe,
Of Sanctitie, and of Religion founde,
Are fhaddowes meere, and with out fubftance goe,
And beinge tri'de, are but diflemblers founde.
    Theife are compar'de, vnto the Oftuche faire,
    Whoe fpreades her winges, yet fealdome flies the aire.

Martialis 7.
Decipis alias verba,
...
...
...

Motto
Nil °penna, sed °usus.

Not the °wing, but the °use.

Picture
An °ostrich with °wings °outstretched.

Epigram
hypocrite   sanctity   religion   shadow
substance   dissembler   ostrich   wing   air
[= fly]

Reference
°Martial 7

Dedicatee
Pr. °Dr.

Fortiſſima minimis interdum cedunt.

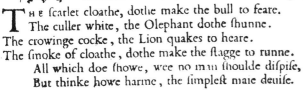

THE ſcarlet cloathe, dothe make the bull to feare.
The culler white, the Olephant dothe ſhunne.
The crowinge cocke, the Lion quakes to heare.
The ſmoke of cloathe, dothe make the ſtagge to runne.
All which doe ſhowe, wee no man ſhoulde diſpiſe,
But thinke howe harme, the ſimpleſt maie deuiſe.

Aelian. De varia hi-
ſtoria lib 5 cap.22.
Ouid. 2. Remed.
Amoris.
Paſſa neuat morſu ſpa-
tiojum vipera taurum:
A cane non magna
ſæpe tenetur aper.

Whitney *Emblemes* London 1586 p.052a

Motto
°Fortissima °minimis interdum °cedunt.

The °strongest sometimes °yield to the °smallest.

Picture
An °elephant frightened by a man holding a °white cloth; a °bull by a man with a °red cloth; a crouching °lion by a °crowing °cock; a °stag flees from a °smoking cloth.

Epigram
scarlet cloth bull fear white elephant shun crowing cocky lion quake smoke cloth stag run despise harm devise

Reference
°Aelian, V H 6, 22
°Ovid, Rem Am 2

Iniuriis, infirmitas subiecta.

T H E mightie fifhe, deuowres the little frie,
  If in the deepe, they venture for to ftaie,
If vp they fwimme, newe foes with watchinge flie,
The caruoraunte, and Seamewe, for theire praie:
    Betweene thefe two, the frie is ftill deftroi'de,
    Ah feeble ftate, on euerie fide anoi'de.

And. Alciat.
ſ.... minuta manens
....que debilitas.

Whitney *Emblemes* London 1586 p.052b

Motto
°Iniuriis, °infirmitas °subiecta.

°Weakness is °subject to °wrongs.

Picture
A °mew or °gull and a °cormorant °fly over a large °fish in pursuit of °three small fishes.

Epigram
mighty   fish   devour   little   swim   foe cormorant   seamew   prey   destroy   feeble state

Reference
Andrea °Alciato [Emblem 170]

Whitney *Emblemes* London 1586 p.053a

In dies meliora.

THE greedie Sowe fo longe as fhee dothe finde,
Some fcatteringes lefte, of haruent vnder foote
She forward goes and neuer lookes behinde,
While anie fweete remayneth for to roote,
   Euen foe wee fhoulde, to goodnes euerie date
   Still further paffe, and not to turne nor ftaie.

Nic Reufnerus.
Sylua iuuat capras:
vnda tutúmque fue

Motto
In °dies °meliora.

°Better °day by day.

Picture
A °pig, or °sow surmounted with the inscription °"ULTERIUS" [Further], roots in
the ground; a man points at the pig with
his °left hand, and with his °right at
°two °columns on a hillock, entwined with
a scroll with the inscription °"PLUS
OLTRE [= ULTRA]" [Still further].

Epigram
greedy sow harvest

Reference
Nicholas °Reusner

Luxuriosorum opes.

On craggie rockes, and haughtie mountaines toppe,
Vntimeliè fruicte, one sower figtree growes:
Whereof, no good mankinde at all doth croppe,
But serues alone, the rauens, and the crowes:
    So fooles, theire goodes vnto no goodnes vse,
    But flatterers feede, or waste them on the stewes.

Whitney *Emblemes* London 1586 p.053b

Motto
°Luxuriosorum °opes.

The °riches of °prodigals.

Picture
°Four °ravens or °crows °fly to °feed on the °fruit of a °fig-tree growing on a °mountain top.

Epigram
rock   mountain   untimely   fruit   fig-tree
raven   crow   fool   goods   flatterer   feed
waste   stews [= brothel]

Agentes, & consentientes, pari pœna puniendi.

A Trompetter, the Captaines captiue leade,
  Whoe pardon crau'de, and saide, he did no harme:
And for his life, with tremblinge longe did pleade,
Whereat, quoth they, and hal'de him by the arme:
    Althoughe, thie hande did neuer strike a stroke,
    Yet with thie winde, thou others did'st prouoke.

Whitney *Emblemes* London 1586 p.054a

Motto
°Agentes, et °consentientes, °pari °poena °puniendi.

Those °acting and those °consenting ought to °bear °equal °punishment.

Picture
°Two °soldiers lead a captive °herald from the °battlefield into a °fortress.

Epigram
trumpeter   captive   pardon   harm   life
plead   provoke

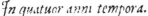

In quatuor anni tempora.

BY fwallowes note, the Springe wee vnderftande,
The Cuckowe comes, ere Sommer doth beginne :
The vinefinche fhowes, that harueft is at hande :
The Chaffinche finges, when winter commeth in :
    Which times they keepe, that man therebie maie knowe,
    Howe Seafons chaunge, and tymes do come and goe.

Nic. Reufnerus de
Ficedula.
Cum me ficus alat :
sü pafcar dulcibus meus:
    Cur potius nomen
non dedit vua mihi ?

Whitney *Emblemes* London 1586 p.054b

Motto
In °quatuor °anni °tempora.

On the °four °seasons of the °year.

Picture
°Three °birds grouped in and around a tree. A °swallow(?) flies towards the tree; a °chaffinch(?) perches on a bare branch; a °cuckoo(?) perches on a rock beneath the tree. There is a °vineyard in the background.

Epigram

swallow	spring	cuckoo	summer	vine
finch	harvest	chaffinch	winter	time
season				

Reference
Nicholas °Reusner

Paruam culinam, duobus ganeonibus non fufficere.

I N fmalle, and little thinges , there is no gaine at all,
One groaue, maie not two redbreaftes ferue, but euermore they brall.

Andr. Alciat.
Arbuftum geminos non
alit erithacos.

Whitney   *Emblemes*   London   1586   p.055a

Motto
Parvam °culinam, °duobus °ganeonibus non sufficere.

A small °kitchen, does not suffice for °two °gluttons.

Picture
One °redbreast °knocks another from a °tree °branch.

Epigram
small   gain   one   grove   two   redbreast brawl

Reference
Andrea °Alciato [Emblem 94]

Cuncta complecti velle, ftultum.

ET TVTTO ABBRACCIO
ET NVLLA STRINGO .

T H E little boyes, that ftriue with all theire mighte,
To catche the belles, or bubbles, as they fall:
In vaine they feeke, for why, they vanifhe righte,
Yet ftill they ftriue, and are deluded all:
     So, they that like all artes, that can bee thoughte,
     Doe comprehende not anie, as they oughte.

Whitney   *Emblemes*   London   1586   p.055b

Motto
Cuncta complecti velle, °stultum.

It is °foolish to wish to encompass all things.

Picture
°Two °boys blow °bubbles; six others try to catch them. Inscription: °"ET TUTTO ABBRACCIO ET NULLA STRINGO" [And all things I embrace and nothing do I hold].

Epigram
boy strive catch bubble vain1 art

Alius peccat, alius plectitur.

Motto
Alius °peccat, alius °plectitur.

One °sins, the other is °beaten.

Picture
A °dog bites a °stone on the ground; a man is about to throw another stone at the dog.

Epigram

angry	dog	stone	bite	ire	pursue
fight	brawl	guiltless	wrath	inflame
mortal	foe	rebuke	shame	rage
innocent				

Reference
Andrea °Alciato [Emblem 175]

THE angrie dogge doth turne vnto the ftone,
When it is cafte, and bytes the fame for ire,
And not purfues, the fame that hathe it throwne,
But with the fame, fulfilleth his defire:
Euen fo, theyr are that doe bothe fighte, and brall,
With guiltleffe men, when wrathe dothe them inflame,
And mortall foes, they deale not with at all,
But let them paffe, to theire rebuke, and fhame

  And in a rage, on innocentes do ronne,
  And turne from them, that all the wronge haue donne.

  Sic plerique finunt veros elabier hoftes,
  Et quos nulla grauat noxia, dente petunt.

And. Alciat.

Æthiopem lauare.

Whitney *Emblemes* London 1586 p.057

Motto
°Aethiopem °lavare.

To °wash an °Ethiopian.

Picture
°Two men °wash a °black °man.

Epigram
blackamoor [= moor1] wash nature power
hue conquer nature vain1 reason

Reference
°Erasmus °Lucian
°Horace, Ep 1, 10
°Aneau, Pict poes

LEAVE of with paine, the blackamore to skowre,
With washinge ofte, and wipinge more then due:
For thou shalt finde, that Nature is of powre,
Doe what thou canste, to keepe his former hue:
Thoughe with a forke, wee Nature thruste awaie,
Shee turnes againe, if wee withdrawe our hande:
And thoughe, wee ofte to conquer her assaie,
Yet all in vaine, shee turnes if still wee stande:
   Then euermore, in what thou doest assaie,
   Let reason rule, and doe the thinges thou maie.

—————— ———— equusq.
Nunquam ex degeneri fiet generosus asello,
Et nunquam ex stolido cordatus fiet ab arte.

Erasmus ex Luciano.
Abluis Æthiopem fru-
stra: quin desinis arte?
Haud unquam efficies
hic sit ut atra, dies.
Horat. 1. Epist. 10.
Naturam expellas fur-
ca tamen usque re-
curret.

Anulus in pict.
poeli.

Non dolo, sed vi.

Motto
Non °dolo, sed °vi.

Not by °deceit, but by °force.

Picture
Two men at a table observe an °ape thrust the °paw of a °dog into the °fire to withdraw °chestnuts from the flames.

Epigram
ape   chestnut   fire   fear   burn   whelp
foot   ember   foul   ambition   heart   king
remorse   subject   famine   sword   fire

Reference
°Aelian, V H 5, 26
°Horace, Ep 1, 2

THE ape, did reache for Cheftnuttes in the fire,
But fearinge muche, the burninge of his toes,
Perforce was bar'de, longe time from his defire:
But at the lengthe, he with a whelpe did clofe,
And thrufte his foote, into the Embers quick,
And made him, pull the Cheftnuttes out perforce:
Which fhewes, when as ambition fowle doth prick,
The hartes of kinges, then there is no remorce,
    But oftentimes, to aunfwere theire defire,
    The fubiectes feele, both famine, fworde, and fire.

Quicquid delirant reges, plectuntur Achiui.

e var.
.ca.26.

ι

Nimium rebus ne fide secundis.

THE loftie Pine, that one the mountaine growes,
  And spreades her armes, with braunches freshe,& greene,
The raginge windes, on sodaine ouerthrowes,
And makes her stoope, that longe a farre was seene :
So they, that truste to muche in fortunes smiles,
Thoughe worlde do laughe, and wealthe doe moste abounde,
When leste they thinke, are often snar'de with wyles,
And from alofte, doo hedlonge fall to grounde:
    Then put no truste, in anie worldlie thinges,
    For frowninge fate, throwes downe the mightie kinges.

       Sæpius ventis agitatur ingens
       Pinus, & celsa grauiore casu
       Decidant turres, feriúntque summos
           Fulmina montes.

       Vt cecidi, cunctíq́, metu fugere ruinam,
         Versáque amicitia terga dedere meæ.

Whitney *Emblemes* London 1586 p.059

Motto
°Nimium °rebus ne °fide °secundis.

Do not °trust °prosperity too much.

Picture
°Pine-trees are °broken by a °wind(?); in the top left, in a °cloud °Jupiter(?) straddles an °eagle; a °rabbit crouches before a °tree °stump in the foreground. In the distance a °horseman.

Epigram
pine mountain branch green rage wind overthrow trust fortune smile laugh wealth snare wile fall trust worldly frowning fate king

Reference
°Horace, C 2, 10
°Ovid, Trist 3, 5

Hor. Carm. 2.
Od. 10.

Ouid. 3. Trist. 5.

Silentium.

Ad D. T. C. M.

PYTHAGORAS, vnto his fchollers gaue,
This leffon firfte, that filence they fhould keepe:
And this, wee reade Philofophers mofte graue,
Yea in theire hartes, this Princes printed deepe:
  VLISSES wordes weare fpare, but rightlie plac'd.
  Thus, NESTOR lik'de LYCVRGVS this imbrac'de.

This, famous made EPAMINONDAS boulde:
By this, great praife did DEMARATVS gaine:
This, Athens made to reuerence ZENO oulde:
SIMONIDES condemned fpeaches vaine,
  Whofe fayinge was, my wordes repentance had,
  But Silence yet, did neuer make mee fad.

And CATO fayeth: That man is next to GOD,
Whofe figures his fpeache, in reafons rightfull frame:
For idle wordes, GOD threatneth with his rodde,
And fayeth, wee mutt giue reckoninge for the fame:
  which PAVLE likewife, this fauce doth fharplie tutche,
  ... fometimes, condemneth babblinge mutche.

... alfo, the tongue, the gate of life, and deathe,
... wifelie vf'd, extolleth men on earthe:
Which lewdlie vf'de, depriueth men of breathe,

Motto
°Silentium.

°Silence.

Picture
A °scholar sits at a table with a °book in his study. He holds a °finger to his °lips making the gesture of °silence. (°Harpocrates)

De laude filentij
Aul. Gel. lib. 1.
cap. 10. idem de va-
niloquio lib. 1.
cap. 15.

Epaminondae ...
Sertor ... Plu...
tum quoque non ia
multa feci ... place
tamen ... ...

Locutu fui ... ali-
cui ... tacuiffe ...
nunquam.

Cato lib. 1
Proximus ille deo, qui
fcit ra... ne tacere.

Cor ... cap ...
Contradi ... ...

Graui ...
Sit vita ... ...
... lingua nocu...

Epigram
Pythagoras scholar silence philosopher prince Ulysses word Nestor Lycurgus Epaminondas praise Demaratus Athens reverence Zeno Simonides condemn speech vain1 Cato God square speech reason idle word God threaten rod Paul fault condemn babble tongue gate life death wisely lewdly deprive breath mourn live mirth evil word pierce sword rue destroy mouth wound woe dumb fool silence wise prate betray babbler despise peace Egyptian nation Harpocrates finger mouth sign

And makes them mourne, whoe might haue liu'de in mirthe:
　　For euell wordes, pierce sharper then a sworde,
　　Which ofte wee rue, thoughe they weare spoke in boorde.

Not that distroyes, into the mowthe that goes,
But that distroyes, that forthe thereof doth comme:
For wordes doe wounde, the inwarde man with woes,
Then wiselie speake, or better to bee domme
　　　The tounge, althowghe it bee a member small,
　　　Of man it is the best, or worste of all.

The foole, is thought with silence to be wise,
But when he prates, him selfe he dothe bewraye:
And wise men still, the babler doe dispise,
Then keepe a watche when thou haste owght to saie,
　　　What labour lesse, then for to houlde thy peace,
　　　Which aged daies, with quiet doth increase.

Th'Ægyptians wise, and other nations farre,
Vnto this ende, HARPOCRATES deuis'de,
Whose finger, still did seeme his mouthe to barre,
To bid them speake, no more then that suffis'de,
　　　Which signe thoughe oulde, wee may not yet detest,
　　　But marke it well, if wee will liue in reste.

Pet. 1. cap. 5.
Qui enim vult vi-
tam diligere, & dies
videre bonos: coer-
ceat linguā à malo.
　Marc. 7.
Nihil est extra ho-
minem introiens ir
eum, quod possit
eū coinquinare, sed
quæ de homine pro
cedunt, &c.

Hor. 1. Serm. 4.
Fingere qui non visa
potest, comissa tacere
Qui nequit: hic niger
est, hunc tu Romane
caueto.

Ouid. 2. Amor. 2
Quis minor est autem
quàm tacui, ssabere?

Horat 1. Ep. 3.
Nec retinent patulæ cō-
missa fideliter aures

Plutarch. in Moral

Reference
°Gellius, N A
°Gellius, N A
°Pindar
°Cato 1
°B Cor 1, 15
°B Tim 2, 1
Guillaume °Roville
°B Pet 1, 3
°B Mk 7
°Horace, Sat 1, 4
°Ovid, Amor 2, 2
°Horace, Ep 1, 13
°Plutarch, Mor

Dedicatee
D.T.C.°M

Written to the like effecte, vppon

Video, & taceo.

Her Maiesties poësie, at the great Lotterie in LONDON, *begon* M. D. LXVIII. *and ended* M. D. LXIX.

I See, and houlde my peace: a Princelie Poëlie righte,
For euerie faulte, ſhoulde not prouoke, a Prince, or man of mighte.
For if that IOVE ſhoulde ſhoote, ſo ofte as men offende,
The Poëttes ſaie, his thunderboltes ſhoulde ſoone bee at an ende.
Then happie wee that haue, a Princeſſe ſo inclin'de.
That when as iuſtice drawes hir ſworde, hath mercie in her minde,
And to declare the ſame, howe prone ſhee is to ſaue:
Her Maieſtie did make her choice, this Poëſie for to haue.

Ouid. 2. Triſt.
Si quoties peccant homines ſua fulmina mittat Iupiter, exiguo tempore inermis erit.

Sed piger ad pœnas princeps, ad præmia velox:
Cuique dolet, quoties cogitur eſſe ferox.

Ouid. 1. Pon

Whitney *Emblemes* London 1586 p.061

Motto
°Video, et °taceo.

I °see, and I am °silent.

Picture
see p. 060

Epigram
see peace [= silence] princely posy [= motto] fault provoke prince might Jove shoot offend thunderbolt princess [= Elizabeth I] justice sword mercy save Majesty [= Elizabeth I]

Reference
°Ovid, Trist 2 °Ovid, Pont 1

Dedicatee
motto of Elizabeth I

Amicitia, etiam poſt mortem durans.

To R. T. and M. C. Eſquiers.

A Withered Elme, whoſe boughes weare bare of leaues
    And ſappe, was ſunke with age into the roote:
A fruictefull vine, vnto her bodie cleaues,
Whoſe grapes did hange, from toppe vnto the foote:
    And when the Elme, was rotten, drie, and dead,
    His braunches ſtill, the vine abowt it ſpread.

Which ſhowes, wee ſhoulde be linck'de with ſuch a frende,
That might reuiue, and helpe when wee bee oulde:
And when wee ſtoope, and drawe vnto our ende,
Our ſtaggering ſtate, to helpe for to vphoulde:
    Yea, when wee ſhall be like a ſenceleſſe block,
    That for our ſakes, will ſtill imbrace our ſtock.

    Ire iubet Pylades charum periturus Oreſtem:
        Hic negat, inꝗ, vicem pugnat vterque mori,
    Extitit hoc vnum quod non conuenerat illis:
        Cætera pars concors, & ſine lite fuit.

Motto

°Amicitia, etiam post °mortem °durans.

°Friendship °enduring even after °death.

Picture

A large °vine laden with °bunches of °grapes °entwined about a °dead °elm-tree.

Epigram

wither elm bough leaf sap age root fruitful vine grape dry dead branch friend help old stoop end1 help senseless block embrace

Reference

°Moecenas °Ovid, Pont 3, 2, 3

Dedicatee

R.°T. and M.°C., esquires

Virgil in Mœcena-
tis obitum.
*Et decus, & certè viuā
tibi ſemper amicus,
    Nec tibi qui mori-
tur, deſinit eſſe tuus:
ipſe ego quicquid ero,
cineres interq; fauillas,
    Tunc quoque non po-
tero non memor eſſe tui.*

Ouid. 3. Pont. 2. 2

Potentiſſimus affeEtus , amor.

Whitney   *Emblemes*   London   1586   p.063

Motto
°Potentissimus °affectus, °amor.

The most °powerful °passion, °love.

Picture
With a °whip in one hand and °reins in
the other, an °Eros °drives the °two
°lions °drawing his °chariot.

Epigram
lion   yield   Cupid   chariot   draw   hand
guide   awe   whip   fierce   cruel   mind
mighty   force   creature   brutish   tame
Jove   remorse   help   feeble   pity   tender
dame   Africa   wild   tyrant   endure

Reference
°Ovid, Ep 5 [Her 9, 26]

THE Lions grimme, behoulde, doe not refiſte,
   But yealde them ſelues, and Cupiddes chariot drawe,
And with one hande, he guydes them where he liſte,
With th'other hande, he keepes them ſtill in awe:
   Theye couche, and drawe, and do the whippe abide,
   And laie theire fierce and crewell mindes aſide.

If Cupid then, bee of ſuch mightie force,
That creatures fierce, and brutiſhe kinde he tames:
Oh mightie I o v e, vouchſafe to ſhowe remorſe,
Helpe feeble man, and pittie tender dames :
   Let Africke wilde, this tyrauntes force indure,
   If not alas, howe can poore man bee ſure.

         Quem non mille fera, quem non Stheneleïus hoſtis,
            Non potuit Iuno vincere, vincit amor.

Ouid. Epiſt. 9

Quæ ante pedes.

To I. I. Esquier.

Whitney   *Emblemes*   London   1586   p.064

Motto
Quae ante °pedes.

Things at our °feet.

Picture
A °hen, perched on the °roof of a °farm-
house, sucks one of her °eggs. Egg shells
roll off the roof.   Below, another hen
also seems to be sucking an egg.   Beside
her   stands   a   °cow(?)   with   a   °feed(?)
basket slung from its neck.

Epigram
friend   country   ungrateful   offspring
blood   waste   substance   beg   sell   land
parent   hen   egg   suck   empty   shell
reproach   shame   heir   decay   name

Reference
°Ovid, A A 1 °Seneca, Hippol 1

NOT for our selues, alone wee are create,
  But for our frendes, and for our countries good:
And thofe, that are vnto theire frendes ingrate,
And not regarde theire offspringe, and theire blood,
Or hee, that waftes his fubftance till he begges,
Or felles his landes, whiche feruide his parentes well:
Is like the henne, when fhee hathe lay'de her egges,
That fuckes them vp and leaues the emptie fhell,
    Euen fo theire fpoile, to theire reproche, and fhame,
    Vndoeth theire heire, and quite decayeth theire name.

Quifquis fecundis rebus exultat nimis,
Fluitq, luxu, femper infolita appetens,
Hunc illa magna dura fortuna comes
Subit libido: non placent fueta dapes,
Non tecta fani moris, aut vilis cibus: &c.

Ouid. 1. Ars.
Sic ne perdiderit non
ceffat perdere lufor,
* Et reuocat cupidas*
alea fæpe manus.

Sen. Hipp. 1.

Dedicatee
J.°J., esquire

Mutuum auxilium.

To R. COTTON *Esquier.*

Motto
°Mutuum °auxilium.

°Mutual °help.

Picture
A °blind man with a °stick carries on his back a °lame man who °points the °way with his °finger.

Epigram

blind	lame	direct	mutual
help	serve	friendly	league
praise	eye	foot	field
street	land	abound	want1
man	rich	scout	great
estate1	despise	poor	work
toil	shoulder	rich	give
food	clothes	lord	assign
friendship	difference		trade
intercourse	borrow	lend	love
truth	kindness		society
proverb	life	death	live
alone			

Reference
°Horace, Sat 1, 2 °Ausonius, Epig

Dedicatee
Richard °Cotton, esquire

T H E blynde, did beare the lame vppon his backe,
The burthen, did directe the bearors waies:
With mutuall helpe, they feru'd eche others lacke,
And euery one, their frendly league did praife:
　　The lame lente eies, the blynde did lend his feete,
　　And fo they fafe, did paffe both feelde, and ftreete.

Some lande aboundes, yet hathe the fame her wante,
Some yeeldes her lacke, and wantes the others ftore:
No man fo ritche, but is in fome thinge fcante,
The greate eftate, muft not difpife the pore:
　　Hee workes, and toyles, and makes his fhowlders beare,
　　The ritche agayne, giues foode, and clothes, to weare.

So without poore, the ritche are like the lame:
And without ritche, the poore are like the blynde:
Let ritche lend eies, the poore his legges wil frame,
Thus fhoulde yt bee. For fo the Lorde affign'd,
　　Whoe at the firfte, for mutuall frendfhip fake,
　　Not all gaue one, but did this difference make.

Whereby, with trade, and intercourfe, in fpace,
And borrowinge heare, and lendinge there agayne:
Such loue, fuch truthe, fuch kyndnes, fhoulde take place,
That frendfhipp, with focietie fhould raigne:
　　The prouerbe faieth, one man is deemed none,
　　And life, is deathe, where men doo liue alone.

Non eft diues opum, diues: nec pauper inopsq̃,
Infelix: alio nec magis alter eget.
Diues eget gemmis; Cereali munere pauper.
Sed cùm egeant ambo, pauper egens minus eft.

Quanta fit mutui au-
xilij neceffitas, cùm in
cômuni hac vitæ hu-
manæ focietate mul-
tis modis intelligi po-
teft: in qua homo
hominis opt maximè
indiget, adeo vt in
prouerbium abierit,
homo homini Deus:
tum verò in ipfa cor-
poris humani confti-
tutione & fabrica lu-
culentiffimè apparet.
Neque enim homo
fubfiftere vlla ratione
poffit, nifi membra
corporis mutuum fi-
bi auxilium præftent.
Quid enim futurum
effet, nifi oculi pedes
ad ingreffum dirige-
rent, nifi rurfum pe-
des corpus mouerent;
nifi manus ori cibũ,
os ventriculo atq̃ he-
pati, hepat per venas
vniuerfo corpot. ali-
mentum fuggereret?
Nihil itaque eft quod
per fe ipfum, fine al-
terius auxilio, confi-
ftare, aut vim fuam
& perpetuitatem con-
feruare poffit.

Hor. 1. ferm. 1.
Nam propria tellus
herum natura neque
illum,
Nec me, nec quenquam
ftatuit, &c.
Aufonius in Epig.

Whitney *Emblemes* London 1586 p.066

In ʊtrumque paratus.
To IOHN PAYTON *Esquier.*

WHEN SANABAL Hierusalem diftreft,
With fharpe affaultes, in NEHEMIAS tyme:
To warre, and worke, the Iewes them felues addreft,
And did repaire theire walles, with ftone, and lime :
    One hande the fworde, againft the foe did fhake,
    The other hande, the trowell vp did take.

Of valiant mindes, loe here, a worthie parte,
That quailed not, with ruine of theire wall:
But Captaines boulde, did prooue the mafons arte,
Which doth inferre, this leffon vnto all:
    That to defende, our countrie deare from harme,
    For warre, or worke, wee eyther hande fhould arme.

2 Efd.cap. 4.

Ouid. 1.Pont.4.
Neſcio qua natale folũ
dulcedine cunctos
Ducit, & immemo-
res non finit effe fui

Motto
In °utrumque °paratus.

°Ready for °both.

Picture
Emerging from a °cloud a right °arm bearing a °sword and a left °arm with a °trowel.

Epigram
Sanabal Jerusalem assault Nehemias war work Jew repair wall stone lime sword foe trowel valiant mind quail ruin wall captain mason art defend country harm war arms

Reference
°B 2 Esd 4 °Ovid, Pont 1, 4

Dedicatee
John °Payton, esquire

Murus æneus, sana conscientia.

To MILES HOBART Esquier.

BOTHE freshe, and greene, the Laurell standeth sounde,
Thoughe lightninges flasshe, and thunderboltes do flie:
Where, other trees are blasted to the grounde,
Yet, not one leafe of it, is withered drie:
Euen so, the man that hathe a conscience cleare,
When wicked men, doe quake at euerie blaste,
Doth constant stande, and dothe no perrilles feare,
When tempestes rage, doe make the worlde agaste :
   Suche men are like vnto the Laurell tree,
   The others, like the blasted boughes that die.

Nic. Reusnerus.
*Missa triumphalem no
tangunt fulmina lauru,
Cingunt hac vates
tempora læta sacri.*

*Integer vita, sceleris̃q; purus.
Non eget Mauri iaculis nec arcu,
Nec venenatis grauida sagittis,
   Fusce pharetra.*

*Sine per Syrtes iter æstuosas
Sine facturus per inhospitalem
Caucasum, vel qua loca fabulosus
   Lambit Hydaspes.*

Hor. 1. Carm. 22

Motto
°Murus °aeneus, °sana °conscientia.

A °wall of °brass is a °clear °conscience.

Picture
°Jupiter with °thunderbolts sits astride his °eagle in a bank of clouds; he looks down upon a man holding onto a °laurel tree in a storm(?)   A °swan(?) with a °laurel °garland about its neck swims on a river in the background.

Epigram
green   laurel   lightning   thunderbolt fly   tree   blast   leaf   wither   dry   man conscience   clear   wicked   quake constant   peril   fear   tempest   rage world   aghast

Reference
Nicholas °Reusner °Horace, C 1, 22

Dedicatee
Miles °Hobart, esquire

Sic discerne.

To Tho. Stvtvile Esquier.

IN fruictefull feilde amid the goodlie croppe,
The hurtfull tares, and dernell ofte doe growe,
And many times, doe mounte aboue the toppe
Of higheft corne: But fkilfull man doth knowe,
    When graine is ripe, with fiue to purge the feedes,
    From chaffe, and dufte, and all the other weedes.

By which is ment, fith wicked men abounde,
That harde it is, the good from bad to trie:
The prudent forte, fhoulde haue fuche iudgement founde,
That ftill the good they fhoulde from bad defcrie:
    And fifte the good, and to difcerne their deedes,
    And weye the bad, noe better then the weedes.

Ouid. 3. Trift. 4.
fiue fine inuidia, mol-
afque inglorius annos
*Exige, commixtus & *
tibi iunge pares.

Whitney   *Emblemes*   London   1586   p.068

Motto
Sic °discerne.

°Winnow it thus.

Picture
°Grain passes through a flat round °sieve hanging from a hook by three ropes.

Epigram
fruitful field crop tare dernel grow corn [= wheat] grain ripe purge seed chaff dust weed wicked prudent judgement deed weight sift

Reference
°Ovid, Trist 3, 4

Dedicatee
Thomas °Stutevile, esquire

Interiora vide.

To GEORGE BROOKE *Esquier.*

THough outwarde thinges, doe trimme, & braue, appeare,
 And fightes at firfte, doe aunfwere thie defire,
Yet, inwarde partes, if that they fhine not cleare,
Sufpecte the fame, and backe in time retire:
　For inwardlie, fuch deadlie foes maie lurke,
　As when wee truft, maie our deftruction worke.

Though bewtie rare, bee farre and neare renoumde,
Though Natures giftes, and fortunes doe excell:
Yet, if the minde, with heinous crimes abounde,
And nothing good with in the fame doe dwell:
　Regarde it not, but fhonne the outward fhowe,
　Vntill, thou doe the inwarde vertues knowe.

　　Virtus omnia in fe habet, omnia adfunt bona, quem
　Pene'ft virtus,

Whitney *Emblemes* London 1586 p.069

Motto
Interiora °vide.

°Look within.

Picture
A man with drawn °sword draws back a window curtain to look into a °house. A °bundle tied with rope lies at his feet.

Epigram
outward inward shine suspect deadly foe lurk trust destruction beauty renown nature gift fortune excel mind heinous crime virtue know

Reference
°Plautus, Amph

Dedicatee
George °Brooke, esquire

Plaut. in Amph.

Whitney   *Emblemes*   London   1586   p.070

Fortuna virtutem superans.

To Fʀ. W. *Esquier.*

WHEN Bʀvtvs knewe, Avgvstvs parte preuail'd
And fawe his frendes, lie bleedinge on the ground
Suche deadlie griefe, his noble harte affail'de,
That with his fworde, hee did him felfe confounde·
   But firfte, his frendes perfwaded him to flee,
   Whoe aunfwer'd thus, my flighte with handes fhalbee.

And bending then to blade, his bared brefte,
Hee did pronounce, theife wordes with courage great
Oh Prowes vaine, I longe did loue thee befte,
But nowe, I fee, thou doeft on fortune waite.
   Wherefore with paine, I nowe doe prooue it true.
   That fortunes force, maie valiant hartes fubdue.

Motto
°Fortuna °virtutem °superans.

°Fortune °vanquishing °virtue.

Picture
°Brutus in °Roman °armour and °helmet, his °shield on the ground, °falls on his °sword.

*Simile de Aiace fe-
ipfum interficiente
(fuper cuius tumu-
lum virtus plorans
pro falfo iudicio)
apparet ante, folio
tricefimo. Nam
cùm Achillis arma
per Agamemnonis
iudicium, Vlyffi ad-
iudicabantur, Aiax
illius iniuriæ impa-
tiens, & poftea in-
fanus, fe.ipfum in-
terficiebat, fic in-
quiens vt Ouid ha-
bet 13. Metamorph.
Hectora qui folus, qui
ferrum, ignémque, Io-
uémque,
Suftinuit toties, vnam
non fuftinet iram:
Inuictúmq. virú vicit
dolor; arripit enfem:
Et meus hic certe eft,
an & hunc fibi pofsit
Vlyffes?
Hoc ait, uédum eft in
me mihi, quiq.ruore
Sæpe Phrygum maduit,
domini nunc cæde ma-
debit,
Ne quifquam Aiacem
pofsit fuperare, nifi
Aiax,
Dixit, & in pectus,
&c.*

Epigram
Brutus   Augustus   prevail   friend   bleed deadly   grief   noble   heart   sword   flee blade   breast   word   courage   prowess vain   love   fortune   valiant   subdue

Reference
°Ovid, Met 13

Dedicatee
Fr. °W., esquire

Fides non apparentiam.

To BARTHRAM CALTHORPE *Esquier.*

Whitney Emblemes London 1586 p.071

Motto
°Fides non °apparentium.

°Faith in things °unseen.

Picture
°Two °fishermen in a °boat haul in a °fishing °net.

Epigram
fisherman net sea hope haul wave trust feed starve constant hope Christian eye faith God word anchor

Reference
°Ovid, Ep 18 [Her 20, 181]

Dedicatee
Barthram °Calthorpe, esquire

THE fiſherman, doth caſte his nettes in ſea,
In hope at lengthe. an happie hale to haue,
And is content, longe time to pauſe, and ſtaie,
Thoughe, nothinge elles hee ſee, beſides the waue:
Yet, onelie truſt for thinges vnſeene dothe ſerue,
Which feedes him ofte, till he doth almoſte ſterue.

If fiſhermen, haue then ſuche conſtant hope,
For hidden thinges, and ſuch as doe decaie,
Let Chriſtians then, the eies of faithe houlde ope,
And thinke not longe, for that which laſtes for aie,
And on GODS worde, theire hope to anchor faſte,
Whereof eache iote, ſhalbee fulfil'de at laſte.

Non boue mactato cœleſtia numina gaudent,
Sed, qua præſtanda eſt & ſine teſte, fide.

Ouid. Epiſt 18.

Whitney   Emblemes   London   1586   p.072

Virtus vnita, valet.

Ornatiß. iuuenibus nouem fratribus GEORGII
BVRGOINE armigeri F. F.

THE furging Sea, doth falte, and fweete remaine,
  And is preferude with working, to and froe:
And not corruptes, nor fuffreth anie ftaine,
Whiles in his boundes, the fame doth ebbe, and flowe:
  But if it wafte, and forth by flufes fall,
  It foone corruptes, and hath no force at all.

The arrowes fharpe, that in one fheafe are bounde,
Are harde to breake, while they are ioined fure,
But feuer them, then feeble are they founde,
So where as loue, and concorde, doth indure:
  A little force, doth mightilie preuaile,
  Where Princes powers, with hate and difcorde quaile.

Motto

°Virtus °unita, °valet.

°Virtue °united, °prevails.

Picture

A °farmer with a spade works the banks of a water-filled °ditch.   The ditch is fed from the °sea by a conduit which passes through a dike.   A °bull or °cow reclines beside a bound °sheaf of °arrows.

Epigram

sea   salt   sweet   corrupt   stain   ebb
flow   sluice   arrow   sharp   sheaf   bind
break   join   sever   feeble   love   concord
prevail   prince   power   hate   discord

Dedicatee

George °Burgoine's nine brothers

Gratiam referendam.

Whitney Emblemes London 1586 p.073

Motto
°Gratiam °referendam.

°Favour to be °repaid.

Picture
A °stork with a °snake in its °beak returns to its °nest on the chimney of a house; °three young storks are in the nest.

Epigram
stork provide care meal hatch brood
old food parent child duty father
provident mild fruit2 age1 grow
child duty reverence help

SEE heare the ſtorke prouides with tender care,
And bringeth meate, vnto her hatched broode:
They like againe, for her they doe prepare,
When ſhee is oulde, and can not get her foode
Which teacheth bothe, the parente and the chide,
Theire duties heare, which eche to other owe:
Firſt, fathers muſt be prouident, and milde,
Vnto theire fruicte, till they of age doe growe:
    And children, muſte with dutie ſtill proceede,
    To reuerence them, and helpe them if they neede.

Defeſſum fertur portare Ciconia patrem,
Hinc illa pietas ſancta notatur aue.

Aelianus lib. 10.
cap. 16.

Idem libro 8.
cap. 22. vbi de
natura Ciconiæ
mira fabula.

Paradiſus poe
ticus.

Reference
°Aelian, N A 10, 16
°Aelian, N A 8, 22
°Reusner, Parad poet

Auaritia.

Whitney Emblemes London 1586 p.074

Motto
°Avaritia.

°Avarice.

Picture
°Tantalus is one of many figures standing in a river up to his shoulders. He looks up at °fruit laden branches of a °tree on the bank. °Flames and °smoke billow up in the background.

HEARE TANTALVS, as Poëttes doe deuine,
This guerdon hathe, for his offence in hell:
The pleafante fruite, dothe to his lippe decline,
A riuer faire vnto his chinne doth fwell :
    Yet, twixt thefe two, for foode the wretche dothe fterue,
    For bothe doe flee, when they his neede fhoulde ferue.

The couetons man, this fable reprehendes,
For chaunge his name, and TANTALVS hee is,
Hee dothe abounde, yet fterues and nothing fpendes,
But keepes his goulde, as if it weare not his :
    With flender fare, he doth his hunger feede,
    And dare not touche his ftore, when hee doth neede.

Ouid. Metam.
lib. 4.

Tantalus à labris fitiens fugientia captat
Flumina, quid rides? mutato nomine de te
Fabula narratur, congeſtis vndique faccis
Indormis inhians: & tanquam parcere facris
Congeris &c.

Horat. ferm. 1
Sat. 1.

Epigram
Tantalus   poet   guerdon   offence   hell
fruit   lip   river   chin   food   wretch
starve   flee   covetous   fable   Tantalus
gold   fare   hunger   feed

Reference
°Ovid, Met 4
°Horace, Sat 1, 1

O vita, misero longa.

Whitney Emblemes London 1586 p.075

Motto
O °vita, °misero °longa.

O °life, °long to the °wretched.

Picture
An °eagle rends the °liver of °Prometheus who is °chained to a °rock.

Epigram
Caucasus Prometheus chain liver die pain torture poet misfortune sorrow slave bind band grief sorrow life death conscience prick care

TO Cawcasus, behoulde PROMETHEVS chain'de,
Whose liuer still, a greedie gripe dothe rente:
He neuer dies, and yet is alwaies pain'de,
With tortures dire, by which the Poëttes ment,
   That hee, that still amid misfortunes standes,
   Is sorrowes slaue, and bounde in lastingo bandes.

For, when that griefe doth grate vppon our gall,
Or surging seas, of sorrowes moste doe swell,
That life is deathe, and is no life at all,
The liuer rente, it dothe the conscience tell:
   Which being launch'de, and prick'd, with inward care,
   Although wee liue, yet still wee dyinge are.

Qualiter in Scythica religatus rupe Prometheus,
Assiduam nimio pectore pauit auem, &c.

De quo, Diodor.
Sicul.lib.6.

Horat. 1. Epist 1.
—hic murus aba-
neus esto,
Nil conscire sibi, nulla
pallescere culpa.

Martial. lib. 2.

Reference
°Diodorus Sic, 6
°Horace, Ep 1, 5
°Martial, I

Concordia.

OF kinges, and Princes greate, lo, Concorde ioynes the handes:
And knittes theire subiectes hartes in one, and wealthie makes
theire Landes.
It bloodie broiles dothe hate, and Enuie doune dothe thruste,
And makes the Souldiour learne to plowghe, and let his armour ruste.

And. Alciat.
Fœderis nae species: id
habet concordia signum,
Vt quo coegit amor,
iungat & ipsa manus.

Whitney   Emblemes   London   1586   p.076a

Motto
°Concordia.

°Concord.

Picture
°Two men in °armour, presumably °kings or °princes shake °right hands. In the background an °encampment and a troop of cavalry.

Epigram

king	prince	concord	join	hand
subject	heart	wealthy	land	bloody
broil	hate	envy	soldier	plough
armour	rust			

Reference
Andrea °Alciato [Emblem 39]

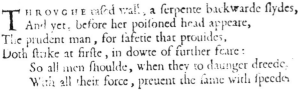

THROVGHE rased wall, a serpente backwarde flydes,
  And yet, before her poisoned head appeare,
The prudent man, for safetie that prouides,
Doth strike at firste, in dowte of further feare:
    So all men shoulde, when they to daunger dreede,
    With all their force, preuent the same with speede.

Quid. 1. Pont. 6.
Cùm poteram recto
tranfire Ceraunia velo
    Vtferā vitarem fi-
xa, monendus eram.
Nunc mihi naufragio
quisprodest dicere facta
  Qui mea mea debuerat
currere cymba via?

Whitney Emblemes London 1586 p.076b

Motto
°Remedium °tempestivum sit.

Let there be a °timely °remedy.

Picture
Amid the ruins of a building, a man raises a °stick to strike a °snake sliding presumably backwards through a crack in a °wall.

Epigram
wall   serpent   slide   poison   head
prudent   safety   strike   fear   danger
force   prevent

Reference
°Ovid, Pont 2, 6

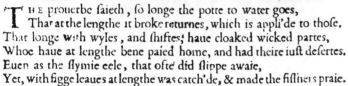

Sero sapiunt Phryges.

THE prouerbe saieth, so longe the potte to water goes,
    That at the lengthe it broke returnes, which is appli'de to those,
That longe with wyles, and shiftes, haue cloaked wicked partes,
Whoe haue at lengthe bene paied home, and had theire iust desertes.
Euen as the slymie eele, that ofte did slippe awaie,
Yet, with figge leaues at lengthe was catch'de, & made the fisshers praie.

Tibul. 1. 9.
*Ah miser, & si quis
prino periuria calat,
Sera tamen tacitis
pæna venit pedibus.*

Whitney Emblemes London 1586 p.077a

Motto
°Sero °sapiunt °Phryges.

The °Phrygians are °wise too °late.

Picture
On the shore of a river lined with buildings and a waterwheel, a °fisherman
grasps an °eel with the help of °fig
°leaves.

Epigram
proverb   pot   water   break   wile   cloak
wicked   just   desert   eel   fig   leaf
catch   fisher   prey

Reference
°Tibullus, I, 9

Dum vivo, prosum.

AN aged tree, whose sappe is almoste spente,
　Yet yeeldes her boughes, to warme vs in the coulde :
And while it growes, her offalles still be lente,
But being falne, to it turneth into moulde,
　　And doth no good : soe ere to graue wee fall,
　　Wee maie do good, but after none at all.

*Da tua, dum tua sunt,
post mortem tunc tua
non sunt.*

Whitney　Emblemes　London　1586　p.077b

Motto
Dum °vivo, °prosum.

While I °live, I do °good.

Picture
A man feeds a °fire with °wood gathered from a °dead °tree.

Epigram
age　tree　sap　bough　warm　cold　grow　fall　mould　grave

Noli altum sapere.

W I T H, lime, and net, the Mauis, and the larke,
  The fowler loe, deceaued by his arte·
But whilſte alofte, he leuel'd at his marke,
And did to highe exalte, his hawghtie harte,
    An adder fell, that in the graſſe did lurke,
    With poiſoned ſtinge, did his deſtruction worke.

Let mortall men, that are but earthe, and duſte,
Not looke to highe, with puffe of wordlie pride:
But ſometime, viewe the place wheretoo they muſte,
And not delighte, the pooreſt to deride:
    Leſte when theire mindes, do mounte vnto the ſkies,
    Their fall is wrought, by thinges they doe diſpiſe.

Some others are, that fitlie this applie,
To thoſe, whoe doe Aſtronomie profeſſe:
Whoe leaue the earthe, and ſtudie on the ſkie,
As if they coulde, all worldlie thinges expreſſe:
    Yet, when to knowe the ſtarres they take in hande,
    Of daungers neare, they doe not vnderſtande.

Whitney   Emblemes   London   1586   p.078

Motto
°Noli °altum °sapere.

Do not °aim at °lofty °things.

Picture
A °snake bites the leg of an °archer who °aims an °arrow at a °bird in flight.

Epigram
lime   net   mavis   lark   fowler   deceive haughty   heart   adder   grass   poison sting   destruction   mortal   earth   dust puff   worldly   pride   mind   sky   fall despise   astronomy   study   sky   star danger

Reference
°Claudian, Ruf 1
°Cato

Claud.x. Ruf.
—iam non ad culmina
rerum,
Iniuſtos creuiſſe que-
rer: tollantur in altũ
Vs lapſu maiore ruant,
&ı.

Cato.
Mitte arcana dei Cæ-
lúmque inquirere
quid ſit.

& alius ſic.
Si Chriſtum bene ſcis,
ſatu eſt ſi catera neſcis.

Sæpius in auro bibitur venenum.

HEARE LAIS fine, doth braue it on the ftage,
With mufkecattes fweete, and all fhee coulde defire :
Her beauties beames, did make the youthe to rage,
And inwardlie Corinthus fet on fire:
    Bothe Princes; Peeres, with learned men, and graue,
    With humble fute, did LAIS fauour craue.

Not euerie one, mighte to Corinthus goe,
The meaninge was, not all mighte LAIS loue:
The manchet fine, on highe eftates beftowe,
The courfer cheate, the bafer forte muft prooue:
    Faire HELEN leaue for MENELAVS grace,
    And CORIDON, let MABLIE ftill imbrace.

And thoughe, the poore maie not prefume alofte,
It is no caufe, they therefore fhoulde difpaire:
For with his choife, doth IRVS ioye as ofte,
As dothe the Prince, that hathe a VENVS faire:
    No highe eftate, can giue a quiet life,
    But GOD it is, that bleffeth man, and wife.

Then make thy choife, amongfte thy equalles ftill,
If thou miflike DIANAS fteppes to trace :
Thoughe PARIS, had his HELEN at his will,
Thinke howe his facte, was ILIONS foule deface.
    And hee, that mofte the houfe of LAIS hauntes,
    The more he lookes, the more her face enchauntes.

Whitney Emblemes London 1586 p.079

Motto
Saepius in °auro °bibitur °venenum.

°Poison is more often °drunk in °gold.

Picture
°Lais, the °courtesan, wearing a sumptuous dress and a fur stole stands in a landscape. She is flanked by two small animals, °muskrats(?)

De Laide Aul. Gel.
lib 1. cap. 8.

Propertius Eleg. 2.
Non ita complebant
Ephyræa Laidos ades,
  Ad cuius sacræi Græ-
cia tota fores.

Horat. Epift. lib. 1.
Epift. 18.
Non cuiuis homini con-
tingit adire Corin-
thum.

Claud. 1. de volupt.
Still. fic,
Blanda quædam vultu,
  fed quæ non tetrior
vlla,
Interius fucata venus,
  & amicta dolofis
Illecebris, &c.

Epigram
Lais stage muscat beauty youth rage Corinth prince peer learned love cheat base Helen Menelaus Coridon Mablie poor despair Iris Venus high estate1 quiet life God bless wife equal Diana Paris Helen Ilion deface Lais face enchant

Reference
°Gellius, N A 1, 8
°Propertius 2
°Horace, Ep 1, 18
°Claudian Stil 2

Præpostera fides.

Whitney Emblemes London 1586 p.080

Motto

°Praepostera °fides.

°Preposterous °faith.

Picture

A °miller and the °wife of °Anellus °embrace before °sacks of °grain stacked against the wall of a °watermill.

Epigram

Anellus	corn [= wheat]	mill	ground
miller	sleight [= trick]	steal	sack
meall	wife night day	strife	spouse
Vulcan	greedy fool	grain	wife
prodigal			

A N E L L V S , sendes his corne vnto the mill,
  Which beinge grounde, he tri de it by the waighte:
And finding not the measure, to his will,
Hee studied longe, to learne, the millers sleighte:
    For noe complaintes, coulde make him leaue to steale,
    Or fill the sacke, with fustie mixed meale.

Wherefore, to mill he sente his dearest wife,
That nighte, and daie, shee mighte the grindinge viewe:
Where shee, (kinde harte,) to ende al former strife,
Did dubbe her Spouse, one of V V L C A N V S crewe:
    Oh greedie foole Anellus, of thy graine,
    And of thy wife, too prodigall, and plaine.

Fatuis leuia committito.

Motto
°Fatuis °levia °committito

°Entrust °trifles to °fools.

Picture
A °naked °child on a °hobby-horse, a °courtier, and a °jester stand before a °crowned °king holding a °sceptre.

Epigram
child   cockhorse   courser [= horse]
idiot   bauble   play   disgrace   motley
coat   coxcomb   bell   jewel   fondling
[= fool]   vain2   honour   prudent   prince
fair   word   humour   infant   hand   razor
unfit   fool   wisdom

THE little childe, is pleaſde with cockhorſe gaie,
Althoughe he aſke a courſer of the beſte:
The ideot likes, with bables for to plaie,
And is diſgrac'de, when he is brauelie dreſte:
    A motley coate, a cockeſcombe, or a bell,
    Hee better likes, then Iewelles that excell.

So fondelinges vaine, that doe for honor ſue,
And ſeeke for roomes, that worthie men deſerue:
The prudent Prince, dothe giue hem ofte their due,
Whiche is faire wordes, that right their humors ſerue:
    For infantes hande, the raſor is vnfitte,
    And fooles vnmeete, in wiſedomes ſeate to ſitte.

Corn. Gall.
Diuerſos diuerſà in-
uant: nò omnibus annis
Omnia conueniunt;
&c.

Reference
Cornelius °Gallus

Homines voluptatibus transformantur.

Whitney Emblemes London 1586 p.082

Motto
°Homines °voluptatibus °transformantur.

°Men are °transformed by °pleasures.

Picture
°Circe touches with her °wand a °pig; nearby a °dog, °ape, a °goat and an °ass, °Ulysses' transformed men.

Epigram
Ulysses man transform goat hog ape ass foolish wicked love thrall beast wisdom Circe burn desire love cross world care Circe cup beware

SEE here VLISSES men, transformed ſtraunge to heare:
Some had the ſhape of Goates, and Hogges, ſome Apes, and
    Aſſes weare.
Who, when they might haue had their former ſhape againe,
They did refuſe, and rather wiſh'd, ſtill brutiſhe to remaine.
Which ſhowes thoſe fooliſhe ſorte, whome wicked loue doth thrall,
Like brutiſhe beaſtes do paſſe theire time, and haue no ſence at all.
And thoughe that wiſedome woulde, they ſhoulde againe retire,
Yet, they had rather CIRCES ſerue, and burne in theire deſire.
Then, loue the onelie croſſe, that clogges the worlde with care,
Oh ſtoppe your eares, and ſhutte your eies, of CIRCES cuppes beware.

Virgil. Aeneid. 7.
Ouid. Metam.
lib. 14.

Sirenum voces, & Circes pocula noſti:
Quæ ſi cum ſociis ſtultus, cupiduſq́, bibiſſet,
Sub domina meretrice fuiſſet turpis, & excors,
Vixiſſet canis immundus, vel amica luto ſus.

Horat. 1. Epiſt. 1.

Reference
°Virgil, Aen 7
°Ovid, Met 14
°Horace, Ep 1, 2

Iudicium Paridis.

To PARIS, here the Goddesses doe pleade:
With kingdomes large, did IVNO make her sute,
And PALLAS nexte, with wisedome him assaide,
But VENVS faire, did winne the goulden fruite.
    No princelie giftes, nor wisedome he did wey,
    For Bewtie, did comaunde him to obey.

The worldlie man, whose sighte is alwaies dimme,
Whose fancie fonde eache pleasure doth entice,
The shaddowes, are like substance vnto him,
And toyes more deare, them thinges of greatest price:
    But yet the wise this iudgement rashe deride,
    And sentence giue on prudent PALLAS side.

Regna Iouis coniux; virtutem filia iactat.
        Et postea ibidem.
Dulcè Venus risit, Nec te Pari munera tangunt,
    Ytraque suspensi plena timoris, ait.

Motto
°Iudicium °Paridis.

The °judgement of °Paris.

Picture
°Paris gives the °golden °apple to °Venus, accompanied by °Eros; at her side stand °Juno and °Athena wearing a °helmet, her °shield on the ground; behind them stands °Mercury.

Epigram

Paris	goddess	kingdom	Juno	suit
Pallas	wisdom	Venus	fair	win	golden
fruit	princely	gift	weight	beauty
obey	worldly	man	fancy	pleasure
entice	shadow	substance	toy	price
judgement	rash	deride	sentence
prudent	Pallas

Reference
°Ovid, Ep 15 [Her 16, 18]

Ouid. Epist. 15.
De iudicio Pa-
ridis.

Ridicula ambitio.

Whitney   Emblemes   London   1586   p.084

Motto
°Ridicula °ambitio.

°Ridiculous °ambition.

Picture
°Hanno releases a °flock of °birds.

Epigram
Hanno   sky   hope   praise   bird   trust
name   teach   fly   god   bird   bondage
release   wood1   lesson cease   sing   flee
fault   ambition shame virtue   love

Reference
°Aelian, V H 14, 30

HEARE HANNO standes, and lookes into the skye,
 And feedes him selfe, with hope of future praise:
Vnto his birdes, he dothe his eare applie,
And trustes in tyme, that they his name should raise:
    For they weare taughte, before they flewe abrode,
    Longe tyme to saie, that HANNO was a God.

But, when the birdes from bondage weare releast,
And in the woodes, with other birdes weare ioin'de,
Then HANNOS name, theire woonted lesson ceaste,
For eache did singe, accordinge to his kinde:
    Then flee this faulte, Ambition workes our shame,
    And vertue loue, which dothe extoll our name.

Aelian. de var.
Histor. lib. 14.
cap. 30.

Desidiam abiiciendam.

Whitney Emblemes London 1586 p.085

Motto
°Desidiam °abiiciendam.

°Sloth to be °rejected.

Picture
°Two °idle men °sit at the foot of a tree.

Epigram
labour leave slothful flee idleness beggar sweat brow meat born labour hand eat praise wanton ease Draco law idle man die Florentine banishment pain Corinth idly warn slay Saint Paul threaten slothful

Reference
°Sabellicus
°B Thess 2
°Ovid, Rem Am 1

Vse labour ftill, and leaue thie flouthfull feate,
Flee Idleneffe, which beggers ftate dothe giue :
With fweate of browe, fee that thou get thy meate,
If thou be borne, with labouring hande to liue :
    And get, to eate. and eate, to liue with praife :
    Liue not to eate, to liue with wanton eafe.

By DRACOES lawes, the idle men fhoulde die,
*The Florentines, made banifhement theire paine :
In Corinthe, thofe that idlie they did fee,
Weare warn'de at firfte, the feconde time were flaine ;
    And eke Sainct Paule, the flothfull thus doth threate,
    Whoe laboreth not, denie him for to eate.

    Quæritur Ægiftus quare fit factus adulter :
    In promptu cauffa eft, defidiofus erat.

* Sabel,
Paul. Thef. 2. ca.,
Neque gratis pa-
nem manducaui-
mus ab aliquo,
fed in labore, &
in fatigatione,
nocte, & die ope-
rantes &c.
  & poftea :
Quoniam fi quis
non vult operari,
nec manducet.

Ouid. 1. Remed.
Amoris.

Mortui diuitiæ.

Ad Reuerendum virum Dn. ALEXANDRVM NOWELL Paulinæ
ecclesiæ Londini Decanum, doctrina & exemplo clarum.

THE Princes greate, and Monarches of the earthe,
　Whoe, while they liu'de, the worlde might not suffice:
Yet can they claime, by greatnesse of their birthe,
To beare from hence, when nature life denies,
　Noe more then they, who for releife did pyne,
　Which is but this, a shrouding sheete of twyne.

Thoughe fewe there bee, while they doe flourishe heere,
That doe regarde the place whereto the muste:
Yet, thoughe theire pride like Lucifers appeere,
They shalbee sure, at lengthe to turne to duste:
　The Prince, the Poore, the Prisoner, and the slaue,
　They all at lengthe, are summon'de to their graue.

Horat. 1. Carm. 4.
Pallida mors aquo pul-
sat pede pauperum ta-
bernas,
　Regumq; turres, &c.

Propertius 2. 28.
Haud ulla portabis apes
Acherontis ad undas:
　Nudus ab inferna
stulte uehere rate.
Victor cum victis pari-
ter miscebitur umbris,
　Consule cum Mario
capte Iugurtha sedes.

Whitney　Emblemes　London　1586　p.086

Motto
°Mortui °divitiae.

A °dead man's °riches.

Picture
A °shirt or °shroud °draped on a °lance and a °crossbar.

Epigram
prince monarch earth world greatness
birth nature shroud twine pride
Lucifer dust prince poor prisoner
slave grave mind mighty Caesar chair
contentment die despair Christian
Turk Saladin sultan Babylon death
time nature shirt spear Aschalon
trumpet herald king east kingdom
clay

Reference
°Horace, C 1, 4
°Propertius, 2, 28

Dedicatee
Alexander °Nowell, Dean of St. Paul's

Whitney   Emblemes   London   1586   p.086

But, hee that printes this deepelie in his minde,
Althoughe he fet in mightie C ÆSARS chaire,
Within this life, fhall contentation finde,
When careleffe men, ofte die in great difpaire:
    Then, let them bluffhe that woulde be Chriftians thought,
    And faile hereof, Sith Turkes the fame haue taught.

As SALADINE, that was the Souldaine greate
Of Babilon, when deathe did him arrefte,
His fubiectes charg'd, when he fhoulde leaue his feats,
And life refigne, to tyme, and natures hefte:
    They fhould prepare, his fhyrte vppon a fpeare,
    And all about forthwith the fame fhoulde beare.

Throughe ASCHALON, the place where he deceafte,   *Vrbs Palæſtinæ.*
With trumpet Sounde, and Heralte to declare,
Theife wordes alowde: *The Kinge of all the Eafte*
Great SALADINE, *beholde is ſtripped bare:*
    Of kingdomes large, and lyes in houſe of claie,
    And this is all, he bare with him awaie.

Quod in te est, prome.

Ad eundem.

THE Pellican, for to reuiue her younge,
   Doth peirce her breſt, and geue them of her blood:
Then ſearche your breſte, and as yow haue with tonge,
With penne proceede to doe our countrie good:
      Your zeale is great, your learning is profounde,
      Then helpe our wantes, with that you doe abounde.

Parad. Poet.
Cor Pharm voſtro ſig's
peiecamus a nobo.)
Et ſ pro nao fa vo-
tat iſ y qui.

Whitney Emblemes London 1586 p.087

Motto
Quod in te est, prome.

Bring forth what is in you.

Picture
In her °nest made of a °crown of °thorns the °pelican with °wings °outspread pierces her °breast with her beak to sprinkle her °three °young1 with °blood.

Epigram

pelican   revive   young1   pierce   breast blood   tongue   pen   country   good   zeal learning   help

Reference
°Reusner, Parad poet

Dedicatee
Alexander °Nowell, Dean of St. Paul's

De paruis, grandis aceruus erit.

To my brother M. BR. WHITNEY.

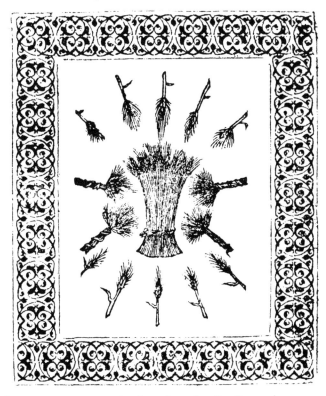

ALTHOVGHE thy ftore bee fmall, for to beginne,
Yet guide it well, and foone it is increafte,
For mightie men, in time there wealthe did winne,
Whoe had at firfte, as little as the lefte:
  Where GOD dothe bleffe, in time aboundance fpringes,
  And heapes are made, of manie little thinges.

Fructibus Agrippa siculis, quos colligis Icci,
Si recté frueris: non est vt copia maior
Ab Ioue donari poßit tibi, tolle querelas.
Pauper enim non est, cui rerum suppetit vsus.

Motto
De °parvis, °grandis °aceruus erit.

From °little things, a °great °sheaf will come.

Picture
In the centre, a large °sheaf of °grain or °wheat(?) encircled by °five single °stalks above and below, and by °two smaller °sheaves on either side.

Epigram
store   small   guide   increase   wealth   win God bless abundance

Ouid. 1. Remed.
Amoris.
Flumina magna vides
parua de fontibus orta:
  Plurima collctu
multiplicantur aquu.

Vt huic vacuo
fpacio aliquid ad-
iiciam, non facilé
occurrit (mi fra-
ter) quod & tibi
(iam patrisfami-
lias) & huic Sym-
bolo magis con-
ueniat, quàm il-
lud Horatianum
ad Iccium.

1. Epift. 12.

Reference
°Ovid, Rem Am 1
°Horace, Ep 1, 12

Dedicatee
Brooke °Whitney

Vita irrequieta.

Ad Doctiß. virum W. M. *fortuna telo ictum.*

THE Apodes, which doe in INDIA breede,
Still flie about, and feldome take theire eafe:
They haue no feete, to refte them as wee reade,
But with theire flighte, do compaffe lande, and feas:
     Vnto this broode, thofe that about doe rome,
     Wee maie compare: that haue no houfe, nor home.

Bothe houfes faire, and citties great, they veiwe,
But Riuers fwifte, theire paffage ftill do let,
They ofte looke backe, and doe theire fortune rue,
Since that therin, they haue no feate to fet:
     Thus, paffe they throughe theire longe vnquiet life,
     Till deathe dothe come, the ende of worldlie ftrife.

        Omne folum forti patria eft, vt pifcibus æquor,
        Vt volucri vacuo quicquid in orbe patet.

Whitney   Emblemes   London   1586   p.089

Motto
°Vita °irrequieta.

A °restless °life.

Picture
A °bird-of-paradise °flies across the sky; a °traveller with a °pack on his back looks towards a °village across a °stream, on which a °swan is feeding.

Epigram
Apodes India breed fly foot rest flight land sea brood house home city river fortune rue life unquiet death end worldly strife

Iuuen. Sat. 10.
*Pauca licet portes ar-
genti vafcula puri,
Nocte iter ingreffus gla-
dium, contumque ti-
mebu,
Et mota ad lunam tre-
pidabis arundinis
vmbram.
Cantabit vacuus co-
latrone viator.*

Ouid. 1. Faft.

Reference
°Juvenal, Sat 10
°Ovid, Fast 1

Dedicatee
W. °M.

In eum qui truculentia suorum perierit.

Ad affinem suum , R. E. medicum insignem.

Motto
In eum qui °truculentia suorum °perierit.

On him who will °perish from the °harshness of his own.

Picture
A °dolphin °flounders on the °sea °shore.

Epigram
dolphin   shore   flood   Neptune   wrong
ship   hope   sea   country   fish   exile
famous   sway   exile   live   poor   Socrates
Tullius   Demosthenes   thousand

THE Dolphin swifte, vpon the shore is throwne,
Thoughe he was bred, and fostered, in the flood:
If NEPTVNE shewe such wronge, vnto his owne,
Then , howe maie man in shippes haue hope of good:
  The raging Sea, our countrie doth declare;
  The Dolphin fishe, those that exiled are.

And thoughe this fishe, was mightie in the sea,
Without regarde, yet was hee caste on shore :
So famous men, that longe did beare the swaie,
Haue bene exil'd, and liud in habit pore :
  This, SOCRATES: and MARCVS TVLLIVS tri'de:
  DEMOSTHENES, and thousandes moe beside.

Aelian. De Ani-
malibus lib. 9.
cap.7. & lib.1 2.
cap. 1 2.
  Alciatus.
Nam si ne proprijs Ne-
ptunus parcit alumnis,
  Quis tutos homines
navibus esse putat?

Fortuna nunquam sistit in eodem statu,
Semper movetur, variat , & mutat vices,
Et summa in imum vertit, ac versa erigit.

Dehis, Petrarcha
lib. vtriusq. for-
tunæ in titulo de
morientibus ex-
tra patriam , lu-
culentei scribit.
Ausonius Epigr.
13 5.

Reference
°Aelian, N A 9, 7
°Aelian, N A 12, 12
°Petrarch, Rem
°Ausonius, Epig 135

Dedicatee R. °E.

Whitney Emblemes London 1586 p.091

Tecum habita.

Ad Agnatum suum R. W. *Coolensem.*

Motto
Tecum °habita.

°Abide by yourself.

Picture
Seated on a °throne, °Jupiter, whose °staff is surmounted by an °eagle, is surrounded by a °deer, a °horse, a °bull, an °ass, a °snail, an °eagle, and a °lion.

Epigram
feast Jupiter beast creature snail blame king house slow home

Dedicatee
Robert °Whitney of Coole

A Solemne feafte great I v p i t e r did make,
And warn'd all beaftes, and creatures to be there:
The preffe was muche, eache one his place did take:
At lengthe, when all weare in there cheifeft cheare:
    At feconde courfe, the fnaile crepte flowlie in,
    Whome I o v e did blame, caufe hee fo flacke had bin.

Who aunfwered thus, oh kinge behoulde the caufe?
I beare my houfe, wherefore my pace is flowe:
Which warneth all, in feafting for to paufe,
And to the fame, with pace of fnaile to goe:
    And further telles, no places maie compare,
    Vnto our homes, where wee commaunders are.

        Admonet hoc, fectanda gradu conuiuia tardo,
        Atque domo propria dulcius effe nihil.

Industria naturam corrigit.

Ad D. H. Wh. patruelis mei F.

THE Lute, whose founde doth moſt delighte the eare,
  Was caſte aſide, and lack'de bothe ſtringes, and frettes:
Whereby, no worthe within it did appeare,
MERCVRIVS càme, and it in order ſettes:
  Which being tun'de, ſuche Harmonie did lende,
  That Poëttes write, the trees theire toppes did bende.

Euen ſo, the man on whome dothe Nature froune,
Whereby, he liues diſpiſ'd of euerie wighte,
Induſtrie yet, maie bringe him to renoume,
And diligence, maie make the crooked righte:
  Then haue no doubt, for arte maie nature helpe.
  Thinke howe the beare doth forme her vglye whelpe.

Si mihi difficilis formam natura negauit;
Ingenio forma damna rependo mea.

Whitney   Emblemes   London   1586   p.092

Motto
°Industria °naturam °corrigit.

°Industry °corrects °nature.

Picture
°Mercury in a °winged °cap repairs the °strings of a °lute; in the background a °woman °dances while another man plays a lute.

Epigram
lute   delight   ear   string   fret   Mercury   tune   harmony   poet   tree   nature   frown   despise   industry   renown   diligence   crooked   art   nature   help   bear   ugly   whelp

Reference
°Ovid Ep 12 [Her 15, 31]

Dedicatee
Hugh °Whitney

Ouid. Epiſt. 12.

Infortunia nostra, alienis collata, leuiora.
Ad eundem.

THE Aſſe, and Ape complaine, and thought theire fortunes bad:
  The Aſſe, for wante of hornes. the Ape, bycauſe no taile he had.
The Mole, then anſwere made: I haue no eyes to ſee,
Then wherefore can you nature blame, if that you looke on mee.
Which biddes vs bee contente, with lot that God doth ſende,
For if wee others wantes do wey, our happes wee maie commende.

Ouid. 9 Metam.
Quódque ego, vult ge-
mìior, vult ipſa ſocir-
que, futuri.
    At non eſt natura,
potentior omnibus iſtu.

Whitney   Emblemes   London   1586   p.093a

Motto
°Infortunia   nostra,   alienis   °collata,
°leviora.

Our °misfortunes, °compared with those of
others, become °lighter.

Picture
An °ape, °ass and a °mole discuss their
lot in life.

Epigram
ass   ape   fortune   bad   horn   tail   mole
eye   nature   blame   content   lot   God

Reference
°Ovid, Met 9

Dedicatee
Hugh °Whitney

Vxoriæ virtutes.
To my Sifter, M. D. COLLEY.

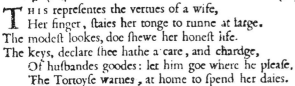

THIS reprefentes the vertues of a wife,
Her finger, ftaies her tonge to runne at large.
The modeft lookes, doe fhewe her honeft life.
The keys, declare fhee hathe a care, and chardge,
Of hufbandes goodes: let him goe where he pleafe.
The Tortoyfe warnes, at home to fpend her daies.

Plautre in Amph.

Whitney Emblemes London 1586 p.093b

Motto
°Uxoriae °virtutes.

The °virtues of °wives.

Picture
°Modesty, a woman, her °finger to her °lips, makes the °Harpocratic gesture of °silence; she holds a ring of °keys and °stands on a °tortoise.

Epigram
virtue wife finger tongue modest
honest life key husband goods
tortoise home

Reference
°Plautus, Amph

Dedicatee
M. D. °Colley, née Whitney

Inuidiae defcriptio.

Ad Ra. W.

Motto
°Invidiae °descriptio.

A °description of °envy.

Picture
°Envy, with °snakes emerging from her °mouth, plucks out her °heart from her breast with her °right hand, as she walks with the help of a °staff.

WHAT hideous hagge with vifage fterne appeares?
Whofe feeble limmes, can fcarce the bodie ftaie:
This, Enuie is: leane, pale, and full of yeares,
Who with the bliffe of other pines awaie.
    And what declares, her eating vipers broode?
    That poyfoned thoughtes, bee euermore her foode.

What meanes her eies? fo bleared, fore, and redd:
Her mourninge ftill, to fee an others gaine.
And what is mente by fnakes vpon her head?
The fruite that fpringes, of fuch a venomed braine.
    But whie, her harte fhee rentes within her breft?
    It fhewes her felfe, doth worke her owne vnreft.

Whie lookes fhee wronge? bicaufe fhee woulde not fee,
An happie wight, which is to her a hell:
What other partes within this furie bee?
Her harte, with gall: her tonge, with ftinges doth fwell.
    And lafte of all, her ftaffe with prickes aboundes:
    Which fhowes her wordes, wherewith the good fhee woundes.

Fertilior feges eft alienis femper in agris,
Vicinumq; pecus grandius yber habet.

Inuidiam Ouid.
defcribit 2. Me-
tamorph.

Lucret. 3.
Macerat Inuidia ante
oculos illũ effe potétem,
Illum adfpectari, clare
qui incedit honore:
Ipfi fe in tenebris voluti,
eumque queruntur.

Ouid. lib. 1. De
Arte Amandi.

Epigram
hog   visage   stern   Envy   lean   pale
bliss   pine1   eat   viper   poison   thought
eye   red   mourn   gain   snake   head   venom
brain   heart   breast   unrest   wrong
happy   hell   fury   heart   gall   tongue
sting   staff   prick   word   wound.

Reference
°Ovid, Met 2   °Lucretius 3
°Ovid, A A 1

Dedicatee
Ralph °Whitney

De Inuido & Auaro, iocosum.

THE Goddes agreed, two men their wifhe fhould haue:
And did decree, who firfte demaunde did make,
Shoulde haue his wifhe: and he that laft did craue,
The others gifte fhoulde double to him take.
　　The Couetous wretche, and the Enuious man:
　　Thefe weare the two, that of this cafe did fcanne.
They longe did ftriue, who fhoulde the firfte demaunde:
The Couetous man refuf'de, bicaufe his mate,
Shoulde haue his gifte then doubled out of hande:
The thought whereof, vppon his harte did grate
　　Wherefore the Goddes, did plague him for his finne,
　　And did commaunde, th'Enuious man beginne.
Who did not craue, what MIDAS cheife did choofe,
Becaufe his frende, the fruite thereof fhould finde:
But onelie wifh'de, that he one eie might loofe,
Vnto the ende, to haue the other blinde:
　　Which beinge fay'd, he did his wifhe obtaine:
　　So but one eye, was lefte vnto them twaine.
See heare how vile, thefe caytiffes doe appeare,
To GOD, and man: but chieflie (as wee fee)
The Couetous man, who hurteth farre, and neare.
Where fpytefull men, theire owne tormentors bee,
　　But bothe be bad, and he that is the befte,
　　GOD keepe him thence, where honeft men doe refte.

Whitney Emblemes London 1586 p.095

Motto
De °Invido et °Avaro, °iocosum.

Of the °envious and the °avaricious, in a °humorous tale.

Picture
An °envious and a °covetous man face each other. The envious man is °blinded in one °eye; the covetous man in both. The covetous(?) man points to three eyes on the ground between them. To the left, an open °treasure °chest.

Auth. de Gueuar
in Epiftolis fuis.

Epigram
God gift covetous envious sin Midas eye lose blind spiteful honest

Reference
Antonio de °Guevara, Ep

Ad ornatiß. virum Dn. PETRVM WITHIPOLE.

Petre, imitare petram.

WHAT IVNIVS fent his fonne, lo, here I fend to thee?
Bycaufe his name, and Nature both, with thyne doe well agree.

Difpife all pleafures vayne, .hould vertue by the hand,
And as in rage of wyndes, and Seas, the Rocke doth firmely ftande.

So ftand thou allwayes fure, that thou maift liue with fame,
Remembring how the Latins founde a Rocke fo like thy name.

Permanet in voto mens' mea 'firma fuo.

Motto
°Petre, °imitare °petram.

°Peter, °imitate the °rock.

Picture
°Four °winds °blow on a °rock which stands in a rough °sea.

Epigram

Junius	son	name	nature	despise
pleasure	vainl	virtue	wind	sea	rock
firmly	live	fame	Latin	

Reference
Hadrianus °Junius, Emblem
°Ovid, Ep 15 [Her 16, 170]

Hadrianus Iu-
nius Harlemen-
fis Medicus cla-
riff. inter Emble-
mata fua, filio
fuo Petro hocin-
fcripfit.

Ouid. Epift. 15.

Dedicatee
Peter °Withipole

Dum potes, viue.

Ad veterem suum amicum Dn. Georgivm Salmon, *qui maximo vitæ periculo Roma euasit.*

THE Cuttle fiſhe, that likes the muddie crickes,
To which, the ſea dothe flowe at euerie tide :
For to eſcape the fiſhers ginnes, and trickes,
Dame nature did this ſtraunge deuiſe prouide :
  That when he ſeeth, his foe to lie in wayte,
  Hee muddes the ſtreame, and ſafelie ſcapes deceyte.

Then man: in whome doth ſacred reaſon reſte,
All waies, and meanes, ſhoulde vſe to ſaue his life :
Not wilfullie, the ſame for to deteſt,
Nor raſhlie runne, when tyrauntes rage with ſtrife :
  But conſtant ſtande, abyding ſweete or ſower,
  Vntill the Lorde appoynte an happie hower.

  *Obſcuri latices me condunt: cernere tectam
  Atramenta vetant: abdita, tuta nato.*

Motto
Dum potes °vive.

Live, °while you can.

Picture
A °fisherman with a °net in his hand kneels on a riverbank. He reaches with his °right hand for a °cuttlefish which is muddying the °water. A °lizard(?) appears to be fleeing on the opposite bank.

Epigram
cuttle-fish muddy creek sea tide
escape fisher gin trick dome nature
devise foe mud stream safely escape
man sacred reason save life rashly
rum tyrant rage strife constant
sweet sour Lord happy hour

Reference
°Ovid, A A 3
°Reusner, Parad poet

Ovid. 3. Art. Amand.
*Nec quæ præterit, cur-
ſu reuocabitur vnda:*
  *Nec quæ præteriit
hora redire poteſt.
Vtendum eſt ætate, cito
pede labitur ætas,*
  *Nec bona tam ſequi-
tur, quam bona prima
fuit.*

Paradiſus poët.
de Sepia.

Dedicatee
George °Salmon

Stultitia sua seipsum saginari.
Ad H. S. communem viduarum procum.

THE Foxe, that longe for grapes did leape in vayne,
  With wearie limmes, at lengthe did sad departe:
And to him selfe quoth hee, I doe disdayne
These grapes I see, bicause their taste is tarte:
    So thou, that hunt'st for that thou longe hast mist,
    Still makes thy boast, thou maist if that thou list.

Whitney Emblemes London 1586 p.098a

Motto
°Stultitia sua seipsum °saginari.

To °glut oneself in one's own° foolish-ness.

Picture
A °fox leaps at bunches of °grapes hang-ing from a trellis.

Epigram
fox   grape   leap   vain1   limb   disdain
taste   tart   boast

Dedicatee
H. °S

Virescit vulnere virtus.

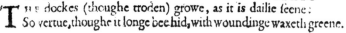
THE dockes (thoughe troden) growe, as it is dailie seene:
  So vertue, thoughe it longe bee hid, with woundinge waxeth greene.

Whitney Emblemes London 1586 p.098b

Motto
°Virescit °vulnere °virtus.

°Virtue °thrives from °wounds.

Picture
A man tramples °docks underfoot.

Epigram
dock   tread   grow   virtue   hide   wound
wax1   green

Impar coniugium.

To *Aphilus.*

Motto
°Impar °coniugium.

An °unequal °marriage.

Picture
From his °throne, °Mezentius with °crown and °sceptre oversees the °binding of a °naked living °body to a naked °corpse.

T H E tyraunt vile M E Z E N T I V S , put in vre,
Amongft the plagues, wherewith hee murthered men:
To binde the quicke, and dead, togeather fure,
And then, to throwe them both into a denne.
    Whereas the quicke, fhould ftill the dead imbrace,
    Vntill with pine, hee turn'd into that cafe.

Thofe wedding webbes, which fome doe weaue with ruthe,
As when the one, with ftraunge difeafe doth pine:
Or when as age, bee coupled vnto youthe,
And thofe that hate, inforced are to ioyne,
    This reprefentes: and doth thofe parentes fhowe,
    Are tyrauntes meere, who ioyne their children foe.

Yet manie are, who not the caufe regarde,
The birthe, the yeares, nor vertues of the minde:
For goulde is firft, with greedie men prefer'de,
And loue is lafte, and likinge fet behinde:
    But parentes harde, that matches make for goodes:
    Can not be free, from guilte of childrens bloodes.

        Quàm malè inæquales veniunt ad aratra iuuenci,
        Tam premitur magno coniuge nupta minor.

Virg. 8. Æneid.
Mortua quinetiã iun-
gebat corpora viuis,
Componens manibúfque
manus atque oribus ora.

Ouid. Epift. 9.

Epigram
tyrant Mezentius plague murder bind
quick1 dead embrace wedding web
weave ruth [= compassion] disease age1
youth hate parent tyrant join child
birth year virtue mind gold greedy
love match goods guilt child blood

Reference
°Virgil, Aen 8
°Ovid, Ep 9 [Her 9, 29]

Frontis nulla fides.

Ad Lecliß. iuuenes Dn. Edm. Freake, & Dn. Anth. Alcock.

THE lions roare : the Bores theire tuſkes do whet.
The Griphins graſpe theire tallantes in theire ire :
The dogges do barke ; the bulles, with hornes doe thret.
The Serpentes hiſſe, with eyes as redde as fire.

But man is made, of ſuche a ſeemelie ſhape,
That frende, or foe, is not diſcern'd by face :
Then harde it is the wickeds wiles to ſcape,
Since that the bad, doe maſke with honeſt grace.

And Hypocrites, haue Godlie wordes at will.
And rauening wolues, in ſkinnes of lambes doe lurke ;
And C A I N doth ſeeke, his brother for to kill,
And ſainctes in ſhewe, with I V D A s hartes doe worke.

Nowe, ſince the good no cognizance doe beare,
To teache vs, whome wee chieflie ſhould imbrace :
But that the ſame the wicked ſorte doe weare,
And ſhewe them ſelues, like them in euerie caſe.

A table lo, herein to you I ſende,
Whereby you might remember ſtill to write,
His wordes, and deedes, that beares the face of frende,
Before you chooſe, ſuche one for your delite.

And if at lengthe, yow trye him by his tuche,
And finde him hault, whereby you ſtand in dout,
No harte, nor hand, ſee that you ioyne with ſuche
But at the firſt, bee bould to raſe him out.
Yet if by proofe, my wordes, and deedes agree,
Then let mee ſtill within your tables bee.

Whitney Emblemes London 1586 p.100

Motto
°Frontis nulla °fides.

No °faith in °appearance.

Picture
A man flees from a °dog and a °bull; in the foreground an °artist draws a figure(?) on a °panel held by a second man.

Epigram
lion roar boar tusk whet griffin talon ire dog bark bull threat horn serpent hiss eye red man friend foe face wicked wile bad mask honest grace hypocrite godly word wolf skin lamb Cain brother kill saint Judas heart good cognisance table1 write word deed bold raze proof

Reference
Pontius °Paulinus, Nol Ep 2
Horace, Sat 1, 3

Dedicatee
Edmund °Freake and Anthony °Alcock

De vera Amicitia
Pontius Paulinus,
Auſon ſcribit Epiſtas
Hŏc hoſtra ceruice mi-
guem non ſana reſoluit

Fabula, non territās-
ſontia longa die mit.
Nec perŏmet, toto licet
abſtrahar orbe, vel auo:
Nunquam animo di-
uiſus agam; prius iſſa
recedet
Corpore vita mea, quā
veſter pectore vultus.

Horara. Serm. 1
At pater vt gnati, ſic
nos debemus amus,
Si quod ſit vitium non
faſtidire, &c.

Animi scrinium seruitus.

Ad ornatum virum, D. ELEISEVM GRYDHITH.

Whitney Emblemes London 1586 p.101

T HE Prouerbe faithe, the bounde muste still obey,
And bondage bringes, the freest man in awe:
Whoe serues must pleafe, and heare what other saye,
And learne to keepe *HARPOCRATES his lawe:
    Then bondage is the Prifon of the minde:
    And makes them mute, where wifedome is by kinde,

The Nightingall, that chaunteth all the springe,
Whofe warblinge notes, throughout the wooddes are harde,
Beinge kepte in cage, she ceafeth for to singe,
And mournes, bicaufe her libertie is barde:
    Oh bondage vile, the worthie mans deface,
    Bee farre from thofe, that learning doe imbrace.

*Silentij deus
apud Aegyptos.

Motto
°Animi °scrinium °servitus.

°Servitude, the °cage of the soul.

Picture
A large °cage containing a °nightingale.

Epigram
proverb bind obey bondage free serve
Harpocrates law prison mind mute
wisdom nightingale chant spring
warble wood1 cage sing mourn liberty
bondage learning

Dedicatee
Ellis °Griffith

In sortis suæ contemptores.

HER DAMOCLES, desirous for to taste,
The princelie fare, of DIONYSIVS kinge,
In royall seate, was at the table plaste,
Where pages braue, all daintie cates did bringe:
   His bed of goulde, with curious coueringes spred,
   And cubbourdes ritche, with plate about his bed.

No where hee stay'de, but musique sweete did sounde;
No where hee went, but hee did odors smell;
Nowe in his pompe, when all thinges did abounde,
Being ask'd, if that this life did please him well:
   Hee aunswere made, it was the heauen alone,
   And that to it, all other liues weare none.

Then, did the king comaunde a naked sworde,
Vnto the roofe, shoulde with a heare bee knit:
That right shoulde hange, when hee was plac'd at bourde,
Aboue his head, where he did vse to sit:
   Which when hee sawe, as one distracte with care,
   Hee had no ioye in mirthe, nor daintie fare.

But did beseech, the Tyraunt for to giue,
His former state, and take his pompe againe:
By which, wee learne, that those who meanely liue,
Haue ofte more ioye, them those who rule and raigne:
   But cheifelye, if like him they doe appeare,
   Who night, and daye, of subiectes stoode in feare.

Cicero Tusc. 5. &
Valer. Max. & Si-
don. Apollinaris.
lib. 2. epist. 13.

Horat. Serm. 1.
Satyra 1.
*Qui fit Mæcenas, vt
nemo, quam sibi sortē
Seu ratio dederit, seu
fors obiecerit, illa
Contentus viuat: laudet
diuersa sequentes?
O fortunati mercato-
res, grauis annis
Miles ait, &c.*

Horat. Carm. 3.
Ode 1.
*Districtus ensis cui su-
per impia
Ceruice pendet, non
Sicula dapes
Dulcem elaborabunt
saporem:
Non animum, cithara'-
que cantus
Somnum reducent, &c.*

Seneca Oed. Act. 3.
*Qui sceptra duro sæuus
imperio regit,
Timet timentes: metus
in auctorem redit.*

Claud. 4. honor.
*Qui terres, plus & ti-
met. sors illa tyrannū
Conuenit, inuideant cla-
rū forēsq; ac trucident,
Munis gladiū viuant,
septique venenis
Ancipites habeant te-
cti, trepidiq; minentur.*

Motto
In °sortis suae °contemptores.

On the °despisers of their own °lot.

Picture
The °sword of °Damocles, here with °wavy °blade, suspended by a thread from a °cloud.

Epigram

Damocles	taste	princely		fare
Dionysius	king	royal	seat	table
page1	cate [= provisions]		bed	gold
cupboard	plate	music	odour	pomp
naked	sword	roof	board1	head
distract	care	joy	mirth	tyrant	rule
reign	subject	fear		

Reference
°Cicero, Tusc 5
°Valerius Maximus
Sidonius °Apollinaris 2, 13
°Horace, Sat 2, 1
°Horace, C 3, 1
°Seneca, Oed 3
°Claudian, IV Hon

Interdum requiescendum.

Ad Dn. PETRVM COLVIVM *Brugenſem.*

CONTINVAL toile, and-labour, is not beſte:
But ſometimes ceaſe, and reſt thy wearie bones,
The daie to worke, the nighte was made to reſte.
And ſtudentes muſt haue paſtimes for the nones:
    Sometime the Lute, the Cheſſe, or Bowe by fittes,
    For ouermuch, dothe dull the fineſt wittes.

For lacke of reſte, the feilde dothe barren growe,
The winter coulde, not all the yeare doth raigne:
And dailie bent, doth weake the ſtrongeſt bowe:
Yea our delightes ſtill vſd, wee doe diſdaine.
    Then reſt by fittes, amongſte your great affaires,
    But not too muche, leſte ſloathe dothe ſet her ſnares.

    ——— *Nec enim facundia ſemper*
Adducta cùm fronte placet: nec ſemper in armis
Bellica turba manet: nec tota claſſicus horror
Nocte dièque gemit: nec ſemper Cnoſſius arcu
Deſtinat, exempto ſed laxat cornua neruo.
Et galea miles caput, & latm enſe reſoluit.

Whitney Emblemes London 1586 p.103

Motto
Interdum °requiescendum.

Sometimes we must °rest.

Picture
At the right °Athene(?) with °helmet, °spear and °shield, stands before a °fruit-tree and °grain °field; at the left she °sits beneath a °barren °tree before a °fallow field.

Periander apud Au-
ſonium.
Multis terribilis cauto
metuet.

Aelianus de tyran-
nis lib. 10. cap. 5. &
lib. 6. cap. 13. De
Var. Hiſt.

Lucanus ad Pi-
ſonem.

Epigram
toil   labour   rest   weary   bone   day
work   night   rest   student   pastime   lute
chess   bow   dull   wit   field   barren
cold   winter   year   reign   bend   low
weaken   disdain   sloth   snare

Reference
°Lucan
°Ausonius
°Aelian, V H 10, 5
°Aelian, V H 6, 13

Dedicatee
Peter °Colvius, of Bruges

Respice, & prospice.

Motto
°Respice, et °prospice.

°Look °backwards and °forwards.

Picture
°Janus with °two °faces, dressed in °Roman °armour holds a °sceptre in his °right hand and a °mirror(?) in his °left hand.

Epigram
Janus   double   year   old   new   fault alter   amend   image   rite   temple   god war   peace   despair   martial   law   time

Reference
°Pliny, H N 4, 7
°Pliny H N 7, 28
°Gellius 2, 11
Cornelius °Nepos
°Eutropius, Pun 2
°Appianus, B Civ 1

THE former parte, nowe paſte, of this my booke,
The ſeconde parte in order doth inſue :
Which, I beginne with IANVS double looke,
That as hee ſees, the yeares both oulde , and newe,
     So, with regarde , I may theſe partes beholde,
     Peruſinge ofte, the newe, and eeke the oulde.

And if, that faulte within vs doe appeare,
Within the yeare, that is alreadie donne,
As IANVS biddes vs alter with the yeare,
And make amendes, within the yeare begonne,
     Euen ſo, my ſelfe ſuruayghinge what is paſt ;
     With greater heede , may take in hande the laſte.

This Image had his rites, and temple faire,
And call'd the GOD of warre, and peace, bicauſe
In warres, hee warn'de of peace not to diſpaire:
And warn'de in peace, to practiſe martiall lawes:
     And furthermore , his lookes did teache this ſomme ;
     To beare in minde, time paſt, and time to comme.

Quid per gemi-
unni Janum ſi-
gnificatur.
Plin. Natur.
Hiſt. lib. :4.
cap. 7.

Mutius Sceuola.

Pietas in patriam.

Whitney   Emblemes   London   1586   p.111

Motto
°Pietas in °patriam.

°Duty towards one's °country.

Picture
A °hand holds a °sword upright over a
°fire.

Epigram
hand   sword   flame   heart   Porsenna   end1
country   fame   life   Scaenola   pain
courage   king   pardon   knight   siege
host1   might   noble   mind   day   fame
live

Reference
Cornelius °Nepos

THIS hande, and sworde, within the furious flame,
  Doth shewe his harte, that sought PORSENNAS ende:
Whose countries good, and eeke perpetuall fame,
Before his life did SCÆVOLA commende:
    No paine, had power his courage highe to quaile,
    But bouldlie spake, when fire did him assaile.

Which sighte, abash'd the lookers on, but moste
Amaz'de the kinge; who pardoned straighte the knight:
And ceasd the siege, and did remooue his hoste,
When that hee sawe one man so muche of mighte:
    Oh noble minde, althoughe thy daies bee paste;
    Thy fame doth liue, and eeke, for aye shall laste.

Corneline Ne
pos.

Habet et bellum suas leges.

CAMILLVS then, that did repulse the Gaules,
And vnto Rome her former state did giue:
When that her foes made spoile within her waules,
Lo here, amongst his actes that still shall liue.
   I made my choice, of this example rare,
   That shall for aye his noble minde declare.
Wherefore, in briefe then this his woorthie parte.
What time he did besiege FALERIA stronge:
A scoolemaster, that bare a IVDAS harte,
Vnto the place where he was fostred longe,
   Ofte walk'd abrode with schollers that hee toughte,
   Whiche cloke hee vsde, so that no harme was thoughte.
At lengthe, with sonnes of all the best, and moste,
Of noble peares, that kepte the towne by mighte:
Hee made his walke into the Romane hoste,
And, when hee came before CAMILLVS sighte,
   Quoth hee, my Lorde, lo these? thy prisoners bee,
   Which beinge kepte, FALERIA yeeldes to thee.
Whereat, a while this noble captaine stay'd,
And pondering well the straungenes of the cause:
Vnto his frendes, this in effecte hee say'd,
Thoughe warres bee ill, yet good mens warres haue lawes,
   And it behooues a Generall good to gaine
   With valiant actes, and not with treacherous traine.
With that, hee caus'de this *SINON to bee striple,
And whippes, and roddes, vnto the schollers gaue:
Whome, backe againe, into the toune they whipte,
Which facte, once knowne vnto their fathers graue:
   With ioyfull hartes, they yeelded vp their Toune:
   An acte moste rare, and glasse of true renoume.

Whitney   Emblemes   London   1586   p.112

Motto
Habet et °bellum suas °leges.

Even °war also has its °laws.

Picture
°Sinon is °whipped by his °pupils back to the °walled °town of °Faleria. The town is °besieged by °Camillus on horseback in the background.

Forius Camillus.

Barba Camilli apud Plutarchum, Xylandro interprete.
Grauis est inquit res bellum, vt quæ multis iniustis multisque violentis factis conficiatur. & tamen apud bonos viros, habentur etiam belli quædam leges, neque tantopere victoria expetenda est, vt non fugienda sint officia quæ per scelus ac malitiam efficiunt, magnum enim imperatorem suæ virtutis, nò alienæ improbitatis fiducia, conuicaat bellum gerere.

Virgil. lib. 2. Aeneid.

Epigram
Camillus Gaul Rome foe live noble mind besiege Faleria schoolmaster Judas heart foster scholar harm son peer town might Roman host prisoner yield captain war ill good law general valiant treacherous Sinon whip rod father yield town glass1 renown

Reference
°Plutarch   °Virgil, Aen 2

M. Valerius Coruinus.
Insperatum auxilium.

IF LIVIES pen haue written but the truthe,
And diuerse mo, that actes of ould declare.
Then knowe, when Gaules did dare the Roman youthe,
VALERIVS, lo, a Roman did prepare
  By dinte of sword, the challenger to trye,
  Who both in armes incountred by and by.
And whilst with force, they proou'd their weapons brighte,
And made the sparkes to flie out of the steele,
A Rauen, straight, vppon VALERIVS lighte,
And made his foe a newe incounter feele:
  Whome hee so sore did damage, and distresse,
  That at the lengthe, the Roman had successe.
For, when his foe his forces at him bente,
With winges all spread the rauen dim'd his sighte:
At lengthe, his face hee scratch'd, and all to rente,
And peck'd his eies, hee coulde not see the lighte,
  Which shewes, the Lorde in daunger doth preserue,
  And rauens raise our worldlie wantes to serue.

Motto
°Insperatum °auxilium.

°Unexpected °help.

Picture
The °head of °Valerius °Corvinus in a °plumed °helmet, the °visor open; a °raven with wings outspread is perched on the visor.

Aul. Gell. lib. 9.
cap. 11.

Eutropius rerum
Romanarum.,
lib. 2.

Epigram
Livy   pen   truth   Gaul   Roman   youth
Valerius   sword   arms   force   weapon
steel   raven   foe   damage   forces   wing
sight   face   eye   Lord   danger   preserve
raven

Reference
°Gellius 9, 11
°Eutropius, R Rom 2

Regulus Attilius.
Hosti etiam seruanda fides.

THE Confull boulde ATTILIVS, here regarde,
That AFRICKE made to tremble at his name;
Who, for his faithe receyued this rewarde,
Two hundreth thoufande men, hee ouercame.
   And three fcore fhippes, and eeke two hundreth townes,
   Yet flattringe fate, in fine vppon him frownes.
For, after by XANTIPPVS ouerthrowne,
To CARTHAGE broughte, in dungeon deepe was cafte;
Yet, with defire for to redeeme their owne,
Their meffenger they made him, at the lafte:
   And in exchaunge, hee vnto Rome was fente,
   For prifoners there, and on his worde he wente.
Who promif'd this, hee woulde retourne to bandes,
If that hee fail'd of that, they did require:
But when hee fawe fo manie in their handes,
Thoughe Romanes glad, did graunt him his defire:
   Yet coulde hee not theretoo, in harte agree,
   Bycaufe for him, fo manie fhoulde bee free.
Thus, countries loue, was dearer then his life,
Who backe retourn'de, to keepe his promife true:
Where hee did tafte longe time of tormentes rife,
But yet, his harte no tortures coulde fubdue.
   His mangled eies, the Sonne all daye affailes;
   And in the ende, was thrufte in tonne with nailes.

Cornelius Nepos.

Eutropius lib. 1. De
Bello punico.

Silius Italicus lib. 6.
Belli Punici, copio-
fiffime pulcherrimis
elegantiffimi.q. ver-
fibus hanc hifto-
riam narrat.

Aul. Gellius lib. 6.
cap. 4.

Whitney Emblemes London 1586 p.114

Motto
°Hosti etiam servanda °fides.

°Faith must be kept even to the °enemy.

Picture
Under a °sun a °bound man, °Attilius, naked to the waist lies on a wooden °stretcher next to an open °barrel riven with °nails; he is observed by a °helmeted °soldier, °battle-axe in hand.

Epigram
consul bold Attilius Africa tremble name faith reward overcome ship town fate frown Xanippus overthrow Carthage dungeon redeem messenger Rome prisoner free country love torture tun nail

Reference
Cornelius °Nepos   °Eutropius, Pun 2
°Silius Italicus, Pun 6   °Gellius 6, 4

Marcus Sergius.

Fortiter & feliciter.

Motto
°Fortiter et °feliciter.

°Bravely and °happily.

Picture
A °left °gauntlet holds a °lance which is ringed by °four °garlands.

Epigram
Marcus Sergius Roman bold foe dismay Hannibal might right2 hand lose left iron Cremona siege defend Placentia sword France triumph success fortune spear crown garland honour

Reference
°Pliny, N H 7, 18

MARC SERGIVS nowe, I maye recorde by righte,
A Romane boulde, whome foes coulde not difmaye:
Gainfte HANNIBAL hee often fhewde his mighte,
Whofe righte hande lofte, his lefte hee did affaye
    Vntill at lengthe an iron hande hee proou'd :
    And after that CREMONA fiege remoou'd.

Then, did defende PLACENTIA in diftreffe,
And wanne twelue houldes, by dinte of fworde in France,
What triumphes great ? were made for his fucceffe,
Vnto what ftate did fortune him aduance ?
    What fpeares ? what crounes ? what garlandes hee poffeft;
    The honours due for them, that did the befte.

Cn. Pompeius Magnus.

Celsa potestatis species.

WHEN POMPEY great, with fortune longe was bleste,
    And did subdue his foes, by lande, and sea,
And conquestes great obtained in the Easte,
And PARTHIANS, and ARABIANS, made obaye,
    And seas, and Iles, did in subiection bringe,
    Whose name with feare, did throughe IVDÆA ringe.

And had restor'de kinge MASINISSAS righte,
And ouercame SERTORIVS with his power:
And made the Kinge of PONTVS knowe his mighte.
Yet, at the lengthe, hee had his haplesse hower:
    For ouercome by CÆSAR, fled for aide,
    To ÆGYPTE lande; wherein hee was betrai'd.

Within whose ringe, this forme aboue was wroughte,
Whereby, his force, and noble minde appeares;
Which, with his head to CÆSAR being broughte,
For inwarde griefe, hee wash'd the same with teares,
    And in a fire with odours, and perfumes:
    This princes head with mourning hee consumes.

Whitney Emblemes London 1586 p.116

Motto
°Celsae °potestatis °species.

The °representation of °exalted °power.

Picture
A °lion °rampant holding an upright °sword.

Epigram
Pompey fortune bless subdue foe land sea conquest East Parthian Arabian obey name fear Judea king Masinissas right3 overcome Sertorius power Pontus might Caesar flee aid Egypt betray noble mind head grief wash tear fire odour perfume prince head mourn consume

Primus in Hircanum, Rubrum, & Arabicum mare. vsque peruenit, Cornelius Nepos.

De cuius maximis victoriis & triumpho longè splendidissimo aetatis suae, anno 15. Appianus libro De Bellis Mithridaticis.

Reference
Cornelius °Nepos
°Appianus, Mithr

Marcus Scæua.

Audaces fortuna iuuat.

Whitney Emblemes London 1586 p.117

Motto
°Audaces °fortuna °iuvat.

°Fortune °helps the °brave.

Picture
A °scrolled °shield pierced by many °arrows.

Epigram
monument   manhood   witness   Marcus
Scaeva   heart   valiance   gain   death
time   blemish   desert   battle   bold   fear
wound   shaft   shield   eye   lose   thigh
soldier   Caesar   host   knight   Roman
author   old

THIS monumente of manhoode, yet remaines,
 A witnes true, of MARCVS SCÆVAS harte:
Whofe valliancie, did purchafe him fuch gaines,
That deathe, nor time, can blemifhe his deferte.
    In battaile, boulde : no feare his harte coulde wounde,
    When fixe-fcore fhaftes within his fhielde weare founde,

And in that fighte, one of his eies hee lofte,
His thighe thruft throughe, and wounded fore befide:
Such fouldiours, had greate CÆSAR in his hofte,
As by him felfe, and others, is difcride.
    But, thofe that would more of thefe Knightes beholde,
    Let them perufe the Roman Aucthours oulde.

Suetonius.

Valerius Maxi-
.mus.

Reference
°Suetonius
°Valerius Maximus

Inuidia integritatis assecla.

Motto
°Invidia °integritatis °assecla.

°Envy the °attendant of °integrity.

Picture
°Frogs and °snakes crowd at the base of a °palm-tree.

Epigram
palm   frog   serpent   poison   tree
destroy   noble   peer   estate1   honour
Envy   Momus   brood   arm   arm1   wound
fame   life   light

Nic. Reusnerus.
Hæc ramis tanquam
iugitu fastigia rediens
Pondribus superum
consurgit ad astra sui.

THE gallant Palme with bodie ſtraighte, and tall,
  That freſhelie ſhowes, with braunches ſweete of ſmelk
Yet, at the foote the frogges, and ſerpentes crall,
With erckſome noiſe, and eke with poiſon fell:
    Who, as it weare, the tree doe ſtill annoye,
    And do their worſte, the ſame for to deſtroye.

When noble peeres, and men of highe eſtate,
By iuſte deſerte, doe liue in honor greate:
Yet, Enuie ſtill dothe waite on them as mate,
And dothe her worſte, to vndermine their ſeate:
    And M o m v s broode dothe arme, with all their mighte,
    To wounde their fame, whoſe life did geue them lighte.

Euſeb. apud Stob
ʒer faciebas per to-
lens, neceſſario co-
mitatur vmbra: iu-
cedentibus verò per
gloriam comitatur
iuvidia.

Reference
Nicholas °Reusner
°Eusebius
°Stobaeus

Ex damno alterius, alterius vtilitas.

Motto
Ex °damno alterius, alterius °utilitas.

One   man's   °loss   is   another   man's °advantage.

Picture
A °vulture watches from a tree as a °lion and a °boar fight.

Epigram

lion	content	vulture	spoil1	hope
prey	blood	rancour	mortal	hate
monarch	gripe	[= covetous man, usurer]		
reign	watch	loss	gain	Suleiman
empire	Christian	king	exile	love
peace				

Reference
Georgius °Sabinus
°Virgil, Aen 10
°Ovid, Met 7

THE Lion fierce, and fauage bore contende,
  The one, his pawes: his tufkes the other tries:
And ere the broile, with bloodie blowes had ende,
A vulture loe, attendes with watchinge eies:
  And of their fpoile, doth hope to præie his fill
  And ioyes, when they eche others blood doe fpill.

When men of mighte, with deadlie rancor fwell,
And mortall hate, twixte mightie Monarches raignes;
Some gripes doe watche, that like the matter well,
And of their loffe, doe raife their priuate gaines:
  So, SOLIMAN his Empire did increafe,
  When chriftian kinges exiled loue, and peace.

Hic magnus fedet Æneas fecumq, volutat
Euentus belli varios, &c.

Et pendebat adhuc belli fortuna, diuq,
Inter vtrumque volat dubiis victoria pennis.

Georgius Sabinus.
Sic modò dum faciant
difcordes prælia reges
  Turcus Europa diri-
pit hoftis opes

Virg. Aeneid. 10

Ouid Metam. 7

Vigilantia, & custodia.

Ad reuerendū Dn. D. GVILELMVM CHATTER-
TONVM Epiſcopum Ceſtrenſem.

T H E Heraulte, that proclaimes the daie at hande,
  The Cocke I meane, that wakés vs out of ſleepe,
On ſteeple highe, doth like a watchman ſtande:
The gate beneath, a Lion ſtill doth keepe.
    And why? theiſe two, did alder time decree,
    That at the Churche, theire places ſtill ſhould bee.

That paſtors, ſhoulde like watchman ſtill be preſte,
To wake the worlde, that ſleepeth in his ſinne,
And rouſe them vp, that longe are rock'd in reſte,
And ſhewe the daie of Chriſte, will ſtraighte beginne:
    And to foretell, and preache, that light deuine,
    Euen as the Cocke doth ſinge, ere daie doth ſhine.

The Lion ſhewes, they ſhoulde of courage bee,
And able to defende, their flocke from foes:
If rauening wolfes, to lie in waite they ſee:
They ſhoulde be ſtronge, and boulde, with them to cloſe:
    And ſo be arm'de with learning, and with life,
    As they might keepe, their charge, from either ſtrife.

Whitney   Emblemes   London   1586   p.120

Motto
°Vigilantia, et °custodia.

°Vigilance and °protection.

Picture
A °lion sits at the entrance to a °church. There is a °weather-vane °cock on the top of the building.

Epigram
cock wake sleep steeple watchman gate lion church pastor world sin Christ preach light divine courage defend flock foe wolf strong bold arm1 learning strife

Reference
°Augustine, Ep 124
Andrea °Alciato [Emblem 15]

Aug. in Epiſt. 124
Epiſcopi munere
in hac vita ni-
hil difficilius, ita
apud Deum nihil
beatius.

Quid per gallum
& leonem ſigni-
ficetur, Claud.
Minos ſuper Al-
ciatum Emb. 15.
accurater ſcribit.

Dedicatee
William °Chatterton, °Bishop of Chester

Festina lente.

Ad amplissimos viros Dn. FRANCISCVM WINDHAM, *& Dn.* EDWARDVM FLOWERDEWE *Iudices integerrimos.*

THIS figure, lo, AVGVSTVS did deuise,
A mirror good, for Iudges iuste to see,
And alwayes fitte, to bee before their eies,
When sentence they, of life, and deathe decree:
Then mute they haste, but verie slowe awaie,
Like butterflie, whome creepinge crabbe dothe staie.

The Prince, or Iudge, maie not with lighte reporte
In doubtfull thinges, giue iudgement touching life:
But trie, and learne the truthe in euerie sorte,
And mercie ioyne, with iustice bloodie knife:
This pleased well AVGVSTVS noble grace,
And Iudges all, within this tracke shoulde trace.

Consulere patriæ, parcere afflictis, fera
Cæde abstinere, tempus atque iræ dare,
Orbi quietem, seculo pacem suo
Hæc summa virtus, petitur hac cœlum via.

Cicero.
Est sapientis [illegible] in hoc, [illegible] non [illegible] tàm quid possit, sed etiam quid debeat, pondere: nec quantum sibi permissum meminerit, sed etiam quatenus commissum sit.

Idem 3 Offic.
Nec contra Remp. nec contra iusiurandum amici causa vir bonus faciet nec [illegible] de [illegible] ponit enim personam amici, cùm induit iudicis [illegible] nia facienda sunt, quæ amici [illegible], non amicitiæ tales, sed coniurationes [illegible] sunt.

Claud. [illegible]
[illegible]

Senec. oct. act. 3.

Whitney Emblemes London 1586 p.121

Motto
°Festina °lente.

°Hasten °slowly.

Picture
A °crab holds a °butterfly in its claws.

Epigram
Augustus mirror judge sentence life death decree haste slow butterfly crab prince truth mercy justice blood knife

Reference
°Cicero
°Claudian
°Seneca, Oct 3

Dedicatee
Francis °Wyndham Edward °Flowerdew

Sine iustitia, confusio.

Ad eosdem Iudices.

WHEN Fire, and Aire, and Earthe, and Water, all weare one:
 Before that worke deuine was wroughte , which nowe wee
 looke vppon.
There was no forme of thinges , but a confused masse :
A lumpe , which CHAOS men did call : wherin no order was.
The Coulde , and Heate , did striue: the Heauie thinges , and Lighte.
The Harde, and Softe, the Wette, and Drye. for none had shape arighte.
But when they weare dispos'd , eache one into his roome: {bloome.
The Fire, had Heate: the Aire, had Lighte: the Earthe, with fruites did
The Sea, had his increase: which thinges, to passe thus broughte:
Beholde, of this vnperfecte masse, the goodly worlde was wroughte.
Then all thinges did abounde, that seru'd the vse of man:
The Riuets greate, with wyne, and oyle, and milke, and honie, ranne.
The Trees did yeeld their fruite: thoughe planting then vnknowne.
And CERES still was in her pompe, thoughe seede weare neuer sowne.
The season , Sommer was: the Groues weare alwayes greene,
And euery banke, did beare the badge, of fragrant FLORA Queene.

Whitney Emblemes London 1586 p.122

Motto
Sine °iustitia, °confusio.

Without °justice, °confusion.

Picture
A representation of °Chaos: the °four °elements -- °fire, °air, °earth and °water -- as a confused mass. Also present are a °crescent °moon, a °sun, a °star and a °wind. In the centre, the inscription °"KAOS" [= "chaos" Gk].

Ouid. in Metam:
Lib. 1.
—quia corpore in vno
Frigida pugnabant ca-
lidu: humentia, siccis:
Mollia, cum duris: sine
pondere, habentia pon-
dus.

Tibul. e. 3.
Non domus vlla fores
habuit, non fixus in agris
Qui regeret certis fini-
bus arua lapis:
Ipsa mella dabat quer-
cus, vltroque ferebant
Obuia securis vbera la-
cte oues;
Non acies, non ira fuit,
non bella, nec ensis,
Immiti saeuus duxerat
arte faber, &c.

Epigram

fire	air	earth	water	one	work
derive	chaos	world	river	wine	oil
milk	honey	tree	fruit	Ceres	seed
sow	season	summer	grove	green	Flora
golden	world	poet	hate		ambition
pride	banish	peace	time		change
silver	age	brass	iron	curse	army
crime	rigour	revenge	evil		poor
oppress	power	law	plough	rich	wife
daughter	goods	life	blood		virtue
vice	wrong	cloak	right1		exile
falsehood	shadow	truth	love		scorn
pity	die	bloodshed	God		Justice
paradise	sacred	goddess	prince		duty
ruin	reign	kingdom	England		

This was the goulden worlde, that Poëttes praiſed moſte,
No hate, was harbor'd then at home: nor hatch'd, in forren coſte.
But after, when the earthe, with people did increaſe:
Ambition, ſtraighte began to ſpringe: and pryde, did baniſhe peace.
For, as all tymes doe change: euen ſo, this age did paſſe.
Then did the ſiluer age inſue. and then, the age of braſſe.
The Iron age was laſte, a fearefull curſed tyme:
Then, armies came of miſchiefes in: and fil'd the worlde with cryme.
Then rigor, and reuenge, did ſpringe in euell howere:
And men of mighte, did manadge all, and poore oppreſt with power.
And hee, that mightie was, his worde, did ſtand for lawe:
And what the poore did ploughe, and ſowe: the ritch away did drawe.
None mighte their wiues inioye, their daughters, or their goodes,
No, not their liues: ſuch tyraunts broode, did ſeeke to ſpill their bloodes.
Then vertues weare defac'd, and dim'd with vices vile,
Then wronge, did maſke in cloke of righte: then bad, did good exile
Then falſhood, ſhadowed truthe: and hate, laugh'd loue to ſkorne:
Then pitie, and compaſſion died: and bloodſhed fowle was borne.
So that no vertues then, their proper ſhapes did beare:
Nor coulde from vices bee decern'd, ſo ſtraunge they mixed weare.
That nowe, into the worlde, an other C H A os came:
But G o D, that of the former heape: the heauen and earthe did frame,
And all thinges plac'd therein, his glorye to declare:
Sente I v s T i c E downe vnto the earthe: ſuch loue to man hee bare
Who, ſo ſuruay'd the world, with ſuch an heauenly vewe:
That quickley vertues ſhee aduanc'd: and vices did ſubdue.
And, of that worlde did make, a paradice, of bliſſe:
By which wee doo inferre: That where this ſacred Goddes is.
That land doth floriſhe ſtill, and gladnes, their doth growe:
Bicauſe that all, to God, and Prince, by her their dewties knowe.
And where her preſence wantes, there ruine raignes, and wracke.
And kingdomes can not longe indure, that doe this ladie lacke.
Then happie England moſt, where I v s T i c E is embrac'd:
And eeke ſo many famous men, within her chaire are plac'd.

——ſed comprime motus,
Nec tibi quid liceat, ſed quid feciſſe licebit,
Occurrat, mentemq̃; domet reſpectus honeſti.

Oukl.1. Metam.
Iamque nocens ferruro, ſerroq̃ nocentius aurum Prodierat, prodit bellū, quid pugnat viroq̃. Sanguineaq̃ manu crepitantia concutit arma, Viuitur ex rapto, non hoſpes ab hoſpite tutus, Non ſoter à genero: fratrum quoque gratia rara eſt, &c.

Iſidor. 3. Ethy.
Factæ ſunt leges, vt earum metu coërceatur audacia, tutaq̃ ſit inter improbos innocentia, & in hſis improbis formidato ſupplicio refrænetur nocendi facultas.

Anſelmus de Iuſtitiæ.
Iuſtitia eſt animi libertas, tribuens vnicuique ſuam propriam dignitatem, maiori reuerentiam, pari concordiam, minori diſciplinā, Deo obedientiam, ſibi ſanctimoniam, inimico patientiam, egeno operoſam miſericordiam.

Imago Iuſtitiæ videtur apud Plutarch. lib. De Iſide & Oſiride, & apud Gell. lib. 14. cap. 4.

De officio optimi Iudicis, Claudianus ad Honorum ſic.

Reference
°Plutarch, De Is et Os
°Gellius, 14, 4
°Claudian, IV Hon
°Ovid, Met 1
°Tibullus 1, 3
°Isidor, Etym 2
°Anselm, Iust

Dedicatee
Francis °Wyndham Edward °Flowerdew

Amicitia fucata vitanda.

Motto
°Amicitia °fucata vitanda.

°Feigned °friendship to be avoided.

Picture
Two men shake °hands; one wears a °fox's °skin over his head and shoulders. A third man watches from behind two trees at the left.

Epigram
foe   arm1   malice   smile   trust   hand
fox   coat   feign   heart   danger   deadly
secret   destruction   Bias   mischief

OF open foes, wee alwaies maie beware,
And arme our selues, theire Malice to withstande:
Yea, thoughe they smile; yet haue wee still a care,
Wee trust them not, althoughe they giue theire hande:
  Theire Foxes coate, theire fained harte bewraies,
  Wee neede not doubt, bicause wee knowe theire waies.

But those, of whome wee must in daunger bee,
Are deadlie foes, that doe in secret lurke,
Whoe lie in waite, when that wee can not see,
And vnawares, doe our destruction worke:
  No foe so fell, (as Bias wise declares)
  As man to man, when mischeife hee prepares.

Permicies homini qua maxima? solus homo alter.

Hor. Arte Poet.
*Nunquam te fallant animus sub vulpe la-
tentes.*

Reference
°Horace, A P
°Bias

Bias.

Sobriè potandum.

A Thirſtie dogge, to N I L V S runnes to drinke,
A Crocodile, was readie in the flood :
Which made the dogge, to lappe harde by the brinke,
As one that much in feare of poiſoning ſtood :
    And ſparingly, began to coole his heate,
    When as hee ſawe, this Serpent lye in waite.

This carefull dogge, condemnes thoſe careles wightes,
Althoughe he bee of brutiſſhe kynde, bycauſe
Thoſe reaſon lacke, that ſpend both daies, and nightes,
Without regard, in keeping B A C C H V S lawes:
    And when throughe drinke, on feete they can not ſtande,
    Yet as they lye, they haue their boales in hande

Cantharon hic retinet : cornu bibit alter adunco :
Concauat ille manus, palmaſ́q, in pocula vertit:
Pronus at ille lacu bibit, & crepitantibus haurit
Muſta labris, &c.

Motto
°Sobrie °potandum.

One should °drink °moderately.

Picture
°Naked °Bacchus, a °wreath of °vines(?) on his head, lies on his stomach on a °river bank. He is °drinking from a °cup. Nearby a °dog leaps in front of a °crocodile waiting in the water.

Epigram
thirsty dog Nile drink crocodile
fear poison serpent reason dog night
Bacchus law drink bowl

De Crocod. Ae-
lian. de Animal.
lib.8. cap.15. &
lib. 9. cap. 3. De
præſcientia eius;
de qua, in prima
parte huius libri,
fol. 3. idem Ael.
lib. 5. cap. 52. &
lib.8. cap. 4.

Contra Ebrieta-
tom.

Paul. { *Gal.cap.5*
         { *Eph.ca.5.*
Pytha. apud Stob.
Primum poculũ
ſanitatis eſt, alte-
rum voluptatis,
tertiũ contume-
liæ, vltimum in-
ſaniæ.
Nemeſ. Eclog.3.
contra potores.

Reference
°Aelian, N A 8, 25
°Aelian, N A 9, 3
°Aelian, N A 5, 52
°Aelian, N A 8, 4
°Nemesianus, Ecl 3
°B Gal 5 °B Eph 5
°Pythagoras
°Stobaeus

Insignia poetarum.

Ad Nobiliss. & doctissvirum Dn. IANVM DOVSAM à NOORTWIICK.

T H E Martiall Captaines ofte, do marche into the fielde,
  With Egles, or with Griphins fierce, or Dragons, in theire shields.
But Phœbus sacred birde, let Poëttes moste commende.
Who, as it were by skill deuine, with songe forshowes his ende.
And as his tune delightes: for rarenes of the same.
So they with sweetenes of theire verse, shoulde winne a lasting name.
And as his colour white: Sincerenes doth declare.
So Poëttes must bee cleane, and pure, and must of crime beware.
For which respectes the Swanne, should in theire Ensigne stande.
No forren fowle, and once suppos'de kinge of L I G V R I A Lande.

    Cura ducum fuerant olim, regumq́, poëta,
      Præmiaq́, antiqui magna tulere chori.
    Sanctaq́, maiestas, & erat venerabile nomen
      Vatibus, & larga sæpè dabantur opes.
    Ennius emeruit Calabris in montibus ortus,
      Contiguus poni Scipio magne tibi,
    Nunc edera sine honore iacent: operataq́, docti
      Cura vigil Musis, nomen inersis habet.
    Sed famam vigilare iuuat, quis nosset Hemerum
      Iliac æternum si latuisset opus.

Ouid. Metam. 1.

Nic. Reusnerus.
Hunc volucrē Phœbo
fertur sacrasse vetustas
Quod referat cantus,
Delphica magna, tuos.

Hor. de arte poët.
Natura fieret laudabile
carmen, an arte,
Quæsitum est. ego nec
studii sine diuite vena,
Nec rude quid prosit
video ingenium: alte-
rius sic
Altera poscit opem res,
& coniurat amice.

Ouid. 3. Art.
ac. 11111.

Whitney   Emblemes   London   1586   p.126

Motto
°Insignia °poetarum.

The °arms1 of the °poets.

Picture
A °shield charged with a °swan1 hangs by a ribbon from the branch of a leafless tree in front of a marsh. °Two °swans float on the waters.

Epigram
captain   eagle   griffin   dragon   shield
Phoebus   sacred   bird   poet   skill
divine   song   end1   time   verse   name
white   sincere   poet   clean   pure   crime
swan   ensign   foreign   king   Liguria

Reference
°Ovid, Met 2
Nicholas °Reusner
°Horace, A P
°Ovid, A A 3

Dedicatee
Janus °Dousa

Cùm larvis non luctandum.

Whitney   Emblemes   London   1586   p.127

Motto
Cum °larvis non °luctandum.

One must not °struggle with °ghosts.

Picture
°Three °hares °bite the head of a °dead supine °lion; a fourth hare runs by.

Epigram
Hector   force   mortal   wound   life   death
Greek   corpse   assail   flee   field1
spite   hare   bite   lion   slander   defame
book   libel   name   fear   skill

Reference
°Virgil, Aen 11 [2]

WHEN Hectors force, throughe mortall wounde did faile,
And life beganne, to dreadefull deathe to yeelde:
The Greekes moste gladde, his dyinge corpes affaile,
Who late did flee before him in the fielde:
    Which when he fawe, quothe hee nowe worke your fpite,
    For fo, the hares the Lion dead doe byte.

Looke here vpon, you that doe wounde the dead,
With flaunders vile, and fpeeches of defame:
Or bookes procure, and libelles to be fpread,
When they bee gone, for to deface theire name:
    Who while they liude, did feare you with theire lookes,
    And for theire fkill, you might not beare their bookes.

Nullum cum victis certamen, & athere caffis.

Virg. Aeneid. II.

Captiuus, ob gulam.

Motto
°Captivus, ob °gulam.

°Captured by °gluttony.

Picture
A °mouse with its head caught in an °oyster °shell on a shell-strewn beach.

Epigram
mouse   oyster   death   guilty   die
glutton   belly   fear   sweet   meat   bait

Reference
°Isidor, S B 1
°Lucan 4

THE mouſe, that longe did feede on daintie crommes,
  And ſafelie ſearch'd the cupborde and the ſhelfe :
At lengthe for chaunge, vnto an Oyſter commes,
Where of his deathe, he guiltie was him ſelfe :
  The Oyſter gap'd, the Mouſe put in his head,
  Where he was catch'd, and cruſh d till he was dead.

Felo de ſe.

The Gluttons fatte, that daintie fare deuoure,
And ſeeke about, to ſatisfie theire taſte :
And what they like, into theire bellies poure,
This iuſtlie blames, for ſurfettes come in haſte :
  And biddes them feare, their ſweete, and dulcet meates,
  For oftentimes, the ſame are deadlie baites.

Iſidorus lib. 1. de ſummo bono. Gulæ ſaturitas nimia acié mentis obtundit ingeniumque euertere facit.

———— *O prodiga rerum*
Luxuries nunquam paruo contenta paratu,
Et quaſitorum terra pelagóque ciborum
ambitoſa fames, & lauta gloria menſa.

Lucanus 4.

ConStanter.

Motto
°Constanter.

°Constantly.

Picture
A °flooded °city; a °wrecked °ship lies on the shore at the left. Various vessels sail on the waters covering the town.

Epigram

sea	world	overthrow	shore	earth	ship
sail	land	town	Lord1	ghostly	foe
soul	siege	pray	fear	sleep	sin
crime					

T H E raging Sea, that roares, with fearefull founde,
  And threatneth all the worlde to ouerflowe:
The fhore fometimes, his billowes doth rebounde,
Though ofte it winnes, and giues the earthe a blowe
    Sometimes, where fhippes did faile: it makes a lande.
    Sometimes againe they faile: where townes did ftande.

So, if the Lorde did not his rage reftraine,
And fet his boundes, fo that it can not paffe:
The worlde fhoulde faile, and man coulde not remaine,
But all that is, fhoulde foone be turn'd to was:
    By raging Sea, is ment our ghoftlie foe,
    By earthe, mans foule: he feekes to ouerthrowe.

And as the furge doth worke both daie, and nighte,
And fhakes the fhore, and ragged rockes doth rente:
So Sathan ftirres, with all his maine, and mighte,
Continuall fiege, our foules to circumuente.
    Then watche, and praie, for feare wee fleepe in finne,
    For ceafe our crime: and hee can nothing winne.

Cicer.2.Off.
Præclara eft in
omni vita æqua-
bilitas, idemque
vultus, eadem-
que frons.

Bern. in Epift.
Perfeuerantia eft
finis virtutum, &
virtus fine qua
nemo videbit
deum.

Reference
°Cicero, Off 2
°Bernard, Ep

Dicta septem sapientum.

To Sir Hvghe Cholmeley *Knight.*

THE sages seuen, whose fame made Grecia glad,
    For wisedome greate, amongst theire sainges wise:
Eache one of them, a goulden sentence had,
And Alciat, did the pictures thus deuise,
    For to obserue the vse of Emblems righte,
    Which represent the meaning to our sighte.
Keepe still the meane, did Cleobulvs teache:
For measure, lo, the ballance ioyn'd thereto.
And *Knowe thy selfe*, did Chilon alwaies preache:
The glasse, behoulde, that thou the same maiste doe.
    Restraine thy wrathe, dothe Periander tell:
    And shewes an hearbe, that choller dothe expell.
Nothinge too mutche, did Pittacvs commende,
Thereto *a flowre, whereof too muche destroyes.
And Solon said, *Remember still thy ende*,
Before the which, none can haue perfect ioyes:
    A piller form'd, declininge downe he snowes,
    Which telles that deathe, the strongest ouerthrowes.
Of wicked men the number dothe exceede:
This Bias vs'd: and cause for foule defame,
Sardinia moste is stained, as we reade,
On asses backe, behoulde one of the same.
    And Thales, laste of all the Sages, say'd:
    Flee sewertiship, for feare thou be betray'd.
And vnderneathe, a birde vpon the net,
That dothe not feare, the craftie foulers call,
Hereby wee ofte, doe paie an others debte,
And free our frendes, and bringe our selues in thrall:
    Which sayinges wise, whoe keepe them in their brestes,
    By proofe shall finde, they harbour happie guestes.

Semen quod dicitur gith, quod pharmacopolæ vocant Nigellam Romanam.

Plutarch. de lib. educand. Cùm reliqua omnia tempore diminuantur, sapientia sola senectute augescit.

Bernard. Sapientiæ otia negotia sunt: & quo otiosior est sapientia, eo exercitatior in suo genere.

Whitney   Emblemes   London   1586   p.130

Motto

°Dicta °septem °sapientium.

The °sayings of the °seven °wise-men.

Picture

°Seven wise-men: °"Cleobulus" and °scales; °"Chilon" and °mirror; °"Periander" and °herb, °pennyroyal(?); °"Pittacus" and °flower, °coriander(?); °"Solon" and an overturned, °armless °statue, a °Term(?); °"Thales" and °bird, °fowler's °net and °cage; °"Bias" and °philosopher on an °ass.

Epigram

sage seven Greece wisdom Alciato
emblem mean Cleobulus measure balance
know self Chiton glass1 restrain
wrath Periander herb choler Pittacus
flower destroy Solon evil pillar
decline death wicked Bias Sardinia
ass Thales flee stewardship fear
betray bird net fowler pay debt
free friend thrall

Reference

°Plutarch, L E
°Bernard

Dedicatee

Sir Hugh °Cholmeley

Scripta manent.
To Sr ARTHVRE MANWARINGE Knight.

IF mightie TROIE, with gates of fteele, and braffe,
Bee worne awaie, with tracte of ftealinge time :
If CARTHAGE, tafte; if THEBES be growne with graffe.
If BABEL ftoope: that to the cloudes did clime:
 If ATHENS, and NVMANTIA fuffered fpoile :
 If ÆGYPT fpires. be euened with the foile.
Then, what maye lafte, which time dothe not impeache,
Since that wee fee, theife monumentes are gone:
Nothinge at all, but time doth ouer reache,
It eates the fteele, and weares the marble ftone;
 But writinges lafte, thoughe yt doe what it can,
 And are preferu'd, euen fince the worlde began.
And fo they fhall, while that they fame dothe lafte,
Which haue declar'd, and fhall to future age:
What thinges before three thoufande yeares haue pafte,
What martiall knightes, haue march'd vppon this ftage:
 Whofe actes, in bookes if writers did not faue,
 Their fame had ceafte, and gone with them to graue.
Of SAMSONS ftrengthe, of worthie IOSVAS might.
Of DAVIDS actes, of ALEXANDERS force,
Of CÆSAR greate; and SCIPIO noble knight,
Howe fhoulde we fpeake, but bookes thereof difcourfe :
 Then fauour them, that learne within their youthe :
 But loue them befte, that learne, and write the truthe.

Whitney Emblemes London 1586 p.131

Motto
°Scripta °manent.

°Writings °remain.

Picture
°Buildings and °towers °collapse about a °table with °three °books; a fourth book on the ground.

Epigram
Troy gate steel grass steal time Carthage rage Thebes grass Babel stoop cloud climb Athens Numantice suffer spoil1 Egypt spire last1 monument marble stone writing fame future age martial knight stage act book save grove Samson strength Joshua David Alexander Caesar Scipio learn youth love truth

Propertius.
Et Theba fteterant, ataque Troia fuit.

Demofth. in Arg. lib. 1.
Clariffimæ olim vrbes, nunc nihil funt, Quæ maxime nunc fuperbiunt eandem aliquando fortunam experientur.

Virg. in Mœcenatis obitu.
Marmora Mæonij vincunt monumenta libelli :
Viuitur ingenio, cetera mortis erunt. & Ouid. 1. Amor. 10.
Scindetur veftes, gemma frangitur & aurū. Carmina quæribuent, fama perennis erit.

Reference
°Propertius
°Demosthenes, Arg 1
°Moecenas
°Ovid A 10

Dedicatee
Sir Arthur °Manwaring

Whitney Emblemes London 1586 p.132

De morte, & amore: Iocosum.
TO EDWARD DYER *Esquier.*

WHILE fúrious Mors, from place, to place did flie,
And here, and there, her fatall dartes did throwe:
    At lengthe fhee mette, with Cupid paffing by,
Who likewife had, bene bufie with his bowe:
    Within one Inne, they bothe togeather ftay'd,
    And for one nighte, awaie theire fhooting lay'd.
The morrowe next, they bothe awaie doe hafte,
And eache by chaunce, the others quiuer takes:
The frozen dartes, on Cupiddes backe weare plac'd,
The fierie dartes, the leane virago fhakes:
    Whereby enfued, fuche alteration ftraunge,
    As all the worlde, did wonder at the chaunge.
For gallant youthes, whome Cupid thoughte to wounde,
Of loue, and life, did make an ende at once.
And aged men, whome deathe woulde bringe to grounde:
Beganne againe to loue, with fighes, and grones;
    Thus natures lawes, this chaunce infringed foe:
    That age did loue, and youthe to graue did goe.
Till at the lafte, as Cupid drewe his bowe,
Before he fhotte: a younglinge thus did crye,
Oh Venus fonne, thy dartes thou dofte not knowe,
They pierce too deepe: for all thou hittes, doe die:
    Oh fpare our age, who honored thee of oulde,
    Thefe dartes are bone, take thou the dartes of goulde.
Which beinge faide, a while did Cupid ftaye,
And fawe, how youthe was almofte cleane extinct:
And age did doate, with garlandes frefhe, and gaye,
And heades all balde, weare newe in wedlocke linckt:
    Wherefore he fhewed, this error vnto Mors,
    Who mifcontent, did chaunge againe perforce.
Yet fo, as bothe fome dartes awaie conuay'd,
Which weare not theirs: yet vnto neither knowne,
Some bonie dartes, in Cupiddes quiuer ftay'd,
Some goulden dartes, had Mors amongft her owne.
    Then, when wee fee, vntimelie deathe appeare:
    Or wanton age: it was this chaunce you heare.

Ioachim. Belleius.
*Mutarunt arma inter
fe Mors atque Cupido
Hic falcem geftat,
geftat at illa facem.
Afficit hæc animum,
corpus fed conficit ille:
Sic moritur iuuenis,
fic moribundus amat.*

Motto
De °morte, et °amore: °Iocosum.

°On °Death and °Love: a humorous tale.

Picture
°Eros and °Death shoot presumably ex-changed °arrows at figures in the land-scape below: a young man, shot by Eros, lies dead at the right; an old man, shot by Death, walks with a woman at the left.

Epigram
Mors fatal dart Cupid bow haste chance quiver frozen fiery virago youth wound love life end1 aged death love nature law Venus son honour dart bone gold age1 garland bald wedlock error

Reference
Joachim du °Bellay

Dedicatee
Edward °Dyer, esquire

Prudentes vino abstinent.

Whitney   Emblemes   London   1586   p.133

Motto
°Prudentes °vino °abstinent.

°Prudent men °abstain from °wine.

Picture
An °olive-tree entwined with a °grape °vine.

Epigram
vine prudent Pallas tree league wise virgin Bacchus friendship flee wine

L o e here the vine dothe clafpe , to prudent Pallas tree,
The league is nought, for virgines wife, doe Bacchus frendfhip flee.

Alciat.   *Quid me vexatis rami? Sum Palladis arbor,*
Auferte hinc botros , virgo fugit Bromium.

Englifhed fo.

Why vexe yee mee yee boughes? fince I am Pallas tree:
Remoue awaie your clufters hence, the virgin wine doth flee.

Max. lib.6.
Mulier quæ vini
vfum immodera-
rè appetit, & vir-
tutibus ianuam
claudit, & deli-
ctis aperit.

Reference
°Maximianus 6
Andrea °Alciato [Emblem 24]

In colores.
TO EDWARDE PASTON Esquier.

T H E dier, loe, in smoke, and heate doth toile,
  Mennes fickle mindes to pleafe, with fundrie hues:
And though hee learne newe collours still to boile,
Yet varijng men, woulde faine fome newer choofe:
    And feeke for that, which arte can not deuife,
    When that the ould, mighte verie well fuffife.
And fome of them, here briefflie to recite,.
And to declare, with whome they best agree:
For mourners, *blacke*, for the religious, *white*.
Which is a figne, of confcience pure, and free.
    The *greene*, agrees with them in hope that liue:
    And eeke to youthe, this colour wee do giue.
The *yelowe* next, vnto the couetous wighte.
And vnto thofe, whome ieloufie doth fret.
The man refuf'd, in *Taunye* doth delite.
The collour *Redde*, let martiall captaine get.
    And little boies, whome fhamefaftnes did grace,
    The Romaines deck'd, in *Scarlet* like their face.
The marriners, the *Blewe* becometh well.
Bicaufe it fhowes the colour of the fea:
And Prophettes, that of thinges deuine foretell,
The men content, like *Violet* arraie.
    And lafte, the poore and meaner forte prouide,
    The *medley*, *graye*, and *ruffet*, neuer dy de.

Whitney Emblemes London 1586 p.134

Motto
In °colores.

On °colours.

Picture
A °dyer at work in his studio; he lifts °cloth from a °vat of dye with a long staff.

Epigram

dyer	toil	fickle	colour	art	mourner
black	religious	white	conscience	pure
free	green	hope	youth	yellow
covetous	jealousy	tawny	red	captain
boy	shamefastness	Roman	scarlet
mariner	blue	sea	prophet	divine
content	violet	poor	gray	russet
nature	tea	thousand	colour	stranger
country	herb	worm	fly1	England
Orient	dye

Ovid de Trist.
Infælix habitum temq
porn humu habe
Nec te purpuree volans
vaccinia fucco:
Non eft confuenuens
luctibus illi color.

  Alciat.
Non fperare docet viri-
dis, fperhcatur effe
In viris quouies irrita
rebro cadit.

Reference
°Ovid, Trist
Andrea °Alciato [Emblem 118]

Loe here, a fewe of colours plaine expreſte,
And eeke the men, with whome they beſt agree:
Yet euerie one, doth thinke his hewe the beſte,
And what one likes, an other lothes to ſee:
    For Nature thoughe ten thouſande colours haue,
    Yet vnto man, more varrijng mindes ſhe gaue.
Nowe ſtraungers, who their countries ſtill commende,
And make vs muſe, with colours they recite:
Maye thinke our lande, ſmall choiſe of hues doth lende.
Bycauſe ſo fewe, of manie I doe write.
    Yet let them knowe, my Auⅽlhor theſe preſentes,
    Inoughe for thoſe, whome reaſon ſtill contentes.
But ſaye wee lacke, their herbes, their wormes, their flies,
And want the meanes: their gallant hues to frame.
Yet Englande, hath her ſtore of orient dies,
And eeke therein, a DYER moſt of fame,
    Who, alwaies hathe ſo fine, and freſhe, a hewe,
    That in their landes, the like is not to vewe.

In ſtudioſum captum amore.

A Reuerend ſage, of wiſedome moſt profounde,
Beganne to doate, and laye awaye his bookes:
For CVPID then, his tender harte did wounde,
That onlie nowe, he likde his ladies lookes:
    Oh VENVS ſtaie? ſince once the price was thine,
    Thou oughſt not ſtill, at PALLAS thus repine.

    Omnes humanos ſanat medicina dolores: Propertꝰ
    Solus amor morbi non amat artificem.

Whitney   Emblemes   London   1586   p.135

Motto
In °studiosum °captum °amore.

A °scholar °captive of °love.

Picture
An enthroned °scholar flanked by °Eros and °Venus at his left and °Athena and a °soldier at his right; he is turned towards Venus.

Epigram
sage wisdom book Cupid heart wound lady Venus prize Pallas

Reference
°Propertius 2

Abstinentia.

Ad ampliſ. virum Dn CAROLVM CALTHORPE *Regia Maſⁿ*
procuratorem in Hibernia, Dn. mihi omnibus modis colendiſſimum.

WHO ſo are plac'd, in ſacred Iuſtice roome,
And haue in charge, her ſtatutes to obſerue:
Let them with care, behoulde this garniſh'd roome,
That ſuche a one, at lengthe they maie deſerue:
Of marble harde, ſuppoſe the ſame to bee,.
An Ewer eeke, vppon one corner ſtandes,
At th'other ende, a baſon wee maie ſee:
With Towell faire, to wipe theire waſhed handes:
Th'effecte whereof, let iudges printe in minde,
That they maie leaue a laſting name behinde.
The marble ſhowes: they muſt bee firme, and ſure,
And not be pierc'd, nor mooued from the truthe:
The reſte declare: they muſt bee cleane, and pure;
And not inclin'd to rigor, or to ruthe.
But, when a cauſe before them ſhalbee harde,
With conſcience cleare, let them the ſame decide:
No Ritche, or Poore, or frend, or foe, regarde,
For feare, they doe throughe their affections ſlide:
But let them waſhe, theire handes from euerie crime,
That GOD maye bleſſe, and here prolonge theire time.

Non prius in dulcem declinat lumina ſomnum,
Omnia quàm longi reputaueris acta diei;
Quæ prætergreſſus? quid geſtum in tempore? quid non?
Cur iſti facto decus abfuit, aut ratio illi?
Quid mihi præteritum: cur hæc ſententia ſedit,
Quam melius mutare fuit? miſeratus egentem,
Cur aliquem fracta perſenſi mente dolerem?

Quid volui, quod nolle bonum foret? vtile honeſto
Cur malus antetuli? num dicto, aut denique vultu
Perſtrictus quiſquam? cur me natura, magis quàs
Diſciplina trahit? ſic acta & facta per omnia
Ingrediens, ortúque à veſpere cuncta reuoluens,
Offenſus prauis, det palmam, & præmia rectis.

Motto
°Abstinentia.

°Abstinence.

Picture
On a °marble °tomb an °ewer next to a
large °basin with folded °towel.

Epigram
sacred Justice statute tomb marble
eewer basin towel wash hand judge
last1 name firm sure truth clean
pure rigour ruth [= pity] conscience
rich poor friend foe fear affection
crime God bless time

Auguſto ſuper Pſal. 37
Apud iuſtum Iudi-
cem ſola conſcientia
propria timenda eſt.

*Auguſt. De cauſa.
vit. Cler.*
Non vos iudicetis
maleuolos eſſe, quã-
do alterius crimen
iudicatis: magis
quippe nocétes iſtis,
& fratres veſtros,
quos iudicando cor-
rigere poteſtis, ta-
cédo perire permit-
tatis.

Stobæus ex Plutar-
chi Serm. 44. retulit
imagines iudicum
apud Thebas eſſe,
ſine manibus, at
ſummi iudicis ima-
ginem clauſis ocu-
lis: Eò quòd iuſtitia
nec muneribus ca-
pi, nec hominum
vultu flecti debeat.

Auſon. de viro bo-
no Edyll. 18.

Reference
°Augustine, In Psa 37
°Augustine, Ep
°Plutarch, Serm 44
°Ausonius, Ed 18
°Stobaeus

Dedicatee
Charles °Calthorpe

Constantia comes victoriæ.
To M I L E S C O R B E T *Esquier.*

T H E ſhippe, that longe vppon the ſea dothe ſaile,
And here, and there, with varnjng windes is toſte :
On rockes, and ſandes, in daunger ofte to quaile.
Yet at the lengthe, obtaines the wiſhed coaſte :
 Which beinge wonne, the trompetts ratlinge blaſte,
 Dothe teare the ſkie, for ioye of perills paſte.

Thoughe maſter reſte, thoughe Pilotte take his eaſe,
Yet nighte, and day, the ship her courſe dothe keepe :
So, whilſt that man dothe ſaile theiſe worldlie ſeas,
His voyage ſhortes : althoughe he wake, or ſleepe.
 And if he keepe his courſe directe, he winnes
 That wiſhed porte, where laſtinge ioye beginnes.

Demetrius Phaler.
Tardè aggredere, quod aggreſſurus ſis perſeueranter proſequere. Nam
vt inquit Greg. lib.1. Mor. Incaſſum bonum agitur, ſi ante vitæ ter-
minum deſeratur : Quia fruſtra velociter currit, qui prius, quàm ad
metas venerit, deſicit.

Whitney Emblemes London 1586 p.137

Motto
°Constantia °comes °victoriae.

°Perseverance a °companion of °victory.

Picture
A °ship in full °sail runs before the °wind on a °sea.

Epigram
ship   sea   sail   wind   rock   sand   danger
coast   trumpet   joy   peril   master   pilot
course   worldly   voyage   wake   sleep
part   last1   joy

Reference
°Aristotle
°Stobaeus
°Demetrius Phalereus

Boni gubernato-
ris eſt, ventorū ſe
flatibus accom-
modare : viri au-
tem ſapiētis, ani-
mi affectibus.
Ariſt. apud Stob.

Dedicatee
Miles °Corbet, esquire

Ex *Bello, pax.*

To HVGHE CHOLMELEY *Esquier.*

THE helmet ftronge, that did the head defende,
Beholde, for hyue, the bees in quiet feru'd:
And when that warres, with bloodie bloes, had ende.
They, hony wroughte, where fouldiour was preferu'd:
    Which doth declare, the bleffed fruites of peace,
    How fweete fhee is, when mortall warres doe ceafe.

Pax me certa ducis placidos curuauit in vfum:
Agricola nunc fum, militis ante fui.

De Falce ex enfe,
Martialis.

Whitney Emblemes London 1586 p.138a

Motto
Ex °bello, °pax.

From °war, °peace.

Picture
A plumed and visored °helmet is used as a °hive by a swarm of °bees.

Epigram
helmet   hive   bee   war   bloody   honey
soldier   fruit   peace   mortal   war

Reference
°Martial, Sat

Dedicatee
Hugh °Cholmeley, esquire

Calumniam contra calumniatorem virtus repellit.

WHO fo with force againft the marble wall,
    Or piller ftronge, doth fhoote, to pierce the fame:
It not preuailes, for doune the arrowes fall,
Or backe rebounde, to him from whence they came:
    So flaunders foule, and wordes like arrowes keene,
    Not vertue hurtes, but turnes her foes to teene.

Whitney Emblemes London 1586 p.138b

Motto
°Calumniam contra calumniatorem °virtus repellit.

°Virtue turns °calumny back against the calumniator.

Picture
An °arrow °broken in two against a °marble °wall.

Epigram
force   marble   wall   pillar   shoot   arrow
slander   word   arrow   virtue   hurt   foe
teen [= injury]

Sic spectanda fides.

To GEORGE MANWARINGE *Esquier.*

THE touche doth trye, the fine, and pureft goulde:
And not the found, or els the goodly fhowe.
So, if mennes wayes, and vertues, wee behoulde,
The worthy men, wee by their workes, fhall knowe.
But gallant lookes, and outward fhowes beguile,
And ofte are clokes to cogitacions vile.

Claud. 1. Stil. de
fide.
Hæc & arcuitua, inaga
poft tempore firmus,
Manfuroque ada tonte
ligat, nec mobile uudct
Ingenium, parus stuo
pitu rec vincularivd
Diffolui patitur me fu
ftidiva pretium
Allicitur vent ha
nouo, &c.

Whitney   Emblemes   London   1586   p.139a

Motto
Sic °spectanda °fides.

Thus °faith is to be °tested.

Picture
A °right hand, surrounded by clouds, a °ring set with a gemstone on its index finger, tests a °coin or °medal on a °touchstone. The coin bears a °shield charged with °three °fleurs-de-lys; the shield surmounted by a °coronet. There is an inscription on the coin.

Epigram
touch1   try1   gold   man   way   virtue
worthy   work   gallant   look   show   beguile
cloak   cogitation   vile

Reference
°Claudian, Stil 2

Dedicatee
George °Manwaring, esquire

Illicitum non ſperandum.

H ERF NEMESIS, and Hope: our deedes doe rightlie trie.
Which warnes vs , not to hope for that , which iuſtice doth
denie.

Alciatus.
Spei ſimul & Nemeſis,
noſt u altaribus adſunt:
Scilicet vt ſperes non
niſi quod liceat.

Whitney Emblemes London 1586 p.139b

Motto

°Illicitum non °sperandum.

The °unlawful should not be °hoped for.

Picture

°Nemesis with her °bridle, stands before a °Hope; Hope, seated on a °barrel, holds a °bow in her °left hand and points with her °right.

Epigram

Nemesis Hope deed try1 hope justice

Reference

Andrea °Alciato [Emblem 46]

Feriunt summos fulmina montes.

To I. T. *Esquier.*

T H E bandogge, fitte to matche the bull, or beare,
  With burthens greate, is loden euery daye:
Or drawes the carte, and forc'd the yoke to weare:
Where littell dogges doe passe their time in playe:
    And ofte, are bould to barke, and eeke to bite,
    When as before, they trembled at his sighte.

Yet, when in bondes they see his thrauled state,
Eache bragginge curre, beginnes to square, and brall:
The freër sorte, doe wonder at his fate,
And thinke them beste, that are of stature small:
    For they maie sleepe vppon their mistris bedde,
    And on their lappes, with daynties still bee fedde.

The loftie pine, with axe is ouerthrowne,
And is prepar'd, to serue the shipmans turne:
When bushes stande, till stormes bee ouerblowne.
And lightninges flashe, the mountaine toppes doth burne.
    All which doe shewe: that pompe, and worldlie power,
    Makes monarches, markes: when varrijnge fate doth lower.

Luxuriant animi rebus plerumque secundis,
    Nec facile est aqua commoda mente pati.

Whitney Emblemes London 1586 p.140

Motto
Feriunt summis °fulmina °montes.

°Lightning strikes the °mountain tops.

Picture
A large °dog pulls a °cart. His driver
brandishes a stick to drive off two
smaller dogs harrassing the cart dog. In
the foreground another small °dog sleeps
in a °woman's lap.

Gregor. in mor.
Cùm quis ponitus
in prosperitate
diligitur, incer-
tum est, vtrum
prosperitas an
persona diligatur.
Amissio autê fœ-
licitatis interro-
gat vim di ectio-
nis: nec prosperi-
tas quidem ami-
cum indicat, nec
aduersitas inimi-
cum celat.

  Eras. in Epist.
Nihil aduersum,
nisi quod nobis
obstat ad æter-
nam fœlicitatem
properantibus:
nihil prosperum,
nisi quod deo
conducit.

Ouid. 1. Art.
Amandi.

Epigram
bandog [= mastiff] bull bear burden
cart yoke dog play bark bite thrall
brag cur brawl free fate sleep
mistress bed lap pine axe shipman
bush storm lightning mountain burn
pomp worldly power monarch fate

Reference
°Gregory, Mor   °Erasmus, Ep
°Ovid, A A 2

Dedicatee
I. °T., esquire.

Perfidus familiaris.

To G. B. Esquier.

WHILE throughe his foes, did boulde BRASIDAS thruste,
And thought with force, their courage to confounde :
Throughe targat faire, wherein he put his trufte,
His manlie corpes receau'd a mortall wounde.
    Beinge afk'd the caufe, before he yeelded ghofte:
    Quoth hee, my fhielde, wherein I trufted mofte.

Euen fo it happes, wee ofte our bayne doe brue,
When ere wee trie, wee truft the gallante fhowe :
When frendes fuppoaf'd, do prooue them felues vntrue,
When SINON falfe, in DAMONS fhape dothe goe :
    Then gulfes of griefe, doe fwallowe vp our mirthe,
    And thoughtes ofte times, doe fhrow'd vs in the earthe.

All is not goulde that glittereth to the eye:
Some poifon ftronge, a fugred tafte doth keepe;
The crabbe ofte times, is beautifull to fee.
The Adder fell, within the flowers doth creepe :
    The braueft tombe, hath ftinking bones within :
    So fawninge mates, haue alwaies faithleffe bin.

Yet, to preuent fuch harmes before they fall,
Thinke howe thy frende, maie liue to bee thy foe :
Then, when your loue exceedeth mofte of all,

Lacedæmoniorum dux apud Plutarchum.

Sæpe fub agnina latet hirtus pelle Lycaon: Subque Catone pio, perfidus ille Nero.

Whitney Emblemes London 1586 p.141

Motto
°Perfidus °familiaris.

The °perfidious °friend.

Picture
°Brasidas points to his °shield which has been °pierced by the °arrow which wounded him.

Epigram
foe	bold Brasidas	force		courage
target	corpse	mortal	wound	shield
trust	bane	friend	Simon false	Damon
gulf	grief	mirth	shroud	earth gold
glitter	poison	sugar	taste	crab
adder	flower	tomb	bone	fawn1 mate
faithless	horn	friend	love	tongue
fear	speech	smart1	Judas	heart weigh
strife	cross	loss	knot	knit Scipio
Lelius	try1 trust			

Reference
°Plutarch °Cato
°Plautus, Capt

Dedicatee
G.°B. esquire

Whitney   Emblemes   London   1586   p.141

Looke that thy tonge, doe not at randonne goe :
   For feare thy fpeeche, doe turne vnto thy fmarte,
   If that thy mate, doe beare a I V D A s harte.

But, if thou doe inioye a faithfull frende,
See that with care, thou keepe him as thy life :
And if perhappes he doe, that maye offende,
Yet waye thy ftende : and fhunne the caufe of ftrife,
   Remembringe ftill, there is no greater croffe;
   Then of a frende, for, to fuftaine the loffe.

Yet, if this knotte of frendfhip be to knitte,
And S c i p i o yet, his L E L I V s can not finde ?
Content thy felfe, till fome occafion fitte,
Allot thee one, according to thy minde :
   Then trie, and trufte : fo maifte thou liue in reft,
   But chieflie fee, thou trufte thy felfe the befte?

Plaut. Capt.
Fac fidelis fis fideli:
caue fluxam fidem
geras.

Cato.
Damnaru nunquã poft
longum tempus amicũ,
Mutauit mores, fed pi-
gnora prima tenento.

In copia minor error.

T н е ape in tree, beganne at foxe beneath to raile :
   And faid , hee was a fhamelefſe beaſt to weare ſo great a taile.
Then aunſwere made the foxe . I maye thee more deride,
Becauſe thou haſte no taile at all, thy fhamelefſe partes to hide.
Which fhewes the bitter fruite , that doth of mocking ſpringe:
The ſcorners ofte, ſuch mates doe meete, that worfe then ſerpentes ſtinge.

Motto
In °copia minor °error.

Lesser °error in °abundance.

Picture
A man observes a seated °fox looking up at an °ape on the branch of a tree; the fox and ape are insulting each other.

Epigram
ape   tree   fox   rail   shameless   tail
deride   hide   bitter   fruit   mock
scorner   mate   serpent   sting

Whitney Emblemes London 1586 p.143

Vindice fato.

To G. B. *sen. Esquier.*

Motto
°Vindice °fato.

With °fate as °protector.

Picture
The °right hand of Emperor °Valens, which has a ring on its index finger, either reaches for or lets fall a °quill °pen. The hand is surrounded by clouds.

Epigram
sentence wrong will rigour Emperor Valens condemn Saint Basil exile pen quill ink hand shake shrink fear writ Lord rash refrain

WHEN ſentence wronge, of will, and rigor vile,
Was framd, to pleaſe the Emperor VALENS minde:
Which ſhoulde condemne Sainct BASIL to exile:
And nothinge lack'd, but that it was not ſign'd:
  Th'Emperor thoughte to take no longer pauſe,
  But tooke his penne, for to confirme the cauſe.

But all in vayne, the quill would take no inke,
Yet ſtill herein, he lewdlie did perſiſte:
Vntill his hande beganne to ſhake, and ſhrinke,
Whereby, the penne did fall out of his fiſte:
  Wherefore for feare, he rente the writte in twaine,
  Then feare the Lorde, and raſhe attemptes refraine.

Valens Imperator, Arrianæ ſe-
ctæ faũtor, tan-
dem per Gothos
victus, in do-
muncula qua ab-
ſconditus erat,
combuſtus anno
Domini 380.
Sabel. & Sex.
Aur.

Reference
°Sabellicus
Sextus °Aurelius Victor

Dedicatee
G. °B. senior, esquire

Homo homini lupus.

Motto
°Homo homini °lupus.

°Man is a °wolf to man.

Picture
°Arion and his °harp are thrown overboard by °sailors; a °dolphin waits at the side of the °ship.   In the background Arion, harp in hand, sits astride a dolphin.

Epigram
mortal	foe	poison	spite	man	mischief
monster	friend	death	kindness		danger
Arion	gold	harp	voice	ship	Corinth
pilot	rob	sea	dolphin	safe	

N O mortall foe fo full of poyfoned fpite,
As man, to man, when mifchiefe he pretendes:
The monfters huge, as druers aucthors write,
Yea Lions wilde, and fifhes weare his frendes:
    And when their deathe, by frendes fuppof'd was fought,
    They kindneffe fhew'd, and them from daunger brought.

A R I O N lo, who gained ftore of goulde,
In countries farre: with harpe, and pleafant voice:
Did fhipping take, and to C O R I N T H V S woulde,
And to his wifhe, of pilottes made his choife:
    Who rob'd the man, and threwe him to the fea,
    A Dolphin, lo, did beare him fafe awaie.

        Quis nefcit vaftas olim delphina per vndas,
         Lefbida cum facro vate tuliffe lyram?

Sicut Rex in imagi-
ne fua honoratur :
fic Deus in homine
diligitur, & oditur.
Non poteft homi-
nem odire, qui deû
amat, nec poteft
deû amare qui ho-
minem odit. Chryf.
fuper Matth 22.

Mira fabula de An-
drode & Leone.
Aul. Gel.li. 5.ca.14.

Item de Arione
lib.16.cap 19.

Parad.poëticus.

Reference
°Chrysostom
°B Matt 22
°Gellius 5, 14
°Gellius 16, 19
°Reusner, Parad poet

In curiosos.

Motto

In °curiosos.

On the °curious.

Picture

An °ape, having tampered with a carpenter's °tools--a °wedge, °axe and °mallet --finds his foot caught in a half-split °log. The workman, at his door, points from the right.

Epigram

maiden sew scholar school Palinurus compass card [= chart] Mars arms1 Vulcan tool Corydon plough Pan pipe bilbo blade grime cool Job whip lash art trade skill workman sleep ape block foot crush stock

LET maidens fowe; let fchollers: plie the fchooles.
Giue PALINVRE: his compaffe, and his carde.
Let MARS, haue armes: let VVLCANE, vfe his tooles.
Giue CORYDON, the ploughe, and harrowe harde.
  Giue PAN, the pipe: giue bilbowe blade, to fwafhe.
  Let Grimme haue coales: and Iobbe his whippe to lafhe.

Let none prefume an others arte to vfe,
But trie the trade, to which he hath bene kept:
But thofe that like a fkill vnknowne to choofe,
Let them beholde: while that the workeman flept,
  The toying ape, was tempringe with his blockes,
  Vntill his foote was crufh'd within the ftockes.

    Nauita de ventis; de tauris narrat arator;
    Enumerat miles vulnera; paftor oues.

Horat. Epift 1.b.2,
cap. 1,
...quid medicorum eft
Promittunt medici,
tractant fabrilia...

Propertius, :

Reference
°Horace, Ep 2, 1
°Propertius, 2, 1

In iuuentam.

Two fonnes of I o v e that beſt of man deſerue,
A p o l l o great, and B a c c h v s, this impartes:
With diet good, the one doth healthe preſerue,
With pleaſante wine, the other cheares our hartes.
    And theiſe, the worlde immortali Goddes would haue,
    Bicauſe longe life, with ſweete delighte, they gaue.

But if theiſe are ſo ſoueraigne vnto man,
That here, with ioye they doe increaſe his daies,
And freſhe doe make the carefull colour wanne:
And keepe him longe from ſicknes, and diſeaſe:
    I graunte, they ought to be renowmed more,
    Then all the Goddes, the Poëttes did adore.

Tu vino curas, tu victu dilue morbos,
Vt lento accedat curua ſenecta pede.

Motto
In °iuventam.

On °youth.

Picture
°Bacchus and °Apollo stand on a °pedestal or °tomb. Bacchus has a °crown of °vine °leaves and a bunch of °grapes; Apollo holds his °lyre.

Epigram

two	son	Jove	Apollo	Bacchus	diet
health	wine	cheer	heart	world	
immortal	god	life	joy	day	colour
sickness	disease	poet			

Reference
Andrea °Alciato [Emblem 100]

Fel in melle.

Whitney   Emblemes   London   1586   p.147

Motto
°Fel in °melle.

°Bitterness in °honey.

Picture
A °bee stung °Eros flies to the arms of a seated °Venus. Bees chase Eros and swarm around two °hives sheltered under an awning at the side of a house in the background.

Epigram
Cupid honey bee power labour sweet sour force arm1 sting hive naked corpse1 wound rash rise joy gallant show nettle rose bait beauty poison

Reference
°Reusner, Parad poet

LO CVPID here, the honie hyes to tafte,
On whome, the bees did ftraight extende their power:
For whilft at will he did their labours wafte,
He founde that fweete, was fauced with the fower:
  And till that time hee thought no little thinges,
  Weare of fuche force: or armed fo with ftinges.

The hyues weare plac'd accordinge to his minde,
The weather warme, the honie did abounde.
And CVPID iudg'd the bees of harmeleffe kinde,
But whilfte he tri'de his naked corpes they wounde:
  And then to late his rafhe attempte hee ru'de,
  When after fweete, fo tarte a tafte infu'de.

So ofte it happes, when wee our fancies feede,
And only ioye in outwarde gallant fhowes.
The inwarde man, if that wee doe not heede,
Wee ofte, doe plucke a nettle for a rofe:
  No baite fo fweete as beautie, to the eie,
  Yet ofte, it hathe worfe poyfon then the bee.

Para l'f. poëtieus.
Melle gerunt verfufa,
gerunt perfufa veneno,
  Et fua fpicula apas,
& fua fpicula amor.

Fere simile ex Theocrito.
To LAVRA.

WHILST CVPID had defire to tafte the honie fweete,
And thruft his hand into the tree, a bee with him did meete.
The boye no harme did doubt, vntill he felt the ftinge:
But after to his mother ranne, and ofte his handes did wringe.
And cry'd to her for helpe, and toulde what hap befell:
Howe that a little beaft with pricke, did make his finger fwell.
Then VENVS fmiling fay'd, if that a little bee?
Doe hurte fo fore: thinke howe thou hurt'ft? that art a childe to fee.
For where the bee can pierce no further then the fkinne:
Thy dartes do giue fo great a wounde, they pierce the harte within.

Cùm quo conuenit aliud ex Anacreonte.

AS VENVS fonne within the rofes play'd,
A bufie bee that crept therein vnfeene,
The wanton wagge with poyfoned ftinge affay'd:
Whereat, aloude he cri'de, throughe fmarte, and teene.
  And fought about, his mother for to finde:
  To whome, with griefe he vttered all his minde.
And fay'd, behoulde, a little creature wilde,
Whome hufbandmen (I heare) doe call a bee,
Hath prick'd mee fore alas: whereat fhee fmil'de,
And fay'd: my childe, if this be griefe to thee,
  Remember then, althoughe thou little arte?
  What greeuous wounde, thou makeft with thy darte.

Whitney Emblemes London 1586 p.148

Motto
Fere simile ex °Theocrito.

Almost the same from °Theocritus.

Picture
°Eros shows his °bee stung °hand to °Venus; bees swarm around the entrance to their °hive, which is in the trunk of a tree in the background.

Epigram
Cupid honey hand bee sting mother cry help prick finger Venus dart wound heart son rose play poison grief husbandman wound

Reference
°Theocritus
°Anacreon

Dedicatee
°Laura

Amor ſui.
To D. E.

The woodcut text in margin:

Ouid. Metam lib. 3.

Anulus in pict.
poët.
Narciſſus liquidu for-
mā ſpeculatus in vndis,
Contemnens alios, arſit
amore ſui, &c.

Terent. And. 1. & 4.
Verum illud verbũ eſt,
vulgo quod dici ſolet
Omnes ſibi malle me-
lius eſſe, quàm alteri.

Suum cuique pul-
chrum eſt, adhuc
neminem cognoui
poëtam, qui ubi nõ
optimus videretur,
ſic res habet, me de-
lectant mea, te tua.
Cicer. 5. Tuſcul.

Nᴀʀᴄɪssᴠs loude, and liked ſo his ſhape,
He died at lengthe with gazinge there vppon:
Which ſhewes ſelfe loue, from which there fewe can ſcape,
A plague too rife : bewitcheth manie a one.
   The ritche, the pore, the learned, and the ſotte,
   Offende therein : and yet they ſee it not.

This, makes vs iudge too well of our deſertes,
When others ſmile, our ignorance to ſee:
And whie? Bicauſe ſelfe loue doth wounde our hartes,
And makes vs thinke, our deedes alone to bee.
   Whiche ſecret ſore, lies hidden from our eyes,
   And yet the ſame, an other plainlie ſees.

What follie more, what dotage like to this?
And doe we ſo our owne deuiſe eſteeme?
Or can we ſee ſo ſoone an others miſſe?
And not our owne? Oh blindnes moſt extreme.
   Affect not then, but trye, and proouc thy deedes,
   For of ſelfe loue, reproche, and ſhame proceedes.

Whitney Emblemes London 1586 p.149

Motto
°Amor °sui.

°Love of °oneself.

Picture
°Narcissus, kneeling at a °stream, admires his own °reflection. °Echo(?),
waving with her °left hand, stands under
a tree in the distance. A °flower, a
°narcissus(?), grows near Narcissus.

Epigram
Narcissus   die   self   love   escape
plague   bewitch   rich   poor   learned   sot
judge   dessert2   ignorance   wound   heart
secret   sore   folly   dotage   devise
esteem   blindness   try1   prove   deed
self   love   reproach   shame

Reference
°Ovid, Met 3
Brthelémy °Aneau, Pict poes
°Terence, And 2, 4
°Cicero, Tusc 5

Dedicatee
D. °E.

Nusquam tuta fides.

Whitney Emblemes London 1586 p.150

Motto
Nusquam °tuta °fides.

Nowhere is °faith °safe.

Picture
A sleeping °elephant rests against a large °tree. The tree has been under-mined by a °hunter with an °axe(?).

NO ſtate ſo ſure, no ſeate within this life
  But that maie fall, thoughe longe the ſame haue ſtoode:
Here fauninge foes, here fained frendes are riſe.
With pickthankes, blabbes, and ſubtill Sinons broode,
  Who when wee truſte, they worke our ouerthrowe,
  And vndermine the grounde, wheron wee goe.

The Olephant ſo huge, and ſtronge to ſee,
No perill fear'd: but thought a ſleepe to gaine
But foes before had vndermin'de the tree,
And downe he falles, and ſo by them was ſlaine:
  Firſt trye, then truſte: like goulde, the copper ſhowes:
  And NERO ofte, in NVMAS clothinge goes.

Fœdera mortales ne ſæuo rumpite ferro,
Sed caſtam ſeruate fidem: fulgentibus oſtro
Hæc potior regnis, &c.

Ælian. de Animal.
lib.13. cap.v. ſcribit
quod Elephāti ſuur,
altitudinis 9. cu-
bitorum, latitud.5.
& lib.17.ca.7.quod
viuunt ad ætatem
200. Annorum &
nonnulli ad 300. &
multa mira de illis,
lib.10. cap.15.

Cato lib.1.
Fiſtula dulce canit vo-
lucrem dum decipit au-
ceps.

Numa Pompilius
Roman. Rex 1.

Silius 11.

Epigram
state   sure   life   fall   fawn1   foe
feign   friend   pickthank [= sycophant]
blab   Sinon   brood   trust   overthrow
elephant   strong   peril   fear   sleep
tree   slay   try1   trust   gold   copper
Nero   Numa   clothing

Reference
°Aelian, N A 13, 8
°Cato
°Silius 1, 3

Quod non capit Christus, rapit fiscus.

WHERE couetoufnes the fcepter doth fupporte,
There, greedie gripes the Kinge dothe ofte extoll:
Bicaufe, he knowes they, doe but make a fporte,
His fubiectes poore, to fhaue, to pill, and poll?
  And when he fees, that they are fatte, and full?
  He cuttes them of, that he maye haue theire wolle?

Vnto a fponge, theife are refembled righte:
Which drie at firfte, when it with water fwelles,
The hande that late did wette it, being lighte:
The fame againe, the moifture quite expelles.
  And to the flood, from whence it latelie came,
  It runnes againe, with wringinge of the fame.

> Orbem iam totum victor Romanus habebat,
> Quà mare, quà terra, quà fidus currit vtrumque,
> Nec fatiatus erat, grauidis freta pulfa carinis,
> Iam peragrabantur, fi quis finus abditus vltra,
> Si qua foret tellus, qua fuluum mitteret aurum, &c

Whitney Emblemes London 1586 p.151

Motto
Quod non capit °Christus, rapit °fiscus.

What °Christ does not take, the °treasury snatches.

Picture
A °king, with °crown and °sceptre, squeezes °water from a °sponge; a crowd watches a °hanging (°gibbet) in the background.

Epigram
covetous sceptre greedy gripe king sport subject poor shave pill poll fat cut wool sponge dry water swell hand

Reference
°Petronius Arb

Petrus Arbiter.

Paupertarem summis ingeniis obesse ne prouehantur.

Ad Doctiß. virum Dn. W. MALIM.

Whitney Emblemes London 1586 p.152

Motto

°Paupertatem summis °ingeniis obesse ne °provehantur.

°Poverty °hinders the greatest °talents from °advancing.

Picture

A man is weighted down by a °stone bound to his °right °arm as he lifts his °winged °left arm and leg skywards towards °God(?). A bank of clouds hides the sun.

Epigram

hand wing fly star win immortal fame necessity bar dust bury name bind stone ground wish will moment want1 woe deny desire wit learning excel high estate1 poverty clog care pull ascend

Reference

°Juvenal

Dedicatee

William °Malim

O NE hande with winges, woulde flie vnto the ftarres,
And raife mee vp to winne immortall fame:
But my defire, neceffitie ftill barres,
And in the dufte doth burie vp my name:
  That hande woulde flie, th'other ftill is bounde,
  With heauie ftone, which houldes it to the ground.

My wifhe, and will, are ftill to mounte alofte.
My wante, and woe, denie me my defire:
I fhewe theire ftate, whofe witte, and learninge, ofte
Excell, and woulde to highe eftate afpire:
  But pouertie, with heauie clogge of care,
  Still pulles them downe, when they afcending are.

Haud facilè emergunt, quorum virtutibus obftat
Res angufta domi, &c.

Iuuenalis.

Pro bono, malum.

T H E ſtagge, that hardly ſkap'd the hunters in the chaſe,
    At lengthe, by ſhadowe of a tree, founde refuge for a ſpace.
And when the eger houndes had lefte their wiſhed praye,
Behoulde, with biting of the boughes, him ſelfe hee did bewraye.
Throughe which, the hunter ſtraight did pierce him to the harte:
Whereat, (quoth hee) this wounde I haue, is iuſtly my deſerte.
For where I good did finde, I ought not ill requite:
But lo, theſe boughes that ſau'd my life, I did vnkindly bite.
Wherefore, althoughe the tree could not reuenge her wronge:
Yet nowe by fates, my fall is wrought, who mighte haue liued longe.

Whitney Emblemes London 1586 p.153a

Motto
Pro °bono, °malum.

°Evil for °good.

Duodecem hæc ſequentia, ob elegantiam, & venuſtatem: è G. Faerni, ſelectis fabulis ſumpta.

Picture
A °stag, hidden in a leafy grove, is struck by an °arrow; a °hunter approaches the grove from the right with °two °dogs. Two other hunters move in from a rise in the background.

Epigram
stag escape hunter chase shadow tree
refuge hound prey betray hunter
pierce heart wound just desert2 good
ill requite bough save life bite
tree revenge wrong fate fall

Reference
Gabriello °Faerno, Fab

In pace de bello.

Whitney Emblemes London 1586 p.153b

T H E bore did whette his tuſkes, the foxe demaunded why :
Since that he had no foes at hande, that ſhould their ſharpnes try.

To which, he anſwere made, when foes doe me beſet,
They all aduantage gladlie take, and giue no leaue to whet.
Which teacheth vs, in peace, our force for warres to frame :
Whereby, we either ſhall ſubdue, or looſe the field with fame.

Motto
In °pace de °bello.

Concerning °war in °peace.

Picture
A °boar, with °tusks sharpened on a tree, faces a °fox.

Epigram
boar   tusks   fox   foe   sharp   try1   peace
force   war   subdue   lose   field1   fame

Aliena pèricula, cautiones noſtræ.

THE lyon, aſſe, and foxe, goe forthe to hunte for pray:
    Which done: the lyon bad the aſſe, the ſpoile in partes to lay.
Then he with greate regarde, three partes alike did ſhare:
Wherat, the lyon in a rage, the aſſe in peeces tare.
The foxe he charged then, for to performe the ſame:
Who, all the beſte, vppon one heape, did for the lyon frame:
And littell of the worſte, did for him ſelfe reſerue:
Then beinge aſk'd, what taughte him ſo vnequally to carue?
This ſpectacle (quoth hee) which I behoulde with care:
Which ſhowes, thoſe happie that can bee by others harmes beware

Whitney   Emblemes   London   1586   p.154

Motto

Aliena °pericula, °cautiones nostrae.

Others' °dangers are our °warnings.

Picture

A °lion and a °fox face each other over their °prey, various animals, including a °stag, in a heap. An °ass, presumably slain by the lion, lies in the background.

Epigram

lion   ass   fox   hunt   prey   spoil1   share
rage   tear1   piece   happy   harm   beware

Indulgentia parentum, filiorum pernicies.

Whitney Emblemes London 1586 p.155

A Theefe, condemn'd to dye, to execution lead:
His wofull mother did beholde, for forowe almofte dead.
And whilst she kiss'd her sonne, whome she did tender deare:
The towarde childe did kiffe with teeth? and off her nose did teare:
Whereat, the standers by exclaymed at his acte:
Then quoth the theefe, my masters marke, I will defend the facte.
My mother, in my youthe, did with my faults difpence:
And euermore did like me best, when I did most offence.
So that, she was the caufe that made me doe amisse:
For if shee had correction vfde, I had not come to this.
Wherefore, I did reuenge my wronge, in what I mighte:
In hope my facte shall mothers warne, that doe behould this fighte.
For if the Children steale, and come vnto the rope:
It often is the parentes faulte, for giuing them much fcope.

Motto
°Indulgentia °parentum, °filiorum °pernicies.

The °indulgence of °parents is the °bane of °children.

Picture
A °thief, escorted to his °hanging by soldiers on foot and on horseback, is met and embraced by his °mother. The °gibbet lies on the ground.

Epigram
thief   condemn   die   execution   mother   sorrow   die   kiss   son   child   teeth   nose   youth   fault   offence   correction   revenge   wrong   hope   warn   steal   rope   parent

Dolor è medicina.

A Purblinde dame agreed with one to helpe her fight;
Who, daylie when he home retorn'd, did fteale what fo he might.
At lengthe when all was gone, the pacient gan to fee:
And then, the falfe Phifition afk'd the price, they did agree.
Whereat quoth fhe, alas, no remedie I finde:
Bycaufe my fences either faile, or ells my eies bee blinde.
For, where my houfe before was garnifh'd euerie nooke:
I, nowe can fee no goodes at all, though rounde about I looke.

Whitney Emblemes London 1586 p.156a

Motto
°Dolor e °medicina.

°Pain from the °medicine.

Picture
A °blind °woman, her eyes bandaged, sits in an armchair in an empty room. A dishonest °doctor, leaves the room with an armful of her possessions.

Epigram
purblind   dame   help   sight   steal
patient1   see   false   physician   price
remedy   sense   fail   eye   blind   house
garnish   goods

Dura vsu molliora.

WHEN firſt the foxe, the lyon did behoulde,
  Hee quak'd for feare, and almoſt dead did fall:
The ſecond time, he waxed ſomewhat boulde;
But at the third, hee had no feare at all.
    Which ſhewes, that artes at firſt moſte harde to ſee,
    With triall oft, both playne, and eaſie bee.

Whitney Emblemes London 1586 p.156b

Motto
°Dura °usu °molliora.

°Difficult things become °easier with
°practice.

Picture
A °fox cowers before a fierce-looking
°lion.

Epigram
fox lion fear dead waxl bold art
hard triall easy

In eos, qui, proximioribus ſpretis, remotiora ſequuntur.

THASTRONOMER, by night beheld the ſtarres to ſhine:
And what ſhould chaunce an other yeare, began for to deuine.
But while too longe in ſkyes, the curious foole did dwell,
As hee was marchinge through the ſhade, he ſlipt into a well.
Then crying out for helpe, had frendes at hand, by chaunce;
And nowe his perill being paſt; they thus at him doe glaunce.
What fooliſhe art is this? (quoth they) thou hould'ſt ſo deare,
That doth forſhowe the perilles farre: but not the daungers neare.

> Saturnus procul eſt, iámque olim cæcus, vt aiunt,
>   Nec propè diſcernens à puero lapidem:
> Luna verecundis formoſa incedit ocellis,
>   Nec niſi virgineum virgo videre poteſt:
> Iupiter Europam, Martem Venus, & Venerem Mars,
>   Daphnen Sol, Herſen Mercurius recolit:
> Hinc factum, Aſtrologe, eſt, tua cùm capit vxor amantes,
>   Sidera ſignificent vt nihil inde tibi.

Motto

In eos, qui, proximioribus °spretis remotiora °sequuntur.

On those who, having °spurned what is more near, °pursue what is more remote.

Picture

An °astronomer, his eyes raised to the °starry °sky, falls into a °well. A fallen °armillary °sphere or °astrolabe lies in the foreground.

Epigram

astronomer   night   star   divine1   chance
year   sky   curious   fool   shade   slip
well   help   friend   peril   art   foreshow
far   danger   near

Reference

°More, Epig

Morus in Epig.

Post fata: uxor morosa, etiam discors.

COLASMVS wife, in raging flood was drown'd?
Who longe did seeke her corpes, againft the ftreame:
His neigbours thought his fences weare not found?
And did deride his madnes moft extreme:
    Who call d aloude, thy wife beneath did fall?
    Then dounwarde.feeke, or feeke thou not at all.

To whome, quoth he, the place belowe I fee,
Yet in her life, gainft reafon fhe did ftriue:
And contrarie to euerie one, woulde bee;
Wherefore, I knowe this way fhe needes muft driue?
    Then leaue, quoth they, and let her ftill be drown'd.
    For fuch a wife is better lofte then founde?

Whitney Emblemes London 1586 p.158

Motto
Post °fata; °uxor °morosa, etiam °discors.

After °death; a °peevish and still °contrary °spouse.

Picture
°Colasmus, who has been searching upriver for his °drowned °wife, is persuaded by four men to follow the current and search downriver.

Epigram
Colasmus wife flood drown corpse stream deride madness reason strive contrary

Dum ætatis ver agitur : consule brumæ.

Whitney   Emblemes   London   1586   p.159

Motto

Dum °aetatis °ver °agitur: °consule °brumae.

°Provide for the °winter of your °life while its °spring is still here.

Picture

The °sun beats down as a °grasshopper watches °ants at work on their stores under barren °trees.

Epigram

winter   cold   tree   bush   bare   frost root   grass   ant   feed   store   summer food   grasshopper   starve   help experience   wise   snow   sing   meadow green   content   chance   dance

IN winter coulde, when tree, and bushe , was bare,
And froſt had nip'd the rootes of tender graſſe :
The antes, with ioye did feede vpon their fare,
Which they had ſtor'de, while ſommers ſeaſon was ·
    To whome, for foode the graſhopper did crie,
    And ſaid ſhe ſtaru'd, if they did helpe denie.

Whereat, an ante, with longe experience wiſe ?
And froſt, and ſnowe, had manie winters ſeene :
Inquired, what in ſommer was her guiſe.
Quoth ſhe, I ſonge, and hop't in meadowes greene :
    Then quoth the ante, content thee with thy chaunce,
    For to thy ſonge, nowe art thou light to daunce?

Bilingues cauendi.

Whitney Emblemes London 1586 p.160

Motto
°Bilingues °cavendi.

One   should   °beware   of   the °double-°tongued.

Picture
A man sits at a °table set with °food under a tree; the man blows on his food to cool it, watched by a °satyr.

Epigram

satyr	host	winter	night	fire	cold
hand	blow	finger	heat	supper	eat
broth	double	mouth	friendship	shun
tongue				

A Satyre, and his hofte , in mid of winters rage,
At night, did hye them to the fire , the could for to aſſwage.
The man with could that quak'd, vpon his handes did blowe:
Which thinge the Satyre marked well, and crau'd the cauſe to knowe.
Who anſwere made , herewith my fingers I doe heate:
At lengthe when ſupper time was come , and bothe ſat downe to eate,
He likewiſe blewe his brothe, he tooke out of the potte:
Being likewiſe aſked why : (quoth hee) bicauſe it is to whotte.
To which the Satyre ſpake, and blow'ſt thou whotte, and coulde:
Hereafter, with ſuch double mouthes , I will no frendſhip houlde.
Which warneth all , to ſhonne a double tonged mate:
And let them neither ſuppe, nor dine , nor come within thy gate.

Ars deluditur arte.

THE sickly foxe, within her hole was hid,
 Where, to the mouthe, the lion ftraight did hye;
And did demaunde moft frendly, how fhee did,
And faide, his tonge woulde helpe her, by and by?
  Bicaufe there was fuch vertue hid therein,
  That all he heal'd, if he did licke their fkinne.

Then quoth the foxe. my Lorde? I doe not doubt,
But that your tonge is foueraigne, as I heare:
But yet, it hath fuch neighbours round about?
It can not helpe, I iudge, while they be neare.
  Wherefore, I wifhe you woulde them banifh all?
  Or ells, I thinke your pacients wilbee finall.

Whitney Emblemes London 1586 p.161

Motto
°Ars °deluditur arte.

°Craft °deceived by craft.

Picture
A °lion with °tongue outstretched stands before a sick °fox crouched in its den.

Epigram
sick fox hole hide lion friendly
tongue help virtue heal lick skin
sovereign patient1

In eos qui multa promittunt, & nihil præstunt.

Whitney   Emblemes   London   1586   p.162

Motto
In   eos   qui   multa   °promittunt,   et   nihil
°praestant.

On those who °promise much and °produce
nothing.

Picture
In a house, a °mother °admonishes with
upraised hand a °child lying in a °bed; a
°wolf lurks outside.

Epigram
cry   baby   mother   threaten   wolf   prey
blood   kill   wolf   wood1

T HE crying babe, the mother fharply threates,
Except he ceaf'd, he fhoulde to wolfe bee throwne:
Which being hard, the wolfe at windowe waites,
And made account that child fhould bee his owne·
    Till at the lengthe, agayne he hard her fay
    Feare not fweete babe, thou fhalt not bee his pray.

For, if he come in hope to fucke thy blood,
Wee wil him kill, before he fhall departe:
With that the wolfe retorned to the wood,
And did exclayme thus wife with heauie hart:
    Oh Iupiter? what people now doe liue,
    That promife much, and yet will nothing giue.

In malis promif-
fis refcinde fidē,
in turpi voto mu-
ta decretū, quod
incautē vouifti,
non facias: im-
pia eft promiffio,
quæ fcelere ad-
impletur Ifid. 1.
Solilo.

Reference
°Isidor, Sol 2

Pietas filiorum in parentes.

Whitney Emblemes London 1586 p.163

Motto
°Pietas °filiorum in °parentes.

The °devotion of °sons towards their °parents.

Picture
°Aeneas carries his °father °Anchises on his back from the burning °city of °Troy.

Epigram

Aeneas	father	Troy	Greek	spoil1
sack1	son	joy	foe	fire	sword
valiant	heart	fear	son	kind1	parent
distress	duty	reverence	reprehend
shame	despise	stock

AENEAS beares his father, out of Troye,
When that the Greekes, the fame did fpoile, and facke:
His father might of fuche a fonne haue ioye,
Who throughe his foes, did beare him on his backe:
    No fier, nor fworde, his valiaunt harte coulde feare,
    To flee awaye, without his father deare.

Which fhowes, that fonnes muft carefull bee, and kinde,
For to releeue their parentes in diftreffe:
And duringe life, that dutie fhoulde them binde,
To reuerence them, that God their daies maie bleffe:
    And reprehendes tenne thowfande to their fhame,
    Who ofte difpife tho ftocke whereof they came.

Hinc fatus Æneas: pietas fpectata per ignes:
Sacra patremq̃, humeris: altera facra, tulit.

Fœlix proles.
qæ efficit vi ge-
nuiffe iuuet, &
generare libeat.
Max. lib 4.

Ouid. 4. Faft.

Reference
°Maximianus 4
°Ovid, Fast 2

Aliquid mali propter vicinum malum.

To my Father M. GEFFREY WHITNEY.

Motto
Aliquid °mali propter °vicinum malum.

°Harm because of an °evil °neighbour.

Picture
A °copper pot and an °earthenware °pot float side by side down a °stream.

Epigram

two	pot	stream	earth	brass	flood
neighbourhood	fear	escape	worldly	sea	
mighty	poor	hurt			

Two pottes, within a runninge ftreame weare tofte,
  The one of yearth, the other, was of braffe :
The brafen potte, who wifh'd the other lofte,
Did bid it ftaie, and neare her fide to paffe.
    Whereby they might, togeather ioyned fure :
    Without all doubt, the force of flood indure.

The earthen potte, then thus did anfweare make,
This neighborhood doth put me much in feare ?
I rather choofe, my chaunce farre of to take,
Then to thy fide, for to be ioyned neare,
    For if wee hitte, my parte fhalbe the wurfte,
    And thou fhalt fcape, when I am all to burfte.

The running ftreame, this worldlie fea dothe fhewe;
The pottes, prefent the mightie, and the pore:
Whoe here, a time are toffed too, and froe,
But if the meane, dwell nighe the mighties dore,
    He maie be hurte, but cannot hurte againe,
    Then like, to like: or befte alone remaine.

Virgilius.
Mantua va mifera nimium vicina Cremona.

Et Angel. Politianus in Manto fua.

Tu tamen ô, mifera nimium vicina Cremona,
Quid fles amiffam:
quad fles mea Mantua campum
Pa'centem niueos herbofo flumine cycnos &c.

Et etiam apud Plautum, pauper Euclio recufat affinitatem cum diuite Megadora facetiffime.

Ecclefiaft. 13.
Et ditiori te ne focius fueris : Quid communicabit cacabus ad ollâ? quando enim fe colliferint, confringetur, Diues iniufte egit, & fremet : pauper aurê lætus, tacebit. &c.

Ouid. 3. Trift. 4.
Viue fine inuidia, mollesque inglorius annos
Exige, amicitias &
tibi iunge pares.

Reference
°Virgil
°Poliziano
°Plautus, Aul
°B Eccl 13
°Ovid, Trist 3, 4

Dedicatee
Geffrey °Whitney,
Whitney's father

Post amara dulcia.
TO M THOMAS MYNORS.

SHARPE prickes preserue the Rose, on euerie parte,
That who in haste to pull the same intendes,
Is like to pricke his fingers, till they smarte?
But being gotte, it makes him straight amendes
It is so freshe, and pleasant to the smell,
Thoughe he was prick'd, he thinkes he ventur'd well.
And he that faine woulde get the gallant rose,
And will not reache, for feare his fingers bleede;
A nettle, is more fitter for his nose?
Or hemblocke meete his appetite to feede?
None merites sweete, who tasted not the sower,
Who feares to climbe, deserues no fruicte, nor flower.
Which showes, we shoulde not fainte for anie paine,
For to atchieue the fruictes of our desire:
But still proceede, and hope at lengthe to gaine,
The thinges wee wishe, and craue with hartes entire:
Which all our toile, and labour, shal requite,
For after paine, comes pleasure, and delighte.
When winter endes, comes in the pleasant springe.
When nighte is done, the gladsome daye appeares.
When greifes be gone, then ioye doth make vs singe.
When stormes be paste, the variing weather cleares.
So after paines, our pleasures make vs glad,
But without sower, the sweete is hardlie had.

Whitney   Emblemes   London   1586   p.165

Motto
Post °amara °dulcia.

°Sweet things come after °bitter things.

Picture
A man points to or is about to touch the °thorns and °flowers of a °rose bush.

Epigram
sharp   prick   rose   finger   pleasant
smell   venture   bleed   nettle   nose
hemlock   appetite   merit   sweet   taste
sour   fear   climb   deserve   fruit   flower
hope   crave   toil   labour   pain   pleasure
delight   winter   spring   night   day
grief joy sing storm weather

Claud. ior epid.
honou.
Non qu. quam frum.
vera odorou.
Hybicos latebra no.
flolsat foxos,
Si fronti caueas, si no.
meat rubos.
Ar. iat spina n.lis,
media teguat apis.

Dulcia no n. .. n. ...
nen fulisa..   ..

Reference
°Claudian, Nupt Hon

Dedicatee
Thomas °Mynors

Veritas inuicta.

To *my vncl:* GEFFREY CARTWRIGHTE.

THOVGHE Sathan ftriue, with all his maine, and mighte,
To hide the truthe, and dimme the lawe deuine:
Yet to his worde, the Lorde doth giue fuch lighte,
That to the Eaſt, and Weſt, the fame doth ſhine:
And thoſe, that are ſo happie for to looke,
Saluation finde, within that bleſſed booke.

Whitney Emblemes London 1586 p.166a

Motto
°Veritas °invicta.

°Unconquered °truth.

Picture
An °open °book; the inscription °"ET USQUE AD NUBES VERITAS TVA" [and your truth (will soar) all the way to the clouds] is surrounded by a blazing °light. The book is surmounted by a °wreath under a pair of outstretched °wings held by a °hand. A °chain, looped and hanging from the book, is pulled by °Satan, watched by two °demons.

Epigram
Satan strive might hide truth dim law divine word Lord light east west shine salvation bless book

Dedicatee
Geffrey °Cartwright,
Whitney's uncle

Si Deus nobiscum, quis contra nos?

Hɪs ſeruauntes Goᴅ preſerues, thoughe they in danger fall
Euen as from vipers deadlie*bite, he kept th'Appoſtle Paule.

Whitney Emblemes London 1586 p.166b

Motto
Si °Deus nobiscum, quis contra nos?

If °God is with us, who can prevail against us?

De Vipera Ae-
liat. lib.15.ca.16
& Plin. De natur.
hiſt. lib.8. ca.39.
& lib.10. cap.61.

Aɛɛ. 28.
Tremellius

Picture
A °right hand, surrounded by °clouds, dangles a twisting °snake, which has bitten into its middle °finger, over an open °fire.

Epigram
servant God preserve danger viper deadly bite apostle Paul

Reference
°Aelian, N A 15,16
°Pliny, H N 8, 39
°Pliny, H N 10, 61
°Tremellius
°B Acts 28

Cum tempore mutamur.

Ad Dn. IOHANNEM CROXTON.

Times change, and wee doe alter in the fame,
  And in one ftaye, there nothing ftill maye bee:
What Monarches greate, that wanne the chiefeft fame,
But ftealinge time, their birthe, and deathe, did fee:
    Firfte NESTOR fuck'd, and HOMER firft was taughte,
    Bothe famous once, yet both to duft are broughte.

Wee firft are younge, and then to age wee yeelde,
Then flit awaye, as we had not bene borne:
No wight fo ftronge, but time doth winne the feelde,
Yea wonders once, are out of memorie worne:
    This Ægypte fpires, and Babell, fawe in fine,
    When they did mounte, and when they did decline.

        Felix qui propriis auum tranfegit in auris,
          Ipfa domus puerum quem videt ipfa fenem;
        Qui baculo nitens, in qua reptauit arena,
          Prius numerat facula longa cafa:
        Illum non vario traxit fortuna tumultu,
          Nec bibit ignotas mobilis hofpes aquas.

Whitney   Emblemes   London   1586   p.167

Motto
Cum °tempore °mutamur.

We °change with °time.

Picture
An °old man on °crutches walks into a room which is empty save for a °swaddled baby in a °cradle.

Epigram
time   change   monarchy   fame   steal
birth   death   Nestor   Homer   famous   dust
young   age   born   strong   field1   Egypt
spire   Babel   mount   decline

Ouid. 6. Faft.
Tempora labuntur ta-
citifq; feneƒcimus annis,
  Et fugiunt frœna non
remoran[t]e diei.

Reference
°Ovid, Fast 6
°Claudian, Sen Ver

Claud. de Senec.
Veronenfi.

  Et paulò pòft.
Ingentem meminit p.n
ue qui gramine querc.
  Æquæuumque videt
conƒenuiƒƒe nemus.

Dedicatee
John °Croxton

Ouid. 2. Art.   *Si nihil attuleris, ibis Homere foras.*

TO M. MATTHEW PATTENSON.

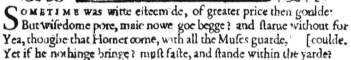

SOMETIME was witte esteem'de, of greater price then goulde:
But wisedome pore, maie nowe goe begge? and starue without for
Yea, thoughe that Homer come, with all the Muses guarde,   [coulde.
Yet if he nothinge bringe? must faste, and stande within the yarde?

Ouid. 2. Amor. 7.
Ingenium quondam fue-
rat preciosius auro.
At nunc barbaria est
grandis, habere nihil.

Whitney   Emblemes   London   1586   p.168a

Motto
Si nihil attuleris, ibis °Homere foras.

If, °Homer, you do not bring anything,
you will go outside.

Picture
°Homer, accompanied by °nine °Muses,
addresses two figures leaning out of a
window over the doorway of a house.

Epigram
wit   esteem   price   gold   wisdom   beg
starve Homer Muse fast1

Reference
°Ovid, A A 2
°Ovid, Am 7

Dedicatee
Matthew °Pattenson

Ingenium superat vires.

MANS wisedome great, doth farre surpasse his strengthe,
For proofe, behoulde, no man coulde bende the bowe:
But yet, his witte deuised at the lengthe,
To winde the stringe so farre as it shoulde goe:
    Then wisedome chiefe, and strengthe, must come behinde,
    But bothe be good, and giftes from God assignde.

Ouid. 1. Pont.
Adde quod ingenuas
deducit fideliter artes,
Emollit mores, nec
sinit esse feros.

Whitney Emblemes London 1586 p.168b

Motto
°Ingenium °superat °vires.

°Talent °overcomes °strength.

Picture
A drawn °cross-bow at an angle to the ground.

Epigram
wisdom surpass strength bend bow wit devise string gift God

Reference
°Ovid, Pont 2

Malè parta malè dilabuntur.
In fœneratores.

Whitney Emblemes London 1586 p.169

Motto
Male parta male dilabuntur.

Ill-gotten, ill-spent.

Picture
An °ape throws °gold °coins from an upper-storey °window of a house; a °table with °two °bags on it can be seen through an open doorway on the ground floor.

Si neceſſariis con-
tenti eſſemus, mini-
mè vſurariorum ge-
nus peſſimum inue-
niretur Plutatch. de
vſur. vit.

Auaritia omnia in
ſe vitia habet. Aut.
Gell. lib. 11 cap. .
Et idem lib. 3. cap..

A N vſerer, whoſe Idol was his goulde,
   Within his houſe, a peeuiſhe ape retain'd:
A ſeruaunt fitte, for ſuche a miſer oulde,
Of whome both mockes, and apiſhe mowes, he gain'd.
   Thus, euerie daie he made his maſter ſporte,
   And to his clogge, was chained in the courte.
At lengthe it hap'd? while greedie graundſir din'de?
The ape got looſe, and founde a windowe ope:
Where in he leap'de, and all about did finde,
The G O D, wherein the Miſer put his hope?
   Which ſoone he broch'd, and forthe with ſpeede did flinge,
   And did delighte on ſtones to heare it ringe?
The ſighte, righte well the paſſers by did pleaſe,
Who did reioyce to finde theſe goulden crommes:
That all their life, their pouertie did eaſe.
Of goodes ill got, loe heere the fruicte that commes.
   Looke herevppon, you that haue M I D A S minte,
   And bee poſſeſte with hartes as harde as flinte.
Shut windowes cloſe, leſte apes doe enter in,
And doe diſperſe your goulde, you doe adore.
But woulde you learne to keepe, that you do winne?
Then get it well, and hourde it not in ſtore.
   If not: no boultes, nor braſen barres will ſerue,
   For G O D will waſte your ſtocke, and make your ſterue.

Epigram
usurer   idol   gold   ape   servant   miser
sport   chain   greedy   dive   poverty
goods   fruit   Midas   mint   heart   hard
flint   adore   hoard   bolt   brazen   bar
God   starve

Reference
°Plutarch
°Gellius 11, 2
°Gellius 3, 1

Fere simile praecedenti, ex Alciato.

THE greedie kyte, so full his gorge had cloy'de,
He coulde not brooke his late deuoured praie :
Wherefore with griefe, vnto his damme hee cry'de,
My bowelles lo, alas doe waste awaie.
    With that quoth shee, why doste thou make thy mone,
    This losse thou haste is nothinge of thy owne.

By which is mente, that they who liue by spoile,
By rapine, thefte, or griping goodes by mighte,
If that with losse they suffer anie foile,
They loose but that, wherein they had no righte?
    Hereof, at firste the prouerbe oulde did growe:
    That goodes ill got, awaie as ill will goe.

Whitney Emblemes London 1586 p.170

Motto
Fere simile praecedenti, ex °Alciato.

Almost the same as the preceding, from °Alciato.

Picture
A °kite, perched on the branch of a tree, regurgitates a long knotted coil. A second kite watches from a rock at the right.

Epigram
greedy kite devour prey grief dame bowel loss spoill rapine theft might lose suffer proverb ill-gotten goods

Reference
°Alciato °Cato, R R

Cato De re Rust.
Peior cuius exhi-
matur fœnerator,
quàm fur.

Di mal gadsin non
gaudet tertius haris.

Usus libri, non lectio prudentes facit.

Ad D. A. P.

Motto
°Usus   °libri,   non   °lectio   °prudentes facit.

The °use, not the °reading, of a °book makes men °wise.

Picture
°Two °scholars stand in a °library: one reads at a °lectern; the second appears to be enumerating on the fingers of his °left hand.

Epigram

volume	fruit	use	reap	toil
fame				
read	practise	drink	Lethe	flood
experience	wisdom	print	mind	book
time	hide			

Reference
°Seneca, Ep 1, 2

Dedicatee
D.A. °P.

THE volumes great, who so doth still peruse,
And dailie turnes, and gazeth on the same,
If that the fruicte thereof, he do not vse,
He reapes but toile, and neuer gaineth fame:
　　Firste reade, then marke, then practise that is good,
　　For without vse, we drinke but LETHE flood.

Of practise longe, experiense doth proceede;
And wisedome then, doth euermore ensue:
Then printe in minde, what wee in printe do reade,
Els loose wee time, and bookes in vaine do vewe:
　　Wee maie not haste, our talent to bestowe,
　　Nor hide it vp, whereby no good shall growe.

Lectio multorum voluminum, & omnis generis auctorum, habet aliquid vagum & instabile: certis ingeniis immorari & innutriri oportet, si ve-his aliquid trahere, quod in animo fideliter sedeat. Senec. 1. Epist. 2.

Studiis inuigilandum.

Ad iuuentutem Schola Aldelemenſis in Anglia.

WHILES prime of youthe, is freſhe within his flower,
  Take houlde of time : for it doth haſte awaye.
Watche, write, and reade, and ſpende no idle hower,
Inritche your mindes with ſome thinge, euerie daye :
    For loſſe of time, all other loſſe exceedes,
    And euermore it late repentaunce breedes.

The idle ſorte, that ignoraunce doe taſte,
Are not eſteem'd, when they in yeares doe growe :
The ſtudious, are with vnderſtanding grac'd,
And ſtill prefer'd, thoughe firſt their caulinge lowe.
    Then haue regarde, to baniſhe idle fittes,
    And in your youthe, with ſkill adorne your wittes.

Whereby, in time ſuch hap maye you aduaunce,
As bothe your Towne, and countrie, you maye frende :
For, what I woulde vnto my ſelfe ſhoulde chaunce :
To you I wiſhe, wheare I my prime did ſpende.
    Wherefore beholde this candle, booke, and glaſſe :
    To vſe your time, and knowe how time dothe paſſe.

Ouid.3.Art.
Nec qua præteriit cur-
ſu, reuocabitur vnda:
  Nec quæ præteriit
hora, redire poteſt.
Vtendū eſt ætate, cito
pede labitur ætas,
  Nec bona tam ſequi-
tur quàm bona prima
fuit.

Studia, quæ ſunt in
adoleſcentia, tan-
quam in herbis ſi-
gnificant, quæ vir-
tutis maturitas, &
quantæ fruges in-
duſtriæ ſint futuræ
Cicero pro Cœlio.

Whitney   Emblemes   London   1586   p.172

Motto
°Studiis invigilandum.

One must pay attention to °studies.

Picture
A °burning °candle, flanked by an °hour-
glass and an °open °book, stands on a
table in a room. The side of the table
bears a °shield charged with a °sheaf of
°wheat(?)

Epigram
youth   fresh   flower   time   haste   write
read   idle   hour   enrich   mind   loss
time   repentance   idle   ignorance
studious   skill   adorn   wit   advance
town   country   candle   book   glass
[= hourglass]   time

Reference
°Ovid, A A 3
°Cicero, Coel

Præcocia non diuturna.

Doctissimo viro D. Stephano Limberto
Nordouicensis Scholæ Magistro.

Thε fruicte that sooneſt ripes, doth sooneſt fade awaie.
And that which ſlowlie hath his time, will not ſo ſoone decaie.
Our writing in the duſte, can not indure a blaſte:
But that, which is in marble wroughte, from age, to age, doth laſte.
Euen ſo it is of wittes, ſome quicke, to put in vre:
Some dull to learne, but oftentimes the ſlowe are ſounde, and ſure.
And thoughe the apte, and prompte: ſoone learne, and ſoone forget.
Yet ofte the dull doe beare in minde, what firſt therein was ſet.
Hereof the prouerbe comes: *Soone ripe, ſoone rotten turnes:*
And greeneſt wood, though kindlinge longe, yet whotteſt moſt it
      burnes.

        O formoſe puer, nimium ne crede colori.
        Alba liguſtra cadunt, vaccinia nigra leguntur.

Omnis profectus ex
lectione et meditatione
procedit_ quæ
enim nescimus, le-
ctione discimus; quæ
didicimus, meditatione
conservamus. Iſid libr; De ſummo bono.

Virg. ...

Whitney   Emblemes   London   1586   p.173

Motto
°Praecocia non diuturna.

°Precocious things do not °last1 long.

Picture
A naked °boy or °Putto(?) sits in a °fruit-tree. An °old °man clad in a coat and barret, a °scholar(?), stands under the tree. He looks at his hands or something in them. °Flowers, some possibly wilted, grow at his feet.

Epigram
fruit	ripe	fade	slow	time	decay
write	dust	blast	marble	age	last1
wit	ure [= practice]	dull	learn	apt	
forget	proverb	soon	ripe	rotten	
green	wood	kindling	hot	burn	

Reference
°Isidor, Sent
°Virgil, Ecl 2

Dedicatee
Stephen °Limbert

In fœcunditatem, sibiipsi damnosam.

IF fence I had, my owne eftate to knowe,
Before all trees, my felfe hath caufe to crie:
In euerie hedge, and common waye, I growe,
Where, I am made a praye, to paffers by:
    And when, they fee my nuttes are ripe, and broune,
    My bowghes are broke, my leaues are beaten doune.

Thus euerie yeare, when I doe yeelde increafe,
My proper fruicte, my ruine doth procure:
If fruictleffe I, then had I growen in peace,
Oh barrennes, of all moft happie, fure
    Which wordes with griefe, did AGRIPPINA grone,
    And mothers more, whofe children made them mone.

       Certè ego ſi nunquam peperiſſem, tutior eſſem:
        Iſta Clytemneſira digna quercia fuit.

Whitney Emblemes London 1586 p.174

Motto
In °foecunditatem, sibi ipsi °damnosam.

On °fertility that is °harmful to itself.

Picture
Two °boys with °rods knock °fruit from the branches of a °nut-tree.

Epigram
tree cry prey nut fruit ruin peace barren happy grief Agrippina mother child

Reference
Andrea °Alciato [Emblem 193]
°Suetonius, Ner
°Ovid

Alciatus.
Quid fterilis poſſes con-
tingere turpius? eheu,
Infelix, fructus in
mea damna fero.

Sueton. in vita
Neronis.

Locus è nuce
Ouidiana.

Otiosi semper egentes.

Whitney Emblemes London 1586 p.175

Motto
°Otiosi semper °egentes.

The °idle are always °needy.

Picture
°Labour, with a °cornucopia and a °crown made of ears of °grain, sits in a °chariot pulled by °ants. She uses a °bundle of stalks of °grain(?) to beat °Idleness, who sits with clasped arms at her feet, weeping.

Epigram
Idleness weep want1 famished labour whip ire Labour chariot ant grasshopper toil deride summer winter song rue food starve youth provide age1

HERE, Idlenes doth weepe amid her wantes,
Neare famifhed: whome, labour whippes for Ire:
Here, labour fittes in chariot drawen with antes:
And dothe abounde with all he can defire.
    The grafhopper, the toyling ante derides,
    In Sommers heate, caufe fhe for coulde prouides.

But when the coulde of winter did increafe,
Out of her hill, the ante did looke for newes:
Whereas fhe harde the grafhopper to ceafe,
And all her fonges, fhee nowe with fighing rues:
    But all to late, for now for foode fhe ftaru'd,
    Whereas the ante had ftore, fhe had preferu'd.

All which doe warne, while that our Sommer laftes,
Which is our youthe: with frefhe, and liuelie ftrengthe.
Wee mufte prouide, for winters bitter blaftes.
Which is our age: that claimes his righte at lengthe.
    Wherefore in youthe, let vs prouide for age;
    For ere wee thinke he ftealeth on the ftage.

Semper præsto esse infortunia.

Whitney Emblemes London 1586 p.176

THREE careleſſe dames, amongſte their wanton toies,
 Did throwe the dice, who firſte of them ſhoulde die:
And ſhee that loſte, did laughe with inwarde ioyes,
For that, ſhee thoughte her terme ſhoulde longer bee:
  But loe, a tyle vppon her head did fall,
  That deathe, with ſpeede, this dame from dice did call

Euen ſo, it falles, while careleſſe times wee ſpende:
That euell happes, vnlooked for doe comme.
But if wee hope, that G o d ſome good wil ſende,
In earneſt praier, then muſt wee not bee domme:
  For bleſſinges good, come ſeild before our praier,
  But euell thinges doe come before we feare.

    Ludit in humanis diuina potentia rebus,
     Et certam præſens vix habet hora fidem.

Motto
Semper praesto esse °infortunia.

°Misfortunes are always at hand.

Picture
°Three °women sit and °gamble with °dice at a table.

Epigram
three   dame   wanton   dice   die   laugh
tile   careless   time   evil   hope   God
good   pray   bless   fear

Reference
°Ovid, Pont 4
°Seneca, Tranq

Cuiuis poteſt ac-
cidere, quod cui-
quam poteſt. Se-
nec. de tranquil.
animi.

Ouid. 4. Pont.

Unica semper auis.
To my countrimen of the Nampcwiche in Cheßhire.

T H E Phœnix rare, with fethers freſhe of hewe,
A R A B I A S righte, and ſacred to the Sonne:
Whome, other birdes with wonder ſeeme to vewe,
Dothe liue vntill a thouſande yeares bee ronne:
    Then makes a pile: which, when with Sonne it burnes
    Shee flies therein, and ſo to aſhes turnes.
Whereof, behoulde, an other Phœnix rare,
With ſpeede dothe riſe moſt beautifull and faire:
And thoughe for truthe, this manie doe declare,
Yet thereunto, I meane not for to ſweare:
    Althoughe I knowe that Auctors witnes true,
    What here I write, bothe of the oulde, and newe.
Which when I wayed, the newe, and eke the oulde,
I thought vppon your towne deſtroyed with fire:
And did in minde, the newe N A M P W I C H E behoulde,
A ſpectacle for anie mans deſire:
    Whoſe buildinges braue, where cinders weare but late,
    Did repreſente (me thought) the Phœnix fate.
And as the oulde, was manie hundreth yeares,
A towne of fame, before it felt that croſſe:
Euen ſo, (I hope) this W I C H E, that nowe appeares,
A Phœnix age ſhall laſte, and knowe no loſſe:
    Which G O D vouchſafe, who make you thankfull, all:
    That ſee this riſe, and ſawe the other fall.

Whitney   Emblemes   London   1586   p.177

Motto
°Unica semper °avis.

The °bird that is ever °unique.

Picture
A °phoenix with wings outstretched rises from the flames of a °fire.

Epigram
phoenix   rare   Arabia   sacred   sun   bird wonder   live   thousand   year   burn   ash Nantwich

Paradiſ. poët.
Solus in Eou ales re-
parabilu oru,
  Igne ſuo vitam dum
rapit, igne capit.

Mart lib. 5. Epigr. 7.
Qualiter Aſſyrios re-
nouant incendia nidos:
  Una dicem quotus
ſecula vixit auis.

Quæ quidem auis
iuxta Plinium, Na-
tural. hiſtor. lib. 10.
cap. 2. viuit ad ſex-
centos ſexaginta an-
nos, quo loco &
alia eiuſdam prode
…

Ouid. Met. lib. 15.
Una est que reparet
…

Reference
°Reusner, Parad poet
°Martial, 5, 7
°Aelian, N A 6, 3
°Ovid, Met 15

Dedicatee
To my countrymen of °Nantwich in °Cheshire

Cælum, non animum.

Hor.lib.1.Ep.11.

To R. P.

WHY fleeft thou throughe the worlde? in hope to alter kinde:
No forren foile, hath anie force to change the inward minde.
Thou dofte but alter aire, thou altereft not thy thoughte:
No diftance farre can wipe awaye, what Nature firft hath wroughte.
The foole, that farre is fente fome wifedome to attaine:
Returnes an Ideot, as he wente, and bringes the foole againe.
Where rancor firfte hathe roote, it growes, liue where wee fhall:
And where as malice is by kinde, no abfence helpes at all.
The catte, in countries kepte, where are no myfe for praye,
Yet, being broughte where they doe breede, her felfe fhee doth bewraye.
The beaftes of crewell kinde, where hate, by nature growes,
Thoughe parted longe, yet when they meete, become moft deadlie foes,
Which prooues, no trauaile farre, no coafte, nor countrie ftraunge:
Hath anie force to alter kinde, or Natures worke to chaunge.

*Quo fugis ah demens? nulla eft fuga: tu licet vfque
Ad Tanaim fugias, vfque fequetur amor.*

Whitney Emblemes London 1586 p.178

Motto
°Caelum, non °animum.

The °clime, not the °mind.

Picture
A spotted cat or °leopard(?) fights with a °lion. °Travellers pass along a roadway nearby. A °flock of °birds flies over the landscape in the background.

Epigram
flee world foreign soil force change mind air thought distance nature fool wisdom idiot rancour root live malice cat mice prey hate grow foe travaill coast country

Propertius 3,7.
Natura fequitur femina quafque fua.

Propert. 2, 30.

Reference
°Horace, Ep 1, 11
°Propertius 2, 30
°Propertius 3, 7

Dedicatee
R. °P.

Auri facra fames quid non?

Motto
°Auri °sacra °fames quid non?

What does °accursed °greed for °gold not
drive men to do?

Picture
A °shipwrecked °traveller, weighted by
the °pack on his back, °swims towards a
shore.

Epigram
desire   endure   labour   rest   merchant
lure   heat   East   gold   travailer
[= labourer]   ship   wreck   venture   life
fardle   hope   love   goods   burden   flood

DESIRE to haue, dothe make vs muche indure,
In trauaile, toile, and labour voide of refte:
The marchant man is caried with this lure,
Throughe fcorching heate, to regions of the Eafte:
  Oh thirfte of goulde, what not? but thou canft do:
  And make mens hartes for to confent thereto.

The trauailer poore, when fhippe doth fuffer wracke,
Who hopes to fwimme vnto the wifhed lande,
Dothe venture life, with fardle on his backe,
That if he fcape, the fame in fteede maye ftande.
  Thus, hope of life, and loue vnto his goods,
  Houldes vp his chinne, with burthen in the floods.

Horat. lib.1. Epift.1.
*Inpiger extremos currit
mercator ad indos,
Per mare pauperiem
fugiens per faxa per
ignes.*

Reference
°Horace, Ep 1, 1

Verbum emiſſum non eſt reuocabile.

Motto
°Verbum °emissum non est °revocabile.

A °word once °spoken can not be °recalled.

Picture
A man runs after and tries to capture a flying °bird.

Epigram

trust	flatter	friend	save	steed	lock
speak	heed	bold	tongue	wit	grief
word	bale [= harm]	breed	wise	man
hatch	door	bird	hand	restrain	fly
vain1					

WHO lookes, maye leape : and ſaue his ſhinnes from
    knockes.
Who tries, maye truſte : els flattringe frendes ſhall finde.
He ſaues the ſteede, that keepes him vnder lockes.
Who ſpeakes with heede, maye bouldlie ſpeake his minde.
    But hee, whoſe tonge before his witte, doth runne,
    Ofte ſpeakes to ſoone, and greeues when he hathe done.

A worde once ſpoke, it can retourne no more,
But flies awaie, and ofte thy bale doth breede :
A wiſe man then, ſettes hatche before the dore,
And while he maye, doth ſquare his ſpeeche with heede.
    The birde in hande, wee maye at will reſtraine,
    But beinge flowen, wee call her backe in vaine.

Praui ſicut in ſenſu
leues, ita ſunt in lo-
cutione præcipites:
Quia quod leuis cõ-
ſcientia concipit, le-
uior protinus lingua
prodit. Greg. Ho-
mil. 5.

Horat. Epiſt. 18.
Et ſemel emiſſum volat
irreuocabile verbum.

Et ſi vtile eſt ſubitò
ſæpe dicere, tamen
illud vtilius, ſumpto
ſpacio ad cogitan-
dum paratius, atque
accuratius dicere.
Cicero 1. De Orator.

Reference
°Gregory, Hom 5
°Horace, Ep 1, 18
°Cicero, Or 2

In occasionem.

To my Kinsman M. GEFFREY WHITNEY.

W H A T creature thou? *Occasion I doe showe.*
    On whirling wheele declare why doste thou stande?
Bicause, I still am tossed too, and froe.
Why doest thou houlde a rasor in thy hande?
    That men maie knowe I cut on euerie side,
    And when I come, I armies can deuide.

But wherefore hast thou winges vppon thy feete?
To showe, how lighte I flie with little winde.
What meanes longe lockes before? *that suche as meete,*
Maye houlde at firste, when they occasion finde.
    Thy head behinde all balde, what telles it more?
    That none shoulde houlde, that let me slippe before.

Why doest thou stande within an open place?
That I maye warne all people not to staye,
But at the firste, occasion to imbrace,
And when shee comes, to meete her by the waye.
    Lysippus so did thinke it best to bee,
    Who did deuise mine image, as you see.

Whitney   Emblemes   London   1586   p.181

Motto
In °occasionem.

On °opportunity.

Picture
Naked °Occasio, with °bald °head, a long °forelock, and a °razor in her raised °right hand, stands on a °wheel in the °sea; her °heels are °winged, and she holds a °scarf in her °left hand.

Horat. lib.1. Ep.11.
ad Bullatium.
Tu quamcumque Deus
tibi fortunauerit hora,
Grata sume manu: nec
dulcia differ in annum.

Epigram
Occasion   wheel   razor   army   divide wing   foot   wind   lock   bald   open   warn Lysippus

Reference
°Horace, Ep 1, 11

Dedicatee
Geffrey °Whitney, kinsman

Potentia amoris.

Palladius Soranus.
Omnia vincit amor,
superum rex magis in
armis,
   Palluit & Titan,
omnia vincit amor.
Omnia vincit amor, fle-
xit Proserpina ditem,
   Martē blandæ Venus,
omnia vincit amor.
Omnis vincit amor,
barbarū Polyphemus,
adornat,
   Pan se vidit aquis,
omnia vincit amor.
Omnia vincit amor,
feruet Neptunus in
undis,
   Neuit & Alcides,
omnia vincit amor.
Omnia vincit amor,
Salomō, & Scipio victi,
   Ilion euersum est,
omnia vincit amor.
Omnia vincit amor ca-
lor, & Tartara, &
vrbes,
   Et nemora, & pif-
ces, omnia vincit amor.

H ERE, naked loue doth sit, with smilinge cheare,
No bended bowe, nor quiuer he doth beare:
One hande, a fishe: the other houldes a flower:
Of Sea, and Lande, to shewe that he hath power.

Motto
°Potentia °amoris.

The °power of °Love.

Picture
Winged, naked °Eros, holding °flowers in his right hand and a °fish in his left hand, is seated on a rock in a landscape.

Epigram
naked love cheer bow quiver fish flower sea land power

Reference
°Palladius Soranus

Pulchritudo vincit.

To the fairest.

WHEN creatures firfte weare form'd, they had by natures lawes,
The bulles, their hornes: the horfes, hoofes: the lions, teeth,
    and pawes.
To hares, fhee fwiftenes gaue: to fifhes, finnes affign'de.
To birdes, their winges: fo no defence was lefte for woman kinde.
But, to fupplie that wante, fhee gaue her fuche a face:
Which makes the boulde, the fierce, the fwifte, to ftoope, and pleade
        for grace.

Whitney   Emblemes   London   1586   p.182b

Motto
°Pulchritudo °vincit.

°Beauty °conquers.

Picture
A °Venus(?) reclines against a basket of °fruit, °Eros(?) stands behind her. Animals populate the scene: a °lion, a °hare, a °horse, a °bird and a °fish.

Epigram
creature   nature   law   bull   horn   horse
hoof   lion   tooth   paw   hare   swift   fish
fin   bird   wing   defence   woman   face
bold   fierce   grace

Qui me alit me extinguit.

E v e n as the waxe dothe feede, and quenche the flame,
So, loue giues life; and loue, difpaire doth giue:
The godlie loue, doth louers croune with fame:
The wicked loue, in fhame dothe make them liue.
   Then leaue to loue, or loue as reafon will,
   For, louers lewde doe vainlie languifhe ftill.

Whitney Emblemes London 1586 p.183a

Motto
Qui me °alit me °extinguit.

The one who nourishes me °extinguishes me.

Picture
An °inverted °burning °torch; a ribbon bearing the inscription °"QUI ME ALIT ME EXTINGUIT" [The one who nourishes me extinguishes me] is curled around its stem.

Epigram
wax feed quench flame love life despair god crown fame wicked shame reason lewd vain1 languish

Scribit in marmore læsus.

I N marble harde our harmes wee alwayes graue,
   Bicaufe, wee ftill will beare the fame in minde :
In dufte wee write the benifittes wee haue,
Where they are foone defaced with the winde.
   So, wronges wee houlde, and neuer will forgiue,
   And foone forget, that ftill with vs fhoulde liue.

Whitney   Emblemes   London   1586   p.183b

Motto

°Scribit in °marmore °laesus.

°Wronged, he °writes on °marble.

Picture

A stone °carver uses a °mallet and
°chisel to incise a marble °tablet; the
inscription reads °"TROIA MIHI LICET
TAMEN" ["Neverthelesss the whore sells
herself to me"; or "For all that I can
buy a whore"]

Epigram

marble	harm	engrave	dust	benefit
deface	wind	wrong	forgive	forget
live				

Whitney Emblemes London 1586 p.184

Nec sibi, nec alteri.

To *Aphilus.*

Motto
Nec sibi, nec alteri.

Neither for himself nor for someone else.

Picture
A °dog, in a °manger built against the wall of a stall, prevents an °ox from reaching his feed.

Epigram
cur manger starve hay meat fang ox hunger spite food covet envy need neighbour groat dog

Reference
°Chrysostom, Hom 41

Dedicatee
°Aphilus

A SNARLINGE curre, did in the manger lie,
Who rather steru'd? then made the haye, his meate,
Yet shew'd his fanges, and offred for to flie
Vppon the oxe, who hungred for to eate.
　　And there throughe spite, did keepe the oxe from foode:
　　Vntill for wante, hee faynted as hee stoode.

The couetous man enuious, here behoulde,
Who hath inowghe, yet vse thereof doth lacke:
And doth enuie his needie neighbour, shoulde
But get a groate, if he coulde houlde it backe?
　　Who, thoughe they doe possesse the diuill, and all?
　　Yet are they like the dogge, in oxes stall?

Inuidus alienas ia-
cturas, suos quæstus
existimat. Chrys.
super Math. Ho-
mil.41.

Scripta non temerè edenda.

Ad doctiß. virum D. St. Bvllvm.

LO, here QVINCTILIVS fittes, a graue and reuerende fire:
And pulles a younglinge by the arme , that did for fame defire.
For, hee with pace of fnayle , proceeded to his pen ;
Left hafte fhoulde make him wifhe (too late) it weare to write againe.
And therfore ftill with care, woulde euerie thinge amende:
Yea, ofte eche worde, and line furuaye, before hee made an ende.
And, yf he any fawe, whofe care to wryte was fmall :
To him , like wordes to thefe hee vf'd , which hee did meane to all.
My fonne , what worke thou writes , correcte, reforme, amende,
But if thou like thy firft affaye, then not QVINCTILIVS frende?.
The fruicte at firfte is fower, till time giue pleafante tafte :
And verie rare is that attempte , that is not harm'd with hafte.
Perfection comes in time, and forme and fafhion giues :
And euer rafhienes, yeeldes repente, and moft difpifed liues.
Then, alter ofte , and chaunge, peruſe, and reade, and marke.
The man that foftlie fettes his fteppes, goes fafeft in the darke.
But if that thirft of fame, doe pricke thee forthe too fafte:
Thou fhalt (when it is all to late) repente therefore at lafte.

*Quin&tilij Var. cen-
fura de fcriptis edē-
dis Horat: Art. poët.*

*Ouid. 3. Faft.
Differ, habent paruæ
commoda magna mora*

*Senec. Agam.
Proinde quicquid eft, da
fpacium, & tempus tibi:
Quod ratio nequit, fa-
pe fanauit mora.*

Whitney   Emblemes   London   1586   p.185

Motto
°Scripta non °temere °edenda.

°Writings   should   not   be   °published °rashly.

Picture
°Quintilius, seated at a table, a °quill in his °right hand, tries to restrain a °youth from handing a hastily written note to °Fame, a °winged figure with a °trumpet.

Epigram
Quintilius   youngling [= youth]   fame desire   snail   pen   haste   write   amend fruit   sour   time   taste   harm perfection   rash   repent   soft   step fast   dark   thirst

Reference
°Horace, A P   °Ovid, Fast 3
°Seneca, Agam

Dedicatee
Stephen °Bull

Orphei Musica.
Ad eundem.

LO, ORPHEVS with his harpe, that sauage kinde did tame:
The Lions fierce,and Leopardes wilde,and birdes about him came.
For, with his muficke fweete , their natures hee fubdu'de :
But if wee thinke his playe fo wroughte, our felues wee doe delude.
For why ? befides his fkill, hee learned was , and wife:
And coulde with fweetenes of his tonge, all fortes of men fuffice.
And thofe that weare moft rude, and knewe no good at all :
And weare of fierce, and cruell mindes, the worlde did brutifhe call.
Yet with perfuafions founde, hoe made their hartes relente,
That meeke,and milde they did become, and followed where he wente.
Lo thefe, the Lions fierce, thefe, Beares, and Tigers weare :
The trees, and rockes, that lefte their roomes, his muficke for to heare.
But, you are happie moft, who in fuche place doe ftaye: [playe.
You neede not THRACIA feeke, to heare fome impe of ORPHEVS
Since, that fo neare your home , Apollos darlinge dwelles;
Who LINVS, & AMPHION ftaynes, and ORPHEVS farre excelles.
For, hartes like marble harde, his harmonie dothe pierce :
And makes them yeelding paffions feele, that are by nature fierce.
But , if his muficke faile: his curtefie is fuche, .
That none fo rude, and bafe of minde,but hee reclaimes them muche.
Nowe fince you, by deferte, for both, commended are :
I choofe you, for a Iudge herein, if truthe I doe declare.
And if you finde I doe, then ofte therefore reioyce :
And thinke,I woulde fuche neighbour haue,if I might make my choice.

Whitney   Emblemes   London   1586   p.186

Motto
°Orphei °Musica.

The °music of °Orpheus.

Picture
A seated °Orpheus plays his °harp,
surrounded by a °vulture, a °stork, a
°stag, a °lion, a °bear, an °antelope,
and an °ape.

Epigram
Orpheus harp tame music lion leopard
bear   tiger   bird   learned   wise   rude
fierce   cruel   brute   savage   wild   heart
relent   meek   tree   rock   Thrace   Apollo
Linus Amphion marble harmony passion
courtesy judge truth

Horat. Art. poët.
Sylueftres homines fa-
cer interprésq.deorum,
Cadibus & fædo victu
deterruit Orpheus ;
Dictus ob hoc lenire ti-
gres, rapidófq. leones.

E. P. Efquier.

Propert. lib. 1.de
Lino.
Tunc ego fim Inachio
notior arte Lino.
De Amphione Ho-
rat. in Art. poët.
Dictus & Amphion
Thebana conditor vrbis
Saxa mouere fono te-
ftudinis, & prece bláda
Ducere quo vellet, &c.

Reference
°Horace, A P
°Propertius 2

Dedicatee
Stephen °Bull

In ſtatuam Bacchi.

Motto
In statuam °Bacchi.

On the statue of °Bacchus.

Picture
°Bacchus, seated under °vines laden with °grapes, beats on a °drum and blows on a °pipe. A °goblet stands on the ground at his side.

Epigram
Semele   drink   belly   cheer   eye   fiery cup   head   crown   grape   pipe   tabret beast   transform   secret   shun   brag friend   join   hand

T HE timelie birthe that S E M E L E did beare,
  See heere, in time howe monſterous he grewe:
With drinkinge muche, and dailie bellie cheare,
His eies weare dimme, and fierie was his hue:
   His cuppe, ſtill full: his head, with grapes was croun'de;
   Thus time he ſpent with pipe, and tabret ſounde.

Which carpes all thoſe, that loue to much the canne,
And dothe deſcribe theire perſonage, and theire guiſe:
For like a beaſte, this doth transforme a man,
And makes him ſpeake that moſte in ſecret lies;
   Then, ſhunne the ſorte that bragge of drinking muche,
   Seeke other frendes, and ioyne not handes with ſuche.

Iunge tibi ſocios pulchræ virtutis amore,
  Nam Venere & Baccho iuncta repentè cadunt.

Vino forma perit, vino corrumpitur ætas,
  Vino ſæpè ſuum neſcit amica virum?

Ouid. 3. Met.

Anac. apud Diog.
Vitis tres vuas fert, primam vo-luptatis; ſecūdam ebrietatis, ter-tiam mœroris.

Chryſ. Ho... 46.
Ebrietas, tempe-ſtas eſt tam in animo, quàm in corpore.

Iohan. Samb. in Epigr.

Propertius.

Reference
°Ovid, Met 3
°Anacreon
°Chrysostom, Hom 46
Joannes °Sambucus
°Propertius
°Diogenes Laert

Cæcus amor prolis.

WITH kindenes, lo, the Ape doth kill her whelpe,
  Throughe clafping harde, and lulling in her armes.
Euen fo, the babes, whofe nature, Arte fhoulde helpe:
The parents fonde doe hazarde them with harmes,
  And worke their fpoile, and bringe them vnto naughte,
  When foolifhe loue forbiddes them to bee taughte

  Admirata putat formofum Simia fœtum :
  Nempe folet· pulchrum cuique placere fuum.

Motto
°Caecus °amor °prolis.

°Love of one's °offspring is °blind.

Picture
A crouching °ape holding its °dead °off-
spring.

In bello ferrum
auro præftat; in vit
autem erudicio di
mitiis. Socrat. apud
Stob.

Nic. Reufnerus.

Epigram
kindness ape kill whelp baby nature
art parent harm spoil fool love
teach

Reference
°Stobaeus
Nicholas °Reusner

Dedicatee
Nicholas °Reusner

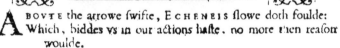

Maturandum.

Aʙᴏᴠᴛᴇ the arrowe ſwifte, Eᴄʜᴇɴᴇɪs ſlowe doth foulde:
Which, biddes vs in our actions haſte, no more then reaſon
woulde.

Whitney   Emblemes   London   1586   p.188b

Gellin lib. 10. ca. 11.
Mature, inquit, eſt
quod neque citius
eſt, neque ſerius, ſed
medium quiddam,
& temperatum eſt:
nam & in frugibus
& in pomis, matura
dicuntur, quæ neq.
cruda & immitia,
neque caduca & ni-
mium cocta, ſed
tempore ſuo tempe-
rate adulta.

Ælian. de Animal.
lib. 2. ca. 17. & Plin.
lib. 9. cap. 25. &
lib 32. cap. 1. vbi
multa mirabilia de
Echeneid-piſce ſcri-
bit. & quædam no-
tatu digna quæ ſua
memoria acciderit.

Motto
°Maturandum.

One must make °haste.

Picture
A downward-pointing °remora encircles the shaft of a downward-pointing °arrow which stands in front of a city in a landscape.

Epigram
arrow   swift   echeneis [= remora]   slow
haste   reason

Reference
°Gellius, 10, 11
°Aelian, N A 2, 17
°Pliny, N H 9, 25
°Pliny, N H 32, 1

In sinu alere serpentem.

Ad Doctiß. V. D. FRANCISCVM RAPHELENGIVM
in obsidione Antverpiana periclitantem.

THOVGHE, cittie stronge the cannons shotte dispise,
    And deadlie foes, beseege the same in vaine :
Yet, in the walles if pining famine rise,
Or elfe fome impe of SINON, there remaine.
    What can preuaile your bulwarkes? and your towers,
    When, all your force, your inwarde foe deuoures.

Whitney   Emblemes   London   1586   p.189a

Motto
In °sinu °alere °serpentem.

To °nourish a °snake in one's °bosom.

Picture
A °man, holding a °snake to his °breast with his °left hand, watches the °siege of a °city in the background.

Epigram
city   cannon   foe   siege   vain1   famine
Sinon   bulwark   tower   force   devour

Dedicatee
Francis °Rapheleng

In desciscentes.

WHEN that with milke, the goate had fil'd the pot,
    Shee brake the same, that all about it ranne.
Wherat, the maide her pacience quite forgot,
And in a rage. the brutishe beaste did banne?
    Which toye, thoughe shorte, yet sharply reprehendes
    Beginnings good, that haue vnhappie endes.

Whitney   Emblemes   London   1586   p.189b

Motto
In °desciscentes.

On those who °degenerate.

Picture
A °goat kicks over and breaks a °jar of °milk; a °milkmaid raises her °hands in anger and despair.

Epigram
goat   milk   pot   maid   patience   forget
rage   ban

Stultorum quantò status sublimior, tantò
manifestior turpitudo.

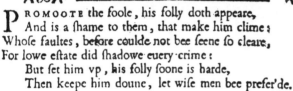

PROMOOTE the foole, his folly doth appeare,
And is a shame to them, that make him clime;
Whose faultes, before coulde not bee seene so cleare,
For lowe estate did shadowe euery crime:
  But set him vp, his folly soone is harde,
  Then keepe him doune, let wise men bee prefer'de.

Whitney Emblemes London 1586 p.190a

Motto
°Stultorum   quanto   °status   sublimior,
tanto manifestior °turpitudo.

The   higher   the   °status   of   °fools,   the
more manifest is their °baseness.

Picture
A   group   of   men   point   to   °two   °apes;   one
climbing   a   tree,   the   other   seated   on   the
ground.

Epigram
fool   shame   climb   estate1   crime
wise-man

Bis dat qui citò dat.

DOE not thine almes deferre, when neede doth bid thee haste:
For why, one gifte is double thought, that in due time is plaste.

Or so.

WHEN to the pore thou giu'st, make speede the same to doe:
Bycause one gifte in time bestowed, is worthe some other two.

Whitney Emblemes London 1586 p.190b

Motto
Bis dat qui °cito °dat.

He gives twice who °gives °quickly.

Picture
A   well-dressed   man   gives   °alms   to   a
seated °poor man.

Epigram
alms   need   haste   gift   poor   speed

Spes vana.

T н я eager haulke, with fodaine fighte of lure
  Doth ftoope, in hope to haue her wifhed praye:
So, manie men do ftoope to fightes vnfure:
And curteous fpeeche, dothe keepe them at the baye.
    Let fuche beware, left frendlie lookes be like,
    The lure, to which the foaring haulke did ftrike?

Ouid. Eplſt. 16.
Fallitur augurio ſpes
bona ſæpe ſuo.

Whitney   Emblemes   London   1586   p.191a

Motto
°Spes °vana.

°Vain °hope

Picture
A feathered °lure, as used in °falconry.

Epigram
hawk lure prey speech friend

Reference
°Ovid, Ep 16 [Her 17, 234]

Audi, tace, fuge.
To my Nephew RO. BORRON.

H EARE much; but little speake, and flee from that is naught:
Which lessons, by these formes in briefe, to euery one are taught.

Whitney   Emblemes   London   1586   p.191b

Motto
°Audi, °tace, °fuge.

°Listen, be °silent, °flee.

Picture
At the left a man points to his huge
°ears; in the centre a man points to his
°mouth with his °left °forefinger
(°Harpocratic gesture); at the right a
man flees from a °snake.

Epigram
hear speak flee naught [= evil]

Dedicatee
Robert °Borron, Whitney's nephew

Importunitas euitanda.

Whitney Emblemes London 1586 p.192

Motto
°Importunitas °evitanda.

°Importunity should be °avoided.

Picture
A man breaks a °sword over an °anvil.

Epigram
force blade anvil hazard strength
stith [= anvil] youth pith love
friend importune

WHO that with force, his burnish'd blade doth trie
On anuill harde, to prooue if it be sure:
Doth Hazarde muche, it shoulde in peeces flie,
Aduentring that, which elfe mighte well indure:
 For, there with strengthe he strikes vppon the stithe,
 That men maye knowe, his youthfull armes haue pithe.

Which warneth thofe, that louinge frendes inioye,
With care, to keepe, and frendlie them to treate,
And not to trye them still, with euerie toye,
Nor preffe them doune, when caufes be too greate,
 Nor in requefts importunate to bee:
 For ouermuche, dothe mer the courfer free?

Strenuorum immortale nomen.

To the honorable Gentleman, Sir WILLIAM RVSSELL Knight.

Whitney Emblemes London 1586 p.193

Motto
°Strenuorum °immortale °nomen.

The °fame of men of °action is °immortal.

Picture
Naked °Thetis in water up to her knees, stands near the °tomb of °Achilles. The tomb, decked with °amaranths, stands beneath a °palm-tree. A °dolphin swims in the waters.

ACHILLES tombe vpon SIGÆA fhore,
This reprefentes: where THETIS ofte was feene:
And for his loffe , did feeme for to deplore,
With gallant flower the fame was alwaies greene:
  And at the toppe, a palme did frefhelie bloome;
  Whofe braunches fweete did ouerfpread the toombe.

Which fhewes, thoughe deathe the valiaunt ouerthrowe,
Yet after fate, their fame remaines behinde:
And triumphes ftill, and dothe no conqueft knowe,
But is the badge of euerie noble minde:
  And when in graue their corpes inclofed lye,
  Their famous actes doe pierce the azure fkye.

Alij in Rhetæo
littore: fed aliter
Claud. Min. fu-
per Alciatū, Em-
blem. 48. & Em-
blem. 135. &
Plin. Natural.
Hiftor. libro 5.
cap. 30.

Nunquam Stygias fertur ad vmbras   *Vos fata trahent: fed cum fuminas*
Inclyta virtus: viuite fortes   *Exiget auras confumpta dies,*
Nec Lethæos fana per amnes   *Iter ad fuperos gloria pandet.*

                                                  Sen. Her. Fur.
                                                  Oct. act. 5.

Epigram
Achilles   tomb   Sigeum   Thetis   gallant
flower   green   palm   death   valiant   fate
fame   triumph   conquest   noble   grave
corpse

Reference
Claude °Mignault
Andrea °Alciato [Emblem 136]
°Pliny, H N 5, 30
°Seneca, Herc Fur
°Seneca, Oct 5

Dedicatee
Sir William °Russell

Vel post mortem formidolosi

To the honorable Sir IOHN NORRIS Knight, Lord president
of Munster in Irelande, and Colonell Generall of the
Englishe Infanterie, in the lowe countries.

A Secret cause, that none can comprehende,
In natures workes is often to bee seene;
As, deathe can not the ancient discorde ende,
That raigneth still, the wolfe, and sheepe betweene:
   The like, beside in many things are knowne,
   The cause reueal'd, to none, but GOD alone.

For, as the wolfe, the sillye sheepe did feare,
And made him still to tremble, at his barke:
So beinge dead, which is moste straunge to heare,
This feare remaynes, as learned men did marke;
   For with their skinnes, if that two drommes bee bounde,
   That, clad with sheepe, doth iarre: and hathe no founde.

And, if that stringes bee of their intrailes wroughte,
And ioyned both, to make a siluer sounde:
No cunninge eare can tune them as they oughte,
But one is harde, the other still is droun'de:
   Or discordes foule, the harmonie doe marre;
   And nothinge can appease this inward warre.

So, ZISCA thoughte when deathe did shorte his daies,
As with his voice, hee erste did daunte his foes;
That after deathe hee shoulde newe terror raise,
And make them flee, as when they felte his bloes.
   Wherefore, hee charg'd that they his skinne shoulde frame,
   To fitte a dromme, and marche forth with the same.

So, HECTORS sighte greate feare in Greekes did worke,
When hee was showed on horsebacke, beeinge dead:
HVNIADES, the terrour of the Turke,
Thoughe layed in graue, yet at his name they fled:
   And cryinge babes, they ceased with the same,
   The like in FRANCE, sometime did TALBOTS name.

Plin. De Nat. Hist.
lio.17. cap.4.

Cladd. Min. super
Alciatum, Emb.:17.

Ænea: Silulur 3.
Commens. De rebus
gestis Alphonso.

Coelius Curio.

Fortes, & magna-
nimi habendi sunt,
non qui faciunt,
sed qui propulsant
iniuriam Cic. 1.
offic.

Whitney Emblemes London 1586 p.194

Motto
Vel post °mortem °formidolosi.

Those °terrifying even after °death.

Picture
°Two °drummers, one beating a large °drum, the other blowing a °horn(?) and beating a smaller drum, stand before an °encampment. A troop of °soldiers in the background.

Epigram

secret	nature	death	discord	wolf
sheep	God	fear	skin	two drum string
entrail	silver	harmony	war	Zizka foe
terror	Hector	Greek	Hunyady	Turk
Talbot	France			

Reference
°Pliny, H N 17, 4
Claude °Mignault
Andrea °Alciato, Emblem 171
Aeneas °Silvius, R G A
Coelius °Curio
°Cicero, Off 1

Dedicatee
Sir John °Norris

Victoria cruenta.

To *Sir* WILLIAM STANDLEY *Knight.*

THE Olephante with ftinge of ferpent fell,
That ftill about his legges, with winding cralles:
Throughe poifon ftronge, his bodie fo did fwell,
That doune he finkes, and on the ferpente falles:
    Which creature huge, did fall vppon him foe.
    That by his deathe, he alfo kill'd his foe.

Thofe fharpe conflictes, thofe broiles and battailes maine,
That are atchieude, with fpoile on either parte:
Where ftreames of blood the hilles, and valleys ftaine,
And what is wonne, the price is deathe, and fmarte:
    This dothe importe: But thofe are captaines good,
    That winne the fielde, with fheddinge leafte of blood.

Whitney   Emblemes   London   1586   p.195

Motto
°Victoria °cruenta.

°Bloody °victory.

Picture
A dead °elephant, poisoned by the bite of a °snake, has fallen and crushed its assailant. In the background a man falls backwards onto °two upright °swords.

Epigram

elephant	sting	snake	poison	death
kill	conflict	battle	spoil	blood
price	captain			

Non eft tanti gaudij excelfa tenere; quanti mœroris eft, de excelfis corruere: nec tanta gloria fequi poteft victoriam, quanta ignominia poteft fequi ruinam. *Ambr.*

Reference
°Ambrose

Dedicatee
Sir William °Stanley

Penne gloria perennis.

To EDWARDE DIER Efquier

Whitney   Emblemes   London   1586   p.196

Motto

°Pennae °gloria perennis.

The °glory everlasting of the °pen.

Picture

Spotted with °mouths(?), °winged °Fame, sounds a °horn as he flies over a °Roman(?) building and °three °Egyptian(?) °pyramids. Fame has a °pen tied to a sling made of °laurel(?) over his shoulder.

WHEN frowning fatall dame, that ftoppes our courfe in fine,
The thred of noble SVRREYS life, made haft for to vntwine.
APOLLO chang'd his cheare, and lay'd awaie his lute,
And PALLAS, and the Mufes fad, did weare a mourninge fute.
And then, the goulden pen, in cafe of fables cladde,
Was lock'd in chifte of Ebonie, and to Parnaffus had.
But, as all times do chaunge, fo paffions haue their fpace;
And cloudie fkies at lengthe are clear'd, with Phœbus chearefull face.
For, when that barren verfe made Mufes voide of mirthe:
Beboulde, LVSINA fweetelie founge, of SIDNEYS ioyfull birthe.
Whome mightie IOVE did bleffe, with graces from aboue:
On whome, did fortune frendlie fmile, and nature moft did loue.
And then, behoulde, the pen, was by MERCVRIVS fente,
Wherewith, hee alfo gaue to him, the gifte for to inuente.
That, when hee firft began, his vayne in verfe to fhowe.
More fweete then honie, was the ftile, that from his penne did flowe.
Wherewith, in youthe hee vfd to bannifhe idle fittes;
That nowe, his workes of endleffe fame, delighte the worthie wittes.

The Erle of Surrey, that wrat the booke of Songes and Sonettes.

Sir Philip Sidney Knighte.

Epigram

fate dame thread Surrey life Apollo lute Pallas Muse mourn gold pen sable chest ebony Parnassus passion cloud sky Phoebus verse mirth Lucina Sidney birth Jove bless grace fortune nature love Mercury gift invent honey youth fame wit Cherillus poet write friend praise dark knight trumpet sky spire pole laurel honour treasure palm Homer book Egypt Rome ruin wheel monarch marble adamant labour brain monument time waste God prince land triumph death corpse grave peace sleep Dyer pear

No haulting verfe hee writes, but matcheth former times,
No°Cherillus, he can abide , nor Poëttes patched rimes.
What volumes hath hee writte, that reft among his frendes,
Which needes no other praife at all, eche worke it felfe comendes.
So, that hee famous liues, at home, and farre , and neare ;
For thofe that liue in other landes, of SIDNEYS giftes doe heare.
And fuche as Mufes ferue, in darkenes meere doe dwell;
If that they haue not feene his workes, they doe fo farre excell.
Wherefore, for to extoll his name in what I might,
This Embleme lo, I did prefent, vnto this woorthie Knight.
Who, did the fame refufe, as not his proper due :
And at the firft , his fentence was, it did belonge tó you.
Wherefore, lo, fame with trompe, that mountes vnto the fkye :
And, farre aboue the higheft fpire, from pole, to pole dothe flye.
Heere houereth at your will , with pen adorn'd with baies :
Which for you bothe, fhee hath prepar'd, vnto your endleffe praife.
The laurell leafe for you, for him, the goulden pen ;
The honours that the Mufes giue, vnto the rareft men.
Wherefore, proceede I praye, vnto your lafting fame ;
For writinges laft when wee bee gonne, and doe preferue our name.
And whilft wee tarrye heere, no treafure can procure,
The palme that waites vpon the pen, which euer doth indure.
Two thoufand yeares, and more, HOMERVS wrat his booke;
And yet, the fame doth ftill remayne, and keepes his former looke.
Wheare Ægypte fpires bee gonne, and ROME doth ruine feele,
Yet, both begonne fince he was borne, thus time doth turne the wheele.
Yea, thoughe fome Monarche greate fome worke fhould take in hand,
Of marble, or of Adamant, that manie worldes fhoulde ftande,
Yet, fhould one only man, with labour of the braine,
Bequeathe the world a monument, that longer fhoulde remaine.
And when that marble waules, with force of time fhould wafte;
It fhould indure from age, to age, and yet no age fhould tafte.
Oh happie you therfore , who fpend your bleffed daies
In feruing GOD, your Prince, your lande, vnto your endleffe praife.
And daily doe proceede, with trauaile of the minde,
To make you famous heere , and eeke, to leaue a fame behinde.
Which is the cheefeft thinge, the greateft Prince can haue,
For, fame doth triumphe ouer deathe, when corpes are clof'd in graue.
Euen fo, your worthie workes, when you in peace fhall fleepe,
Shall make reporte of your defertes, and DIERS name fhall keepe.
Whome, I doe reuerence ftill, as one of PALLAS peares:
And praye the Lorde, with ioyfull dayes for to prolonge your yeares.

Side notes:

*Horat. lib. 2. Epift. 1. ad Auguftum.

Reference
°Horace, Ep 2, 1
°Gellius 17, 21
°Pliny, H N 7, 16
°Pliny, H N 36, 12
Cornelius °Nepos
°Herodotus

Dedicatee
Edward °Dyer, esquire

Homerus vixit, poft Romam conditam, fed natus ante, Aul. Gell. lib. 17. cap. 11.

Sed Plinius fecúdus, qui ante Gellium, tempore Vefpafiani Imperatoris vixit : De Homeri ætate, lib. 7. ca 16. Natur. Hiftor. fic fcribit: Iam verò antè annos propè mille, vates illa Homerus non ceffauit, &c. Et Cornelius Nepos primo Chronicorum ante Romam , Homerum vixiffe fcribit.

De Pyramidum ætate, incertum, Plin. Natural hift. lib. 36. cap. 12. tamen quafdam poft Homerum conditas, probabile. De his, Herodotus.

Animus, non res.
To EDWARD PASTON Esquier.

IN chriſtall towers, and turrets richlie ſette
With glittering gemmes, that ſhine againſt the ſonne:
In regall roomes of Iaſper, and of Iette,
Contente of minde, not alwaies likes to wonne:
    But oftentimes, it pleaſeth her to ſtaye
    In ſimple cotes, cloſ'de in with walles of claye.

DIOGENES, within a tonne did dwell,
No choice of place, nor ſtore of pelfe he had;
And all his goodes, coulde BIAS beare right well,
And CODRVS had ſmall cates, his harte to gladde:
    His meate was rootes: his table, was a ſtoole.
    Yet theſe for witte, did ſet the worlde to ſcoole?

Who couettes ſtill, or hee that liues in feare,
As much delighte is wealthe vnto his minde,
As muſicke is to him, that can not heare,
Or pleaſante ſhowes, and pictures, to the blinde:
    Then ſweete content, ofte likes the meane eſtate,
    Which is exempte, and free, from feare, and hate.

What man is ritche? not he that doth abounde.
What man is pore? not hee that hath no ſtore.
But he is ritche, that makes content his grounde.
And he is pore, that couettes more and more.
    Which proues: the man was ritcher in the tonne,
    Then was the Kinge, that manie laudes had wonne.

If then, content the chiefeſt riches bee,
And greedie gripes, that doe abounde be pore,
Since that, inoughe allotted is to thee,
Embrace content, then CÆSAR hath no more.
    Giue MIDAS, goulde: and let him pine with ſhame.
    Vſe you, your goodes, to liue, and die, with fame.

Eraſm. Chiliad. 61.
Centuria 8. de Dio-
gene, & quid per
vitam doliarem:
ſignificatur.

Iuuenalis:
Tota domus Codri rheda
componitur una.

Horat.lib.1.epiſt.2.
Qui cupit, aut metuit,
iuuat illum ſic domus,
aut res;
Vt lippum picta tabula,
fomenta podagram;
Auriculas cithara col-
lecta ſorde dolentes.

Quis diues? quid mi
cupias. quis pauper?
auarus.
Biantis dictum per
Antonium.

Claud. 1. Ruf.
.. Contentus honeſta
Fabricius parui ſperne-
bat munera regum:
Sudabat fine graui con-
ſul Serranus aratro:
& raſa pugnaces Curios
anguſta tenebat.

Whitney Emblemes London 1586 p.198

Motto
°Animus, non °res

°Mind, not °property.

Picture
°Diogenes, seated in his °barrel, converses through the open doorway with °Alexander, with °crown and °sceptre.

Epigram
crystal tower turret rich gem sun jasper jet regal content mind cote clay Diogenes tun pelf Bias Codrus cate [= provisions] meat root table stool wit school covet fear wealth music hear picture blind estate1 hate poor king greed Caesar Midas gold Shame live die fame

Reference
°Erasmus, Chil 61 [= Adag. 1, 8, 61]
°Juvenal °Horace, Ep 1, 2
°Ausonius °Claudian, In Ruf 1

Dedicatee
Edward °Paston, esquire

Quae sequimur fugimus.
TO THOMAS WILBRAHAM *Esquier.*

WE flee, from that wee seeke; & followe, that wee leaue: [weaue,
    And, whilst wee thinke our webbe to skante, & larger still would
Lo, Time dothe cut vs of, amid our carke : and care.
Which warneth all, that haue enoughe, and not contented are,
For to inioye their goodes, their howses, and their landes :
Bicause the Lorde vnto that end, commits them to their handes.
Yet, those whose greedie mindes : enoughe, doe thinke too small :
Whilst that with care they seeke for more, oft times are reu'd of all,
Wherefore all such (I wishe) that spare, where is no neede :
To vse their goodes whilst that they may, for time apace doth speede.
And since, by proofe I knowe, you hourde not vp your store;
Whose gate, is open to your frende : and purce, vnto the pore :
And spend vnto your praise, what GOD dothe largely lende :
I chiefly made any choice of this, which I to you commende.
In hope, all those that see your name, aboue the head :
Will at your lampe, their owne come light, within your steppes to tread,
Whose daily studie is, your countrie to adorne :
And for to keepe a worthie house, in place where you weare borne.

Whitney   Emblemes   London   1586   p.199

Motto
Quae °sequimur °fugimus.

We °flee what we °follow.

Picture
A °couple walk away from a large building; the man points back to an open °treasure °chest. °Winged °Time, with a °scythe, in a bank of clouds above, pursues the couple.

Epigram
flee   seek   web   weave   Time   cut   goods
house   land   Lord   greedy   mind   hoard
gate   purse   poor   spend   God   land
country

Plautus Rud.
Rape quod here sit,
haud perit.

Reference
°Plautus, Rud

Dedicatee
Thomas °Wilbraham

Patria cuique chara.
To RICHARDE COTTON *Esquier.*

THE bees at lengthe retourne into their hiue,
When they haue suck'd the sweete of FLORAS bloomes;
And with one minde their worke they doe contriue,
And laden come with honie to their roomes:
 A worke of arte; and yet no arte of man,
 Can worke, this worke; these little creatures can.

The maister bee, within the midst dothe liue,
In fairest roome, and most of stature is;
And euerie one to him dothe reuerence giue,
And in the hiue with him doe liue in blisse:
 Hee hath no stinge, yet none can doe him harme,
 For with their strengthe, the rest about him swarme.

Lo, natures force within these creatures small,
Some, all the daye the honie home doe beare.
And some, farre off on flowers freshe doe fall,
Yet all at nighte vnto their home repaire:
 And euerie one, her proper hiue doth knowe,
 Althoughe there stande a thousande on a rowe.

Whitney Emblemes London 1586 p.200

Motto
°Patria cuique °chara.

One's °homeland is °dear to each.

Picture
A swarm of °bees returning to its °hive.

Epigram

bee	hive	Flora	work	honey	art	man
master	reverence		bliss	sting	harm
strength	nature		force		flower
commonwealth	rule	obey	head	Lord
Combermere	Jove	horn	plenty	fish
fowl	cattle	crystal	spring1	fertile
field	meadow	grain	water	wood1	gold
time	praise	country	tenant	desire
stranger	parent	love	wing

Aelian. de animal. lib. 1. ca. 59.
& 60. Et lib. 5.
cap. 11.
Et Plin. Natural.
hist. lib. 11. cap. 5.
& 16.

Reference
°Aelian, N A 1, 59 and 60
°Aelian, N A 5, 11
°Pliny, H N 11, 5 and 16
°Ovid, Pont 1, 4
°Ambrose

Dedicatee
Richard °Cotton, esquire

Whitney   Emblemes   London   1586   p.200

A Comon-wealthe, by this, is right expreſte;
Bothe him, that rules, and thoſe, that doe obaye:
Or ſuche, as are the heads aboue the reſt,
Whome here, the Lorde in highe eſtate dothe ſtaye:
    By whoſe ſupporte, the meaner ſorte doe liue,
    And vnto them all reuerence dulie giue.

Plin. Natural.
Hiſt. li.11.cap.5.

Which when I waied: I call'd vnto my minde
Your C v m b e r m a i r e, that fame ſo farre commendes:
A ſtately ſeate, whoſe like is harde to finde,
Where mightie I o v e the horne of plentie lendes:
    With fiſhe, and foule, and cattaile ſondrie flockes,
    Where chriſtall ſpringes doe guſhe out of the rockes.

There, fertile fieldes; there, meadowes large extende:
There, ſtore of grayne: with water, and with wood.
And, in this place, your goulden time you ſpende,
Vnto your praiſe, and to your countries good:
    This is the hiue; your tennaunts, are the bees:
    And in the ſame, haue places by degrees.

And as the bees, that farre and neare doe ſtraye,
And yet come home, when honie they haue founde:
So, thoughe ſome men doe linger longe awaye,
Yet loue they beſt their natiue countries grounde.
    And from the ſame, the more they abſent bee,
    With more deſire, they wiſhe the ſame to ſee.

Ouid. 1. Pont. 4.
Rurſus amor pa-
tria ratione va-
lentior omni, &c.

Euen ſo my ſelfe; throughe abſence manie a yeare,
A ſtraunger meere, where I did ſpend my prime.
Nowe, parentes loue dothe hale mee by the eare,
And ſayeth, come home, deferre no longer time:
    Wherefore, when happe, ſome goulden honie bringes?
    I will retorne, and reſt my wearie winges.

Primus gradus
pietatis eſt iſte,
vt quos auctores
tibi voluit eſſe
deus, honores
obſequiis, abſti-
neas cōtumeliis,
nec vultu læden-
da eſt pietas pa-
rentum. Amb.

                    Ouid. 1. Pont. 4.

        Quid melius Roma? Scythico quid frigore peius:
          Huc tamen ex illa barbarus vrbe fugit.

Aurea compedes.

To G. M. *Efquier.*

I T better is (wee fay) a cotage poore to houlde,
Then for to lye in prifon ftronge, with fetters made of goulde.
Which fhewes, that bondage is the prifon of the minde.:
And libertie the happie life, that is to man affign'de,
And thoughe that fome preferre their bondage, for their gaines:
And richely are adorn'd in filkes, and prefte with maffie chaines.
Yet manie others liue, that are accompted wife:
Who libertie doe chiefely choofe, thoughe clad in gounes of frife
And waighe not POMPEYS porte, nor yet LVCVLLVS fare:
So that they may adorne their mindes, they well contented are.
Yea, rather doe accepte his dwelling in the tonne,
And for to liue with CODRYS cates; a roote, and barly bonne.
Where freedome they inioye, and vncontrolled liue:
Then with the chiefeft fare of all, attendance for to geue.
And, if I fhould bee afk'd, which life doth pleafe mee befte:
I like the goulden libertie, let goulden bondage refte.

Whitney Emblemes London 1586 p.202

Motto
°Aureae °compedes.

°Golden °shackles.

Picture
A well-dressed man or °courtier(?) sits in leg °stocks.

Epigram
poor cottage strong prison fetter gold bondage mind liberty life gain rich silk chain wise Pompey Lucillus dwelling tun Codrus freedom

Erafmus Chi-
liad. 1. Centur.4.
Adag 25.

Diogenes dicebat
Ariftippum (philo-
fophum aulicum)
aureis teneri compe-
dibus ne poflet ex-
ire.

Tertullianus lib. 6.
De habitu muliebri
cap. 4. Apud Barba-
ros quofdam (quia
vernaculum eft au-
rum)auro vinctos in
ergaftulis habent.
idem narrat in lib.
De cultu feminar.
Plutarchus fcribit
autem in Erotico
apud Aethiopas hoc
in vfu efle.
De quo etiam Aul.
Gell. lib.11. cap. 18.

Erafmus Chiliad.1.
Centuria 6.Adag.76
de Codro.

Reference
°Erasmus, Chil [= Adag] 2, 4, 25
°Erasmus, Chil [=Adag] 1, 6, 76
°Tertullian, Apolog 6, 4
°Plutarch, Ama
°Gellius 11, 18

Dedicatee
G.°M., esquire

Whitney   Emblemes   London   1586   p.203

Auxilio divino.

To RICHARD DRAKE Esquier, *in praise of*
Sir FRANCIS DRAKE *Knight.*

THROVGHE ſcorchinge heate, throughe coulde, in ſtormes, and
    tempeſts force,
By ragged rocks, by ſhelſes, & ſandes: this Knighte did keepe his courſe.
By gapinge gulſes hee paſſ'd, by monſters of the flood,
By pirattes, theeues, and cruell foes, that long'd to ſpill his blood.
That wonder greate to ſcape: but, GOD was on his ſide,
And throughe them all, in ſpite of all, his ſhaken ſhippe did guide.
And, to requite his paines: *By helpe of power deuine.*
His happe, at lengthe did aunſwere hope, to finde the goulden-mine.
Let GRÆCIA then forbeare, to praiſe her IASON boulde?
Who throughe the watchfull dragons paſſ'd, to win the fleece of goulde,
Since by MÆDEAS helpe, they weare inchaunted all,
And IASON without perrilles, paſſ'd: the conqueſte therfore ſmall?
But, hee, of whome I write, this noble minded DRAKE,
Did bringe away his goulden fleece, when thouſand eies did wake.
Wherefore, yee woorthie wightes, that ſeeke for forreine ſandes:
Yſ that you can, come alwaiſe home, by GANGES goulden ſandes.
And you, that liue at home, and can not brooke the flood,
Geue praiſe to them, that paſſe the waues, to doe their countrie good.
Before which ſorte, as chiefe: in tempeſte, and in calme,
Sir FRANCIS DRAKE, by due deſerte, may weare the goulden palme.

Motto
°Auxilio °divino.

With °divine °aid.

Picture
A three masted °sailing °ship rests on a °world °globe. The globe is surrounded by °clouds, °stars, the °sun and a crescent °moon. A °right hand emerging from the clouds at the top left holds a °bridle, which, fastened to the bow of the ship, encircles the globe.

Epigram
heat   cold   storm   rock   sand   knight
course   gulf   monster   flood   pirate
thief   foe   blood   God   ship   help   power
hope   gold   mine   Greece   Jason   dragon
fleece   Medea   peril   conquest   foreign
land   Ganges   praise   wave   country   palm
Francis Drake

Ouid. Met. 7.

Reference
°Ovid, Met 7

Dedicatee
Richard °Drake, esquire

Auaritia huius saeculi.

10 ARTHVRE BOVRCHIER *Esquier.*

WITH double dore this Pallace loe, doth ope;
The one, vnto the gallant roomes doth shewe,
Whereas the ritche with goulden giftes haue scope;
The other, to an emptie benche doth goe,
   And there, the pore haue leaue for to resorte,
   But not presume vnto the other porte.

For, alwaies that is shutte vnto the pore,
But ope to them, that haue the mines of goulde:
Then; thoughe the worlde of Poëttes haue no store,
No maruaile tho, sith bountie is so coulde;
   For, if there did MECOENAS giftes abounde,
   Newe HORACE soone, & VIRGIL should be founde.

   Ingenium sacri miraris abesse Maronis,
      Nec quenquam tanta bella sonare tuba:
   Sint Mecenates, non deerunt Flacce, Marones;
      Virgiliumq; tibi vel tua rura dabunt.

Whitney Emblemes London 1586 p.204

Motto
°Avaritia huius °saeculi.

The °avarice of this °generation.

Picture
°Three °rich men and °two °poor men enter a °palace through two different °doors set in an archway.

Epigram
door palace rich gold gift bench poor mine poet bounty Mycenas Horace Virgil

Reference
°Ovid, A A 2
°Martial 8, 55

Dedicatee
Arthur °Bourchier, esquire

Ovid. 1. Art.
carmina laudantur sed munera magna petuntur.
   Dummodo sit diues barbarus, ille placet.

Martial. lib. 8.
Epig. 55. ad Flac-
cum.

Pulchritudo sine fructu.

To ARTHVRE STARKEY *Esquier.*

Motto
°Pulchritudo sine °fructu.

°Beauty without °fruit.

Picture
A °cypress tree.

Epigram
cypress   green   sweet   smell   fruit
gallant courtesy fawn1 deed barren

Dedicatee
Arthur °Starkey, esquire

THE Cipreſſe tree is pleaſinge to the ſighte,
Straighte, tall, and greene, and ſweete vnto the ſmell:
Yet, yeeldes no fruicte vnto the trauaylinge wighte,
But naughte, and bad, experience dothe vs tell:
    Where, other trees that make not ſuche a ſhowe,
    Yeelde pleaſante fruicte, and plentifullie growe.

This gallante tree that good, and fruictfull ſeemes,
In couerte ſorte, a kinde of men doth checke:
Whoſe curteſie, no man but much eſteemes,
Who promiſe muche, and faune about our necke:
    But if wee trie, their deedes wee barren finde,
    Or yeelde but fruicte, like to the Cipreſſe kinde.

Pulchra coma eſt, pulchro digeſtaq̧, ordine frondes;
ſed fructus nullos hæc coma pulchra gerit.

Tempore cuncta mitiora.

IANO DOVSÆ, *nobiliß. viri,* Dn. IANI DOVSÆ
à *Noortwijck* F.

THE grapes not ripe, the trauailinge man doth wafte,
  And vnder foote doth treade, as fower, and naughte:
Which, being ripe, had fweete, and pleafaunte tafte
Whereby, wee maie this leffon true be taughte.
    Howe fimple men, doe fimplie iudge of thinges.
    And doe not waighe that time perfection bringes.

For in this worlde, the thinges moft faire, and rare,
Are harde at firfte, and feeme both harfhe, and fower:
But yet in time, they fweete and eafie are,
Then ftaie for time, which giues both fruite and flower?
    And vfe our time, and let vs ftill fuppofe
    No greater loffe, then time that wee doe lofe.

        Nam mora dat vires, teneras mora percoquit vuas,   Ouid.1. Remed.
          Et validas fegetes, quod fuit herba facit.

Motto
°Tempore cuncta °mitiora.

Everything becomes more °mellower with °time.

Picture
A man in rags °tramples °grapes under his °right °foot while reaching for another °bunch with his °left hand. The °vine grows against the brick wall of a building. A patch of stucco on the wall bears °astrological symbols, and a signboard bears a crescent °moon. A °woman, standing next to the man, holds a bunch of °grapes away from her with her °left hand. Overhead part of a °zodical °circle with a nude °Virgo, her °right hand pointing at the grapes held by the woman.

Epigram
grape ripe travail sour sweet time perfection fruit flower

Reference
°Ovid, Rem Am 1

Dedicatee
Janus °Dousa

Imparilitas.

To M. William Harebrowne, *at Conſtantinople.*

Whitney   Emblemes   London   1586   p.207

Motto
°Imparilitas.

°Inequality.

Picture
°Two °ducks and two °geese hunt for food in a °pond(?) edged with reeds.   A °falcon flies overhead.

Epigram
falcon   sky   duck   goose   ditch   prince
fame   world   home   native   country

Reference
Andrea °Alciato [Emblem 140]

Dedicatee
William °Harebrowne

THE faulcon mountes alofte vnto the ſkie,
  And ouer hilles, and dales, dothe make her flighte;
The duckes, and geeſe, about the houſe doe flie,
And in eche diche, and muddie lake doe lighte,
  They ſeeke their foode in puddles, and in pittes,
  While that alofte, the princelie faulcon ſittes.

Suche difference is in men, as maye appeare;
Some, throughe the worlde doe paſſe by lande, and ſea:
And by deſerte are famous farre, and neare,
So, all their life at home, ſome others ſtaie:
  And nothinge can to trauaile them prouoke,
  Beyonde the ſmell of natiue countries ſmoke.

In ſublime volans tenuem ſecat aëra falco :
Sed paſcuntur humi graculus, anſer, anas.

Alciatus.

Tunc tua res agitur, paries cùm proximus ardet

To M. THOMAS WHETELEY.

A WAKE from fleepe fecure, when perrill doth appeare :
No wifedome then to take our eafe, and not the worft to feare.
Still ARCHIMEDES wroughte , when foes had wonne the⁎towne,
And woulde not leaue his worke in hande, till he was beaten downe.
No furetie is within , when roofe alofte doth flame :
It is a madnes then to ftaye , till wee haue donne our game.
Yea, thofe that helpe deferre, when neighbours houfe doth burne:
Are like with griefe, to fee their owne , with fpeede to cinders turne.
Then, cut of all delaies when daungers are begonne,
For if beginnings wee withftande, the conqueft fooner wonne.

> *Temporis officium eft folatia dicere certi,*
> *Dum dolor in curfu eft, dum petit æger opem.*

Whitney   Emblemes   London   1586   p.208

Motto
Tunc tua °res agitur, °paries cum proximus °ardet.

Then your °property is in °danger, when the nearest wall is °burning.

Picture
A °young man and an °older one sit at a table over a °game of °draughts or °chess. The younger man is intent on the game, while the older points at the °flames which engulf the building behind them.

Horat. lib.1. Ep.19.

°Syracufa.

Plutarch. in vita
Marcelli.
Plin. lib 7. cap. 37.

Vegetius.
Nunquam impera-
tor i a paci credat,
vt non fe præparet
bello. Et Bern, in
Nat. Dom Ser.6.
Ex confideratione
remedij , periculi
æftimatur quantitas.

Ouid. 4. Pont. 11.

Epigram
awaken   sleep   secure   peril   wisdom fear   Archimedes   foe   town   roof   flame mad   game   neighbour   house   burn   grief cinder   delay   danger   conquest

Reference
°Horace, Ep 1, 19   °Plutarch, Vit Marc
°Pliny, N H 7, 37   °Vegetius
°Ovid, Pont 4, 11   °Bernard, Ser 6

Dedicatee
Thomas °Wheatley

Ex morbo medicina.
To W. Ro.

WHEN that OPIMIVS ritche, had fcraped manie a pounde;
And fil'd his baggs, & cofers full, that wealthe did moft abounde.
Yet liu'd hee ftill in awe, as if it weare offence
To ope his purce, for any neede; hee fpared fo his pence.
At lengthe, this greedie carle the Lythergie poffefte:
That vnneth hee could ftere a foote, with fleepe fo fore opprefte.
And languifhinge therein, not like for to efcape:
His heire, was ioyfull of that fighte, who for his goodes did gape.
But, when that nothinge coulde OPIMIVS fleepinge let,
The quicke Phifition did commaunde, that tables fhoulde bee fet
About the mifers bed, and budgettes forthe to bringe,
And poure the goulde vppon the bourde, that hee mighte heare it ringe.
And bad the heire to tell, and all the ftanders bye:
With that, hee to the ficke man call'de, what meane you thus to lye?
And will not haue regarde your treafure to preferue:
B-houlde your heire, and all the refte, howe largely nowe they carue?
With that, hee ftarted vp; halfe dead, and halfe a liue;
And ftaringe on his heapes of goulde, longe time for life did ftriue.
So that, when nothinge coulde his droufie eies awake,
Such vertue, had the fighte of goulde, that fleepe did him forfake.
Which fhowes, when dreadfull deathe prefentes the laftinge fleepe:
They hardly can departe in peace, whofe goulde is rooted deepe.

Effigiem Rex Crœfe tuã ditiffime Regum   Nunc profunt Regum Rex ò ditiffime cùm fis
Vidit apud Manes, Diogenes Cynicus.   Stuut ego folus, me quoque pauperiori
Cõftitit vtq; procul folito maiore cachinno   Nã quacunq. habui, mecü fero, cùm nihil ipfe
Concuffus, dixit. quid tibi diuitia   Ex tantis tecum Crœfe feras apibus.

Horat. Serm. lib. 2.
Satyra 3.
Demefth. apud Velat.
Qui animum curat,
feipfum curat: qui
corpus, non fe fed
fua curat: qui pe-
cuniam, non fe, nec
fua curat, fed valdè
aliena curat.
Plut. de Polit.
Maiori odio diui-
tem populus perfe-
qui folet, nihil per
benignitaté & gra-
tiam depromentem,
quàm inopem, qui
bona fubripiat pub-
lica. hoc enim ne-
ceffitate domina'fti-
muiante, illud ma-
lignitate, atq. con-
temptu fieri arbi-
tratur.
Grigor. in Homil.
Res fuas, eu ... no-
reretur, diue ... um
.olleret, fi ad peten-
tis vocem, cùm vi-
uerет, tuliffet: nam
terrena omnia, quæ
feruando amitti-
mus, largiendo fer-
uamus.
Aufon. Epig 55.

Whitney   Emblemes   London   1586   p.209

Motto
Ex °morbo °medicina.

°Remedy from °disease.

Picture
°Opimius, the °miser, languishes in his sick-bed. His °physician supervises two men who are emptying Opimius's °chests of °gold onto a table in the hope that the sound of the falling gold will revive the patient.

Epigram

Opimius	rich	coffer
wealth	purse	greed
lethargy	sleep	languish
heir	physician	table
miser	gold	sick	treasure
life	virtue	death	place

Reference
°Horace, Sat 2, 3
Raffaele °Maffei, Pol
°Gregory, Hom
°Ausonius, Epigr 55

Dedicatee
W. °Ro.

Fraus meretur fraudem.

Whitney Emblemes London 1586 p.210

Motto
°Fraus meretur fraudem.

°Deceit deserves deceit.

Picture
An old °lion, feigning °sickness, lies in a cave. A °fox stands at the mouth of the den. The ground at the entrance is marked with foot prints, all of which lead into the lair.

Epigram
lion prey feign sick fox step secret mischief threat den

Horat. Epift.
lib.1. Epift. 1.

Reference
°Horace, Ep 1, 1

T H E Lion oulde that coulde not get his praye,
 By fwifte purfute, as he had done of late:
Did faigne him ficke, and in his denne did ftaye,
And præde on thofe, that came to fee his ftate:
    At lengthe, the foxe his dutie to declare,
    Came to the dore, to knowe howe he did fare.

Who anfwered, ficke, my oulde beloued frende?
Come in, and fee, and feele my pulfes beate:
To whome, quoth he, I dare not now intende,
Bicaufe, thefe fteppes fome fecret mifchiefe threate:
    For, all I fee haue gone into thy denne,
    But none I finde, that haue retorn'd againe.

Zelotypia.

Motto
°Zelotypia.

°Jealousy.

Picture
°Procris collapses, struck in the breast by an °arrow. °Cephalus, who shot the arrow, stands poised at the left. A small °dog runs towards the dying Procris.

Epigram

sick	secret	wound	heart	force
despair	jealousy	hell	pain	Pluto
passion	beauty	foe	marry	envy	fury
Procris	bane	gall	mourn	husband	bow
prey				

Reference
°Ovid, Met 7
°Plutarch, Mor

A Sicknes fore, that dothe in fecret wounde,
  And gripes the harte, thoughe outward nothing fhowe;
The force whereof, the paciente doth confounde,
That oftentimes, difpaire therof doth growe:
   And Ieloufie, this ficknes hathe to name,
   An hellifhe paine, that firfte from PLVTO came.

Which paffion ftraunge, is alwaies beauties foe,
And mofte of all, the married forte enuies:
Oh happie they, that liue in wedlocke foe,
That in their breftes this furie neuer rife:
   For, when it once doth harbour in the harte,
   It foiournes ftill, and doth too late departe.

Lo PROCRIS heare, when wounded therwithall,
Did breede her bane, who mighte haue bath'de in bliffe:
This corfie fharpe fo fedde vppon her gall,
That all to late fhee mourn'd, for her amiffe:
   For, whilft fhee watch'd her hufbandes wires to knowe,
   Shee vnawares, was praye vnto his bowe.

Ouid. Metam.
lib. 7.

Similem de vxo-
re Cyanippi, &c.
hic Plutarchus in
Moral.

Medici Icon.

Ad ornatiß. viros D. IOANNEM IAMES, *&* LANCE-
LOTTVM BROWNE. *Medicos celeberrimos.*

THIS portrature, dothe ÆSCVLAPIVS tell.
The laurell crowne, the fame of phifike fhowes:
The bearde, declares his longe experience well:
And grauitie therewith that alwaie goes.
   The fcepter, tells he ruleth like a kinge
   Amongft the ficke; commaunding euerie thinge.

The knotted ftaffe, declares the crabbed fkill
Mofte harde t'attaine; that doth fupporte his ftate:
His fittinge, fhewes he muft be fetled ftill,
With conftant minde, and rafhe proceedinge hate:
   The Dragon, tells he doth our age renewe,
   And foone decerne, to giue the ficke his dewe.

The cocke, dothe teache his watchinge, and his care,
To vifite ofte his pacientes, in their paine:
The couchinge dogge, dothe lafte of all declare,
That faithfulnes, and loue, fhoulde ftill remaine:
   Within their breftes, that Phifike doe profeffe.
   Which partes, they all fhoulde in their deedes expreffe.

Ouid.3. Pont.4.
*Ad medicam du-
bius confugit æger
opem.*

Hier. in Epift.
Corporis debilitas
nimia, etiam animi
vires frangit, mentis
quoque ingenium
marcefcere facit:
quicquid cum mo-
do, & temperamen-
to fit, falubre fit.

Motto
°Medici °Icon.

The °image of a °physician.

Picture
A bearded °Aesculapius, wearing a °laurel °garland, a °sceptre in his °right hand and a knotted °staff in his °left hand, sits on a °throne, supported by two °eagles, under a canopy. There are a °snake at his right, a °dog lying in front of him and a °cock at his left.

Epigram
Aesculapius laurel crown fame physic beard experience gravity sceptre rule king sick staff skill sit constant mind rash hate dragon age cock care patient dog faith love

Reference
°Ovid, Pont 3, 4
°Jerome, Ep

Dedicatee
John °James and Lancelot °Browne

Inanis impetus.

Clariſ. omni�q̃, doctrina & virtutꝰ laude ornatiſſimo
viro D. IVSTO LIPSIO.

BY ſhininge lighte, of wanniſhe CYNTHIAS raies,
The dogge behouldes his ſhaddowe to appeare :
Wherefore, in vaine aloude he barkes, and baies,
And alwaies thoughte, an other dogge was there :
　　But yet the Moone, who did not heare his queſte,
　　Hir woonted courſe, did keepe vnto the weſte.

This reprehendes, thoſe fooles which baule, and barke,
At learned men, that ſhine aboue the reſte :
With due regarde, that they their deedes ſhould marke,
And reuerence them, that are with wiſedome bleſte :
　　But if they ſtriue, in vaine their winde they ſpende,
　　For woorthie nien, the Lorde doth ſtill defende.

　　　Eſſe quid hoc dicam, viuis quod fama negatur,
　　　　Et ſua quod rarus tempora lector amat?
　　　Hi ſunt innidia nimirum Regule mores ;
　　　　Præferat antiquos ſemper vt illa nouis.

Whitney Emblemes London 1586 p.213

Motto
°Inanis °impetus.

A °futile °effort.

Picture
A crouching °dog bays at a full °moon. The moon is surrounded by stars and a bank of clouds.

Epigram
Cynthia ray light dog shadow vain1 bark moon fool learned man revere wisdom Lord defend

Reference
°Ovid, Rem Am 1
°Martial, Sat
Justus °Lipsius

Ouid. 1. Remed
Ingenium luor no ne.
detreɟtat Homeri,
　　Quiſquis es, ex illo
Zoile nomen habes.

Martial. lib. 1.
ad Regulum.

In diuitem, indoctum.

ON goulden fleece, did Phryxus paſſe the waue,
  And landèd ſafe, within the wiſhed baie:
By which is ment, the fooles that riches haue,
Supported are, and borne throughe Lande, and Sea:
  And thoſe enrich'de by wife, or ſeruauntes goodds,
  Are borne by them like Phryxus through the floodds.

An other of the like argument.
To M. I. E.

A Leaden ſworde, within a goulden ſheathe,
  Is like a foole of natures fineſt moulde:
To whome, ſhee did her rareſt giftes bequethe.
Or like a ſheepe, within a fleece of goulde.
  Or like a clothe, whome colours braue adorne,
  When as the grounde, is patched, rente, and torne.

For, if the minde the chiefeſt treaſures lacke,
Thoughe nature bothe, and fortune, bee our frende;
Thoughe goulde wee weare, and purple on our backe,
Yet are wee poore, and none will vs comende
  But onlie fooles; and flatterers, for theire gaine:
  For other men, will ride vs with diſdaine.

Whitney Emblemes London 1586 p.214

Motto
In °divitem,°indoctum.

On the °ignorant °rich man.

Picture
°Phrixus crosses the °Hellespont on the
back of the °golden °ram. His eyes and
his °right arm are raised to the heavens.

Epigram

gold	fleece	Phrixus	wave	fool	rich
land	sea	wife	servant	flood	lead
sword	gold	sheath	fool	nature	gift
sheep	fleece	cloth	colour	mind
treasure	fortune	friend	purple	poor
flatter	disdain

Plaut. in poem.
°Pulcrum ornatum tur-
pes mores peius caeno
collinunt,
lapidi mores turpem
ornatum facile factis
comprobant.

Bern. in Epiſt.
Decor, qui cum
veſte induitur, &
cum veſte depo-
nitur: veſtimenti
eſt, non veſtiti.

Reference
°Plautus, Poen
°Bernard, Ep

Dedicatee
M.I.°E.

Interminabilis humanæ vitæ labor.

TO M. IOHN GOSTLINGE.

Motto
Interminabilis humanae °vitae °labor.

The unending °labour of human °life.

Picture
°Sisyphus pushes a °stone up a °hill.

Epigram
Sisyphus   stone   hill   toil   wretch   work
Adam   race1

L OE SISYPHVS, that roles the reſtleſſe ſtone
To toppe of hill, with endleſſe toile, and paine:
Which beinge there, it tumbleth doune alone,
And then, the wretche muſt force it vp againe:
    And as it falles, he makes it ſtill aſcende;
    And yet, no toile can bringe this worke to ende.

This SISYPHVS: preſenteth Adams race.
The reſtleſſe ſtone: their trauaile, and their toile:
The hill, dothe ſhewe the daye, and eeke the ſpace,
Wherein they ſtill doe labour, worke, and moile.
    And thoughe till nighte they ſtriue the hill to clime,
    Yet vp againe, the morning nexte betime.

Vita humana propriè vti ferrum eſt: Ferrum ſi exerceas, conteritur: ſi non exerceas, tamen rubigo interficit. Item homines exercendo videmus conteri. Si
nihil exerceas, inertia atque torpedo plus detrimenti facit, quàm exercitatio.

Ouid. Metam.
lib. 4.

Plat. de proſper.
Hanc rationem deus
ſequitur in bonis vi-
ris, quàm in diſcipu-
lis ſuis præceptores;
qui plus laboris ab
his exigunt, in qui-
bus certior ſpes eſt.

Aul. Gell. lib. 11. c. 1.

Reference
°Ovid, Met 4
Bartolomeo °Platina(?), D P
°Gellius 11, 1

Dedicatee
John °Gostling

Qui se exaltat, humiliabitur. Luc. cap. 18.

T H E boylinge brothe, aboue the brinke dothe swell,
And comes to naughte, with falling in the fire:
So reaching heads that thinke them neuer well, .
Doe headlonge fall , for pride hathe ofte that hire: *
And where before their frendes they did difpife,
Nowe beinge falne, none helpe them for to rife.

Whitney   Emblemes   London   1586   p.216a

Motto
Qui se °exaltat, °humiliabitur.

He who °exalts himself will be °humbled.

Picture
Boiling °broth overflows a °cauldron and spills into the °fire below.

Epigram
boil   broth   brink   fall   fire   head
pride friend despise rise

Reference
°Lucan 18

Sol non occidat super iracundiam vestram.   Ephef. cap. 4.

CASTE fwordes awaye, take laurell in your handes.
Let not the Sonne goe downe vppon your ire.
Let hartes relente, and breake oulde rancors bandes,
And frendfhippes force fubdue your rafhe defire.
    Let defperate wightes, and ruffians, thirft for blood;
    Winne foes, with loue; and thinke your conqueft good.   Roman. 12.

Whitney   Emblemes   London   1586   p.216b

Motto
°Sol non occidat super °iracundiam vestram.

Let the °sun not set on your °anger.

Picture
°Two °men, each with °laurel °branches in both hands, °embrace each other; their °swords lie on the ground behind them. A °palm-tree stands at the left, and the °sun sets in the background at the right.

Epigram
sword   laurel   sun   ire   heart   relent rancour   friend   ruffian

Reference
°B Eph 4
°B Rom 12

Omnis caro faenum.

To M. ELCOCKE *Preacher.*

ALL fleſhe, is graſſe; and withereth like the haie:
To daie, man laughes, to morrowe, lies in claie.
Then, let him marke the frailtie of his kinde,
For here his tearme is like a puffe of winde,
Like bubbles ſmalle, that on the waters riſe:
Or like the flowers, whome FLORA freſhlie dies.
Yet, in one daie their glorie all is gone:
So, worldlie pompe, which here we gaze vppon.
Which warneth all, that here their pageantes plaie,
Howe, well to liue: but not how longe to waie.

Inter ſpem curamq̃, timores inter & iras,
Omnem crede diem tibi diluxiſſe ſupremam.
Grata ſuperueniet, qua non ſperabitur, hora.

Whitney Emblemes London 1586 p.217

Motto
Omnis °caro °foenum.

All °flesh is °hay.

Picture
A bundle of °hay hanging from an upright °staff.

Epigram

flesh	grass	hay	laugh	clay	wind
bubble	flower	Flora	glory	pomp	
pageant					

Reference
°B Isa 41
°Cicero, Phil 11
°Horace, Ep 1

Eſaie 41.

Quis eſt, quamuis
ſit adoleſcens qui
exploratum habeat
ſe ad veſperum eſſe
victurum?

Senſim ſine ſenſu
ætas ſeneſcit, nec °
ſubito frangitur, ſed
diuturnitate extin-
guitur. Cicer. Phi
lip. 11.

Horat. 1. Ep. 1.

Dedicatee
Thomas °Elcock, preacher

Peruerſa iudicia.

PRESVMPTVOVS PAN, did ſtriue APOLLOS ſkill to paſſe:
  But MIDAS gaue the palme to PAN: wherefore the eares of aſſe
APOLLO gaue the Iudge: which doth all Iudges teache ;
To iudge with knowledge, and aduiſe, in matters paſte their reache.

Ouid. Metam.
lib. 11.

Whitney   Emblemes   London   1586   p.218a

Motto
°Perversa °iudicia.

°Perverse °judgements.

Picture
°Apollo and °Pan sit on a bench making music; Apollo plucks a °viola(?), Pan blows °bagpipes. °Midas, reclining on the ground in front of them points to Pan. Midas has sprouted the °ears of an °ass.

Epigram
Pan Apollo Midas palm ear ass judge knowledge

Reference
°Ovid, Met 11

Mulier umbra viri.

Oᵥʀ ſhadowe flies, if wee the ſame purſue:
But if wee flie, it followeth at the heele.
So, he throughe loue that moſte dothe ſerue, and ſue,
Is furtheſt off his miſtreſſe harte is ſteele.
But if hee flie, and turne awaie his face;
Shee followeth ſtraight, and grones to him for grace.

Whitney   Emblemes   London   1586   p.218b

Motto
°Mulier °umbra °viri.

A °woman is the °shadow of her °husband.

Picture
Two °men run in a landscape under a blazing °sun; one flees his own °shadow, the other chases his.

Epigram
shadow   love   mistress   heart   steel
grace

In amore tormentum.

E V E N as the gnattes, that flie into the blaze,
Doe burne their winges and fall into the fire:
So, those too muche on gallant showes that gaze,
Are captiues caught, and burne in their desire:
   And suche as once doe feele this inwarde warre,
   Thoughe they bee cur'de, yet still appeares the scarre.

For wanton L o v e althoughe hee promise ioies,
Yet hee that yeeldes in hope to finde it true,
His pleasures shalbee mated with annoyes;
And sweetes suppos'de, bee mix'd, with bitter rue:
   Bicause, his dartes not all alike, doe wounde:
   For so the frendes of coye A s p a s i a founde.

They lou'd, shee loth'de: they crau'd, shee still deni'de.
They sigh'd, shee songe: they spake, shee stopt her eare.
They walk'd, shee satte: they set, awaye shee hi'de.
Lo this their bale, which was her blisse, you heare.
   O loue, a plague, thoughe grac'd with gallant glosse,
   For in thy seates a snake is in the mosse.

Then stoppe your eares, and like V l i s s e s waulke,
The S y r e e n e s tunes, the carelesse often heares:
*C r o c v t a killes when shee doth frendly taulke:
The Crocodile, hathe treason in her teares.
   In gallant fruicte, the core is ofte decav'd;
   Yea poison ofte in cuppe of goulde allay'd.

Then, in your waies let reason strike the stroke,
A s p a s i a shonne, althoughe her face doe shine:
But, if you like of H y m e n æ v s yoke,
P e n e l o p e preferre, thoughe spinninge twine,
   Yet if you like, how most to liue in rest,
   H i p p o l y t v s his life, suppose the best.

*De malignitate
Crocutæ feræ Æl.
lib.7. cap. 21. &
Plin. lib. 8. cap. 30.

Motto
In °amore °tormentum.

°Torment in °love.

Picture
°Gnats °fly into the °flame of a °candle. The °candlestick is placed in the centre of a cloth covered plinth which bears the inscription °"COSI DE BEN AMAR/PORTO TORMENTO" [Thus from a great love I bear torment] The base is flanked by °two °fires: a °woman holds her hands over the one at the left; a second woman kneels beside the one at the right.

Epigram
gnat   fire   captive   burn   desire   war scar   Love   wanton   hope   rue   dart wound   Aspasia   plague   snake   moss Ulysses   Siren   crocutta [= hyena] crocodile   treason   tear   fruit   decay poison   gold   cup   Hymen   Penelope Hippolytus

Reference
°Pliny, N H 8, 30

Vincit qui patitur.

Whitney Emblemes London 1586 p.220

THE mightie oke, that fhrinkes not with a blafte,
But ftillie ftandes, when Boreas mofte doth blowe,
With rage thereof, is broken downe at lafte,
When bending reedes, that couche in tempeftes lowe
With yeelding ftill, doe fafe, and founde appeare:
And looke alofte, when that the cloudes be cleare.

When Enuie, Hate, Contempte, and Slaunder, rage:
Which are the ftormes, and tempeftes, of this life;
With patience then, wee muft the combat wage,
And not with force refift their deadlie ftrife
But fuffer ftill, and then wee fhall in fine,
Our foes fubdue, when they with fhame fhall pine.

Motto
°Vincit qui °patitur.

He °conquers who °suffers.

Picture
The °wind, °Boreas, blows on a landscape beside a sea from a bank of clouds. °Reeds in the water bend, while an °oak on shore breaks, under the force of the wind.

Epigram

oak	Boreas	bend	reed	tempest	yield
envy	hate	contempt	slander	patience
combat	force	strife	suffer	foe
subdue	shame			

Erafm. in Epift.
Vere magni ani-
mi eft, quafdam
iniurias neglige-
re, nec ad quo-
rundam conuitia
aures, vel lin-
guam habere.

Reference
°Erasmus, Ep

Aculei irriti.

Whitney   Emblemes   London   1586   p.221

Motto
°Aculei irriti.

Ineffectual °stings.

Picture
A °lily grows and blooms in a thicket of °briars and °thorns.

Epigram
virtue   vice   wicked   sting   wit
learning   folly   ignorance   lily   bloom
thorn   briar

WHERE as the good, do liue amongſt the bad:
  And vertue growes, where ſeede of vices ſpringes:
The wicked ſorte to wounde the good, are glad:
And vices thruſt at vertue, all their ſtinges:
    The like, where witte, and learning doe remaine,
    Where follie rules, and ignoraunce doth raigne.

Yet as wee ſee, the lillie freſhlie bloomes,
Though thornes, and briers, encloſe it round aboute:
So with the good, thoughe wicked haue their roomes,
They are preſeru'd, in ſpite of all their route:
    And learning liues, and vertue ſtill doth ſhine,
    When follie dies, and ignoraunce doth pine.

Neglecta virescunt.
To M. RAWLINS *Preacher.*

THE Iuie greene that dothe difpifed growe,
And none doth plante, or trimme the fame at all,
Althoughe a while it fpreades it felfe belowe,
In time it mountes, with creepinge vp the wall.
So, thoughe the worlde the vertuons men difpife,
Yet vp alofte in fpite of them they rife.

Whitney Emblemes London 1586 p.222a

Motto
Neglecta °virescunt.

Neglected things °flourish.

Picture
°Virtue(?) or °Athena(?), sits on a bench outside a building. She wears a °helmet, holds a °lance with her °right hand, and cradles a sceptre(?) or °mace(?) with her °left. Her °right °foot rests on a °tortoise(?). °Ivy and °two °snakes scale the walls to her left.

Epigram
ivy green despise grow wall virtuous despise rise

Dedicatee
? °Rawlins, preacher

Impunitas ferociæ parens.
To M. STEEVENSON *Preacher.*

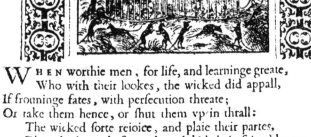

WHEN worthie men, for life, and learninge greate,
Who with their lookes, the wicked did appall,
If frouninge fates, with perfecution threate;
Or take them hence, or fhut them vp in thrall:
The wicked forte reioice, and plaie their partes,
Thoughe longe before, they clok'd their fained hartes.

Whitney Emblemes London 1586 p.222b

Motto
°Impunitas °ferociae °parens.

°Impunity is the °parent of °ferocity.

Picture
°Mice gambol around °two °cats in °cages.

Epigram
learning wicked fate persecute thrall cloak heart

Dedicatee
? °Stevenson, preacher

Nemo potest duobus dominis seruire.

To M. KNEWSTVB *Preacher.*

HERE, man who first should heauenlie thinges attaine,
And then, to world his fences should incline :
First, vndergoes the worlde with might, and maine,
And then, at foote doth drawe the lawes deuine.
     Thus GOD hee beares, and Mammon in his minde:
     But Mammon first, and GOD doth come behinde.

Oh worldlinges fonde, that ioyne these two so ill,
The league is nought, throwe doune the world which speede:
Take vp the lawe, according to his will.
First seeke for heauen, and then for wordly neede.
     But those that first their wordlie wishe doe serue,
     Their gaine, is losse, and seeke their soules to sterue.

Whitney   Emblemes   London   1586   p.223

Motto
Nemo potest °duobus °dominis °servire.

No one can °serve °two °masters.

Picture
A man walks through a landscape carrying a °globe of the °world on his shoulders; he drags behind him the °tablets of the °commandments, tied to his °right ankle.

Epigram
heaven world law divine God Mammon worldling gain loss soul

Reference
°B Matt 6

Luc. 16.

Matth. 6.
Non potestis deo seruire & Mammonæ.

Primum quærite regnum dei, &c
Ibidem.

Dedicatee
John °Knewstub, preacher, chaplain to the Earl of Leicester

Sic probantur. *Luk. 24.*

To M. ANDREWES *Preacher.*

THROVGHE tormentes ſtraunge, and perſecutions dire,
The Chriſtians paſſe, with paçience in their paine:
And ende their courſe, ſometime with ſworde, and fire,
And conſtant ſtand, and like to lambes are ſlaine.
Bycauſe, when all their martirdome is paſt,
They hope to gaine a glorious çroune at laſt.

Whitney Emblemes London 1586 p.224a

Motto
Sic °probantur.

Thus are they °tested.

Picture
°Three °Christian °martyrs stand with their hands clasped in °prayer before a °fire. They are being harassed by two men with °swords and by two °dogs. A °left hand, extended from a bank of °clouds, holds a °garland over the three martyrs.

Epigram
torment persecution Christian patience sword fire constant lamb slay martyrdom glorious crown

Reference
°B Matt 24

Dedicatee
Bartimæus °Andrewes, preacher

Noli tuba canere Eleemoſynam.

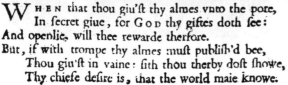

WHEN that thou giu'ſt thy almes vnto the pore,
    In ſecret giue, for GOD thy giftes doth ſee:
And openlie, will thee rewarde therfore.
But, if with trompe thy almes muſt publiſh'd bee,
    Thou giu'ſt in vaine: ſith thou therby doſt ſhowe,
    Thy chiefe deſire is, that the world maie knowe.

Whitney   Emblemes   London   1586   p.224b

Motto
Noli °tuba canere °Eleemosynam.

Do no °trumpet your °charity.

Picture
A well dressed man blows a °trumpet as he gives °alms to a °beggar who is seated under a tree.

Epigram

alms   poor   secret   God   gift   reward
trumpet vain1   world

Amico ficto nulla fit iniuria.

SINCE fauninge lookes, and fugred fpeache preuaile,
Take heede betime : and linke thee not with theife.
The gallant clokes, doe hollowe hartes conceile,
And goodlie fhowes, are miftes before our eies :
    But whome thou find'ft with guile, difguifed fo:
    No wronge thou doeft, to vfe him as thy foe.

Whitney Emblemes London 1586 p.226a

Motto
°Amico °ficto nulla fit °iniuria.

There is no °wrong done to a °false °friend.

Picture
Two well dressed men face each other; the man on the °left strikes the other on the forehead with a °sword.

Epigram
fawn1   sugar   speech   gallant   cloak
hollow   heart   mist   guile   foe

Ferè fimile, in Hypocritas.

A Face deform'de, a vifor faire dothe hide,
That none can fee his vglie fhape within ;
To Ipocrites, the fame maie bee applide,
With outward fhowes, who all their credit winne :
    Yet giue no heate, but like a painted fire;
    And, all their zeale, is : as the times require.

Whitney Emblemes London 1586 p.226b

Motto
Fere simile, in °Hypocritas.

Almost the same, on °hypocrites.

Picture
Two well dressed men face each other; the man on the °left strikes the other on the forehead with a °sword.

Epigram
face   deform   visor   fair   hypocrite
show   heat   fire   zeal

Superest quod suprà est.

Motto
°Superest quod supra est.

What is above °lives on.

Picture
A °traveller dressed as a °pilgrim, walks past a °globe of the °world with the inscription °"EUROPA" and °"AFRICA". He is looking up at the °tetragrammaton which blazes in a bank of °clouds above.

A D V E *deceiptfull worlde, thy pleasures I detest:*
Nowe, *others with thy showes delude; my hope in heauen doth rest.*

Peregrinus Chri-
stianus loquitur.

Inlarged as followeth.

E V E N as a flower, or like vnto the grasse,
Which now dothe stande, and straight with sithe dothe fall;
So is our state: now here, now hence wee passe:
For, time attendes with shredding sithe for all.
   And deathe at lengthe, both oulde, and yonge, doth strike:
   And into dust dothe turne vs all alike.

Iacob. 1.
Ecclesiast. 14
Isaia 40.

Yet, if wee marke how swifte our race dothe ronne,
And waighe the cause, why wee created bee:
Then shall wee know, when that this life is donne,
Wee shall bee sure our countrie right to see.
   For, here wee are but straungers, that must flitte:
   The nearer home, the nearer to the pitte.

2 Corinth. 5.

O happie they, that pondering this arighte,
Before that here their pilgrimage bee past,
Resigne this worlde: and marche with all their mighte
Within that pathe, that leades where ioyes shall last.
   And whilst they maye, there, treasure vp their store,
   Where, without rust, it lastes for euermore.

Via veritas vita.
Ioan. 14
Matth. 6

This worlde must chaunge: That worlde, shall still indure.
Here, pleasures fade: There, shall they endlesse bee.
Here, man doth sinne: And there, hee shalbee pure
Here, deathe hee tastes: And there, shall neuer die.
   Here, hathe hee griefe: And there shall ioyes possesse,
   As none hath seene, nor anie harte can geffe.

Apocal. 6.
Apocal. 11.

2 Corinth. 15.
Apocal. 21.
1 Corinth. 2.

Epigram

deceit	world	pleasure
delude	hope	heaven
flower	grass	state1 fall
death	old	young dust
race	life	country
stranger	pilgrim	path
treasure	rust	sin grief

Reference
°B Jac 1
°B Eccl 14
°B Isa 40
°B 2 Cor 5
°B Jn 14
°B Matt 6

Sic ætas fugit.

To M. IAMES IONSON.

Two horfes free, a thirde doe fwiftlie chace,
The one, is white, the other, blacke of hewe:
None, bridles haue for to reftraine their pace,
And thus, they bothe, the other ftill purfue:
  And, neuer ceafe continuall courfe to make,
  Vntill at lengthe, the firft, they ouertake.

This formoft horfe, that ronnes fo faft awaye,
It is our time; while heere, our race wee ronne:
The blacke, and white, prefenteth nighte, and daye:
Who after halt, vntill the goale bee wonne,
  And leaue vs not, but followe from our birthe,
  Vntill wee yeelde, and turne againe to earthe.

Labitur occulte, fallitq; volatilis ætas,
Et celer admiſsis labitur annus equis.

Pfalm 89.

Ouid.1.Amo1.8.

Whitney   Emblemes   London   1586   p.227

Motto
Sic °aetas °fugit.

Thus does °life °flee.

Picture
°Two °horsemen, brandishing °whips, ride bareback in pursuit of a riderless °horse towards a °standard fixed in the   ground at the right.

Epigram
two   horse   three   white   black   bridle pursue   night   day   goal   birth   earth

Reference
°B Ps 89
°Ovid, Am 1, 8

Dedicatee
James °Jonson

Soli Deo gloria.

To M. HOWLTE *Preacher.*

HERE, man with axe doth cut the boughe in twaine,
And without him, the axe, coulde nothing doe
Within the toole, there doth no force remaine;
But man it is, that mighte doth put thereto
   Like to this axe, is man, in all his deeds;
   Who hath no strength, but what from GOD proceedes

Then, let him not make vaunt of his desert,
Nor bragge thereof, when hee good deedes hath donne
For, it is GOD that worketh in his harte,
And with his grace, to good, doth make him ronne:
   And of him selfe, hee weake thereto, doth liue;
   And GOD giues power, to whome all glorie giue.   Iud. Epiſt.

Whitney   Emblemes   London   1586   p.228

Motto
Soli °Deo °gloria.

°Glory to °God alone.

Picture
A °woodsman is at work with his °axe at the base of a °tree.

Epigram

axe	bough	tool	force	man	deed
strength	brag	God	heart	grace	power
glory					

Reference
°B Jud

Dedicatee
? °Howlte, preacher

Dominus viuit & videt.

Whitney   Emblemes   London   1586   p.229a

BEHINDE a figtree great, him felfe did A D A M hide: fefpide.
And thought from G o D hee there might lurke, & fhould not bee
Oh foole, no corners feeke, thoughe thou a finner bee;
For none but G o D can thee forgiue, who all thy waies doth fee.

Genef. 3

Motto
°Dominus °vivit et °videt.

The °Lord °lives and °sees.

Picture
°Adam, clad with a °fig-leaf, hides his face with his hand as he crouches at the right behind a °tree. The inscription °"UBI ES" [Where are you?] blazes in the sky at the top left.

Epigram
fig-tree   Adam   hide   God   fool   sinner   forgive

Reference
°B Gen 3

Ex maximo minimum.

WHERE liuely once, GODS image was expreſte,
   Wherin, ſometime was ſacred reaſon plac'de,
The head, I meane, that is ſo ritchly bleſte,
With ſighte, with ſmell, with hearinge, and with taſte.
   Lo, nowe a ſkull, both rotten, bare, and drye,
   A relike meete in charnell houſe to lye,

Nic. Reuſnerus.
Vt roſa mane viget,
ro mox veſpere langueſ:
Sic modo qui flumbæ
erat laudatue: a ſumus.

Whitney   Emblemes   London   1586   p.229b

Motto
Ex maximo minimum.

The least from the greatest.

Picture
A °skull, rests on the ground. A °bone lies in front of it and a °flower grows to the left.

Epigram
God image sacred reason head sight smell hearing taste skull charnel house

Reference
Nicholas °Reusner

CONCLVSIO OPERIS

Ad Illustrissimum Heroem D. Robertum Dudlæum, Comitem Leicestriæ, *Baronem de Denbighe, &/c. Dominum meum vnicè colendum.*

Tempus omnia terminat.

THE *longest daye, in time resignes to nighte.*
  The greatest oke, in time to duste doth turne..
The Rauen dies, the Egle failes of flighte.
The Phœnix rare, in time her selfe doth burne.
  The princelie stagge at lengthe his race doth ronne.
  And all must ende, that euer was begonne.

Euen so, I, here doe ende this simple booke,
And offer it vnto your Lorshippes sighte:
Which, if you shall receiue with pleasinge looke,
I shall reioyce, and thinke my labour lighte.
  And pray the Lorde your honour to preserue,
  Our noble Queene, and countrie long to serue.

FINIS.

Whitney Emblemes London 1586 p.230

Motto
°Tempus omnia °terminat.

°Time °ends all things.

Picture
°Two °oak-trees grow on an embankment on a sea shore; a third oak lies on the ground near them. The °sun sets on the horizon .

Epigram
day time night oak dust raven die eagle phoenix burn stag race book Lord1 [= Earl of Leicester] labour honour queen [= Elizabeth I] country serve

Dedicatee
Robert °Dudley, Earl of °Leicester

THE EMBLEMS OF JAN VAN DER NOOT

CONCORDANCES, INDEXES, AND LISTS

Prepared by Peter M. Daly

PICTURE INDEX

angel: An °angel flies before the °sun and sends forth
 °birds after the routed °soldiers. The fleeing men and
 the °seven °headed °beast with °crowns fall into a
 °pit of °fire.
 Van der Noot, Theatre, London, 1569, Diiii^v

angel: On a °cliff one of the °angels of the °plagues
 stands holding a °staff in its °right hand.
 Van der Noot, Theatre, London, 1569, Dv^v

apocalyptic: The °winged and °crowned °apocalyptic
 °woman, in the °orans position, stands on a °crescent
 °moon. Her head is encircled by °stars. She is
 surrounded by a °mandorla.
 Van der Noot, Theatre, London, 1569, Dii^v

arch: A °triumphal °arch, the front decorated with °two
 °Victories. A plaque is inscribed °"CIV[ITAS]
 AVGV[STO] CAES[ARI] SEMP[ER] CONS[ULI]" [THE
 CITY TO AUGUSTUS CAESAR FOREVER CONSUL].
 Van der Noot, Theatre, London, 1569, Cii^v

archangel: The °archangel °Michael, °staff in hand, flies
 over a °seven °headed °beast, casting floods of
 °water out of its mouth.
 Van der Noot, Theatre, London, 1569, Dii^v

armour: °Statue of °charioteer, in °Roman °armour, with
 a °palm °branch in his °right hand.
 Van der Noot, Theatre, London, 1569, Cii^v

armour: °Echidna, in °armour and a °helmet, stands with
 a °globe in her raised °left hand and supports a
 °standard of °trophies with her °right.
 Van der Noot, Theatre, London, 1569, Di^v

armour: °Five men in °armour, one a °king wearing a
 °crown, kneel before the crowned °Whore of
 °Babylon.
 Van der Noot, Theatre, London, 1569, Diii^v

arrow: The trophies are °shields, °arrows, and a °cuirass.
 Van der Noot, Theatre, London, 1569, Di^v

baby [= Romulus and Remus]: A °wolf suckles °two
 °babies.
 Van der Noot, Theatre, London, 1569, Cv^v

bear: The °beast from the °sea, with °seven °heads and
 °ten °horns bearing °ten crowns, is like a °leopard
 with feet of a °bear and mouth of a °lion and is
 worshipped by a man in °papal °regalia.
 Van der Noot, Theatre, London, 1569, Dii^v

bearded: °God, as a °bearded °old-man lifts up a °child.
 Van der Noot, Theatre, London, 1569, Dii^v

beast: The °archangel °Michael, °staff in hand, flies over
 a °seven °headed °beast, casting floods of °water out
 of its mouth.
 Van der Noot, Theatre, London, 1569, Dii^v

beast: A °beast with °horns of a °lamb [= °ram].
 Van der Noot, Theatre, London, 1569, Dii^v

beast: The °beast from the °sea, with °seven °heads and
 °ten °horns bearing °ten crowns, is like a °leopard
 with feet of a °bear and mouth of a °lion and is
 worshipped by a man in °papal °regalia.
 Van der Noot, Theatre, London, 1569, Dii^v

beast: °Whore of °Babylon, seated on a °seven °headed
 °beast.
 Van der Noot, Theatre, London, 1569, Diii^v

beast: Fleeing men and the °seven °headed °beast with
 °crowns fall into a °pit of °fire.
 Van der Noot, Theatre, London, 1569, Diiii^v

bird: A °laurel-tree, °birds on its branches, grows in a
 °circular enclosure.
 Van der Noot, Theatre, London, 1569, Biii^v

bird: An °angel flies before the °sun and sends forth
 °birds after the routed °soldiers. The fleeing men and
 the °seven °headed °beast with °crowns fall into a
 °pit of °fire.
 Van der Noot, Theatre, London, 1569, Diiii^v

blood: A °crested °phoenix stands on a mound. A second
 phoenix, °wings displayed, pecks its °breast so that
 the °blood gushes onto the ground.

book: °Four °nymphs, °Naiads, sit under trees. Three
 huddle over an °open °book. A °spring[1] rises from
 the ground.
 Van der Noot, Theatre, London, 1569, Biv^v

book: °Eight °Naiads flee the attack of °three °satyrs.
 There is a °spring[1] nearby. A °horn, a °lute, and a
 °musical score °book lie at the right.
 Van der Noot, Theatre, London, 1569, Cviii^v

branch: °Statue of °charioteer, in °Roman °armour, with
 a °palm °branch in his °right hand.
 Van der Noot, Theatre, London, 1569, Cii^v

breast: A second phoenix, °wings displayed, pecks its
 °breast so that the °blood gushes onto the ground.
 Van der Noot, Theatre, London, 1569, Bv^v

broken: An °obelisk with °hieroglyphs, supported by
 °four °lions °sejant on a °pedestal, supports an °urn.
 The obelisk lies °broken on the ground under °rain
 and °clouds.
 Van der Noot, Theatre, London, 1569, Ci^v

building: A °Roman °building with °Doric °columns.
 Van der Noot, Theatre, London, 1569, Bviii^v

bull: A °Roman °building with °Doric °columns, the
 °metopes charged with °bulls' heads alternating with
 °discs.
 Van der Noot, Theatre, London, 1569, Bviii^v

cedar: An °eagle rises to °heaven in the °smoke of a
 °fire fuelled by °cedar logs.
 Van der Noot, Theatre, London, 1569, Cvii^v

chariot: °Statue of °charioteer, in °Roman °armour, with
 a °palm °branch in his °right hand stands in a
 °chariot drawn by °three °horses.
 Van der Noot, Theatre, London, 1569, Cii^v

charioteer: °Statue of °charioteer, in °Roman °armour,
 with a °palm °branch in his °right hand.
 Van der Noot, Theatre, London, 1569, Cii^v

child: The °winged and °crowned °apocalyptic °woman;
 °God, as a °bearded °old-man lifts up her °child by
 the hands.
 Van der Noot, Theatre, London, 1569, Dii^v

circular: A °laurel-tree, °birds on its branches, grows in
 a °circular enclosure.
 Van der Noot, Theatre, London, 1569, Biii^v

cliff: On a °cliff one of the °angels of the °plagues
 stands holding a °staff in its °right hand.
 Van der Noot, Theatre, London, 1569, Dv^v

cloud: A °woman her head surrounded by dark °cloud;
 °snake bites her °left °heel.
 Van der Noot, Theatre, London, 1569, Bvi^v

cloud: An °obelisk lies °broken on the ground under
 °rain and °clouds.
 Van der Noot, Theatre, London, 1569, Ci^v

cloud: An °eagle flies towards the °sun. It falls through
 °clouds emitting °flames.
 Van der Noot, Theatre, London, 1569, Ciiii^v

cloud: An °eagle rises to °heaven in the °smoke of a
 °fire fuelled by °cedar logs. Dark °clouds, pouring
 out °rain, approach the fire.
 Van der Noot, Theatre, London, 1569, Cvii^v

cloud: The °archangel °Michael, °staff in hand, flies
 over a °seven °headed °beast. °Flames issue from
 °clouds.
 Van der Noot, Theatre, London, 1569, Dii^v

column: A °Roman °building with °Doric °columns.
 Van der Noot, Theatre, London, 1569, Bviii^v

crescent: The °winged and °crowned °apocalyptic
 °woman, in the °orans position, stands on a
 °crescent °moon.
 Van der Noot, Theatre, London, 1569, Dii^v

crested: A °crested °phoenix stands on a mound.
 Van der Noot, Theatre, London, 1569, Bv^v

crown: The °winged and °crowned °apocalyptic °woman,
 in the °orans position, stands on a °crescent °moon.
 Van der Noot, Theatre, London, 1569, Dii^v

crown: °Five men in °armour, one a °king wearing a

˚crown, kneel before the crowned ˚Whore of
˚Babylon.
Van der Noot, Theatre, London, 1569, Diii[V]

crown: A ˚man with many ˚crowns rides a ˚horse, a
˚sword issuing from his ˚mouth. An ˚angel flies
before the ˚sun.
Van der Noot, Theatre, London, 1569, Diiii[V]

crown: Fleeing men and the ˚seven ˚headed ˚beast with
˚crowns fall into a ˚pit of ˚fire.
Van der Noot, Theatre, London, 1569, Diiii[V]

crown: The bound figures of ˚naked but ˚crowned kings.
Van der Noot, Theatre, London, 1569, Di[V]

crown: The ˚winged and ˚crowned ˚apocalyptic ˚woman,
in the ˚orans position, stands on a ˚crescent ˚moon.
Van der Noot, Theatre, London, 1569, Dii[V]

crown: The ˚Whore of ˚Babylon, seated on a ˚seven
˚headed ˚beast. The heads are ˚crowned.
Van der Noot, Theatre, London, 1569, Diii[V]

cuirass: The trophies are ˚shields, ˚arrows, and a
˚cuirass.
Van der Noot, Theatre, London, 1569, Di[V]

cup: ˚Whore of ˚Babylon, seated on a ˚seven ˚headed
˚beast, holds up a ˚cup in her ˚right hand.
Van der Noot, Theatre, London, 1569, Diii[V]

dead: A phoenix pecks its ˚breast so that the ˚blood
gushes onto the ground. It stands beside a ˚dead
˚tree. Nearby, a ˚dead ˚spring[1].
Van der Noot, Theatre, London, 1569, Bv[V]

dead: A ˚phoenix pecks its ˚breast so that the ˚blood
gushes onto the ground. It stands beside a ˚dead
˚tree. Nearby, a ˚dead ˚spring[1].
Van der Noot, Theatre, London, 1569, Bv[V]

destroy: A ˚palm-tree grows on top of ˚seven ˚hills
[= ˚Rome] by a ˚river[= ˚Tiber]. On the far shore,
˚four men ˚destroy the palm-tree by uprooting it.
Van der Noot, Theatre, London, 1569, Ciii[V]

disc: A ˚Roman ˚building with ˚Doric ˚columns,the
˚metopes charged with ˚bulls' heads alternating with
˚discs.
Van der Noot, Theatre, London, 1569, Bviii[V]

dog: A ˚hind is chased by ˚two ˚dogs. Collapsed against
a ˚rock, its hindquarters torn by the dogs.
Van der Noot, Theatre, London, 1569, Bi[V]

eagle: An ˚eagle flies towards the ˚sun. It falls through
˚clouds emitting ˚flames.On the ground, the eagle or
˚phoenix(?) sits in the midst of a ˚fire.
Van der Noot, Theatre, London, 1569, Ciiii[V]

eagle: An ˚eagle rises to ˚heaven in the ˚smoke of a
˚fire fuelled by ˚cedar logs.
Van der Noot, Theatre, London, 1569, Cvii[V]

eight: ˚Eight ˚Naiads flee the attack of ˚three ˚satyrs.
Van der Noot, Theatre, London, 1569, Cviii[V]

fence: A ˚laurel-tree, ˚birds on its branches, grows in a
˚circular enclosure; birds on the ˚fence and ground.
The fence and laurel-tree are broken by a ˚storm,
bringing ˚rain.
Van der Noot, Theatre, London, 1569, Biii[V]

fire: On the ground, the eagle or ˚phoenix(?) sits in the
midst of a ˚fire.
Van der Noot, Theatre, London, 1569, Ciiii[V]

fire: An ˚eagle rises to ˚heaven in the ˚smoke of a ˚fire
fuelled by ˚cedar logs.
Van der Noot, Theatre, London, 1569, Cvii[V]

fire: Fleeing men and the ˚seven ˚headed ˚beast with
˚crowns fall into a ˚pit of ˚fire.
Van der Noot, Theatre, London, 1569, Diiii[V]

five: ˚Five men in ˚armour, one a ˚king wearing a
˚crown, kneel before the crowned ˚Whore of
˚Babylon.
Van der Noot, Theatre, London, 1569, Diii[V]

flame: An ˚eagle flies towards the ˚sun. It falls through
˚clouds emitting ˚flames.
Van der Noot, Theatre, London, 1569, Ciiii[V]

flame: The ˚archangel ˚Michael flies over a ˚seven
˚headed ˚beast, casting floods of ˚water out of its

mouth. ˚Flames issue from ˚clouds.
Van der Noot, Theatre, London, 1569, Dii[V]

flower: A bare breasted ˚woman, her ˚right hand to her
breasts and eyes downcast, walks on a mound
covered with ˚herbs and ˚flowers.
Van der Noot, Theatre, London, 1569, Bvi[V]

four: ˚Four ˚nymphs, ˚Naiads, sit under trees.
Van der Noot, Theatre, London, 1569, Biv[V]

four: An ˚obelisk with ˚hieroglyphs, supported by ˚four
˚lions ˚sejant on a ˚pedestal, supports an ˚urn.
Van der Noot, Theatre, London, 1569, Ci[V]

four: A ˚palm-tree grows on top of ˚seven ˚hills
[= ˚Rome] by a ˚river [= ˚Tiber]. On the far shore,
˚four men ˚destroy the palm-tree by uprooting it.
Van der Noot, Theatre, London, 1569, Ciii[V]

garland: A ˚river ˚god reclines against a ˚pot. He
wears a ˚laurel ˚garland and holds a ˚palm branch in
his ˚right hand and an ˚olive branch in his ˚left.
Van der Noot, Theatre, London, 1569, Cv[V]

globe: ˚Echidna, in ˚armour and a ˚helmet, stands with
a ˚globe in her raised ˚left hand and supports a
˚standard of ˚trophies with her ˚right.
Van der Noot, Theatre, London, 1569, Di[V]

god: A ˚river ˚god reclines against a ˚pot.
Van der Noot, Theatre, London, 1569, Cv[V]

head: The ˚beast from the ˚sea, with ˚seven ˚heads and
˚ten ˚horns bearing ˚ten crowns.
Van der Noot, Theatre, London, 1569, Dii[V]

head: The ˚archangel ˚Michael, ˚staff in hand, flies
over a ˚seven ˚headed ˚beast, casting floods of
˚water out of its mouth.
Van der Noot, Theatre, London, 1569, Dii[V]

head: The crowned ˚Whore of ˚Babylon, seated on a
˚seven ˚headed ˚beast. The heads are ˚crowned.
Van der Noot, Theatre, London, 1569, Diii[V]

head: Fleeing men and the ˚seven ˚headed ˚beast with
˚crowns fall into a ˚pit of ˚fire.
Van der Noot, Theatre, London, 1569, Diiii[V]

heaven: An ˚eagle rises to ˚heaven in the ˚smoke of a
˚fire fuelled by ˚cedar logs.
Van der Noot, Theatre, London, 1569, Cvii[V]

heel: A woman, looking over her ˚left shoulder, walks
with raised hands. A ˚snake bites her ˚left ˚heel.
Van der Noot, Theatre, London, 1569, Bvi[V]

helmet: ˚Echidna, in ˚armour and a ˚helmet, stands with
a ˚globe in her raised ˚left hand and supports a
˚standard of ˚trophies.
Van der Noot, Theatre, London, 1569, Di[V]

herb: A bare breasted ˚woman, her ˚right hand to her
breasts and eyes downcast, walks on a mound
covered with ˚herbs and ˚flowers.
Van der Noot, Theatre, London, 1569, Bvi[V]

hieroglyph: An ˚obelisk with ˚hieroglyphs, supported by
˚four ˚lions ˚sejant on a ˚pedestal, supports an ˚urn.
Van der Noot, Theatre, London, 1569, Ci[V]

hill [= ˚Rome]: A ˚palm-tree grows on top of ˚seven
˚hills [= ˚Rome] by a ˚river [= ˚Tiber].
Van der Noot, Theatre, London, 1569, Ciii[V]

hind: A ˚hind is chased by ˚two ˚dogs. Collapsed
against a ˚rock, its hindquarters torn by the dogs.
Van der Noot, Theatre, London, 1569, Bi[V]

horn: ˚Eight ˚Naiads flee the attack of ˚three ˚satyrs.
A ˚horn, a ˚lute, and a ˚musical score ˚book lie at
the right.
Van der Noot, Theatre, London, 1569, Cviii[V]

horn: A ˚beast with ˚horns of a ˚lamb [= ˚ram].
Van der Noot, Theatre, London, 1569, Dii[V]

horn: The ˚beast from the ˚sea, with ˚seven ˚heads and
˚ten ˚horns bearing ˚ten crowns, is like a ˚leopard
with feet of a ˚bear and mouth of a ˚lion and is
worshipped by a man in ˚papal ˚regalia.
Van der Noot, Theatre, London, 1569, Dii[V]

horse: ˚Statue of ˚charioteer, in ˚Roman ˚armour, with
a ˚palm ˚branch in his ˚right hand stands in a
˚chariot drawn by ˚three ˚horses.

˚discs. The ˚pediment is inscribed ˚"SPQR".
Van der Noot, Theatre, London, 1569, Bviii^v

phoenix: A ˚crested ˚phoenix stands on a mound. A
second phoenix, ˚wings displayed, pecks its ˚breast so
that the ˚blood gushes onto the ground.
Van der Noot, Theatre, London, 1569, Bv^v

phoenix(?): An ˚eagle flies towards the ˚sun. It falls
through ˚clouds emitting ˚flames.On the ground, the
eagle or ˚phoenix(?) sits in the midst of a ˚fire.
Van der Noot, Theatre, London, 1569, Ciiii^v

pit: Fleeing men and the ˚seven ˚headed ˚beast with
˚crowns fall into a ˚pit of ˚fire.
Van der Noot, Theatre, London, 1569, Diiii^v

plague: On a ˚cliff one of the ˚angels of the ˚plagues
stands holding a ˚staff in its ˚right hand.
Van der Noot, Theatre, London, 1569, Dv^v

pot: A ˚river ˚god reclines against a ˚pot. He wears a
˚laurel ˚garland and holds a ˚palm branch in his
˚right hand and an ˚olive branch in his ˚left. ˚Water
flows from his pot into the ˚river [= ˚Tiber].
Van der Noot, Theatre, London, 1569, Cv^v

pray: The ˚praying figure of ˚St John. In the valley is
the heavenly city of ˚Jerusalem.
Van der Noot, Theatre, London, 1569, Dv^v

rain: Fence and laurel-tree are broken by a ˚storm,
bringing ˚rain.
Van der Noot, Theatre, London, 1569, Biii^v

rain: Obelisk lies ˚broken on the ground under ˚rain and
˚clouds.
Van der Noot, Theatre, London, 1569, Ci^v

rain: An ˚eagle rises to ˚heaven in the ˚smoke of a ˚fire
fuelled by ˚cedar logs. Dark ˚clouds, pouring out
˚rain, approach the fire.
Van der Noot, Theatre, London, 1569, Cvii^v

ram [= lamb]: A ˚beast with ˚horns of a ˚lamb [= ˚ram].
The ˚beast from the ˚sea, with ˚seven ˚heads and
˚ten ˚horns bearing ˚ten crowns, is like a ˚leopard
with feet of a ˚bear and mouth of a ˚lion and is
worshipped by a man in ˚papal ˚regalia.
Van der Noot, Theatre, London, 1569, Dii^v

regalia: The ˚beast from the ˚sea, with ˚seven ˚heads
and ˚ten ˚horns bearing ˚ten crowns, is worshipped
by a man in ˚papal ˚regalia.
Van der Noot, Theatre, London, 1569, Dii^v

right: A bare breasted ˚woman, her ˚right hand to her
breasts and eyes downcast, walks on a mound covered
with ˚herbs and ˚flowers.
Van der Noot, Theatre, London, 1569, Bvi^v

right: ˚Statue of ˚charioteer, in ˚Roman ˚armour, with a
˚palm ˚branch in his ˚right hand.
Van der Noot, Theatre, London, 1569, Cii^v

right: A ˚river ˚god reclines against a ˚pot. He wears a
˚laurel ˚garland and holds a ˚palm branch in his
˚right hand and an ˚olive branch in his ˚left.
Van der Noot, Theatre, London, 1569, Cv^v

right: ˚Echidna, in ˚armour and a ˚helmet, stands with a
˚globe in her raised ˚left hand and supports a
˚standard of ˚trophies with her ˚right.
Van der Noot, Theatre, London, 1569, Di^v

right: ˚Whore of ˚Babylon, seated on a ˚seven ˚headed
˚beast, holds up a ˚cup in her ˚right hand.
Van der Noot, Theatre, London, 1569, Diii^v

right: One of the ˚angels of the ˚plagues stands holding
a ˚staff in its ˚right hand, pointing upwards with his
˚left.
Van der Noot, Theatre, London, 1569, Dv^v

river: A ˚river ˚god reclines against a ˚pot. ˚Water flows
from his pot into the ˚river [= ˚Tiber].
Van der Noot, Theatre, London, 1569, Cv^v

river [= Tiber]: A ˚palm-tree grows on top of ˚seven
˚hills [= ˚Rome] by a ˚river [= ˚Tiber].
Van der Noot, Theatre, London, 1569, Ciii^v

river [= Tiber]: A ˚river ˚god reclines against a ˚pot.
˚Water flows from his pot into the ˚river [= ˚Tiber].
At his feet a ˚wolf suckles ˚two ˚babies [= ˚Romulus

and ˚Remus].
Van der Noot, Theatre, London, 1569, Cv^v

river [= Tiber]: A ˚Naiad, seated on a ˚river [= ˚Tiber]
bank, ˚laments.
Van der Noot, Theatre, London, 1569, Cvi^v

rock: A ˚hind is chased by ˚two ˚dogs. Collapsed
against a ˚rock, its hindquarters torn by the dogs.
Van der Noot, Theatre, London, 1569, Bi^v

rock: A ˚ship, with billowing ˚sails, runs before the
˚wind. The ship is ˚wrecked on the ˚rocks.
Van der Noot, Theatre, London, 1569, Bii^v

sail: A ˚ship, with billowing ˚sails, runs before the
˚wind. The ship is ˚wrecked on the ˚rocks.
Van der Noot, Theatre, London, 1569, Bii^v

satyr: ˚Eight ˚Naiads flee the attack of ˚three ˚satyrs.
Van der Noot, Theatre, London, 1569, Cviii^v

sea: The ˚beast from the ˚sea, with ˚seven ˚heads and
˚ten ˚horns bearing ˚ten crowns, is like a ˚leopard
with feet of a ˚bear and mouth of a ˚lion and is
worshipped by a man in ˚papal ˚regalia.
Van der Noot, Theatre, London, 1569, Dii^v

sejant: An ˚obelisk with ˚hieroglyphs, supported by
˚four ˚lions ˚sejant on a ˚pedestal.
Van der Noot, Theatre, London, 1569, Ci^v

seven: A ˚palm-tree grows on top of ˚seven ˚hills
[= ˚Rome] by a ˚river [= ˚Tiber]. On the far shore,
˚four men ˚destroy the palm-tree by uprooting it.
Van der Noot, Theatre, London, 1569, Ciii^v

seven: The ˚archangel ˚Michael, ˚staff in hand, flies
over a ˚seven ˚headed ˚beast, casting floods of
˚water out of its mouth.
Van der Noot, Theatre, London, 1569, Dii^v

seven: The ˚beast from the ˚sea, with ˚seven ˚heads
and ˚ten ˚horns bearing ˚ten crowns, is like a
˚leopard with feet of a ˚bear and mouth of a ˚lion
and is worshipped by a man in ˚papal ˚regalia.
Van der Noot, Theatre, London, 1569, Dii^v

seven: ˚Whore of ˚Babylon, seated on a ˚seven ˚headed
˚beast. The heads are ˚crowned.
Van der Noot, Theatre, London, 1569, Diii^v

seven: Fleeing men and the ˚seven ˚headed ˚beast with
˚crowns fall into a ˚pit of ˚fire.
Van der Noot, Theatre, London, 1569, Diiii^v

shield: The trophies are ˚shields, ˚arrows, and a
˚cuirass.
Van der Noot, Theatre, London, 1569, Di^v

ship: A ˚ship, with billowing ˚sails, runs before the
˚wind. The ship is ˚wrecked on the ˚rocks.
Van der Noot, Theatre, London, 1569, Bii^v

smoke: An ˚eagle rises to ˚heaven in the ˚smoke of a
˚fire fuelled by ˚cedar logs.
Van der Noot, Theatre, London, 1569, Cvii^v

snake: A bare breasted ˚woman, looking over her ˚left
shoulder, walks with raised hands. A ˚snake bites
her ˚left ˚heel.
Van der Noot, Theatre, London, 1569, Bvi^v

soldier: An ˚angel flies before the ˚sun and sends forth
˚birds after the routed ˚soldiers. The fleeing men
and the ˚seven ˚headed ˚beast with ˚crowns fall into
a ˚pit of ˚fire.
Van der Noot, Theatre, London, 1569, Diiii^v

spring¹ = stream

spring¹: ˚Four ˚nymphs, ˚Naiads, sit under trees. Three
huddle over an ˚open ˚book. A ˚spring¹ rises from
the ground.
Van der Noot, Theatre, London, 1569, Biv^v

spring¹: A phoenix, ˚wings displayed, pecks its ˚breast
so that the ˚blood gushes onto the ground. Nearby,
a ˚dead ˚spring¹.
Van der Noot, Theatre, London, 1569, Bv^v

spring¹: ˚Eight ˚Naiads flee the attack of ˚three
˚satyrs. There is a ˚spring¹ nearby.
Van der Noot, Theatre, London, 1569, Cviii^v

staff: The ˚archangel ˚Michael, ˚staff in hand, flies
over a ˚seven ˚headed ˚beast.

Van der Noot, Theatre, London, 1569, Dii[v]
staff: On a ˚cliff one of the ˚angels of the ˚plagues
stands holding a ˚staff in its ˚right hand.
Van der Noot, Theatre, London, 1569, Dv[v]
standard: ˚Echidna, in ˚armour and a ˚helmet, stands
with a ˚globe in her raised ˚left hand and supports a
˚standard of ˚trophies with her ˚right.
Van der Noot, Theatre, London, 1569, Di[v]
star: The ˚winged and ˚crowned ˚apocalyptic ˚woman, in
the ˚orans position, stands on a ˚crescent ˚moon.
Her head is encircled by ˚stars.
Van der Noot, Theatre, London, 1569, Dii[v]
statue: ˚Statue of ˚charioteer in ˚Roman ˚armour.
Van der Noot, Theatre, London, 1569, Cii[v]
storm: A ˚laurel-tree in a ˚circular enclosure is broken
by a ˚storm, bringing ˚rain.
Van der Noot, Theatre, London, 1569, Biii[v]
sun: An ˚eagle flies towards the ˚sun. It falls through
˚clouds emitting ˚flames. On the ground, the eagle or
˚phoenix(?) sits in the midst of a ˚fire.
Van der Noot, Theatre, London, 1569, Ciiii[v]
sun: An ˚angel flies before the ˚sun and sends forth
˚birds after the routed ˚soldiers. The fleeing men and
the ˚seven ˚headed ˚beast with ˚crowns fall into a
˚pit of ˚fire.
Van der Noot, Theatre, London, 1569, Diiii[v]
sword: A ˚man with many ˚crowns rides a ˚horse, a
˚sword issuing from his ˚mouth. An ˚angel flies
before the ˚sun and sends forth ˚birds after the
routed ˚soldiers.
Van der Noot, Theatre, London, 1569, Diiii[v]
ten: The ˚beast from the ˚sea, with ˚seven ˚heads and
˚ten ˚horns bearing ˚ten crowns, is like a ˚leopard
with feet of a ˚bear and mouth of a ˚lion and is
worshipped by a man in ˚papal ˚regalia.
Van der Noot, Theatre, London, 1569, Dii[v]
three: ˚Statue of ˚charioteer, in ˚Roman ˚armour, with a
˚palm ˚branch in his ˚right hand stands in a ˚chariot
drawn by ˚three ˚horses.
Van der Noot, Theatre, London, 1569, Cii[v]
three: ˚Eight ˚Naiads flee the attack of ˚three ˚satyrs.
Van der Noot, Theatre, London, 1569, Cviii[v]
tree: A phoenix, ˚wings displayed, pecks its ˚breast so
that the ˚blood gushes onto the ground. It stands
beside a ˚dead ˚tree. Nearby, a ˚dead ˚spring[1].
Van der Noot, Theatre, London, 1569, Bv[v]
triumphal: A ˚triumphal ˚arch, the front decorated with
˚two ˚Victories. A plaque is inscribed ˚"CIV[ITAS]
AVGV[STO] CAES[ARI] SEMP[ER] CONS[ULI]" [THE
CITY TO AUGUSTUS CAESAR FOREVER CONSUL].
Van der Noot, Theatre, London, 1569, Cii[v]
trophy: ˚Echidna, in ˚armour and a ˚helmet, stands with
a ˚globe in her raised ˚left hand and supports a
˚standard of ˚trophies.
Van der Noot, Theatre, London, 1569, Di[v]
two: A ˚hind is chased by ˚two ˚dogs. Collapsed against
a ˚rock, its hindquarters torn by the dogs.
Van der Noot, Theatre, London, 1569, Bi[v]
two: A ˚triumphal ˚arch, the front decorated with ˚two
˚Victories.
Van der Noot, Theatre, London, 1569, Cii[v]
two: ˚Four men ˚destroy the palm-tree by uprooting it.
˚Two other ˚palms grow beside it.
Van der Noot, Theatre, London, 1569, Ciii[v]
two: A ˚wolf suckles ˚two ˚babies [= ˚Romulus and
˚Remus].
Van der Noot, Theatre, London, 1569, Cv[v]
urn: An ˚obelisk with ˚hieroglyphs, supported by ˚four
˚lions ˚sejant on a ˚pedestal, supports an ˚urn.
Van der Noot, Theatre, London, 1569, Ci[v]
water: A ˚river ˚god reclines against a ˚pot from which
˚water flows into the ˚river [= ˚Tiber].
Van der Noot, Theatre, London, 1569, Cv[v]
water: The ˚archangel ˚Michael, ˚staff in hand, flies over
a ˚seven ˚headed ˚beast, casting floods of ˚water out

of its mouth.
Van der Noot, Theatre, London, 1569, Dii[v]
wind: A ˚ship, with billowing ˚sails, runs before the
˚wind. The ship is ˚wrecked on the ˚rocks.
Van der Noot, Theatre, London, 1569, Bii[v]
wing: A phoenix, ˚wings displayed, pecks its ˚breast so
that the ˚blood gushes onto the ground.
Van der Noot, Theatre, London, 1569, Bv[v]
winged: The ˚winged and ˚crowned ˚apocalyptic ˚woman,
in the ˚orans position, stands on a ˚crescent ˚moon.
Van der Noot, Theatre, London, 1569, Dii[v]
wolf: A ˚wolf suckles ˚two ˚babies [= ˚Romulus and
˚Remus].
Van der Noot, Theatre, London, 1569, Cv[v]
woman: A bare breasted ˚woman, her ˚right hand to her
breasts and eyes downcast, walks on a mound
covered with ˚herbs and ˚flowers.
Van der Noot, Theatre, London, 1569, Bvi[v]
woman: The ˚winged and ˚crowned ˚apocalyptic ˚woman,
in the ˚orans position, stands on a ˚crescent ˚moon.
Van der Noot, Theatre, London, 1569, Dii[v]
wreck: A ˚ship, with billowing ˚sails, runs before the
˚wind. The ship is ˚wrecked on the ˚rocks.
Van der Noot, Theatre, London, 1569, Bii[v]

PROPER NOUN INDEX (PICTURE)

Babylon: ˚Five men kneel before the crowned ˚Whore of
˚Babylon, seated on a ˚seven ˚headed ˚beast.
Van der Noot, Theatre, London, 1569, Diii[v]
Doric: A ˚Roman ˚building with ˚Doric ˚columns,the
˚metopes charged with ˚bulls' heads alternating with
˚discs.
Van der Noot, Theatre, London, 1569, Bviii[v]
Echidna: ˚Echidna, in ˚armour and a ˚helmet, stands
with a ˚globe in her raised ˚left hand and supports a
˚standard of ˚trophies.
Van der Noot, Theatre, London, 1569, Di[v]
God: ˚God, as a ˚bearded ˚old-man lifts up by the
hands the ˚child of the ˚Whore of ˚Babylon.
Van der Noot, Theatre, London, 1569, Dii[v]
Jerusalem: One of the ˚angels of the ˚plagues, beside
him ˚St John. In the valley is the heavenly city of
˚Jerusalem.
Van der Noot, Theatre, London, 1569, Dv[v]
Michael: The ˚archangel ˚Michael, ˚staff in hand, flies
over a ˚seven ˚headed ˚beast, casting floods of
˚water out of its mouth. ˚Flames issue from ˚clouds.
Van der Noot, Theatre, London, 1569, Dii[v]
Naiad: ˚Four ˚nymphs, ˚Naiads, sit under trees. Three
huddle over an ˚open ˚book. A ˚spring[1] rises from
the ground.
Van der Noot, Theatre, London, 1569, Biv[v]
Naiad: A ˚Naiad, seated on a ˚river [= ˚Tiber] bank,
˚laments.
Van der Noot, Theatre, London, 1569, Cvi[v]
Naiad: ˚Eight ˚Naiads flee the attack of ˚three ˚satyrs.
Van der Noot, Theatre, London, 1569, Cviii[v]
Roman: A ˚Roman ˚building with ˚Doric ˚columns,the
˚metopes charged with ˚bulls' heads alternating with
˚discs. The ˚pediment is inscribed ˚"SPQR". An
˚earthquake brings ˚fire and ˚destruction.
Van der Noot, Theatre, London, 1569, Bviii[v]
Roman: ˚Statue of ˚charioteer, in ˚Roman ˚armour, with
a ˚palm ˚branch in his ˚right hand stands in a
˚chariot drawnby ˚three ˚horses.
Van der Noot, Theatre, London, 1569, Cii[v]
Rome [= hills]: A ˚palm-tree grows on top of ˚seven
˚hills [= ˚Rome] by a ˚river [= ˚Tiber].
Van der Noot, Theatre, London, 1569, Ciii[v]
Romulus and Remus [= baby]: A ˚river ˚god reclines
against a ˚pot from which ˚water flows into the
˚river [= ˚Tiber]. At his feet a ˚wolf suckles ˚two
˚babies[= ˚Romulus and ˚Remus].

Van der Noot, *Theatre*, London, 1569, Cv^v
Saint John: On a ˚cliff one of the ˚angels of the
     ˚plagues stands holding a ˚staff in its ˚right hand,
     pointing upwards with his ˚left. Beside him ˚kneels
     the ˚praying figure of ˚St John. In the valley is the
     heavenly city of ˚Jerusalem.
     Van der Noot, *Theatre*, London, 1569, Dv^v
Tiber [= river]: A ˚palm-tree grows on top of ˚seven
     ˚hills [= ˚Rome] by a ˚river [= ˚Tiber].
     Van der Noot, *Theatre*, London, 1569, Ciii^v
Tiber [= river]: A ˚river ˚god reclines against a ˚pot.
     He wears a ˚laurel ˚garland and holds a ˚palm branch
     in his ˚right hand and an ˚olive branch in his ˚left.
     ˚Water flows from his pot into the ˚river [= ˚Tiber].
     Van der Noot, *Theatre*, London, 1569, Cv^v
Tiber [= river]: A ˚Naiad, seated on a ˚river [= ˚Tiber]
     bank, ˚laments.
     Van der Noot, *Theatre*, London, 1569, Cvi^v
Victory: A ˚triumphal ˚arch, the front decorated with
     ˚two ˚Victories. A plaque is inscribed ˚"CIV[ITAS]
     AVGV[STO] CAES[ARI] SEMP[ER] CONS[ULI]" [THE
     CITY TO AUGUSTUS CAESAR FOREVER CONSUL].
     Van der Noot, *Theatre*, London, 1569, Cii^v
Whore of Babylon: ˚Five men in ˚armour, one a ˚king
     wearing a ˚crown, kneel before the crowned ˚Whore
     of ˚Babylon, seated on a ˚seven ˚headed ˚beast. The
     heads are ˚crowned. The whore holds up a ˚cup in
     her ˚right hand.
     Van der Noot, *Theatre*, London, 1569, Diii^v

PICTURE INSCRIPTIONS

"CIVITAS AUGUSTO CAESARI SEMPER CONSULI" [The
     city to Augustus Caesar forever Consul]
     Van der Noot, *Theatre*, London, 1569, Cii^v
"SPQR"
     Van der Noot, *Theatre*, London, 1569, Bviii^v

EPIGRAM INDEX

endure→corpse→world→grief
  Van der Noot, Theatre, 1569, Ci^v
eye→art→nature→pleasure
  Van der Noot, Theatre, 1569, Cviii^v
faith→white→horse→man
  Van der Noot, Theatre, 1569, Diiii^v
fall→fire→heaven→dust→sudden
  Van der Noot, Theatre, 1569, Cii^v
fall→green→laurel→die→olive
  Van der Noot, Theatre, 1569, Cv^v
fall→heaven→Babylon
  Van der Noot, Theatre, 1569, Diii^v
fear→war→thunder→wonder→shame
  Van der Noot, Theatre, 1569, Di^v
fight→Aeneas [= duke]→duke
  [= Aeneas]→Turnus
  Van der Noot, Theatre, 1569, Cv^v
fire→heaven→dust→sudden→fall
  Van der Noot, Theatre, 1569, Cii^v
fire→body→dust→temple→god
  Van der Noot, Theatre, 1569, Ciiii^v
fire→ray→melody→smoke
  Van der Noot, Theatre, 1569, Cvii^v
fire→adore→beast→image
  Van der Noot, Theatre, 1569, Dii^v
fire→beast→flee→pit
  Van der Noot, Theatre, 1569, Diiii^v
fire [= lightning]→royal→tree→root→
  lightning [= fire]
  Van der Noot, Theatre, 1569, Biii^v
flame→triple→heaven→hill
  Van der Noot, Theatre, 1569, Cvii^v
flame→countenance→word→God
  Van der Noot, Theatre, 1569, Diiii^v
flee→pit→fire→beast
  Van der Noot, Theatre, 1569, Diiii^v
flesh→war→king→eat
  Van der Noot, Theatre, 1569, Diiii^v
floor→step→parget→ceiling
  Van der Noot, Theatre, 1569, Bviii^v
flower→love→lady→herb
  Van der Noot, Theatre, 1569, Bvi^v
fly→throne→god→sing
  Van der Noot, Theatre, 1569, Cvii^v
foot→water→foul→naked→Faun
  Van der Noot, Theatre, 1569, Cviii^v
foot→arms→hundred→vanquish→king
  Van der Noot, Theatre, 1569, Di^v
foot→bear→cruel→leopard
  Van der Noot, Theatre, 1569, Dii^v
force→dog→black→white
  Van der Noot, Theatre, 1569, Bi^v
force→blood→wound→honour
  Van der Noot, Theatre, 1569, Dii^v
foresake→white→robe→proudly
  Van der Noot, Theatre, 1569, Bvi^v
foul→naked→Faun→foot→water
  Van der Noot, Theatre, 1569, Cviii^v
four→lion→worthy→tomb
  Van der Noot, Theatre, 1569, Ci^v
fowl→light→ash→phoenix(?)
  [= worm]→worm [= phoenix(?)]
  Van der Noot, Theatre, 1569, Ciiii^v
freight→storm→rock→water→treasure
  Van der Noot, Theatre, 1569, Bii^v
frieze→crystal→chapter→alabaster
  Van der Noot, Theatre, 1569, Cii^v
fruit→Church→triumph→seat→life
  Van der Noot, Theatre, 1569, Dv^v
gate→pearl→house→gold
  Van der Noot, Theatre, 1569, Dv^v
gentle→hind→pursue→two
  Van der Noot, Theatre, 1569, Bi^v
ghost [= rivergod Tiber]→beard→
  Saturn→rivergod Tiber [= ghost]
  Van der Noot, Theatre, 1569, Cv^v

glory→Rome→lord→dart→Jupiter
  Van der Noot, Theatre, 1569, Cii^v
glory→praise→god→worship
  Van der Noot, Theatre, 1569, Cvi^v
glory→scarlet→pearl→gold
  Van der Noot, Theatre, 1569, Diii^v
god→fire→body→dust→temple
  Van der Noot, Theatre, 1569, Ciiii^v
god→worship→glory→praise
  Van der Noot, Theatre, 1569, Cvi^v
god→sing→fly→throne
  Van der Noot, Theatre, 1569, Cvii^v
god→sister→morion→majesty
  Van der Noot, Theatre, 1569, Di^v
gold→white→ivory→sail
  Van der Noot, Theatre, 1569, Bii^v
gold→crest→break→tree
  Van der Noot, Theatre, 1569, Bv^v
gold→waist→cloud→snow
  Van der Noot, Theatre, 1569, Bvi^v
gold→crystal→thousand→ray
  Van der Noot, Theatre, 1569, Bviii^v
gold→vessel→ash→emperor
  Van der Noot, Theatre, 1569, Ci^v
gold→pillar→ivory→base
  Van der Noot, Theatre, 1569, Cii^v
gold→hair→Rome→honour
  Van der Noot, Theatre, 1569, Cvi^v
gold→shower→grief→change
  Van der Noot, Theatre, 1569, Cvii^v
gold→Pactol→plain→yellow
  Van der Noot, Theatre, 1569, Cviii^v
gold→glory→scarlet→pearl
  Van der Noot, Theatre, 1569, Diii^v
gold→gate→pearl→house
  Van der Noot, Theatre, 1569, Dv^v
golden→triumph→arch→Victory
  Van der Noot, Theatre, 1569, Cii^v
green→wood→branch→laurel-tree
  Van der Noot, Theatre, 1569, Biii^v
green→laurel→die→olive→fall
  Van der Noot, Theatre, 1569, Cv^v
grief→lose→drown→rich→misfortune
  Van der Noot, Theatre, 1569, Bii^v
grief→heart→joy→earth→bitter
  Van der Noot, Theatre, 1569, Bvi^v
grief→endure→corpse→world
  Van der Noot, Theatre, 1569, Ci^v
grief→change→gold→shower
  Van der Noot, Theatre, 1569, Cvii^v
grieve→delight→earth→devour→
  spring
  Van der Noot, Theatre, 1569, Biv^v
hair→Rome→honour→gold
  Van der Noot, Theatre, 1569, Cvi^v
hair→blasphemy→pride→beast
  Van der Noot, Theatre, 1569, Diii^v
head→crime→Nero→Caligula→rule
  Van der Noot, Theatre, 1569, Cvi^v
head→beast→sea→seven
  Van der Noot, Theatre, 1569, Dii^v
head→ten→horn→seven
  Van der Noot, Theatre, 1569, Diiii^v
heart→rejoice→accord→tune→voice
  Van der Noot, Theatre, 1569, Biv^v
heart→burn→pain→love
  Van der Noot, Theatre, 1569, Bv^v
heart→joy→earth→bitter→grief
  Van der Noot, Theatre, 1569, Bvi^v
heart→wine→whoredom→cup
  Van der Noot, Theatre, 1569, Diii^v
heaven→sky→dark→welkin
  Van der Noot, Theatre, 1569, Biii^v
heaven→noble→monument→tempest→
  stick
  Van der Noot, Theatre, 1569, Ci^v

heaven→dust→sudden→fall→fire
  Van der Noot, Theatre, 1569, Cii^v
heaven→eagle(?) [= bird]→bird
  [= eagle(?)]→sun
  Van der Noot, Theatre, 1569, Ciiii^v
heaven→hill→flame→triple
  Van der Noot, Theatre, 1569, Cvii^v
heaven→Typhoeus→Morpheus→
  inconstancy
  Van der Noot, Theatre, 1569, Di^v
heaven→Babylon→fall
  Van der Noot, Theatre, 1569, Diii^v
heaven→army→angel→bird
  Van der Noot, Theatre, 1569, Diiii^v
heaven→Saint→John→earth
  Van der Noot, Theatre, 1569, Dv^v
heben [= ebony]→sea→ship→ebony
  [= heben]
  Van der Noot, Theatre, 1569, Bii^v
heel→languish→shroud→serpent
  Van der Noot, Theatre, 1569, Bvi^v
herb→flower→love→lady
  Van der Noot, Theatre, 1569, Bvi^v
hill→hundred→pillar→diamond
  Van der Noot, Theatre, 1569, Bviii^v
hill→shade→conqueror→oak [= leaf]
  Van der Noot, Theatre, 1569, Ciii^v
hill→flame→triple→heaven
  Van der Noot, Theatre, 1569, Cvii^v
hill→ivory→hundred→nymph
  Van der Noot, Theatre, 1569, Cviii^v
hind→pursue→two→gentle
  Van der Noot, Theatre, 1569, Bi^v
holy→city→Lord→sea
  Van der Noot, Theatre, 1569, Dv^v
honour→noble→bough→outrage
  Van der Noot, Theatre, 1569, Ciii^v
honour→gold→hair→Rome
  Van der Noot, Theatre, 1569, Cvi^v
honour→force→blood→wound
  Van der Noot, Theatre, 1569, Dii^v
horn→blasphemy→ten→crown
  Van der Noot, Theatre, 1569, Dii^v
horn→seven→head→ten
  Van der Noot, Theatre, 1569, Diiii^v
horse→man→faith→white
  Van der Noot, Theatre, 1569, Diiii^v
house→gold→gate→pearl
  Van der Noot, Theatre, 1569, Dv^v
hundred→pillar→diamond→hill
  Van der Noot, Theatre, 1569, Bviii^v
hundred→nymph→hill→ivory
  Van der Noot, Theatre, 1569, Cviii^v
hundred→vanquish→king→foot→arms
  Van der Noot, Theatre, 1569, Di^v
image→fire→adore→beast
  Van der Noot, Theatre, 1569, Dii^v
incense→cedar→balm→odour
  Van der Noot, Theatre, 1569, Cvii^v
inconstancy→heaven→Typhoeus→
  Morpheus
  Van der Noot, Theatre, 1569, Di^v
ivory→sail→gold→white
  Van der Noot, Theatre, 1569, Bii^v
ivory→base→gold→pillar
  Van der Noot, Theatre, 1569, Cii^v
ivory→hundred→nymph→hill
  Van der Noot, Theatre, 1569, Cviii^v
joy→earth→bitter→grief→heart
  Van der Noot, Theatre, 1569, Bvi^v
king→foot→arms→hundred→vanquish
  Van der Noot, Theatre, 1569, Di^v
king→eat→flesh→war
  Van der Noot, Theatre, 1569, Diiii^v
lady→herb→flower→love
  Van der Noot, Theatre, 1569, Bvi^v

Van der Noot, Theatre, 1569, Diii^V
shade→melody→spirit→ravish
Van der Noot, Theatre, 1569, Biii^V
shade→conqueror→oak [= leaf]→hill
Van der Noot, Theatre, 1569, Ciii^V
shake→building→stone→earthquake
Van der Noot, Theatre, 1569, Bviii^V
shame→fear→war→thunder→wonder
Van der Noot, Theatre, 1569, Di^V
shepherd→clown→Muse→nymph
Van der Noot, Theatre, 1569, Biv^V
ship→ebony [= heben]→heben
 [= ebony]→sea
Van der Noot, Theatre, 1569, Bii^V
shore→trophy→world→stream
Van der Noot, Theatre, 1569, Di^V
shower→grief→change→gold
Van der Noot, Theatre, 1569, Cvii^V
shroud→serpent→heel→languish
Van der Noot, Theatre, 1569, Bvi^V
sign→race^1→trophy→spoil^1
Van der Noot, Theatre, 1569, Ciii^V
silk→tackle→wind→sky
Van der Noot, Theatre, 1569, Bii^V
sing→fly→throne→god
Van der Noot, Theatre, 1569, Cvii^V
sister→morion→majesty→god
Van der Noot, Theatre, 1569, Di^V
sky→silk→tackle→wind
Van der Noot, Theatre, 1569, Bii^V
sky→dark→welkin→heaven
Van der Noot, Theatre, 1569, Biii^V
sleep→accord→mermaid→song
Van der Noot, Theatre, 1569, Cviii^V
smell→scent→sulphur→corrupt
Van der Noot, Theatre, 1569, Cvii^V
smite→die→pity→phoenix
Van der Noot, Theatre, 1569, Bv^V
smoke→fire→ray→melody
Van der Noot, Theatre, 1569, Cvii^V
snow→gold→waist→cloud
Van der Noot, Theatre, 1569, Bvi^V
song→sleep→accord→mermaid
Van der Noot, Theatre, 1569, Cviii^V
spire→diamond→archer→pot
Van der Noot, Theatre, 1569, Ci^V
spirit→ravish→shade→melody
Van der Noot, Theatre, 1569, Biii^V
spoil^1 = booty
spoil^1→sign→race^1→trophy
Van der Noot, Theatre, 1569, Ciii^V
spouse→abode→God→man
Van der Noot, Theatre, 1569, Dv^V
spring→grieve→delight→earth→
 devour
Van der Noot, Theatre, 1569, Biv^V
spring^1 = stream
spring^1→water→wood^1→rock
Van der Noot, Theatre, 1569, Biv^V
spring^1→devour→water→dry
Van der Noot, Theatre, 1569, Bv^V
spring^1→rock→crystal→sun
Van der Noot, Theatre, 1569, Cviii^V
square→city→twelve→tear
Van der Noot, Theatre, 1569, Dv^V
step→parget→ceiling→floor
Van der Noot, Theatre, 1569, Bviii^V
stick→heaven→noble→monument→
 tempest
Van der Noot, Theatre, 1569, Ci^V
stone→earthquake→shake→building
Van der Noot, Theatre, 1569, Bviii^V
stone^1 = precious stone
stone^1→stream→crystal→pavement
Van der Noot, Theatre, 1569, Dv^V
storm→rock→water→treasure→freight

Van der Noot, Theatre, 1569, Bii^V
stream→ancient→leaf [= oak]→Italy
Van der Noot, Theatre, 1569, Ciii^V
stream→Trojan→pot→water
Van der Noot, Theatre, 1569, Cv^V
stream→shore→trophy→world
Van der Noot, Theatre, 1569, Di^V
stream→crystal→pavement→stone^1
Van der Noot, Theatre, 1569, Dv^V
suck→two→bitch→wolf
Van der Noot, Theatre, 1569, Cv^V
sudden→fall→fire→heaven→dust
Van der Noot, Theatre, 1569, Cii^V
sulphur→corrupt→smell→scent
Van der Noot, Theatre, 1569, Cvii^V
sun→heaven→eagle(?) [= bird]→bird
 [= eagle(?)]
Van der Noot, Theatre, 1569, Ciiii^V
sun→spring^1→rock→crystal
Van der Noot, Theatre, 1569, Cviii^V
tackle→wind→sky→silk
Van der Noot, Theatre, 1569, Bii^V
tear→square→city→twelve
Van der Noot, Theatre, 1569, Dv^V
tempest→stick→heaven→noble→
 monument
Van der Noot, Theatre, 1569, Ci^V
temple→god→fire→body→dust
Van der Noot, Theatre, 1569, Ciiii^V
ten→crown→horn→blasphemy
Van der Noot, Theatre, 1569, Dii^V
ten→horn→seven→head
Van der Noot, Theatre, 1569, Diii^V
thousand→ray→gold→crystal
Van der Noot, Theatre, 1569, Bviii^V
throat→dragon→power→lion
Van der Noot, Theatre, 1569, Dii^V
throne→god→sing→fly
Van der Noot, Theatre, 1569, Cvii^V
thunder→wonder→shame→fear→war
Van der Noot, Theatre, 1569, Di^V
tomb→four→lion→worthy
Van der Noot, Theatre, 1569, Ci^V
treasure→freight→storm→rock→water
Van der Noot, Theatre, 1569, Bii^V
tree→root→lightning [= fire]→fire
 [= lightning]→royal
Van der Noot, Theatre, 1569, Biii^V
tree→gold→crest→break
Van der Noot, Theatre, 1569, Bv^V
tree→trunk→root→disdain→twin
Van der Noot, Theatre, 1569, Ciii^V
tree [= oak]→seven→Dodona→oak
 [= tree]
Van der Noot, Theatre, 1569, Ciii^V
tree [= olive]→Romulus and Remus
 [= baby]→baby [= Romulus and
 Remus]→olive [= tree]
Van der Noot, Theatre, 1569, Cv^V
triple→heaven→hill→flame
Van der Noot, Theatre, 1569, Cvii^V
triumph→arch→Victory→golden
Van der Noot, Theatre, 1569, Cii^V
triumph→seat→life→fruit→Church
Van der Noot, Theatre, 1569, Dv^V
trophy→spoil^1→sign→race
Van der Noot, Theatre, 1569, Ciii^V
trophy→world→stream→shore
Van der Noot, Theatre, 1569, Di^V
trunk→root→disdain→twin→tree
Van der Noot, Theatre, 1569, Ciii^V
trust→wing→dam^1→cloud
Van der Noot, Theatre, 1569, Ciiii^V
tune→voice→heart→rejoice→accord
Van der Noot, Theatre, 1569, Biv^V
twelve→tear→square→city

Van der Noot, Theatre, 1569, Dv^V
twin→tree→trunk→root→disdain
Van der Noot, Theatre, 1569, Ciii^V
two→gentle→hind→pursue
Van der Noot, Theatre, 1569, Bi^V
two→bitch→wolf→suck
Van der Noot, Theatre, 1569, Cv^V
vanity→lapis-lazuli→emerald→world
Van der Noot, Theatre, 1569, Bviii^V
vanquish→noble→beauty→wail→
 destiny
Van der Noot, Theatre, 1569, Bi^V
vanquish→king→foot→arms→hundred
Van der Noot, Theatre, 1569, Di^V
vessel→ash→emperor→gold
Van der Noot, Theatre, 1569, Ci^V
villain→Trojan→blood→barbarous
Van der Noot, Theatre, 1569, Ciii^V
voice→heart→rejoice→accord→tune
Van der Noot, Theatre, 1569, Biv^V
wail→destiny→vanquish→noble→
 beauty
Van der Noot, Theatre, 1569, Bi^V
wail→nymph→Tiber [= river]→river
 [= Tiber]
Van der Noot, Theatre, 1569, Cvi^V
waist→cloud→snow→gold
Van der Noot, Theatre, 1569, Bvi^V
wall→Doric→brick→marble
Van der Noot, Theatre, 1569, Bviii^V
war→thunder→wonder→shame→fear
Van der Noot, Theatre, 1569, Di^V
war→king→eat→flesh
Van der Noot, Theatre, 1569, Diiii^V
water→treasure→freight→storm→rock
Van der Noot, Theatre, 1569, Bii^V
water→wood^1→rock→spring^1
Van der Noot, Theatre, 1569, Biv^V
water→dry→spring^1→devour
Van der Noot, Theatre, 1569, Bv^V
water→stream→Trojan→pot
Van der Noot, Theatre, 1569, Cv^V
water→foul→naked→Faun→foot
Van der Noot, Theatre, 1569, Cviii^V
welkin→heaven→sky→dark
Van der Noot, Theatre, 1569, Biii^V
white→force→dog→black
Van der Noot, Theatre, 1569, Bi^V
white→ivory→sail→gold
Van der Noot, Theatre, 1569, Bii^V
white→robe→proudly→foresake
Van der Noot, Theatre, 1569, Bvi^V
white→bird→wing→perfume
Van der Noot, Theatre, 1569, Cvii^V
white→horse→man→faith
Van der Noot, Theatre, 1569, Diiii^V
whoredom→cup→heart→wine
Van der Noot, Theatre, 1569, Diii^V
wind→sky→silk→tackle
Van der Noot, Theatre, 1569, Bii^V
wine→whoredom→cup→heart
Van der Noot, Theatre, 1569, Diii^V
wing→phoenix→wood^1→purple
Van der Noot, Theatre, 1569, Bv^V
wing→nymph→chariot [= chair]→chair
 [= chariot]
Van der Noot, Theatre, 1569, Cii^V
wing→dam^1→cloud→trust
Van der Noot, Theatre, 1569, Ciiii^V
wing→perfume→white→bird
Van der Noot, Theatre, 1569, Cvii^V
wolf→suck→two→bitch
Van der Noot, Theatre, 1569, Cv^V
woman [= Whore of Babylon]→beast→
 orange→Whore of Babylon
 [= woman]

Van der Noot, Theatre, 1569, Diii^V
wonder→shame→fear→war→thunder
   Van der Noot, Theatre, 1569, Di^V
wood¹ = forest
wood¹→branch→laurel-tree→green
   Van der Noot, Theatre, 1569, Biii^V
wood¹→rock→spring¹→water
   Van der Noot, Theatre, 1569, Biv^V
wood¹→purple→wing→phoenix
   Van der Noot, Theatre, 1569, Bv^V
word→God→flame→countenance
   Van der Noot, Theatre, 1569, Diiii^V
world→vanity→lapis-lazuli→emerald
   Van der Noot, Theatre, 1569, Bviii^V
world→grief→endure→corpse
   Van der Noot, Theatre, 1569, Ci^V
world→stream→shore→trophy
   Van der Noot, Theatre, 1569, Di^V
worm [= phoenix(?)]→fowl→light→
   ash→phoenix(?) [= worm]
   Van der Noot, Theatre, 1569, Ciiii^V
worship→glory→praise→god
   Van der Noot, Theatre, 1569, Cvi^V
worthy→tomb→four→lion
   Van der Noot, Theatre, 1569, Ci^V
wound→honour→force→blood
   Van der Noot, Theatre, 1569, Dii^V
yellow→gold→Pactol→plain
   Van der Noot, Theatre, 1569, Cviii^V

PROPER NOUN INDEX (EPIGRAM)

Aeneas [= duke]→duke [= Aeneas]→
   Turnus→fight
   Van der Noot, Theatre, 1569, Cv^V
Babylon→fall→heaven
   Van der Noot, Theatre, 1569, Diii^V
Caligula→rule→head→crime→Nero
   Van der Noot, Theatre, 1569, Cvi^V
Church→triumph→seat→life→fruit
   Van der Noot, Theatre, 1569, Dv^V
Dodona→oak [= tree]→tree [= oak]→
   seven
   Van der Noot, Theatre, 1569, Ciii^V
Doric→brick→marble→wall
   Van der Noot, Theatre, 1569, Bviii^V
Faun→foot→water→foul→naked
   Van der Noot, Theatre, 1569, Cviii^V
God→flame→countenance→word
   Van der Noot, Theatre, 1569, Diiii^V
God→man→spouse→abode
   Van der Noot, Theatre, 1569, Dv^V
Hercules→seven→booty→Hydra
   Van der Noot, Theatre, 1569, Cvi^V
Hydra→Hercules→seven→booty
   Van der Noot, Theatre, 1569, Cvi^V
Italy→stream→ancient→leaf [= oak]
   Van der Noot, Theatre, 1569, Ciii^V
John→earth→heaven→Saint
   Van der Noot, Theatre, 1569, Dv^V
Jupiter→glory→Rome→lord→dart
   Van der Noot, Theatre, 1569, Cii^V
Lord→sea→holy→city
   Van der Noot, Theatre, 1569, Dv^V
Morpheus→inconstancy→heaven→
   Typhoeus
   Van der Noot, Theatre, 1569, Di^V
Muse→nymph→shepherd→clown
   Van der Noot, Theatre, 1569, Biv^V
Nero→Caligula→rule→head→crime
   Van der Noot, Theatre, 1569, Cvi^V
Pactolus→plain→yellow→gold
   Van der Noot, Theatre, 1569, Cviii^V
Rome→lord→dart→Jupiter→glory

Van der Noot, Theatre, 1569, Cii^V
Rome→honour→gold→hair
   Van der Noot, Theatre, 1569, Cvi^V
Romulus and Remus [= baby]→baby
   [= Romulus and Remus]→olive
   [= tree]→tree [= olive]
   Van der Noot, Theatre, 1569, Cv^V
Saint→John→earth→heaven
   Van der Noot, Theatre, 1569, Dv^V
Saturn→rivergod Tiber [= ghost]→
   ghost [= rivergod Tiber]→beard
   Van der Noot, Theatre, 1569, Cv^V
Tiber [= river]→river [= Tiber]→wail→
   nymph
   Van der Noot, Theatre, 1569, Cvi^V
Trojan→blood→barbarous→villain
   Van der Noot, Theatre, 1569, Ciii^V
Trojan→pot→water→stream
   Van der Noot, Theatre, 1569, Cv^V
Turnus→fight→Aeneas [= duke]→duke
   [= Aeneas]
   Van der Noot, Theatre, 1569, Cv^V
Typhoeus→Morpheus→inconstancy→
   heaven
   Van der Noot, Theatre, 1569, Di^V
Victory→golden→triumph→arch
   Van der Noot, Theatre, 1569, Cii^V
Whore of Babylon [= woman]→woman
   [= Whore of Babylon]→beast→
   orange
   Van der Noot, Theatre, 1569, Diii^V

THE IMPRESE OF PAOLO GIOVIO

CONCORDANCES, INDEXES, AND LISTS

Prepared by Peter M. Daly

PICTURE INDEX

account: A °closed °account °book with °flames rising
    from margins, inscribed °"1485".
    Giovio, Imprese, London, 1585, Cv^v
agate: The °descent of the °Holy °Ghost upon the
    °twelve °apostles in an °agate.
    Giovio, Imprese, London, 1585, Bvii^r
altar: A °hand burning in °fire on an °altar.
    Giovio, Imprese, London, 1585, Dvii^v
altar: The °temple of °Juno °Lucina and within, an °altar
    with a °fire.
    Giovio, Imprese, London, 1585, Fvi^r
altar: °Mount °Olympus with the °altar of °faith.
    Giovio, Imprese, London, 1585, Giiii^r
aperture: A °metal °globe containing °flames issuing
    through °apertures.
    Giovio, Imprese, London, 1585, Eii^r
apostle: The °descent of the °Holy °Ghost upon the
    °twelve °apostles in an °agate.
    Giovio, Imprese, London, 1585, Bvii^r
argent: A °griffin °argent in a °field^2 °gueles.
    Giovio, Imprese, London, 1585, Evi^r
argent: A °lion °rampant in a °field^2 °argent, all sown
    with °buckles.
    Giovio, Imprese, London, 1585, Fi^v
armelin: An °armelin, or °ermine surrounded by a °ring
    of °dung.
    Giovio, Imprese, London, 1585, Cv^r
arrow: An °arrow hits the °white^1 of a °target.
    Giovio, Imprese, London, 1585, Gii^r
azure: A clear °sky; upon a calm °sea a °nest with birds
    looking out; °halcyons are °azure, °red, °white,
    °green, °yellow.
    Giovio, Imprese, London, 1585, Ev^r
azure: A clear °azure °sky with °stars above a °compass
    °needle and compass, set upon a °sea °card or °chart.
    Giovio, Imprese, London, 1585, Ev^v
azure: The °sun, °or, surrounded by thick °clouds in a
    °field^2, °azure.
    Giovio, Imprese, London, 1585, Fi^r
balance: A °balance or °scales.
    Giovio, Imprese, London, 1585, Fiii^v
beak: An °eagle holding a °crown in its °beak.
    Giovio, Imprese, London, 1585, Diiii^r
beam: The °sun with °beams shining through a °crystal
    °lens, producing °flames, all set in a °white °hood.
    Giovio, Imprese, London, 1585, Di^r
beaver: A °beaver.
    Giovio, Imprese, London, 1585, Gvii^v
bee: A °hive of °bees with °honey.
    Giovio, Imprese, London, 1585, Gvii^r
billet: °Billets of °green °wood stacked; °smoke and
    °flame issuing from within.
    Giovio, Imprese, London, 1585, Cviii^v
black: Many °black °numbers scattered in a °field^2 or
    °border.
    Giovio, Imprese, London, 1585, Eiii^v
black: A °pot full of °black °stones and °one °white
    stone.
    Giovio, Imprese, London, 1585, Gvi^v
block: A °palm-tree weighted down with a °marble °block
    tied to the top.
    Giovio, Imprese, London, 1585, Eii^v
block [= quadret]: A °marble °block or °quadret with an
    iron °stile inset, opposite the °sun.
    Giovio, Imprese, London, 1585, Eii^r
bloody: A °wolf with °bloody °lamb looking back at °two
    °mastiffs.
    Giovio, Imprese, London, 1585, Hii^r
body: °Cattle ... without °body.
    Giovio, Imprese, London, 1585, Giiii^r
book: An °open °book.
    Giovio, Imprese, London, 1585, Ciiii^v
book: A °closed °account °book with °flames rising from

margins, inscribed °"1485".
    Giovio, Imprese, London, 1585, Cv^v
border: Many °black °numbers scattered in a °field^2 or
    °border.
    Giovio, Imprese, London, 1585, Eiii^v
bough: A °golden °bough.
    Giovio, Imprese, London, 1585, Diiii^r
branch: A °laurel-tree with °branches cut off; one °twig
    grows to a great height.
    Giovio, Imprese, London, 1585, Giiii^r
brazen: The °brazen °bull of °Perillus.
    Giovio, Imprese, London, 1585, Dvi^r
bucket: A °wheel with °buckets for drawing °water.
    Giovio, Imprese, London, 1585, Ciiii^r
bucket: A °firebrand and °bucket of °water.
    Giovio, Imprese, London, 1585, Giiii^r
buckle: A °lion °rampant in a °field^2 °argent, all sown
    with °buckles.
    Giovio, Imprese, London, 1585, Fi^v
bull: The °brazen °bull of °Perillus.
    Giovio, Imprese, London, 1585, Dvi^r
bullrush: °Bullrushes in a °river.
    Giovio, Imprese, London, 1585, Dviii^r
bundle: A °bundle of °javelins.
    Giovio, Imprese, London, 1585, Fiii^r
bundle: °Two °bundles of °ripe °millet.
    Giovio, Imprese, London, 1585, Fv^r
bundle: A °bundle of °darts.
    Giovio, Imprese, London, 1585, Giiii^r
burn: The slopes of the °volcano, °Mount °Aetna, are
    covered with °snow, °burnt °stones, and °fertile
    °fields.
    Giovio, Imprese, London, 1585, Fiiii^r
caduceus: The °caduceus of °Mercury with a
    °cornucopia.
    Giovio, Imprese, London, 1585, Gvii^v
camel: A °camel disturbing the °river °water.
    Giovio, Imprese, London, 1585, Dv^v
camel: A °kneeling °camel.
    Giovio, Imprese, London, 1585, Gi^v
candle: A °white wax °candle, worn in a cap.
    Giovio, Imprese, London, 1585, Bvi^v
candleflye [= moth]: °Gold °candleflyes [= °moths]
    dispersed.
    Giovio, Imprese, London, 1585, Biiii^v
candlestick: A °triangular °candlestick.
    Giovio, Imprese, London, 1585, Giii^v
capricorn: A °capricorn.
    Giovio, Imprese, London, 1585, Diii^v
card [= chart]: A clear °azure °sky with °stars above a
    °compass °needle and compass, set upon a °sea °card
    or °chart.
    Giovio, Imprese, London, 1585, Ev^v
cattle: °Cattle ... without °body.
    Giovio, Imprese, London, 1585, Giiii^r
chair: °Florence sitting on a °chair, a °yoke under her
    feet.
    Giovio, Imprese, London, 1585, Cvii^v
chariot: A °triumphal °chariot, drawn by °five °white
    °horses, °emperor within, a °slave holding °laurel
    °garland.
    Giovio, Imprese, London, 1585, Gi^r
chart [= card]: A clear °azure °sky with °stars above a
    °compass °needle and compass, set upon a °sea °card
    or °chart.
    Giovio, Imprese, London, 1585, Ev^v
chimney: A large °chimney with a °fire within.
    Giovio, Imprese, London, 1585, Fv^v
circle: A °round °shield, °fringed; °four °circles, one at
    each side, bound by a °laurel °wreath. In each
    circle an °impresa.
    Giovio, Imprese, London, 1585, Giiii^r
claw: A °crane holds in his °left °claw a °stone.
    Giovio, Imprese, London, 1585, Fiii^r
clock: A °falcon holding in her °talons the

˚counterweight of a ˚clock.
Giovio, Imprese, London, 1585, Gi^r

closed: A ˚closed ˚account ˚book with ˚flames rising
from margins, inscribed ˚"1485".
Giovio, Imprese, London, 1585, Cv^v

cloud: A ˚heron with the ˚sun above and ˚clouds below;
˚marsh and ˚sedge; possibly ˚rain and ˚hail falling.
Giovio, Imprese, London, 1585, Dvii^r

cloud: The ˚sun, ˚or, surrounded by thick ˚clouds in a
˚field², ˚azure.
Giovio, Imprese, London, 1585, Fi^r

club: A ˚wild ˚man with a ˚club in one hand.
Giovio, Imprese, London, 1585, Fi^v

collar: An ˚iron ˚dog's ˚collar with ˚spikes.
Giovio, Imprese, London, 1585, Dv^v

collar: A spiked ˚iron ˚collar grasped by ˚two ˚hands
pierced by the ˚spikes; in the middle of the collar, a
˚rose.
Giovio, Imprese, London, 1585, Dv^v

comet: A ˚comet.
Giovio, Imprese, London, 1585, Dii^r

compass: A clear ˚azure ˚sky with ˚stars above a
˚compass ˚needle and compass, set upon a ˚sea ˚card
or ˚chart.
Giovio, Imprese, London, 1585, Ev^v

corn [= wheat]: ˚Five ˚ears of ˚corn, ˚wheat.
Giovio, Imprese, London, 1585, Fv^r

corn [= wheat]: ˚Two ˚sheaves of ˚ripe ˚corn, ˚wheat.
Giovio, Imprese, London, 1585, Fvi^r

cornucopia: The ˚caduceus of ˚Mercury with a
˚cornucopia.
Giovio, Imprese, London, 1585, Gvii^v

counterweight: A ˚falcon holding in her ˚talons the
˚counterweight of a ˚clock.
Giovio, Imprese, London, 1585, Gi^r

crane: A ˚crane holds in his ˚left ˚claw a ˚stone.
Giovio, Imprese, London, 1585, Fiii^r

crescent: The ˚crescent ˚moon.
Giovio, Imprese, London, 1585, Cii^v

crocodile: A ˚crocodile.
Giovio, Imprese, London, 1585, Gii^r

cross: ˚St. George on ˚horseback in a ˚white ˚shield,
parted with a ˚red ˚cross.
Giovio, Imprese, London, 1585, Ci^v

crown: An ˚eagle holding a ˚crown in its ˚beak.
Giovio, Imprese, London, 1585, Diiii^r

crowned: A ˚hedgehog ˚crowned.
Giovio, Imprese, London, 1585, Cii^r

crystal: The ˚sun with ˚beams shining through a ˚crystal
˚lens, producing ˚flames, all set in a ˚white ˚hood.
Giovio, Imprese, London, 1585, Di^r

cursant: An ˚ostrich ˚cursant.
Giovio, Imprese, London, 1585, Evii^r

cypress: A ˚palm branch wreathed with ˚cypress.
Giovio, Imprese, London, 1585, Dvi^v

dart: A ˚bundle of ˚darts.
Giovio, Imprese, London, 1585, Giiii^r

descent: The ˚descent of the ˚Holy ˚Ghost upon the
˚twelve ˚apostles in an ˚agate.
Giovio, Imprese, London, 1585, Bvii^r

diadem: ˚Three ˚saints' ˚diadems linked, with ˚"valer" in
the middle.
Giovio, Imprese, London, 1585, Cv^v

diamond: A ˚mountain of ˚diamonds.
Giovio, Imprese, London, 1585, Cv^v

diamond: ˚Three ˚diamonds.
Giovio, Imprese, London, 1585, Cviii^r

diamond: A ˚diamond between ˚three ˚feathers, ˚green,
˚white and ˚red.
Giovio, Imprese, London, 1585, Cviii^r

diamond: A ˚falcon grasping ˚diamonds in its ˚talons.
Giovio, Imprese, London, 1585, Cviii^r

dog: An ˚iron ˚dog's ˚collar with ˚spikes.
Giovio, Imprese, London, 1585, Dv^v

dragon: An ˚elephant attacked by a ˚dragon.

Giovio, Imprese, London, 1585, Eiiii^v

duck: A ˚duck.
Giovio, Imprese, London, 1585, Ciii^v

dung: An ˚armelin, or ˚ermine surrounded by a ˚ring of
˚dung.
Giovio, Imprese, London, 1585, Cv^r

eagle: An ˚eagle holding a ˚crown in its ˚beak.
Giovio, Imprese, London, 1585, Diiii^r

ear: ˚Five ˚ears of ˚corn, ˚wheat.
Giovio, Imprese, London, 1585, Fv^r

eclipse: The ˚moon, ˚eclipsed.
Giovio, Imprese, London, 1585, Dii^v

eclipse: The ˚sun, ˚eclipsed by the ˚moon.
Giovio, Imprese, London, 1585, Gi^v

egg: Two ˚ostriches look at their ˚eggs, ˚hatched by
the ˚rays from their ˚eyes.
Giovio, Imprese, London, 1585, Eviii^r

element: The ˚spheres of the ˚four ˚elements.
Giovio, Imprese, London, 1585, Fvi^v

elephant: An ˚elephant attacked by a ˚dragon.
Giovio, Imprese, London, 1585, Eiiii^v

emperor: A ˚triumphal ˚chariot, drawn by ˚five ˚white
˚horses, ˚emperor within, a ˚slave holding ˚laurel
˚garland.
Giovio, Imprese, London, 1585, Gi^r

ermine: An ˚armelin, or ˚ermine surrounded by a ˚ring
of ˚dung.
Giovio, Imprese, London, 1585, Cv^r

eye: Two ˚ostriches look at their ˚eggs, ˚hatched by
the ˚rays from their ˚eyes.
Giovio, Imprese, London, 1585, Eviii^r

faith: ˚Mount ˚Olympus with the ˚altar of ˚faith.
Giovio, Imprese, London, 1585, Giiii^r

falcon: A ˚falcon grasping ˚diamonds in its ˚talons.
Giovio, Imprese, London, 1585, Cviii^r

falcon: A ˚falcon holding in her ˚talons the
˚counterweight of a ˚clock.
Giovio, Imprese, London, 1585, Gi^r

farrier: A ˚harness used by ˚farrier to ˚shoe wild
˚horses.
Giovio, Imprese, London, 1585, Fi^v

feather: A ˚diamond between ˚three ˚feathers, ˚green,
˚white and ˚red.
Giovio, Imprese, London, 1585, Cviii^r

fertile: The slopes of the ˚volcano, ˚Mount ˚Aetna, are
covered with ˚snow, ˚burnt ˚stones, and ˚fertile
˚fields.
Giovio, Imprese, London, 1585, Fiiii^r

field: The slopes of the ˚volcano, ˚Mount ˚Aetna, are
covered with ˚snow, ˚burnt ˚stones, and ˚fertile
˚fields.
Giovio, Imprese, London, 1585, Fiiii^r

field² = heraldic

field²: Many ˚black ˚numbers scattered in a ˚field² or
˚border.
Giovio, Imprese, London, 1585, Ejii^v

field²: A ˚griffin ˚argent in a ˚field² ˚gueles.
Giovio, Imprese, London, 1585, Evi^r

field²: The ˚sun, ˚or, surrounded by thick ˚clouds in a
˚field², ˚azure.
Giovio, Imprese, London, 1585, Fi^r

field²: A ˚lion ˚rampant in a ˚field² ˚argent, all sown
with ˚buckles.
Giovio, Imprese, London, 1585, Fi^v

field²: ˚Quinces, ˚or, in a ˚field², ˚gueles.
Giovio, Imprese, London, 1585, Fviii^r

field²: A ˚lion ˚rampant in a ˚field² ˚gueles holding a
˚sword in his ˚paw.
Giovio, Imprese, London, 1585, Gv^v

fig-tree: A block of ˚marble split by a ˚fig-tree.
Giovio, Imprese, London, 1585, Gv^r

fire: A ˚salamander in a ˚fire.
Giovio, Imprese, London, 1585, Cii^r

fire: A ˚helmeted ˚lion sitting on a ˚fire.
Giovio, Imprese, London, 1585, Cvi^v

fire: A ˚vesture or ˚garment in the midst of a ˚fire.
Giovio, Imprese, London, 1585, Dvii^v

fire: A ˚hand burning in ˚fire on an ˚altar.
Giovio, Imprese, London, 1585, Dvii^v

fire: ˚Gold in a ˚furnace ˚fire.
Giovio, Imprese, London, 1585, Ei^v

fire: A large ˚chimney with a ˚fire within.
Giovio, Imprese, London, 1585, Fv^v

fire: The ˚temple of ˚Juno ˚Lucina and within, an ˚altar with a ˚fire.
Giovio, Imprese, London, 1585, Fvi^r

firebrand: A ˚firebrand and ˚bucket of ˚water.
Giovio, Imprese, London, 1585, Giiii^v

five: ˚Five ˚ears of ˚corn, ˚wheat.
Giovio, Imprese, London, 1585, Fv^r

five: A ˚triumphal ˚chariot, drawn by ˚five ˚white ˚horses, ˚emperor within, a ˚slave holding ˚laurel ˚garland.
Giovio, Imprese, London, 1585, Gi^r

flame: A ˚closed ˚account ˚book with ˚flames rising from margins, inscribed ˚"1485".
Giovio, Imprese, London, 1585, Cv^v

flame: ˚Billets of ˚green ˚wood stacked; ˚smoke and ˚flame issuing from within.
Giovio, Imprese, London, 1585, Cviii^v

flame: The ˚sun with ˚beams shining through a ˚crystal ˚lens, producing ˚flames, all set in a ˚white ˚hood.
Giovio, Imprese, London, 1585, Di^r

flame: A ˚metal ˚globe containing ˚flames issuing through ˚apertures.
Giovio, Imprese, London, 1585, Eii^r

fountain: A ˚fountain surrounded by ˚toads and ˚snakes; a ˚unicorn puts its ˚horn in the ˚water.
Giovio, Imprese, London, 1585, Dviii^v

four: The ˚spheres of the ˚four ˚elements.
Giovio, Imprese, London, 1585, Fvi^v

four: A ˚round ˚shield, ˚fringed; ˚four ˚circles, one at each side, bound by a ˚laurel ˚wreath. In each circle an ˚impresa.
Giovio, Imprese, London, 1585, Giiii^r

fox: A ˚fox with bared ˚teeth.
Giovio, Imprese, London, 1585, Hi^v

fringed: A ˚round ˚shield, ˚fringed; ˚four ˚circles, one at each side, bound by a ˚laurel ˚wreath. In each circle an ˚impresa.
Giovio, Imprese, London, 1585, Giiii^r

fruit: A ˚peach-tree laden with ˚fruit.
Giovio, Imprese, London, 1585, Gviii^v

full: A ˚full ˚moon.
Giovio, Imprese, London, 1585, Cii^v

furnace: ˚Gold in a ˚furnace ˚fire.
Giovio, Imprese, London, 1585, Ei^v

furnace: A ˚furnace ˚testing ˚gold.
Giovio, Imprese, London, 1585, Giiii^r

gander: A ˚gander among ˚swans.
Giovio, Imprese, London, 1585, Ei^r

garland: A ˚triumphal ˚chariot, drawn by ˚five ˚white ˚horses, ˚emperor within, a ˚slave holding ˚laurel ˚garland.
Giovio, Imprese, London, 1585, Gi^r

garment [= vesture]: A ˚vesture or ˚garment in the midst of a ˚fire.
Giovio, Imprese, London, 1585, Dvii^v

globe: A ˚metal ˚globe containing ˚flames issuing through ˚apertures.
Giovio, Imprese, London, 1585, Eii^r

god: The ˚god ˚Terminus.
Giovio, Imprese, London, 1585, Gvii^r

gold: ˚Gold ˚candleflyes[= ˚moths] dispersed.
Giovio, Imprese, London, 1585, Biiii^v

gold: ˚Gold in a ˚furnace ˚fire.
Giovio, Imprese, London, 1585, Ei^v

gold: A ˚furnace ˚testing ˚gold.
Giovio, Imprese, London, 1585, Giiii^r

golden: A ˚golden ˚bough.

Giovio, Imprese, London, 1585, Diiii^r

graft: A ˚tree with ˚grafts.
Giovio, Imprese, London, 1585, Gviii^r

green: A bush of ˚green ˚mallows.
Giovio, Imprese, London, 1585, Ciii^v

green: A ˚diamond between ˚three ˚feathers, ˚green, ˚white and ˚red.
Giovio, Imprese, London, 1585, Cviii^r

green: ˚Billets of ˚green ˚wood stacked; ˚smoke and ˚flame issuing from within.
Giovio, Imprese, London, 1585, Cviii^v

green: A clear ˚sky; upon a calm ˚sea a ˚nest with birds looking out; ˚halcyons are ˚azure, ˚red, ˚white, ˚green, ˚yellow.
Giovio, Imprese, London, 1585, Ev^r

greyhound: A ˚mastiff or ˚greyhound crouching under a ˚pine ˚tree.
Giovio, Imprese, London, 1585, Cvi^r

griffin: A ˚griffin ˚argent in a ˚field[2] ˚gueles.
Giovio, Imprese, London, 1585, Evj^r

gueles: A ˚griffin ˚argent in a ˚field[2] ˚gueles.
Giovio, Imprese, London, 1585, Evi^r

gueles: ˚Quinces, ˚or, in a ˚field[2], ˚gueles.
Giovio, Imprese, London, 1585, Fviii^r

gueles: A ˚lion ˚rampant in a ˚field[2] ˚gueles holding a ˚sword in his ˚paw.
Giovio, Imprese, London, 1585, Gv^v

hail: A ˚heron with the ˚sun above and ˚clouds below; ˚marsh and ˚sedge; possibly ˚rain and ˚hail falling.
Giovio, Imprese, London, 1585, Dvii^r

halcyon: A clear ˚sky; upon a calm ˚sea a ˚nest with birds looking out; ˚halcyons are ˚azure, ˚red, ˚white, ˚green, ˚yellow.
Giovio, Imprese, London, 1585, Ev^r

hand: A spiked ˚iron ˚collar grasped by ˚two ˚hands pierced by the ˚spikes; in the middle of the collar, a ˚rose.
Giovio, Imprese, London, 1585, Dv^v

hand: A ˚hand burning in ˚fire on an ˚altar.
Giovio, Imprese, London, 1585, Dvii^v

harness: A ˚harness used by ˚farrier to ˚shoe wild ˚horses.
Giovio, Imprese, London, 1585, Fi^v

hart: A ˚winged ˚hart.
Giovio, Imprese, London, 1585, Biiii^r

hart: A ˚winged ˚hart.
Giovio, Imprese, London, 1585, Biiii^r

hatch: Two ˚ostriches look at their ˚eggs, ˚hatched by the ˚rays from their ˚eyes.
Giovio, Imprese, London, 1585, Eviii^r

heaven: ˚Atlas bearing the ˚heavens with the ˚zodiac and ˚signs.
Giovio, Imprese, London, 1585, Giiii^r

hedgehog: A ˚hedgehog ˚crowned.
Giovio, Imprese, London, 1585, Cii^r

helmet: A ˚helmeted ˚lion sitting on a ˚fire.
Giovio, Imprese, London, 1585, Cvi^v

heron: A ˚heron with the ˚sun above and ˚clouds below; ˚marsh and ˚sedge; possibly ˚rain and ˚hail falling.
Giovio, Imprese, London, 1585, Dvii^r

hive: A ˚hive of ˚bees with ˚honey.
Giovio, Imprese, London, 1585, Gvii^r

honey: A ˚hive of ˚bees with ˚honey.
Giovio, Imprese, London, 1585, Gvii^r

hood: The ˚sun with ˚beams shining through a ˚crystal ˚lens, producing ˚flames, all set in a ˚white ˚hood.
Giovio, Imprese, London, 1585, Di^r

horn: A ˚fountain surrounded by ˚toads and ˚snakes; a ˚unicorn puts its ˚horn in the ˚water.
Giovio, Imprese, London, 1585, Dviii^v

horse: A ˚harness used by ˚farrier to ˚shoe wild ˚horses.
Giovio, Imprese, London, 1585, Fi^v

horse: A ˚triumphal ˚chariot, drawn by ˚five ˚white ˚horses, ˚emperor within, a ˚slave holding ˚laurel

˚garland.
Giovio, Imprese, London, 1585, Gi^r
horseback: ˚St. George on ˚horseback in a ˚white
˚shield, parted with a ˚red ˚cross.
Giovio, Imprese, London, 1585, Ci^v
horseshoe: An ˚ostrich devouring a ˚horseshoe ˚nail.
Giovio, Imprese, London, 1585, Evi^v
impresa: A ˚round ˚shield, ˚fringed; ˚four ˚circles, one
at each side, bound by a ˚laurel ˚wreath. In each
circle an ˚impresa.
Giovio, Imprese, London, 1585, Giiii^r
iron: An ˚iron ˚dog's ˚collar with ˚spikes.
Giovio, Imprese, London, 1585, Dv^v
iron: A spiked ˚iron ˚collar grasped by ˚two ˚hands
pierced by the ˚spikes; in the middle of the collar, a
˚rose.
Giovio, Imprese, London, 1585, Dv^v
javelin: A ˚bundle of ˚javelins.
Giovio, Imprese, London, 1585, Fiii^r
kneel: A ˚kneeling ˚camel.
Giovio, Imprese, London, 1585, Gi^v
knot: The ˚Gordian ˚knot.
Giovio, Imprese, London, 1585, Ciii^r
lamb: A ˚wolf with ˚bloody ˚lamb looking back at ˚two
˚mastiffs.
Giovio, Imprese, London, 1585, Hii^r
laurel: A ˚triumphal ˚chariot, drawn by ˚five ˚white
˚horses, ˚emperor within, a ˚slave holding ˚laurel
˚garland.
Giovio, Imprese, London, 1585, Gi^r
laurel: A ˚round ˚shield, ˚fringed; ˚four ˚circles, one at
each side, bound by a ˚laurel ˚wreath. In each circle
an ˚impresa.
Giovio, Imprese, London, 1585, Giiii^r
laurel-tree: A ˚laurel-tree between ˚two ˚lions.
Giovio, Imprese, London, 1585, Bv^v
laurel-tree: A ˚laurel-tree with ˚branches cut off; one
˚twig grows to a great height.
Giovio, Imprese, London, 1585, Giiii^r
left: A ˚crane holds in his ˚left ˚claw a ˚stone.
Giovio, Imprese, London, 1585, Fiii^r
lens: The ˚sun with ˚beams shining through a ˚crystal
˚lens, producing ˚flames, all set in a ˚white ˚hood.
Giovio, Imprese, London, 1585, Di^r
lightning: The ˚mountain ˚Chimera or ˚Acroceraunia
struck by ˚lightning.
Giovio, Imprese, London, 1585, Biiii^r
lightning: ˚Jupiter's ˚lightning.
Giovio, Imprese, London, 1585, Eiiii^r
lightning: ˚Jupiter's ˚triple forked ˚lightning.
Giovio, Imprese, London, 1585, Gii^v
lion: A ˚laurel-tree between ˚two ˚lions.
Giovio, Imprese, London, 1585, Bv^v
lion: A ˚helmeted ˚lion sitting on a ˚fire.
Giovio, Imprese, London, 1585, Cvi^v
lion: A ˚lion ˚rampant in a ˚field^2 ˚argent, all sown with
˚buckles.
Giovio, Imprese, London, 1585, Fi^v
lion: A ˚lion ˚rampant in a ˚field^2 ˚gueles holding a
˚sword in his ˚paw.
Giovio, Imprese, London, 1585, Gv^v
mallow: A bush of ˚green ˚mallows.
Giovio, Imprese, London, 1585, Ciii^v
man: A ˚wild ˚man with a ˚club in one hand.
Giovio, Imprese, London, 1585, Fi^v
marble: A ˚marble ˚block or ˚quadret with an iron ˚stile
inset, opposite the ˚sun.
Giovio, Imprese, London, 1585, Eii^r
marble: A ˚palm-tree weighted down with a ˚marble
˚block tied to the top.
Giovio, Imprese, London, 1585, Eii^v
marble: A block of ˚marble split by a ˚fig-tree.
Giovio, Imprese, London, 1585, Gv^r
marsh: A ˚heron with the ˚sun above and ˚clouds below;
˚marsh and ˚sedge; possibly ˚rain and ˚hail falling.

Giovio, Imprese, London, 1585, Dvii^r
mastiff: A ˚mastiff or ˚greyhound crouching under a
˚pine ˚tree.
Giovio, Imprese, London, 1585, Cvi^r
mastiff: A ˚wolf with ˚bloody ˚lamb looking back at
˚two ˚mastiffs.
Giovio, Imprese, London, 1585, Hii^r
metal: A ˚metal ˚globe containing ˚flames issuing
through ˚apertures.
Giovio, Imprese, London, 1585, Eii^r
millet: ˚Two ˚bundles of ˚ripe ˚millet.
Giovio, Imprese, London, 1585, Fv^r
moon: The ˚crescent ˚moon.
Giovio, Imprese, London, 1585, Cii^v
moon: A ˚full ˚moon.
Giovio, Imprese, London, 1585, Cii^v
moon: The ˚moon, ˚eclipsed.
Giovio, Imprese, London, 1585, Dii^v
moon: The ˚sun, ˚eclipsed by the ˚moon.
Giovio, Imprese, London, 1585, Gi^v
moth [= candleflye]: ˚Gold ˚candleflyes [= ˚moths]
dispersed.
Giovio, Imprese, London, 1585, Biiii^v
mountain: The ˚mountain ˚Chimera or ˚Acroceraunia
struck by ˚lightning.
Giovio, Imprese, London, 1585, Biiii^r
mountain: A ˚mountain of ˚diamonds.
Giovio, Imprese, London, 1585, Cv^v
mulberry-tree: A ˚mulberry-tree.
Giovio, Imprese, London, 1585, Cvi^v
nail: An ˚ostrich devouring a ˚horseshoe ˚nail.
Giovio, Imprese, London, 1585, Evi^v
needle: A clear ˚azure ˚sky with ˚stars above a
˚compass ˚needle and compass, set upon a ˚sea ˚card
or ˚chart.
Giovio, Imprese, London, 1585, Ev^v
nest: A clear ˚sky; upon a calm ˚sea a ˚nest with birds
looking out; ˚halcyons are ˚azure, ˚red, ˚white,
˚green, ˚yellow.
Giovio, Imprese, London, 1585, Ev^r
number: Many ˚black ˚numbers scattered in a ˚field^2 or
˚border.
Giovio, Imprese, London, 1585, Eiii^v
one: A ˚pot full of ˚black ˚stones and ˚one ˚white
stone.
Giovio, Imprese, London, 1585, Gvi^v
open: An ˚open ˚book.
Giovio, Imprese, London, 1585, Ciiii^v
or: The ˚sun, ˚or, surrounded by thick ˚clouds in a
˚field^2, ˚azure.
Giovio, Imprese, London, 1585, Fi^r
or: ˚Quinces, ˚or, in a ˚field^2, ˚gueles.
Giovio, Imprese, London, 1585, Fviii^r
ostrich: An ˚ostrich devouring a ˚horseshoe ˚nail.
Giovio, Imprese, London, 1585, Evi^v
ostrich: An ˚ostrich ˚cursant.
Giovio, Imprese, London, 1585, Evii^r
ostrich: Two ˚ostriches look at their ˚eggs, ˚hatched by
the ˚rays from their ˚eyes.
Giovio, Imprese, London, 1585, Eviii^r
painting: ˚Apelles ˚painting.
Giovio, Imprese, London, 1585, Gvii^r
palm: A ˚palm branch wreathed with ˚cypress.
Giovio, Imprese, London, 1585, Dvi^v
palm-tree: A ˚palm-tree weighted down with a ˚marble
˚block tied to the top.
Giovio, Imprese, London, 1585, Eii^v
paper: A ˚scroll of ˚white ˚paper.
Giovio, Imprese, London, 1585, Gii^v
paw: A ˚lion ˚rampant in a ˚field^2 ˚gueles holding a
˚sword in his ˚paw.
Giovio, Imprese, London, 1585, Gv^v
peach-tree: A ˚peach-tree laden with ˚fruit.
Giovio, Imprese, London, 1585, Gviii^v
peahen: A ˚peahen sheltering under her ˚wings ˚six of

her °young[1].
   Giovio, Imprese, London, 1585, Gvi^r
pillar: The °pillars of °Hercules.
   Giovio, Imprese, London, 1585, Bviii^r
pine: A °mastiff or °greyhound crouching under a °pine
   °tree.
   Giovio, Imprese, London, 1585, Cvi^r
plowshare: A °plowshare.
   Giovio, Imprese, London, 1585, Gviii^v
pot: A °pot full of °black °stones and °one °white stone.
   Giovio, Imprese, London, 1585, Gvi^v
quadret [= block]: A °marble °block or °quadret with an
   iron °stile inset, opposite the °sun.
   Giovio, Imprese, London, 1585, Eii^r
quince: °Quinces, °or, in a °field[2], °gueles.
   Giovio, Imprese, London, 1585, Fviii^r
rain: A °heron with the °sun above and °clouds below;
   °marsh and °sedge; possibly °rain and °hail falling.
   Giovio, Imprese, London, 1585, Dvii^r
rampant: A °lion °rampant in a °field[2] °argent, all sown
   with °buckles.
   Giovio, Imprese, London, 1585, Fi^v
rampant: A °lion °rampant in a °field[2] °gueles holding a
   °sword in his °paw.
   Giovio, Imprese, London, 1585, Gv^v
rattle: A °rattle.
   Giovio, Imprese, London, 1585, Fviii^r
raven: A °raven.
   Giovio, Imprese, London, 1585, Gv^v
ray: Two °ostriches look at their °eggs, °hatched by the
   °rays from their °eyes.
   Giovio, Imprese, London, 1585, Eviii^r
red: °St. George on °horseback in a °white °shield,
   parted with a °red °cross.
   Giovio, Imprese, London, 1585, Ci^v
red: A °diamond between °three °feathers, °green, °white
   and °red.
   Giovio, Imprese, London, 1585, Cviii^r
red: A clear °sky; upon a calm °sea a °nest with birds
   looking out; °halcyons are °azure, °red, °white,
   °green, °yellow.
   Giovio, Imprese, London, 1585, Ev^r
rhinoceros: A °rhinoceros.
   Giovio, Imprese, London, 1585, Diii^r
ring: An °armelin, or °ermine surrounded by a °ring of
   °dung.
   Giovio, Imprese, London, 1585, Cv^r
ripe: °Two °bundles of °ripe °millet.
   Giovio, Imprese, London, 1585, Fv^r
ripe: °Two °sheaves of °ripe °corn, °wheat.
   Giovio, Imprese, London, 1585, Fvi^r
river: A °camel disturbing the °river °water.
   Giovio, Imprese, London, 1585, Dv^v
river: °Bullrushes in a °river.
   Giovio, Imprese, London, 1585, Dviii^r
rock: °Rocks in a °turbulent °sea.
   Giovio, Imprese, London, 1585, Fiiii^v
rose: A spiked °iron °collar grasped by °two °hands
   pierced by the °spikes; in the middle of the collar, a
   °rose.
   Giovio, Imprese, London, 1585, Dv^v
round: A °round °shield, °fringed; °four °circles, one at
   each side, bound by a °laurel °wreath. In each circle
   an °impresa.
   Giovio, Imprese, London, 1585, Giiii^r
saint: °Three °saints' °diadems linked, with °"valer" in
   the middle.
   Giovio, Imprese, London, 1585, Cv^v
salamander: A °salamander in a °fire.
   Giovio, Imprese, London, 1585, Cii^r
scale: A °balance or °scales.
   Giovio, Imprese, London, 1585, Fiii^v
scorpion: A °scorpion.
   Giovio, Imprese, London, 1585, Fvii^r
scroll: A °scroll of °white °paper.

   Giovio, Imprese, London, 1585, Gii^v
sea: A clear °sky; upon a calm °sea a °nest with birds
   looking out; °halcyons are °azure, °red, °white,
   °green, °yellow.
   Giovio, Imprese, London, 1585, Ev^r
sea: A clear °azure °sky with °stars above a °compass
   °needle and compass, set upon a °sea °card or
   °chart.
   Giovio, Imprese, London, 1585, Ev^v
sea: °Rocks in a °turbulent °sea.
   Giovio, Imprese, London, 1585, Fiiii^v
sedge: A °heron with the °sun above and °clouds below;
   °marsh and °sedge; possibly °rain and °hail falling.
   Giovio, Imprese, London, 1585, Dvii^r
sheaf: °Two °sheaves of °ripe °corn, °wheat.
   Giovio, Imprese, London, 1585, Fvi^r
shield: °St. George on °horseback in a °white °shield,
   parted with a °red °cross.
   Giovio, Imprese, London, 1585, Ci^v
shield: A °Spartan °shield.
   Giovio, Imprese, London, 1585, Eviii^r
shield: A °round °shield, °fringed; °four °circles, one at
   each side, bound by a °laurel °wreath. In each
   circle an °impresa.
   Giovio, Imprese, London, 1585, Giiii^r
ship: The °stern of a °ship.
   Giovio, Imprese, London, 1585, Bvi^r
shoe: A °harness used by °farrier to °shoe wild °horses.
   Giovio, Imprese, London, 1585, Fi^v
sign: °Atlas bearing the °heavens with the °zodiac and
   °signs.
   Giovio, Imprese, London, 1585, Giii^r
six: A °peahen sheltering under her °wings °six of her
   °young[1].
   Giovio, Imprese, London, 1585, Gvi^r
sky: A clear °sky; upon a calm °sea a °nest with birds
   looking out; °halcyons are °azure, °red, °white,
   °green, °yellow.
   Giovio, Imprese, London, 1585, Ev^r
sky: A clear °azure °sky with °stars above a °compass
   °needle and compass, set upon a °sea °card or
   °chart.
   Giovio, Imprese, London, 1585, Ev^v
slave: A °triumphal °chariot, drawn by °five °white
   °horses, °emperor within, a °slave holding °laurel
   °garland.
   Giovio, Imprese, London, 1585, Gi^r
smoke: °Billets of °green °wood stacked; °smoke and
   °flame issuing from within.
   Giovio, Imprese, London, 1585, Cviii^v
snake: A °fountain surrounded by °toads and °snakes; a
   °unicorn puts its °horn in the °water.
   Giovio, Imprese, London, 1585, Dviii^r
snow: The slopes of the °volcano, °Mount °Aetna, are
   covered with °snow, °burnt °stones, and °fertile
   °fields.
   Giovio, Imprese, London, 1585, Fiiii^r
sphere: The °spheres of the °four °elements.
   Giovio, Imprese, London, 1585, Fvi^v
spike: An °iron °dog's °collar with °spikes.
   Giovio, Imprese, London, 1585, Dv^v
spike: A spiked °iron °collar grasped by °two °hands
   pierced by the °spikes; in the middle of the collar,
   a °rose.
   Giovio, Imprese, London, 1585, Dv^v
star: A clear °azure °sky with °stars above a °compass
   °needle and compass, set upon a °sea °card or
   °chart.
   Giovio, Imprese, London, 1585, Ev^v
stern: The °stern of a °ship.
   Giovio, Imprese, London, 1585, Bvi^r
stile: A °marble °block or °quadret with an iron °stile
   inset, opposite the °sun.
   Giovio, Imprese, London, 1585, Eii^r
stone: A °crane holds in his °left °claw a °stone.

stone: The ˚slopes of the ˚volcano, ˚Mount ˚Aetna, are covered with ˚snow, ˚burnt ˚stones, and ˚fertile ˚fields.
   Giovio, Imprese, London, 1585, Fiii[r]

stone: A ˚pot full of ˚black ˚stones and ˚one ˚white stone.
   Giovio, Imprese, London, 1585, Gvi[v]

stone: A ˚pot full of ˚black ˚stones and ˚one ˚white stone.
   Giovio, Imprese, London, 1585, Gvi[v]

sun: The ˚sun with ˚beams shining through a ˚crystal ˚lens, producing ˚flames, all set in a ˚white ˚hood.
   Giovio, Imprese, London, 1585, Di[r]

sun: A ˚heron with the ˚sun above and ˚clouds below; ˚marsh and ˚sedge; possibly ˚rain and ˚hail falling.
   Giovio, Imprese, London, 1585, Dvii[r]

sun: A ˚marble ˚block or ˚quadret with an iron ˚stile inset, opposite the ˚sun.
   Giovio, Imprese, London, 1585, Eii[r]

sun: The ˚sun, or, surrounded by thick ˚clouds in a ˚field^2, ˚azure.
   Giovio, Imprese, London, 1585, Fi[r]

sun: The ˚sun, ˚eclipsed by the ˚moon.
   Giovio, Imprese, London, 1585, Gi[v]

swan: A ˚gander among ˚swans.
   Giovio, Imprese, London, 1585, Ei[r]

sword: A ˚lion ˚rampant in a ˚field^2 ˚gueles holding a ˚sword in his ˚paw.
   Giovio, Imprese, London, 1585, Gv[v]

tablet: A ˚white ˚tablet.
   Giovio, Imprese, London, 1585, Gii[r]

talon: A ˚falcon grasping ˚diamonds in its ˚talons.
   Giovio, Imprese, London, 1585, Cviii[r]

talon: A ˚falcon holding in her ˚talons the ˚counterweight of a ˚clock.
   Giovio, Imprese, London, 1585, Gi[r]

target: An ˚arrow hits the ˚white[1] of a ˚target.
   Giovio, Imprese, London, 1585, Gii[r]

temple: The ˚temple of ˚Juno ˚Lucina and within, an ˚altar with a ˚fire.
   Giovio, Imprese, London, 1585, Fvi[r]

temple: The ˚temple of ˚Diana at ˚Ephesus.
   Giovio, Imprese, London, 1585, Fvii[v]

test: A ˚furnace ˚testing ˚gold.
   Giovio, Imprese, London, 1585, Giiii[r]

three: ˚Three ˚saints' ˚diadems linked, with ˚"valer" in the middle.
   Giovio, Imprese, London, 1585, Cv[v]

three: ˚Three ˚diamonds.
   Giovio, Imprese, London, 1585, Cviii[r]

three: A ˚diamond between ˚three ˚feathers, ˚green, ˚white and ˚red.
   Giovio, Imprese, London, 1585, Cviii[r]

tinderbox: A ˚tinderbox.
   Giovio, Imprese, London, 1585, Bviii[r]

toad: A ˚fountain surrounded by ˚toads and ˚snakes; a ˚unicorn puts its ˚horn in the ˚water.
   Giovio, Imprese, London, 1585, Dviii[v]

tooth: A ˚fox with bared ˚teeth.
   Giovio, Imprese, London, 1585, Hi[v]

touchstone: A ˚touchstone.
   Giovio, Imprese, London, 1585, Dvi[v]

tree: A ˚mastiff or ˚greyhound crouching under a ˚pine ˚tree.
   Giovio, Imprese, London, 1585, Cvi[r]

tree: A ˚tree with ˚grafts.
   Giovio, Imprese, London, 1585, Gviii[r]

triangular: A ˚triangular ˚candlestick.
   Giovio, Imprese, London, 1585, Giii[v]

triple-forked: ˚Jupiter's ˚triple forked ˚lightning.
   Giovio, Imprese, London, 1585, Gii[v]

triumphal: A ˚triumphal ˚chariot, drawn by ˚five ˚white ˚horses, ˚emperor within, a ˚slave holding ˚laurel ˚garland.

Giovio, Imprese, London, 1585, Gi[r]

turbulent: ˚Rocks in a ˚turbulent ˚sea.
   Giovio, Imprese, London, 1585, Fiiii[v]

twelve: The ˚descent of the ˚Holy ˚Ghost upon the ˚twelve ˚apostles in an ˚agate.
   Giovio, Imprese, London, 1585, Bvii[r]

twig: A ˚laurel-tree with ˚branches cut off; one ˚twig grows to a great height.
   Giovio, Imprese, London, 1585, Giiii[r]

two: A ˚laurel-tree between ˚two ˚lions.
   Giovio, Imprese, London, 1585, Bv[v]

two: A spiked ˚iron ˚collar grasped by ˚two ˚hands pierced by the ˚spikes; in the middle of the collar, a ˚rose.
   Giovio, Imprese, London, 1585, Dv[v]

two: ˚Two ˚bundles of ˚ripe ˚millet.
   Giovio, Imprese, London, 1585, Fv[r]

two: ˚Two ˚sheaves of ˚ripe ˚corn, ˚wheat.
   Giovio, Imprese, London, 1585, Fvi[r]

two: A ˚wolf with ˚bloody ˚lamb looking back at ˚two ˚mastiffs.
   Giovio, Imprese, London, 1585, Hii[r]

udder: A ˚wolf with distended ˚udder.
   Giovio, Imprese, London, 1585, Gv[v]

unicorn: A ˚fountain surrounded by ˚toads and ˚snakes; a ˚unicorn puts its ˚horn in the ˚water.
   Giovio, Imprese, London, 1585, Dviii[v]

urn(?) [= vessel]: An antique ˚vessel, or ˚urn(?).
   Giovio, Imprese, London, 1585, Dvi[v]

vessel [= urn(?)]: An antique ˚vessel, or ˚urn(?).
   Giovio, Imprese, London, 1585, Dvi[v]

vesture [= garment]: A ˚vesture or ˚garment in the midst of a ˚fire.
   Giovio, Imprese, London, 1585, Dvii[v]

volcano: The ˚slopes of the ˚volcano, ˚Mount ˚Aetna, are covered with ˚snow, ˚burnt ˚stones, and ˚fertile ˚fields.
   Giovio, Imprese, London, 1585, Fiiii[r]

water: A ˚wheel with ˚buckets for drawing ˚water.
   Giovio, Imprese, London, 1585, Ciiii[r]

water: A ˚camel disturbing the ˚river ˚water.
   Giovio, Imprese, London, 1585, Dv[v]

water: A ˚fountain surrounded by ˚toads and ˚snakes; a ˚unicorn puts its ˚horn in the ˚water.
   Giovio, Imprese, London, 1585, Dviii[v]

water: A ˚firebrand and ˚bucket of ˚water.
   Giovio, Imprese, London, 1585, Giiii[v]

wheat [= corn]: ˚Five ˚ears of ˚corn, ˚wheat.
   Giovio, Imprese, London, 1585, Fv[r]

wheat [= corn]: ˚Two ˚sheaves of ˚ripe ˚corn, ˚wheat.
   Giovio, Imprese, London, 1585, Fvi[r]

wheel: A ˚wheel with ˚buckets for drawing ˚water.
   Giovio, Imprese, London, 1585, Ciiii[r]

wheel: A ˚wheel.
   Giovio, Imprese, London, 1585, Eviii[v]

white: A ˚white wax ˚candle, worn in a cap.
   Giovio, Imprese, London, 1585, Bvi[v]

white: ˚St. George on ˚horseback in a ˚white ˚shield, parted with a ˚red ˚cross.
   Giovio, Imprese, London, 1585, Ci[v]

white: A ˚diamond between ˚three ˚feathers, ˚green, ˚white and ˚red.
   Giovio, Imprese, London, 1585, Cviii[r]

white: The ˚sun with ˚beams shining through a ˚crystal ˚lens, producing ˚flames, all set in a ˚white ˚hood.
   Giovio, Imprese, London, 1585, Di[r]

white: A clear ˚sky; upon a calm ˚sea a ˚nest with birds looking out; ˚halcyons are ˚azure, ˚red, ˚white, ˚green, ˚yellow.
   Giovio, Imprese, London, 1585, Ev[r]

white: A ˚triumphal ˚chariot, drawn by ˚five ˚white ˚horses, ˚emperor within, a ˚slave holding ˚laurel ˚garland.
   Giovio, Imprese, London, 1585, Gi[r]

white: A ˚white ˚tablet.

PROPER NOUN INDEX (PICTURE)

PICTURE INSCRIPTIONS

LATIN MOTTO INDEX

armatus: Unguibus et rostro, atque alis armatus in
  hostem.
  Giovio, Imprese, London, 1585, Evi^r
ars: Naturae non artis opus.
  Giovio, Imprese, London, 1585, Cv^v
astus: Simul astu et dentibus utor.
  Giovio, Imprese, London, 1585, Hi^v
aurum: Samnitico non capitur auro.
  Giovio, Imprese, London, 1585, Dvi^v
bonum: Pro bono malum.
  Giovio, Imprese, London, 1585, Gvii^r
bonus: Alterutra clarescere fama. Sive bonum, sive malum,
  fama est.
  Giovio, Imprese, London, 1585, Fvii^v
candidus: Aequabit nigras candida una dies.
  Giovio, Imprese, London, 1585, Gvi^v
candor: Candor illesus.
  Giovio, Imprese, London, 1585, Di^r
canis: Pavent oves, Timent canes, intrepidus maneo.
  Giovio, Imprese, London, 1585, Hii^r
capio: Samnitico non capitur auro.
  Giovio, Imprese, London, 1585, Dvi^v
caprificus: Ingentia marmora findit caprificus.
  Giovio, Imprese, London, 1585, Gv^r
cedo: Non cedit umbra soli.
  Giovio, Imprese, London, 1585, Eii^r
cedo: Vel Iovi cedere nescit.
  Giovio, Imprese, London, 1585, Gvii^r
cognosco: Probasti me Domine, et cognovisti.
  Giovio, Imprese, London, 1585, Ei^v
comes: Virtuti fortuna comes.
  Giovio, Imprese, London, 1585, Bv^r
comminus: Comminus et eminus.
  Giovio, Imprese, London, 1585, Cii^r
contemno: Contemnit tuta procellas.
  Giovio, Imprese, London, 1585, Gvi^r
coquo: Spiritus durissima coquit.
  Giovio, Imprese, London, 1585, Evi^v
crepito: Cum crepitat, sonora silent.
  Giovio, Imprese, London, 1585, Fviii^r
crocodilus: Crocodili lachrymae.
  Giovio, Imprese, London, 1585, Gii^r
currus: Servus curru portatur eodem.
  Giovio, Imprese, London, 1585, Gi^r
cursus: Cursum intendimus alis. [ironic attribution]
  Giovio, Imprese, London, 1585, Biiii^r
cursus: Si sursum non efferor alis, saltem cursu
  praetervehor omnes.
  Giovio, Imprese, London, 1585, Evii^r
defendo: Sauciat et defendit.
  Giovio, Imprese, London, 1585, Dv^v
degener: Virtutis trophaea novae non degener addet.
  Giovio, Imprese, London, 1585, Giiii^r
dens: Simul astu et dentibus utor.
  Giovio, Imprese, London, 1585, Hi^v
desum: Fortibus non deerunt.
  Giovio, Imprese, London, 1585, Fiii^r
desum: Fortibus non deerunt.
  Giovio, Imprese, London, 1585, Giiii^r
dicatus: Iunoni Lucinae dicatum.
  Giovio, Imprese, London, 1585, Fvi^r
dies: Aequabit nigras candida una dies.
  Giovio, Imprese, London, 1585, Gvi^v
dies: Nulla dies sine linea. [inferred]
  Giovio, Imprese, London, 1585, Gvii^r
distans: Distantia iungit.
  Giovio, Imprese, London, 1585, Fi^v
doceo: Officium natura docet.
  Giovio, Imprese, London, 1585, Fiii^r
dominus: Probasti me domine.
  Giovio, Imprese, London, 1585, Giiii^r
durus: Spiritus durissima coquit.
  Giovio, Imprese, London, 1585, Evi^v
eluctor: Hinc aliquando eluctabor.
  Giovio, Imprese, London, 1585, Dii^v

eminus: Comminus et eminus.
  Giovio, Imprese, London, 1585, Cii^r
emulus: Cum plena est, sit emula Solis.
  Giovio, Imprese, London, 1585, Cii^v
experior: Ingenio experior funera digna meo.
  Giovio, Imprese, London, 1585, Dvi^r
expio: Expiabit aut obruet.
  Giovio, Imprese, London, 1585, Eiiii^r
exuro: In viridi teneras exurit flamma medullas.
  Giovio, Imprese, London, 1585, Cviii^v
fallo: Prius mori quam fidem fallere.
  Giovio, Imprese, London, 1585, Dv^v
fama: Alterutra clarescere fama. Sive bonum, sive
  malum, fama est.
  Giovio, Imprese, London, 1585, Fvii^v
fatisco: Sustinet nec fatiscit.
  Giovio, Imprese, London, 1585, Giii^r
fatum: Fidem fati virtute sequemur.
  Giovio, Imprese, London, 1585, Diii^v
fatum: Votis subscribunt fata secundis.
  Giovio, Imprese, London, 1585, Gii^v
ferio: Feriunt summos fulmina montes.
  Giovio, Imprese, London, 1585, Biiii^r
fero: Natura dictante feror.
  Giovio, Imprese, London, 1585, Dvii^r
fides: Fidem fati virtute sequemur.
  Giovio, Imprese, London, 1585, Diii^v
fides: Prius mori quam fidem fallere.
  Giovio, Imprese, London, 1585, Dv^v
fides: Fides hoc uno, virtusque probantur.
  Giovio, Imprese, London, 1585, Dvi^v
flamma: In viridi teneras exurit flamma medullas.
  Giovio, Imprese, London, 1585, Cviii^v
flecto: Flectimur non frangimur undis.
  Giovio, Imprese, London, 1585, Dviii^r
foecunditas: Cum pudore laeta foecunditas.
  Giovio, Imprese, London, 1585, Gvi^r
foedo: Malo mori quam foedari.
  Giovio, Imprese, London, 1585, Cv^r
fortis: Fortia facere et pati Romanum est.
  Giovio, Imprese, London, 1585, Dvii^v
fortis: Fortibus non deerunt.
  Giovio, Imprese, London, 1585, Fiii^r
fortis: Fortibus non deerunt.
  Giovio, Imprese, London, 1585, Giiii^r
fortuna: Virtuti fortuna comes.
  Giovio, Imprese, London, 1585, Bv^r
fortuna: Melior fortuna notabit.
  Giovio, Imprese, London, 1585, Gii^r
fragrans: Fragrantia durant Herculea collecta manu.
  Giovio, Imprese, London, 1585, Fviii^r
frango: Flectimur non frangimur undis.
  Giovio, Imprese, London, 1585, Dviii^r
frango: Conantia frangere frangunt.
  Giovio, Imprese, London, 1585, Fiiii^v
fulmen: Feriunt summos fulmina montes.
  Giovio, Imprese, London, 1585, Biiii^r
funus: Ingenio experior funera digna meo.
  Giovio, Imprese, London, 1585, Dvi^r
generosus: Non deest generoso in pectore virtus.
  Giovio, Imprese, London, 1585, Gv^v
hostis: Rhinoceros nunquam victus ab hoste cedit.
  Giovio, Imprese, London, 1585, Diii^r
hostis: Unguibus et rostro, atque alis armatus in hostem.
  Giovio, Imprese, London, 1585, Evi^r
illesus: Candor illesus.
  Giovio, Imprese, London, 1585, Di^r
impune: Quietum nemo impune lacesset.
  Giovio, Imprese, London, 1585, Cvi^r
incertus: Incerta animi decreta resolvet.
  Giovio, Imprese, London, 1585, Gvii^r
inclinatus: Inclinata resurgit.
  Giovio, Imprese, London, 1585, Eii^v
ingenium: Ingenio experior funera digna meo.
  Giovio, Imprese, London, 1585, Dvi^r

ingratus: Totum adimit quo ingrata refulget.
　Giovio, Imprese, London, 1585, Gi^v
intrepidus: Pavent oves, Timent canes, intrepidus maneo.
　Giovio, Imprese, London, 1585, Hii^r
iungo: Distantia iungit.
　Giovio, Imprese, London, 1585, Fi^v
labor: Finiunt pariter renovantque labores.
　Giovio, Imprese, London, 1585, Fvi^r
lacesso: Quietum nemo impune lacesset.
　Giovio, Imprese, London, 1585, Cvi^r
lachryma: Crocodili lachrymae.
　Giovio, Imprese, London, 1585, Gii^r
laedo: Qui vivens laedit morte medetur.
　Giovio, Imprese, London, 1585, Fvii^r
linea: Nulla dies sine linea. [inferred]
　Giovio, Imprese, London, 1585, Gvii^r
locus: Loco et tempore. [later changed to: A lieu et temps.]
　Giovio, Imprese, London, 1585, Eii^r
maior: Natura maiora facit.
　Giovio, Imprese, London, 1585, Fiiii^r
malum: Pro bono malum.
　Giovio, Imprese, London, 1585, Gvii^r
malus: Alterutra clarescere fama. Sive bonum, sive malum, fama est.
　Giovio, Imprese, London, 1585, Fvii^v
manus: Fragrantia durant Herculea collecta manu.
　Giovio, Imprese, London, 1585, Fviii^r
marmor: Ingentia marmora findit caprificus.
　Giovio, Imprese, London, 1585, Gv^r
maximus: Hoc per se nihil est, sed si minimum addideris maximum fiet [=fieret].
　Giovio, Imprese, London, 1585, Eiii^v
medeor: Qui vivens laedit morte medetur.
　Giovio, Imprese, London, 1585, Fvii^r
medulla: In viridi teneras exurit flamma medullas.
　Giovio, Imprese, London, 1585, Cviii^v
merces: Erit altera merces.
　Giovio, Imprese, London, 1585, Dvi^v
mereo: Jupiter merentibus offert.
　Giovio, Imprese, London, 1585, Diiii^r
metus: Nec spe, nec metu.
　Giovio, Imprese, London, 1585, Giiii^r
minimus: Hoc per se nihil est, sed si minimum addideris maximum fiet [=fieret].
　Giovio, Imprese, London, 1585, Eiii^v
mitis: Mitem animum agresti sub tegmine servo.
　Giovio, Imprese, London, 1585, Fi^v
mons: Feriunt summos fulmina montes.
　Giovio, Imprese, London, 1585, Biiii^r
morior: Malo mori quam foedari.
　Giovio, Imprese, London, 1585, Cv^r
morior: Prius mori quam fidem fallere.
　Giovio, Imprese, London, 1585, Dv^v
mors: Qui vivens laedit morte medetur.
　Giovio, Imprese, London, 1585, Fvii^r
natura: Naturae non artis opus.
　Giovio, Imprese, London, 1585, Cv^v
natura: Natura dictante feror.
　Giovio, Imprese, London, 1585, Dvii^r
natura: Officium natura docet.
　Giovio, Imprese, London, 1585, Fiii^r
natura: Natura maiora facit.
　Giovio, Imprese, London, 1585, Fiiii^r
niger: Aequabit nigras candida una dies.
　Giovio, Imprese, London, 1585, Gvi^v
nihil: Hoc per se nihil est, sed si minimum addideris maximum fiet [=fieret].
　Giovio, Imprese, London, 1585, Eiii^v
noto: Melior fortuna notabit.
　Giovio, Imprese, London, 1585, Gii^r
nubilum: Obstantia nubila solvet.
　Giovio, Imprese, London, 1585, Fi^r
nutrisco: Mi nutrisco.
　Giovio, Imprese, London, 1585, Cii^r

nutrisco: Sina alienaque pignora nutrit.
　Giovio, Imprese, London, 1585, Gv^v
obruo: Expiabit aut obruet.
　Giovio, Imprese, London, 1585, Eiiii^r
obsto: Obstantia nubila solvet.
　Giovio, Imprese, London, 1585, Fi^r
obstrepo: Obstrepuit inter olores.
　Giovio, Imprese, London, 1585, Ei^r
offero: Jupiter merentibus offert.
　Giovio, Imprese, London, 1585, Diiii^r
officium: Officium natura docet.
　Giovio, Imprese, London, 1585, Fiii^r
olor: Obstrepuit inter olores.
　Giovio, Imprese, London, 1585, Ei^r
opus: Hoc opus.
　Giovio, Imprese, London, 1585, Bvi^r
opus: Naturae non artis opus.
　Giovio, Imprese, London, 1585, Cv^v
orbis: Donec totum impleat orbem.
　Giovio, Imprese, London, 1585, Cii^v
ovis: Pavent oves, Timent canes, intrepidus maneo.
　Giovio, Imprese, London, 1585, Hii^r
patior: Fortia facere et pati Romanum est.
　Giovio, Imprese, London, 1585, Dvii^v
paveo: Pavent oves, Timent canes, intrepidus maneo.
　Giovio, Imprese, London, 1585, Hii^r
pectus: Non deest generoso in pectore virtus.
　Giovio, Imprese, London, 1585, Gv^v
pello: Venena pello.
　Giovio, Imprese, London, 1585, Dviii^v
pertinax: Semper pertinax.
　Giovio, Imprese, London, 1585, Dvii^v
pignus: Sina alienaque pignora nutrit.
　Giovio, Imprese, London, 1585, Gv^v
plenus: Cum plena est, sit emula Solis.
　Giovio, Imprese, London, 1585, Cii^v
porto: Servus curru portatur eodem.
　Giovio, Imprese, London, 1585, Gi^r
probo: Fides hoc uno, virtusque probantur.
　Giovio, Imprese, London, 1585, Dvi^v
probo: Probasti me Domine, et cognovisti.
　Giovio, Imprese, London, 1585, Ei^v
probo: Probasti me domine.
　Giovio, Imprese, London, 1585, Giiii^r
procella: Contemnit tuta procellas.
　Giovio, Imprese, London, 1585, Gvi^r
proficio: Translata proficit arbos.
　Giovio, Imprese, London, 1585, Gviii^v
pudor: Cum pudore laeta foecunditas.
　Giovio, Imprese, London, 1585, Gvi^r
quietus: Quietum nemo impune lacesset.
　Giovio, Imprese, London, 1585, Cvi^r
recedo: Recedant vetera.
　Giovio, Imprese, London, 1585, Cv^v
refulgeo: Totum adimit quo ingrata refulget.
　Giovio, Imprese, London, 1585, Gi^v
renovo: Finiunt pariter renovantque labores.
　Giovio, Imprese, London, 1585, Fvi^r
resolvo: Incerta animi decreta resolvet.
　Giovio, Imprese, London, 1585, Gvii^r
rhinoceros: Rhinoceros nunquam victus ab hoste cedit.
　Giovio, Imprese, London, 1585, Diii^r
rostrum: Unguibus et rostro, atque alis armatus in hostem.
　Giovio, Imprese, London, 1585, Evi^r
saucio: Sauciat et defendit.
　Giovio, Imprese, London, 1585, Dv^v
sequor: Fidem fati virtute sequemur.
　Giovio, Imprese, London, 1585, Diii^v
servo: Servari et servare meum est.
　Giovio, Imprese, London, 1585, Fv^r
servus: Servus curru portatur eodem.
　Giovio, Imprese, London, 1585, Gi^r
silent: Cum crepitat, sonora silent.
　Giovio, Imprese, London, 1585, Fviii^r

PROPER NOUN INDEX (LATIN MOTTO)

FRENCH MOTTO INDEX

GERMAN MOTTO INDEX

Gott: Wan Got will.
    Giovio, Imprese, London, 1585, Gviii^r
wollen: Wan Got will.
    Giovio, Imprese, London, 1585, Gviii^r

GREEK MOTTO INDEX

ballo: Ball' ontos.
    Giovio, Imprese, London, 1585, Gii^r

ITALIAN MOTTO INDEX

adorare: Margherita te adoro. [understood]
    Giovio, Imprese, London, 1585, Bvi^v
amare: Margherita Te suola di cuor' amo. [understood]
    Giovio, Imprese, London, 1585, Bvi^v
corna: Porto le corna ch'ogni Huomo le vede, e qualch'
    Altro le porta che nol crede.
    Giovio, Imprese, London, 1585, Bvii^v
credere: Porto le corna ch'ogni Huomo le vede, e qualch'
    Altro le porta che nol crede.
    Giovio, Imprese, London, 1585, Bvii^v
dio: Egli e como dio vuole.
    Giovio, Imprese, London, 1585, Bvii^v
dio: E sara quel che dio vorra.
    Giovio, Imprese, London, 1585, Bvii^v
fumo: Dov' é gran fuoco é gran fumo.
    Giovio, Imprese, London, 1585, Fv^v
fuoco: Dov' é gran fuoco é gran fumo.
    Giovio, Imprese, London, 1585, Fv^v
tempo: Fal con tempo. [understood: pun on picture]
    Giovio, Imprese, London, 1585, Gi^r
vedere: Porto le corna ch'ogni Huomo le vede, e qualch'
    Altro le porta che nol crede.
    Giovio, Imprese, London, 1585, Bvii^v
volere: Egli e como dio vuole.
    Giovio, Imprese, London, 1585, Bvii^v
volere: E sara quel che dio vorra.
    Giovio, Imprese, London, 1585, Bvii^v

PROPER NOUN INDEX (GREEK MOTTO)

Margherita: Margherita Te suola di cuor' amo.
    [understood]
    Giovio, Imprese, London, 1585, Bvi^v
Margherita: Margherita te adoro. [understood]
    Giovio, Imprese, London, 1585, Bvi^v

SPANISH MOTTO INDEX

alabar: Non vos alabereis.
    Giovio, Imprese, London, 1585, Eiiii^v
dia: Dia de mas valer. [understood; pun on "diadem"]
    Giovio, Imprese, London, 1585, Cv^v
dolor: Los llenos de dolor y, Los vazios de speranza.
    Giovio, Imprese, London, 1585, Ciiii^r
lleno: Los llenos de dolor y, Los vazios de speranza.
    Giovio, Imprese, London, 1585, Ciiii^r
male: mal va. [understood]
    Giovio, Imprese, London, 1585, Ciii^v
montar: Tanto monta.
    Giovio, Imprese, London, 1585, Ciii^r
speranza: Los llenos de dolor y, Los vazios de speranza.
    Giovio, Imprese, London, 1585, Ciiii^r
sufrir: Non suefro mas de lo que puedo.
    Giovio, Imprese, London, 1585, Gi^v
vacio: Los llenos de dolor y, Los vazios de speranza.
    Giovio, Imprese, London, 1585, Ciiii^r
valer: Dia de mas valer. [understood; pun on "diadem"]
    Giovio, Imprese, London, 1585, Cv^v

PROPER NOUN INDEX (SPANISH MOTTO)

Anna: Anna di no. [understood]
    Giovio, Imprese, London, 1585, Ciii^v

ENGLISH MOTTO INDEX (TRANSLATIONS)

adore: Margherita, I adore thee.
    Giovio, Imprese, London, 1585, Bvi^v
aim: Aim true.
    Giovio, Imprese, London, 1585, Gii^r
appearance: I have a soft soul beneath a rough
    appearance.
    Giovio, Imprese, London, 1585, Fi^v
armed: Armed with nails, beak, and wings against the
    enemy.
    Giovio, Imprese, London, 1585, Evi^r
art: A work of nature, not of art.
    Giovio, Imprese, London, 1585, Cv^v
attack: Though I am peaceful, no one will attack me
    with impunity.
    Giovio, Imprese, London, 1585, Cvi^r
bad: To become famous in one way or the other,
    whether it be good or bad, it is fame.
    Giovio, Imprese, London, 1585, Fvii^v
banish: I banish poisons.
    Giovio, Imprese, London, 1585, Dviii^v
beak: Armed with nails, beak, and wings against the
    enemy.
    Giovio, Imprese, London, 1585, Evi^r
believe: I bear horns that everyone can see. Someone
    else bears them too, but does not believe it.
    Giovio, Imprese, London, 1585, Bvii^v
bent: We are bent but not broken by waves.
    Giovio, Imprese, London, 1585, Dviii^r
betray: Die rather than betray trust.
    Giovio, Imprese, London, 1585, Dv^v
black: One single bright day will equal the black ones.
    Giovio, Imprese, London, 1585, Gvi^v
boast: You shall not boast.
    Giovio, Imprese, London, 1585, Eiiii^v
brave: To do brave deeds and to suffer is Roman.
    Giovio, Imprese, London, 1585, Dvii^v
brave: The brave will not lack them.
    Giovio, Imprese, London, 1585, Fiii^r
brave: The brave will not lack them.
    Giovio, Imprese, London, 1585, Giiii^r
break: They break those which are trying to break
    them.
    Giovio, Imprese, London, 1585, Fiiii^v
breast: Her breasts nourish also an offspring not her
    own.
    Giovio, Imprese, London, 1585, Gv^v
bright: One single bright day will equal the black ones.
    Giovio, Imprese, London, 1585, Gvi^v
broken: We are bent but not broken by waves.
    Giovio, Imprese, London, 1585, Dviii^r
chariot: The slave rides in the same chariot.
    Giovio, Imprese, London, 1585, Gi^r
clamor: It clamored among the swans.
    Giovio, Imprese, London, 1585, Ei^r
cloud: It will disolve confronting clouds.
    Giovio, Imprese, London, 1585, Fi^r
companion: Fortune, companion of virtue.
    Giovio, Imprese, London, 1585, Bv^r
confront: It will disolve confronting clouds.
    Giovio, Imprese, London, 1585, Fi^r
consume: In the green, the flame consumes their tender
    marrows.
    Giovio, Imprese, London, 1585, Cviii^v
corrupted: He is not corrupted by Samnitic gold.

height: Rising from triumphal stock it seeks the heights.
    Giovio, Imprese, London, 1585, Giiii[r]
hold: He holds up and does not weary.
    Giovio, Imprese, London, 1585, Giii[r]
hope: Those that are full contain sorrow, those that are
    empty, hope.
    Giovio, Imprese, London, 1585, Ciiii[r]
hope: Without hope or fear.
    Giovio, Imprese, London, 1585, Giiii[r]
horn: I bear horns that everyone can see. Someone else
    bears them too, but does not believe it.
    Giovio, Imprese, London, 1585, Bvii[v]
hurt: He who hurts in life, heals in death.
    Giovio, Imprese, London, 1585, Fvii[r]
ill[1] = wrong, harm
ill[1]: It goes ill.
    Giovio, Imprese, London, 1585, Ciii[v]
impunity: Though I am peaceful, no one will attack me
    with impunity.
    Giovio, Imprese, London, 1585, Cvi[r]
injury: A noble mind digests even the most painful
    injuries.
    Giovio, Imprese, London, 1585, Evi[v]
intrepid: The sheep are frightened, the dogs fear, I stand
    intrepid.
    Giovio, Imprese, London, 1585, Hii[r]
invention: I suffer ruin worthy of my own invention.
    Giovio, Imprese, London, 1585, Dvi[r]
know: You tested me, O Lord, and knew me.
    Giovio, Imprese, London, 1585, Ei[v]
know: We know well the time.
    Giovio, Imprese, London, 1585, Ev[r]
labour: They finish at the same time and renew their
    labour.
    Giovio, Imprese, London, 1585, Fvi[r]
lack: The brave will not lack them.
    Giovio, Imprese, London, 1585, Fiii[r]
lack: The brave will not lack them.
    Giovio, Imprese, London, 1585, Giiii[r]
lady: I repent me the cost of my lady. [understood; pun
    on Pentecost depicted in picture]
    Giovio, Imprese, London, 1585, Bvii[r]
least: This by itself is nothing, but if you should add
    even the least to it, it would become the greatest.
    Giovio, Imprese, London, 1585, Eiii[v]
leave: Margherita, I adore thee.
    Giovio, Imprese, London, 1585, Bvi[v]
life: He who hurts in life, heals in death.
    Giovio, Imprese, London, 1585, Fvii[r]
lightning: Lightning strikes the mountain tops.
    Giovio, Imprese, London, 1585, Biiii[r]
line: Not a day without a line.
    Giovio, Imprese, London, 1585, Gvii[r]
live: Do this and you shall live.
    Giovio, Imprese, London, 1585, Fiii[v]
love: Margherita, I solely love thee.
    Giovio, Imprese, London, 1585, Bvi[v]
marble: The fig-tree splits huge blocks of marble.
    Giovio, Imprese, London, 1585, Gv[r]
marrow: In the green, the flame consumes their tender
    marrows.
    Giovio, Imprese, London, 1585, Cviii[v]
mind: A noble mind digests even the most painful
    injuries.
    Giovio, Imprese, London, 1585, Evi[v]
mind: She will dispel the uncertainties of the mind.
    Giovio, Imprese, London, 1585, Gvii[r]
modesty: Happy fecundity accompanied by modesty.
    Giovio, Imprese, London, 1585, Gvi[r]
mountain: Lightning strikes the mountain tops.
    Giovio, Imprese, London, 1585, Biiii[r]
nail: Armed with nails, beak, and wings against the
    enemy.
    Giovio, Imprese, London, 1585, Evi[r]
nature: A work of nature, not of art.

    Giovio, Imprese, London, 1585, Cv[v]
nature: I fly where nature bids me.
    Giovio, Imprese, London, 1585, Dvii[r]
nature: Nature teaches one's duty.
    Giovio, Imprese, London, 1585, Fiii[r]
nature: Nature does greater things.
    Giovio, Imprese, London, 1585, Fiiii[r]
near: Near and far.
    Giovio, Imprese, London, 1585, Cii[r]
noble: A noble mind digests even the most painful
    injuries.
    Giovio, Imprese, London, 1585, Evi[v]
noble: There is no lack of courage in a noble heart.
    Giovio, Imprese, London, 1585, Gv[v]
nothing: This by itself is nothing, but if you should add
    even the least to it, it would become the greatest.
    Giovio, Imprese, London, 1585, Eiii[v]
nourish: I nourish myself on it.
    Giovio, Imprese, London, 1585, Cii[r]
nourish: Her breasts nourish also an offspring not her
    own.
    Giovio, Imprese, London, 1585, Gv[v]
offence: Let old [offences] be forgiven.
    Giovio, Imprese, London, 1585, Cv[v]
offspring: Her breasts nourish also an offspring not her
    own.
    Giovio, Imprese, London, 1585, Gv[v]
old: Let old [offences] be forgiven.
    Giovio, Imprese, London, 1585, Cv[v]
one: It sees one only.
    Giovio, Imprese, London, 1585, Ev[v]
one: One suffices in darkness.
    Giovio, Imprese, London, 1585, Giii[v]
path: Without straying from the path.
    Giovio, Imprese, London, 1585, Eviii[v]
peaceful: Though I am peaceful, no one will attack me
    with impunity.
    Giovio, Imprese, London, 1585, Cvi[r]
pertinacious: Always pertinacious.
    Giovio, Imprese, London, 1585, Dvii[v]
place: In place and time.
    Giovio, Imprese, London, 1585, Eii[r]
please: Trouble pleases me.
    Giovio, Imprese, London, 1585, Dv[v]
poison: I banish poisons.
    Giovio, Imprese, London, 1585, Dviii[v]
pressed: When pressed down, it raises itself again.
    Giovio, Imprese, London, 1585, Eii[v]
progress: A tree makes progress when transplanted.
    Giovio, Imprese, London, 1585, Gviii[v]
promise: With my own virtue I shall strive to achieve
    the promise given to me by destiny.
    Giovio, Imprese, London, 1585, Diii[v]
punish: With this alone Jupiter punishes.
    Giovio, Imprese, London, 1585, Gii[v]
purge: It will purge or cause ruin.
    Giovio, Imprese, London, 1585, Eiiii[r]
purity: Purity unharmed.
    Giovio, Imprese, London, 1585, Di[r]
raise: When pressed down, it raises itself again.
    Giovio, Imprese, London, 1585, Eii[v]
rattle: When it rattles, loud words subside.
    Giovio, Imprese, London, 1585, Fviii[r]
renew: They finish at the same time and renew their
    labour.
    Giovio, Imprese, London, 1585, Fvi[r]
repent: I repent me the cost of my lady. [understood;
    pun on Pentecost depicted in picture]
    Giovio, Imprese, London, 1585, Bvii[r]
reward: Jupiter rewards the deserving.
    Giovio, Imprese, London, 1585, Diiii[r]
reward: The one or the other will be my reward.
    Giovio, Imprese, London, 1585, Dvi[v]
rhinoceros: The rhinoceros never turns away defeated
    from the enemy.

Giovio, Imprese, London, 1585, Diii[r]
rides: The slave rides in the same chariot.
    Giovio, Imprese, London, 1585, Gi[r]
rise: Rising from triumphal stock it seeks the heights.
    Giovio, Imprese, London, 1585, Giiii[r]
rival: When full, she may rival the sun.
    Giovio, Imprese, London, 1585, Cii[v]
rough: I have a soft soul beneath a rough appearance.
    Giovio, Imprese, London, 1585, Fi[v]
ruin: I suffer ruin worthy of my own invention.
    Giovio, Imprese, London, 1585, Dvi[r]
ruin: It will purge or cause ruin.
    Giovio, Imprese, London, 1585, Eiiii[r]
run: Though I do not soar high on my wings, I outstrip all in running.
    Giovio, Imprese, London, 1585, Evii[r]
secure: Secure, she despises storms.
    Giovio, Imprese, London, 1585, Gvi[r]
see: I bear horns that everyone can see. Someone else bears them too, but does not believe it.
    Giovio, Imprese, London, 1585, Bvii[v]
shade: Shade does not yield to the sun.
    Giovio, Imprese, London, 1585, Eii[r]
sheep: The sheep are frightened, the dogs fear, I stand intrepid.
    Giovio, Imprese, London, 1585, Hii[r]
shine: The ungrateful takes away all with which she shines.
    Giovio, Imprese, London, 1585, Gi[v]
shine: With long use it shines.
    Giovio, Imprese, London, 1585, Gviii[v]
skill: We are strong because our skill differs from theirs.
    Giovio, Imprese, London, 1585, Eviii[r]
slave: The slave rides in the same chariot.
    Giovio, Imprese, London, 1585, Gi[r]
smoke: Where there is great fire, there is great smoke.
    Giovio, Imprese, London, 1585, Fv[v]
soar: Though I do not soar high on my wings, I outstrip all in running.
    Giovio, Imprese, London, 1585, Evii[r]
soft: I have a soft soul beneath a rough appearance.
    Giovio, Imprese, London, 1585, Fi[v]
sorrow: Those that are full contain sorrow, those that are empty, hope.
    Giovio, Imprese, London, 1585, Ciiii[r]
soul: I have a soft soul beneath a rough appearance.
    Giovio, Imprese, London, 1585, Fi[v]
stock: Rising from triumphal stock it seeks the heights.
    Giovio, Imprese, London, 1585, Giiii[r]
storm: Secure, she despises storms.
    Giovio, Imprese, London, 1585, Gvi[r]
stray: Without straying from the path.
    Giovio, Imprese, London, 1585, Eviii[v]
strike: Lightning strikes the mountain tops.
    Giovio, Imprese, London, 1585, Biiii[r]
strive: With my own virtue I shall strive to achieve the promise given to me by destiny.
    Giovio, Imprese, London, 1585, Diii[v]
strong: We are strong because our skill differs from theirs.
    Giovio, Imprese, London, 1585, Eviii[r]
struggle: Sometime I shall struggle out of here.
    Giovio, Imprese, London, 1585, Dii[v]
subside: When it rattles, loud words subside.
    Giovio, Imprese, London, 1585, Fviii[r]
suffer: I suffer ruin worthy of my own invention.
    Giovio, Imprese, London, 1585, Dvi[r]
suffer: To do brave deeds and to suffer is Roman.
    Giovio, Imprese, London, 1585, Dvii[v]
suffer: I suffer no more than I am able.
    Giovio, Imprese, London, 1585, Gi[v]
suffice: One suffices in darkness.
    Giovio, Imprese, London, 1585, Giii[v]
sun: When full, she may rival the sun.
    Giovio, Imprese, London, 1585, Cii[v]

sun: Shade does not yield to the sun.
    Giovio, Imprese, London, 1585, Eii[r]
swan: It clamored among the swans.
    Giovio, Imprese, London, 1585, Ei[r]
tame: To tame folly.
    Giovio, Imprese, London, 1585, Fi[v]
teach: Nature teaches one's duty.
    Giovio, Imprese, London, 1585, Fiii[r]
tear: Tears of the crocodile.
    Giovio, Imprese, London, 1585, Gii[r]
test: Virtue and faith are tested by this alone.
    Giovio, Imprese, London, 1585, Dvi[v]
test: You tested me, O Lord, and knew me.
    Giovio, Imprese, London, 1585, Ei[v]
test: You tested me, O Lord.
    Giovio, Imprese, London, 1585, Giiii[r]
think: Let him be dishonoured who thinks evil of it.
    Giovio, Imprese, London, 1585, Ci[v]
time: In place and time.
    Giovio, Imprese, London, 1585, Eii[r]
time: We know well the time.
    Giovio, Imprese, London, 1585, Ev[r]
time: Do it in time.
    Giovio, Imprese, London, 1585, Gi[r]
tooth: I use my cunning and my teeth simultaneously.
    Giovio, Imprese, London, 1585, Hi[v]
transplanted: A tree makes progress when transplanted.
    Giovio, Imprese, London, 1585, Gviii[v]
tree: A tree makes progress when transplanted.
    Giovio, Imprese, London, 1585, Gviii[v]
triumphal: Rising from triumphal stock it seeks the heights.
    Giovio, Imprese, London, 1585, Giiii[r]
trophy: In keeping with family tradition, he will add new trophies of valour.
    Giovio, Imprese, London, 1585, Giiii[r]
trouble: Trouble pleases me.
    Giovio, Imprese, London, 1585, Dv[v]
trust: Die rather than betray trust.
    Giovio, Imprese, London, 1585, Dv[v]
uncertainty: She will dispel the uncertainties of the mind.
    Giovio, Imprese, London, 1585, Gvii[r]
ungrateful: The ungrateful takes away all with which she shines.
    Giovio, Imprese, London, 1585, Gi[v]
unharmed: Purity unharmed.
    Giovio, Imprese, London, 1585, Di[r]
united: It holds distant things united.
    Giovio, Imprese, London, 1585, Fi[v]
use: With long use it shines.
    Giovio, Imprese, London, 1585, Gviii[v]
valour: In keeping with family tradition, he will add new trophies of valour.
    Giovio, Imprese, London, 1585, Giiii[r]
virtue: Fortune, companion of virtue.
    Giovio, Imprese, London, 1585, Bv[r]
virtue: Thus also virtue.
    Giovio, Imprese, London, 1585, Bv[v]
virtue: With my own virtue I shall strive to achieve the promise given to me by destiny.
    Giovio, Imprese, London, 1585, Diii[v]
virtue: Virtue and faith are tested by this alone.
    Giovio, Imprese, London, 1585, Dvi[v]
virtue: When separated, each has its own virtue.
    Giovio, Imprese, London, 1585, Fvi[v]
wave: We are bent but not broken by waves.
    Giovio, Imprese, London, 1585, Dviii[r]
way: We wing our way.
    Giovio, Imprese, London, 1585, Biiii[r]
weary: He holds up and does not weary.
    Giovio, Imprese, London, 1585, Giii[r]
will: He is as God wills.
    Giovio, Imprese, London, 1585, Bvii[v]
will: It shall be as God wills.

Giovio, Imprese, London, 1585, Bvii^v
will: When God wills.
Giovio, Imprese, London, 1585, Gviii^r
wing: We wing our way.
Giovio, Imprese, London, 1585, Biiii^r
wing: Armed with nails, beak, and wings against the enemy.
Giovio, Imprese, London, 1585, Evi^r
wing: Though I do not soar high on my wings, I outstrip all in running.
Giovio, Imprese, London, 1585, Evii^r
wish: Destiny makes wishes come true.
Giovio, Imprese, London, 1585, Gii^v
word: When it rattles, loud words subside.
Giovio, Imprese, London, 1585, Fviii^r
work: A work of nature, not of art.
Giovio, Imprese, London, 1585, Cv^v
world: Until it fills the whole world.
Giovio, Imprese, London, 1585, Cii^v
worth: A day of more worth.
Giovio, Imprese, London, 1585, Cv^v
wound: It wounds and defends.
Giovio, Imprese, London, 1585, Dv^v
write: Better fortune will write on it.
Giovio, Imprese, London, 1585, Gii^r
yield: Shade does not yield to the sun.
Giovio, Imprese, London, 1585, Eii^r
yield: He does not yield, even to Jupiter.
Giovio, Imprese, London, 1585, Gvii^r

PROPER NOUN INDEX (ENGLISH MOTTO TRANSLATION)

Anna: Anna say no.
Giovio, Imprese, London, 1585, Ciii^v
Caesar: Caesar or nothing.
Giovio, Imprese, London, 1585, Biiii^r
God: He is as God wills.
Giovio, Imprese, London, 1585, Bvii^v
God: It shall be as God wills.
Giovio, Imprese, London, 1585, Bvii^v
God: When God wills.
Giovio, Imprese, London, 1585, Gviii^r
Hercules: When gathered by Hercules' hand, they keep their fragrance.
Giovio, Imprese, London, 1585, Fviii^r
Juno: Dedicated to Juno Lucina.
Giovio, Imprese, London, 1585, Fvi^r
Jupiter: Jupiter rewards the deserving.
Giovio, Imprese, London, 1585, Diiii^r
Jupiter: With this alone Jupiter punishes.
Giovio, Imprese, London, 1585, Gii^v
Jupiter: He does not yield, even to Jupiter.
Giovio, Imprese, London, 1585, Gvii^r
Lord: You tested me, O Lord, and knew me.
Giovio, Imprese, London, 1585, Ei^v
Lord: You tested me, O Lord.
Giovio, Imprese, London, 1585, Giiii^r
Lucina: Dedicated to Juno Lucina.
Giovio, Imprese, London, 1585, Fvi^r
Margherita: Margherita, I solely love thee.
Giovio, Imprese, London, 1585, Bvi^v
Margherita: Margherita, I adore thee.
Giovio, Imprese, London, 1585, Bvi^v
Roman: To do brave deeds and to suffer is Roman.
Giovio, Imprese, London, 1585, Dvii^v
Samnitic: He is not corrupted by Samnitic gold.
Giovio, Imprese, London, 1585, Dvi^v

MOTTO (ALPHABETICAL LIST)

Aequabit nigras candida una dies.
One single bright day will equal the black ones.

Giovio, Imprese, London, 1585, Gvi^v
Alterutra clarescere fama. Sive bonum, sive malum, fama est.
To become famous in one way or the other, whether it be good or bad, it is fame.
Giovio, Imprese, London, 1585, Fvii^v
Anna di no. [understood]
Anna say no.
Giovio, Imprese, London, 1585, Ciii^v
Aspicit unam.
It sees one only.
Giovio, Imprese, London, 1585, Ev^v
Aut Caesar aut nihil.
Caesar or nothing.
Giovio, Imprese, London, 1585, Biiii^r
Aut cum hoc aut in hoc.
Either with this or on this.
Giovio, Imprese, London, 1585, Eviii^r
Ball'[Gk] ontos[Gk]
Aim true.
Giovio, Imprese, London, 1585, Gii^r
Candor illesus.
Purity unharmed.
Giovio, Imprese, London, 1585, Di^r
Comminus et eminus.
Near and far.
Giovio, Imprese, London, 1585, Cii^r
Conantia frangere frangunt.
They break those which are trying to break them.
Giovio, Imprese, London, 1585, Fiiii^v
Contemnit tuta procellas.
Secure, she despises storms.
Giovio, Imprese, London, 1585, Gvi^r
Crocodili lachrymae.
Tears of the crocodile.
Giovio, Imprese, London, 1585, Gii^r
Cum crepitat, sonora silent.
When it rattles, loud words subside.
Giovio, Imprese, London, 1585, Fviii^r
Cum plena est, sit emula Solis.
When full, she may rival the sun.
Giovio, Imprese, London, 1585, Cii^v
Cum pudore laeta foecunditas.
Happy fecundity accompanied by modesty.
Giovio, Imprese, London, 1585, Gvi^r
Cursum intendimus alis. [ironic attribution]
We wing our way.
Giovio, Imprese, London, 1585, Biiii^r
Dia de mas valer. [understood; pun on "diadem"]
A day of more worth.
Giovio, Imprese, London, 1585, Cv^v
Discretis sua virtus inest.
When separated, each has its own virtue.
Giovio, Imprese, London, 1585, Fvi^v
Distantia iungit.
It holds distant things united.
Giovio, Imprese, London, 1585, Fi^v
Diversa ab illis virtute valemus.
We are strong because our skill differs from theirs.
Giovio, Imprese, London, 1585, Eviii^r
Donec totum impleat orbem.
Until it fills the whole world.
Giovio, Imprese, London, 1585, Cii^v
Dov' é gran fuoco é gran fumo.
Where there is great fire, there is great smoke.
Giovio, Imprese, London, 1585, Fv^v
E sara quel che dio vorra.
It shall be as God wills.
Giovio, Imprese, London, 1585, Bvii^v
Egli e como dio vuole.
He is as God wills.
Giovio, Imprese, London, 1585, Bvii^v
Erit altera merces.
The one or the other will be my reward.
Giovio, Imprese, London, 1585, Dvi^v

Expiabit aut obruet.
It will purge or cause ruin.
Giovio, Imprese, London, 1585, Eiiii^r

Fal con tempo. [understood: pun on picture]
Do it in time.
Giovio, Imprese, London, 1585, Gi^r

Feriunt summos fulmina montes.
Lightning strikes the mountain tops.
Giovio, Imprese, London, 1585, Biiii^r

Fidem fati virtute sequemur.
With my own virtue I shall strive to achieve the
promise given to me by destiny.
Giovio, Imprese, London, 1585, Diii^v

Fides hoc uno, virtusque probantur.
Virtue and faith are tested by this alone.
Giovio, Imprese, London, 1585, Dvi^v

Finiunt pariter renovantque labores.
They finish at the same time and renew their labour.
Giovio, Imprese, London, 1585, Fvi^r

Flectimur non frangimur undis.
We are bent but not broken by waves.
Giovio, Imprese, London, 1585, Dviii^r

Fortia facere et pati Romanum est.
To do brave deeds and to suffer is Roman.
Giovio, Imprese, London, 1585, Dvii^v

Fortibus non deerunt.
The brave will not lack them.
Giovio, Imprese, London, 1585, Fiii^r

Fortibus non deerunt.
The brave will not lack them.
Giovio, Imprese, London, 1585, Giiii^r

Fragrantia durant Herculea collecta manu.
When gathered by Hercules' hand, they keep their
fragrance.
Giovio, Imprese, London, 1585, Fviii^r

Hinc aliquando eluctabor.
Sometime I shall struggle out of here.
Giovio, Imprese, London, 1585, Dii^v

Hoc fac et vives.
Do this and you shall live.
Giovio, Imprese, London, 1585, Fiii^v

Hoc opus.
This is my work.
Giovio, Imprese, London, 1585, Bvi^r

Hoc per se nihil est, sed si minimum addideris maximum
fiet [=fieret].
This by itself is nothing, but if you should add even
the least to it, it would become the greatest.
Giovio, Imprese, London, 1585, Eiii^v

Hoc uno Iupiter ultor.
With this alone Jupiter punishes.
Giovio, Imprese, London, 1585, Gii^v

Honni soit qui mal y pense.
Let him be dishonoured who thinks evil of it.
Giovio, Imprese, London, 1585, Ci^v

I repent me the cost of my lady. [understood; pun on
Pentecost depicted in picture]
Giovio, Imprese, London, 1585, Bvii^r

Il me plait le trouble.
Trouble pleases me.
Giovio, Imprese, London, 1585, Dv^v

In viridi teneras exurit flamma medullas.
In the green, the flame consumes their tender
marrows.
Giovio, Imprese, London, 1585, Cviii^v

Incerta animi decreta resolvet.
She will dispel the uncertainties of the mind.
Giovio, Imprese, London, 1585, Gvii^r

Inclinata resurgit.
When pressed down, it raises itself again.
Giovio, Imprese, London, 1585, Eii^v

Ingenio experior funera digna meo.
I suffer ruin worthy of my own invention.
Giovio, Imprese, London, 1585, Dvi^r

Ingentia marmora findit caprificus.
The fig-tree splits huge blocks of marble.
Giovio, Imprese, London, 1585, Gv^r

Inter omnes.
Among all.
Giovio, Imprese, London, 1585, Dii^r

Ita et virtus.
Thus also virtue.
Giovio, Imprese, London, 1585, Bv^v

Iunoni Lucinae dicatum.
Dedicated to Juno Lucina.
Giovio, Imprese, London, 1585, Fvi^r

Jupiter merentibus offert.
Jupiter rewards the deserving.
Giovio, Imprese, London, 1585, Diiii^r

Loco et tempore. [later changed to: A lieu et temps.]
In place and time.
Giovio, Imprese, London, 1585, Eii^r

Longo splendescit in usu.
With long use it shines.
Giovio, Imprese, London, 1585, Gviii^v

Los llenos de dolor y, Los vazios de speranza.
Those that are full contain sorrow, those that are
empty, hope.
Giovio, Imprese, London, 1585, Ciiii^r

Mal va. [understood]
It goes ill.
Giovio, Imprese, London, 1585, Ciii^v

Malo mori quam foedari.
I prefer to die than to be dishonoured.
Giovio, Imprese, London, 1585, Cv^r

Margherita te adoro. [understood]
Margherita, I adore thee.
Giovio, Imprese, London, 1585, Bvi^v

Margherita Te suola di cuor' amo. [understood]
Margherita, I solely love thee.
Giovio, Imprese, London, 1585, Bvi^v

Melior fortuna notabit.
Better fortune will write on it.
Giovio, Imprese, London, 1585, Gii^r

Mi nutrisco.
I nourish myself on it.
Giovio, Imprese, London, 1585, Cii^r

Mitem animum agresti sub tegmine servo.
I have a soft soul beneath a rough appearance.
Giovio, Imprese, London, 1585, Fi^v

Natura dictante feror.
I fly where nature bids me.
Giovio, Imprese, London, 1585, Dvii^r

Natura maiora facit.
Nature does greater things.
Giovio, Imprese, London, 1585, Fiiii^r

Naturae non artis opus.
A work of nature, not of art.
Giovio, Imprese, London, 1585, Cv^v

Nec spe, nec metu.
Without hope or fear.
Giovio, Imprese, London, 1585, Giiii^r

Non cedit umbra soli.
Shade does not yield to the sun.
Giovio, Imprese, London, 1585, Eii^r

Non deest generoso in pectore virtus.
There is no lack of courage in a noble heart.
Giovio, Imprese, London, 1585, Gv^v

Non suefro mas de lo que puedo.
I suffer no more than I am able.
Giovio, Imprese, London, 1585, Gi^v

Non vos alabereis.
You shall not boast.
Giovio, Imprese, London, 1585, Eiiii^v

Nous scavons bien le temps.
We know well the time.
Giovio, Imprese, London, 1585, Ev^r

Nulla dies sine linea. [inferred]
Not a day without a line.
Giovio, Imprese, London, 1585, Gvii^r

Obstantia nubila solvet.
   It will dissolve confronting clouds.
      Giovio, Imprese, London, 1585, Fi^r
Obstrepuit inter olores.
   It clamored among the swans.
      Giovio, Imprese, London, 1585, Ei^r
Officium natura docet.
   Nature teaches one's duty.
      Giovio, Imprese, London, 1585, Fiii^r
Pavent oves, Timent canes, intrepidus maneo.
   The sheep are frightened, the dogs fear, I stand
   intrepid.
      Giovio, Imprese, London, 1585, Hii^r
Plus ultra.
   Further.
      Giovio, Imprese, London, 1585, Bviii^r
Porto le corna ch'ogni Huomo le vede, e qualch' Altro le
   porta che nol crede.
   I bear horns that everyone can see. Someone else
   bears them too, but does not believe it.
      Giovio, Imprese, London, 1585, Bvii^v
Pour dompter folie.
   To tame folly.
      Giovio, Imprese, London, 1585, Fi^v
Prius mori quam fidem fallere.
   Die rather than betray trust.
      Giovio, Imprese, London, 1585, Dv^v
Pro bono malum.
   Evil for good.
      Giovio, Imprese, London, 1585, Gvii^r
Probasti me Domine, et cognovisti.
   You tested me, O Lord, and knew me.
      Giovio, Imprese, London, 1585, Ei^v
Probasti me domine.
   You tested me, O Lord.
      Giovio, Imprese, London, 1585, Giiii^r
Qui vivens laedit morte medetur.
   He who hurts in life, heals in death.
      Giovio, Imprese, London, 1585, Fvii^r
Quietum nemo impune lacesset.
   Though I am peaceful, no one will attack me with
   impunity.
      Giovio, Imprese, London, 1585, Cvi^r
Recedant vetera.
   Let old [offences] be forgiven.
      Giovio, Imprese, London, 1585, Cv^v
Rhinoceros nunquam victus ab hoste cedit.
   The rhinoceros never turns away defeated from the
   enemy.
      Giovio, Imprese, London, 1585, Diii^r
Samnitico non capitur auro.
   He is not corrupted by Samnitic gold.
      Giovio, Imprese, London, 1585, Dvi^v
Sans point sortir hors de l'orniére.
   Without straying from the path.
      Giovio, Imprese, London, 1585, Eviii^v
Sauciat et defendit.
   It wounds and defends.
      Giovio, Imprese, London, 1585, Dv^v
Semper
   Forever.
      Giovio, Imprese, London, 1585, Cviii^r
Semper pertinax.
   Always pertinacious.
      Giovio, Imprese, London, 1585, Dvii^v
Semper.
   For ever.
      Giovio, Imprese, London, 1585, Cviii^r
Servari et servare meum est.
   My duty is to guard myself and others.
      Giovio, Imprese, London, 1585, Fv^r
Servus curru portatur eodem.
   The slave rides in the same chariot.
      Giovio, Imprese, London, 1585, Gi^r
Si sursum non efferor alis, saltem cursu praetervehor

omnes.
   Though I do not soar high on my wings, I outstrip
   all in running.
      Giovio, Imprese, London, 1585, Evii^r
Sic vos non vobis.
   Thus you [fight] not for yourselves.
      Giovio, Imprese, London, 1585, Ciiii^r
Simul astu et dentibus utor.
   I use my cunning and my teeth simultaneously.
      Giovio, Imprese, London, 1585, Hi^v
Sina alienaque pignora nutrit.
   Her breasts nourish also an offspring not her own.
      Giovio, Imprese, London, 1585, Gv^v
Spiritus durissima coquit.
   A noble mind digests even the most painful injuries.
      Giovio, Imprese, London, 1585, Evi^v
Suave.
   Gentle.
      Giovio, Imprese, London, 1585, Cvii^v
Sufficit unum in tenebris.
   One suffices in darkness.
      Giovio, Imprese, London, 1585, Giii^v
Sustinet nec fatiscit.
   He holds up and does not weary.
      Giovio, Imprese, London, 1585, Giii^r
Tanto monta.
   So much does he excel.
      Giovio, Imprese, London, 1585, Ciii^r
Totum adimit quo ingrata refulget.
   The ungrateful takes away all with which she shines.
      Giovio, Imprese, London, 1585, Gi^v
Translata proficit arbos.
   A tree makes progress when transplanted.
      Giovio, Imprese, London, 1585, Gviii^v
Triumphali e stipite surgens alta petit.
   Rising from triumphal stock it seeks the heights.
      Giovio, Imprese, London, 1585, Giiii^r
Unguibus et rostro, atque alis armatus in hostem.
   Armed with nails, beak, and wings against the enemy.
      Giovio, Imprese, London, 1585, Evi^r
Uno avulso non deficit alter.
   When one is torn away, a second does not fail.
      Giovio, Imprese, London, 1585, Diiii^r
Vel Iovi cedere nescit.
   He does not yield, even to Jupiter.
      Giovio, Imprese, London, 1585, Gvii^r
Venena pello.
   I banish poisons.
      Giovio, Imprese, London, 1585, Dviii^v
Virtuti fortuna comes.
   Fortune, companion of virtue.
      Giovio, Imprese, London, 1585, Bv^r
Virtutis trophaea novae non degener addet.
   In keeping with family tradition, he will add new
   trophies of valour.
      Giovio, Imprese, London, 1585, Giiii^r
Votis subscribunt fata secundis.
   Destiny makes wishes come true.
      Giovio, Imprese, London, 1585, Gii^v
Wan Got will.
   When God wills.
      Giovio, Imprese, London, 1585, Gviii^r

REFERENCE INDEX

Ariosto: Ariosto
   Giovio, Imprese, London, 1585, Eii^r
B Matt 10, 20:
   Giovio, Imprese, London, 1585, Cvii^v
Cicero: Cicero
   Giovio, Imprese, London, 1585, Cvii^v
Colonna: arms of the house of Colonna.
   Giovio, Imprese, London, 1585, Gvi^r
Diocletian: figure on the gate of the baths of

THE IMPRESE OF LODOVICO DOMENICHI

CONCORDANCES, INDEXES, AND LISTS

Prepared by Peter M. Daly

Domenichi, Devises, [London, 1585], Hvi[V]
ship: A ˚remora staying a ˚ship under ˚sail.
Domenichi, Devises, [London, 1585], Hv[V]
silk-worm: A ˚silk-worm.
Domenichi, Devises, [London, 1585], Hiii[r]
snail: A ˚snail, its ˚head out of ˚shell, ˚wounded with an
˚arrow.
Domenichi, Devises, [London, 1585], Hiii[V]
snail: A ˚snail in its ˚shell.
Domenichi, Devises, [London, 1585], Hvi[V]
stockdove [= pigeon]: A ˚stockdove [= wild ˚pigeon] with
a ˚diamond in its ˚bill.
Domenichi, Devises, [London, 1585], Hiii[r]
sun: An ˚eagle ˚flying near ˚sun, ˚burning its ˚feathers.
Domenichi, Devises, [London, 1585], Hv[r]
sun: A ˚marigold turning towards ˚sun.
Domenichi, Devises, [London, 1585], Hvi[r]
sword: A ˚sword.
Domenichi, Devises, [London, 1585], Hv[r]
sword: A ˚sword entwined by a ˚serpent holding in its
mouth a ˚garland of ˚laurel.
Domenichi, Devises, [London, 1585], Hv[V]
sword: A ˚sword.
Domenichi, Devises, [London, 1585], Hviii[r]
talon: An ˚eagle, possibly carrying ˚Jupiter's ˚lightning
˚bolts in his ˚talons.
Domenichi, Devises, [London, 1585], Hvi[V]
torch: A ˚burning ˚torch, ˚inverted, the ˚flames
˚extinguished by ˚melting ˚wax.
Domenichi, Devises, [London, 1585], Hvii[V]
tusk: An ˚elephant, without ˚tusks.
Domenichi, Devises, [London, 1585], Hv[r]
two: ˚Two ˚palm-trees, ˚male and ˚female.
Domenichi, Devises, [London, 1585], Hiii[V]
wax: A ˚burning ˚torch, ˚inverted, the ˚flames
˚extinguished by ˚melting ˚wax.
Domenichi, Devises, [London, 1585], Hvii[V]
wounded: A ˚snail, its ˚head out of ˚shell, ˚wounded
with an ˚arrow.
Domenichi, Devises, [London, 1585], Hiii[V]
wounded: An ˚hart ˚wounded by an ˚arrow, with the
˚herb ˚dictamnum in its ˚mouth.
Domenichi, Devises, [London, 1585], Hvii[r]

PROPER NOUN INDEX (PICTURE)

Argus: ˚Argus guarding ˚Io as a ˚cow.
Domenichi, Devises, [London, 1585], Hvi[r]
Caesar: Julius ˚Caesar's ˚horse with ˚human ˚forefeet.
Domenichi, Devises, [London, 1585], Hvii[V]
Io: ˚Argus guarding ˚Io as a ˚cow.
Domenichi, Devises, [London, 1585], Hvi[r]
Jupiter: An ˚eagle, possibly carrying ˚Jupiter's ˚lightning
˚bolts in his ˚talons.
Domenichi, Devises, [London, 1585], Hvi[V]

LATIN MOTTO INDEX

aeternus: In aeternum.
Domenichi, Devises, [London, 1585], Hiii[r]
alo: Quod me alit me extinguit.
Domenichi, Devises, [London, 1585], Hvii[V]
audeo: Aude aliquid dignum.
Domenichi, Devises, [London, 1585], Hv[r]
dignus: Aude aliquid dignum.
Domenichi, Devises, [London, 1585], Hv[r]
dux: His ducibus.
Domenichi, Devises, [London, 1585], Hv[V]
elevo: Perculsus elevor.
Domenichi, Devises, [London, 1585], Hiii[V]
extinguo: Quod me alit me extinguit.
Domenichi, Devises, [London, 1585], Hvii[V]
fatum: Nec sorte, nec fato.

Domenichi, Devises, [London, 1585], Hii[V]
flecto: Flectimur obsequio non viribus.
Domenichi, Devises, [London, 1585], Hv[V]
foecunditas: Mutua foecunditas.
Domenichi, Devises, [London, 1585], Hii[V]
fortuna: In utraque fortuna.
Domenichi, Devises, [London, 1585], Hiii[r]
frustra: Sic frustra.
Domenichi, Devises, [London, 1585], Hv[V]
frustra: Frustra vigilant.
Domenichi, Devises, [London, 1585], Hvi[r]
ingenium: Ingenium superat vires.
Domenichi, Devises, [London, 1585], Hvii[r]
lascivia: Lasciviae penitentia.
Domenichi, Devises, [London, 1585], Hvii[r]
mutus: Mutua foecunditas.
Domenichi, Devises, [London, 1585], Hii[V]
obsequium: Flectimur obsequio non viribus.
Domenichi, Devises, [London, 1585], Hv[V]
penitentia: Lasciviae penitentia.
Domenichi, Devises, [London, 1585], Hvii[r]
perculsus: Perculsus elevor.
Domenichi, Devises, [London, 1585], Hiii[V]
proprius: Proprio alitur succo.
Domenichi, Devises, [London, 1585], Hvi[V]
salus: Hinc sola salus.
Domenichi, Devises, [London, 1585], Hv[r]
sol: Vertitur ad solem.
Domenichi, Devises, [London, 1585], Hvi[r]
sors: Nec sorte, nec fato.
Domenichi, Devises, [London, 1585], Hii[V]
sors: Est mihi sorte datum.
Domenichi, Devises, [London, 1585], Hvi[V]
succus: Proprio alitur succo.
Domenichi, Devises, [London, 1585], Hvi[V]
supero: Ingenium superat vires.
Domenichi, Devises, [London, 1585], Hvii[r]
torqueo: Quod huic deest me torquet.
Domenichi, Devises, [London, 1585], Hiii[V]
verto: Vertitur ad solem.
Domenichi, Devises, [London, 1585], Hvi[r]
vigilo: Frustra vigilant.
Domenichi, Devises, [London, 1585], Hvi[r]
vis: Flectimur obsequio non viribus.
Domenichi, Devises, [London, 1585], Hv[V]
vis: Ingenium superat vires.
Domenichi, Devises, [London, 1585], Hvii[r]

PROPER NOUN INDEX (LATIN MOTTO)

Caesar: Soli Caesari.
Domenichi, Devises, [London, 1585], Hvii[V]

GREEK MOTTO INDEX

parameno: Pistos soi parameno[Gk]
Domenichi, Devises, [London, 1585], Hviii[r]
pistos: Pistos soi parameno[Gk]
Domenichi, Devises, [London, 1585], Hviii[r]

HEBREW MOTTO INDEX

lamazabatani: Lamazabatani.
Domenichi, Devises, [London, 1585], Hiiii[V]

ITALIAN MOTTO INDEX

amante: Di amante falso. [understood pun on "false
diamond"]
Domenichi, Devises, [London, 1585], Hiiii[V]
amore: Trovommi amor del tutto disarmato.

Domenichi, Devises, [London, 1585], Hiii^v
disarmato: Trovommi amor del tutto disarmato.
   Domenichi, Devises, [London, 1585], Hiii^v
falso: Di amante falso. [understood pun on "false
   diamond"]
   Domenichi, Devises, [London, 1585], Hiiii^v
lasciare: Lasciai di me la meglior parte a dietro.
   Domenichi, Devises, [London, 1585], Hv^r
vivere: Suol di cilo vivo.
   Domenichi, Devises, [London, 1585], Hiiii^r

SPANISH MOTTO INDEX

remedio: Esto tiene su remedio y non yo.
   Domenichi, Devises, [London, 1585], Hvii^r

ENGLISH MOTTO INDEX (TRANSLATIONS)

bend: We bend out of compliance and not because of
   force.
   Domenichi, Devises, [London, 1585], Hv^v
chance: Not by chance nor by fate.
   Domenichi, Devises, [London, 1585], Hii^v
chance: It is given to me by chance.
   Domenichi, Devises, [London, 1585], Hvi^v
compliance: We bend out of compliance and not because
   of force.
   Domenichi, Devises, [London, 1585], Hv^v
dare: Dare something worthy.
   Domenichi, Devises, [London, 1585], Hv^r
disarmed: Love found me completely disarmed.
   Domenichi, Devises, [London, 1585], Hiiii^v
extinguish: That which nourishes me extinguishes me.
   Domenichi, Devises, [London, 1585], Hvii^v
faithfully: I shall remain faithfully with you.
   Domenichi, Devises, [London, 1585], Hviii^r
false: Say, false lover.
   Domenichi, Devises, [London, 1585], Hiiii^v
fate: Not by chance nor by fate.
   Domenichi, Devises, [London, 1585], Hii^v
fecundity: Mutual fecundity.
   Domenichi, Devises, [London, 1585], Hii^v
force: We bend out of compliance and not because of
   force.
   Domenichi, Devises, [London, 1585], Hv^v
forever: Forever.
   Domenichi, Devises, [London, 1585], Hiii^r
forsaken: Why have you forsaken me?
   Domenichi, Devises, [London, 1585], Hiiii^v
guard: They stand guard in vain.
   Domenichi, Devises, [London, 1585], Hvi^r
guide: With these as guides.
   Domenichi, Devises, [London, 1585], Hv^v
lasciviousness: Penitence for lasciviousness.
   Domenichi, Devises, [London, 1585], Hvii^r
live: Only of this do I live.
   Domenichi, Devises, [London, 1585], Hiii^r
love: Love found me completely disarmed.
   Domenichi, Devises, [London, 1585], Hiiii^v
lover: Say, false lover.
   Domenichi, Devises, [London, 1585], Hiiii^v
moisture: It nourishes itself from its own moisture.
   Domenichi, Devises, [London, 1585], Hvi^v
mutual: Mutual fecundity.
   Domenichi, Devises, [London, 1585], Hii^v
nourish: It nourishes itself from its own moisture.
   Domenichi, Devises, [London, 1585], Hvi^v
nourish: That which nourishes me extinguishes me.
   Domenichi, Devises, [London, 1585], Hvii^v
overcome: Talent overcomes strength.
   Domenichi, Devises, [London, 1585], Hvii^r
penitence: Penitence for lasciviousness.

Domenichi, Devises, [London, 1585], Hvii^r
prosper: I prosper either way.
   Domenichi, Devises, [London, 1585], Hiii^r
raised: Though struck I am raised.
   Domenichi, Devises, [London, 1585], Hiiii^v
remain: I shall remain faithfully with you.
   Domenichi, Devises, [London, 1585], Hviii^r
remedy: This creature has his remedy, but I do not.
   Domenichi, Devises, [London, 1585], Hvii^r
salvation: This is my only salvation.
   Domenichi, Devises, [London, 1585], Hv^r
strength: Talent overcomes strength.
   Domenichi, Devises, [London, 1585], Hvii^r
strike: Though struck I am raised.
   Domenichi, Devises, [London, 1585], Hiiii^v
sun: It terns towards the sun.
   Domenichi, Devises, [London, 1585], Hvi^r
talent: Talent overcomes strength.
   Domenichi, Devises, [London, 1585], Hvii^r
torment: What this creature lacks torments me.
   Domenichi, Devises, [London, 1585], Hiiii^v
vain[1] = futile, idle
vain[1]: Thus in vain.
   Domenichi, Devises, [London, 1585], Hv^v
vain[1]: They stand guard in vain.
   Domenichi, Devises, [London, 1585], Hvi^r
worthy: Dare something worthy.
   Domenichi, Devises, [London, 1585], Hv^r

PROPER NOUN INDEX (ENGLISH MOTTO TRANSLATION)

Caesar: To Caesar alone.
   Domenichi, Devises, [London, 1585], Hvii^v

MOTTO (ALPHABETICAL LIST)

Aude aliquid dignum.
   Dare something worthy.
   Domenichi, Devises, [London, 1585], Hv^r
Di amante falso. [understood pun on "false diamond"]
   Say, false lover.
   Domenichi, Devises, [London, 1585], Hiiii^v
Est mihi sorte datum.
   It is given to me by chance.
   Domenichi, Devises, [London, 1585], Hvi^v
Esto tiene su remedio y non yo.
   This creature has his remedy, but I do not.
   Domenichi, Devises, [London, 1585], Hvii^r
Ex hoc in hoc.
   For this reason.
   Domenichi, Devises, [London, 1585], Hv^r
Flectimur obsequio non viribus.
   We bend out of compliance and not because of force.
   Domenichi, Devises, [London, 1585], Hv^v
Frustra vigilant.
   They stand guard in vain[1].
   Domenichi, Devises, [London, 1585], Hvi^r
Hinc sola salus.
   This is my only salvation.
   Domenichi, Devises, [London, 1585], Hv^r
His ducibus.
   With these as guides.
   Domenichi, Devises, [London, 1585], Hv^v
In aeternum.
   Forever.
   Domenichi, Devises, [London, 1585], Hiiii^r
In utraque fortuna.
   I prosper either way.
   Domenichi, Devises, [London, 1585], Hiii^r
Ingenium superat vires.
   Talent overcomes strength.
   Domenichi, Devises, [London, 1585], Hvii^r

Lamazabatani. [Hebrew]
    Why have you forsaken me?
        Domenichi, Devises, [London, 1585], Hiiii[v]
Lasciai di me la meglior parte a dietro.
    I left the better part of me behind.
        Domenichi, Devises, [London, 1585], Hv[r]
Lasciviae penitentia.
    Penitence for lasciviousness.
        Domenichi, Devises, [London, 1585], Hvii[r]
Mutua foecunditas.
    Mutual fecundity.
        Domenichi, Devises, [London, 1585], Hii[v]
Nec sorte, nec fato.
    Not by chance nor by fate.
        Domenichi, Devises, [London, 1585], Hii[v]
Perculsus elevor.
    Though struck I am raised.
        Domenichi, Devises, [London, 1585], Hiiii[v]
Pistos soi parameno[Gk].
    I shall remain faithfully with you.
        Domenichi, Devises, [London, 1585], Hviii[r]
Proprio alitur succo.
    It nourishes itself from its own moisture.
        Domenichi, Devises, [London, 1585], Hvi[v]
Quod huic deest me torquet.
    What this creature lacks torments me.
        Domenichi, Devises, [London, 1585], Hiiii[v]
Quod me alit me extinguit.
    That which nourishes me extinguishes me.
        Domenichi, Devises, [London, 1585], Hvii[v]
Sic frustra.
    Thus in vain[1].
        Domenichi, Devises, [London, 1585], Hv[v]
Soli Caesari.
    To Caesar alone.
        Domenichi, Devises, [London, 1585], Hvii[v]
Suol di cilo vivo.
    Only of this do I live.
        Domenichi, Devises, [London, 1585], Hiiii[r]
Trovommi amor del tutto disarmato.
    Love found me completely disarmed.
        Domenichi, Devises, [London, 1585], Hiiii[v]
Vertitur ad solem.
    It terns towards the sun.
        Domenichi, Devises, [London, 1585], Hvi[r]

REFERENCE INDEX

B Matt 17, 26
    Domenichi, Devises, [London, 1585], Hiiii[v]
Ovid: Ovid
    Domenichi, Devises, [London, 1585], Hvii[r]
Petrarch: Petrarch
    Domenichi, Devises, [London, 1585], Hiiii[v]
Petrarch: Petrarch
    Domenichi, Devises, [London, 1585], Hv[r]
Pliny: Pliny
    Domenichi, Devises, [London, 1585], Hii[v]
Pliny: Pliny
    Domenichi, Devises, [London, 1585], Hv[r]
Pliny: Pliny
    Domenichi, Devises, [London, 1585], Hv[v]
Pliny: Pliny
    Domenichi, Devises, [London, 1585], Hvii[v]

BEARER INDEX

Bottigella: Giovanni Battista Bottigella
    Domenichi, Devises, [London, 1585], Hv[v]
Dutch: Dutch gentleman living in Naples
    Domenichi, Devises, [London, 1585], Hvii[r]
Fernando: Consalvo Fernando
    Domenichi, Devises, [London, 1585], Hvii[r]
Girami: Ippolito Girami

Domenichi, Devises, [London, 1585], Hv[v]
Gonzaga: Frederico Gonzaga, Duke of Mantua
    Domenichi, Devises, [London, 1585], Hiii[v]
Lodron: Count Battista di Lodron
    Domenichi, Devises, [London, 1585], Hiii[r]
Maino: Gasparo de Maino
    Domenichi, Devises, [London, 1585], Hiii[r]
Milan: amorous gentleman of Milan
    Domenichi, Devises, [London, 1585], Hvii[v]
Naples: unnamed Dutch gentleman living in Naples.
    Domenichi, Devises, [London, 1585], Hvii[r]
Pallavicino: Girolamo Pallavicino
    Domenichi, Devises, [London, 1585], Hvi[v]
Pietra: Count Maurizio Pietra
    Domenichi, Devises, [London, 1585], Hiii[v]
Pietro: Count Clemente Pietro
    Domenichi, Devises, [London, 1585], Hv[r]
Pietro: Count Clemente Pietro
    Domenichi, Devises, [London, 1585], Hv[r]
Pietro: Count Clemente Pietro
    Domenichi, Devises, [London, 1585], Hv[r]
Pietro: Count Clemente Pietro
    Domenichi, Devises, [London, 1585], Hv[r]
Salerno: anonymous young gallant of Salerno
    Domenichi, Devises, [London, 1585], Hiiii[v]
Salerno: anonymous young gallant of Salerno.
    Domenichi, Devises, [London, 1585], Hiiii[v]
Stampo: Count Massimiliano Stampo
    Domenichi, Devises, [London, 1585], Hiii[r]
Stampo: Hermet Stampo
    Domenichi, Devises, [London, 1585], Hii[v]
Stampo: Hermet Stampo, Marquis of Sonomo(?)
    Domenichi, Devises, [London, 1585], Hii[v]
Stipiciana: Pyrho di Stipiciana
    Domenichi, Devises, [London, 1585], Hvii[v]
Tormiella: Livia Tormiella
    Domenichi, Devises, [London, 1585], Hvi[r]
Ursino: Carlo Ursino
    Domenichi, Devises, [London, 1585], Hiii[v]

COMMENTARY INDEX

Moronna, Anna: The mulberry in Lombardy is called
    mora [punning allusion to name of the lady Anna
    Moronna].
        Domenichi, Devises, [London, 1585], Hiii[r]
lizard: The lizard, unlike other creatures, does not love.
    Domenichi, Devises, [London, 1585], Hiii[v]
love: The lizard, unlike other creatures, does not love.
    Domenichi, Devises, [London, 1585], Hiii[v]
mora: The mulberry in Lombardy is called mora [punning
    allusion to name of the lady Anna Moronna].
        Domenichi, Devises, [London, 1585], Hiii[r]
mulberry: The mulberry in Lombardy is called mora
    [punning allusion to name of the lady Anna
    Moronna].
        Domenichi, Devises, [London, 1585], Hiii[r]

THE EMBLEMS OF GEFFREY WHITNEY

INDEXES AND LISTS

Prepared by Peter M. Daly

PICTURE INDEX

admonish: A ˚mother ˚admonishes a ˚child in ˚bed; a
˚wolf lurks outside.
Whitney, Emblemes, Leyden, 1586, p.162

aim: A ˚snake bites an ˚archer ˚aiming an ˚arrow at a
˚bird in flight.
Whitney, Emblemes, Leyden, 1586, p.078

air: ˚Chaos: ˚four ˚elements -- ˚fire, ˚air, ˚earth and
˚water -- in confusion. A ˚crescent ˚moon, ˚sun,
˚star and ˚wind. The inscription ˚"KAOS" [="chaos"].
Whitney, Emblemes, Leyden, 1586, p.122

alms: A man gives ˚alms to a ˚poor man.
Whitney, Emblemes, Leyden, 1586, p.190b

alms: A man blows a ˚trumpet as he gives ˚alms to a
˚beggar.
Whitney, Emblemes, Leyden, 1586, p.224b

amaranth: ˚Thetis stands by the ˚tomb of ˚Achilles,
which is decked with ˚amaranths.
Whitney, Emblemes, Leyden, 1586, p.193

animal: A ˚lion ˚devours its ˚prey, observed by an
˚envious ˚dog. ˚Animals nearby.
Whitney, Emblemes, Leyden, 1586, p.044

ant: The ˚sun beats down as a ˚grasshopper watches
˚ants work under barren ˚trees.
Whitney, Emblemes, Leyden, 1586, p.159

ant: ˚Labour, with ˚cornucopia and ˚crown of ears of
˚grain, sits in a ˚chariot pulled by ˚ants.
Whitney, Emblemes, Leyden, 1586, p.175

antelope: ˚Orpheus plays his ˚harp, surrounded by a
˚vulture, ˚stork, ˚stag, ˚lion, ˚bear, ˚antelope, and
˚ape.
Whitney, Emblemes, Leyden, 1586, p.186

anvil: A man breaks a ˚sword over an ˚anvil.
Whitney, Emblemes, Leyden, 1586, p.192

ape: An ˚ape thrusts the ˚paw of a ˚dog into the ˚fire
to withdraw ˚chestnuts.
Whitney, Emblemes, Leyden, 1586, p.058

ape: ˚Circe touches with her ˚wand a ˚pig; nearby a
˚dog, ˚ape, ˚goat and ˚ass, ˚Ulysses's transformed
men.
Whitney, Emblemes, Leyden, 1586, p.082

ape: An ˚ape, ˚ass and ˚mole discuss their lot in life.
Whitney, Emblemes, Leyden, 1586, p.093a

ape: A ˚fox and an ˚ape exchange insults.
Whitney, Emblemes, Leyden, 1586, p.142

ape: An ˚ape, tampering with a carpenter's ˚tools -- a
˚wedge, ˚axe and ˚mallet -- catches his foot in a
˚log.
Whitney, Emblemes, Leyden, 1586, p.145

ape: An ˚ape throws ˚gold ˚coins from a ˚window.
Whitney, Emblemes, Leyden, 1586, p.169

ape: ˚Orpheus plays his ˚harp, surrounded by a ˚vulture,
˚stork, ˚stag, ˚lion, ˚bear, ˚antelope, and ˚ape.
Whitney, Emblemes, Leyden, 1586, p.186

ape: A ˚ape holding its ˚dead ˚offspring.
Whitney, Emblemes, Leyden, 1586, p.188a

ape: ˚Two ˚apes.
Whitney, Emblemes, Leyden, 1586, p.190a

apple: ˚Paris gives the ˚golden ˚apple to ˚Venus,
accompanied by ˚Eros.
Whitney, Emblemes, Leyden, 1586, p.083

archer: A ˚snake bites an ˚archer ˚aiming an ˚arrow at a
˚bird in flight.
Whitney, Emblemes, Leyden, 1586, p.078

archway: ˚Three ˚rich and ˚two ˚poor men enter a
˚palace through two different ˚doors.
Whitney, Emblemes, Leyden, 1586, p.204

arm: From a ˚cloud a right ˚arm bearing a ˚sword and a
left ˚arm with a ˚trowel.
Whitney, Emblemes, Leyden, 1586, p.066

arm: From a ˚cloud a right ˚arm bearing a ˚sword and a
left ˚arm with a ˚trowel.
Whitney, Emblemes, Leyden, 1586, p.066

arm: A man is weighted down by a ˚stone bound to his

˚right ˚arm as he lifts his ˚winged ˚left arm and leg
skywards towards ˚God(?).
Whitney, Emblemes, Leyden, 1586, p.152

armed: ˚Armed ˚Pygmies ˚attack ˚Hercules, who sleeps
˚club in hand.
Whitney, Emblemes, Leyden, 1586, p.016

armillary sphere: An ˚astronomer, looking at the ˚starry
˚sky, falls into a ˚well; an ˚armillary ˚sphere or
˚astrolabe on the ground.
Whitney, Emblemes, Leyden, 1586, p.157

armour: ˚Brutus in ˚Roman ˚armour and ˚helmet, ˚shield
on the ground, ˚falls on his ˚sword.
Whitney, Emblemes, Leyden, 1586, p.070

armour: ˚Two ˚kings or ˚princes in ˚armour shake
˚right hands; nearby, cavalry and an ˚encampment.
Whitney, Emblemes, Leyden, 1586, p.076a

armour: ˚Janus with ˚two ˚faces, in ˚Roman ˚armour
holds a ˚sceptre in his ˚right hand and a ˚mirror(?)
in his ˚left.
Whitney, Emblemes, Leyden, 1586, p.108

arrow: ˚Apollo and ˚Diana kill ˚Niobe's ˚children with
˚arrows.
Whitney, Emblemes, Leyden, 1586, p.013

arrow: A ˚snake bites an ˚archer ˚aiming an ˚arrow at
a ˚bird in flight.
Whitney, Emblemes, Leyden, 1586, p.078

arrow: A ˚scrolled ˚shield pierced by ˚arrows.
Whitney, Emblemes, Leyden, 1586, p.117

arrow: ˚Eros and ˚Death shoot exchanged ˚arrows.
Whitney, Emblemes, Leyden, 1586, p.132

arrow: An ˚arrow ˚broken in two against a ˚marble
˚wall.
Whitney, Emblemes, Leyden, 1586, p.138b

arrow: ˚Brasidas points to his ˚shield, ˚pierced by the
˚arrow that wounded him.
Whitney, Emblemes, Leyden, 1586, p.141

arrow: A ˚stag is struck by an ˚arrow; a ˚hunter
approaches with ˚two ˚dogs.
Whitney, Emblemes, Leyden, 1586, p.153a

arrow: A ˚remora encircles an ˚arrow.
Whitney, Emblemes, Leyden, 1586, p.188b

arrow: ˚Procris is struck by an ˚arrow, shot by
˚Cephalus.
Whitney, Emblemes, Leyden, 1586, p.211

arrow: A ˚farmer works the banks of a ˚ditch, fed by
the ˚sea; a ˚bull or ˚cow beside a bound ˚sheaf of
˚arrows.
Whitney, Emblemes, Leyden, 1586, p.072

arsonist: An ˚arsonist sets ˚fire to a ˚house; a man,
carrying a ˚bucket of ˚oil, scales a ˚ladder placed
against the burning house. A third man ˚stabs
another man.
Whitney, Emblemes, Leyden, 1586, p.007

artist: A man flees from a ˚dog and a ˚bull; an ˚artist
draws a figure(?) on a ˚panel.
Whitney, Emblemes, Leyden, 1586, p.100

ass: ˚Worshippers kneel in ˚reverence before an ˚ass
bearing a ˚statue of ˚Isis; the ˚driver ˚beats the ass
with a ˚stick.
Whitney, Emblemes, Leyden, 1586, p.008

ass: An ˚ass, laden with ˚foodstuffs: ˚jugs, a ˚cask(?),
bags with ˚bread(?), a spitted ˚fowl, and a ˚rabbit,
˚eats ˚thistles.
Whitney, Emblemes, Leyden, 1586, p.018

ass: ˚Ocnus and a ˚ropemaker make a ˚rope from
grasses. An ˚ass eats the rope.
Whitney, Emblemes, Leyden, 1586, p.048

ass: ˚Circe touches with her ˚wand a ˚pig; nearby a
˚dog, ˚ape, ˚goat and ˚ass, ˚Ulysses's transformed
men.
Whitney, Emblemes, Leyden, 1586, p.082

ass: Seated on a ˚throne, ˚Jupiter, whose ˚staff is
surmounted by an ˚eagle, is surrounded by a ˚deer,
˚horse, ˚bull, ˚ass, ˚snail, ˚eagle, and ˚lion.
Whitney, Emblemes, Leyden, 1586, p.091

ass: An ˚ape, ˚ass and ˚mole discuss their lot in life.
Whitney, Emblemes, Leyden, 1586, p.093a

ass: A ˚lion and a ˚fox face each other over their ˚prey,
including a ˚stag. A dead ˚ass lies nearby.
Whitney, Emblemes, Leyden, 1586, p.154

ass: ˚Apollo and ˚Pan making music on ˚viola(?) and
˚bagpipes. ˚Midas has ˚ears of an ˚ass.
Whitney, Emblemes, Leyden, 1586, p.218a

astrolabe: An ˚astronomer, looking at the ˚starry ˚sky,
falls into a ˚well; an ˚armillary ˚sphere or ˚astrolabe
on the ground.
Whitney, Emblemes, Leyden, 1586, p.157

astrolobe: A ˚king with ˚crown and ˚sceptre on a ˚horse
watches a ˚ploughman give his ˚harrow to an
˚astronomer in exchange for a ˚sphere(?) or
˚astrolobe and the ˚doctor's ˚robe.
Whitney, Emblemes, Leyden, 1586, p.009

astrological: A ˚vine grows on a wall with ˚astrological
symbols and a ˚moon. A ˚woman holds grapes away
from her with her ˚left hand. Above ˚zodiacal ˚circle
with ˚Virgo, her ˚right hand pointing at grapes held
by the woman.
Whitney, Emblemes, Leyden, 1586, p.206

astronomer: A ˚king with ˚crown and ˚sceptre on a
˚horse watches a ˚ploughman give his ˚harrow to an
˚astronomer in exchange for a ˚sphere(?) or
˚astrolobe and the ˚doctor's ˚robe.
Whitney, Emblemes, Leyden, 1586, p.009

astronomer: An ˚astronomer, looking at the ˚starry ˚sky,
falls into a ˚well; an ˚armillary ˚sphere or ˚astrolabe
on the ground.
Whitney, Emblemes, Leyden, 1586, p.157

attack: ˚Armed ˚Pygmies ˚attack ˚Hercules, who sleeps
˚club in hand.
Whitney, Emblemes, Leyden, 1586, p.016

awaken: A ˚sleeping man is ˚awakened by a ˚swallow
chattering in its ˚nest.
Whitney, Emblemes, Leyden, 1586, p.050a

axe: An ˚ape, tampering with a carpenter's ˚tools -- a
˚wedge, ˚axe and ˚mallet -- catches his foot in a
˚log.
Whitney, Emblemes, Leyden, 1586, p.145

axe: A ˚woodsman is at work with his ˚axe at the base
of a ˚tree.
Whitney, Emblemes, Leyden, 1586, p.228

axe(?): An ˚elephant rests against a ˚tree, undermined by
a ˚hunter with an ˚axe(?).
Whitney, Emblemes, Leyden, 1586, p.150

backgammon: Four ˚men sit at a table; one ˚drinks from
a ˚mug; a second watches two argue over a ˚game of
˚backgammon.
Whitney, Emblemes, Leyden, 1586, p.017

bag: An ˚ape throws ˚gold ˚coins from a ˚window; ˚table
with ˚two ˚bags on it.
Whitney, Emblemes, Leyden, 1586, p.169

bagpipes: ˚Apollo and ˚Pan making music on ˚viola(?) and
˚bagpipes.
Whitney, Emblemes, Leyden, 1586, p.218a

bald: ˚Naked ˚Occasio, with ˚bald ˚head, long ˚forelock,
and ˚razor in her raised ˚right hand, stands on a
˚wheel in the ˚sea.
Whitney, Emblemes, Leyden, 1586, p.181

bare: ˚Bare ˚breasted ˚Prowess ˚tears out her ˚hair as
she sits on the ˚tomb of ˚Ajax.
Whitney, Emblemes, Leyden, 1586, p.030

barrel: A ˚barrel with small ˚holes ˚discharges ˚water on
all sides.
Whitney, Emblemes, Leyden, 1586, p.012

barrel: Under a ˚sun, a ˚bound ˚Attilius, lies on a
˚stretcher near an open ˚barrel riven with ˚nails.
Whitney, Emblemes, Leyden, 1586, p.114

barrel: ˚Nemesis with ˚bridle, stands before ˚Hope,
seated on a ˚barrel.
Whitney, Emblemes, Leyden, 1586, p.139b

barrel: ˚Diogenes in his ˚barrel, talks with ˚Alexander.

Whitney, Emblemes, Leyden, 1586, p.198

barren: ˚Athene(?) ˚sits under a ˚barren ˚tree before a
˚fallow field.
Whitney, Emblemes, Leyden, 1586, p.103

basin: On a ˚marble ˚tomb an ˚ewer and ˚basin with
folded ˚towel.
Whitney, Emblemes, Leyden, 1586, p.136

battle-axe: ˚bound ˚Attilius, lies on a ˚stretcher near an
open ˚barrel riven with ˚nails; he is observed by a
˚helmeted ˚soldier with a ˚battle-axe.
Whitney, Emblemes, Leyden, 1586, p.114

battlefield: ˚Two ˚soldiers lead a captive ˚herald from
the ˚battlefield into a ˚fortress.
Whitney, Emblemes, Leyden, 1586, p.054a

beak: A ˚swallow with a ˚grasshopper in its ˚beak
returns to its ˚nest in the ˚ruins of a ˚palace.
Whitney, Emblemes, Leyden, 1586, p.005

beak: A ˚stork with a ˚snake in its ˚beak returns to its
˚nest with ˚three young.
Whitney, Emblemes, Leyden, 1586, p.072

bear: ˚Orpheus plays his ˚harp, surrounded by a
˚vulture, ˚stork, ˚stag, ˚lion, ˚bear, ˚antelope, and
˚ape.
Whitney, Emblemes, Leyden, 1586, p.186

beat: ˚Worshippers kneel in ˚reverence before an ˚ass
bearing a ˚statue of ˚Isis; the ˚driver ˚beats the ass
with a ˚stick.
Whitney, Emblemes, Leyden, 1586, p.008

beaver: A ˚beaver tears off his ˚testicles, ˚pursued by a
˚hunter and ˚two ˚hounds.
Whitney, Emblemes, Leyden, 1586, p.035

bed: ˚Glory ˚flees through a ˚doorway from ˚naked
˚couple on a ˚bed; beside them stands a ˚table with
˚food and ˚drink.
Whitney, Emblemes, Leyden, 1586, p.042

bed: A ˚mother ˚admonishes a ˚child in ˚bed; a ˚wolf
lurks outside.
Whitney, Emblemes, Leyden, 1586, p.162

bee: A ˚flower gives ˚honey to a ˚bee and ˚poison to a
˚spider.
Whitney, Emblemes, Leyden, 1586, p.051a

bee: A ˚helmet is used as a ˚hive by ˚bees.
Whitney, Emblemes, Leyden, 1586, p.138a

bee: A ˚bee stung ˚Eros flies to ˚Venus. Bees swarm
around two ˚hives.
Whitney, Emblemes, Leyden, 1586, p.147

bee: ˚Eros shows his ˚bee stung ˚hand to ˚Venus; bees
swarm around their ˚hive.
Whitney, Emblemes, Leyden, 1586, p.148

bee: ˚Bees return to the ˚hive.
Whitney, Emblemes, Leyden, 1586, p.200

beggar: A man blows a ˚trumpet as he gives ˚alms to a
˚beggar.
Whitney, Emblemes, Leyden, 1586, p.224b

bellows: ˚Strife stands on a ˚bellows, holding an
˚inverted ˚torch.
Whitney, Emblemes, Leyden, 1586, p.004

bind: From his ˚throne, ˚Mezentius with ˚crown and
˚sceptre overseee the ˚binding of a ˚naked ˚body to
a naked ˚corpse.
Whitney, Emblemes, Leyden, 1586, p.099

bird: ˚Two ˚fowlers watch as ˚four ˚birds, ˚ducks, are
˚lured into the ˚net by a live ˚decoy.
Whitney, Emblemes, Leyden, 1586, p.027

bird: ˚Three ˚birds: ˚swallow(?), cuckoo(?), and
˚chaffinch(?). A ˚vineyard nearby.
Whitney, Emblemes, Leyden, 1586, p.054b

bird: A ˚snake bites an ˚archer ˚aiming an ˚arrow at a
˚bird in flight.
Whitney, Emblemes, Leyden, 1586, p.078

bird: ˚Hanno releases a ˚flock of ˚birds.
Whitney, Emblemes, Leyden, 1586, p.084

bird: A ˚leopard(?) fights with a ˚lion. ˚Travellers pass
nearby. A ˚flock of ˚birds flies over head.
Whitney, Emblemes, Leyden, 1586, p.178

bird: A man tries to capture a flying ˚bird.
  Whitney, Emblemes, Leyden, 1586, p.180
bird: A ˚Venus(?) with basket of ˚fruit, and ˚Eros(?);
  animals nearby: ˚lion, ˚hare, ˚horse, ˚bird and ˚fish.
  Whitney, Emblemes, Leyden, 1586, p.182b
bird-of-paradise: A ˚bird-of-paradise ˚flies by; a
  ˚traveller with a back ˚pack looks towards a ˚village
  across a ˚stream, where a ˚swan is feeding.
  Whitney, Emblemes, Leyden, 1586, p.089
bit: ˚Nemesis holds a ˚bit and ˚bridle.
  Whitney, Emblemes, Leyden, 1586, p.019
bite: ˚Three ˚hares ˚bite the head of a ˚dead supine
  ˚lion; a fourth hare runs by.
  Whitney, Emblemes, Leyden, 1586, p.127
black: ˚Two men ˚wash a ˚black ˚man.
  Whitney, Emblemes, Leyden, 1586, p.057
blade: The ˚sword of ˚Damocles, with ˚wavy ˚blade,
  suspended from a ˚cloud.
  Whitney, Emblemes, Leyden, 1586, p.102
blind: A ˚blind man with a ˚stick carries a ˚lame man
  who ˚points the ˚way with his ˚finger.
  Whitney, Emblemes, Leyden, 1586, p.065
blind: A ˚blind ˚woman sits in an armchair in an empty
  room. A ˚doctor leaves the room with an armful of
  her possessions.
  Whitney, Emblemes, Leyden, 1586, p.156a
blind: An ˚envious man, ˚blind in one ˚eye and a
  ˚covetous man, blind in both; the covetous man points
  to three eyes on the ground. Nearby, a ˚treasure
  ˚chest.
  Whitney, Emblemes, Leyden, 1586, p.095
blood: In a ˚nest made of a ˚crown of ˚thorns,the
  ˚pelican with ˚wings ˚outspread, pierces her ˚breast
  with her beak to sprinkle her ˚three ˚young¹ with
  ˚blood.
  Whitney, Emblemes, Leyden, 1586, p.087
blow: ˚Four ˚winds ˚blow on a ˚rock in a rough ˚sea.
  Whitney, Emblemes, Leyden, 1586, p.096
boar: A ˚vulture watches a ˚lion and a ˚boar fighting.
  Whitney, Emblemes, Leyden, 1586, p.119
boar: A ˚boar with ˚tusks sharpened faces a ˚fox.
  Whitney, Emblemes, Leyden, 1586, p.153b
boat: ˚Two ˚fishermen in a ˚boat haul in a ˚fishing ˚net.
  Whitney, Emblemes, Leyden, 1586, p.071
body: From his ˚throne, ˚Mezentius with ˚crown and
  ˚sceptre overseee the ˚binding of a ˚naked ˚body to a
  naked ˚corpse.
  Whitney, Emblemes, Leyden, 1586, p.099
bone: A ˚dog, his ˚muzzle and front ˚paws in a ˚stream,
  searches for his ˚bone.
  Whitney, Emblemes, Leyden, 1586, p.039
bone: A ˚skull, a ˚bone and a ˚flower.
  Whitney, Emblemes, Leyden, 1586, p.229b
book: ˚Laughing ˚Democritus and ˚weeping ˚Heraclitus,
  with two ˚books, face each other.
  Whitney, Emblemes, Leyden, 1586, p.014
book: A ˚scholar with a ˚book in his study. He holds a
  ˚finger to his ˚lips in a gesture of ˚silence.
  (˚Harpocrates)
  Whitney, Emblemes, Leyden, 1586, p.060
book: ˚Buildings and ˚towers ˚collapse about a ˚table
  with ˚three ˚books.
  Whitney, Emblemes, Leyden, 1586, p.131
book: An ˚open ˚book, inscribed ˚"ET USQUE AD NUBES
  VERITAS TVA" [And your truth (will soar) all the
  way to the clouds] is surrounded by ˚light. The book
  is surmounted by a ˚wreath under a pair of ˚wings
  held by a ˚hand. A ˚chain, hanging from the book, is
  pulled by ˚Satan, watched by two ˚demons.
  Whitney, Emblemes, Leyden, 1586, p.166a
book: A ˚burning ˚candle, flanked by an ˚hourglass and
  an ˚open ˚book,stands on a table in a room.
  Whitney, Emblemes, Leyden, 1586, p.172
bound: Under a ˚sun, a ˚bound ˚Attilius, lies on a
  ˚stretcher near an open ˚barrel riven with ˚nails.

  Whitney, Emblemes, Leyden, 1586, p.114
bow: ˚Nemesis with ˚bridle, stands before ˚Hope, seated
  on a ˚barrel, a ˚bow in her ˚left hand, pointing with
  her ˚right.
  Whitney, Emblemes, Leyden, 1586, p.139b
boy: ˚Two ˚boys blow ˚bubbles; six others try to catch
  them. Inscription: ˚"ET TUTTO ABBRACCIO ET
  NULLA STRINGO" [And all things I embrace and
  nothing do I hold].
  Whitney, Emblemes, Leyden, 1586, p.055b
boy: A naked ˚boy or ˚Putto(?) sits in a ˚fruit-tree; an
  ˚old ˚man, ˚scholar(?); ˚Flowers, some wilted, grow
  nearby.
  Whitney, Emblemes, Leyden, 1586, p.173
boy: Two ˚boys with ˚rods knock ˚fruit from a
  ˚nut-tree.
  Whitney, Emblemes, Leyden, 1586, p.174
branch: One ˚redbreast ˚knocks another from a ˚tree
  ˚branch.
  Whitney, Emblemes, Leyden, 1586, p.055a
branch: ˚Two ˚men with ˚laurel ˚branches ˚embrace;
  ˚swords lie on the ground. A ˚palm-tree and ˚sun
  set.
  Whitney, Emblemes, Leyden, 1586, p.216b
bread(?): An ˚ass, laden with ˚foodstuffs: ˚jugs, a
  ˚cask(?), bags with ˚bread(?), a spitted ˚fowl, and a
  ˚rabbit, ˚eats ˚thistles.
  Whitney, Emblemes, Leyden, 1586, p.018
breast: ˚Bare ˚breasted ˚Prowess ˚tears out her ˚hair as
  she sits on the ˚tomb of ˚Ajax, inscribed ˚"D
  AIACIS."
  Whitney, Emblemes, Leyden, 1586, p.030
breast: In a ˚nest made of a ˚crown of ˚thorns,the
  ˚pelican with ˚wings ˚outspread, pierces her ˚breast
  with her beak to sprinkle her ˚three ˚young¹ with
  ˚blood.
  Whitney, Emblemes, Leyden, 1586, p.087
breast: A ˚man, holding a ˚snake to his ˚breast with his
  ˚left hand, watches a ˚siege.
  Whitney, Emblemes, Leyden, 1586, p.189a
briar: A ˚lily blooms in ˚briars and ˚thorns.
  Whitney, Emblemes, Leyden, 1586, p.221
bridle: ˚Nemesis holds a ˚bit and ˚bridle.
  Whitney, Emblemes, Leyden, 1586, p.019
bridle: ˚Nemesis with ˚bridle, stands before ˚Hope,
  seated on a ˚barrel, a ˚bow in her ˚left hand,
  pointing with her ˚right.
  Whitney, Emblemes, Leyden, 1586, p.139b
bridle: A ˚sailing ˚ship on a ˚world ˚globe, surrounded
  by ˚clouds, ˚stars, ˚sun and crescent ˚moon. A
  ˚right hand holds a ˚bridle, which encircles the
  globe.
  Whitney, Emblemes, Leyden, 1586, p.203
broken: ˚Pine-trees are ˚broken by a ˚wind(?); in a
  ˚cloud ˚Jupiter(?) sits astride an ˚eagle; a ˚rabbit
  crouches before a ˚tree ˚stump; a ˚horseman nearby.
  Whitney, Emblemes, Leyden, 1586, p.059
broken: An ˚arrow ˚broken in two against a ˚marble
  ˚wall.
  Whitney, Emblemes, Leyden, 1586, p.138b
broth: Boiling ˚broth overflows a ˚cauldron into the
  ˚fire.
  Whitney, Emblemes, Leyden, 1586, p.216a
bubble: ˚Two ˚boys blow ˚bubbles; six others try to
  catch them. Inscription: ˚"ET TUTTO ABBRACCIO ET
  NULLA STRINGO" [And all things I embrace and
  nothing do I hold].
  Whitney, Emblemes, Leyden, 1586, p.055b
bucket: An ˚arsonist sets ˚fire to a ˚house; a man,
  carrying a ˚bucket of ˚oil, scales a ˚ladder placed
  against the burning house. A third man ˚stabs
  another man.
  Whitney, Emblemes, Leyden, 1586, p.007
building: ˚Buildings and ˚towers ˚collapse about a ˚table
  with ˚three ˚books.

Whitney, Emblemes, Leyden, 1586, p.131
bull: An ˚elephant is frightened by a ˚white cloth; a ˚bull by a ˚red cloth; a ˚lion by a crowing ˚cock; a ˚stag flees from a ˚smoking cloth.
Whitney, Emblemes, Leyden, 1586, p.052a
bull: A ˚farmer works the banks of a ˚ditch, fed by the ˚sea; a ˚bull or ˚cow beside a bound ˚sheaf of ˚arrows.
Whitney, Emblemes, Leyden, 1586, p.072
bull: Seated on a ˚throne, ˚Jupiter, whose ˚staff is surmounted by an ˚eagle, is surrounded by a ˚deer, ˚horse, ˚bull, ˚ass, ˚snail, ˚eagle, and ˚lion.
Whitney, Emblemes, Leyden, 1586, p.091
bull: A man flees from a ˚dog and a ˚bull; an ˚artist draws a figure(?) on a ˚panel.
Whitney, Emblemes, Leyden, 1586, p.100
bunch: A ˚vine laden with ˚bunches of ˚grapes ˚entwined about a ˚dead ˚elm-tree.
Whitney, Emblemes, Leyden, 1586, p.062
bunch: ˚Bacchus with a ˚crown of ˚vine ˚leaves and ˚grapes, and ˚Apollo with his ˚lyre stand on a ˚pedestal or ˚tomb.
Whitney, Emblemes, Leyden, 1586, p.146
bunch: A man ˚tramples ˚grapes under his ˚right ˚foot, reaching for a ˚bunch with his ˚left hand.
Whitney, Emblemes, Leyden, 1586, p.206
bundle: A man with drawn ˚sword looks into a ˚house; a ˚bundle at his feet.
Whitney, Emblemes, Leyden, 1586, p.069
bundle: ˚Labour, with ˚cornucopia and ˚crown of ears of ˚grain, sits in a ˚chariot pulled by ˚ants. She uses a ˚bundle of stalks of ˚grain(?) to beat ˚Idleness.
Whitney, Emblemes, Leyden, 1586, p.175
burn: An ˚envious man covers his ˚eyes and pulls his companion away from a ˚burning ˚house.
Whitney, Emblemes, Leyden, 1586, p.031
burn: A ˚burning ˚candle, flanked by an ˚hourglass and an ˚open ˚book, stands on a table in a room.
Whitney, Emblemes, Leyden, 1586, p.172
burn: An ˚inverted ˚burning ˚torch inscribed ˚"QUI ME ALIT ME EXTINGUIT" [The one who nourishes me extinguishes me].
Whitney, Emblemes, Leyden, 1586, p.183a
butterfly: A ˚crab holds a ˚butterfly in its claws.
Whitney, Emblemes, Leyden, 1586, p.121
caduceus: Wearing a ˚winged ˚helmet and holding a ˚caduceus, ˚Mercury points to the ˚path at his feet; a ˚traveller with a ˚staff.
Whitney, Emblemes, Leyden, 1586, p.002
cage: A child and a man observe a ˚parrot in a ˚cage.
Whitney, Emblemes, Leyden, 1586, p.036
cage: A large ˚cage with a ˚nightingale.
Whitney, Emblemes, Leyden, 1586, p.101
cage: ˚Mice play; ˚two ˚cats in ˚cages.
Whitney, Emblemes, Leyden, 1586, p.222b
candle: A ˚burning ˚candle, flanked by an ˚hourglass and an ˚open ˚book,stands on a table in a room.
Whitney, Emblemes, Leyden, 1586, p.172
candle: ˚Gnats ˚fly into a ˚candle ˚flame; the ˚candlestick is on a plinth inscribed ˚"COSI DE BEN AMAR PORTO TORMENTO" [Thus from a great love I bear torment] The plinth is flanked by ˚two ˚fires, ˚women nearby.
Whitney, Emblemes, Leyden, 1586, p.219
candlestick: ˚Gnats ˚fly into a ˚candle ˚flame; the ˚candlestick is on a plinth inscribed ˚"COSI DE BEN AMAR PORTO TORMENTO" [Thus from a great love I bear torment] The plinth is flanked by ˚two ˚fires, ˚women nearby.
Whitney, Emblemes, Leyden, 1586, p.219
cap: A ˚scholar in a ˚philosopher's ˚cap, ˚Diomedes or ˚Cicero, a ˚tablet under his arm talks with a ˚soldier in a ˚helmet with ˚sword, ˚shield and ˚spear, ˚Ulysses or ˚Caesar.
Whitney, Emblemes, Leyden, 1586, p.047

cap: ˚Mercury in a ˚winged ˚cap repairs the ˚strings of a ˚lute.
Whitney, Emblemes, Leyden, 1586, p.092
cart: A ˚dog pulls a ˚cart, harrassed by two smaller dogs. Another small ˚dog sleeps in a ˚woman's lap.
Whitney, Emblemes, Leyden, 1586, p.140
carver: A ˚carver uses a ˚mallet and ˚chisel to incise a ˚tablet with ˚"TROIA MIHI LICET TAMEN" [Never-the-less the whore sells herself to me].
Whitney, Emblemes, Leyden, 1586, p.183b
cask(?): An ˚ass, laden with ˚foodstuffs: ˚jugs, a ˚cask(?), bags with ˚bread(?), a spitted ˚fowl, and a ˚rabbit, ˚eats ˚thistles.
Whitney, Emblemes, Leyden, 1586, p.018
cat: ˚Mice play; ˚two ˚cats in ˚cages.
Whitney, Emblemes, Leyden, 1586, p.222b
cauldron: Boiling ˚broth overflows a ˚cauldron into the ˚fire.
Whitney, Emblemes, Leyden, 1586, p.216a
chaffinch(?): ˚Three ˚birds: ˚swallow(?), cuckoo(?),and ˚chaffinch(?). A ˚vineyard nearby.
Whitney, Emblemes, Leyden, 1586, p.054b
chain: An ˚eagle rends the ˚liver of ˚Prometheus, ˚chained to a ˚rock.
Whitney, Emblemes, Leyden, 1586, p.075
chaos: ˚Chaos: ˚four ˚elements-- ˚fire, ˚air, ˚earth and ˚water-- in confusion. A ˚crescent ˚moon, ˚sun, ˚star and ˚wind. The inscription ˚"KAOS" [="chaos"].
Whitney, Emblemes, Leyden, 1586, p.122
chapel: A ˚woman collects ˚skulls into her apron; ˚horse is ˚trotting on a hill; ˚skulls piled beside a ˚chapel.
Whitney, Emblemes, Leyden, 1586, p.046
chariot: A ˚charioteer with a ˚whip tries to ˚rein in the ˚two galloping ˚horses pulling his ˚chariot.
Whitney, Emblemes, Leyden, 1586, p.006
chariot: With ˚whip and ˚reins, ˚Eros ˚drives the ˚two ˚lions ˚drawing his ˚chariot.
Whitney, Emblemes, Leyden, 1586, p.063
chariot: ˚Labour, with ˚cornucopia and ˚crown of ears of ˚grain, sits in a ˚chariot pulled by ˚ants.
Whitney, Emblemes, Leyden, 1586, p.175
charioteer: A ˚charioteer with a ˚whip tries to ˚rein in the ˚two galloping ˚horses pulling his ˚chariot.
Whitney, Emblemes, Leyden, 1586, p.006
chart: A man ˚kneeling before a ˚chart holds a ˚compass to the ˚stars; below a ˚stag ˚drinks from a ˚stream.
Whitney, Emblemes, Leyden, 1586, p.043
chess: A ˚young man and an ˚older over a ˚game of ˚draughts or ˚chess; ˚flames engulf the building behind them.
Whitney, Emblemes, Leyden, 1586, p.208
chest: An ˚envious man, ˚blind in one ˚eye and a ˚covetous man, blind in both; the covetous man points to three eyes on the ground. Nearby, a ˚treasure ˚chest.
Whitney, Emblemes, Leyden, 1586, p.095
chest: A ˚couple walk from a building, the man points to an open ˚treasure chest. ˚Winged ˚Time, with a ˚scythe, pursues the couple.
Whitney, Emblemes, Leyden, 1586, p.199
chest: ˚Opimius, the ˚miser, in his sick-bed. The ˚physician supervises the emptying of his ˚chests of ˚gold onto a table.
Whitney, Emblemes, Leyden, 1586, p.209
chestnut: An ˚ape thrusts the ˚paw of a ˚dog into the ˚fire to withdraw ˚chestnuts.
Whitney, Emblemes, Leyden, 1586, p.058
child: ˚Apollo and ˚Diana kill ˚Niobe's ˚children with ˚arrows. Niobe is turned to ˚stone.
Whitney, Emblemes, Leyden, 1586, p.013
child: A ˚swallow approaches its ˚nest in a niche with a ˚statue of ˚Medea ˚killing her ˚child with a ˚sword.
Whitney, Emblemes, Leyden, 1586, p.033

crown: A ˙king with ˙crown and ˙sceptre on a ˙horse
watches a ˙ploughman give his ˙harrow to an
˙astronomer in exchange for a ˙sphere(?) or
˙astrolobe and the ˙doctor's ˙robe.
Whitney, Emblemes, Leyden, 1586, p.009

crown: ˙Agamemnon, with ˙crown, ˙sword, and ˙shield
inscribed ˙"Agamemnon" bearing a ˙lion[1] ˙rampant.
˙Troy in ˙flames.
Whitney, Emblemes, Leyden, 1586, p.045

crown: In a ˙nest made of a ˙crown of ˙thorns,the
˙pelican with ˙wings ˙outspread, pierces her ˙breast
with her beak to sprinkle her ˙three ˙young[1] with
˙blood.
Whitney, Emblemes, Leyden, 1586, p.087

crown: From his ˙throne, ˙Mezentius with ˙crown and
˙sceptre oversees the ˙binding of a ˙naked ˙body to a
naked ˙corpse.
Whitney, Emblemes, Leyden, 1586, p.099

crown: ˙Bacchus with a ˙crown of ˙vine ˙leaves and
˙grapes, and ˙Apollo with his ˙lyre stand on a
˙pedestal or ˙tomb.
Whitney, Emblemes, Leyden, 1586, p.146

crown: A ˙king, with ˙crown and ˙sceptre, squeezes
˙water from a ˙sponge; a crowd watches a ˙hanging
(˙gibbet).
Whitney, Emblemes, Leyden, 1586, p.151

crown: ˙Labour, with ˙cornucopia and ˙crown of ears of
˙grain, sits in a ˙chariot pulled by ˙ants. She uses a
˙bundle of stalks of ˙grain(?) to beat ˙Idleness.
Whitney, Emblemes, Leyden, 1586, p.175

crown: ˙Diogenes in his ˙barrel, talks with ˙Alexander
with ˙crown and ˙sceptre.
Whitney, Emblemes, Leyden, 1586, p.198

crown: A ˙naked ˙child on a ˙hobby-horse, a ˙courtier,
and a ˙jester stand before a ˙crowned ˙king holding a
˙sceptre.
Whitney, Emblemes, Leyden, 1586, p.081

crutch: An ˙old man on ˙crutches enters a room with a
˙swaddled baby in a ˙cradle.
Whitney, Emblemes, Leyden, 1586, p.167

cub: A ˙goat ˙suckles a ˙wolf ˙cub.
Whitney, Emblemes, Leyden, 1586, p.049

cuckoo(?): ˙Three ˙birds: ˙swallow(?), cuckoo(?),and
˙chaffinch(?). A ˙vineyard nearby.
Whitney, Emblemes, Leyden, 1586, p.054b

cup: ˙Naked ˙Bacchus, a ˙wreath of ˙vines(?) on his
head, lies on a ˙river bank, ˙drinking from a ˙cup. A
˙dog leaps in front of a ˙crocodile in the water.
Whitney, Emblemes, Leyden, 1586, p.125

cuttlefish: A ˙fisherman with a ˙net reaches with his
˙right hand for a ˙cuttlefish muddying the ˙water. A
˙lizard(?) flees on the opposite bank.
Whitney, Emblemes, Leyden, 1586, p.097

cypress: A ˙cypress tree.
Whitney, Emblemes, Leyden, 1586, p.205

dance: ˙Mercury in a ˙winged ˙cap repairs the ˙strings
of a ˙lute; a ˙woman ˙dances while another man plays
a lute.
Whitney, Emblemes, Leyden, 1586, p.092

dead: A ˙vine laden with ˙bunches of ˙grapes ˙entwined
about a ˙dead ˙elm-tree.
Whitney, Emblemes, Leyden, 1586, p.062

dead: A ˙fire fed with ˙wood from a ˙dead ˙tree.
Whitney, Emblemes, Leyden, 1586, p.077b

dead: ˙Three ˙hares ˙bite the head of a ˙dead supine
˙lion; a fourth hare runs by.
Whitney, Emblemes, Leyden, 1586, p.127

dead: A ˙ape holding its ˙dead ˙offspring.
Whitney, Emblemes, Leyden, 1586, p.188a

decoy: ˙Two ˙fowlers watch as ˙four ˙birds, ˙ducks, are
˙lured into the ˙net by a live ˙decoy.
Whitney, Emblemes, Leyden, 1586, p.027

deer: Seated on a ˙throne, ˙Jupiter, whose ˙staff is
surmounted by an ˙eagle, is surrounded by a ˙deer,

˙horse, ˙bull, ˙ass, ˙snail, ˙eagle, and ˙lion.
Whitney, Emblemes, Leyden, 1586, p.091

devour: A ˙lion ˙devours its ˙prey, observed by an
˙envious ˙dog. ˙Animals nearby.
Whitney, Emblemes, Leyden, 1586, p.044

dice: ˙Three ˙women ˙gamble with ˙dice.
Whitney, Emblemes, Leyden, 1586, p.176

discharge: A ˙barrel with small ˙holes ˙discharges
˙water on all sides.
Whitney, Emblemes, Leyden, 1586, p.012

ditch: A ˙farmer works the banks of a ˙ditch, fed by
the ˙sea; a ˙bull or ˙cow beside a bound ˙sheaf of
˙arrows.
Whitney, Emblemes, Leyden, 1586, p.072

dock: A man tramples ˙docks underfoot.
Whitney, Emblemes, Leyden, 1586, p.098b

doctor: A ˙king watches a ˙ploughman give his ˙harrow
to an ˙astronomer in exchange for a ˙sphere(?) or
˙astrolobe and the ˙doctor's ˙robe.
Whitney, Emblemes, Leyden, 1586, p.009

doctor: A ˙blind ˙woman sits in an armchair in an
empty room. A ˙doctor leaves the room with an
armful of her possessions.
Whitney, Emblemes, Leyden, 1586, p.156a

dog: A ˙dog, his ˙muzzle and front ˙paws in a ˙stream,
searches for his ˙bone.
Whitney, Emblemes, Leyden, 1586, p.039

dog: A ˙lion ˙devours its ˙prey, observed by an
˙envious ˙dog. ˙Animals nearby.
Whitney, Emblemes, Leyden, 1586, p.044

dog: A ˙dog bites a ˙stone; a man is about to throw
another stone at the dog.
Whitney, Emblemes, Leyden, 1586, p.056

dog: An ˙ape thrusts the ˙paw of a ˙dog into the ˙fire
to withdraw ˙chestnuts.
Whitney, Emblemes, Leyden, 1586, p.058

dog: ˙Circe touches with her ˙wand a ˙pig; nearby a
˙dog, ˙ape, ˙goat and ˙ass, ˙Ulysses's transformed
men.
Whitney, Emblemes, Leyden, 1586, p.082

dog: A man flees from a ˙dog and a ˙bull; an ˙artist
draws a figure(?) on a ˙panel.
Whitney, Emblemes, Leyden, 1586, p.100

dog: ˙Naked ˙Bacchus lies on a ˙river bank, ˙drinking
from a ˙cup. A ˙dog leaps in front of a ˙crocodile in
the water.
Whitney, Emblemes, Leyden, 1586, p.125

dog: A ˙dog pulls a ˙cart, harrassed by two smaller
dogs. Another small ˙dog sleeps in a ˙woman's lap.
Whitney, Emblemes, Leyden, 1586, p.140

dog: A ˙stag is struck by an ˙arrow; a ˙hunter
approaches with ˙two ˙dogs.
Whitney, Emblemes, Leyden, 1586, p.153a

dog: A ˙dog in a ˙manger prevents an ˙ox from feeding.
Whitney, Emblemes, Leyden, 1586, p.184

dog: ˙Procris is struck by an ˙arrow, shot by ˙Cephalus.
A ˙dog runs towards her.
Whitney, Emblemes, Leyden, 1586, p.211

dog: ˙Aesculapius on a ˙throne, supported by two
˙eagles. Nearby a ˙snake, ˙dog and ˙cock.
Whitney, Emblemes, Leyden, 1586, p.212

dog: A ˙dog bays at a full ˙moon.
Whitney, Emblemes, Leyden, 1586, p.213

dog: ˙Three ˙Christian ˙martyrs in ˙prayer before a
˙fire are harassed by men with ˙swords and ˙dogs.
Whitney, Emblemes, Leyden, 1586, p.224a

dolphin: A ˙dolphin ˙flounders on the ˙sea ˙shore.
Whitney, Emblemes, Leyden, 1586, p.090

dolphin: ˙Arion and his ˙harp thrown overboard by
˙sailors; a ˙dolphin waits near the ˙ship.
Whitney, Emblemes, Leyden, 1586, p.144

dolphin: ˙Thetis stands by the ˙tomb of ˙Achilles, which
is decked with ˙amaranths, and stands under a
˙palm-tree. A ˙dolphin nearby.
Whitney, Emblemes, Leyden, 1586, p.193

door: `Three `rich and `two `poor men enter a `palace
through two different `doors.
Whitney, Emblemes, Leyden, 1586, p.204

doorway: `Glory `flees through a `doorway from `naked
`couple on a `bed.
Whitney, Emblemes, Leyden, 1586, p.042

drape: A `shirt or `shroud `draped on a `lance and a
`crossbar.
Whitney, Emblemes, Leyden, 1586, p.086

draughts: A `young man and an `older over a `game of
`draughts or `chess; `flames engulf the building
behind them.
Whitney, Emblemes, Leyden, 1586, p.208

draw: With `whip and `reins, `Eros `drives the `two
`lions `drawing his `chariot.
Whitney, Emblemes, Leyden, 1586, p.063

drink: Four `men sit at a table; one `drinks from a
`mug; a second watches the remaining two argue over
a `game of `backgammon. Two other men `wrestle.
Whitney, Emblemes, Leyden, 1586, p.017

drink: `Glory `flees through a `doorway from `naked
`couple on a `bed; beside them stands a `table with
`food and `drink.
Whitney, Emblemes, Leyden, 1586, p.042

drink: A man `kneeling before a `chart holds a `compass
to the `stars; below a `stag `drinks from a `stream.
Whitney, Emblemes, Leyden, 1586, p.043

drink: `Naked `Bacchus, a `wreath of `vines(?) on his
head, lies on a `river bank, `drinking from a `cup.
Whitney, Emblemes, Leyden, 1586, p.125

drive: With `whip and `reins, `Eros `drives the `two
`lions `drawing his `chariot.
Whitney, Emblemes, Leyden, 1586, p.063

driver: `Worshippers kneel in `reverence before an `ass
bearing a `statue of `Isis; the `driver `beats the ass
with a `stick.
Whitney, Emblemes, Leyden, 1586, p.008

drown: `Colasmus searches for his `drowned `wife.
Whitney, Emblemes, Leyden, 1586, p.158

drum: `Bacchus, under `vines with `grapes, beats a `drum
and blows a `pipe; nearby a `goblet.
Whitney, Emblemes, Leyden, 1586, p.187

drum: `Two `drummers with `drum and `horn(?) before
an `encampment with `soldiers.
Whitney, Emblemes, Leyden, 1586, p.194

drummer: `Two `drummers with `drum and `horn(?)
before an `encampment with `soldiers.
Whitney, Emblemes, Leyden, 1586, p.194

duck: `Two `fowlers watch as `four `birds, `ducks, are
`lured into the `net by a live `decoy.
Whitney, Emblemes, Leyden, 1586, p.027

duck: `Two `ducks and two `geese hunt for food in a
`pond(?). A `falcon overhead.
Whitney, Emblemes, Leyden, 1586, p.207

dung-beetle: A `scarab or `dung-beetle in the centre of
a `rose.
Whitney, Emblemes, Leyden, 1586, p.021

dyer: A `dyer lifts `cloth from a `vat.
Whitney, Emblemes, Leyden, 1586, p.134

eagle: A man with `upraised `sword takes fright at his
`shadow. `Jupiter sits astride an `eagle in a bank of
clouds.
Whitney, Emblemes, Leyden, 1586, p.032

eagle: `Pine-trees are `broken by a `wind(?); in a `cloud
`Jupiter(?) sits astride an `eagle; a `rabbit crouches
before a `tree `stump; a `horseman nearby.
Whitney, Emblemes, Leyden, 1586, p.059

eagle: `Jupiter with `thunderbolts sits on his `eagle; a
man holds onto a `laurel tree in a storm(?); a
`swan(?) with a `laurel `garland about its neck.
Whitney, Emblemes, Leyden, 1586, p.067

eagle: An `eagle rends the `liver of `Prometheus,
`chained to a `rock.
Whitney, Emblemes, Leyden, 1586, p.075

eagle: Seated on a `throne, `Jupiter, whose `staff is

surmounted by an `eagle, is surrounded by a `deer,
`horse, `bull, `ass, `snail, `eagle, and `lion.
Whitney, Emblemes, Leyden, 1586, p.091

eagle: `Aesculapius, with a `laurel `garland, a `sceptre
in his `right hand and a `staff in his `left, on a
`throne, supported by two `eagles. Nearby a `snake,
`dog and `cock.
Whitney, Emblemes, Leyden, 1586, p.212

ear: A man with huge `ears; another points to his
`mouth with his `left `forefinger (`Harpocratic
gesture); a man flees from a `snake.
Whitney, Emblemes, Leyden, 1586, p.191b

ear: `Apollo and `Pan making music on `viola(?) and
`bagpipes. `Midas has `ears of an `ass.
Whitney, Emblemes, Leyden, 1586, p.218a

earth: `Chaos: `four `elements-- `fire, `air, `earth and
`water-- in confusion. A `crescent `moon, `sun,
`star and `wind.
Whitney, Emblemes, Leyden, 1586, p.122

earthenware: A `copper pot and an `earthenware `pot
float side by side down a `stream.
Whitney, Emblemes, Leyden, 1586, p.164

eat: An `ass, laden with `foodstuffs: `jugs, a `cask(?),
bags with `bread(?), a spitted `fowl, and a `rabbit,
`eats `thistles.
Whitney, Emblemes, Leyden, 1586, p.018

eel: A `fisherman grasps an `eel with the help of `fig
`leaves.
Whitney, Emblemes, Leyden, 1586, p.077a

egg: A `crocodile laying her `eggs, on the bank of the
`river `Nile.
Whitney, Emblemes, Leyden, 1586, p.003

egg: A `hen on the `roof of a `farmhouse sucks an
`egg; nearby a `cow(?) with a `feed(?) basket slung
from its neck.
Whitney, Emblemes, Leyden, 1586, p.064

element: `Chaos: `four `elements-- `fire, `air, `earth and
`water --in confusion.
Whitney, Emblemes, Leyden, 1586, p.122

elephant: An `elephant is frightened by a `white cloth;
a `bull by a `red cloth; a `lion by a crowing `cock;
a `stag flees from a `smoking cloth.
Whitney, Emblemes, Leyden, 1586, p.052a

elephant: An `elephant rests against a `tree, undermined
by a `hunter with an `axe(?).
Whitney, Emblemes, Leyden, 1586, p.150

elephant: A dead `elephant, poisoned by a `snake,
crushes it; man falls on `two `swords.
Whitney, Emblemes, Leyden, 1586, p.195

elm-tree: A `vine laden with `bunches of `grapes
`entwined about a `dead `elm-tree.
Whitney, Emblemes, Leyden, 1586, p.062

embrace: A `miller and the `wife of `Anellus `embrace
before `sacks of `grain at a `watermill.
Whitney, Emblemes, Leyden, 1586, p.080

embrace: `Two `men with `laurel `branches `embrace;
`swords lie on the ground. A `palm-tree and `sun
set.
Whitney, Emblemes, Leyden, 1586, p.216b

encampment: `Two `kings or `princes in `armour shake
`right hands; nearby, cavalry and an `encampment.
Whitney, Emblemes, Leyden, 1586, p.076a

encampment: `Two `drummers with `drum and `horn(?)
before an `encampment with `soldiers.
Whitney, Emblemes, Leyden, 1586, p.194

entwine: A `vine laden with `bunches of `grapes
`entwined about a `dead `elm-tree.
Whitney, Emblemes, Leyden, 1586, p.062

envious: An `envious man covers his `eyes and pulls his
companion away from a `burning `house. A third
man battles the `fire consuming his house.
Whitney, Emblemes, Leyden, 1586, p.031

envious: A `lion `devours its `prey, observed by an
`envious `dog. `Animals nearby.
Whitney, Emblemes, Leyden, 1586, p.044

envious: An ˚envious man, ˚blind in one ˚eye and a
 ˚covetous man, blind in both; the covetous man points
 to three eyes on the ground. Nearby, a ˚treasure
 ˚chest.
 Whitney, Emblemes, Leyden, 1586, p.095
ewer: On a ˚marble ˚tomb an ˚ewer and ˚basin with
 folded ˚towel.
 Whitney, Emblemes, Leyden, 1586, p.136
exchange: ˚Ajax and ˚Hector ˚exchange a ˚sword and
 ˚girdle.
 Whitney, Emblemes, Leyden, 1586, p.037
eye: An ˚envious man covers his ˚eyes and pulls his
 companion away from a ˚burning ˚house.
 Whitney, Emblemes, Leyden, 1586, p.031
eye: An ˚envious man, ˚blind in one ˚eye and a
 ˚covetous man, blind in both; the covetous man points
 to three eyes on the ground. Nearby, a ˚treasure
 ˚chest.
 Whitney, Emblemes, Leyden, 1586, p.095
face: ˚Janus with ˚two ˚faces, in ˚Roman ˚armour holds
 a ˚sceptre in his ˚right hand and a ˚mirror(?) in his
 ˚left.
 Whitney, Emblemes, Leyden, 1586, p.108
falcon: ˚Diana, with ˚laurel ˚wreath, ˚falcon, and ˚staff,
 ˚watches as a ˚stag-headed ˚Actaeon is attacked by
 ˚three ˚hounds.
 Whitney, Emblemes, Leyden, 1586, p.015
falcon: ˚Two ˚ducks and two ˚geese hunt for food in a
 ˚pond(?). A ˚falcon overhead.
 Whitney, Emblemes, Leyden, 1586, p.207
falconry: A feathered ˚lure for ˚falconry.
 Whitney, Emblemes, Leyden, 1586, p.191a
fall: A man clutches his breast as ˚Pliny ˚falls into the
 volcano.
 Whitney, Emblemes, Leyden, 1586, p.025
fall: ˚Icarus ˚falls into the ˚sea after the ˚sun has
 melted the wax binding the ˚feathers of his ˚wings.
 Whitney, Emblemes, Leyden, 1586, p.028
fall: ˚Brutus in ˚Roman ˚armour and ˚helmet, ˚shield on
 the ground, ˚falls on his ˚sword.
 Whitney, Emblemes, Leyden, 1586, p.070
fallow: ˚Athene(?) ˚sits under a ˚barren ˚tree before a
 ˚fallow field.
 Whitney, Emblemes, Leyden, 1586, p.103
farmer: A ˚farmer works the banks of a ˚ditch, fed by
 the ˚sea; a ˚bull or ˚cow beside a bound ˚sheaf of
 ˚arrows.
 Whitney, Emblemes, Leyden, 1586, p.072
farmhouse: A ˚hen on the ˚roof of a ˚farmhouse sucks
 an ˚egg; nearby a ˚cow(?) with a ˚feed(?) basket
 slung from its neck.
 Whitney, Emblemes, Leyden, 1586, p.064
father: ˚Aeneas carries his ˚father ˚Anchises from the
 burning ˚city of ˚Troy.
 Whitney, Emblemes, Leyden, 1586, p.163
feather: ˚Icarus ˚falls into the ˚sea after the ˚sun has
 melted the wax binding the ˚feathers of his ˚wings.
 Whitney, Emblemes, Leyden, 1586, p.028
feed: ˚Four ˚ravens or ˚crows ˚fly to ˚feed on the ˚fruit
 of a ˚fig-tree on a ˚mountain.
 Whitney, Emblemes, Leyden, 1586, p.053b
feed(?): A ˚hen on the ˚roof of a ˚farmhouse sucks an
 ˚egg; nearby a ˚cow(?) with a ˚feed(?) basket slung
 from its neck.
 Whitney, Emblemes, Leyden, 1586, p.064
field: An ˚old man ˚sits at ˚table; outside a ˚young man
 ˚labours in the ˚field.
 Whitney, Emblemes, Leyden, 1586, p.050b
field: ˚Athene(?) with ˚helmet, ˚spear and ˚shield, stands
 before a ˚grain ˚field and ˚fruit-tree; at the left, she
 ˚sits under a ˚barren ˚tree before a ˚fallow field.
 Whitney, Emblemes, Leyden, 1586, p.103
fig: A ˚fisherman grasps an ˚eel with the help of ˚fig
 ˚leaves.
 Whitney, Emblemes, Leyden, 1586, p.077a

fig-leaf: ˚Adam, in a ˚fig-leaf, hides behind a ˚tree.
 The inscription ˚"UBI ES" [Where are you?] blazes in
 the sky.
 Whitney, Emblemes, Leyden, 1586, p.229a
fig-tree: ˚Four ˚ravens or ˚crows ˚fly to ˚feed on the
 ˚fruit of a ˚fig-tree on a ˚mountain.
 Whitney, Emblemes, Leyden, 1586, p.053b
figure: A ˚winged ˚figure ˚reclines at the foot of the
 ˚volcano ˚Vesuvius. At the top a man clutches his
 breast as ˚Pliny ˚falls into the volcano.
 Whitney, Emblemes, Leyden, 1586, p.025
finger: A ˚scholar with a ˚book in his study. He holds a
 ˚finger to his ˚lips in a gesture of ˚silence.
 (˚Harpocrates)
 Whitney, Emblemes, Leyden, 1586, p.060
finger: A ˚blind man with a ˚stick carries a ˚lame man
 who ˚points the ˚way with his ˚finger.
 Whitney, Emblemes, Leyden, 1586, p.065
finger: ˚Modesty, her ˚finger to her ˚lips in the
 ˚Harpocratic gesture of ˚silence, holds ˚keys and
 ˚stands on a ˚tortoise.
 Whitney, Emblemes, Leyden, 1586, p.093b
finger: A ˚right hand, surrounded by ˚clouds, dangles a
 ˚snake, which has bitten into its middle ˚finger, over
 an open ˚fire.
 Whitney, Emblemes, Leyden, 1586, p.166b
fire: An ˚arsonist sets ˚fire to a ˚house; a man,
 carrying a ˚bucket of ˚oil, scales a ˚ladder placed
 against the burning house. A third man ˚stabs
 another man.
 Whitney, Emblemes, Leyden, 1586, p.007
fire: An ˚envious man covers his ˚eyes and pulls his
 companion away from a ˚burning ˚house. A third
 man battles the ˚fire consuming his house.
 Whitney, Emblemes, Leyden, 1586, p.031
fire: An ˚ape thrusts the ˚paw of a ˚dog into the ˚fire
 to withdraw ˚chestnuts.
 Whitney, Emblemes, Leyden, 1586, p.058
fire: A ˚fire fed with ˚wood from a ˚dead ˚tree.
 Whitney, Emblemes, Leyden, 1586, p.077b
fire: A ˚hand holds a ˚sword over a ˚fire.
 Whitney, Emblemes, Leyden, 1586, p.111
fire: ˚Chaos: ˚four ˚elements -- ˚fire, ˚air, ˚earth and
 ˚water -- in confusion.
 Whitney, Emblemes, Leyden, 1586, p.122
fire: A ˚right hand, surrounded by ˚clouds, dangles a
 ˚snake, which has bitten into its middle ˚finger, over
 an open ˚fire.
 Whitney, Emblemes, Leyden, 1586, p.166b
fire: A ˚phoenix rises from the flames of a ˚fire.
 Whitney, Emblemes, Leyden, 1586, p.177
fire: Boiling ˚broth overflows a ˚cauldron into the ˚fire.
 Whitney, Emblemes, Leyden, 1586, p.216a
fire: ˚Three ˚Christian ˚martyrs in ˚prayer before a
 ˚fire are harassed by men with ˚swords and ˚dogs. A
 ˚left hand from the ˚clouds holds a ˚garland over
 them.
 Whitney, Emblemes, Leyden, 1586, p.224a
fish: A ˚mew or ˚gull and a ˚cormorant ˚fly in pursuit
 of ˚three small ˚fishes.
 Whitney, Emblemes, Leyden, 1586, p.052b
fish: ˚Two ˚fishermen in a ˚boat haul in a ˚fishing
 ˚net.
 Whitney, Emblemes, Leyden, 1586, p.071
fish: ˚Eros, holding ˚flowers and a ˚fish.
 Whitney, Emblemes, Leyden, 1586, p.182a
fish: A ˚Venus(?) with basket of ˚fruit, and ˚Eros(?);
 animals nearby: ˚lion, ˚hare, ˚horse, ˚bird and ˚fish.
 Whitney, Emblemes, Leyden, 1586, p.182b
fisherman: A ˚fisherman grasps an ˚eel with the help of
 ˚fig ˚leaves.
 Whitney, Emblemes, Leyden, 1586, p.077a
fisherman: A ˚fisherman with a ˚net reaches with his
 ˚right hand for a ˚cuttlefish muddying the ˚water.
 A ˚lizard(?) flees on the opposite bank.

Whitney, Emblemes, Leyden, 1586, p.097
fisherman: ˙Two ˙fishermen in a ˙boat haul in a ˙fishing ˙net.
Whitney, Emblemes, Leyden, 1586, p.071
five: A large ˙sheaf of ˙grain or ˙wheat(?) encircled by ˙five single ˙stalks, and by ˙two smaller ˙sheaves.
Whitney, Emblemes, Leyden, 1586, p.088
flame: ˙Tantalus stands in a river, looking up at ˙fruit laden ˙tree. ˙Flames and ˙smoke billow up in the background.
Whitney, Emblemes, Leyden, 1586, p.074
flame: A ˙young man and an ˙older over a ˙game of ˙draughts or ˙chess; ˙flames engulf the building behind them.
Whitney, Emblemes, Leyden, 1586, p.208
flame: ˙Gnats ˙fly into a ˙candle ˙flame; the ˙candlestick is on a plinth inscribed ˙"COSI DE BEN AMAR PORTO TORMENTO" [Thus from a great love I bear torment] The plinth is flanked by ˙two ˙fires, ˙women nearby.
Whitney, Emblemes, Leyden, 1586, p.219
flee: ˙Glory ˙flees through a ˙doorway from ˙naked ˙couple on a ˙bed; beside them stands a ˙table with ˙food and ˙drink.
Whitney, Emblemes, Leyden, 1586, p.042
fleur-de-lys: A coin bears a ˙shield with ˙three ˙fleurs-de-lys, surmounted by a ˙coronet.
Whitney, Emblemes, Leyden, 1586, p.139a
flock: ˙Hanno releases a ˙flock of ˙birds.
Whitney, Emblemes, Leyden, 1586, p.084
flock: A ˙leopard(?) fights with a ˙lion. ˙Travellers pass nearby. A ˙flock of ˙birds flies over head.
Whitney, Emblemes, Leyden, 1586, p.178
flood: A ˙flooded ˙city and a ˙wrecked ˙ship.
Whitney, Emblemes, Leyden, 1586, p.129
flounder: A sailing ship ˙flounders in the ˙sea off the ˙shore; the ˙sun's rays melt ˙snow on ˙mountains.
Whitney, Emblemes, Leyden, 1586, p.011
flounder: A ˙dolphin ˙flounders on the ˙sea ˙shore.
Whitney, Emblemes, Leyden, 1586, p.090
flower: A ˙flower gives ˙honey to a ˙bee and ˙poison to a ˙spider.
Whitney, Emblemes, Leyden, 1586, p.051a
flower: ˙Narcissus admires his ˙reflection in a ˙stream; ˙Echo(?) waves her ˙left hand; A ˙flower, ˙narcissus(?), grows nearby.
Whitney, Emblemes, Leyden, 1586, p.149
flower: A man touches the ˙thorns and ˙flowers of a ˙rose bush.
Whitney, Emblemes, Leyden, 1586, p.165
flower: A naked ˙boy or ˙Putto(?) sits in a ˙fruit-tree; an ˙old ˙man, ˙scholar(?); ˙Flowers, some wilted, grow nearby.
Whitney, Emblemes, Leyden, 1586, p.173
flower: ˙Eros, holding ˙flowers and a ˙fish.
Whitney, Emblemes, Leyden, 1586, p.182a
flower: A ˙skull, a ˙bone and a ˙flower.
Whitney, Emblemes, Leyden, 1586, p.229b
fly: A ˙mew or ˙gull and a ˙cormorant ˙fly in pursuit of ˙three small ˙fishes.
Whitney, Emblemes, Leyden, 1586, p.052b
fly: ˙Four ˙ravens or ˙crows ˙fly to ˙feed on the ˙fruit of a ˙fig-tree on a ˙mountain.
Whitney, Emblemes, Leyden, 1586, p.053b
fly: A ˙bird-of-paradise ˙flies by; a ˙traveller with a back ˙pack looks towards a ˙village across a ˙stream, where a ˙swan is feeding.
Whitney, Emblemes, Leyden, 1586, p.089
fly: ˙Gnats ˙fly into a ˙candle ˙flame; the ˙candlestick is on a plinth inscribed ˙"COSI DE BEN AMAR PORTO TORMENTO" [Thus from a great love I bear torment]. The plinth is flanked by ˙two ˙fires, ˙women nearby.
Whitney, Emblemes, Leyden, 1586, p.219
food: ˙Glory ˙flees through a ˙doorway from ˙naked ˙couple on a ˙bed; beside them stands a ˙table with ˙food and ˙drink.
Whitney, Emblemes, Leyden, 1586, p.042
food: A man at ˙table blows his ˙food to cool it, watched by a ˙satyr.
Whitney, Emblemes, Leyden, 1586, p.160
foodstuff: An ˙ass, laden with ˙foodstuffs: ˙jugs, a ˙cask(?), bags with ˙bread(?), a spitted ˙fowl, and a ˙rabbit, ˙eats ˙thistles.
Whitney, Emblemes, Leyden, 1586, p.018
foot: A man ˙tramples ˙grapes under his ˙right ˙foot, reaching for a ˙bunch with his ˙left hand.
Whitney, Emblemes, Leyden, 1586, p.206
foot: Virtue(?) or ˙Athene(?) wears a ˙helmet, a ˙lance with her ˙right hand, a sceptre(?) or ˙mace(?) in her ˙left; her ˙right ˙foot on a ˙tortoise(?).
Whitney, Emblemes, Leyden, 1586, p.222a
forefinger: A man with huge ˙ears; another points to his ˙mouth with his ˙left ˙forefinger (˙Harpocratic gesture); a man flees from a ˙snake.
Whitney, Emblemes, Leyden, 1586, p.191b
forelock: ˙Naked ˙Occasio, with ˙bald ˙head, long ˙forelock, and ˙razor in her raised ˙right hand, stands on a ˙wheel in the ˙sea.
Whitney, Emblemes, Leyden, 1586, p.181
fortress: ˙Two ˙soldiers lead a captive ˙herald from the ˙battlefield into a ˙fortress.
Whitney, Emblemes, Leyden, 1586, p.054a
four: ˙Two ˙fowlers watch as ˙four ˙birds, ˙ducks, are ˙lured into the ˙net by a live ˙decoy.
Whitney, Emblemes, Leyden, 1586, p.027
four: ˙Four ˙ravens or ˙crows ˙fly to ˙feed on the ˙fruit of a ˙fig-tree on a ˙mountain.
Whitney, Emblemes, Leyden, 1586, p.053b
four: ˙Four ˙winds ˙blow on a ˙rock in a rough ˙sea.
Whitney, Emblemes, Leyden, 1586, p.096
four: A ˙left ˙gauntlet holds a ˙lance which is ringed by ˙four ˙garlands.
Whitney, Emblemes, Leyden, 1586, p.115
four: ˙Chaos: ˙four ˙elements-- ˙fire, ˙air, ˙earth and ˙water-- in confusion.
Whitney, Emblemes, Leyden, 1586, p.122
fowl: An ˙ass, laden with ˙foodstuffs: ˙jugs, a ˙cask(?), bags with ˙bread(?), a spitted ˙fowl, and a ˙rabbit, ˙eats ˙thistles.
Whitney, Emblemes, Leyden, 1586, p.018
fowler: ˙Two ˙fowlers watch as ˙four ˙birds, ˙ducks, are ˙lured into the ˙net by a live ˙decoy.
Whitney, Emblemes, Leyden, 1586, p.027
fox: A ˙fox on an ˙ice-flow floats down a ˙river (˙Danube) past a ˙town (˙Regensburg).
Whitney, Emblemes, Leyden, 1586, p.022
fox: A ˙fox leaps after bunches of ˙grapes.
Whitney, Emblemes, Leyden, 1586, p.098a
fox: Two men shake ˙hands; one wears a ˙fox's ˙skin over his head.
Whitney, Emblemes, Leyden, 1586, p.124
fox: A ˙fox and an ˙ape exchange insults.
Whitney, Emblemes, Leyden, 1586, p.142
fox: A ˙boar with ˙tusks sharpened faces a ˙fox.
Whitney, Emblemes, Leyden, 1586, p.153b
fox: A ˙lion and a ˙fox face each other over their ˙prey, including a ˙stag. A dead ˙ass lies nearby.
Whitney, Emblemes, Leyden, 1586, p.154
fox: A ˙fox cowers before a ˙lion.
Whitney, Emblemes, Leyden, 1586, p.156b
fox: A ˙lion with ˙tongue outstretched stands before a sick ˙fox in its den.
Whitney, Emblemes, Leyden, 1586, p.161
fox: An old ˙lion, feigning ˙sickness, lies in a cave; a ˙fox at the entrance.
Whitney, Emblemes, Leyden, 1586, p.210
frog: ˙Frogs and ˙snakes crowd at the base of a ˙palm-tree.
Whitney, Emblemes, Leyden, 1586, p.118
fruit: ˙Four ˙ravens or ˙crows ˙fly to ˙feed on the

˙fruit of a ˙fig-tree on a ˙mountain.
Whitney, Emblemes, Leyden, 1586, p.053b

fruit: ˙Tantalus stands in a river, looking up at ˙fruit
laden ˙tree. ˙Flames and ˙smoke billow up in the
background.
Whitney, Emblemes, Leyden, 1586, p.074

fruit: Two ˙boys with ˙rods knock ˙fruit from a
˙nut-tree.
Whitney, Emblemes, Leyden, 1586, p.174

fruit: A ˙Venus(?) with basket of ˙fruit, and ˙Eros(?);
animals nearby: ˙lion, ˙hare, ˙horse, ˙bird and ˙fish.
Whitney, Emblemes, Leyden, 1586, p.182b

fruit-tree: ˙Athene(?) with ˙helmet, ˙spear and ˙shield,
stands before a ˙grain ˙field and ˙fruit-tree.
Whitney, Emblemes, Leyden, 1586, p.103

fruit-tree: A naked ˙boy or ˙Putto(?) sits in a
˙fruit-tree; an ˙old ˙man, ˙scholar(?); ˙Flowers, some
wilted, grow nearby.
Whitney, Emblemes, Leyden, 1586, p.173

galley: ˙Three ˙mermaids with a ˙lyre and a ˙woodwind
instrument, watch a ˙galley, with ˙Ulysses tied to the
mast.
Whitney, Emblemes, Leyden, 1586, p.010

gamble: ˙Three ˙women ˙gamble with ˙dice.
Whitney, Emblemes, Leyden, 1586, p.176

game: Four ˙men sit at a table; one ˙drinks from a ˙mug;
a second watches the remaining two argue over a
˙game of ˙backgammon.
Whitney, Emblemes, Leyden, 1586, p.017

game: A ˙young man and an ˙older over a ˙game of
˙draughts or ˙chess; ˙flames engulf the building
behind them.
Whitney, Emblemes, Leyden, 1586, p.208

garland: ˙Jupiter with ˙thunderbolts sits on his ˙eagle; a
man holds onto a ˙laurel tree in a storm(?); a
˙swan(?) with a ˙laurel ˙garland about its neck.
Whitney, Emblemes, Leyden, 1586, p.067

garland: A ˙left ˙gauntlet holds a ˙lance which is ringed
by ˙four ˙garlands.
Whitney, Emblemes, Leyden, 1586, p.115

garland: ˙Aesculapius, with a ˙laurel ˙garland, a ˙sceptre
in his ˙right hand and a ˙staff in his ˙left, on a
˙throne.
Whitney, Emblemes, Leyden, 1586, p.212

garland: ˙Three ˙Christian ˙martyrs in ˙prayer before a
˙fire are harassed by men with ˙swords and ˙dogs. A
˙left hand from the ˙clouds holds a ˙garland over
them.
Whitney, Emblemes, Leyden, 1586, p.224a

gauntlet: A ˙left ˙gauntlet holds a ˙lance which is ringed
by ˙four ˙garlands.
Whitney, Emblemes, Leyden, 1586, p.115

gibbet: A ˙king, with ˙crown and ˙sceptre, squeezes
˙water from a ˙sponge; a crowd watches a ˙hanging
(˙gibbet).
Whitney, Emblemes, Leyden, 1586, p.151

gibbet: A ˙thief, escorted to his ˙hanging by soldiers, is
embraced by his ˙mother. The ˙gibbet lies on the
ground.
Whitney, Emblemes, Leyden, 1586, p.155

girdle: ˙Ajax and ˙Hector ˙exchange a ˙sword and
˙girdle.
Whitney, Emblemes, Leyden, 1586, p.037

globe: A ˙sailing ˙ship on a ˙world ˙globe, surrounded by
˙clouds, ˙stars, ˙sun and crescent ˙moon. A ˙right
hand holds a ˙bridle, which encircles the globe.
Whitney, Emblemes, Leyden, 1586, p.203

globe: A man with a ˙world ˙globe on his back drags the
˙tablets of the ˙commandments tied to his ˙right
ankle.
Whitney, Emblemes, Leyden, 1586, p.223

globe: A ˙traveller or ˙pilgrim walks past a ˙world
˙globe inscribed ˙"EUROPA" and ˙"AFRICA". The
˙tetragrammaton blazes in ˙clouds above.
Whitney, Emblemes, Leyden, 1586, p.225

gnat: ˙Gnats ˙fly into a ˙candle ˙flame; the ˙candlestick
is on a plinth inscribed ˙"COSI DE BEN AMAR
PORTO TORMENTO" [Thus from a great love I bear
torment]. The plinth is flanked by ˙two ˙fires,
˙women nearby.
Whitney, Emblemes, Leyden, 1586, p.219

goat: A man with a ˙staff climbs a ˙snow covered
˙mountain. A ˙goat stands on the top of the
mountain.
Whitney, Emblemes, Leyden, 1586, p.020

goat: A ˙goat ˙suckles a ˙wolf ˙cub.
Whitney, Emblemes, Leyden, 1586, p.049

goat: ˙Circe touches with her ˙wand a ˙pig; nearby a
˙dog, ˙ape, ˙goat and ˙ass, ˙Ulysses's transformed
men.
Whitney, Emblemes, Leyden, 1586, p.082

goat: A ˙goat kicks over a ˙jar of ˙milk; a ˙milkmaid
raises her ˙hands in anger.
Whitney, Emblemes, Leyden, 1586, p.189b

goblet: ˙Bacchus, under ˙vines with ˙grapes, beats a
˙drum and blows a ˙pipe; nearby a ˙goblet.
Whitney, Emblemes, Leyden, 1586, p.187

gold: An ˙ape throws ˙gold ˙coins from a ˙window.
Whitney, Emblemes, Leyden, 1586, p.169

gold: ˙Opimius, the ˙miser, in his sick-bed. The
˙physician supervises the emptying of his ˙chests of
˙gold onto a table.
Whitney, Emblemes, Leyden, 1586, p.209

golden: ˙Paris gives the ˙golden ˙apple to ˙Venus,
accompanied by ˙Eros.
Whitney, Emblemes, Leyden, 1586, p.083

golden: ˙Phrixus crosses ˙Hellespont on the ˙golden
˙ram, eyes and ˙right arm raised to the heavens.
Whitney, Emblemes, Leyden, 1586, p.214

goose: ˙Two ˙ducks and two ˙geese hunt for food in a
˙pond(?). A ˙falcon overhead.
Whitney, Emblemes, Leyden, 1586, p.207

gourd: A leafy ˙vine laden with ˙gourds climbs the
trunk of a ˙pine tree.
Whitney, Emblemes, Leyden, 1586, p.034

grain: A ˙sheaf of ˙grain (˙wheat).
Whitney, Emblemes, Leyden, 1586, p.023

grain: ˙Grain passes through a ˙sieve.
Whitney, Emblemes, Leyden, 1586, p.068

grain: A ˙miller and the ˙wife of ˙Anellus ˙embrace
before ˙sacks of ˙grain at a ˙watermill.
Whitney, Emblemes, Leyden, 1586, p.080

grain: A large ˙sheaf of ˙grain or ˙wheat(?) encircled
by ˙five single ˙stalks, and by ˙two smaller ˙sheaves.
Whitney, Emblemes, Leyden, 1586, p.088

grain: ˙Athene(?) with ˙helmet, ˙spear and ˙shield,
stands before a ˙grain ˙field and ˙fruit-tree.
Whitney, Emblemes, Leyden, 1586, p.103

grain: ˙Labour, with ˙cornucopia and ˙crown of ears of
˙grain, sits in a ˙chariot pulled by ˙ants. She uses
a ˙bundle of stalks of ˙grain(?) to beat ˙Idleness.
Whitney, Emblemes, Leyden, 1586, p.175

grain(?): ˙Labour, with ˙cornucopia and ˙crown of ears
of ˙grain, sits in a ˙chariot pulled by ˙ants. She
uses a ˙bundle of stalks of ˙grain(?) to beat
˙Idleness.
Whitney, Emblemes, Leyden, 1586, p.175

grape: A ˙vine laden with ˙bunches of ˙grapes
˙entwined about a ˙dead ˙elm-tree.
Whitney, Emblemes, Leyden, 1586, p.062

grape: A ˙fox leaps after bunches of ˙grapes.
Whitney, Emblemes, Leyden, 1586, p.098a

grape: An ˙olive-tree entwined by a ˙grape ˙vine.
Whitney, Emblemes, Leyden, 1586, p.133

grape: ˙Bacchus with a ˙crown of ˙vine ˙leaves and
˙grapes, and ˙Apollo with his ˙lyre stand on a
˙pedestal or ˙tomb.
Whitney, Emblemes, Leyden, 1586, p.146

grape: ˙Bacchus, under ˙vines with ˙grapes, beats a
˙drum and blows a ˙pipe; nearby a ˙goblet.

Whitney, Emblemes, Leyden, 1586, p.187
grape: A *man *tramples *grapes under his *right *foot,
　reaching for a *bunch with his *left hand. A *vine
　grows on a wall with *astrological symbols and a
　*moon. A *woman holds grapes away from her with
　her *left hand. Above *zodiacal *circle with *Virgo,
　her *right hand pointing at grapes held by the
　woman.
Whitney, Emblemes, Leyden, 1586, p.206
grass: *Ocnus and a *ropemaker make a *rope from
　*grasses. An *ass eats the rope.
Whitney, Emblemes, Leyden, 1586, p.048
grasshopper: A *swallow with a *grasshopper in its *beak
　returns to its *nest in the *ruins of a *palace.
Whitney, Emblemes, Leyden, 1586, p.005
grasshopper: The *sun beats down as a *grasshopper
　watches *ants work under barren *trees.
Whitney, Emblemes, Leyden, 1586, p.159
gull: A *mew or *gull and a *cormorant *fly in pursuit
　of *three small *fishes.
Whitney, Emblemes, Leyden, 1586, p.052b
hair: *Bare *breasted *Prowess *tears out her *hair as
　she sits on the *tomb of *Ajax, inscribed *"D
　AIACIS."
Whitney, Emblemes, Leyden, 1586, p.030
hand: *Slander, holding an *torch, has her hand on a
　kneeling figure, her *hands clasped in *supplication.
Whitney, Emblemes, Leyden, 1586, p.004
hand: A *hand holds a *sword over a *fire.
Whitney, Emblemes, Leyden, 1586, p.111
hand: Two men shake *hands; one wears a *fox's *skin
　over his head.
Whitney, Emblemes, Leyden, 1586, p.124
hand: *Eros shows his *bee stung *hand to *Venus; bees
　swarm around their *hive.
Whitney, Emblemes, Leyden, 1586, p.148
hand: A *goat kicks over a *jar of *milk; a *milkmaid
　raises her *hands in anger.
Whitney, Emblemes, Leyden, 1586, p.189b
hang: A *king, with *crown and *sceptre, squeezes
　*water from a *sponge; a crowd watches a *hanging
　(*gibbet).
Whitney, Emblemes, Leyden, 1586, p.151
hang: A *thief, escorted to his *hanging by soldiers, is
　embraced by his *mother. The *gibbet lies on the
　ground.
Whitney, Emblemes, Leyden, 1586, p.155
hare: *Three *hares *bite the head of a *dead supine
　*lion; a fourth hare runs by.
Whitney, Emblemes, Leyden, 1586, p.127
hare: A *Venus(?) with basket of *fruit, and *Eros(?);
　animals nearby: *lion, *hare, *horse, *bird and *fish.
Whitney, Emblemes, Leyden, 1586, p.182b
harp: *Arion and his *harp thrown overboard by *sailors;
　a *dolphin waits near the *ship.
Whitney, Emblemes, Leyden, 1586, p.144
harp: *Orpheus plays his *harp, surrounded by a *vulture,
　*stork, *stag, *lion, *bear, *antelope, and *ape.
Whitney, Emblemes, Leyden, 1586, p.186
harrow: A *king with *crown and *sceptre on a *horse
　watches a *ploughman give his *harrow to an
　*astronomer in exchange for a *sphere(?) or
　*astrolabe and the *doctor's *robe.
Whitney, Emblemes, Leyden, 1586, p.009
hay: A bundle of *hay hangs from an *staff.
Whitney, Emblemes, Leyden, 1586, p.217
head: The *head of *Valerius *Corvinus in a *plumed
　*helmet, the *visor open; a *raven is perched on the
　visor.
Whitney, Emblemes, Leyden, 1586, p.113
head: *Naked *Occasio, with *bald *head, long *forelock,
　and *razor in her raised *right hand, stands on a
　*wheel in the *sea.
Whitney, Emblemes, Leyden, 1586, p.181
heart: *Snake-haired *Envy eats her *heart.

Whitney, Emblemes, Leyden, 1586, p.004
heart: *Envy, with *snakes emerging from her *mouth,
　plucks out her *heart with her *right hand, walking
　with a *staff.
Whitney, Emblemes, Leyden, 1586, p.094
heel: *Naked *Occasio, with *bald *head, long *forelock,
　and *razor in her raised *right hand, stands on a
　*wheel in the *sea; her *heels are *winged.
Whitney, Emblemes, Leyden, 1586, p.181
helmet: Wearing a *winged *helmet and holding a
　*caduceus, *Mercury points to the *path at his feet;
　a *traveller with a *staff.
Whitney, Emblemes, Leyden, 1586, p.002
helmet: *Hercules stands between *Virtue, *Athena with
　*helmet, *shield and *spear and *Vice, *Venus with
　*Eros.
Whitney, Emblemes, Leyden, 1586, p.040
helmet: A *scholar in a *philosopher's *cap, *Diomedes
　or *Cicero, a *tablet under his arm talks with a
　*soldier in a *helmet with *sword, *shield and
　*spear, *Ulysses or *Caesar.
Whitney, Emblemes, Leyden, 1586, p.047
helmet: *Brutus in *Roman *armour and *helmet, *shield
　on the ground, *falls on his *sword.
Whitney, Emblemes, Leyden, 1586, p.070
helmet: *Paris gives the *golden *apple to *Venus,
　accompanied by *Eros; nearby, *Juno and *Athena
　with a *helmet and *shield.
Whitney, Emblemes, Leyden, 1586, p.083
helmet: *Athene(?) with *helmet, *spear and *shield,
　stands before a *grain *field and *fruit-tree.
Whitney, Emblemes, Leyden, 1586, p.103
helmet: The *head of *Valerius *Corvinus in a *plumed
　*helmet, the *visor open; a *raven is perched on
　the visor.
Whitney, Emblemes, Leyden, 1586, p.113
helmet: *Bound *Attilius on a *stretcher near an open
　*barrel riven with *nails is observed by a *helmeted
　*soldier with a *battle-axe.
Whitney, Emblemes, Leyden, 1586, p.114
helmet: A *helmet is used as a *hive by *bees.
Whitney, Emblemes, Leyden, 1586, p.138a
helmet: Virtue(?) or *Athene(?) wears a *helmet, a
　*lance with her *right hand, a sceptre(?) or *mace(?)
　in her *left; her *right *foot on a *tortoise(?).
Whitney, Emblemes, Leyden, 1586, p.222a
hen: A *hen on the *roof of a *farmhouse sucks an
　*egg; nearby a *cow(?) with a *feed(?) basket slung
　from its neck.
Whitney, Emblemes, Leyden, 1586, p.064
herald: Two *soldiers lead a captive *herald from the
　*battlefield into a *fortress.
Whitney, Emblemes, Leyden, 1586, p.054a
hill: *Sisyphus pushes a *stone up a *hill.
Whitney, Emblemes, Leyden, 1586, p.215
hive: A *helmet is used as a *hive by *bees.
Whitney, Emblemes, Leyden, 1586, p.138a
hive: A *bee stung *Eros flies to *Venus. Bees swarm
　around two *hives.
Whitney, Emblemes, Leyden, 1586, p.147
hive: *Eros shows his *bee stung *hand to *Venus; bees
　swarm around their *hive.
Whitney, Emblemes, Leyden, 1586, p.148
hive: *Bees return to the *hive.
Whitney, Emblemes, Leyden, 1586, p.200
hobby-horse: A *naked *child on a *hobby-horse, a
　*courtier, and a *jester stand before a *crowned
　*king holding a *sceptre.
Whitney, Emblemes, Leyden, 1586, p.081
hole: A *barrel with small *holes *discharges *water on
　all sides.
Whitney, Emblemes, Leyden, 1586, p.012
honey: A *flower gives *honey to a *bee and *poison to
　a *spider.
Whitney, Emblemes, Leyden, 1586, p.051a

horn: Spotted with ˚mouths(?), ˚winged ˚Fame, sounds a
˚horn as he flies over a ˚Roman(?) building and
˚three ˚Egyptian(?) ˚pyramids.
Whitney, Emblemes, Leyden, 1586, p.196

horn(?): ˚Two ˚drummers with ˚drum and ˚horn(?) before
an ˚encampment with ˚soldiers.
Whitney, Emblemes, Leyden, 1586, p.194

horse: A ˚charioteer with a ˚whip tries to ˚rein in the
˚two galloping ˚horses pulling his ˚chariot.
Whitney, Emblemes, Leyden, 1586, p.006

horse: A ˚king with ˚crown and ˚sceptre on a ˚horse
watches a ˚ploughman give his ˚harrow to an
˚astronomer in exchange for a ˚sphere(?) or
˚astrolobe and the ˚doctor's ˚robe.
Whitney, Emblemes, Leyden, 1586, p.009

horse: A ˚horseman on a ˚rearing ˚horse.
Whitney, Emblemes, Leyden, 1586, p.038

horse: A ˚woman collects ˚skulls into her apron; ˚horse
is ˚trotting on a hill; ˚skulls piled beside a ˚chapel.
Whitney, Emblemes, Leyden, 1586, p.046

horse: Seated on a ˚throne, ˚Jupiter, whose ˚staff is
surmounted by an ˚eagle, is surrounded by a ˚deer,
˚horse, ˚bull, ˚ass, ˚snail, ˚eagle, and ˚lion.
Whitney, Emblemes, Leyden, 1586, p.091

horse: A ˚Venus(?) with basket of ˚fruit, and ˚Eros(?);
animals nearby: ˚lion, ˚hare, ˚horse, ˚bird and ˚fish.
Whitney, Emblemes, Leyden, 1586, p.182b

horse: ˚Two ˚horsemen with ˚whips pursue a riderless
˚horse towards a ˚standard.
Whitney, Emblemes, Leyden, 1586, p.227

horseman: A ˚horseman on a ˚rearing ˚horse.
Whitney, Emblemes, Leyden, 1586, p.038

horseman: ˚Pine-trees are ˚broken by a ˚wind(?); in a
˚cloud ˚Jupiter(?) sits astride an ˚eagle; a ˚rabbit
crouches before a ˚tree ˚stump; a ˚horseman nearby.
Whitney, Emblemes, Leyden, 1586, p.059

horseman: ˚Two ˚horsemen with ˚whips pursue a riderless
˚horse towards a ˚standard.
Whitney, Emblemes, Leyden, 1586, p.227

hound: ˚Diana, with ˚laurel ˚wreath, ˚falcon, and ˚staff,
˚watches as a ˚stag-headed ˚Actaeon is attacked by
˚three ˚hounds.
Whitney, Emblemes, Leyden, 1586, p.015

hound: A ˚beaver tears off his ˚testicles, ˚pursued by a
˚hunter and ˚two ˚hounds.
Whitney, Emblemes, Leyden, 1586, p.035

hourglass: A ˚burning ˚candle, flanked by an ˚hourglass
and an ˚open ˚book, stands on a table in a room.
Whitney, Emblemes, Leyden, 1586, p.172

house: An ˚arsonist sets ˚fire to a ˚house; a man,
carrying a ˚bucket of ˚oil, scales a ˚ladder placed
against the burning house. A third man ˚stabs another
man.
Whitney, Emblemes, Leyden, 1586, p.007

house: An ˚envious man covers his ˚eyes and pulls his
companion away from a ˚burning ˚house. A third man
battles the ˚fire consuming his house.
Whitney, Emblemes, Leyden, 1586, p.031

house: A man with drawn ˚sword looks into a ˚house; a
˚bundle at his feet.
Whitney, Emblemes, Leyden, 1586, p.069

hull: ˚Three ˚mermaids with a ˚lyre and a ˚woodwind
instrument, watch a ˚galley, with ˚Ulysses tied to the
mast. A ˚wrecked ˚hull lies in the distance.
Whitney, Emblemes, Leyden, 1586, p.010

hunter: A ˚beaver tears off his ˚testicles, ˚pursued by a
˚hunter and ˚two ˚hounds.
Whitney, Emblemes, Leyden, 1586, p.035

hunter: An ˚elephant rests against a ˚tree, undermined
by a ˚hunter with an ˚axe(?).
Whitney, Emblemes, Leyden, 1586, p.150

hunter: A ˚stag is struck by an ˚arrow; a ˚hunter
approaches with ˚two ˚dogs.
Whitney, Emblemes, Leyden, 1586, p.153a

ice-flow: A ˚fox on an ˚ice-flow floats down a ˚river

(˚Danube) past a ˚town (˚Regensburg).
Whitney, Emblemes, Leyden, 1586, p.022

idle: ˚Two ˚idle men ˚sit by a tree.
Whitney, Emblemes, Leyden, 1586, p.085

inverted: ˚Strife stands on a ˚bellows, holding an
˚inverted ˚torch.
Whitney, Emblemes, Leyden, 1586, p.004

inverted: An ˚inverted ˚burning ˚torch inscribed ˚"QUI
ME ALIT ME EXTINGUIT" [The one who nourishes
me extinguishes me].
Whitney, Emblemes, Leyden, 1586, p.183

ivy: A ˚spire or pointed ˚obelisk, set on a ˚plinth,
entwined with ˚ivy.
Whitney, Emblemes, Leyden, 1586, p.001

ivy: Virtue(?) or ˚Athene(?), her ˚right ˚foot on a
˚tortoise(?). ˚Ivy and ˚two ˚snakes scale the wall.
Whitney, Emblemes, Leyden, 1586, p.222a

jar: A ˚goat kicks over a ˚jar of ˚milk; a ˚milkmaid
raises her ˚hands in anger.
Whitney, Emblemes, Leyden, 1586, p.189b

jester: A ˚naked ˚child on a ˚hobby-horse, a ˚courtier,
and a ˚jester stand before a ˚crowned ˚king holding
a ˚sceptre.
Whitney, Emblemes, Leyden, 1586, p.081

jug: An ˚ass, laden with ˚foodstuffs: ˚jugs, a ˚cask(?),
bags with ˚bread(?), a spitted ˚fowl, and a ˚rabbit,
˚eats ˚thistles.
Whitney, Emblemes, Leyden, 1586, p.018

key: ˚Modesty, her ˚finger to her ˚lips in the
˚Harpocratic gesture of ˚silence, holds ˚keys and
˚stands on a ˚tortoise.
Whitney, Emblemes, Leyden, 1586, p.093b

kill: A ˚swallow approaches its ˚nest in a niche with a
˚statue of ˚Medea ˚killing her ˚child with a ˚sword.
Whitney, Emblemes, Leyden, 1586, p.033

king: A ˚king with ˚crown and ˚sceptre on a ˚horse
watches a ˚ploughman give his ˚harrow to an
˚astronomer in exchange for a ˚sphere(?) or
˚astrolobe and the ˚doctor's ˚robe.
Whitney, Emblemes, Leyden, 1586, p.009

king: ˚Two ˚kings or ˚princes in ˚armour shake ˚right
hands; nearby, cavalry and an ˚encampment.
Whitney, Emblemes, Leyden, 1586, p.076a

king: A ˚naked ˚child on a ˚hobby-horse, a ˚courtier,
and a ˚jester stand before a ˚crowned ˚king holding
a ˚sceptre.
Whitney, Emblemes, Leyden, 1586, p.081

king: A ˚king, with ˚crown and ˚sceptre, squeezes
˚water from a ˚sponge; a crowd watches a ˚hanging
(˚gibbet).
Whitney, Emblemes, Leyden, 1586, p.151

kite: A ˚kite regurgiates a knotted coil.
Whitney, Emblemes, Leyden, 1586, p.170

kneel: A man ˚kneeling before a ˚chart holds a
˚compass to the ˚stars; below a ˚stag ˚drinks from a
˚stream.
Whitney, Emblemes, Leyden, 1586, p.043

knock: One ˚redbreast ˚knocks another from a ˚tree
˚branch.
Whitney, Emblemes, Leyden, 1586, p.055a

labour: An ˚old man ˚sits at ˚table; outside a ˚young
man ˚labours in the ˚field.
Whitney, Emblemes, Leyden, 1586, p.050b

ladder: An ˚arsonist sets ˚fire to a ˚house; a man,
carrying a ˚bucket of ˚oil, scales a ˚ladder placed
against the burning house.
Whitney, Emblemes, Leyden, 1586, p.007

lame: A ˚blind man with a ˚stick carries a ˚lame man
who ˚points the ˚way with his ˚finger.
Whitney, Emblemes, Leyden, 1586, p.065

lance: A ˚shirt or ˚shroud ˚draped on a ˚lance and a
˚crossbar.
Whitney, Emblemes, Leyden, 1586, p.086

lance: A ˚left ˚gauntlet holds a ˚lance which is ringed
by ˚four ˚garlands.

Whitney, Emblemes, Leyden, 1586, p.115
lance: Virtue(?) or *Athene(?) wears a *helmet, a *lance with her *right hand, a sceptre(?) or *mace(?) in her *left; her *right *foot on a *tortoise(?).
Whitney, Emblemes, Leyden, 1586, p.222a
laugh: *Laughing *Democritus and *weeping *Heraclitus, with two *books, face each other.
Whitney, Emblemes, Leyden, 1586, p.014
laurel: *Diana, with *laurel *wreath, *falcon, and *staff, *watches as a *stag-headed *Actaeon is attacked by *three *hounds.
Whitney, Emblemes, Leyden, 1586, p.015
laurel: *Jupiter with *thunderbolts sits on his *eagle; a man holds onto a *laurel tree in a storm(?); a *swan(?) with a *laurel *garland about its neck.
Whitney, Emblemes, Leyden, 1586, p.067
laurel: *Aesculapius, with a *laurel *garland, a *sceptre in his *right hand and a *staff in his *left, on a *throne.
Whitney, Emblemes, Leyden, 1586, p.212
laurel: *Two *men with *laurel *branches *embrace; *swords lie on the ground. A *palm-tree and *sun set.
Whitney, Emblemes, Leyden, 1586, p.216b
laurel(?): Spotted with *mouths(?), *winged *Fame, sounds a *horn; he has a *pen tied to a sling made of *laurel(?) over his shoulder.
Whitney, Emblemes, Leyden, 1586, p.196
leaf: A *fisherman grasps an *eel with the help of *fig *leaves.
Whitney, Emblemes, Leyden, 1586, p.077a
leaf: *Bacchus with a *crown of *vine *leaves and *grapes, and *Apollo with his *lyre stand on a *pedestal or *tomb.
Whitney, Emblemes, Leyden, 1586, p.146
leafless: A *ringdove broods on a *nest in a *leafless *tree.
Whitney, Emblemes, Leyden, 1586, p.029
lectern: *Two *scholars in a *library: one reads at a *lectern.
Whitney, Emblemes, Leyden, 1586, p.171
left: *Janus with *two *faces, in *Roman *armour holds a *sceptre in his *right hand and a *mirror(?) in his *left.
Whitney, Emblemes, Leyden, 1586, p.108
left: A *left *gauntlet holds a *lance which is ringed by *four *garlands.
Whitney, Emblemes, Leyden, 1586, p.115
left: *Nemesis with *bridle, stands before *Hope, seated on a *barrel, a *bow in her *left hand, pointing with her *right.
Whitney, Emblemes, Leyden, 1586, p.139b
left: *Narcissus admires his *reflection in a *stream; *Echo(?) waves her *left hand.
Whitney, Emblemes, Leyden, 1586, p.149
left: A man is weighted down by a *stone bound to his *right *arm as he lifts his *winged *left arm and leg skywards towards *God(?).
Whitney, Emblemes, Leyden, 1586, p.152
left: *Two *scholars in a *library: one reads at a *lectern; the second counts on the fingers of his *left hand.
Whitney, Emblemes, Leyden, 1586, p.171
left: *Naked *Occasio holds a *scarf in her *left hand.
Whitney, Emblemes, Leyden, 1586, p.181
left: A *man, holding a *snake to his *breast with his *left hand, watches a *siege.
Whitney, Emblemes, Leyden, 1586, p.189a
left: A man with huge *ears; another points to his *mouth with his *left *forefinger (*Harpocratic gesture).
Whitney, Emblemes, Leyden, 1586, p.191b
left: A man *tramples *grapes under his *right *foot, reaching for a *bunch with his *left hand. A *vine grows on a wall with *astrological symbols and a *moon. A *woman holds grapes away from her with

her *left hand.
Whitney, Emblemes, Leyden, 1586, p.206
left: *Aesculapius, with a *laurel *garland, a *sceptre in his *right hand and a *staff in his *left, on a *throne.
Whitney, Emblemes, Leyden, 1586, p.212
left: Virtue(?) or *Athene(?) wears a *helmet, a *lance with her *right hand, a sceptre(?) or *mace(?) in her *left.
Whitney, Emblemes, Leyden, 1586, p.222a
left: *Three *Christian *martyrs in *prayer before a *fire are harassed by men with *swords and *dogs. A *left hand from the *clouds holds a *garland over them.
Whitney, Emblemes, Leyden, 1586, p.224a
left: One man on the *left strikes another on the forehead with a *sword.
Whitney, Emblemes, Leyden, 1586, p.226a
left: One man on the *left strikes another on the forehead with a *sword.
Whitney, Emblemes, Leyden, 1586, p.226b
leopard(?): A *leopard(?) fights with a *lion. *Travellers pass nearby. A *flock of *birds flies over head.
Whitney, Emblemes, Leyden, 1586, p.178
library: *Two *scholars in a *library.
Whitney, Emblemes, Leyden, 1586, p.171
lily: A *lily blooms in *briars and *thorns.
Whitney, Emblemes, Leyden, 1586, p.221
lion: A *lion *devours its *prey, observed by an *envious *dog. *Animals nearby.
Whitney, Emblemes, Leyden, 1586, p.044
lion: An *elephant is frightened by a *white cloth; a *bull by a *red cloth; a *lion by a crowing *cock; a *stag flees from a *smoking cloth.
Whitney, Emblemes, Leyden, 1586, p.052a
lion: With *whip and *reins, *Eros *drives the *two *lions *drawing his *chariot.
Whitney, Emblemes, Leyden, 1586, p.063
lion: Seated on a *throne, *Jupiter, whose *staff is surmounted by an *eagle, is surrounded by a *deer, *horse, *bull, *ass, *snail, *eagle, and *lion.
Whitney, Emblemes, Leyden, 1586, p.091
lion: A *vulture watches a *lion and a *boar fighting.
Whitney, Emblemes, Leyden, 1586, p.119
lion: A *lion sits at a *church entrance; *weather-vane *cock on the roof.
Whitney, Emblemes, Leyden, 1586, p.120
lion: *Three *hares *bite the head of a *dead supine *lion; a fourth hare runs by.
Whitney, Emblemes, Leyden, 1586, p.127
lion: A *lion and a *fox face each other over their *prey, including a *stag. A dead *ass lies nearby.
Whitney, Emblemes, Leyden, 1586, p.154
lion: A *fox cowers before a *lion.
Whitney, Emblemes, Leyden, 1586, p.156b
lion: A *lion with *tongue outstretched stands before a sick *fox in its den.
Whitney, Emblemes, Leyden, 1586, p.161
lion: A *leopard(?) fights with a *lion. *Travellers pass nearby. A *flock of *birds flies over head.
Whitney, Emblemes, Leyden, 1586, p.178
lion: A *Venus(?) with basket of *fruit, and *Eros(?); animals nearby: *lion, *hare, *horse, *bird and *fish.
Whitney, Emblemes, Leyden, 1586, p.182b
lion: *Orpheus plays his *harp, surrounded by a *vulture, *stork, *stag, *lion, *bear, *antelope, and *ape.
Whitney, Emblemes, Leyden, 1586, p.186
lion: An old *lion, feigning *sickness, lies in a cave; a *fox at the entrance.
Whitney, Emblemes, Leyden, 1586, p.210
lion[1] = heraldic
lion[1]: A *lion *rampant holding an upright *sword.
Whitney, Emblemes, Leyden, 1586, p.116

lip: A ˙scholar with a ˙book in his study. He holds a
 ˙finger to his ˙lips in a gesture of ˙silence.
 (˙Harpocrates)
    Whitney, Emblemes, Leyden, 1586, p.060
lip: ˙Modesty, her ˙finger to her ˙lips in the
 ˙Harpocratic gesture of ˙silence, holds ˙keys and
 ˙stands on a ˙tortoise.
    Whitney, Emblemes, Leyden, 1586, p.093b
liver: An ˙eagle rends the ˙liver of ˙Prometheus,
 ˙chained to a ˙rock.
    Whitney, Emblemes, Leyden, 1586, p.075
lizard(?): A ˙fisherman with a ˙net reaches with his
 ˙right hand for a ˙cuttlefish muddying the ˙water. A
 ˙lizard(?) flees on the opposite bank.
    Whitney, Emblemes, Leyden, 1586, p.097
log: An ˙ape, tampering with a carpenter's ˙tools -- a
 ˙wedge, ˙axe and ˙mallet -- catches his foot in a
 ˙log.
    Whitney, Emblemes, Leyden, 1586, p.145
lure: A feathered ˙lure for ˙falconry.
    Whitney, Emblemes, Leyden, 1586, p.191a
lure: ˙Two ˙fowlers watch as ˙four ˙birds, ˙ducks, are
 ˙lured into the ˙net by a live ˙decoy.
    Whitney, Emblemes, Leyden, 1586, p.027
lute: ˙Mercury in a ˙winged ˙cap repairs the ˙strings of
 a ˙lute; a ˙woman ˙dances while another man plays a
 lute.
    Whitney, Emblemes, Leyden, 1586, p.092
lyre: ˙Three ˙mermaids with a ˙lyre and a ˙woodwind
 instrument, watch a ˙galley, with ˙Ulysses tied to the
 mast.
    Whitney, Emblemes, Leyden, 1586, p.010
lyre: ˙Bacchus with a ˙crown of ˙vine ˙leaves and
 ˙grapes, and ˙Apollo with his ˙lyre stand on a
 ˙pedestal or ˙tomb.
    Whitney, Emblemes, Leyden, 1586, p.146
mace(?): Virtue(?) or ˙Athene(?) wears a ˙helmet, a
 ˙lance with her ˙right hand, a sceptre(?) or ˙mace(?)
 in her ˙left.
    Whitney, Emblemes, Leyden, 1586, p.222a
mallet: An ˙ape, tampering with a carpenter's ˙tools -- a
 ˙wedge, ˙axe and ˙mallet -- catches his foot in a
 ˙log.
    Whitney, Emblemes, Leyden, 1586, p.145
mallet: A ˙carver uses a ˙mallet and ˙chisel to incise a
 ˙tablet with ˙"TROIA MIHI LICET TAMEN"
 [Never-the-less the whore sells herself to me].
    Whitney, Emblemes, Leyden, 1586, p.183b
man: Four ˙men sit at a table; one ˙drinks from a ˙mug;
 a second watches the remaining two argue over a
 ˙game of ˙backgammon. Two other men ˙wrestle.
    Whitney, Emblemes, Leyden, 1586, p.017
man: ˙Two men ˙wash a ˙black ˙man.
    Whitney, Emblemes, Leyden, 1586, p.057
man: A naked ˙boy or ˙Putto(?) sits in a ˙fruit-tree; an
 ˙old ˙man, ˙scholar(?); ˙Flowers, some wilted, grow
 nearby.
    Whitney, Emblemes, Leyden, 1586, p.173
man: A ˙man, holding a ˙snake to his ˙breast with his
 ˙left hand, watches a ˙siege.
    Whitney, Emblemes, Leyden, 1586, p.189a
man: ˙Two ˙men with ˙laurel ˙branches ˙embrace;
 ˙swords lie on the ground. A ˙palm-tree and ˙sun set.
    Whitney, Emblemes, Leyden, 1586, p.216b
man: Two ˙men under a blazing ˙sun; one flees, the
 other chases his ˙shadow.
    Whitney, Emblemes, Leyden, 1586, p.218b
manger: A ˙dog in a ˙manger prevents an ˙ox from
 feeding.
    Whitney, Emblemes, Leyden, 1586, p.184
marble: On a ˙marble ˙tomb an ˙ewer and ˙basin with
 folded ˙towel.
    Whitney, Emblemes, Leyden, 1586, p.136
marble: An ˙arrow ˙broken in two against a ˙marble
 ˙wall.

Whitney, Emblemes, Leyden, 1586, p.138b
martyr: ˙Three ˙Christian ˙martyrs in ˙prayer before a
 ˙fire are harassed by men with ˙swords and ˙dogs. A
 ˙left hand from the ˙clouds holds a ˙garland over
 them.
    Whitney, Emblemes, Leyden, 1586, p.224a
meat: A ˙thief is ˙strangled in ˙sleep by the ˙sack of
 ˙stolen ˙meats about his ˙neck.
    Whitney, Emblemes, Leyden, 1586, p.041
medal: A ˙right hand, wearing a ˙ring, tests a ˙coin or
 ˙medal on a ˙touchstone. The coin bears a ˙shield
 with ˙three ˙fleurs-de-lys, surmounted by a ˙coronet.
    Whitney, Emblemes, Leyden, 1586, p.139a
melt: A man with a ˙staff climbs a ˙snow covered
 ˙mountain. The ˙sun has ˙melted the snow from the
 peak.
    Whitney, Emblemes, Leyden, 1586, p.020
mermaid: ˙Three ˙mermaids with a ˙lyre and a
 ˙woodwind instrument, watch a ˙galley, with ˙Ulysses
 tied to the mast. A ˙wrecked ˙hull lies in the
 distance.
    Whitney, Emblemes, Leyden, 1586, p.010
mew: A ˙mew or ˙gull and a ˙cormorant ˙fly in pursuit
 of ˙three small ˙fishes.
    Whitney, Emblemes, Leyden, 1586, p.052b
milk: A ˙goat kicks over a ˙jar of ˙milk; a ˙milkmaid
 raises her ˙hands in anger.
    Whitney, Emblemes, Leyden, 1586, p.189b
milkmaid: A ˙goat kicks over a ˙jar of ˙milk; a
 ˙milkmaid raises her ˙hands in anger.
    Whitney, Emblemes, Leyden, 1586, p.189b
miller: A ˙miller sleeps by a ˙windmill. A man with a
 sack stands on the steps of the mill, watching for
 ˙wind.
    Whitney, Emblemes, Leyden, 1586, p.026
miller: A ˙miller and the ˙wife of ˙Anellus ˙embrace
 before ˙sacks of ˙grain at a ˙watermill.
    Whitney, Emblemes, Leyden, 1586, p.080
mirror(?): ˙Janus with ˙two ˙faces, in ˙Roman ˙armour
 holds a ˙sceptre in his ˙right hand and a ˙mirror(?)
 in his ˙left.
    Whitney, Emblemes, Leyden, 1586, p.108
miser: ˙Opimius, the ˙miser, in his sick-bed. The
 ˙physician supervises the emptying of his ˙chests of
 ˙gold onto a table.
    Whitney, Emblemes, Leyden, 1586, p.209
mole: An ˙ape, ˙ass and ˙mole discuss their lot in life.
    Whitney, Emblemes, Leyden, 1586, p.093a
moon: ˙Chaos: ˙four ˙elements -- ˙fire, ˙air, ˙earth and
 ˙water -- in confusion. A ˙crescent ˙moon, ˙sun,
 ˙star and ˙wind.
    Whitney, Emblemes, Leyden, 1586, p.122
moon: A ˙sailing ˙ship on a ˙world ˙globe, surrounded
 by ˙clouds, ˙stars, ˙sun and crescent ˙moon.
    Whitney, Emblemes, Leyden, 1586, p.203
moon: A ˙vine grows on a wall with ˙astrological
 symbols and a ˙moon.
    Whitney, Emblemes, Leyden, 1586, p.206
moon: A ˙dog bays at a full ˙moon.
    Whitney, Emblemes, Leyden, 1586, p.213
mother: A ˙thief, escorted to his ˙hanging by soldiers,
 is embraced by his ˙mother. The ˙gibbet lies on the
 ground.
    Whitney, Emblemes, Leyden, 1586, p.155
mother: A ˙mother ˙admonishes a ˙child in ˙bed; a
 ˙wolf lurks outside.
    Whitney, Emblemes, Leyden, 1586, p.162
mountain: A sailing ship ˙flounders in the ˙sea off the
 ˙shore; the ˙sun's rays melt ˙snow on ˙mountains.
    Whitney, Emblemes, Leyden, 1586, p.011
mountain: A man with a ˙staff climbs a ˙snow covered
 ˙mountain. A ˙goat stands on top of the mountain.
 The ˙sun has ˙melted the snow from the peak.
    Whitney, Emblemes, Leyden, 1586, p.020
mountain: ˙Four ˙ravens or ˙crows ˙fly to ˙feed on the

˚fruit of a ˚fig-tree on a ˚mountain.
Whitney, Emblemes, Leyden, 1586, p.053b
mouse: A ˚mouse, its head caught in an ˚oyster ˚shell,
on a shell-strewn beach.
Whitney, Emblemes, Leyden, 1586, p.128
mouse: ˚Mice play; ˚two ˚cats in ˚cages.
Whitney, Emblemes, Leyden, 1586, p.222b
mouth: ˚Envy, with ˚snakes emerging from her ˚mouth,
plucks out her ˚heart with her ˚right hand, walking
with a ˚staff.
Whitney, Emblemes, Leyden, 1586, p.094
mouth: A man with huge ˚ears; another points to his
˚mouth with his ˚left ˚forefinger (˚Harpocratic
gesture); a man flees from a ˚snake.
Whitney, Emblemes, Leyden, 1586, p.191b
mouth(?): Spotted with ˚mouths(?), ˚winged ˚Fame,
sounds a ˚horn as he flies over a ˚Roman(?) building
and ˚three ˚Egyptian(?) ˚pyramids.
Whitney, Emblemes, Leyden, 1586, p.196
mug: Four ˚men sit at a table; one ˚drinks from a ˚mug;
a second watches the remaining two argue over a
˚game of ˚backgammon. Two other mem ˚wrestle.
Whitney, Emblemes, Leyden, 1586, p.017
muskrat(?): ˚Lais, the ˚courtesan with ˚muskrats(?).
Whitney, Emblemes, Leyden, 1586, p.079
muzzle: A ˚dog, his ˚muzzle and front ˚paws in a
˚stream, searches for his ˚bone.
Whitney, Emblemes, Leyden, 1586, p.039
nail: Under a ˚sun, a ˚bound ˚Attilius, lies on a
˚stretcher near an open ˚barrel riven with ˚nails.
Whitney, Emblemes, Leyden, 1586, p.114
naked: ˚Glory ˚flees through a ˚doorway from ˚naked
˚couple on a ˚bed; beside them stands a ˚table with
˚food and ˚drink.
Whitney, Emblemes, Leyden, 1586, p.042
naked: A ˚naked ˚child on a ˚hobby-horse, a ˚courtier,
and a ˚jester stand before a ˚crowned ˚king holding a
˚sceptre.
Whitney, Emblemes, Leyden, 1586, p.081
naked: From his ˚throne, ˚Mezentius with ˚crown and
˚sceptre overseee the ˚binding of a ˚naked ˚body to a
naked ˚corpse.
Whitney, Emblemes, Leyden, 1586, p.099
naked: ˚Naked ˚Bacchus, a ˚wreath of ˚vines(?) on his
head, lies on a ˚river bank, ˚drinking from a ˚cup.
Whitney, Emblemes, Leyden, 1586, p.125
naked: ˚Naked ˚Occasio stands on a ˚wheel in the ˚sea.
Whitney, Emblemes, Leyden, 1586, p.181
narcissus(?): ˚Narcissus admires his ˚reflection in a
˚stream; a ˚flower, ˚narcissus(?), grows nearby.
Whitney, Emblemes, Leyden, 1586, p.149
neck: A ˚thief is ˚strangled in ˚sleep by the ˚sack of
˚stolen ˚meats about his ˚neck.
Whitney, Emblemes, Leyden, 1586, p.041
nest: A ˚swallow with a ˚grasshopper in its ˚beak
returns to its ˚nest in the ˚ruins of a ˚palace.
Whitney, Emblemes, Leyden, 1586, p.005
nest: A ˚ringdove broods on a ˚nest in a ˚leafless ˚tree.
Whitney, Emblemes, Leyden, 1586, p.029
nest: A ˚swallow approaches its ˚nest in a niche with a
˚statue of ˚Medea ˚killing her ˚child with a ˚sword.
Whitney, Emblemes, Leyden, 1586, p.033
nest: A ˚sleeping man is ˚awakened by a ˚swallow
chattering in its ˚nest.
Whitney, Emblemes, Leyden, 1586, p.050a
nest: In a ˚nest made of a ˚crown of ˚thorns,the
˚pelican with ˚wings ˚outspread, pierces her ˚breast
with her beak to sprinkle her ˚three ˚young[1] with
˚blood.
Whitney, Emblemes, Leyden, 1586, p.087
nest: A ˚stork with a ˚snake in its ˚beak returns to its
˚nest with ˚three young.
Whitney, Emblemes, Leyden, 1586, p.072
net: ˚Two ˚fowlers watch as ˚four ˚birds, ˚ducks, are
˚lured into the ˚net by a live ˚decoy.

Whitney, Emblemes, Leyden, 1586, p.027
net: ˚Two ˚fishermen in a ˚boat haul in a ˚fishing ˚net.
Whitney, Emblemes, Leyden, 1586, p.071
net: A ˚fisherman with a ˚net reaches with his ˚right
hand for a ˚cuttlefish muddying the ˚water.
Whitney, Emblemes, Leyden, 1586, p.097
nightingale: A large ˚cage with a ˚nightingale.
Whitney, Emblemes, Leyden, 1586, p.101
nine: ˚Homer with the ˚nine ˚Muses.
Whitney, Emblemes, Leyden, 1586, p.168a
nut-tree: Two ˚boys with ˚rods knock ˚fruit from a
˚nut-tree.
Whitney, Emblemes, Leyden, 1586, p.174
oak: The ˚wind, ˚Boreas, blows; ˚reeds in the water
bend, while an ˚oak breaks.
Whitney, Emblemes, Leyden, 1586, p.220
oak-tree: ˚Two ˚oak-trees grow on a sea shore; a third
lies on the ground. ˚Sun set.
Whitney, Emblemes, Leyden, 1586, p.230
obelisk: A ˚spire or pointed ˚obelisk, set on a ˚plinth,
entwined with ˚ivy.
Whitney, Emblemes, Leyden, 1586, p.001
offspring: A ˚ape holding its ˚dead ˚offspring.
Whitney, Emblemes, Leyden, 1586, p.188a
oil: An ˚arsonist sets ˚fire to a ˚house; a man, carrying
a ˚bucket of ˚oil, scales a ˚ladder placed against the
burning house.
Whitney, Emblemes, Leyden, 1586, p.007
old: An ˚old man ˚sits at ˚table; outside a ˚young man
˚labours in the ˚field.
Whitney, Emblemes, Leyden, 1586, p.050b
old: An ˚old man on ˚crutches enters a room with a
˚swaddled baby in a ˚cradle.
Whitney, Emblemes, Leyden, 1586, p.167
old: A naked ˚boy or ˚Putto(?) sits in a ˚fruit-tree; an
˚old ˚man, ˚scholar(?); ˚Flowers, some wilted, grow
nearby.
Whitney, Emblemes, Leyden, 1586, p.173
old: A ˚young man and an ˚older man over a ˚game of
˚draughts or ˚chess; ˚flames engulf the building
behind them.
Whitney, Emblemes, Leyden, 1586, p.208
olive-tree: An ˚olive-tree entwined by a ˚grape ˚vine.
Whitney, Emblemes, Leyden, 1586, p.133
open: An ˚open ˚book, inscribed ˚"ET USQUE AD
NUBES VERITAS TVA" [And your truth (will soar)
all the way to the clouds] is surrounded by ˚light.
Whitney, Emblemes, Leyden, 1586, p.166a
open: A ˚burning ˚candle, flanked by an ˚hourglass and
an ˚open ˚book, stands on a table in a room.
Whitney, Emblemes, Leyden, 1586, p.172
ostrich: An ˚ostrich with ˚wings ˚outstretched.
Whitney, Emblemes, Leyden, 1586, p.051b
outspread: The ˚pelican with ˚wings ˚outspread, pierces
her ˚breast with her beak to sprinkle her ˚three
˚young[1] with ˚blood.
Whitney, Emblemes, Leyden, 1586, p.087
outstretched: An ˚ostrich with ˚wings ˚outstretched.
Whitney, Emblemes, Leyden, 1586, p.051b
ox: A ˚dog in a ˚manger prevents an ˚ox from feeding.
Whitney, Emblemes, Leyden, 1586, p.184
oyster: A ˚mouse, its head caught in an ˚oyster ˚shell,
on a shell-strewn beach.
Whitney, Emblemes, Leyden, 1586, p.128
pack: A ˚bird-of-paradise ˚flies by; a ˚traveller with a
back ˚pack looks towards a ˚village across a
˚stream.
Whitney, Emblemes, Leyden, 1586, p.089
pack: A ˚shipwrecked ˚traveller, a ˚pack on his back,
˚swims to shore.
Whitney, Emblemes, Leyden, 1586, p.179
palace: A ˚swallow with a ˚grasshopper in its ˚beak
returns to its ˚nest in the ˚ruins of a ˚palace.
Whitney, Emblemes, Leyden, 1586, p.005
palace: ˚Three ˚rich and ˚two ˚poor men enter a

`palace through two different `doors.
Whitney, Emblemes, Leyden, 1586, p.204

palm-tree: `Frogs and `snakes crowd at the base of a
  `palm-tree.
Whitney, Emblemes, Leyden, 1586, p.118

palm-tree: `Thetis stands by the `tomb of `Achilles,
  which is decked with `amaranths, and stands under a
  `palm-tree.
Whitney, Emblemes, Leyden, 1586, p.193

palm-tree: `Two `men with `laurel `branches `embrace;
  `swords lie on the ground. A `palm-tree and `sun set.
Whitney, Emblemes, Leyden, 1586, p.216b

panel: A man flees from a `dog and a `bull; an `artist
  draws a figure(?) on a `panel.
Whitney, Emblemes, Leyden, 1586, p.100

parrot: A child and a man observe a `parrot in a `cage.
Whitney, Emblemes, Leyden, 1586, p.036

path: Wearing a `winged `helmet and holding a
  `caduceus, `Mercury points to the `path at his feet; a
  `traveller with a `staff.
Whitney, Emblemes, Leyden, 1586, p.002

paw: A `dog, his `muzzle and front `paws in a `stream,
  searches for his `bone.
Whitney, Emblemes, Leyden, 1586, p.039

paw: An `ape thrusts the `paw of a `dog into the `fire
  to withdraw `chestnuts.
Whitney, Emblemes, Leyden, 1586, p.058

pedestal: `Bacchus with a `crown of `vine `leaves and
  `grapes, and `Apollo with his `lyre stand on a
  `pedestal or `tomb.
Whitney, Emblemes, Leyden, 1586, p.146

pelican: In a `nest made of a `crown of `thorns,the
  `pelican with `wings `outspread, pierces her `breast
  with her beak to sprinkle her `three `young[1] with
  `blood.
Whitney, Emblemes, Leyden, 1586, p.087

pen: The `right hand of Emperor `Valens, reaches for or
  lets fall a `quill `pen.
Whitney, Emblemes, Leyden, 1586, p.143

pen: `Winged `Fame has a `pen tied to a sling made of
  `laurel(?) over his shoulder.
Whitney, Emblemes, Leyden, 1586, p.196

philosopher: A `scholar in a `philosopher's `cap,
  `Diomedes or `Cicero, a `tablet under his arm talks
  with a `soldier..
Whitney, Emblemes, Leyden, 1586, p.047

phoenix: A `phoenix rises from the flames of a `fire.
Whitney, Emblemes, Leyden, 1586, p.177

physician: `Opimius, the `miser, in his sick-bed. The
  `physician supervises the emptying of his `chests of
  `gold onto a table.
Whitney, Emblemes, Leyden, 1586, p.209

pierce: `Brasidas points to his `shield, `pierced by the
  `arrow that wounded him.
Whitney, Emblemes, Leyden, 1586, p.141

pig: A `pig, or `sow with the inscription `"ULTERIUS"
  [Further]; a man points at the pig with his `left
  hand, and with his `right at `two `columns entwined
  with a scroll inscribed `"PLUS OLTRE [= ULTRA]"
  [Still further].
Whitney, Emblemes, Leyden, 1586, p.053a

pig: `Circe touches with her `wand a `pig; nearby a
  `dog, `ape, `goat and `ass, `Ulysses's transformed
  men.
Whitney, Emblemes, Leyden, 1586, p.082

pilgrim: A `traveller or `pilgrim walks past a `world
  `globe inscribed `"EUROPA" and `"AFRICA". The
  `tetragrammaton blazes in `clouds above.
Whitney, Emblemes, Leyden, 1586, p.225

pine-tree: A leafy `vine laden with `gourds climbs the
  trunk of a `pine-tree.
Whitney, Emblemes, Leyden, 1586, p.034

pine-tree: `Pine-trees are `broken by a `wind(?); in a
  `cloud `Jupiter(?) sits astride an `eagle; a `rabbit
  crouches before a `tree `stump; a `horseman nearby.

Whitney, Emblemes, Leyden, 1586, p.059

pipe: `Bacchus, under `vines with `grapes, beats a
  `drum and blows a `pipe; nearby a `goblet.
Whitney, Emblemes, Leyden, 1586, p.187

plinth: A `spire or pointed `obelisk, set on a `plinth,
  entwined with `ivy.
Whitney, Emblemes, Leyden, 1586, p.001

ploughman: A `king with `crown and `sceptre on a
  `horse watches a `ploughman give his `harrow to an
  `astronomer in exchange for a `sphere(?) or
  `astrolobe and the `doctor's `robe.
Whitney, Emblemes, Leyden, 1586, p.009

plumed: The `head of `Valerius `Corvinus in a `plumed
  `helmet.
Whitney, Emblemes, Leyden, 1586, p.113

point: A `blind man with a `stick carries a `lame man
  who `points the `way with his `finger.
Whitney, Emblemes, Leyden, 1586, p.065

poison: A `flower gives `honey to a `bee and `poison to
  a `spider.
Whitney, Emblemes, Leyden, 1586, p.051a

pond(?): `Two `ducks and two `geese hunt for food in a
  `pond(?). A `falcon overhead.
Whitney, Emblemes, Leyden, 1586, p.207

poor: A man gives `alms to a `poor man.
Whitney, Emblemes, Leyden, 1586, p.190b

poor: `Three `rich and `two `poor men enter a `palace
  through two different `doors.
Whitney, Emblemes, Leyden, 1586, p.204

pot: A `copper pot and an `earthenware `pot float side
  by side down a `stream.
Whitney, Emblemes, Leyden, 1586, p.164

prayer: `Three `Christian `martyrs in `prayer before a
  `fire are harassed by men with `swords and `dogs. A
  `left hand from the `clouds holds a `garland over
  them.
Whitney, Emblemes, Leyden, 1586, p.224a

prey: A `lion `devours its `prey, observed by an
  `envious `dog. `Animals nearby.
Whitney, Emblemes, Leyden, 1586, p.044

prey: A `lion and a `fox face each other over their
  `prey, including a `stag. A dead `ass lies nearby.
Whitney, Emblemes, Leyden, 1586, p.154

prince: `Two `kings or `princes in `armour shake `right
  hands.
Whitney, Emblemes, Leyden, 1586, p.076a

pupil: `Sinon is `whipped by his `pupils back to `the
  Faleria; the `walled `town is `besieged by `Camillus
  on horseback.
Whitney, Emblemes, Leyden, 1586, p.112

pursue: A `beaver tears off his `testicles, `pursued by a
  `hunter and `two `hounds.
Whitney, Emblemes, Leyden, 1586, p.035

pyramid: `Winged `Fame, sounds a `horn as he flies
  over a `Roman(?) building and `three `Egyptian(?)
  `pyramids.
Whitney, Emblemes, Leyden, 1586, p.196

quill: The `right hand of Emperor `Valens, reaches for
  or lets fall a `quill `pen.
Whitney, Emblemes, Leyden, 1586, p.143

quill: `Quintilius, a `quill in his `right hand, restrains a
  `youth from handing a note to `winged `Fame with a
  `trumpet.
Whitney, Emblemes, Leyden, 1586, p.185

rabbit: An `ass, laden with `foodstuffs: `jugs, a
  `cask(?), bags with `bread(?), a spitted `fowl, and a
  `rabbit, `eats `thistles.
Whitney, Emblemes, Leyden, 1586, p.018

rabbit: `Pine-trees are `broken by a `wind(?); in a
  `cloud `Jupiter(?) sits astride an `eagle; a `rabbit
  crouches before a `tree `stump; a `horseman nearby.
Whitney, Emblemes, Leyden, 1586, p.059

ram: `Phrixus crosses `Hellespont on the `golden `ram,
  eyes and `right arm raised to the heavens.
Whitney, Emblemes, Leyden, 1586, p.214

rampant: A ˚lion ˚rampant holding an upright ˚sword.
  Whitney, Emblemes, Leyden, 1586, p.116
raven: ˚Four ˚ravens or ˚crows ˚fly to ˚feed on the
  ˚fruit of a ˚fig-tree on a ˚mountain.
  Whitney, Emblemes, Leyden, 1586, p.053b
raven: The ˚head of ˚Valerius ˚Corvinus in a ˚plumed
  ˚helmet, the ˚visor open; a ˚raven is perched on the
  visor.
  Whitney, Emblemes, Leyden, 1586, p.113
razor: ˚Naked ˚Occasio, with ˚bald ˚head, long ˚forelock,
  and ˚razor in her raised ˚right hand, stands on a
  ˚wheel in the ˚sea.
  Whitney, Emblemes, Leyden, 1586, p.181
rear: A ˚horseman on a ˚rearing ˚horse.
  Whitney, Emblemes, Leyden, 1586, p.038
recline: A ˚winged ˚figure ˚reclines at the foot of the
  ˚volcano ˚Vesuvius. At the top a man clutches his
  breast as ˚Pliny ˚falls into the volcano.
  Whitney, Emblemes, Leyden, 1586, p.025
red: An ˚elephant is frightened by a ˚white cloth; a ˚bull
  by a ˚red cloth; a ˚lion by a crowing ˚cock.
  Whitney, Emblemes, Leyden, 1586, p.052a
redbreast: One ˚redbreast ˚knocks another from a ˚tree
  ˚branch.
  Whitney, Emblemes, Leyden, 1586, p.055a
reed: The ˚wind, ˚Boreas, blows; ˚reeds in the water
  bend, while an ˚oak breaks.
  Whitney, Emblemes, Leyden, 1586, p.220
reflection: ˚Narcissus admires his ˚reflection in a
  ˚stream.
  Whitney, Emblemes, Leyden, 1586, p.149
rein: A ˚charioteer with a ˚whip tries to ˚rein in the
  ˚two galloping ˚horses pulling his ˚chariot.
  Whitney, Emblemes, Leyden, 1586, p.006
rein: With ˚whip and ˚reins, ˚Eros ˚drives the ˚two
  ˚lions ˚drawing his ˚chariot.
  Whitney, Emblemes, Leyden, 1586, p.063
remora: A ˚remora encircles an ˚arrow.
  Whitney, Emblemes, Leyden, 1586, p.188b
reverence: ˚Worshippers kneel in ˚reverence before an
  ˚ass bearing a ˚statue of ˚Isis.
  Whitney, Emblemes, Leyden, 1586, p.008
rich: ˚Three ˚rich and ˚two ˚poor men enter a ˚palace
  through two different ˚doors.
  Whitney, Emblemes, Leyden, 1586, p.204
right: ˚Two ˚kings or ˚princes in ˚armour shake ˚right
  hands.
  Whitney, Emblemes, Leyden, 1586, p.076a
right: ˚Envy, with ˚snakes emerging from her ˚mouth,
  plucks out her ˚heart with her ˚right hand, walking
  with a ˚staff.
  Whitney, Emblemes, Leyden, 1586, p.094
right: A ˚fisherman with a ˚net reaches with his ˚right
  hand for a ˚cuttlefish muddying the ˚water.
  Whitney, Emblemes, Leyden, 1586, p.097
right: ˚Janus with ˚two ˚faces, in ˚Roman ˚armour holds
  a ˚sceptre in his ˚right hand and a ˚mirror(?) in his
  ˚left.
  Whitney, Emblemes, Leyden, 1586, p.108
right: A ˚right hand, wearing a ˚ring, tests a ˚coin or
  ˚medal on a ˚touchstone.
  Whitney, Emblemes, Leyden, 1586, p.139a
right: ˚Nemesis with ˚bridle, stands before ˚Hope, seated
  on a ˚barrel, a ˚bow in her ˚left hand, pointing with
  her ˚right.
  Whitney, Emblemes, Leyden, 1586, p.139b
right: The ˚right hand of Emperor ˚Valens, reaches for
  or lets fall a ˚quill ˚pen.
  Whitney, Emblemes, Leyden, 1586, p.143
right: A man is weighted down by a ˚stone bound to his
  ˚right ˚arm as he lifts his ˚winged ˚left arm and leg
  skywards towards ˚God(?).
  Whitney, Emblemes, Leyden, 1586, p.152
right: A ˚right hand, surrounded by ˚clouds, dangles a
  ˚snake, which has bitten into its middle ˚finger, over

an open ˚fire.
  Whitney, Emblemes, Leyden, 1586, p.166b
right: ˚Naked ˚Occasio, a ˚razor in her raised ˚right
  hand, stands on a ˚wheel in the ˚sea.
  Whitney, Emblemes, Leyden, 1586, p.181
right: ˚Quintilius, a ˚quill in his ˚right hand, restrains a
  ˚youth from handing a note to ˚winged ˚Fame with a
  ˚trumpet.
  Whitney, Emblemes, Leyden, 1586, p.185
right: A ˚sailing ˚ship on a ˚world ˚globe; a ˚right hand
  holds a ˚bridle, which encircles the globe.
  Whitney, Emblemes, Leyden, 1586, p.203
right: A man ˚tramples ˚grapes under his ˚right ˚foot,
  reaching for a ˚bunch with his ˚left hand. A ˚vine
  grows on a wall with ˚astrological symbols and a
  ˚moon. A ˚woman holds grapes away from her with
  her ˚left hand. Above ˚zodiacal ˚circle with ˚Virgo,
  her ˚right hand pointing at grapes held by the
  woman.
  Whitney, Emblemes, Leyden, 1586, p.206
right: ˚Aesculapius, with a ˚laurel ˚garland, a ˚sceptre
  in his ˚right hand and a ˚staff in his ˚left, on a
  ˚throne.
  Whitney, Emblemes, Leyden, 1586, p.212
right: ˚Phrixus crosses ˚Hellespont on the ˚golden ˚ram,
  eyes and ˚right arm raised to the heavens.
  Whitney, Emblemes, Leyden, 1586, p.214
right: Virtue(?) or ˚Athene(?) wears a ˚helmet, a ˚lance
  with her ˚right hand, a sceptre(?) or ˚mace(?) in her
  ˚left; her ˚right ˚foot on a ˚tortoise(?).
  Whitney, Emblemes, Leyden, 1586, p.222a
right: A man with a ˚world ˚globe on his back drags
  the ˚tablets of the ˚commandments tied to his ˚right
  ankle.
  Whitney, Emblemes, Leyden, 1586, p.223
ring: A ˚right hand, wearing a ˚ring, tests a ˚coin or
  ˚medal on a ˚touchstone.
  Whitney, Emblemes, Leyden, 1586, p.139a
ringdove: A ˚ringdove broods on a ˚nest in a ˚leafless
  ˚tree.
  Whitney, Emblemes, Leyden, 1586, p.029
river: A ˚crocodile laying her ˚eggs, on the bank of the
  ˚river ˚Nile.
  Whitney, Emblemes, Leyden, 1586, p.003
river: A ˚fox on an ˚ice-flow floats down a ˚river
  (˚Danube) past a ˚town (˚Regensburg).
  Whitney, Emblemes, Leyden, 1586, p.022
river: ˚Naked ˚Bacchus lies on a ˚river bank, ˚drinking
  from a ˚cup. A ˚dog leaps in front of a ˚crocodile in
  the water.
  Whitney, Emblemes, Leyden, 1586, p.125
robe: A ˚king watches a ˚ploughman give his ˚harrow to
  an ˚astronomer in exchange for an ˚astrolobe and
  the ˚doctor's ˚robe.
  Whitney, Emblemes, Leyden, 1586, p.009
rock: An ˚eagle rends the ˚liver of ˚Prometheus,
  ˚chained to a ˚rock.
  Whitney, Emblemes, Leyden, 1586, p.075
rock: ˚Four ˚winds ˚blow on a ˚rock in a rough ˚sea.
  Whitney, Emblemes, Leyden, 1586, p.096
rod: Two ˚boys with ˚rods knock ˚fruit from a
  ˚nut-tree.
  Whitney, Emblemes, Leyden, 1586, p.174
roof: A ˚hen on the ˚roof of a ˚farmhouse sucks an
  ˚egg.
  Whitney, Emblemes, Leyden, 1586, p.064
rope: ˚Ocnus and a ˚ropemaker make a ˚rope from
  ˚grasses. An ˚ass eats the rope.
  Whitney, Emblemes, Leyden, 1586, p.048
ropemaker: ˚Ocnus and a ˚ropemaker make a ˚rope from
  ˚grasses. An ˚ass eats the rope.
  Whitney, Emblemes, Leyden, 1586, p.048
rose: A ˚scarab or ˚dung-beetle in the centre of a
  ˚rose.
  Whitney, Emblemes, Leyden, 1586, p.021

rose: A man touches the ˙thorns and ˙flowers of a ˙rose
  bush.
  Whitney, Emblemes, Leyden, 1586, p.165
ruin: A ˙swallow with a ˙grasshopper in its ˙beak returns
  to its ˙nest in the ˙ruins of a ˙palace.
  Whitney, Emblemes, Leyden, 1586, p.005
sack: A ˙thief is ˙strangled in ˙sleep by the ˙sack of
  ˙stolen ˙meats about his ˙neck.
  Whitney, Emblemes, Leyden, 1586, p.041
sack: A ˙miller and the ˙wife of ˙Anellus ˙embrace
  before ˙sacks of ˙grain at a ˙watermill.
  Whitney, Emblemes, Leyden, 1586, p.080
sail: A ˙ship in full ˙sail runs before the ˙wind on a
  ˙sea.
  Whitney, Emblemes, Leyden, 1586, p.137
sail: A ˙sailing ˙ship on a ˙world ˙globe; a ˙right hand
  holds a ˙bridle, which encircles the globe.
  Whitney, Emblemes, Leyden, 1586, p.203
sailor: ˙Arion and his ˙harp thrown overboard by
  ˙sailors; a ˙dolphin waits near the ˙ship.
  Whitney, Emblemes, Leyden, 1586, p.144
satyr: A man at ˙table blows his ˙food to cool it,
  watched by a ˙satyr.
  Whitney, Emblemes, Leyden, 1586, p.160
scarab: A ˙scarab or ˙dung-beetle in the centre of a
  ˙rose.
  Whitney, Emblemes, Leyden, 1586, p.021
scarf: ˙Naked ˙Occasio holds a ˙scarf in her ˙left hand.
  Whitney, Emblemes, Leyden, 1586, p.181
sceptre: A ˙king with ˙crown and ˙sceptre on a ˙horse.
  Whitney, Emblemes, Leyden, 1586, p.009
sceptre: A ˙naked ˙child on a ˙hobby-horse, a ˙courtier,
  and a ˙jester stand before a ˙crowned ˙king holding a
  ˙sceptre.
  Whitney, Emblemes, Leyden, 1586, p.081
sceptre: From his ˙throne, ˙Mezentius with ˙crown and
  ˙sceptre overseee the ˙binding of a ˙naked ˙body to a
  naked ˙corpse.
  Whitney, Emblemes, Leyden, 1586, p.099
sceptre: ˙Janus with ˙two ˙faces, in ˙Roman ˙armour
  holds a ˙sceptre in his ˙right hand and a ˙mirror(?)
  in his ˙left.
  Whitney, Emblemes, Leyden, 1586, p.108
sceptre: A ˙king, with ˙crown and ˙sceptre, squeezes
  ˙water from a ˙sponge; a crowd watches a ˙hanging
  (˙gibbet).
  Whitney, Emblemes, Leyden, 1586, p.151
sceptre: ˙Diogenes in his ˙barrel, talks with ˙Alexander
  with ˙crown and ˙sceptre.
  Whitney, Emblemes, Leyden, 1586, p.198
sceptre: ˙Aesculapius, with a ˙laurel ˙garland, holds a
  ˙sceptre in his ˙right hand and a ˙staff in his ˙left.
  Whitney, Emblemes, Leyden, 1586, p.212
scholar: A ˙scholar in a ˙philosopher's ˙cap talks with a
  ˙soldier.
  Whitney, Emblemes, Leyden, 1586, p.047
scholar: A ˙scholar with a ˙book in his study. He holds a
  ˙finger to his ˙lips in a gesture of ˙silence.
  (˙Harpocrates)
  Whitney, Emblemes, Leyden, 1586, p.060
scholar: A ˙scholar flanked by ˙Eros and ˙Venus,and by
  ˙Athena and a ˙soldier.
  Whitney, Emblemes, Leyden, 1586, p.135
scholar: ˙Two ˙scholars in a ˙library.
  Whitney, Emblemes, Leyden, 1586, p.171
scholar(?): A naked ˙boy or ˙Putto(?) sits in a
  ˙fruit-tree; an ˙old ˙man, ˙scholar(?); ˙Flowers, some
  wilted, grow nearby.
  Whitney, Emblemes, Leyden, 1586, p.173
scroll: A ˙scrolled ˙shield pierced by ˙arrows.
  Whitney, Emblemes, Leyden, 1586, p.117
scythe: ˙Winged ˙Time with a ˙scythe liberates ˙Truth.
  Whitney, Emblemes, Leyden, 1586, p.004
scythe: ˙Winged ˙Time, with a ˙scythe, pursues a couple.
  Whitney, Emblemes, Leyden, 1586, p.199

sea: A sailing ship ˙flounders in the ˙sea off the
  ˙shore.
  Whitney, Emblemes, Leyden, 1586, p.011
sea: ˙Icarus ˙falls into the ˙sea after the ˙sun has
  melted the wax binding the ˙feathers of his ˙wings.
  Whitney, Emblemes, Leyden, 1586, p.028
sea: A ˙farmer works the banks of a ˙ditch, fed by the
  ˙sea.
  Whitney, Emblemes, Leyden, 1586, p.072
sea: A ˙dolphin ˙flounders on the ˙sea ˙shore.
  Whitney, Emblemes, Leyden, 1586, p.090
sea: ˙Four ˙winds ˙blow on a ˙rock in a rough ˙sea.
  Whitney, Emblemes, Leyden, 1586, p.096
sea: A ˙ship in full ˙sail runs before the ˙wind on a
  ˙sea.
  Whitney, Emblemes, Leyden, 1586, p.137
sea: ˙Naked ˙Occasio stands on a ˙wheel in the ˙sea.
  Whitney, Emblemes, Leyden, 1586, p.181
seven: ˙Seven ˙wise-men of Greece.
  Whitney, Emblemes, Leyden, 1586, p.130
shadow: A man with ˙upraised ˙sword takes fright at
  his ˙shadow. ˙Jupiter sits astride an ˙eagle in a bank
  of clouds.·
  Whitney, Emblemes, Leyden, 1586, p.032
shadow: Two ˙men under a blazing ˙sun; one flees, the
  other chases his ˙shadow.
  Whitney, Emblemes, Leyden, 1586, p.218b
sheaf: A ˙sheaf of ˙grain (˙wheat).
  Whitney, Emblemes, Leyden, 1586, p.023
sheaf: A large ˙sheaf of ˙grain or ˙wheat(?) encircled
  by ˙five single ˙stalks, and by ˙two smaller ˙sheaves.
  Whitney, Emblemes, Leyden, 1586, p.088
sheaf: A large ˙sheaf of ˙grain or ˙wheat(?) encircled
  by ˙five single ˙stalks, and by ˙two smaller ˙sheaves.
  Whitney, Emblemes, Leyden, 1586, p.088
sheaf: A ˙burning ˙candle, an ˙hourglass and an ˙open
  ˙book, stand on a table; the side of the table bears
  a ˙shield charged with a ˙sheaf of ˙wheat(?).
  Whitney, Emblemes, Leyden, 1586, p.172
sheaf: A ˙farmer works the banks of a ˙ditch, fed by
  the ˙sea; a ˙bull or ˙cow beside a bound ˙sheaf of
  ˙arrows.
  Whitney, Emblemes, Leyden, 1586, p.072
shell: A ˙mouse, its head caught in an ˙oyster ˙shell, on
  a shell-strewn beach.
  Whitney, Emblemes, Leyden, 1586, p.128
shield: ˙Hercules stands between ˙Virtue, ˙Athena with
  ˙helmet, ˙shield and ˙spear and ˙Vice, ˙Venus with
  ˙Eros.
  Whitney, Emblemes, Leyden, 1586, p.040
shield: ˙Agamemnon, with ˙crown, ˙sword, and ˙shield
  inscribed ˙"Agamemnon" bearing a ˙lion[1] ˙rampant.
  ˙Troy in ˙flames.
  Whitney, Emblemes, Leyden, 1586, p.045
shield: A ˙scholar in a ˙philosopher's ˙cap talks with a
  ˙soldier in a ˙helmet with ˙sword, ˙shield and
  ˙spear.
  Whitney, Emblemes, Leyden, 1586, p.047
shield: ˙Brutus in ˙Roman ˙armour and ˙helmet, ˙shield
  on the ground, ˙falls on his ˙sword.
  Whitney, Emblemes, Leyden, 1586, p.070
shield: ˙Paris gives the ˙golden ˙apple to ˙Venus;
  nearby, ˙Juno and ˙Athena with a ˙helmet and
  ˙shield.
  Whitney, Emblemes, Leyden, 1586, p.083
shield: ˙Athene(?) with ˙helmet, ˙spear and ˙shield,
  stands before a ˙grain ˙field and ˙fruit-tree.
  Whitney, Emblemes, Leyden, 1586, p.103
shield: A ˙scrolled ˙shield pierced by ˙arrows.
  Whitney, Emblemes, Leyden, 1586, p.117
shield: A ˙shield charged with a ˙swan[1] hangs from a
  tree; ˙two ˙swans on the waters.
  Whitney, Emblemes, Leyden, 1586, p.126
shield: A ˙right hand tests a ˙coin or ˙medal on a
  ˙touchstone. The coin bears a ˙shield with ˙three

*fleurs-de-lys, surmounted by a *coronet.
  Whitney, Emblemes, Leyden, 1586, p.139a
shield: *Brasidas points to his *shield, *pierced by the
  *arrow that wounded him.
  Whitney, Emblemes, Leyden, 1586, p.141
shield: The side of the table bears a *shield charged with
  a *sheaf of *wheat(?).
  Whitney, Emblemes, Leyden, 1586, p.172
ship: A *flooded *city and a *wrecked *ship.
  Whitney, Emblemes, Leyden, 1586, p.129
ship: A *ship in full *sail runs before the *wind on a
  *sea.
  Whitney, Emblemes, Leyden, 1586, p.137
ship: *Arion and his *harp thrown overboard by *sailors;
  a *dolphin waits near the *ship.
  Whitney, Emblemes, Leyden, 1586, p.144
ship: A *sailing *ship on a *world *globe; a *right hand
  holds a *bridle, which encircles the globe.
  Whitney, Emblemes, Leyden, 1586, p.203
shipwreck: A *shipwrecked *traveller, a *pack on his
  back, *swims to shore.
  Whitney, Emblemes, Leyden, 1586, p.179
shirt: A *shirt or *shroud *draped on a *lance and a
  *crossbar.
  Whitney, Emblemes, Leyden, 1586, p.086
shore: A sailing ship *flounders in the *sea off the
  *shore.
  Whitney, Emblemes, Leyden, 1586, p.011
shore: A *dolphin *flounders on the *sea *shore.
  Whitney, Emblemes, Leyden, 1586, p.090
shroud: A *shirt or *shroud *draped on a *lance and a
  *crossbar.
  Whitney, Emblemes, Leyden, 1586, p.086
sickness: An old *lion, feigning *sickness, lies in a cave;
  a *fox at the entrance.
  Whitney, Emblemes, Leyden, 1586, p.210
siege: *Sinon is *whipped by his *pupils back to *the
  Faleria; the *walled *town is *besieged by *Camillus
  on horseback.
  Whitney, Emblemes, Leyden, 1586, p.112
siege: A *man, holding a *snake to his *breast with his
  *left hand, watches a *siege.
  Whitney, Emblemes, Leyden, 1586, p.189a
sieve: *Grain passes through a *sieve.
  Whitney, Emblemes, Leyden, 1586, p.068
silence: A *scholar with a *book in his study. He holds a
  *finger to his *lips in a gesture of *silence.
  (*Harpocrates)
  Whitney, Emblemes, Leyden, 1586, p.060
silence: *Modesty, her *finger to her *lips in the
  *Harpocratic gesture of *silence, holds *keys and
  *stands on a *tortoise.
  Whitney, Emblemes, Leyden, 1586, p.093b
sit: An *old man *sits at *table; outside a *young man
  *labours in the *field.
  Whitney, Emblemes, Leyden, 1586, p.050b
sit: *Two *idle men *sit by a tree.
  Whitney, Emblemes, Leyden, 1586, p.085
skin: Two men shake *hands; one wears a *fox's *skin
  over his head.
  Whitney, Emblemes, Leyden, 1586, p.124
skull: A *woman collects *skulls into her apron; *skulls
  piled beside a *chapel.
  Whitney, Emblemes, Leyden, 1586, p.046
skull: A *skull, a *bone and a *flower.
  Whitney, Emblemes, Leyden, 1586, p.229b
sky: An *astronomer, looking at the *starry *sky, falls
  into a *well.
  Whitney, Emblemes, Leyden, 1586, p.157
sleep: A *thief is *strangled in *sleep by the *sack of
  *stolen *meats about his *neck.
  Whitney, Emblemes, Leyden, 1586, p.041
sleep: A *sleeping man is *awakened by a *swallow
  chattering in its *nest.
  Whitney, Emblemes, Leyden, 1586, p.050a

smoke: A *stag flees from a *smoking cloth.
  Whitney, Emblemes, Leyden, 1586, p.052a
smoke: *Tantalus stands in a river, looking up at *fruit
  laden *tree. *Flames and *smoke billow up in the
  background.
  Whitney, Emblemes, Leyden, 1586, p.074
snail: Seated on a *throne, *Jupiter is surrounded by a
  *deer, *horse, *bull, *ass, *snail, *eagle, and *lion.
  Whitney, Emblemes, Leyden, 1586, p.091
snake: A *snake *coils up *strawberry plants.
  Whitney, Emblemes, Leyden, 1586, p.024
snake: A *stork with a *snake in its *beak returns to
  its *nest with *three young.
  Whitney, Emblemes, Leyden, 1586, p.072
snake: A man with a *stick strikes a *snake sliding
  through a crack in a *wall.
  Whitney, Emblemes, Leyden, 1586, p.076b
snake: A *snake bites an *archer *aiming an *arrow at
  a *bird in flight.
  Whitney, Emblemes, Leyden, 1586, p.078
snake: *Envy, with *snakes emerging from her *mouth,
  plucks out her *heart.
  Whitney, Emblemes, Leyden, 1586, p.094
snake: *Frogs and *snakes crowd at the base of a
  *palm-tree.
  Whitney, Emblemes, Leyden, 1586, p.118
snake: A *right hand, surrounded by *clouds, dangles a
  *snake, which has bitten into its middle *finger, over
  an open *fire.
  Whitney, Emblemes, Leyden, 1586, p.166b
snake: A *man, holding a *snake to his *breast with his
  *left hand, watches a *siege.
  Whitney, Emblemes, Leyden, 1586, p.189a
snake: A man with huge *ears; another points to his
  *mouth with his *left *forefinger (*Harpocratic gesture);
  a man flees from a *snake.
  Whitney, Emblemes, Leyden, 1586, p.191b
snake: A dead *elephant, poisoned by a *snake, crushes
  it.
  Whitney, Emblemes, Leyden, 1586, p.195
snake: *Aesculapius; nearby a *snake, *dog and *cock.
  Whitney, Emblemes, Leyden, 1586, p.212
snake: Virtue(?) or *Athene(?); *ivy and *two *snakes
  scale the wall.
  Whitney, Emblemes, Leyden, 1586, p.222a
snake-haired: *Snake-haired *Envy eats her *heart.
  Whitney, Emblemes, Leyden, 1586, p.004
snow: A sailing ship *flounders in the *sea off the
  *shore; the *sun's rays melt *snow on *mountains.
  Whitney, Emblemes, Leyden, 1586, p.011
snow: A man with a *staff climbs a *snow covered
  *mountain. The *sun has *melted the snow from the
  peak.
  Whitney, Emblemes, Leyden, 1586, p.020
soldier: A *scholar talks with a *soldier in a *helmet
  with *sword, *shield and *spear.
  Whitney, Emblemes, Leyden, 1586, p.047
soldier: *Two *soldiers lead a captive *herald from the
  *battlefield into a *fortress.
  Whitney, Emblemes, Leyden, 1586, p.054a
soldier: *Attilius, on a *stretcher near an open *barrel
  riven with *nails, is observed by a *soldier with a
  *battle-axe.
  Whitney, Emblemes, Leyden, 1586, p.114
soldier: A *scholar flanked by *Eros and *Venus, and by
  *Athena and a *soldier.
  Whitney, Emblemes, Leyden, 1586, p.135
soldier: *Two *drummers with *drum and *horn(?) before
  an *encampment with *soldiers.
  Whitney, Emblemes, Leyden, 1586, p.194
sow: A *pig, or *sow with the inscription *"ULTERIUS"
  [Further]; *two *columns entwined with a scroll
  inscribed *"PLUS OLTRE [= ULTRA]" [Still further].
  Whitney, Emblemes, Leyden, 1586, p.053a
spear: *Hercules stands between *Virtue, *Athena with

helmet, shield and spear and Vice, Venus with Eros.
Whitney, Emblemes, Leyden, 1586, p.040

spear: A scholar talks with a soldier in a helmet with sword, shield and spear.
Whitney, Emblemes, Leyden, 1586, p.047

spear: Athene(?) with helmet, spear and shield, stands before a grain field and fruit-tree.
Whitney, Emblemes, Leyden, 1586, p.103

sphere(?): A king watches a ploughman give his harrow to an astronomer in exchange for a sphere(?) or astrolobe.
Whitney, Emblemes, Leyden, 1586, p.009

sphere, armillary: An astronomer, looking at the starry sky, falls into a well; an armillary sphere or astrolabe on the ground.
Whitney, Emblemes, Leyden, 1586, p.157

spider: A flower gives honey to a bee and poison to a spider.
Whitney, Emblemes, Leyden, 1586, p.051a

spire: A spire or pointed obelisk, set on a plinth, entwined with ivy.
Whitney, Emblemes, Leyden, 1586, p.001

sponge: A king, with crown and sceptre, squeezes water from a sponge; a crowd watches a hanging (gibbet).
Whitney, Emblemes, Leyden, 1586, p.151

stab: An arsonist sets fire to a house; a man stabs another.
Whitney, Emblemes, Leyden, 1586, p.007

staff: Mercury points to the path at his feet; a traveller with a staff.
Whitney, Emblemes, Leyden, 1586, p.002

staff: Diana, with laurel wreath, falcon, and staff, watches as Actaeon is attacked by three hounds.
Whitney, Emblemes, Leyden, 1586, p.015

staff: A man with a staff climbs a snow covered mountain.
Whitney, Emblemes, Leyden, 1586, p.020

staff: Jupiter's staff is surmounted by an eagle.
Whitney, Emblemes, Leyden, 1586, p.091

staff: Envy with a staff.
Whitney, Emblemes, Leyden, 1586, p.094

staff: Aesculapius, with a laurel garland, a sceptre and a staff, on a throne, supported by two eagles.
Whitney, Emblemes, Leyden, 1586, p.212

staff: A bundle of hay hangs from an staff.
Whitney, Emblemes, Leyden, 1586, p.217

stag: A man kneeling before a chart holds a compass to the stars; below a stag drinks from a stream.
Whitney, Emblemes, Leyden, 1586, p.043

stag: a stag flees from a smoking cloth.
Whitney, Emblemes, Leyden, 1586, p.052a

stag: A stag is struck by an arrow.
Whitney, Emblemes, Leyden, 1586, p.153a

stag: A lion and a fox face each other over their prey, including a stag.
Whitney, Emblemes, Leyden, 1586, p.154

stag: Orpheus plays his harp, surrounded by a vulture, stork, stag, lion, bear, antelope, and ape.
Whitney, Emblemes, Leyden, 1586, p.186

stag-headed: Diana watches as a stag-headed Actaeon is attacked by three hounds.
Whitney, Emblemes, Leyden, 1586, p.015

stalk: A large sheaf of grain or wheat(?) encircled by five single stalks, and by two smaller sheaves.
Whitney, Emblemes, Leyden, 1586, p.088

stand: Modesty, her finger to her lips in the Harpocratic gesture of silence, holds keys and stands on a tortoise.
Whitney, Emblemes, Leyden, 1586, p.093b

standard: Two horsemen with whips pursue a riderless horse towards a standard.
Whitney, Emblemes, Leyden, 1586, p.227

star: A man kneeling before a chart holds a compass to the stars; below a stag drinks from a stream.
Whitney, Emblemes, Leyden, 1586, p.043

star: Chaos: four elements -- fire, air, earth and water -- in confusion. A crescent moon, sun, star and wind.
Whitney, Emblemes, Leyden, 1586, p.122

star: A sailing ship on a world globe, surrounded by clouds, stars, sun and crescent moon.
Whitney, Emblemes, Leyden, 1586, p.203

star: An astronomer, looking at the starry sky, falls into a well; an armillary sphere or astrolabe on the ground.
Whitney, Emblemes, Leyden, 1586, p.157

statue: Worshippers kneel in reverence before an ass bearing a statue of Isis; the driver beats the ass with a stick.
Whitney, Emblemes, Leyden, 1586, p.008

statue: A swallow approaches its nest in a niche with a statue of Medea killing her child with a sword.
Whitney, Emblemes, Leyden, 1586, p.033

stick: Worshippers kneel in reverence before an ass bearing a statue of Isis; the driver beats the ass with a stick.
Whitney, Emblemes, Leyden, 1586, p.008

stick: A blind man with a stick carries a lame man who points the way with his finger.
Whitney, Emblemes, Leyden, 1586, p.065

stick: A man with a stick strikes a snake sliding through a crack in a wall.
Whitney, Emblemes, Leyden, 1586, p.076b

stocks: A courtier(?) sits in leg stocks.
Whitney, Emblemes, Leyden, 1586, p.202

stolen: A thief is strangled in sleep by the sack of stolen meats about his neck.
Whitney, Emblemes, Leyden, 1586, p.041

stone: Apollo and Diana kill Niobe's children with arrows. Niobe is turned to stone.
Whitney, Emblemes, Leyden, 1586, p.013

stone: A dog bites a stone; a man is about to throw another stone at the dog.
Whitney, Emblemes, Leyden, 1586, p.056

stone: A man is weighted down by a stone bound to his right arm as he lifts his winged left arm and leg skywards.
Whitney, Emblemes, Leyden, 1586, p.152

stone: Sisyphus pushes a stone up a hill.
Whitney, Emblemes, Leyden, 1586, p.215

stork: Orpheus plays his harp, surrounded by a vulture, stork, stag, lion, bear, antelope, and ape.
Whitney, Emblemes, Leyden, 1586, p.186

stork: A stork with a snake in its beak returns to its nest with three young.
Whitney, Emblemes, Leyden, 1586, p.072

strangle: A thief is strangled in sleep by the sack of stolen meats about his neck.
Whitney, Emblemes, Leyden, 1586, p.041

strawberry: A snake coils up strawberry plants.
Whitney, Emblemes, Leyden, 1586, p.024

stream: A dog, his muzzle and front paws in a stream, searches for his bone.
Whitney, Emblemes, Leyden, 1586, p.039

stream: A man kneeling before a chart holds a compass to the stars; below a stag drinks from a stream.
Whitney, Emblemes, Leyden, 1586, p.043

stream: a traveller with a back pack looks towards a village across a stream, where a swan is feeding.
Whitney, Emblemes, Leyden, 1586, p.089

stream: Narcissus admires his reflection in a stream.
Whitney, Emblemes, Leyden, 1586, p.149

stream: A copper pot and an earthenware pot float side by side down a stream.
Whitney, Emblemes, Leyden, 1586, p.164

stretcher: `Bound `Attilius, lies on a `stretcher near an
    open `barrel riven with `nails.
    Whitney, Emblemes, Leyden, 1586, p.114
string: `Mercury in a `winged `cap repairs the `strings
    of a `lute; a `woman `dances while another man plays
    a lute.
    Whitney, Emblemes, Leyden, 1586, p.092
stump: `Pine-trees are `broken by a `wind(?); a `rabbit
    crouches before a `tree `stump; a `horseman nearby.
    Whitney, Emblemes, Leyden, 1586, p.059
suckle: A `goat `suckles a `wolf `cub.
    Whitney, Emblemes, Leyden, 1586, p.049
sun: A sailing ship `flounders in the `sea off the `shore;
    the `sun's rays melt `snow on `mountains.
    Whitney, Emblemes, Leyden, 1586, p.011
sun: A man with a `staff climbs a `snow covered
    `mountain. The `sun has `melted the snow from the
    peak.
    Whitney, Emblemes, Leyden, 1586, p.020
sun: `Icarus `falls into the `sea after the `sun has
    melted the wax binding the `feathers of his `wings.
    Whitney, Emblemes, Leyden, 1586, p.028
sun: Under a `sun, a `bound `Attilius, lies on a
    `stretcher near an open `barrel riven with `nails.
    Whitney, Emblemes, Leyden, 1586, p.114
sun: `Chaos: `four `elements -- `fire, `air, `earth and
    `water -- in confusion. A `crescent `moon, `sun,
    `star and `wind.
    Whitney, Emblemes, Leyden, 1586, p.122
sun: The `sun beats down as a `grasshopper watches
    `ants work under barren `trees.
    Whitney, Emblemes, Leyden, 1586, p.159
sun: A `sailing `ship on a `world `globe, surrounded by
    `clouds, `stars, `sun and crescent `moon.
    Whitney, Emblemes, Leyden, 1586, p.203
sun: `Two `men with `laurel `branches `embrace; `swords
    lie on the ground. A `palm-tree and `sun set.
    Whitney, Emblemes, Leyden, 1586, p.216b
sun: Two `men under a blazing `sun; one flees, the other
    chases his `shadow.
    Whitney, Emblemes, Leyden, 1586, p.218b
sun: `Two `oak-trees grow on a sea shore; a third lies
    on the ground. `Sun set.
    Whitney, Emblemes, Leyden, 1586, p.230
supplication: `Slander, holding an `torch, has her hand
    on a kneeling figure, her `hands clasped in
    `supplication.
    Whitney, Emblemes, Leyden, 1586, p.004
swaddled: An `old man on `crutches enters a room with
    a `swaddled baby in a `cradle.
    Whitney, Emblemes, Leyden, 1586, p.167
swallow: A `swallow with a `grasshopper in its `beak
    returns to its `nest in the `ruins of a `palace.
    Whitney, Emblemes, Leyden, 1586, p.005
swallow: A `swallow approaches its `nest in a niche with
    a `statue of `Medea `killing her `child with a `sword.
    Whitney, Emblemes, Leyden, 1586, p.033
swallow: A `sleeping man is `awakened by a `swallow
    chattering in its `nest.
    Whitney, Emblemes, Leyden, 1586, p.050a
swallow(?): `Three `birds: `swallow(?), cuckoo(?), and
    `chaffinch(?). A `vineyard nearby.
    Whitney, Emblemes, Leyden, 1586, p.054b
swan: A `bird-of-paradise `flies by; a `traveller with a
    back `pack looks towards a `village across a `stream,
    where a `swan is feeding.
    Whitney, Emblemes, Leyden, 1586, p.089
swan: A `shield charged with a `swan[1] hangs from a
    tree; `two `swans on the waters.
    Whitney, Emblemes, Leyden, 1586, p.126
swan(?): `Jupiter with `thunderbolts sits on his `eagle; a
    man holds onto a `laurel tree in a storm(?); a
    `swan(?) with a `laurel `garland about its neck.
    Whitney, Emblemes, Leyden, 1586, p.067
swan[1] = heraldic

swan[1]: A `shield charged with a `swan[1] hangs from a
    tree; `two `swans on the waters.
    Whitney, Emblemes, Leyden, 1586, p.126
swim: A `shipwrecked `traveller, a `pack on his back,
    `swims to shore.
    Whitney, Emblemes, Leyden, 1586, p.179
sword: A man with `upraised `sword takes fright at his
    `shadow. `Jupiter sits astride an `eagle in a bank of
    clouds.
    Whitney, Emblemes, Leyden, 1586, p.032
sword: A `swallow approaches its `nest in a niche with
    a `statue of `Medea `killing her `child with a
    `sword.
    Whitney, Emblemes, Leyden, 1586, p.033
sword: `Ajax and `Hector `exchange a `sword and
    `girdle.
    Whitney, Emblemes, Leyden, 1586, p.037
sword: `Agamemnon, with `crown, `sword, and `shield
    inscribed `"Agamemnon" bearing a `lion[1] `rampant.
    Whitney, Emblemes, Leyden, 1586, p.045
sword: A `scholar talks with a `soldier in a `helmet
    with `sword, `shield and `spear.
    Whitney, Emblemes, Leyden, 1586, p.047
sword: From a `cloud a right `arm bearing a `sword and
    a left `arm with a `trowel.
    Whitney, Emblemes, Leyden, 1586, p.066
sword: A man with drawn `sword looks into a `house; a
    `bundle at his feet.
    Whitney, Emblemes, Leyden, 1586, p.069
sword: `Brutus in `Roman `armour and `helmet, `shield
    on the ground, `falls on his `sword.
    Whitney, Emblemes, Leyden, 1586, p.070
sword: The `sword of `Damocles, with `wavy `blade,
    suspended from a `cloud.
    Whitney, Emblemes, Leyden, 1586, p.102
sword: A `hand holds a `sword over a `fire.
    Whitney, Emblemes, Leyden, 1586, p.111
sword: A `lion `rampant holding an upright `sword.
    Whitney, Emblemes, Leyden, 1586, p.116
sword: A man breaks a `sword over an `anvil.
    Whitney, Emblemes, Leyden, 1586, p.192
sword: A dead `elephant, poisoned by a `snake, crushes
    it; man falls on `two `swords.
    Whitney, Emblemes, Leyden, 1586, p.195
sword: `Two `men with `laurel `branches `embrace;
    `swords lie on the ground. A `palm-tree and `sun
    set.
    Whitney, Emblemes, Leyden, 1586, p.216b
sword: `Three `Christian `martyrs in `prayer before a
    `fire are harassed by men with `swords and `dogs.
    Whitney, Emblemes, Leyden, 1586, p.224a
sword: One man on the `left strikes another on the
    forehead with a `sword.
    Whitney, Emblemes, Leyden, 1586, p.226a
sword: One man on the `left strikes another on the
    forehead with a `sword.
    Whitney, Emblemes, Leyden, 1586, p.226b
table: `Glory `flees through a `doorway from `naked
    `couple on a `bed; beside them stands a `table with
    `food and `drink.
    Whitney, Emblemes, Leyden, 1586, p.042
table: An `old man `sits at `table; outside a `young man
    `labours in the `field.
    Whitney, Emblemes, Leyden, 1586, p.050b
table: `Buildings and `towers `collapse about a `table
    with `three `books.
    Whitney, Emblemes, Leyden, 1586, p.131
table: A man at `table blows his `food to cool it,
    watched by a `satyr.
    Whitney, Emblemes, Leyden, 1586, p.160
table: An `ape throws `gold `coins from a `window;
    `table with `two `bags on it.
    Whitney, Emblemes, Leyden, 1586, p.169
tablet: A `scholar in a `philosopher's `cap, a `tablet
    under his arm talks with a `soldier.

Whitney, Emblemes, Leyden, 1586, p.047
tablet: A ˙carver incises a ˙tablet with ˙"TROIA MIHI LICET TAMEN" [Never-the-less the whore sells herself to me].
Whitney, Emblemes, Leyden, 1586, p.183b
tablet: A man with a ˙world ˙globe on his back drags the ˙tablets of the ˙commandments tied to his ˙right ankle.
Whitney, Emblemes, Leyden, 1586, p.223
tear[1] = to rip
tear[1]: ˙Bare ˙breasted ˙Prowess ˙tears out her ˙hair as she sits on the ˙tomb of ˙Ajax, inscribed ˙"D AIACIS."
Whitney, Emblemes, Leyden, 1586, p.030
testicle: A ˙beaver tears off his ˙testicles, ˙pursued by a ˙hunter and ˙two ˙hounds.
Whitney, Emblemes, Leyden, 1586, p.035
thief: A ˙thief is ˙strangled in ˙sleep by the ˙sack of ˙stolen ˙meats about his ˙neck.
Whitney, Emblemes, Leyden, 1586, p.041
thief: A ˙thief, escorted to his ˙hanging by soldiers, is embraced by his ˙mother.
Whitney, Emblemes, Leyden, 1586, p.155
thistle: An ˙ass, laden with ˙foodstuffs, ˙eats ˙thistles.
Whitney, Emblemes, Leyden, 1586, p.018
thorn: In a ˙nest made of a ˙crown of ˙thorns, the ˙pelican pierces her ˙breast to sprinkle her ˙young[1] with ˙blood.
Whitney, Emblemes, Leyden, 1586, p.087
thorn: A man touches the ˙thorns and ˙flowers of a ˙rose bush.
Whitney, Emblemes, Leyden, 1586, p.165
thorn: A ˙lily blooms in ˙briars and ˙thorns.
Whitney, Emblemes, Leyden, 1586, p.221
three: ˙Three ˙mermaids with a ˙lyre and a ˙woodwind instrument, watch a ˙galley, with ˙Ulysses tied to the mast.
Whitney, Emblemes, Leyden, 1586, p.010
three: ˙Diana ˙watches as a ˙stag-headed ˙Actaeon is attacked by ˙three ˙hounds.
Whitney, Emblemes, Leyden, 1586, p.015
three: A ˙mew or ˙gull and a ˙cormorant ˙fly in pursuit of ˙three small ˙fishes.
Whitney, Emblemes, Leyden, 1586, p.052b
three: ˙Three ˙birds: ˙swallow(?), cuckoo(?),and ˙chaffinch(?). A ˙vineyard nearby.
Whitney, Emblemes, Leyden, 1586, p.054b
three: The ˙pelican pierces her ˙breast with her beak to sprinkle her ˙three ˙young[1] with ˙blood.
Whitney, Emblemes, Leyden, 1586, p.087
three: ˙Three ˙hares ˙bite the head of a ˙dead supine ˙lion; a fourth hare runs by.
Whitney, Emblemes, Leyden, 1586, p.127
three: ˙Buildings and ˙towers ˙collapse about a ˙table with ˙three ˙books.
Whitney, Emblemes, Leyden, 1586, p.131
three: A ˙right hand tests a ˙coin or ˙medal on a ˙touchstone. The coin bears a ˙shield with ˙three ˙fleurs-de-lys, surmounted by a ˙coronet.
Whitney, Emblemes, Leyden, 1586, p.139a
three: ˙Three ˙women ˙gamble with ˙dice.
Whitney, Emblemes, Leyden, 1586, p.176
three: ˙Winged ˙Fame, sounds a ˙horn as he flies over a ˙Roman(?) building and ˙three ˙Egyptian(?) ˙pyramids.
Whitney, Emblemes, Leyden, 1586, p.196
three: ˙Three ˙rich and ˙two ˙poor men enter a ˙palace through two different ˙doors.
Whitney, Emblemes, Leyden, 1586, p.204
three: ˙Three ˙Christian ˙martyrs in ˙prayer before a ˙fire are harassed by men with ˙swords and ˙dogs. A ˙left hand from the ˙clouds holds a ˙garland over them.
Whitney, Emblemes, Leyden, 1586, p.224a
three: A ˙stork with a ˙snake in its ˙beak returns to its ˙nest with ˙three young.

Whitney, Emblemes, Leyden, 1586, p.072
throne: Seated on a ˙throne, ˙Jupiter is surrounded by a ˙deer, ˙horse, ˙bull, ˙ass, ˙snail, ˙eagle, and ˙lion.
Whitney, Emblemes, Leyden, 1586, p.091
throne: From his ˙throne, ˙Mezentius with ˙crown and ˙sceptre overseee the ˙binding of a ˙naked ˙body to a naked ˙corpse.
Whitney, Emblemes, Leyden, 1586, p.099
throne: ˙Aesculapius, a ˙sceptre in his ˙right hand and a ˙staff in his ˙left, on a ˙throne, supported by two ˙eagles.
Whitney, Emblemes, Leyden, 1586, p.212
thunderbolt: ˙Jupiter with ˙thunderbolts sits on his ˙eagle; a man holds onto a ˙laurel tree in a storm(?); a ˙swan(?) with a ˙laurel ˙garland about its neck.
Whitney, Emblemes, Leyden, 1586, p.067
tomb: ˙Bare ˙breasted ˙Prowess ˙tears out her ˙hair as she sits on the ˙tomb of ˙Ajax, inscribed ˙"D AIACIS."
Whitney, Emblemes, Leyden, 1586, p.030
tomb: On a ˙marble ˙tomb an ˙ewer and ˙basin with folded ˙towel.
Whitney, Emblemes, Leyden, 1586, p.136
tomb: ˙Bacchus with a ˙crown of ˙vine ˙leaves and ˙grapes, and ˙Apollo with his ˙lyre stand on a ˙pedestal or ˙tomb.
Whitney, Emblemes, Leyden, 1586, p.146
tomb: ˙Thetis stands by the ˙tomb of ˙Achilles, which is decked with ˙amaranths, and stands under a ˙palm-tree.
Whitney, Emblemes, Leyden, 1586, p.193
tongue: A ˙lion with ˙tongue outstretched stands before a sick ˙fox in its den.
Whitney, Emblemes, Leyden, 1586, p.161
tool: An ˙ape, tampering with a carpenter's ˙tools -- a ˙wedge, ˙axe and ˙mallet -- catches his foot in a ˙log.
Whitney, Emblemes, Leyden, 1586, p.145
torch: ˙Strife stands on a ˙bellows, holding an ˙inverted ˙torch.
Whitney, Emblemes, Leyden, 1586, p.004
torch: ˙Slander, holding an ˙torch, has her hand on a kneeling figure, her ˙hands clasped in ˙supplication.
Whitney, Emblemes, Leyden, 1586, p.004
torch: An ˙inverted ˙burning ˙torch inscribed ˙"QUI ME ALIT ME EXTINGUIT" [The one who nourishes me extinguishes me].
Whitney, Emblemes, Leyden, 1586, p.183a
tortoise: ˙Modesty, her ˙finger to her ˙lips in the ˙Harpocratic gesture of ˙silence, holds ˙keys and ˙stands on a ˙tortoise.
Whitney, Emblemes, Leyden, 1586, p.093b
tortoise(?): Virtue(?) or ˙Athene(?) wears a ˙helmet, a ˙lance with her ˙right hand, a sceptre(?) or ˙mace(?) in her ˙left; her ˙right ˙foot on a ˙tortoise(?).
Whitney, Emblemes, Leyden, 1586, p.222a
touchstone: A ˙right hand, wearing a ˙ring, tests a ˙coin or ˙medal on a ˙touchstone.
Whitney, Emblemes, Leyden, 1586, p.139a
towel: On a ˙marble ˙tomb an ˙ewer and ˙basin with folded ˙towel.
Whitney, Emblemes, Leyden, 1586, p.136
tower: ˙Buildings and ˙towers ˙collapse about a ˙table with ˙three ˙books.
Whitney, Emblemes, Leyden, 1586, p.131
town: A ˙fox on an ˙ice-flow floats down a ˙river (˙Danube) past a ˙town (˙Regensburg).
Whitney, Emblemes, Leyden, 1586, p.022
town: ˙Sinon is ˙whipped by his ˙pupils back to ˙the Faleria; the ˙walled ˙town is ˙besieged by ˙Camillus on horseback.
Whitney, Emblemes, Leyden, 1586, p.112
trample: A man ˙tramples ˙grapes under his ˙right ˙foot, reaching for a ˙bunch with his ˙left hand.
Whitney, Emblemes, Leyden, 1586, p.206

traveller: °Mercury points to the °path at his feet; a
     °traveller with a °staff.
     Whitney, Emblemes, Leyden, 1586, p.002
traveller: A °bird-of-paradise °flies by; a °traveller with
     a back °pack looks towards a °village.
     Whitney, Emblemes, Leyden, 1586, p.089
traveller: A °leopard(?) fights with a °lion. °Travellers
     pass nearby. A °flock of °birds flies over head.
     Whitney, Emblemes, Leyden, 1586, p.178
traveller: A °shipwrecked °traveller, a °pack on his back,
     °swims to shore.
     Whitney, Emblemes, Leyden, 1586, p.179
traveller: A °traveller walks past a °world °globe
     inscribed °"EUROPA" and °"AFRICA". The
     °tetragrammaton blazes in °clouds.
     Whitney, Emblemes, Leyden, 1586, p.225
treasure: An °envious man, °blind in one °eye and a
     °covetous man, blind in both; nearby, a °treasure
     °chest.
     Whitney, Emblemes, Leyden, 1586, p.095
treasure: A °couple walk from a building, the man points
     to an open °treasure chest. °Winged °Time, with a
     °scythe, pursues the couple.
     Whitney, Emblemes, Leyden, 1586, p.199
tree: A °ringdove broods on a °nest in a °leafless °tree.
     Whitney, Emblemes, Leyden, 1586, p.029
tree: One °redbreast °knocks another from a °tree
     °branch.
     Whitney, Emblemes, Leyden, 1586, p.055a
tree: °Pine-trees are °broken by a °wind(?); in a °cloud
     °Jupiter(?) sits astride an °eagle.
     Whitney, Emblemes, Leyden, 1586, p.059
tree: °Tantalus stands in a river, looking up at °fruit
     laden °tree. °Flames and °smoke billow up in the
     background.
     Whitney, Emblemes, Leyden, 1586, p.074
tree: A °fire fed with °wood from a °dead °tree.
     Whitney, Emblemes, Leyden, 1586, p.077b
tree: °Athene(?) stands before a °grain °field and
     °fruit-tree; at the left, she °sits under a °barren
     °tree.
     Whitney, Emblemes, Leyden, 1586, p.103
tree: An °elephant rests against a °tree, undermined by a
     °hunter with an °axe(?).
     Whitney, Emblemes, Leyden, 1586, p.150
tree: The °sun beats down as a °grasshopper watches
     °ants work under barren °trees.
     Whitney, Emblemes, Leyden, 1586, p.159
tree: A °woodsman is at work with his °axe at the base
     of a °tree.
     Whitney, Emblemes, Leyden, 1586, p.228
tree: °Adam, in a °fig-leaf, hides behind a °tree. The
     inscription °"UBI ES" [Where are you?] blazes in the
     sky.
     Whitney, Emblemes, Leyden, 1586, p.229a
trot: A °woman collects °skulls into her apron; °horse
     is °trotting on a hill; °skulls piled beside a °chapel.
     Whitney, Emblemes, Leyden, 1586, p.046
trowel: From a °cloud a right °arm bearing a °sword and
     a left °arm with a °trowel.
     Whitney, Emblemes, Leyden, 1586, p.066
trumpet: °Quintilius, a °quill in his °right hand, restrains
     a °youth from handing a note to °winged °Fame with
     a °trumpet.
     Whitney, Emblemes, Leyden, 1586, p.185
trumpet: A man blows a °trumpet as he gives °alms to a
     °beggar.
     Whitney, Emblemes, Leyden, 1586, p.224b
tusk: A °boar with °tusks sharpened faces a °fox.
     Whitney, Emblemes, Leyden, 1586, p.153b
two: A °charioteer with a °whip tries to °rein in the
     °two galloping °horses pulling his °chariot.
     Whitney, Emblemes, Leyden, 1586, p.006
two: °Two °fowlers watch as °four °birds, °ducks, are
     °lured into the °net by a live °decoy.

Whitney, Emblemes, Leyden, 1586, p.027
two: A °beaver tears off his °testicles, °pursued by a
     °hunter and °two °hounds.
     Whitney, Emblemes, Leyden, 1586, p.035
two: °Two °soldiers lead a captive °herald from the
     °battlefield into a °fortress.
     Whitney, Emblemes, Leyden, 1586, p.054a
two: °Two °boys blow °bubbles; six others try to catch
     them.
     Whitney, Emblemes, Leyden, 1586, p.055b
two: °Two men °wash a °black °man.
     Whitney, Emblemes, Leyden, 1586, p.057
two: °Eros °drives the °two °lions °drawing his
     °chariot.
     Whitney, Emblemes, Leyden, 1586, p.063
two: °Two °fishermen in a °boat haul in a °fishing
     °net.
     Whitney, Emblemes, Leyden, 1586, p.071
two: °Two °kings or °princes in °armour shake °right
     hands; nearby, cavalry and an °encampment.
     Whitney, Emblemes, Leyden, 1586, p.076a
two: °Two °idle men °sit by a tree.
     Whitney, Emblemes, Leyden, 1586, p.085
two: A large °sheaf of °grain or °wheat(?) encircled by
     °five single °stalks, and by °two smaller °sheaves.
     Whitney, Emblemes, Leyden, 1586, p.088
two: °Janus with °two °faces.
     Whitney, Emblemes, Leyden, 1586, p.108
two: A °shield charged with a °swan¹ hangs from a
     tree; °two °swans on the waters.
     Whitney, Emblemes, Leyden, 1586, p.126
two: A °stag is struck by an °arrow; a °hunter
     approaches with °two °dogs.
     Whitney, Emblemes, Leyden, 1586, p.153a
two: An °ape throws °gold °coins from a °window;
     °table with °two °bags on it.
     Whitney, Emblemes, Leyden, 1586, p.169
two: °Two °scholars in a °library.
     Whitney, Emblemes, Leyden, 1586, p.171
two: °Two °apes.
     Whitney, Emblemes, Leyden, 1586, p.190a
two: °Two °drummers before an °encampment.
     Whitney, Emblemes, Leyden, 1586, p.194
two: man falls on °two °swords.
     Whitney, Emblemes, Leyden, 1586, p.195
two: °Three °rich and °two °poor men enter a °palace
     through two different °doors.
     Whitney, Emblemes, Leyden, 1586, p.204
two: °Two °ducks and two °geese hunt for food in a
     °pond(?).
     Whitney, Emblemes, Leyden, 1586, p.207
two: °Two °men with °laurel °branches °embrace;
     °swords lie on the ground. A °palm-tree and °sun
     set.
     Whitney, Emblemes, Leyden, 1586, p.216b
two: Virtue(?) or °Athene(?) armed, her °right °foot on
     a °tortoise(?). °Ivy and °two °snakes scale the wall.
     Whitney, Emblemes, Leyden, 1586, p.222a
two: °Mice play; °two °cats in °cages.
     Whitney, Emblemes, Leyden, 1586, p.222b
two: °Two °horsemen pursue a riderless °horse.
     Whitney, Emblemes, Leyden, 1586, p.227
two: °Two °oak-trees grow on a sea shore; a third lies
     on the ground. °Sun set.
     Whitney, Emblemes, Leyden, 1586, p.230
upraised: A man with °upraised °sword takes fright at
     his °shadow. °Jupiter sits astride an °eagle in a bank
     of clouds.
     Whitney, Emblemes, Leyden, 1586, p.032
vat: A °dyer lifts °cloth from a °vat.
     Whitney, Emblemes, Leyden, 1586, p.134
village: A °bird-of-paradise °flies by; a °traveller with a
     back °pack looks towards a °village across a
     °stream, where a °swan is feeding.
     Whitney, Emblemes, Leyden, 1586, p.089

vine: A leafy °vine laden with °gourds climbs the trunk of a °pine tree.
Whitney, Emblemes, Leyden, 1586, p.034

vine: A °vine laden with °bunches of °grapes °entwined about a °dead °elm-tree.
Whitney, Emblemes, Leyden, 1586, p.062

vine: An °olive-tree entwined by a °grape °vine.
Whitney, Emblemes, Leyden, 1586, p.133

vine: °Bacchus with a °crown of °vine °leaves and °grapes, and °Apollo with his °lyre stand on a °pedestal or °tomb.
Whitney, Emblemes, Leyden, 1586, p.146

vine: °Bacchus, under °vines with °grapes, beats a °drum and blows a °pipe; nearby a °goblet.
Whitney, Emblemes, Leyden, 1586, p.187

vine: A °vine grows on a wall with °astrological symbols and a °moon.
Whitney, Emblemes, Leyden, 1586, p.206

vine(?): °Naked °Bacchus, a °wreath of °vines(?) on his head, lies on a °river bank, °drinking from a °cup.
Whitney, Emblemes, Leyden, 1586, p.125

vineyard: °Three °birds: °swallow(?), cuckoo(?),and °chaffinch(?). A °vineyard nearby.
Whitney, Emblemes, Leyden, 1586, p.054b

viola(?): °Apollo and °Pan making music on °viola(?) and °bagpipes. °Midas has °ears of an °ass.
Whitney, Emblemes, Leyden, 1586, p.218a

visor: The °head of °Valerius °Corvinus in a °plumed °helmet, the °visor open; a °raven is perched on the visor.
Whitney, Emblemes, Leyden, 1586, p.113

volcano: A °winged °figure °reclines at the foot of the °volcano °Vesuvius; °Pliny °falls into the volcano.
Whitney, Emblemes, Leyden, 1586, p.025

vulture: A °vulture watches a °lion and a °boar fighting.
Whitney, Emblemes, Leyden, 1586, p.119

vulture: °Orpheus plays his °harp, surrounded by a °vulture, °stork, °stag, °lion, °bear, °antelope, and °ape.
Whitney, Emblemes, Leyden, 1586, p.186

wall: A man with a °stick strikes a °snake sliding through a crack in a °wall.
Whitney, Emblemes, Leyden, 1586, p.076b

wall: An °arrow °broken in two against a °marble °wall.
Whitney, Emblemes, Leyden, 1586, p.138b

wall: °Sinon is °whipped by his °pupils back to °the Faleria; the °walled °town is °besieged by °Camillus on horseback.
Whitney, Emblemes, Leyden, 1586, p.112

wand: °Circe touches with her °wand a °pig; nearby a °dog, °ape, °goat and °ass, °Ulysses's transformed men.
Whitney, Emblemes, Leyden, 1586, p.082

wash: °Two men °wash a °black °man.
Whitney, Emblemes, Leyden, 1586, p.057

watch: °Diana °watches as a °stag-headed °Actaeon is attacked by °three °hounds.
Whitney, Emblemes, Leyden, 1586, p.015

water: A °barrel with small °holes °discharges °water.
Whitney, Emblemes, Leyden, 1586, p.012

water: A °fisherman with a °net reaches with his °right hand for a °cuttlefish muddying the °water.
Whitney, Emblemes, Leyden, 1586, p.097

water: °Chaos: °four °elements -- °fire, °air, °earth and °water -- in confusion. A °crescent °moon, °sun, °star and °wind.
Whitney, Emblemes, Leyden, 1586, p.122

water: A °king, with °crown and °sceptre, squeezes °water from a °sponge; a crowd watches a °hanging (°gibbet).
Whitney, Emblemes, Leyden, 1586, p.151

watermill: A °miller and the °wife of °Anellus °embrace before °sacks of °grain at a °watermill.
Whitney, Emblemes, Leyden, 1586, p.080

wavy: The °sword of °Damocles, with °wavy °blade,

suspended from a °cloud.
Whitney, Emblemes, Leyden, 1586, p.102

way: A °blind man with a °stick carries a °lame man who °points the °way with his °finger.
Whitney, Emblemes, Leyden, 1586, p.065

weather-vane: A °lion sits at a °church entrance; °weather-vane °cock on the roof.
Whitney, Emblemes, Leyden, 1586, p.120

wedge: An °ape, tampering with a carpenter's °tools -- a °wedge, °axe and °mallet -- catches his foot in a °log.
Whitney, Emblemes, Leyden, 1586, p.145

weep: °Laughing °Democritus and °weeping °Heraclitus, with two °books, face each other.
Whitney, Emblemes, Leyden, 1586, p.014

well: An °astronomer, looking at the °stars, falls into a °well.
Whitney, Emblemes, Leyden, 1586, p.157

wheat: A °sheaf of °grain (°wheat).
Whitney, Emblemes, Leyden, 1586, p.023

wheat(?): A large °sheaf of °grain or °wheat(?) encircled by °five single °stalks, and by °two smaller °sheaves.
Whitney, Emblemes, Leyden, 1586, p.088

wheat(?): The side of the table bears a °shield charged with a °sheaf of °wheat(?).
Whitney, Emblemes, Leyden, 1586, p.172

wheel: °Naked °Occasio stands on a °wheel in the °sea.
Whitney, Emblemes, Leyden, 1586, p.181

whip: A °charioteer with a °whip tries to °rein in the °two galloping °horses pulling his °chariot.
Whitney, Emblemes, Leyden, 1586, p.006

whip: With °whip and °reins, °Eros °drives the °two °lions °drawing his °chariot.
Whitney, Emblemes, Leyden, 1586, p.063

whip: °Two °horsemen with °whips pursue a riderless °horse towards a °standard.
Whitney, Emblemes, Leyden, 1586, p.227

whip: °Sinon is °whipped by his °pupils back to °the Faleria; the °walled °town is °besieged by °Camillus on horseback.
Whitney, Emblemes, Leyden, 1586, p.112

white: An °elephant is frightened by a °white cloth.
Whitney, Emblemes, Leyden, 1586, p.052a

wife: A °miller and the °wife of °Anellus °embrace before °sacks of °grain at a °watermill.
Whitney, Emblemes, Leyden, 1586, p.080

wife: °Colasmus searches for his °drowned °wife.
Whitney, Emblemes, Leyden, 1586, p.158

wind: A °miller sleeps by a °windmill. A man with a sack stands on the steps of the mill, watching for °wind.
Whitney, Emblemes, Leyden, 1586, p.026

wind: °Four °winds °blow on a °rock in a rough °sea.
Whitney, Emblemes, Leyden, 1586, p.096

wind: °Chaos: °four °elements -- °fire, °air, °earth and °water -- in confusion.
Whitney, Emblemes, Leyden, 1586, p.122

wind: A °ship in full °sail runs before the °wind on a °sea.
Whitney, Emblemes, Leyden, 1586, p.137

wind: The °wind, °Boreas, blows; °reeds in the water bend, while an °oak breaks.
Whitney, Emblemes, Leyden, 1586, p.220

wind(?): °Pine-trees are °broken by a °wind(?); in a °cloud °Jupiter(?) sits astride an °eagle.
Whitney, Emblemes, Leyden, 1586, p.059

windmill: A °miller sleeps by a °windmill. A man with a sack stands on the steps of the mill, watching for °wind.
Whitney, Emblemes, Leyden, 1586, p.026

window: An °ape throws °gold °coins from a °window; °table with °two °bags on it.
Whitney, Emblemes, Leyden, 1586, p.169

wing (see also: Eros, angel, bird)

wing: ˙Icarus ˙falls into the ˙sea after the ˙sun has melted the wax binding the ˙feathers of his ˙wings.
Whitney, Emblemes, Leyden, 1586, p.028

wing: An ˙ostrich with ˙wings ˙outstretched.
Whitney, Emblemes, Leyden, 1586, p.051b

wing: The ˙pelican with ˙wings ˙outspread, pierces her ˙breast with her beak to sprinkle her ˙three ˙young[1] with ˙blood.
Whitney, Emblemes, Leyden, 1586, p.087

wing: Wearing a ˙winged ˙helmet and holding a ˙caduceus, ˙Mercury points to the ˙path at his feet; a ˙traveller with a ˙staff.
Whitney, Emblemes, Leyden, 1586, p.002

wing: ˙Winged ˙Time with a ˙scythe liberates ˙Truth.
Whitney, Emblemes, Leyden, 1586, p.004

wing: A ˙winged ˙figure ˙reclines at the foot of the ˙volcano ˙Vesuvius as ˙Pliny ˙falls into the volcano.
Whitney, Emblemes, Leyden, 1586, p.025

wing: ˙Mercury in a ˙winged ˙cap repairs the ˙strings of a ˙lute.
Whitney, Emblemes, Leyden, 1586, p.092

wing: A man is weighted down by a ˙stone bound to his ˙right ˙arm as he lifts his ˙winged ˙left arm and leg towards ˙God(?).
Whitney, Emblemes, Leyden, 1586, p.152

wing: ˙Naked ˙Occasio, her ˙heels ˙winged, holds a ˙scarf.
Whitney, Emblemes, Leyden, 1586, p.181

wing: ˙Quintilius, a ˙quill in his ˙right hand, restrains a ˙youth from handing a note to ˙winged ˙Fame with a ˙trumpet.
Whitney, Emblemes, Leyden, 1586, p.185

wing: ˙Winged ˙Fame, sounds a ˙horn as he flies over a ˙Roman(?) building and ˙three ˙Egyptian(?) ˙pyramids.
Whitney, Emblemes, Leyden, 1586, p.196

wing: ˙Winged ˙Time, with a ˙scythe, pursues a couple.
Whitney, Emblemes, Leyden, 1586, p.199

wise-man: ˙Seven ˙wise-men: ˙"Cleobulus" and ˙scales; ˙"Chilon" and ˙mirror; ˙"Periander" and ˙herb, ˙pennyroyal(?); ˙"Pitac" and ˙flower, ˙coriander(?); ˙"Solon" and ˙statue, a ˙Term(?); ˙"Thales" and ˙bird, ˙fowler's ˙net and ˙cage; ˙"Bias" and ˙philosopher on ˙ass.
Whitney, Emblemes, Leyden, 1586, p.130

wolf: A ˙goat ˙suckles a ˙wolf ˙cub.
Whitney, Emblemes, Leyden, 1586, p.049

wolf: A ˙mother ˙admonishes a ˙child in ˙bed; a ˙wolf lurks outside.
Whitney, Emblemes, Leyden, 1586, p.162

woman: A ˙woman collects ˙skulls into her apron; ˙horse is ˙trotting on a hill; ˙skulls piled beside a ˙chapel.
Whitney, Emblemes, Leyden, 1586, p.046

woman: ˙Mercury in a ˙winged ˙cap repairs the ˙strings of a ˙lute; a ˙woman ˙dances while another man plays a lute.
Whitney, Emblemes, Leyden, 1586, p.092

woman: A small ˙dog sleeps in a ˙woman's lap.
Whitney, Emblemes, Leyden, 1586, p.140

woman: A ˙blind ˙woman sits in an armchair in an empty room. A ˙doctor leaves the room with an armful of her possessions.
Whitney, Emblemes, Leyden, 1586, p.156a

woman: ˙Three ˙women ˙gamble with ˙dice.
Whitney, Emblemes, Leyden, 1586, p.176

woman: A ˙woman holds grapes away from her with her ˙left hand.
Whitney, Emblemes, Leyden, 1586, p.206

wood: A ˙fire fed with ˙wood from a ˙dead ˙tree.
Whitney, Emblemes, Leyden, 1586, p.077b

woodsman: A ˙woodsman works with his ˙axe at the base of a ˙tree.
Whitney, Emblemes, Leyden, 1586, p.228

woodwind: ˙Three ˙mermaids with a ˙lyre and a ˙woodwind instrument, watch a ˙galley, with ˙Ulysses

tied to the mast.
Whitney, Emblemes, Leyden, 1586, p.010

world: A ˙sailing ˙ship on a ˙world ˙globe; a ˙right hand holds a ˙bridle, which encircles the globe.
Whitney, Emblemes, Leyden, 1586, p.203

world: A man with a ˙world ˙globe on his back drags the ˙tablets of the ˙commandments tied to his ˙right ankle.
Whitney, Emblemes, Leyden, 1586, p.223

world: A ˙traveller or ˙pilgrim walks past a ˙world ˙globe inscribed ˙"EUROPA" and ˙"AFRICA".
Whitney, Emblemes, Leyden, 1586, p.225

worshipper: ˙Worshippers kneel in ˙reverence before an ˙ass bearing a ˙statue of ˙Isis.
Whitney, Emblemes, Leyden, 1586, p.008

wreath: ˙Diana, with ˙laurel ˙wreath, ˙falcon, and ˙staff, ˙watches as ˙Actaeon is attacked by ˙three ˙hounds.
Whitney, Emblemes, Leyden, 1586, p.015

wreath: ˙Naked ˙Bacchus, a ˙wreath of ˙vines(?) on his head, lies on a ˙river bank, ˙drinking from a ˙cup.
Whitney, Emblemes, Leyden, 1586, p.125

wreck: ˙Three ˙mermaids watch a ˙galley, with ˙Ulysses tied to the mast. A ˙wrecked ˙hull lies in the distance.
Whitney, Emblemes, Leyden, 1586, p.010

wreck: A ˙flooded ˙city and a ˙wrecked ˙ship.
Whitney, Emblemes, Leyden, 1586, p.129

wrestle: Four ˙men sit at a table; one ˙drinks; two argue over a ˙game of ˙backgammon. Two other men ˙wrestle.
Whitney, Emblemes, Leyden, 1586, p.017

young: An ˙old man ˙sits at ˙table; outside a ˙young man ˙labours in the ˙field.
Whitney, Emblemes, Leyden, 1586, p.050b

young: A ˙young man and an ˙older over a ˙game of ˙draughts or ˙chess; ˙flames engulf the building behind them.
Whitney, Emblemes, Leyden, 1586, p.208

young[1] = offspring

young[1]: The ˙pelican with ˙wings ˙outspread, pierces her ˙breast with her beak to sprinkle her ˙three ˙young[1] with ˙blood.
Whitney, Emblemes, Leyden, 1586, p.087

youth: ˙Quintilius, a ˙quill in his ˙right hand, restrains a ˙youth from handing a note to ˙winged ˙Fame with a ˙trumpet.
Whitney, Emblemes, Leyden, 1586, p.185

zodiacal: A ˙vine grows on a wall with ˙astrological symbols and a ˙moon. Above, a ˙zodiacal ˙circle with ˙Virgo, her ˙right hand pointing at grapes held by a woman.
Whitney, Emblemes, Leyden, 1586, p.206

PROPER NOUN INDEX (PICTURE)

Achilles: ˙Thetis stands by the ˙tomb of ˙Achilles, which is decked with ˙amaranths, and stands under a ˙palm-tree. A ˙dolphin nearby.
Whitney, Emblemes, Leyden, 1586, p.193

Actaeon: ˙Diana ˙watches as a ˙stag-headed ˙Actaeon is attacked by ˙three ˙hounds.
Whitney, Emblemes, Leyden, 1586, p.015

Adam: ˙Adam, in a ˙fig-leaf, hides behind a ˙tree. The inscription ˙"UBI ES" [Where are you?] blazes in the sky.
Whitney, Emblemes, Leyden, 1586, p.229a

Aeneas: ˙Aeneas carries his ˙father ˙Anchises from the burning ˙city of ˙Troy.
Whitney, Emblemes, Leyden, 1586, p.163

Aesculapius: ˙Aesculapius, with a ˙laurel ˙garland, a ˙sceptre in his ˙right hand and a ˙staff in his ˙left, on a ˙throne, supported by two ˙eagles. Nearby a ˙snake, ˙dog and ˙cock.

Whitney, Emblemes, Leyden, 1586, p.212
Agamemnon: ˙Agamemnon, with ˙crown, ˙sword, and
˙shield inscribed ˙"Agamemnon" bearing a ˙lion[1]
˙rampant. ˙Troy in ˙flames.
Whitney, Emblemes, Leyden, 1586, p.045
Ajax: ˙Bare ˙breasted ˙Prowess ˙tears out her ˙hair as
she sits on the ˙tomb of ˙Ajax, inscribed ˙"D
AIACIS."
Whitney, Emblemes, Leyden, 1586, p.030
Ajax: ˙Ajax and ˙Hector ˙exchange a ˙sword and ˙girdle.
Whitney, Emblemes, Leyden, 1586, p.037
Alexander: ˙Diogenes in his ˙barrel talks with
˙Alexander.
Whitney, Emblemes, Leyden, 1586, p.198
Anchises: ˙Aeneas carries his ˙father ˙Anchises from the
burning ˙city of ˙Troy.
Whitney, Emblemes, Leyden, 1586, p.163
Anellus: A ˙miller and the ˙wife of ˙Anellus ˙embrace
before ˙sacks of ˙grain at a ˙watermill.
Whitney, Emblemes, Leyden, 1586, p.080
Apollo: ˙Apollo and ˙Diana kill ˙Niobe's ˙children with
˙arrows. Niobe is turned to ˙stone.
Whitney, Emblemes, Leyden, 1586, p.013
Apollo: ˙Bacchus with a ˙crown of ˙vine ˙leaves and
˙grapes, and ˙Apollo with his ˙lyre stand on a
˙pedestal or ˙tomb.
Whitney, Emblemes, Leyden, 1586, p.146
Apollo: ˙Bacchus with a ˙crown of ˙vine ˙leaves and
˙grapes, and ˙Apollo with his ˙lyre stand on a
˙pedestal or ˙tomb.
Whitney, Emblemes, Leyden, 1586, p.146
Apollo: ˙Apollo and ˙Pan making music on ˙viola(?) and
˙bagpipes. ˙Midas has ˙ears of an ˙ass.
Whitney, Emblemes, Leyden, 1586, p.218a
Arion: ˙Arion and his ˙harp thrown overboard by
˙sailors; a ˙dolphin waits near the ˙ship.
Whitney, Emblemes, Leyden, 1586, p.144
Athena: ˙Hercules stands between ˙Virtue, ˙Athena with
˙helmet, ˙shield and ˙spear and ˙Vice, ˙Venus with
˙Eros.
Whitney, Emblemes, Leyden, 1586, p.040
Athena: ˙Paris gives the ˙golden ˙apple to ˙Venus,
accompanied by ˙Eros; nearby, ˙Juno and ˙Athena
with a ˙helmet and ˙shield; behind them stands
˙Mercury.
Whitney, Emblemes, Leyden, 1586, p.083
Athena: A ˙scholar flanked by ˙Eros and ˙Venus, and by
˙Athena and a ˙soldier.
Whitney, Emblemes, Leyden, 1586, p.135
Athena(?): ˙Athena(?) with ˙helmet, ˙spear and ˙shield,
stands before a ˙grain ˙field and ˙fruit-tree; at the
left, she ˙sits under a ˙barren ˙tree before a ˙fallow
field.
Whitney, Emblemes, Leyden, 1586, p.103
Athena(?): Virtue(?) or ˙Athena(?) wears a ˙helmet, a
˙lance with her ˙right hand, a sceptre(?) or ˙mace(?)
in her ˙left; her ˙right ˙foot on a ˙tortoise(?). ˙Ivy
and ˙two ˙snakes scale the wall.
Whitney, Emblemes, Leyden, 1586, p.222a
Attilius: ˙Bound ˙Attilius lies on a ˙stretcher near an
open ˙barrel riven with ˙nails.
Whitney, Emblemes, Leyden, 1586, p.114
Bacchus: ˙Naked ˙Bacchus, a ˙wreath of ˙vines(?) on his
head, lies on a ˙river bank, ˙drinking from a ˙cup.
Whitney, Emblemes, Leyden, 1586, p.125
Bacchus: ˙Bacchus with a ˙crown of ˙vine ˙leaves and
˙grapes, and ˙Apollo with his ˙lyre stand on a
˙pedestal or ˙tomb.
Whitney, Emblemes, Leyden, 1586, p.146
Bacchus: ˙Bacchus with a ˙crown of ˙vine ˙leaves and
˙grapes, and ˙Apollo with his ˙lyre stand on a
˙pedestal or ˙tomb.
Whitney, Emblemes, Leyden, 1586, p.146
Bacchus: ˙Bacchus, under ˙vines with ˙grapes, beats a
˙drum and blows a ˙pipe; nearby a ˙goblet.

Whitney, Emblemes, Leyden, 1586, p.187
Boreas: The ˙wind, ˙Boreas, blows; ˙reeds in the water
bend, while an ˙oak breaks.
Whitney, Emblemes, Leyden, 1586, p.220
Brasidas: ˙Brasidas points to his ˙shield, ˙pierced by the
˙arrow that wounded him.
Whitney, Emblemes, Leyden, 1586, p.141
Brutus: ˙Brutus in ˙Roman ˙armour and ˙helmet, ˙shield
on the ground, ˙falls on his ˙sword.
Whitney, Emblemes, Leyden, 1586, p.070
Caesar: A ˙scholar talks with a ˙soldier in a ˙helmet
with ˙sword, ˙shield and ˙spear, ˙Ulysses or ˙Caesar.
Whitney, Emblemes, Leyden, 1586, p.047
Camillus: ˙Sinon is ˙whipped by his ˙pupils back to ˙the
Faleria; the ˙walled ˙town is ˙besieged by ˙Camillus
on horseback.
Whitney, Emblemes, Leyden, 1586, p.112
Cephalus: ˙Procris is struck by an ˙arrow, shot by
˙Cephalus. A ˙dog runs towards her.
Whitney, Emblemes, Leyden, 1586, p.211
Christian: ˙Three ˙Christian ˙martyrs in ˙prayer before
a ˙fire are harassed by men with ˙swords and ˙dogs.
A ˙left hand from the ˙clouds holds a ˙garland over
them.
Whitney, Emblemes, Leyden, 1586, p.224a
Cicero: A ˙scholar, ˙Diomedes or ˙Cicero, a ˙tablet
under his arm talks with a ˙soldier, ˙Ulysses or
˙Caesar.
Whitney, Emblemes, Leyden, 1586, p.047
Circe: ˙Circe touches with her ˙wand a ˙pig; nearby a
˙dog, ˙ape, ˙goat and ˙ass, ˙Ulysses's transformed
men.
Whitney, Emblemes, Leyden, 1586, p.082
Colasmus: ˙Colasmus searches for his ˙drowned ˙wife.
Whitney, Emblemes, Leyden, 1586, p.158
Corvinus: The ˙head of ˙Valerius ˙Corvinus in a ˙plumed
˙helmet, the ˙visor open; a ˙raven is perched on
the visor.
Whitney, Emblemes, Leyden, 1586, p.113
Damocles: The ˙sword of ˙Damocles, with ˙wavy ˙blade,
suspended from a ˙cloud.
Whitney, Emblemes, Leyden, 1586, p.102
Danube: A ˙fox on an ˙ice-flow floats down a ˙river
(˙Danube) past a ˙town (˙Regensburg).
Whitney, Emblemes, Leyden, 1586, p.022
Death: ˙Eros and ˙Death shoot exchanged ˙arrows.
Whitney, Emblemes, Leyden, 1586, p.132
Democritus: ˙Laughing ˙Democritus and ˙weeping
˙Heraclitus, with two ˙books, face each other.
Whitney, Emblemes, Leyden, 1586, p.014
Diana: ˙Apollo and ˙Diana kill ˙Niobe's ˙children with
˙arrows. Niobe is turned to ˙stone.
Whitney, Emblemes, Leyden, 1586, p.013
Diana: ˙Diana, with ˙laurel ˙wreath, ˙falcon, and ˙staff,
˙watches as ˙Actaeon is attacked by ˙three ˙hounds.
Whitney, Emblemes, Leyden, 1586, p.015
Diogenes: ˙Diogenes in his ˙barrel, talks with
˙Alexander.
Whitney, Emblemes, Leyden, 1586, p.198
Diomedes: A ˙scholar, ˙Diomedes or ˙Cicero, a ˙tablet
under his arm talks with a ˙soldier, ˙Ulysses or
˙Caesar.
Whitney, Emblemes, Leyden, 1586, p.047
Echo(?): ˙Narcissus admires his ˙reflection in a ˙stream;
˙Echo(?) waves her ˙left hand.
Whitney, Emblemes, Leyden, 1586, p.149
Egyptian(?): ˙Winged ˙Fame, sounds a ˙horn as he flies
over a ˙Roman(?) building and ˙three ˙Egyptian(?)
˙pyramids.
Whitney, Emblemes, Leyden, 1586, p.196
Envy: ˙Time liberates ˙Truth. ˙Snake-haired ˙Envy eats
her ˙heart; ˙Strife stands on a ˙bellows, holding an
˙inverted ˙torch. ˙Slander, holding an ˙torch, has
her hand on a kneeling figure, her ˙hands clasped in
˙supplication.

Whitney, Emblemes, Leyden, 1586, p.004
Envy: ˚Envy, with ˚snakes emerging from her ˚mouth, plucks out her ˚heart with her ˚right hand, walking with a ˚staff.
Whitney, Emblemes, Leyden, 1586, p.094
Eros: ˚Hercules stands between ˚Virtue, ˚Athena with ˚helmet, ˚shield and ˚spear and ˚Vice, ˚Venus with ˚Eros.
Whitney, Emblemes, Leyden, 1586, p.040
Eros: With ˚whip and ˚reins, ˚Eros ˚drives the ˚two ˚lions ˚drawing his ˚chariot.
Whitney, Emblemes, Leyden, 1586, p.063
Eros: ˚Paris gives the ˚golden ˚apple to ˚Venus, accompanied by ˚Eros.
Whitney, Emblemes, Leyden, 1586, p.083
Eros: ˚Eros and ˚Death shoot exchanged ˚arrows.
Whitney, Emblemes, Leyden, 1586, p.132
Eros: A ˚scholar flanked by ˚Eros and ˚Venus, and by ˚Athena and a ˚soldier.
Whitney, Emblemes, Leyden, 1586, p.135
Eros: A ˚bee stung ˚Eros flies to ˚Venus. Bees swarm around two ˚hives.
Whitney, Emblemes, Leyden, 1586, p.147
Eros: A ˚bee stung ˚Eros flies to ˚Venus. Bees swarm around two ˚hives.
Whitney, Emblemes, Leyden, 1586, p.147
Eros: ˚Eros shows his ˚bee stung ˚hand to ˚Venus; bees swarm around their ˚hive.
Whitney, Emblemes, Leyden, 1586, p.148
Eros: ˚Eros, holding ˚flowers and a ˚fish.
Whitney, Emblemes, Leyden, 1586, p.182a
Eros(?): A ˚Venus(?) with basket of ˚fruit, and ˚Eros(?); animals nearby: ˚lion, ˚hare, ˚horse, ˚bird and ˚fish.
Whitney, Emblemes, Leyden, 1586, p.182b
Faleria: ˚Sinon is ˚whipped by his ˚pupils back to ˚the Faleria; the ˚walled ˚town is ˚besieged by ˚Camillus on horseback.
Whitney, Emblemes, Leyden, 1586, p.112
Fame: ˚Quintilius, a ˚quill in his ˚right hand, restrains a ˚youth from handing a note to ˚winged ˚Fame with a ˚trumpet.
Whitney, Emblemes, Leyden, 1586, p.185
Fame: Spotted with ˚mouths(?), ˚winged ˚Fame, sounds a ˚horn as he flies over a ˚Roman(?) building and ˚three ˚Egyptian(?) ˚pyramids. Fame has a ˚pen tied to a sling made of ˚laurel(?) over his shoulder.
Whitney, Emblemes, Leyden, 1586, p.196
Glory: ˚Glory ˚flees through a ˚doorway from ˚naked ˚couple on a ˚bed; beside them stands a ˚table with ˚food and ˚drink.
Whitney, Emblemes, Leyden, 1586, p.042
God(?): A man is weighted down by a ˚stone bound to his ˚right ˚arm as he lifts his ˚winged ˚left arm and leg towards ˚God(?).
Whitney, Emblemes, Leyden, 1586, p.152
Hanno: ˚Hanno releases a ˚flock of ˚birds.
Whitney, Emblemes, Leyden, 1586, p.084
Harpocrates: A ˚scholar with a ˚book in his study. He holds a ˚finger to his ˚lips in a gesture of ˚silence. (˚Harpocrates)
Whitney, Emblemes, Leyden, 1586, p.060
Harpocratic: ˚Modesty, her ˚finger to her ˚lips in the ˚Harpocratic gesture of ˚silence, holds ˚keys and ˚stands on a ˚tortoise.
Whitney, Emblemes, Leyden, 1586, p.093b
Harpocratic: A man with huge ˚ears; another points to his ˚mouth with his ˚left ˚forefinger (˚Harpocratic gesture); a man flees from a ˚snake.
Whitney, Emblemes, Leyden, 1586, p.191b
Hector: ˚Ajax and ˚Hector ˚exchange a ˚sword and ˚girdle.
Whitney, Emblemes, Leyden, 1586, p.037
Hellespont: ˚Phrixus crosses ˚Hellespont on the ˚golden ˚ram, eyes and ˚right arm raised to the heavens.
Whitney, Emblemes, Leyden, 1586, p.214

Heraclitus: ˚Laughing ˚Democritus and ˚weeping ˚Heraclitus, with two ˚books, face each other.
Whitney, Emblemes, Leyden, 1586, p.014
Hercules: ˚Armed ˚Pygmies ˚attack ˚Hercules, who sleeps ˚club in hand.
Whitney, Emblemes, Leyden, 1586, p.016
Hercules: ˚Hercules stands between ˚Virtue, ˚Athena with ˚helmet, ˚shield and ˚spear and ˚Vice, ˚Venus with ˚Eros.
Whitney, Emblemes, Leyden, 1586, p.040
Homer: ˚Homer with the ˚nine ˚Muses.
Whitney, Emblemes, Leyden, 1586, p.168a
Hope: ˚Nemesis with ˚bridle, stands before ˚Hope, seated on a ˚barrel, a ˚bow in her ˚left hand, pointing with her ˚right.
Whitney, Emblemes, Leyden, 1586, p.139b
Icarus: ˚Icarus ˚falls into the ˚sea after the ˚sun has melted the wax binding the ˚feathers of his ˚wings.
Whitney, Emblemes, Leyden, 1586, p.028
Idleness: ˚Labour, with ˚cornucopia and ˚crown of ears of ˚grain, sits in a ˚chariot pulled by ˚ants. She uses a ˚bundle of stalks of ˚grain(?) to beat ˚Idleness.
Whitney, Emblemes, Leyden, 1586, p.175
Isis: ˚Worshippers kneel in ˚reverence before an ˚ass bearing a ˚statue of ˚Isis; the ˚driver ˚beats the ass with a ˚stick.
Whitney, Emblemes, Leyden, 1586, p.008
Janus: ˚Janus with ˚two ˚faces, in ˚Roman ˚armour holds a ˚sceptre in his ˚right hand and a ˚mirror(?) in his ˚left.
Whitney, Emblemes, Leyden, 1586, p.108
Juno: ˚Paris gives the ˚golden ˚apple to ˚Venus, accompanied by ˚Eros; nearby, ˚Juno and ˚Athena; behind them stands ˚Mercury.
Whitney, Emblemes, Leyden, 1586, p.083
Jupiter: A man with ˚upraised ˚sword takes fright at his ˚shadow. ˚Jupiter sits astride an ˚eagle in a bank of clouds.
Whitney, Emblemes, Leyden, 1586, p.032
Jupiter: ˚Jupiter with ˚thunderbolts sits on his ˚eagle; a man holds onto a ˚laurel tree in a storm(?).
Whitney, Emblemes, Leyden, 1586, p.067
Jupiter: Seated on a ˚throne, ˚Jupiter, whose ˚staff is surmounted by an ˚eagle, is surrounded by a ˚deer, ˚horse, ˚bull, ˚ass, ˚snail, ˚eagle, and ˚lion.
Whitney, Emblemes, Leyden, 1586, p.091
Jupiter(?): ˚Pine-trees are ˚broken by a ˚wind(?); in a ˚cloud ˚Jupiter(?) sits astride an ˚eagle.
Whitney, Emblemes, Leyden, 1586, p.059
Labour: ˚Labour, with ˚cornucopia and ˚crown of ears of ˚grain, sits in a ˚chariot pulled by ˚ants. She uses a ˚bundle of stalks of ˚grain(?) to beat ˚Idleness.
Whitney, Emblemes, Leyden, 1586, p.175
Lais: ˚Lais, the ˚courtesan with small animals, ˚muskrats(?).
Whitney, Emblemes, Leyden, 1586, p.079
Medea: A ˚swallow approaches its ˚nest in a niche with a ˚statue of ˚Medea ˚killing her ˚child with a ˚sword.
Whitney, Emblemes, Leyden, 1586, p.033
Mercury: Wearing a ˚winged ˚helmet and holding a ˚caduceus, ˚Mercury points to the ˚path at his feet; a ˚traveller with a ˚staff.
Whitney, Emblemes, Leyden, 1586, p.002
Mercury: ˚Paris gives the ˚golden ˚apple to ˚Venus, accompanied by ˚Eros; nearby, ˚Juno and ˚Athena; behind them stands ˚Mercury.
Whitney, Emblemes, Leyden, 1586, p.083
Mercury: ˚Mercury in a ˚winged ˚cap repairs the ˚strings of a ˚lute; a ˚woman ˚dances while another man plays a lute.
Whitney, Emblemes, Leyden, 1586, p.092
Mezentius: From his ˚throne, ˚Mezentius with ˚crown

and ˙sceptre overseee the ˙binding of a ˙naked ˙body
to a naked ˙corpse.
  Whitney, Emblemes, Leyden, 1586, p.099
Midas: ˙Apollo and ˙Pan making music on ˙viola(?) and
  ˙bagpipes. ˙Midas has ˙ears of an ˙ass.
  Whitney, Emblemes, Leyden, 1586, p.218a
Modesty: ˙Modesty, her ˙finger to her ˙lips in the
  ˙Harpocratic gesture of ˙silence, holds ˙keys and
  ˙stands on a ˙tortoise.
  Whitney, Emblemes, Leyden, 1586, p.093b
Muse: ˙Homer with the ˙nine ˙Muses.
  Whitney, Emblemes, Leyden, 1586, p.168a
Narcissus: ˙Narcissus admires his ˙reflection in a
  ˙stream; ˙Echo(?) waves her ˙left hand; a
  ˙narcissus(?), grows nearby.
  Whitney, Emblemes, Leyden, 1586, p.149
Nemesis: ˙Nemesis holds a ˙bit and ˙bridle.
  Whitney, Emblemes, Leyden, 1586, p.019
Nemesis: ˙Nemesis with ˙bridle, stands before ˙Hope,
  seated on a ˙barrel, a ˙bow in her ˙left hand,
  pointing with her ˙right.
  Whitney, Emblemes, Leyden, 1586, p.139b
Nile: A ˙crocodile laying her ˙eggs, on the bank of the
  ˙river ˙Nile.
  Whitney, Emblemes, Leyden, 1586, p.003
Niobe: ˙Apollo and ˙Diana kill ˙Niobe's ˙children with
  ˙arrows. Niobe is turned to ˙stone.
  Whitney, Emblemes, Leyden, 1586, p.013
Occasio: ˙Naked ˙Occasio, with ˙bald ˙head, long
  ˙forelock, and ˙razor in her raised ˙right hand,
  stands on a ˙wheel in the ˙sea; her ˙heels are
  ˙winged, and she holds a ˙scarf in her ˙left hand.
  Whitney, Emblemes, Leyden, 1586, p.181
Ocnus: ˙Ocnus and a ˙ropemaker make a ˙rope from
  ˙grasses. An ˙ass eats the rope.
  Whitney, Emblemes, Leyden, 1586, p.048
Opimius: ˙Opimius, the ˙miser, in his sick-bed. The
  ˙physician supervises the emptying of his ˙chests of
  ˙gold onto a table.
  Whitney, Emblemes, Leyden, 1586, p.209
Orpheus: ˙Orpheus plays his ˙harp, surrounded by a
  ˙vulture, ˙stork, ˙stag, ˙lion, ˙bear, ˙antelope, and
  ˙ape.
  Whitney, Emblemes, Leyden, 1586, p.186
Pan: ˙Apollo and ˙Pan making music on ˙viola(?) and
  ˙bagpipes. ˙Midas has ˙ears of an ˙ass.
  Whitney, Emblemes, Leyden, 1586, p.218a
Paris: ˙Paris gives the ˙golden ˙apple to ˙Venus.
  Whitney, Emblemes, Leyden, 1586, p.083
Phrixus: ˙Phrixus crosses ˙Hellespont on the ˙golden
  ˙ram, eyes and ˙right arm raised to the heavens.
  Whitney, Emblemes, Leyden, 1586, p.214
Pliny: A ˙winged ˙figure ˙reclines at the foot of the
  ˙volcano ˙Vesuvius as ˙Pliny ˙falls into the volcano.
  Whitney, Emblemes, Leyden, 1586, p.025
Procris: ˙Procris is struck by an ˙arrow, shot by
  ˙Cephalus. A ˙dog runs towards her.
  Whitney, Emblemes, Leyden, 1586, p.211
Prometheus: An ˙eagle rends the ˙liver of ˙Prometheus,
  ˙chained to a ˙rock.
  Whitney, Emblemes, Leyden, 1586, p.075
Prowess: ˙Bare ˙breasted ˙Prowess ˙tears out her ˙hair
  as she sits on the ˙tomb of ˙Ajax, inscribed ˙"D
  AIACIS."
  Whitney, Emblemes, Leyden, 1586, p.030
Putto(?): A naked ˙boy or ˙Putto(?) sits in a ˙fruit-tree;
  an ˙old ˙man, ˙scholar(?); ˙Flowers, some wilted,
  grow nearby.
  Whitney, Emblemes, Leyden, 1586, p.173
Pygmy: ˙Armed ˙Pygmies ˙attack ˙Hercules, who sleeps
  ˙club in hand.
  Whitney, Emblemes, Leyden, 1586, p.016
Quintilius: ˙Quintilius, a ˙quill in his ˙right hand,
  restrains a ˙youth from handing a note to ˙winged
  ˙Fame with a ˙trumpet.

Whitney, Emblemes, Leyden, 1586, p.185
Regensburg: A ˙fox on an ˙ice-flow floats down a ˙river
  (˙Danube) past a ˙town (˙Regensburg).
  Whitney, Emblemes, Leyden, 1586, p.022
Roman: ˙Brutus in ˙Roman ˙armour and ˙helmet, ˙shield
  on the ground, ˙falls on his ˙sword.
  Whitney, Emblemes, Leyden, 1586, p.070
Roman: ˙Janus with ˙two ˙faces, in ˙Roman ˙armour
  holds a ˙sceptre in his ˙right hand and a ˙mirror(?)
  in his ˙left.
  Whitney, Emblemes, Leyden, 1586, p.108
Roman(?): ˙Winged ˙Fame sounds a ˙horn as he flies
  over a ˙Roman(?) building and ˙three ˙Egyptian(?)
  ˙pyramids.
  Whitney, Emblemes, Leyden, 1586, p.196
Sinon: ˙Sinon is ˙whipped by his ˙pupils back to ˙the
  Faleria; the ˙walled ˙town is ˙besieged by ˙Camillus
  on horseback.
  Whitney, Emblemes, Leyden, 1586, p.112
Sisyphus: ˙Sisyphus pushes a ˙stone up a ˙hill.
  Whitney, Emblemes, Leyden, 1586, p.215
Slander: ˙Winged ˙Time with a ˙scythe liberates ˙Truth.
  ˙Snake-haired ˙Envy eats her ˙heart; ˙Strife stands
  on a ˙bellows, holding an ˙inverted ˙torch. ˙Slander,
  holding an ˙torch, has her hand on a kneeling
  figure, her ˙hands clasped in ˙supplication.
  Whitney, Emblemes, Leyden, 1586, p.004
Strife: ˙Winged ˙Time with a ˙scythe liberates ˙Truth.
  ˙Snake-haired ˙Envy eats her ˙heart; ˙Strife stands
  on a ˙bellows, holding an ˙inverted ˙torch. ˙Slander,
  holding an ˙torch, has her hand on a kneeling
  figure, her ˙hands clasped in ˙supplication.
  Whitney, Emblemes, Leyden, 1586, p.004
Tantalus: ˙Tantalus stands in a river, looking up at
  ˙fruit laden ˙tree. ˙Flames and ˙smoke billow up in
  the background.
  Whitney, Emblemes, Leyden, 1586, p.074
Thetis: ˙Thetis stands by the ˙tomb of ˙Achilles, which
  is decked with ˙amaranths, and stands under a
  ˙palm-tree.
  Whitney, Emblemes, Leyden, 1586, p.193
Time: ˙Winged ˙Time with a ˙scythe liberates ˙Truth.
  Whitney, Emblemes, Leyden, 1586, p.004
Time: A ˙couple walk from a building, the man points to
  an open ˙treasure chest. ˙Winged ˙Time, with a
  ˙scythe, pursues the couple.
  Whitney, Emblemes, Leyden, 1586, p.199
Troy: ˙Aeneas carries his ˙father ˙Anchises from the
  burning ˙city of ˙Troy.
  Whitney, Emblemes, Leyden, 1586, p.163
Truth: ˙Winged ˙Time with a ˙scythe liberates ˙Truth.
  Whitney, Emblemes, Leyden, 1586, p.004
Ulysses: ˙Three ˙mermaids with a ˙lyre and a
  ˙woodwind instrument, watch a ˙galley with ˙Ulysses
  tied to the mast.
  Whitney, Emblemes, Leyden, 1586, p.010
Ulysses: A ˙scholar talks with a ˙soldier in a ˙helmet
  with ˙sword, ˙shield and ˙spear, ˙Ulysses or ˙Caesar.
  Whitney, Emblemes, Leyden, 1586, p.047
Ulysses: ˙Circe touches with her ˙wand a ˙pig; nearby
  a ˙dog, ˙ape, ˙goat and ˙ass, ˙Ulysses's transformed
  men.
  Whitney, Emblemes, Leyden, 1586, p.082
Valens: The ˙right hand of Emperor ˙Valens, reaches for
  or lets fall a ˙quill ˙pen.
  Whitney, Emblemes, Leyden, 1586, p.143
Valerius: The ˙head of ˙Valerius ˙Corvinus in a ˙plumed
  ˙helmet, the ˙visor open; a ˙raven is perched on
  the visor.
  Whitney, Emblemes, Leyden, 1586, p.113
Venus: ˙Hercules stands between ˙Virtue, ˙Athena with
  ˙helmet, ˙shield and ˙spear and ˙Vice, ˙Venus with
  ˙Eros.
  Whitney, Emblemes, Leyden, 1586, p.040
Venus: ˙Paris gives the ˙golden ˙apple to ˙Venus,

accompanied by `Eros; nearby, `Juno and `Athena;
behind them stands `Mercury.
   Whitney, Emblemes, Leyden, 1586, p.083
Venus: A `scholar flanked by `Eros and `Venus, and by
   `Athena and a `soldier.
   Whitney, Emblemes, Leyden, 1586, p.135
Venus: A `bee stung `Eros flies to `Venus. Bees swarm
   around two `hives.
   Whitney, Emblemes, Leyden, 1586, p.147
Venus: `Eros shows his `bee stung `hand to `Venus; bees
   swarm around their `hive.
   Whitney, Emblemes, Leyden, 1586, p.148
Venus(?): A `Venus(?) with basket of `fruit, and
   `Eros(?); animals nearby: `lion, `hare, `horse, `bird
   and `fish.
   Whitney, Emblemes, Leyden, 1586, p.182b
Vesuvius: A `winged `figure `reclines at the foot of
   `Vesuvius. `Pliny `falls into the volcano.
   Whitney, Emblemes, Leyden, 1586, p.025
Vice: `Hercules stands between `Virtue, `Athena with
   `helmet, `shield and `spear and `Vice, `Venus with
   `Eros.
   Whitney, Emblemes, Leyden, 1586, p.040
Virgo: A `vine grows on a wall with `astrological
   symbols and a `moon. Above, `zodiacal `circle with
   `Virgo, her `right hand pointing at grapes held by a
   woman.
   Whitney, Emblemes, Leyden, 1586, p.206
Virtue: `Hercules stands between `Virtue, `Athena with
   `helmet, `shield and `spear and `Vice, `Venus with
   `Eros.
   Whitney, Emblemes, Leyden, 1586, p.040
Virtue(?): Virtue(?) or `Athene(?) wears a `helmet, a
   `lance with her `right hand, a sceptre(?) or `mace(?)
   in her `left; her `right `foot on a `tortoise(?). `Ivy
   and `two `snakes scale the wall.
   Whitney, Emblemes, Leyden, 1586, p.222a

PICTURE INSCRIPTIONS

"Agamemnon"
   Whitney, Emblemes, Leyden, 1586, p.045
"Bias"
   Whitney, Emblemes, Leyden, 1586, p.130
"Chilon"
   Whitney, Emblemes, Leyden, 1586, p.130
"COSI DE BEN AMAR / PORTO TORMENTO"
   [Thus from a great love I bear the torment]
   Whitney, Emblemes, Leyden, 1586, p.219
"Cleobulus"
   Whitney, Emblemes, Leyden, 1586, p.130
"D AIACIS."
   Whitney, Emblemes, Leyden, 1586, p.030
"ET TUTTO ABBRACCIO ET NULLA STRINGO"
   [And all things I embrace and nothing do I hold]
   Whitney, Emblemes, Leyden, 1586, p.055b
"ET USQUE AD NUBES VERITAS TVA"
   [And your truth (will soar) all the way to the clouds]
   Whitney, Emblemes, Leyden, 1586, p.166a
"EUROPA"
   Whitney, Emblemes, Leyden, 1586, p.225
"KAOS" [= chaos (Gk)]
   Whitney, Emblemes, Leyden, 1586, p.122
"Periander"
   Whitney, Emblemes, Leyden, 1586, p.130
"Pittacus"
   Whitney, Emblemes, Leyden, 1586, p.130
"PLUS OLTRE [= ULTRA]" [Still further]
   Whitney, Emblemes, Leyden, 1586, p.183a
"QUI ME ALIT ME EXTINGUIT"
   [The one who nourishes me extinguishes me]
   Whitney, Emblemes, Leyden, 1586, p.183a
"Solon"
   Whitney, Emblemes, Leyden, 1586, p.130

"Thales"
   Whitney, Emblemes, Leyden, 1586, p.130
"TROIA MIHI LICET TAMEN"
   [Nevertheless the whore sells herself to me] or [For
   all that I can buy a whore]
   Whitney, Emblemes, Leyden, 1586, p.183b
"UBI ES" [Where are you?]
   Whitney, Emblemes, Leyden, 1586, p.229a
"ULTERIUS" [Further]
   Whitney, Emblemes, Leyden, 1586, p.053a

LATIN MOTTO INDEX

abjicio: Desidiam abiiciendam.
   Whitney, Emblemes, Leyden, 1586, p.085
abstinentia: Abstinentia.
   Whitney, Emblemes, Leyden, 1586, p.136
abstineo: Prudentes vino abstinent.
   Whitney, Emblemes, Leyden, 1586, p.133
acervus: De parvis, grandis aceruus erit.
   Whitney, Emblemes, Leyden, 1586, p.088
aculeus: Aculei irriti.
   Whitney, Emblemes, Leyden, 1586, p.221
adolescens: Quaere adolescens, utere senex.
   Whitney, Emblemes, Leyden, 1586, p.050b
aeneus: Murus aeneus, sana conscientia.
   Whitney, Emblemes, Leyden, 1586, p.067
aequalis: Dissidia inter aequales, pessima.
   Whitney, Emblemes, Leyden, 1586, p.005
aerumnosus: Voluptas aerumnosa.
   Whitney, Emblemes, Leyden, 1586, p.015
aes: Aere quandoque salutem redimendam.
   Whitney, Emblemes, Leyden, 1586, p.035
aetas: Dum aetatis ver agitur: consule brumae.
   Whitney, Emblemes, Leyden, 1586, p.159
aetas: Sic aetas fugit.
   Whitney, Emblemes, Leyden, 1586, p.227
affectus: Potentissimus affectus, amor.
   Whitney, Emblemes, Leyden, 1586, p.063
ago: Agentes, et consentientes, pari poena puniendi.
   Whitney, Emblemes, Leyden, 1586, p.054a
ago: Dum aetatis ver agitur: consule brumae.
   Whitney, Emblemes, Leyden, 1586, p.159
alo: Qui me alit me extinguit.
   Whitney, Emblemes, Leyden, 1586, p.183a
alo: In sinu alere serpentem.
   Whitney, Emblemes, Leyden, 1586, p.189a
altus: Noli altum sapere.
   Whitney, Emblemes, Leyden, 1586, p.078
amarus: Post amara dulcia.
   Whitney, Emblemes, Leyden, 1586, p.165
ambitio: Ridicula ambitio.
   Whitney, Emblemes, Leyden, 1586, p.084
amicitia: Amicitia, etiam post mortem durans.
   Whitney, Emblemes, Leyden, 1586, p.062
amicitia: Amicitia fucata vitanda.
   Whitney, Emblemes, Leyden, 1586, p.124
amicus: Amico ficto nulla fit iniuria.
   Whitney, Emblemes, Leyden, 1586, p.226a
amor: Amor in filios.
   Whitney, Emblemes, Leyden, 1586, p.029
amor: Potentissimus affectus, amor.
   Whitney, Emblemes, Leyden, 1586, p.063
amor: In studiosum captum amore.
   Whitney, Emblemes, Leyden, 1586, p.135
amor: Amor sui.
   Whitney, Emblemes, Leyden, 1586, p.149
amor: Caecus amor prolis.
   Whitney, Emblemes, Leyden, 1586, p.188a
amor: In amore tormentum.
   Whitney, Emblemes, Leyden, 1586, p.219
anguis: Latet anguis in herba.
   Whitney, Emblemes, Leyden, 1586, p.024
animus: Animi scrinium servitus.

Whitney, Emblemes, Leyden, 1586, p.044
desidia: Desidiam abiiciendam.
Whitney, Emblemes, Leyden, 1586, p.085
deus: Qua dij vocant, eundum.
Whitney, Emblemes, Leyden, 1586, p.002
dictum: Dicta septem sapientium.
Whitney, Emblemes, Leyden, 1586, p.130
dies: In dies meliora.
Whitney, Emblemes, Leyden, 1586, p.053a
discerno: Sic discerne.
Whitney, Emblemes, Leyden, 1586, p.068
discors: Post fata; uxor morosa, etiam discors.
Whitney, Emblemes, Leyden, 1586, p.158
dissidia: Dissidia inter aequales, pessima.
Whitney, Emblemes, Leyden, 1586, p.005
dives: In divitem,indoctum.
Whitney, Emblemes, Leyden, 1586, p.214
divinus: Auxilio divino.
Whitney, Emblemes, Leyden, 1586, p.203
divitiae: Mortui divitiae.
Whitney, Emblemes, Leyden, 1586, p.086
do: Bis dat qui cito dat.
Whitney, Emblemes, Leyden, 1586, p.190b
doceo: Experientia docet.
Whitney, Emblemes, Leyden, 1586, p.009
dolor: Dolor e medicina.
Whitney, Emblemes, Leyden, 1586, p.156a
dolus: Nullus dolus contra Casum.
Whitney, Emblemes, Leyden, 1586, p.022
dolus: Dolus in suos.
Whitney, Emblemes, Leyden, 1586, p.027
dolus: In victoriam dolo partam.
Whitney, Emblemes, Leyden, 1586, p.030
dolus: Non dolo, sed vi.
Whitney, Emblemes, Leyden, 1586, p.058
dominus: Nemo potest duobus dominis servire.
Whitney, Emblemes, Leyden, 1586, p.223
donum: Inimicorum dona, infausta.
Whitney, Emblemes, Leyden, 1586, p.037
dulcis: Post amara dulcia.
Whitney, Emblemes, Leyden, 1586, p.165
duo: Parvam culinam, duobus ganeonibus non sufficere.
Whitney, Emblemes, Leyden, 1586, p.055a
duo: Nemo potest duobus dominis servire.
Whitney, Emblemes, Leyden, 1586, p.223
duro: Amicitia, etiam post mortem durans.
Whitney, Emblemes, Leyden, 1586, p.062
durus: Durum telum necessitas.
Whitney, Emblemes, Leyden, 1586, p.036
durus: Dura usu molliora.
Whitney, Emblemes, Leyden, 1586, p.156b
edo: Scripta non temere edenda.
Whitney, Emblemes, Leyden, 1586, p.185
egeo: Otiosi semper egentes.
Whitney, Emblemes, Leyden, 1586, p.175
eleemosyna: Noli tuba canere Eleemosynam.
Whitney, Emblemes, Leyden, 1586, p.224b
emitto: Verbum emissum non est revocabile.
Whitney, Emblemes, Leyden, 1586, p.180
eo: Qua dij vocant, eundum.
Whitney, Emblemes, Leyden, 1586, p.002
error: In copia minor error.
Whitney, Emblemes, Leyden, 1586, p.142
evito: Importunitas evitanda.
Whitney, Emblemes, Leyden, 1586, p.192
exalto: Qui se exaltat, humiliabitur.
Whitney, Emblemes, Leyden, 1586, p.216a
exitium: Turpibus exitium.
Whitney, Emblemes, Leyden, 1586, p.021
experientia: Experientia docet.
Whitney, Emblemes, Leyden, 1586, p.009
exspecto: Otium sortem exspectat.
Whitney, Emblemes, Leyden, 1586, p.026
extinguo: Qui me alit me extinguit.
Whitney, Emblemes, Leyden, 1586, p.183a

factum: Nec verbo, nec facto, quenquam laedendum.
Whitney, Emblemes, Leyden, 1586, p.019
fama: Minuit praesentia famam.
Whitney, Emblemes, Leyden, 1586, p.020
familiaris: Perfidus familiaris.
Whitney, Emblemes, Leyden, 1586, p.141
famis: Auri sacra fames quid non?
Whitney, Emblemes, Leyden, 1586, p.179
fatum: Vindice fato.
Whitney, Emblemes, Leyden, 1586, p.143
fatum: Post fata; uxor morosa, etiam discors.
Whitney, Emblemes, Leyden, 1586, p.158
fatuus: Fatuis levia committito
Whitney, Emblemes, Leyden, 1586, p.081
fel: Fel in melle.
Whitney, Emblemes, Leyden, 1586, p.147
felicitas: In momentaneam felicitatem.
Whitney, Emblemes, Leyden, 1586, p.034
feliciter: Fortiter et feliciter.
Whitney, Emblemes, Leyden, 1586, p.115
ferocia: Impunitas ferociae parens.
Whitney, Emblemes, Leyden, 1586, p.222b
festino: Festina lente.
Whitney, Emblemes, Leyden, 1586, p.121
fictus: Amico ficto nulla fit iniuria.
Whitney, Emblemes, Leyden, 1586, p.226a
fides: Fides non apparentium.
Whitney, Emblemes, Leyden, 1586, p.071
fides: Praepostera fides.
Whitney, Emblemes, Leyden, 1586, p.080
fides: Frontis nulla fides.
Whitney, Emblemes, Leyden, 1586, p.100
fides: Hosti etiam servanda fides.
Whitney, Emblemes, Leyden, 1586, p.114
fides: Sic spectanda fides.
Whitney, Emblemes, Leyden, 1586, p.139a
fides: Nusquam tuta fides.
Whitney, Emblemes, Leyden, 1586, p.150
fido: Nimium rebus ne fide secundis.
Whitney, Emblemes, Leyden, 1586, p.059
filia: Veritas temporis filia.
Whitney, Emblemes, Leyden, 1586, p.004
filius: Amor in filios.
Whitney, Emblemes, Leyden, 1586, p.029
filius: Indulgentia parentum, filiorum pernicies.
Whitney, Emblemes, Leyden, 1586, p.155
filius: Pietas filiorum in parentes.
Whitney, Emblemes, Leyden, 1586, p.163
fiscus: Quod non capit Christus, rapit fiscus.
Whitney, Emblemes, Leyden, 1586, p.151
foecunditas: In foecunditatem, sibi ipsi damnosam.
Whitney, Emblemes, Leyden, 1586, p.174
foenum: Omnis caro foenum.
Whitney, Emblemes, Leyden, 1586, p.217
formidolosus: Vel post mortem formidolosi.
Whitney, Emblemes, Leyden, 1586, p.194
fortis: Fortissima minimis interdum cedunt.
Whitney, Emblemes, Leyden, 1586, p.052a
fortiter: Fortiter et feliciter.
Whitney, Emblemes, Leyden, 1586, p.115
fortuna: Fortuna virtutem superans.
Whitney, Emblemes, Leyden, 1586, p.070
fortuna: Audaces fortuna iuvat.
Whitney, Emblemes, Leyden, 1586, p.117
fraus: Fraus meretur fraudem.
Whitney, Emblemes, Leyden, 1586, p.210
frons: Frontis nulla fides.
Whitney, Emblemes, Leyden, 1586, p.100
fructus: Pulchritudo sine fructu.
Whitney, Emblemes, Leyden, 1586, p.205
frustra: Frustra.
Whitney, Emblemes, Leyden, 1586, p.012
fucatus: Amicitia fucata vitanda.
Whitney, Emblemes, Leyden, 1586, p.124
fugio: Venter, pluma, Venus, laudem fugiunt.

locus: Non locus virum, sed vir locum ornat.
  Whitney, Emblemes, Leyden, 1586, p.038
locus: Non locus virum, sed vir locum ornat.
  Whitney, Emblemes, Leyden, 1586, p.038
longus: O vita, misero longa.
  Whitney, Emblemes, Leyden, 1586, p.075
lucto: Cum larvis non luctandum.
  Whitney, Emblemes, Leyden, 1586, p.127
luctus: Ludus, luctus, luxus.
  Whitney, Emblemes, Leyden, 1586, p.017
ludus: Ludus, luctus, luxus.
  Whitney, Emblemes, Leyden, 1586, p.017
lupus: Homo homini lupus.
  Whitney, Emblemes, Leyden, 1586, p.144
luxuriosus: Luxuriosorum opes.
  Whitney, Emblemes, Leyden, 1586, p.053b
luxus: Ludus, luctus, luxus.
  Whitney, Emblemes, Leyden, 1586, p.017
luxus: Mihi pondera, luxus.
  Whitney, Emblemes, Leyden, 1586, p.023
malum: Pro bono, malum.
  Whitney, Emblemes, Leyden, 1586, p.153a
malus: Aliquid mali propter vicinum malum.
  Whitney, Emblemes, Leyden, 1586, p.164
maneo: Mens immota manet.
  Whitney, Emblemes, Leyden, 1586, p.043
maneo: Scripta manent.
  Whitney, Emblemes, Leyden, 1586, p.131
marmor: Scribit in marmore laesus.
  Whitney, Emblemes, Leyden, 1586, p.183b
maturo: Maturandum.
  Whitney, Emblemes, Leyden, 1586, p.188b
medicina: Dolor e medicina.
  Whitney, Emblemes, Leyden, 1586, p.156a
medicina: Ex morbo medicina.
  Whitney, Emblemes, Leyden, 1586, p.209
medicus: Medici Icon.
  Whitney, Emblemes, Leyden, 1586, p.212
mediocris: Mediocribus utere partis.
  Whitney, Emblemes, Leyden, 1586, p.039
mel: Fel in melle.
  Whitney, Emblemes, Leyden, 1586, p.147
melior: In dies meliora.
  Whitney, Emblemes, Leyden, 1586, p.053a
mens: Mens immota manet.
  Whitney, Emblemes, Leyden, 1586, p.043
minimus: Fortissima minimis interdum cedunt.
  Whitney, Emblemes, Leyden, 1586, p.052a
minuo: Minuit praesentia famam.
  Whitney, Emblemes, Leyden, 1586, p.020
miser: O vita, misero longa.
  Whitney, Emblemes, Leyden, 1586, p.075
mitis: Tempore cuncta mitiora.
  Whitney, Emblemes, Leyden, 1586, p.206
mollior: Dura usu molliora.
  Whitney, Emblemes, Leyden, 1586, p.156b
momentaneus: In momentaneam felicitatem.
  Whitney, Emblemes, Leyden, 1586, p.034
mons: Feriunt summis fulmina montes.
  Whitney, Emblemes, Leyden, 1586, p.140
morbus: Ex morbo medicina.
  Whitney, Emblemes, Leyden, 1586, p.209
morosus: Post fata; uxor morosa, etiam discors.
  Whitney, Emblemes, Leyden, 1586, p.158
mors: Vitae, aut morti.
  Whitney, Emblemes, Leyden, 1586, p.051a
mors: Amicitia, etiam post mortem durans.
  Whitney, Emblemes, Leyden, 1586, p.062
mors: Vel post mortem formidolosi.
  Whitney, Emblemes, Leyden, 1586, p.194
mortuus: Mortui divitiae.
  Whitney, Emblemes, Leyden, 1586, p.086
mulier: Mulier umbra viri.
  Whitney, Emblemes, Leyden, 1586, p.218b
murus: Murus aeneus, sana conscientia.

  Whitney, Emblemes, Leyden, 1586, p.067
musica: Orphei Musica.
  Whitney, Emblemes, Leyden, 1586, p.186
muto: Cum tempore mutamur.
  Whitney, Emblemes, Leyden, 1586, p.167
mutuus: Mutuum auxilium.
  Whitney, Emblemes, Leyden, 1586, p.065
natura: Industria naturam corrigit.
  Whitney, Emblemes, Leyden, 1586, p.092
necessitas: Durum telum necessitas.
  Whitney, Emblemes, Leyden, 1586, p.036
nimium: Nimium rebus ne fide secundis.
  Whitney, Emblemes, Leyden, 1586, p.059
nolo: Noli altum sapere.
  Whitney, Emblemes, Leyden, 1586, p.078
nomen: Strenuorum immortale nomen.
  Whitney, Emblemes, Leyden, 1586, p.193
occasio: In occasionem.
  Whitney, Emblemes, Leyden, 1586, p.181
odium: Caecum odium.
  Whitney, Emblemes, Leyden, 1586, p.031
opes: Luxuriosorum opes.
  Whitney, Emblemes, Leyden, 1586, p.053b
oportet: Ei, qui semel sua prodegerit, aliena credi non
    oportere.
  Whitney, Emblemes, Leyden, 1586, p.033
orno: Non locus virum, sed vir locum ornat.
  Whitney, Emblemes, Leyden, 1586, p.038
otiosus: Otiosi semper egentes.
  Whitney, Emblemes, Leyden, 1586, p.175
otium: Otium sortem exspectat.
  Whitney, Emblemes, Leyden, 1586, p.026
paratus: In utrumque paratus.
  Whitney, Emblemes, Leyden, 1586, p.066
parens: Indulgentia parentum, filiorum pernicies.
  Whitney, Emblemes, Leyden, 1586, p.155
parens: Pietas filiorum in parentes.
  Whitney, Emblemes, Leyden, 1586, p.163
parens: Impunitas ferociae parens.
  Whitney, Emblemes, Leyden, 1586, p.222b
paries: Tunc tua res agitur, paries cum proximus ardet.
  Whitney, Emblemes, Leyden, 1586, p.208
paris: Agentes, et consentientes, pari poena puniendi.
  Whitney, Emblemes, Leyden, 1586, p.054a
partio: Mediocribus utere partis.
  Whitney, Emblemes, Leyden, 1586, p.039
parvus: De parvis, grandis aceruus erit.
  Whitney, Emblemes, Leyden, 1586, p.088
patior: Vincit qui patitur.
  Whitney, Emblemes, Leyden, 1586, p.220
patria: Pietas in patriam.
  Whitney, Emblemes, Leyden, 1586, p.111
patria: Patria cuique chara.
  Whitney, Emblemes, Leyden, 1586, p.200
paupertas: Paupertatem summis ingeniis obesse ne
    provehantur.
  Whitney, Emblemes, Leyden, 1586, p.152
pax: Ex bello, pax.
  Whitney, Emblemes, Leyden, 1586, p.138a
pax: In pace de bello.
  Whitney, Emblemes, Leyden, 1586, p.153b
pecco: Alius peccat, alius plectitur.
  Whitney, Emblemes, Leyden, 1586, p.056
penna: Nil penna, sed usus.
  Whitney, Emblemes, Leyden, 1586, p.051b
penna: Pennae gloria perennis.
  Whitney, Emblemes, Leyden, 1586, p.196
pereo: In eum qui truculentia suorum perierit.
  Whitney, Emblemes, Leyden, 1586, p.090
perfidus: Perfidus familiaris.
  Whitney, Emblemes, Leyden, 1586, p.141
periculum: Aliena pericula, cautiones nostrae.
  Whitney, Emblemes, Leyden, 1586, p.154
pernicies: Indulgentia parentum, filiorum pernicies.
  Whitney, Emblemes, Leyden, 1586, p.155

perversus: Perversa iudicia.
  Whitney, Emblemes, Leyden, 1586, p.218a
pes: Quae ante pedes.
  Whitney, Emblemes, Leyden, 1586, p.064
pessimus: Dissidia inter aequales, pessima.
  Whitney, Emblemes, Leyden, 1586, p.005
petra: Petre, imitare petram.
  Whitney, Emblemes, Leyden, 1586, p.096
pietas: Pietas in patriam.
  Whitney, Emblemes, Leyden, 1586, p.111
pietas: Pietas filiorum in parentes.
  Whitney, Emblemes, Leyden, 1586, p.163
plecto: Alius peccat, alius plectitur.
  Whitney, Emblemes, Leyden, 1586, p.056
pluma: Venter, pluma, Venus, laudem fugiunt.
  Whitney, Emblemes, Leyden, 1586, p.042
poena: In poenam sectatur et umbra.
  Whitney, Emblemes, Leyden, 1586, p.032
poena: Poena sequens.
  Whitney, Emblemes, Leyden, 1586, p.041
poena: Agentes, et consentientes, pari poena puniendi.
  Whitney, Emblemes, Leyden, 1586, p.054a
poeta: Insignia poetarum.
  Whitney, Emblemes, Leyden, 1586, p.126
pondus: Mihi pondera, luxus.
  Whitney, Emblemes, Leyden, 1586, p.023
potens: Potentissimus affectus, amor.
  Whitney, Emblemes, Leyden, 1586, p.063
potentia: Potentia amoris.
  Whitney, Emblemes, Leyden, 1586, p.182a
potestas: Celsae potestatis species.
  Whitney, Emblemes, Leyden, 1586, p.116
poto: Sobrie potandum.
  Whitney, Emblemes, Leyden, 1586, p.125
praecox: Praecocia non diuturna.
  Whitney, Emblemes, Leyden, 1586, p.173
praeposterus: Praepostera fides.
  Whitney, Emblemes, Leyden, 1586, p.080
praesentia: Minuit praesentia famam.
  Whitney, Emblemes, Leyden, 1586, p.020
praesto: In eos qui multa promittunt, et nihil praestant.
  Whitney, Emblemes, Leyden, 1586, p.162
probo: Sic probantur.
  Whitney, Emblemes, Leyden, 1586, p.224a
prodigo: Ei, qui semel sua prodegerit, aliena credi non
    oportere.
  Whitney, Emblemes, Leyden, 1586, p.033
proles: Caecus amor prolis.
  Whitney, Emblemes, Leyden, 1586, p.188a
promitto: In eos qui multa promittunt, et nihil praestant.
  Whitney, Emblemes, Leyden, 1586, p.162
prospicio: Respice, et prospice.
  Whitney, Emblemes, Leyden, 1586, p.108
prosum: Dum vivo, prosum.
  Whitney, Emblemes, Leyden, 1586, p.077b
proveho: Paupertatem summis ingeniis obesse ne
    provehantur.
  Whitney, Emblemes, Leyden, 1586, p.152
providentia: Providentia.
  Whitney, Emblemes, Leyden, 1586, p.003
prudens: Prudentes vino abstinent.
  Whitney, Emblemes, Leyden, 1586, p.133
prudens: Usus libri, non lectio prudentes facit.
  Whitney, Emblemes, Leyden, 1586, p.171
pulchritudo: Pulchritudo vincit.
  Whitney, Emblemes, Leyden, 1586, p.182b
pulchritudo: Pulchritudo sine fructu.
  Whitney, Emblemes, Leyden, 1586, p.205
punio: Agentes, et consentientes, pari poena puniendi.
  Whitney, Emblemes, Leyden, 1586, p.054a
quaero: Quaere adolescens, utere senex.
  Whitney, Emblemes, Leyden, 1586, p.050b
quatuor: In quatuor anni tempora.
  Whitney, Emblemes, Leyden, 1586, p.054b
rabies: Furor et rabies.

Whitney, Emblemes, Leyden, 1586, p.045
redimo: Aere quandoque salutem redimendam.
  Whitney, Emblemes, Leyden, 1586, p.035
referendo:
  Whitney, Emblemes, Leyden, 1586,
religio: Non tibi, sed Religioni.
  Whitney, Emblemes, Leyden, 1586, p.008
remedium: Remedium tempestivum sit.
  Whitney, Emblemes, Leyden, 1586, p.076b
requiesco: Interdum requiescendum.
  Whitney, Emblemes, Leyden, 1586, p.103
res: Nimium rebus ne fide secundis.
  Whitney, Emblemes, Leyden, 1586, p.059
res: Animus, non res.
  Whitney, Emblemes, Leyden, 1586, p.198
res: Tunc tua res agitur, paries cum proximus ardet.
  Whitney, Emblemes, Leyden, 1586, p.208
respicio: Respice, et prospice.
  Whitney, Emblemes, Leyden, 1586, p.108
revocabilis: Verbum emissum non est revocabile.
  Whitney, Emblemes, Leyden, 1586, p.180
ridiculus: Ridicula ambitio.
  Whitney, Emblemes, Leyden, 1586, p.084
sacer: Auri sacra fames quid non?
  Whitney, Emblemes, Leyden, 1586, p.179
saeculum: Avaritia huius saeculi.
  Whitney, Emblemes, Leyden, 1586, p.204
sagino: Stultitia sua seipsum saginari.
  Whitney, Emblemes, Leyden, 1586, p.098a
salus: Aere quandoque salutem redimendam.
  Whitney, Emblemes, Leyden, 1586, p.035
sanus: Murus aeneus, sana conscientia.
  Whitney, Emblemes, Leyden, 1586, p.067
sapiens: Dicta septem sapientium.
  Whitney, Emblemes, Leyden, 1586, p.130
sapio: Sero sapiunt Phryges.
  Whitney, Emblemes, Leyden, 1586, p.077a
sapio: Noli altum sapere.
  Whitney, Emblemes, Leyden, 1586, p.078
scribo: Scribit in marmore laesus.
  Whitney, Emblemes, Leyden, 1586, p.183b
scrinium: Animi scrinium servitus.
  Whitney, Emblemes, Leyden, 1586, p.101
scriptum: Scripta manent.
  Whitney, Emblemes, Leyden, 1586, p.131
scriptum: Scripta non temere edenda.
  Whitney, Emblemes, Leyden, 1586, p.185
secto: In poenam sectatur et umbra.
  Whitney, Emblemes, Leyden, 1586, p.032
secundus: Nimium rebus ne fide secundis.
  Whitney, Emblemes, Leyden, 1586, p.059
senex: Quaere adolescens, utere senex.
  Whitney, Emblemes, Leyden, 1586, p.050b
sensus: Varii hominum sensus.
  Whitney, Emblemes, Leyden, 1586, p.046
septem: Dicta septem sapientium.
  Whitney, Emblemes, Leyden, 1586, p.130
sequor: Poena sequens.
  Whitney, Emblemes, Leyden, 1586, p.041
sequor: In eos, qui, proximioribus spretis remotiora
    sequuntur.
  Whitney, Emblemes, Leyden, 1586, p.157
sequor: Quae sequimur fugimus.
  Whitney, Emblemes, Leyden, 1586, p.199
sero: Sero sapiunt Phryges.
  Whitney, Emblemes, Leyden, 1586, p.077a
serpens: In sinu alere serpentem.
  Whitney, Emblemes, Leyden, 1586, p.189a
servio: Nemo potest duobus dominis servire.
  Whitney, Emblemes, Leyden, 1586, p.223
servitus: Animi scrinium servitus.
  Whitney, Emblemes, Leyden, 1586, p.101
silentium: Silentium.
  Whitney, Emblemes, Leyden, 1586, p.060
simultas: Intestinae simultates.

Whitney, Emblemes, Leyden, 1586, p.007
sinus: In sinu alere serpentem.

Whitney, Emblemes, Leyden, 1586, p.189a
sobrie: Sobrie potandum.

Whitney, Emblemes, Leyden, 1586, p.125
sol: Sol non occidat super iracundiam vestram.

Whitney, Emblemes, Leyden, 1586, p.216b
sors: Otium sortem exspectat.

Whitney, Emblemes, Leyden, 1586, p.026
sors: In sortis suae contemptores.

Whitney, Emblemes, Leyden, 1586, p.102
species: Celsae potestatis species.

Whitney, Emblemes, Leyden, 1586, p.116
specto: Sic spectanda fides.

Whitney, Emblemes, Leyden, 1586, p.139a
sperno: In eos, qui, proximioribus spretis remotiora
   sequuntur.

Whitney, Emblemes, Leyden, 1586, p.157
spero: Illicitum non sperandum.

Whitney, Emblemes, Leyden, 1586, p.139b
spes: Desiderium spe vacuum.

Whitney, Emblemes, Leyden, 1586, p.044
spes: Spes vana.

Whitney, Emblemes, Leyden, 1586, p.191a
status: Stultorum quanto status sublimior, tanto
   manifestior turpitudo.

Whitney, Emblemes, Leyden, 1586, p.190a
sto: Te stante, virebo.

Whitney, Emblemes, Leyden, 1586, p.001
strenuus: Strenuorum immortale nomen.

Whitney, Emblemes, Leyden, 1586, p.193
studiosus: In studiosum captum amore.

Whitney, Emblemes, Leyden, 1586, p.135
studium: Studiis invigilandum.

Whitney, Emblemes, Leyden, 1586, p.172
stultitia: Stultitia sua seipsum saginari.

Whitney, Emblemes, Leyden, 1586, p.098a
stultus: Cuncta complecti velle, stultum.

Whitney, Emblemes, Leyden, 1586, p.055b
stultus: Stultorum quanto status sublimior, tanto
   manifestior turpitudo.

Whitney, Emblemes, Leyden, 1586, p.190a
subicio: Iniuriis, infirmitas subiecta.

Whitney, Emblemes, Leyden, 1586, p.052b
sui: Amor sui.

Whitney, Emblemes, Leyden, 1586, p.149
summus: Res humanae in summo declinant.

Whitney, Emblemes, Leyden, 1586, p.011
superbia: Superbiae ultio.

Whitney, Emblemes, Leyden, 1586, p.013
supero: Fortuna virtutem superans.

Whitney, Emblemes, Leyden, 1586, p.070
supersum: Superest quod supra est.

Whitney, Emblemes, Leyden, 1586, p.225
tabesco: Curis tabescimus omnes.

Whitney, Emblemes, Leyden, 1586, p.025
taceo: Video, et taceo.

Whitney, Emblemes, Leyden, 1586, p.061
taceo: Audi, tace, fuge.

Whitney, Emblemes, Leyden, 1586, p.191b
telum: Durum telum necessitas.

Whitney, Emblemes, Leyden, 1586, p.036
temere: Scripta non temere edenda.

Whitney, Emblemes, Leyden, 1586, p.185
temeritas: Temeritas.

Whitney, Emblemes, Leyden, 1586, p.006
tempestivus: Remedium tempestivum sit.

Whitney, Emblemes, Leyden, 1586, p.076b
tempus: Veritas temporis filia.

Whitney, Emblemes, Leyden, 1586, p.004
tempus: In quatuor anni tempora.

Whitney, Emblemes, Leyden, 1586, p.054b
tempus: Cum tempore mutamur.

Whitney, Emblemes, Leyden, 1586, p.167
tempus: Tempore cuncta mitiora.

Whitney, Emblemes, Leyden, 1586, p.206
tempus: Tempus omnia terminat.

Whitney, Emblemes, Leyden, 1586, p.230
termino: Tempus omnia terminat.

Whitney, Emblemes, Leyden, 1586, p.230
tormentum: In amore tormentum.

Whitney, Emblemes, Leyden, 1586, p.219
transformo: Homines voluptatibus transformantur.

Whitney, Emblemes, Leyden, 1586, p.082
truculentia: In eum qui truculentia suorum perierit.

Whitney, Emblemes, Leyden, 1586, p.090
tu: Non tibi, sed Religioni.

Whitney, Emblemes, Leyden, 1586, p.008
tuba: Noli tuba canere Eleemosynam.

Whitney, Emblemes, Leyden, 1586, p.224b
turpis: Turpibus exitium.

Whitney, Emblemes, Leyden, 1586, p.021
turpitudo: Stultorum quanto status sublimior, tanto
   manifestior turpitudo.

Whitney, Emblemes, Leyden, 1586, p.190a
tutus: Nusquam tuta fides.

Whitney, Emblemes, Leyden, 1586, p.150
ultio: Superbiae ultio.

Whitney, Emblemes, Leyden, 1586, p.013
umbra: In poenam sectatur et umbra.

Whitney, Emblemes, Leyden, 1586, p.032
umbra: Mulier umbra viri.

Whitney, Emblemes, Leyden, 1586, p.218b
unicus: Unica semper avis.

Whitney, Emblemes, Leyden, 1586, p.177
unitus: Virtus unita, valet.

Whitney, Emblemes, Leyden, 1586, p.072
usus: Nil penna, sed usus.

Whitney, Emblemes, Leyden, 1586, p.051b
usus: Dura usu molliora.

Whitney, Emblemes, Leyden, 1586, p.156b
usus: Usus libri, non lectio prudentes facit.

Whitney, Emblemes, Leyden, 1586, p.171
uterque: In utrumque paratus.

Whitney, Emblemes, Leyden, 1586, p.066
utilitas: Ex damno alterius, alterius utilitas.

Whitney, Emblemes, Leyden, 1586, p.119
utor: Mediocribus utere partis.

Whitney, Emblemes, Leyden, 1586, p.039
utor: Quaere adolescens, utere senex.

Whitney, Emblemes, Leyden, 1586, p.050b
uxor: Post fata; uxor morosa, etiam discors.

Whitney, Emblemes, Leyden, 1586, p.158
uxorius: Uxoriae virtutes.

Whitney, Emblemes, Leyden, 1586, p.093b
vacuus: Desiderium spe vacuum.

Whitney, Emblemes, Leyden, 1586, p.044
valeo: Virtus unita, valet.

Whitney, Emblemes, Leyden, 1586, p.072
vanus: Spes vana.

Whitney, Emblemes, Leyden, 1586, p.191a
varius: Varii hominum sensus.

Whitney, Emblemes, Leyden, 1586, p.046
venenum: Saepius in auro bibitur venenum.

Whitney, Emblemes, Leyden, 1586, p.079
venter: Venter, pluma, Venus, laudem fugiunt.

Whitney, Emblemes, Leyden, 1586, p.042
ver: Dum aetatis ver agitur: consule brumae.

Whitney, Emblemes, Leyden, 1586, p.159
verbum: Nec verbo, nec facto, quenquam laedendum.

Whitney, Emblemes, Leyden, 1586, p.019
verbum: Verbum emissum non est revocabile.

Whitney, Emblemes, Leyden, 1586, p.180
veritas: Veritas invicta.

Whitney, Emblemes, Leyden, 1586, p.166a
vicinus: Aliquid mali propter vicinum malum.

Whitney, Emblemes, Leyden, 1586, p.164
victoria: In victoriam dolo partam.

Whitney, Emblemes, Leyden, 1586, p.030
victoria: Constantia comes victoriae.

PROPER NOUN INDEX (LATIN MOTTO)

ENGLISH MOTTO INDEX (TRANSLATIONS)

fool: Entrust trifles to fools.
Whitney, Emblemes, Leyden, 1586, p.081
fool: The higher the status of fools, the more manifest
is their baseness.
Whitney, Emblemes, Leyden, 1586, p.190a
foolish: It is foolish to wish to encompass all things.
Whitney, Emblemes, Leyden, 1586, p.055b
foolishness: To glut oneself in one's own foolishness.
Whitney, Emblemes, Leyden, 1586, p.098a
foot: Things at our feet.
Whitney, Emblemes, Leyden, 1586, p.064
force: Not by deceit, but by force.
Whitney, Emblemes, Leyden, 1586, p.058
foresight: Foresight.
Whitney, Emblemes, Leyden, 1586, p.003
fortune: Fortune vanquishing virtue.
Whitney, Emblemes, Leyden, 1586, p.070
fortune: Fortune helps the brave.
Whitney, Emblemes, Leyden, 1586, p.117
forwards: Look backwards and forwards.
Whitney, Emblemes, Leyden, 1586, p.108
four: On the four seasons of the year.
Whitney, Emblemes, Leyden, 1586, p.054b
friend: The perfidious friend.
Whitney, Emblemes, Leyden, 1586, p.141
friend: There is no wrong done to a false friend.
Whitney, Emblemes, Leyden, 1586, p.226a
friendship: Friendship enduring even after death.
Whitney, Emblemes, Leyden, 1586, p.062
friendship: Feigned friendship to be avoided.
Whitney, Emblemes, Leyden, 1586, p.124
fruit: Beauty without fruit.
Whitney, Emblemes, Leyden, 1586, p.205
fury: Fury and madness.
Whitney, Emblemes, Leyden, 1586, p.045
futile: A futile effort.
Whitney, Emblemes, Leyden, 1586, p.213
game: Gaming, grief, gluttony.
Whitney, Emblemes, Leyden, 1586, p.017
garrulousness: Garrulousness.
Whitney, Emblemes, Leyden, 1586, p.050a
generation: The avarice of this generation.
Whitney, Emblemes, Leyden, 1586, p.204
ghost: One must not struggle with ghosts.
Whitney, Emblemes, Leyden, 1586, p.127
gift: Gifts of enemies are unlucky.
Whitney, Emblemes, Leyden, 1586, p.037
give: He gives twice who gives quickly.
Whitney, Emblemes, Leyden, 1586, p.190b
glory: The glory everlasting of the pen.
Whitney, Emblemes, Leyden, 1586, p.196
glory: Glory to God alone.
Whitney, Emblemes, Leyden, 1586, p.228
glut: To glut oneself in one's own foolishness.
Whitney, Emblemes, Leyden, 1586, p.098a
glutton: A small kitchen, does not suffice for two
gluttons.
Whitney, Emblemes, Leyden, 1586, p.055a
gluttony: Gaming, grief, gluttony.
Whitney, Emblemes, Leyden, 1586, p.017
gluttony: Captured by gluttony.
Whitney, Emblemes, Leyden, 1586, p.128
go: Where the gods call, we must go.
Whitney, Emblemes, Leyden, 1586, p.002
god: Where the gods call, we must go.
Whitney, Emblemes, Leyden, 1586, p.002
gold: Poison is more often drunk in gold.
Whitney, Emblemes, Leyden, 1586, p.079
gold: What does accursed greed for gold not drive men to
do?
Whitney, Emblemes, Leyden, 1586, p.179
golden: Golden shackles.
Whitney, Emblemes, Leyden, 1586, p.202
good: While I live, I do good.
Whitney, Emblemes, Leyden, 1586, p.077b

good: Evil for good.
Whitney, Emblemes, Leyden, 1586, p.153a
grass: The snake hides in the grass.
Whitney, Emblemes, Leyden, 1586, p.024
great: From little things, a great sheaf will come.
Whitney, Emblemes, Leyden, 1586, p.088
greed: What does accursed greed for gold not drive men
to do?
Whitney, Emblemes, Leyden, 1586, p.179
grief: Gaming, grief, gluttony.
Whitney, Emblemes, Leyden, 1586, p.017
guile: On victory gained by guile.
Whitney, Emblemes, Leyden, 1586, p.030
happily: Bravely and happily.
Whitney, Emblemes, Leyden, 1586, p.115
happiness: On momentary happiness.
Whitney, Emblemes, Leyden, 1586, p.034
hard: Necessity is a hard weapon.
Whitney, Emblemes, Leyden, 1586, p.036
harm: Harm because of an evil neighbour.
Whitney, Emblemes, Leyden, 1586, p.164
harmful: On fertility that is harmful to itself.
Whitney, Emblemes, Leyden, 1586, p.174
harshness: On him who will perish from the harshness
of his own.
Whitney, Emblemes, Leyden, 1586, p.090
haste: Hasten slowly.
Whitney, Emblemes, Leyden, 1586, p.121
haste: One must make haste.
Whitney, Emblemes, Leyden, 1586, p.188b
hatred: Blind hatred.
Whitney, Emblemes, Leyden, 1586, p.031
hay: All flesh is hay.
Whitney, Emblemes, Leyden, 1586, p.217
help: Mutual help.
Whitney, Emblemes, Leyden, 1586, p.065
help: Unexpected help.
Whitney, Emblemes, Leyden, 1586, p.113
help: Fortune helps the brave.
Whitney, Emblemes, Leyden, 1586, p.117
hide: The snake hides in the grass.
Whitney, Emblemes, Leyden, 1586, p.024
hinder: Poverty hinders the greatest talents from
advancing.
Whitney, Emblemes, Leyden, 1586, p.152
homeland: One's homeland is dear to each.
Whitney, Emblemes, Leyden, 1586, p.200
honey: Bitterness in honey.
Whitney, Emblemes, Leyden, 1586, p.147
hope: Desire void of hope.
Whitney, Emblemes, Leyden, 1586, p.044
hope: The unlawful should not be hoped for.
Whitney, Emblemes, Leyden, 1586, p.139b
hope: Vain hope .
Whitney, Emblemes, Leyden, 1586, p.191a
human: At their summit, human affairs decline.
Whitney, Emblemes, Leyden, 1586, p.011
human: On human life.
Whitney, Emblemes, Leyden, 1586, p.014
humbled: He who exalts himself will be humbled.
Whitney, Emblemes, Leyden, 1586, p.216a
humorous: Of the envious and the avaricious, in a
humorous tale.
Whitney, Emblemes, Leyden, 1586, p.095
husband: A woman is the shadow of her husband.
Whitney, Emblemes, Leyden, 1586, p.218b
hypocrite: Almost the same, on hypocrites.
Whitney, Emblemes, Leyden, 1586, p.226b
idle: The idle are always needy.
Whitney, Emblemes, Leyden, 1586, p.175
idleness: Idleness awaits its destiny.
Whitney, Emblemes, Leyden, 1586, p.026
ignorant: On the ignorant rich man.
Whitney, Emblemes, Leyden, 1586, p.214
image: The image of a physician.

music: The music of Orpheus.
    Whitney, Emblemes, Leyden, 1586, p.186
mutual: Mutual help.
    Whitney, Emblemes, Leyden, 1586, p.065
nature: Industry corrects nature.
    Whitney, Emblemes, Leyden, 1586, p.092
necessity: Necessity is a hard weapon.
    Whitney, Emblemes, Leyden, 1586, p.036
needy: The idle are always needy.
    Whitney, Emblemes, Leyden, 1586, p.175
neighbour: Harm because of an evil neighbour.
    Whitney, Emblemes, Leyden, 1586, p.164
nourish: To nourish a snake in one's bosom.
    Whitney, Emblemes, Leyden, 1586, p.189a
offspring: Love for offspring.
    Whitney, Emblemes, Leyden, 1586, p.029
offspring: Love of one's offspring is blind.
    Whitney, Emblemes, Leyden, 1586, p.188a
old: Youth seek, the old man use.
    Whitney, Emblemes, Leyden, 1586, p.050b
oneself: Love of oneself.
    Whitney, Emblemes, Leyden, 1586, p.149
opinion: Various are the opinions of men.
    Whitney, Emblemes, Leyden, 1586, p.046
opportunity: On opportunity.
    Whitney, Emblemes, Leyden, 1586, p.181
pain: Pain from the medicine.
    Whitney, Emblemes, Leyden, 1586, p.156a
parent: The indulgence of parents is the bane of
    children.
    Whitney, Emblemes, Leyden, 1586, p.155
parent: The devotion of sons towards their parents.
    Whitney, Emblemes, Leyden, 1586, p.163
parent: Impunity is the parent of ferocity.
    Whitney, Emblemes, Leyden, 1586, p.222b
passion: The most powerful passion, love.
    Whitney, Emblemes, Leyden, 1586, p.063
peace: From war, peace.
    Whitney, Emblemes, Leyden, 1586, p.138a
peace: Concerning war in peace.
    Whitney, Emblemes, Leyden, 1586, p.153b
peevish: After death; a peevish and still contrary
    spouse.
    Whitney, Emblemes, Leyden, 1586, p.158
pen: The glory everlasting of the pen.
    Whitney, Emblemes, Leyden, 1586, p.196
perfidious: The perfidious friend.
    Whitney, Emblemes, Leyden, 1586, p.141
perish: On him who will perish from the harshness of his
    own.
    Whitney, Emblemes, Leyden, 1586, p.090
perseverance: Perseverance a companion of victory.
    Whitney, Emblemes, Leyden, 1586, p.137
perverse: Perverse judgements.
    Whitney, Emblemes, Leyden, 1586, p.218a
physician: The image of a physician.
    Whitney, Emblemes, Leyden, 1586, p.212
place: Not the place the men, but the man adorns the
    place.
    Whitney, Emblemes, Leyden, 1586, p.038
pleasure: Sorrowful pleasure.
    Whitney, Emblemes, Leyden, 1586, p.015
pleasure: Men are transformed by pleasures.
    Whitney, Emblemes, Leyden, 1586, p.082
poet: The arms of the poets.
    Whitney, Emblemes, Leyden, 1586, p.126
poison: Poison is more often drunk in gold.
    Whitney, Emblemes, Leyden, 1586, p.079
possession: Accept moderate possessions.
    Whitney, Emblemes, Leyden, 1586, p.039
poverty: Poverty hinders the greatest talents from
    advancing.
    Whitney, Emblemes, Leyden, 1586, p.152
power: The representation of exalted power.
    Whitney, Emblemes, Leyden, 1586, p.116

power: The power of love.
    Whitney, Emblemes, Leyden, 1586, p.182a
powerful: The most powerful passion, love.
    Whitney, Emblemes, Leyden, 1586, p.063
practice: Difficult things become easier with practice.
    Whitney, Emblemes, Leyden, 1586, p.156b
praise: The stomach, feather-bed and Venus run away
    from praise.
    Whitney, Emblemes, Leyden, 1586, p.042
precocious: Precocious things do not last long.
    Whitney, Emblemes, Leyden, 1586, p.173
preposterous: Preposterous faith.
    Whitney, Emblemes, Leyden, 1586, p.080
presence: Presence diminishes fame.
    Whitney, Emblemes, Leyden, 1586, p.020
prevail: Virtue united, prevails.
    Whitney, Emblemes, Leyden, 1586, p.072
pride: Vengeance on pride.
    Whitney, Emblemes, Leyden, 1586, p.013
prodigal: The riches of prodigals.
    Whitney, Emblemes, Leyden, 1586, p.053b
produce: On those who promise much and produce
    nothing.
    Whitney, Emblemes, Leyden, 1586, p.162
promise: On those who promise much and produce
    nothing.
    Whitney, Emblemes, Leyden, 1586, p.162
property: Mind, not property.
    Whitney, Emblemes, Leyden, 1586, p.198
property: Then your property is in danger, when the
    nearest wall is burning.
    Whitney, Emblemes, Leyden, 1586, p.208
prosperity: Do not trust prosperity too much.
    Whitney, Emblemes, Leyden, 1586, p.059
protection: Vigilance and protection.
    Whitney, Emblemes, Leyden, 1586, p.120
protector: With fate as protector.
    Whitney, Emblemes, Leyden, 1586, p.143
provide: Provide for the winter of your life while its
    spring is still here.
    Whitney, Emblemes, Leyden, 1586, p.159
prudent: Prudent men abstain from wine.
    Whitney, Emblemes, Leyden, 1586, p.133
publish: Writings should not be published rashly.
    Whitney, Emblemes, Leyden, 1586, p.185
punishment: For punishment even a shadow is pursued.
    Whitney, Emblemes, Leyden, 1586, p.032
punishment: Punishment following.
    Whitney, Emblemes, Leyden, 1586, p.041
punishment: Those acting and those consenting ought to
    bear equal punishment.
    Whitney, Emblemes, Leyden, 1586, p.054a
pursue: For punishment even a shadow is pursued.
    Whitney, Emblemes, Leyden, 1586, p.032
pursue: On those who, having spurned what is more
    near, pursue what is more remote.
    Whitney, Emblemes, Leyden, 1586, p.157
quickly: He gives twice who gives quickly.
    Whitney, Emblemes, Leyden, 1586, p.190b
rashly: Writings should not be published rashly.
    Whitney, Emblemes, Leyden, 1586, p.185
rashness: Rashness.
    Whitney, Emblemes, Leyden, 1586, p.006
read: The use, not the reading, of a book makes men
    wise.
    Whitney, Emblemes, Leyden, 1586, p.171
ready: Ready for both.
    Whitney, Emblemes, Leyden, 1586, p.066
recall: A word once spoken can not be recalled.
    Whitney, Emblemes, Leyden, 1586, p.180
rejected: Sloth to be rejected.
    Whitney, Emblemes, Leyden, 1586, p.085
religion: Not for you, but for religion.
    Whitney, Emblemes, Leyden, 1586, p.008
remain: The mind unmoved remains.

Whitney, Emblemes, Leyden, 1586, p.008
youth: Youth seek, the old man use.
Whitney, Emblemes, Leyden, 1586, p.050b
youth: On youth.
Whitney, Emblemes, Leyden, 1586, p.146

PROPER NOUN INDEX (ENGLISH MOTTO TRANSLATION)

Alciato: Almost the same as the preceding, from Alciato.
Whitney, Emblemes, Leyden, 1586, p.170
Bacchus: On the statue of Bacchus.
Whitney, Emblemes, Leyden, 1586, p.187
Christ: What Christ does not take, the treasury snatches.
Whitney, Emblemes, Leyden, 1586, p.151
Death: Jesting about death and love.
Whitney, Emblemes, Leyden, 1586, p.132
Ethiopian: To wash an Ethiopian.
Whitney, Emblemes, Leyden, 1586, p.057
God: If God is with us, who can prevail against us?
Whitney, Emblemes, Leyden, 1586, p.166b
God: Glory to God alone.
Whitney, Emblemes, Leyden, 1586, p.228
Homer: If, Homer, you do not bring anything, you will go outside.
Whitney, Emblemes, Leyden, 1586, p.168a
Lord: The Lord lives and sees.
Whitney, Emblemes, Leyden, 1586, p.229a
Love: Jesting about death and love.
Whitney, Emblemes, Leyden, 1586, p.132
Love: The power of love.
Whitney, Emblemes, Leyden, 1586, p.182a
Mars: By Mars and by art.
Whitney, Emblemes, Leyden, 1586, p.047
Orpheus: The music of Orpheus.
Whitney, Emblemes, Leyden, 1586, p.186
Paris: The judgment of Paris.
Whitney, Emblemes, Leyden, 1586, p.083
Peter: Peter, imitate the rock.
Whitney, Emblemes, Leyden, 1586, p.096
Phrygian: The Phrygians are wise too late.
Whitney, Emblemes, Leyden, 1586, p.077a
Siren: Sirens.
Whitney, Emblemes, Leyden, 1586, p.010
Theocritus: Almost the same from Theocritus.
Whitney, Emblemes, Leyden, 1586, p.148
Time: Truth, the daughter of Time.
Whitney, Emblemes, Leyden, 1586, p.004
Truth: Truth, the daughter of Time.
Whitney, Emblemes, Leyden, 1586, p.004
Venus: The stomach, feather-bed and Venus run away from praise.
Whitney, Emblemes, Leyden, 1586, p.042

MOTTO (ALPHABETICAL LIST)

Abstinentia.
Abstinence.
Whitney, Emblemes, Leyden, 1586, p.136
Aculei irriti.
Ineffectual stings.
Whitney, Emblemes, Leyden, 1586, p.221
Aere quandoque salutem redimendam.
Safety must sometimes be bought with money.
Whitney, Emblemes, Leyden, 1586, p.035
Aethiopem lavare.
To wash an Ethiopian.
Whitney, Emblemes, Leyden, 1586, p.057
Agentes, et consentientes, pari poena puniendi.
Those acting and those consenting ought to bear equal punishment.
Whitney, Emblemes, Leyden, 1586, p.054a
Aliena pericula, cautiones nostrae.

Others' dangers are our warnings.
Whitney, Emblemes, Leyden, 1586, p.154
Aliquid mali propter vicinum malum.
Harm because of an evil neighbour.
Whitney, Emblemes, Leyden, 1586, p.164
Alius peccat, alius plectitur.
One sins, the other is beaten.
Whitney, Emblemes, Leyden, 1586, p.056
Amicitia fucata vitanda.
Feigned friendship to be avoided.
Whitney, Emblemes, Leyden, 1586, p.124
Amicitia, etiam post mortem durans.
Friendship enduring even after death.
Whitney, Emblemes, Leyden, 1586, p.062
Amico ficto nulla fit iniuria.
There is no wrong done to a false friend.
Whitney, Emblemes, Leyden, 1586, p.226a
Amor in filios.
Love for offspring.
Whitney, Emblemes, Leyden, 1586, p.029
Amor sui.
Love of oneself.
Whitney, Emblemes, Leyden, 1586, p.149
Animi scrinium servitus.
Servitude, the cage of the soul.
Whitney, Emblemes, Leyden, 1586, p.101
Animus, non res.
Mind, not property.
Whitney, Emblemes, Leyden, 1586, p.198
Ars deluditur arte.
Craft deceived by craft.
Whitney, Emblemes, Leyden, 1586, p.161
Audaces fortuna iuvat.
Fortune helps the brave.
Whitney, Emblemes, Leyden, 1586, p.117
Audi, tace, fuge.
Listen, be silent, flee.
Whitney, Emblemes, Leyden, 1586, p.191b
Aureae compedes.
Golden shackles.
Whitney, Emblemes, Leyden, 1586, p.202
Auri sacra fames quid non?
What does accursed greed for gold not drive men to do?
Whitney, Emblemes, Leyden, 1586, p.179
Auxilio divino.
With divine aid.
Whitney, Emblemes, Leyden, 1586, p.203
Avaritia huius saeculi.
The avarice of this generation.
Whitney, Emblemes, Leyden, 1586, p.204
Avaritia.
Avarice.
Whitney, Emblemes, Leyden, 1586, p.074
Bilingues cavendi.
One should beware of the double-tongued.
Whitney, Emblemes, Leyden, 1586, p.160
Bis dat qui cito dat.
He gives twice who gives quickly.
Whitney, Emblemes, Leyden, 1586, p.190b
Bivium virtutis et vitii.
The crossroads of virtue and vice.
Whitney, Emblemes, Leyden, 1586, p.040
Caecum odium.
Blind hatred.
Whitney, Emblemes, Leyden, 1586, p.031
Caecus amor prolis.
Love of one's offspring is blind.
Whitney, Emblemes, Leyden, 1586, p.188a
Caelum, non animum.
The clime, not the mind.
Whitney, Emblemes, Leyden, 1586, p.178
Calumniam contra calumniatorem virtus repellit.
Virtue turns calumny back against the calumniator.
Whitney, Emblemes, Leyden, 1586, p.138b

Captivus, ob gulam.
   Captured by gluttony.
   Whitney, Emblemes, Leyden, 1586, p.128
Celsae potestatis species.
   The representation of exalted power.
   Whitney, Emblemes, Leyden, 1586, p.116
Concordia.
   Concord.
   Whitney, Emblemes, Leyden, 1586, p.076a
Constanter.
   Constantly.
   Whitney, Emblemes, Leyden, 1586, p.129
Constantia comes victoriae.
   Perseverance a companion of victory.
   Whitney, Emblemes, Leyden, 1586, p.137
Cum larvis non luctandum.
   One must not struggle with ghosts.
   Whitney, Emblemes, Leyden, 1586, p.127
Cum tempore mutamur.
   We change with time.
   Whitney, Emblemes, Leyden, 1586, p.167
Cuncta complecti velle, stultum.
   It is foolish to wish to encompass all things.
   Whitney, Emblemes, Leyden, 1586, p.055b
Curis tabescimus omnes.
   We are all consumed by cares.
   Whitney, Emblemes, Leyden, 1586, p.025
De Invido et Avaro, iocosum.
   Of the envious and the avaricious, in a humorous tale.
   Whitney, Emblemes, Leyden, 1586, p.095
De morte, et amore: Iocosum.
   Jesting about Death and Love.
   Whitney, Emblemes, Leyden, 1586, p.132
De parvis, grandis aceruus erit.
   From little things, a great sheaf will come.
   Whitney, Emblemes, Leyden, 1586, p.088
Desiderium spe vacuum.
   Desire void of hope.
   Whitney, Emblemes, Leyden, 1586, p.044
Desidiam abiiciendam.
   Sloth to be rejected.
   Whitney, Emblemes, Leyden, 1586, p.085
Dicta septem sapientium.
   The sayings of the seven wise-men.
   Whitney, Emblemes, Leyden, 1586, p.130
Dissidia inter aequales, pessima.
   Dissensions among equals are the worst.
   Whitney, Emblemes, Leyden, 1586, p.005
Dolor e medicina.
   Pain from the medicine.
   Whitney, Emblemes, Leyden, 1586, p.156a
Dolus in suos.
   Treachery towards one's own.
   Whitney, Emblemes, Leyden, 1586, p.027
Dominus vivit et videt.
   The Lord lives and sees.
   Whitney, Emblemes, Leyden, 1586, p.229a
Dum aetatis ver agitur: consule brumae.
   Provide for the winter of your life while its spring is
   still here.
   Whitney, Emblemes, Leyden, 1586, p.159
Dum potes vive.
   Live, while you can.
   Whitney, Emblemes, Leyden, 1586, p.097
Dum vivo, prosum.
   While I live, I do good.
   Whitney, Emblemes, Leyden, 1586, p.077b
Dura usu molliora.
   Difficult things become easier with practice.
   Whitney, Emblemes, Leyden, 1586, p.156b
Durum telum necessitas.
   Necessity is a hard weapon.
   Whitney, Emblemes, Leyden, 1586, p.036
Ei, qui semel sua prodegerit, aliena credi non oportere.
   He who has once squandered his own, ought not to be

trusted with another's.
   Whitney, Emblemes, Leyden, 1586, p.033
Ex bello, pax.
   From war, peace.
   Whitney, Emblemes, Leyden, 1586, p.138a
Ex damno alterius, alterius utilitas.
   One man's loss is another man's advantage.
   Whitney, Emblemes, Leyden, 1586, p.119
Ex maximo minimum.
   The least from the greatest.
   Whitney, Emblemes, Leyden, 1586, p.229b
Ex morbo medicina.
   Remedy from disease.
   Whitney, Emblemes, Leyden, 1586, p.209
Experientia docet.
   Experience teaches.
   Whitney, Emblemes, Leyden, 1586, p.009
Fatuis levia committito.
   Entrust trifles to fools.
   Whitney, Emblemes, Leyden, 1586, p.081
Fel in melle.
   Bitterness in honey.
   Whitney, Emblemes, Leyden, 1586, p.147
Fere simile ex Theocrito.
   Almost the same from Theocritus.
   Whitney, Emblemes, Leyden, 1586, p.148
Fere simile praecedenti, ex Alciato.
   Almost the same as the preceding, from Alciato.
   Whitney, Emblemes, Leyden, 1586, p.170
Fere simile, in Hypocritas.
   Almost the same, on hypocrites.
   Whitney, Emblemes, Leyden, 1586, p.226b
Feriunt summis fulmina montes.
   Lightning strikes the mountain tops.
   Whitney, Emblemes, Leyden, 1586, p.140
Festina lente.
   Hasten slowly.
   Whitney, Emblemes, Leyden, 1586, p.121
Fides non apparentium.
   Faith in things unseen.
   Whitney, Emblemes, Leyden, 1586, p.071
Fortissima minimis interdum cedunt.
   The strongest sometimes yield to the smallest.
   Whitney, Emblemes, Leyden, 1586, p.052a
Fortiter et feliciter.
   Bravely and happily.
   Whitney, Emblemes, Leyden, 1586, p.115
Fortuna virtutem superans.
   Fortune vanquishing virtue.
   Whitney, Emblemes, Leyden, 1586, p.070
Fraus meretur fraudem.
   Deceit deserves deceit.
   Whitney, Emblemes, Leyden, 1586, p.210
Frontis nulla fides.
   No faith in appearance.
   Whitney, Emblemes, Leyden, 1586, p.100
Frustra.
   In vain[1].
   Whitney, Emblemes, Leyden, 1586, p.012
Furor et rabies.
   Fury and madness.
   Whitney, Emblemes, Leyden, 1586, p.045
Garrulitas.
   Garrulousness.
   Whitney, Emblemes, Leyden, 1586, p.050a
Gratiam referendam.
   Favour to be repaid.
   Whitney, Emblemes, Leyden, 1586, p.073
Habet et bellum suas leges.
   Even war also has its laws.
   Whitney, Emblemes, Leyden, 1586, p.112
Homines voluptatibus transformantur.
   Men are transformed by pleasures.
   Whitney, Emblemes, Leyden, 1586, p.082
Homo homini lupus.

Man is a wolf to man.
Whitney, Emblemes, Leyden, 1586, p.144
Hosti etiam servanda fides.
Faith must be kept even to the enemy.
Whitney, Emblemes, Leyden, 1586, p.114
Illicitum non sperandum.
The unlawful should not be hoped for.
Whitney, Emblemes, Leyden, 1586, p.139b
Impar coniugium.
An unequal marriage.
Whitney, Emblemes, Leyden, 1586, p.099
Imparilitas.
Inequality.
Whitney, Emblemes, Leyden, 1586, p.207
Importunitas evitanda.
Importunity should be avoided.
Whitney, Emblemes, Leyden, 1586, p.192
Impunitas ferociae parens.
Impunity is the parent of ferocity.
Whitney, Emblemes, Leyden, 1586, p.222b
In amore tormentum.
Torment in love.
Whitney, Emblemes, Leyden, 1586, p.219
In Astrologos.
Against astrologers.
Whitney, Emblemes, Leyden, 1586, p.028
In auaros.
On misers.
Whitney, Emblemes, Leyden, 1586, p.018
In colores.
On colours
Whitney, Emblemes, Leyden, 1586, p.134
In copia minor error.
Lesser error in abundance.
Whitney, Emblemes, Leyden, 1586, p.142
In curiosos.
On the curious.
Whitney, Emblemes, Leyden, 1586, p.145
In desciscentes.
On those who degenerate.
Whitney, Emblemes, Leyden, 1586, p.189b
In dies meliora.
Better day by day.
Whitney, Emblemes, Leyden, 1586, p.053a
In divitem,indoctum.
On the ignorant rich man.
Whitney, Emblemes, Leyden, 1586, p.214
In eos qui multa promittunt, et nihil praestant.
On those who promise much and produce nothing.
Whitney, Emblemes, Leyden, 1586, p.162
In eos, qui, proximioribus spretis remotiora sequuntur.
On those who, having spurned what is more near,
pursue what is more remote.
Whitney, Emblemes, Leyden, 1586, p.157
In eum qui sibi ipsi damnum apparat.
On him who prepares loss for himself.
Whitney, Emblemes, Leyden, 1586, p.049
In eum qui truculentia suorum perierit.
On him who will perish from the harshness of his
own.
Whitney, Emblemes, Leyden, 1586, p.090
In foecunditatem, sibi ipsi damnosam.
On fertility that is harmful to itself.
Whitney, Emblemes, Leyden, 1586, p.174
In iuventam.
On youth.
Whitney, Emblemes, Leyden, 1586, p.146
In momentaneam felicitatem.
On momentary happiness.
Whitney, Emblemes, Leyden, 1586, p.034
In occasionem.
On opportunity.
Whitney, Emblemes, Leyden, 1586, p.181
In pace de bello.
Concerning war in peace.

Whitney, Emblemes, Leyden, 1586, p.153b
In poenam sectatur et umbra.
For punishment even a shadow is pursued.
Whitney, Emblemes, Leyden, 1586, p.032
In quatuor anni tempora.
On the four seasons of the year.
Whitney, Emblemes, Leyden, 1586, p.054b
In sinu alere serpentem.
To nourish a snake in one's bosom.
Whitney, Emblemes, Leyden, 1586, p.189a
In sortis suae contemptores.
On the despisers of their own lot.
Whitney, Emblemes, Leyden, 1586, p.102
In statuam Bacchi.
On the statue of Bacchus.
Whitney, Emblemes, Leyden, 1586, p.187
In studiosum captum amore.
A scholar captive of love.
Whitney, Emblemes, Leyden, 1586, p.135
In utrumque paratus.
Ready for both.
Whitney, Emblemes, Leyden, 1586, p.066
In victoriam dolo partam.
On victory gained by guile.
Whitney, Emblemes, Leyden, 1586, p.030
In vitam humanam.
On human life.
Whitney, Emblemes, Leyden, 1586, p.014
Inanis impetus.
A futile effort.
Whitney, Emblemes, Leyden, 1586, p.213
Indulgentia parentum, filiorum pernicies.
The indulgence of parents is the bane of children.
Whitney, Emblemes, Leyden, 1586, p.155
Industria naturam corrigit.
Industry corrects nature.
Whitney, Emblemes, Leyden, 1586, p.092
Infortunia nostra, alienis collata, leviora.
Our misfortunes, compared with those of others,
become lighter.
Whitney, Emblemes, Leyden, 1586, p.093a
Ingenium superat vires.
Talent overcomes strength.
Whitney, Emblemes, Leyden, 1586, p.168b
Inimicorum dona, infausta.
Gifts of enemies are unlucky.
Whitney, Emblemes, Leyden, 1586, p.037
Iniuriis, infirmitas subiecta.
Weakness is subject to wrongs.
Whitney, Emblemes, Leyden, 1586, p.052b
Insignia poetarum.
The arms[1] of the poets.
Whitney, Emblemes, Leyden, 1586, p.126
Insperatum auxilium.
Unexpected help.
Whitney, Emblemes, Leyden, 1586, p.113
Interdum requiescendum.
Sometimes we must rest.
Whitney, Emblemes, Leyden, 1586, p.103
Interiora vide.
Look within.
Whitney, Emblemes, Leyden, 1586, p.069
Interminabilis humanae vitae labor.
The unending labour of human life.
Whitney, Emblemes, Leyden, 1586, p.215
Intestinae simultates.
Internal dissensions.
Whitney, Emblemes, Leyden, 1586, p.007
Invidia integritatis assecla.
Envy the attendant of integrity.
Whitney, Emblemes, Leyden, 1586, p.118
Invidiae descriptio.
A description of envy.
Whitney, Emblemes, Leyden, 1586, p.094
Iudicium Paridis.

The judgement of Paris.
Whitney, Emblemes, Leyden, 1586, p.083
Labor irritus.
Labour in vain[1].
Whitney, Emblemes, Leyden, 1586, p.048
Latet anguis in herba.
The snake hides in the grass.
Whitney, Emblemes, Leyden, 1586, p.024
Ludus, luctus, luxus.
Gaming, grief, gluttony.
Whitney, Emblemes, Leyden, 1586, p.017
Luxuriosorum opes.
The riches of prodigals.
Whitney, Emblemes, Leyden, 1586, p.053b
Male parta male dilabuntur.
Ill-gotten, ill-spent.
Whitney, Emblemes, Leyden, 1586, p.169
Marte et arte.
By Mars and by art.
Whitney, Emblemes, Leyden, 1586, p.047
Maturandum.
One must make haste.
Whitney, Emblemes, Leyden, 1586, p.188b
Medici Icon.
The image of a physician.
Whitney, Emblemes, Leyden, 1586, p.212
Mediocribus utere partis.
Accept moderate possessions.
Whitney, Emblemes, Leyden, 1586, p.039
Mens immota manet.
The mind unmoved remains.
Whitney, Emblemes, Leyden, 1586, p.043
Mihi pondera, luxus.
Excess is a burden to me.
Whitney, Emblemes, Leyden, 1586, p.023
Minuit praesentia famam.
Presence diminishes fame.
Whitney, Emblemes, Leyden, 1586, p.020
Mortui divitiae.
A dead man's riches.
Whitney, Emblemes, Leyden, 1586, p.086
Mulier umbra viri.
A woman is the shadow of her husband.
Whitney, Emblemes, Leyden, 1586, p.218b
Murus aeneus, sana conscientia.
A wall of brass is a clear conscience.
Whitney, Emblemes, Leyden, 1586, p.067
Mutuum auxilium.
Mutual help.
Whitney, Emblemes, Leyden, 1586, p.065
Nec sibi, nec alteri.
Neither for himself nor for someone else.
Whitney, Emblemes, Leyden, 1586, p.184
Nec verbo, nec facto, quenquam laedendum.
Neither in word nor in deed should anyone be injured.
Whitney, Emblemes, Leyden, 1586, p.019
Neglecta virescunt.
Neglected things flourish.
Whitney, Emblemes, Leyden, 1586, p.222a
Nemo potest duobus dominis servire.
No one can serve two masters.
Whitney, Emblemes, Leyden, 1586, p.223
Nil penna, sed usus.
Not the wing, but the use.
Whitney, Emblemes, Leyden, 1586, p.051b
Nimium rebus ne fide secundis.
Do not trust prosperity too much.
Whitney, Emblemes, Leyden, 1586, p.059
Noli altum sapere.
Do not aim at lofty things.
Whitney, Emblemes, Leyden, 1586, p.078
Noli tuba canere Eleemosynam.
Do no trumpet your charity.
Whitney, Emblemes, Leyden, 1586, p.224b
Non dolo, sed vi.

Not by deceit, but by force.
Whitney, Emblemes, Leyden, 1586, p.058
Non locus virum, sed vir locum ornat.
Not the place the men, but the man adorns the place.
Whitney, Emblemes, Leyden, 1586, p.038
Non tibi, sed Religioni.
Not for you, but for religion.
Whitney, Emblemes, Leyden, 1586, p.008
Nullus dolus contra Casum.
No cunning against chance.
Whitney, Emblemes, Leyden, 1586, p.022
Nusquam tuta fides.
Nowhere is faith safe.
Whitney, Emblemes, Leyden, 1586, p.150
O vita, misero longa.
O life, long to the wretched.
Whitney, Emblemes, Leyden, 1586, p.075
Omnis caro foenum.
All flesh is hay.
Whitney, Emblemes, Leyden, 1586, p.217
Orphei Musica.
The music of Orpheus
Whitney, Emblemes, Leyden, 1586, p.186
Otiosi semper egentes.
The idle are always needy.
Whitney, Emblemes, Leyden, 1586, p.175
Otium sortem exspectat.
Idleness awaits its destiny.
Whitney, Emblemes, Leyden, 1586, p.026
Parvam culinam, duobus ganeonibus non sufficere.
A small kitchen, does not suffice for two gluttons.
Whitney, Emblemes, Leyden, 1586, p.055a
Patria cuique chara.
One's homeland is dear to each.
Whitney, Emblemes, Leyden, 1586, p.200
Paupertatem summis ingeniis obesse ne provehantur.
Poverty hinders the greatest talents from advancing.
Whitney, Emblemes, Leyden, 1586, p.152
Pennae gloria perennis.
The glory everlasting of the pen.
Whitney, Emblemes, Leyden, 1586, p.196
Perfidus familiaris.
The perfidious friend.
Whitney, Emblemes, Leyden, 1586, p.141
Perversa iudicia.
Perverse judgements.
Whitney, Emblemes, Leyden, 1586, p.218a
Petre, imitare petram.
Peter, imitate the rock.
Whitney, Emblemes, Leyden, 1586, p.096
Pietas filiorum in parentes.
The devotion of sons towards their parents.
Whitney, Emblemes, Leyden, 1586, p.163
Pietas in patriam.
Duty towards one's country.
Whitney, Emblemes, Leyden, 1586, p.111
Poena sequens.
Punishment following.
Whitney, Emblemes, Leyden, 1586, p.041
Post amara dulcia.
Sweet things come after bitter things.
Whitney, Emblemes, Leyden, 1586, p.165
Post fata; uxor morosa, etiam discors.
After death; a peevish and still contrary spouse.
Whitney, Emblemes, Leyden, 1586, p.158
Potentia amoris.
The power of Love.
Whitney, Emblemes, Leyden, 1586, p.182a
Potentissimus affectus, amor.
The most powerful passion, love.
Whitney, Emblemes, Leyden, 1586, p.063
Praecocia non diuturna.
Precocious things do not last[1] long.
Whitney, Emblemes, Leyden, 1586, p.173

Praepostera fides.
Preposterous faith.
Whitney, Emblemes, Leyden, 1586, p.080

Pro bono, malum.
Evil for good.
Whitney, Emblemes, Leyden, 1586, p.153a

Providentia.
Foresight.
Whitney, Emblemes, Leyden, 1586, p.003

Prudentes vino abstinent.
Prudent men abstain from wine.
Whitney, Emblemes, Leyden, 1586, p.133

Pulchritudo sine fructu.
Beauty without fruit.
Whitney, Emblemes, Leyden, 1586, p.205

Pulchritudo vincit.
Beauty conquers.
Whitney, Emblemes, Leyden, 1586, p.182b

Qua dij vocant, eundum.
Where the gods call, we must go.
Whitney, Emblemes, Leyden, 1586, p.002

Quae ante pedes.
Things at our feet.
Whitney, Emblemes, Leyden, 1586, p.064

Quae sequimur fugimus.
We flee what we follow.
Whitney, Emblemes, Leyden, 1586, p.199

Quaere adolescens, utere senex.
Youth seek, the old man use.
Whitney, Emblemes, Leyden, 1586, p.050b

Qui me alit me extinguit.
The one who nourishes me extinguishes me.
Whitney, Emblemes, Leyden, 1586, p.183a

Qui se exaltat, humiliabitur.
He who exalts himself will be humbled.
Whitney, Emblemes, Leyden, 1586, p.216a

Quod in te est, prome.
Bring forth what is in you.
Whitney, Emblemes, Leyden, 1586, p.087

Quod non capit Christus, rapit fiscus.
What Christ does not take, the treasury snatches.
Whitney, Emblemes, Leyden, 1586, p.151

Quod potes, tenta.
Try what you can.
Whitney, Emblemes, Leyden, 1586, p.016

Remedium tempestivum sit.
Let there be a timely remedy.
Whitney, Emblemes, Leyden, 1586, p.076b

Res humanae in summo declinant.
At their summit, human affairs decline.
Whitney, Emblemes, Leyden, 1586, p.011

Respice, et prospice.
Look backwards and forwards.
Whitney, Emblemes, Leyden, 1586, p.108

Ridicula ambitio.
Ridiculous ambition.
Whitney, Emblemes, Leyden, 1586, p.084

Saepius in auro bibitur venenum.
Poison is more often drunk in gold.
Whitney, Emblemes, Leyden, 1586, p.079

Scribit in marmore laesus.
Wronged, he writes on marble.
Whitney, Emblemes, Leyden, 1586, p.183b

Scripta manent.
Writings remain.
Whitney, Emblemes, Leyden, 1586, p.131

Scripta non temere edenda.
Writings should not be published rashly.
Whitney, Emblemes, Leyden, 1586, p.185

Semper praesto esse infortunia.
Misfortunes are always at hand.
Whitney, Emblemes, Leyden, 1586, p.176

Sero sapiunt Phryges.
The Phrygians are wise too late.
Whitney, Emblemes, Leyden, 1586, p.077a

Si Deus nobiscum, quis contra nos?
If God is with us, who can prevail against us?
Whitney, Emblemes, Leyden, 1586, p.166b

Si nihil attuleris, ibis Homere foras.
If, Homer, you do not bring anything, you will go
outside.
Whitney, Emblemes, Leyden, 1586, p.168a

Sic aetas fugit.
Thus does life flee.
Whitney, Emblemes, Leyden, 1586, p.227

Sic discerne.
Winnow it thus.
Whitney, Emblemes, Leyden, 1586, p.068

Sic probantur.
Thus are they tested.
Whitney, Emblemes, Leyden, 1586, p.224a

Sic spectanda fides.
Thus faith is to be tested.
Whitney, Emblemes, Leyden, 1586, p.139a

Silentium.
Silence.
Whitney, Emblemes, Leyden, 1586, p.060

Sine iustitia, confusio.
Without justice, confusion.
Whitney, Emblemes, Leyden, 1586, p.122

Sirenes.
Sirens.
Whitney, Emblemes, Leyden, 1586, p.010

Sobrie potandum.
One should drink moderately.
Whitney, Emblemes, Leyden, 1586, p.125

Sol non occidat super iracundiam vestram.
Let the sun not set on your anger.
Whitney, Emblemes, Leyden, 1586, p.216b

Soli Deo gloria.
Glory to God alone.
Whitney, Emblemes, Leyden, 1586, p.228

Spes vana.
Vain[1] hope .
Whitney, Emblemes, Leyden, 1586, p.191a

Strenuorum immortale nomen.
The fame of men of action is immortal.
Whitney, Emblemes, Leyden, 1586, p.193

Studiis invigilandum.
One must pay attention to studies.
Whitney, Emblemes, Leyden, 1586, p.172

Stultitia sua seipsum saginari.
To glut oneself in one's own foolishness.
Whitney, Emblemes, Leyden, 1586, p.098a

Stultorum quanto status sublimior, tanto manifestior
turpitudo.
The higher the status of fools, the more manifest is
their baseness.
Whitney, Emblemes, Leyden, 1586, p.190a

Superbiae ultio.
Vengeance on pride.
Whitney, Emblemes, Leyden, 1586, p.013

Superest quod supra est.
What is above lives on.
Whitney, Emblemes, Leyden, 1586, p.225

Te stante, virebo
With you standing, I shall flourish.
Whitney, Emblemes, Leyden, 1586, p.001

Tecum habita.
Abide by yourself.
Whitney, Emblemes, Leyden, 1586, p.091

Temeritas.
Rashness.
Whitney, Emblemes, Leyden, 1586, p.006

Tempore cuncta mitiora.
Everything becomes more mellower with time.
Whitney, Emblemes, Leyden, 1586, p.206

Tempus omnia terminat.
Time ends all things.
Whitney, Emblemes, Leyden, 1586, p.230

Tunc tua res agitur, paries cum proximus ardet.
>Then your property is in danger, when the nearest
>wall is burning.
>Whitney, Emblemes, Leyden, 1586, p.208

Turpibus exitium.
>Destruction to the shameless.
>Whitney, Emblemes, Leyden, 1586, p.021

Unica semper avis.
>The bird that is ever unique.
>Whitney, Emblemes, Leyden, 1586, p.177

Usus libri, non lectio prudentes facit.
>The use, not the reading, of a book makes men wise.
>Whitney, Emblemes, Leyden, 1586, p.171

Uxoriae virtutes.
>The virtues of wives.
>Whitney, Emblemes, Leyden, 1586, p.093b

Varii hominum sensus.
>Various are the opinions of men.
>Whitney, Emblemes, Leyden, 1586, p.046

Vel post mortem formidolosi.
>Those terrifying even after death.
>Whitney, Emblemes, Leyden, 1586, p.194

Venter, pluma, Venus, laudem fugiunt.
>The stomach, feather-bed and Venus run away from
>praise.
>Whitney, Emblemes, Leyden, 1586, p.042

Verbum emissum non est revocabile.
>A word once spoken can not be recalled.
>Whitney, Emblemes, Leyden, 1586, p.180

Veritas invicta.
>Unconquered truth.
>Whitney, Emblemes, Leyden, 1586, p.166a

Veritas temporis filia.
>Truth, the daughter of Time.
>Whitney, Emblemes, Leyden, 1586, p.004

Victoria cruenta.
>Bloody victory.
>Whitney, Emblemes, Leyden, 1586, p.195

Video, et taceo.
>I see, and I am silent.
>Whitney, Emblemes, Leyden, 1586, p.061

Vigilantia, et custodia.
>Vigilance and protection.
>Whitney, Emblemes, Leyden, 1586, p.120

Vincit qui patitur.
>He conquers who suffers.
>Whitney, Emblemes, Leyden, 1586, p.220

Vindice fato.
>With fate as protector.
>Whitney, Emblemes, Leyden, 1586, p.143

Virescit vulnere virtus.
>Virtue thrives from wounds.
>Whitney, Emblemes, Leyden, 1586, p.098b

Virtus unita, valet.
>Virtue united, prevails.
>Whitney, Emblemes, Leyden, 1586, p.072

Vita irrequieta.
>A restless life.
>Whitney, Emblemes, Leyden, 1586, p.089

Vitae, aut morti.
>For life, or for death.
>Whitney, Emblemes, Leyden, 1586, p.051a

Voluptas aerumnosa.
>Sorrowful pleasure.
>Whitney, Emblemes, Leyden, 1586, p.015

Zelotypia.
>Jealousy.
>Whitney, Emblemes, Leyden, 1586, p.211

bird→slay→deceive→warning→destroy
  Whitney, Emblemes, 1586, p.033
bird→necessity→popinjay→prate
  Whitney, Emblemes, 1586, p.036
bird→trust→name→teach
  Whitney, Emblemes, 1586, p.084
bird→bondage→fly→god
  Whitney, Emblemes, 1586, p.084
bird→shield→Phoebus→sacred
  Whitney, Emblemes, 1586, p.126
bird→net→fowler→pay
  Whitney, Emblemes, 1586, p.130
bird→wonder→live→sun
  Whitney, Emblemes, 1586, p.177
bird→hand→restrain→fly→vain[1]
  Whitney, Emblemes, 1586, p.180
bird→wing→defence→fish→fin
  Whitney, Emblemes, 1586, p.182b
bird→learned→wise→rude
  Whitney, Emblemes, 1586, p.186
birth→nature→shroud→greatness
  Whitney, Emblemes, 1586, p.086
birth→year→virtue→child
  Whitney, Emblemes, 1586, p.099
birth→death→Nestor→steal
  Whitney, Emblemes, 1586, p.167
birth→Jove→bless→grace
  Whitney, Emblemes, 1586, p.196
birth→earth→day→goal
  Whitney, Emblemes, 1586, p.227
bit→measure→way→rein
  Whitney, Emblemes, 1586, p.019
bit→rider→fool→steed
  Whitney, Emblemes, 1586, p.038
bite→angry→dog→stone
  Whitney, Emblemes, 1586, p.056
bite→lion→slander→defame→hare
  Whitney, Emblemes, 1586, p.127
bite→thrall→play→bark
  Whitney, Emblemes, 1586, p.140
bite→tree→save→life
  Whitney, Emblemes, 1586, p.153a
bite→apostle→Paul→viper→deadly
  Whitney, Emblemes, 1586, p.166b
bitter→fruit→mock→scorner
  Whitney, Emblemes, 1586, p.142
blab→secret→suffice
  Whitney, Emblemes, 1586, p.012
blab→Sinon→sycophant [= pickthank]→
  pickthank [= sycophant]
  Whitney, Emblemes, 1586, p.150
black→religious→art→mourner
  Whitney, Emblemes, 1586, p.134
black→bridle→pursue→night
  Whitney, Emblemes, 1586, p.227
blackamoor [= moor[1]]→wash→nature→
  power→moor[1] [= blackamoor]
  Whitney, Emblemes, 1586, p.057
blade→cutthroat→pay→swear
  Whitney, Emblemes, 1586, p.017
blade→heart→sword→flee
  Whitney, Emblemes, 1586, p.070
blade→grime→cool→bilbo
  Whitney, Emblemes, 1586, p.145
blade→anvil→hazard→force
  Whitney, Emblemes, 1586, p.192
blame→mother→tyrant→serpent
  Whitney, Emblemes, 1586, p.029
blame→king→house→slow→home
  Whitney, Emblemes, 1586, p.091
blame→content→lot→God→nature
  Whitney, Emblemes, 1586, p.093a
blast→leaf→fly→tree
  Whitney, Emblemes, 1586, p.067
blast→marble→age→last[1]
  Whitney, Emblemes, 1586, p.173

bleed→deadly→grief→noble
  Whitney, Emblemes, 1586, p.070
bleed→pleasant→smell→venture
  Whitney, Emblemes, 1586, p.165
blemish→desert→death→time
  Whitney, Emblemes, 1586, p.117
bless→patient→Job→dunghill→God
  Whitney, Emblemes, 1586, p.035
bless→wife→life→God
  Whitney, Emblemes, 1586, p.079
bless→abundance→wealth→win→God
  Whitney, Emblemes, 1586, p.088
bless→subdue→Pompey→fortune
  Whitney, Emblemes, 1586, p.116
bless→time→crime→God
  Whitney, Emblemes, 1586, p.136
bless→book→west→shine→salvation
  Whitney, Emblemes, 1586, p.166a
bless→fear→good→pray
  Whitney, Emblemes, 1586, p.176
bless→grace→birth→Jove
  Whitney, Emblemes, 1586, p.196
blind→Ajax→sword→Lynceus→eye
  Whitney, Emblemes, 1586, p.037
blind→lame→direct→mutual
  Whitney, Emblemes, 1586, p.065
blind→spiteful→honest
  Whitney, Emblemes, 1586, p.095
blind→house→garnish→goods→eye
  Whitney, Emblemes, 1586, p.156a
blind→estate[1]→hate→poor
  Whitney, Emblemes, 1586, p.198
blindness→try[1]→prove→devise→
  esteem
  Whitney, Emblemes, 1586, p.149
bliss→virtue→port
  Whitney, Emblemes, 1586, p.043
bliss→pine[1]→lean→pale
  Whitney, Emblemes, 1586, p.094
bliss→sting→harm→reverence
  Whitney, Emblemes, 1586, p.200
block→embrace→end[1]→help→
  senseless
  Whitney, Emblemes, 1586, p.062
block→foot→crush→stock→ape
  Whitney, Emblemes, 1586, p.145
blood→care→forget→spill
  Whitney, Emblemes, 1586, p.049
blood→waste→substance→beg
  Whitney, Emblemes, 1586, p.064
blood→tongue→pen→breast
  Whitney, Emblemes, 1586, p.087
blood→match→goods→guilt→child
  Whitney, Emblemes, 1586, p.099
blood→rancour→hope→prey
  Whitney, Emblemes, 1586, p.119
blood→knife→truth→mercy→justice
  Whitney, Emblemes, 1586, p.121
blood→virtue→goods→life
  Whitney, Emblemes, 1586, p.122
blood→kill→wolf→wood[1]→prey
  Whitney, Emblemes, 1586, p.162
blood→price→captain→spoil
  Whitney, Emblemes, 1586, p.195
blood→God→ship→foe
  Whitney, Emblemes, 1586, p.203
blood [= offspring]→good→trust→
  hate→offspring [= blood]
  Whitney, Emblemes, 1586, p.033
bloodshed→God→Justice→paradise
  Whitney, Emblemes, 1586, p.122
bloody→home→civil→sword
  Whitney, Emblemes, 1586, p.007
bloody→thought→Agamemnon→shield
  Whitney, Emblemes, 1586, p.045
bloody→broil→hate→land

  Whitney, Emblemes, 1586, p.076a
bloody→honey→soldier→fruit
  Whitney, Emblemes, 1586, p.138a
bloom→pillar→spire→ivy
  Whitney, Emblemes, 1586, p.001
bloom→root→rot→frost
  Whitney, Emblemes, 1586, p.034
bloom→thorn→briar→lily
  Whitney, Emblemes, 1586, p.221
blow→fire→cold→hand
  Whitney, Emblemes, 1586, p.160
blue→sea→scarlet→mariner
  Whitney, Emblemes, 1586, p.134
boar→tusk→lion→roar
  Whitney, Emblemes, 1586, p.100
boar→tusk→fox→foe
  Whitney, Emblemes, 1586, p.153b
board[1]→head→sword→roof
  Whitney, Emblemes, 1586, p.102
boast→fade→fortune→wheel
  Whitney, Emblemes, 1586, p.034
boast→limb→disdain→taste→tart
  Whitney, Emblemes, 1586, p.098a
boil→broth→brink→fall→fire
  Whitney, Emblemes, 1586, p.216a
bold→stag→transform→hound
  Whitney, Emblemes, 1586, p.015
bold→raze→proof→deed
  Whitney, Emblemes, 1586, p.100
bold→Attilius→Africa→consul
  Whitney, Emblemes, 1586, p.114
bold→Marcus→Sergius→Roman
  Whitney, Emblemes, 1586, p.115
bold→fear→wound→battle
  Whitney, Emblemes, 1586, p.117
bold→arm[1]→learning→strife→strong
  Whitney, Emblemes, 1586, p.120
bold→Brasidas→force→foe
  Whitney, Emblemes, 1586, p.141
bold→art→hard→trial[1]→easy
  Whitney, Emblemes, 1586, p.156b
bold→tongue→wit→grief
  Whitney, Emblemes, 1586, p.180
bold→fierce→grace→woman→face
  Whitney, Emblemes, 1586, p.182b
bolt→brazen→bar→God→starve
  Whitney, Emblemes, 1586, p.169
bondage→fly→god→bird
  Whitney, Emblemes, 1586, p.084
bondage→proverb→bind→obey
  Whitney, Emblemes, 1586, p.101
bondage→learning→liberty
  Whitney, Emblemes, 1586, p.101
bondage→mind→fetter→gold
  Whitney, Emblemes, 1586, p.202
bone→moan→brook→deceive→shadow
  Whitney, Emblemes, 1586, p.039
bone→day→work→night
  Whitney, Emblemes, 1586, p.103
bone→gold→age[1]→dart
  Whitney, Emblemes, 1586, p.132
bone→fawn[1]→flower→tomb
  Whitney, Emblemes, 1586, p.141
book→libel→name→fear→skill
  Whitney, Emblemes, 1586, p.127
book→save→grove→Samson
  Whitney, Emblemes, 1586, p.131
book→Cupid→heart→sage→wisdom
  Whitney, Emblemes, 1586, p.135
book→west→shine→salvation→bless
  Whitney, Emblemes, 1586, p.166a
book→time→hide→print→mind
  Whitney, Emblemes, 1586, p.171
book→hourglass [= glass]→glass
  [= hourglass]→time
  Whitney, Emblemes, 1586, p.172

card [= chart]→Palinurus→compass→
   chart [= card]
     Whitney, Emblemes, 1586, p.145
care→escape→viper→promise
     Whitney, Emblemes, 1586, p.024
care→grief→harbour→breast
     Whitney, Emblemes, 1586, p.025
care→young[1]→foolish→bird
     Whitney, Emblemes, 1586, p.033
care→place→skull→men
     Whitney, Emblemes, 1586, p.046
care→forget→spill→blood
     Whitney, Emblemes, 1586, p.049
care→meal→stork→provide
     Whitney, Emblemes, 1586, p.073
care→death→conscience→prick
     Whitney, Emblemes, 1586, p.075
care→love→cross→world
     Whitney, Emblemes, 1586, p.082
care→joy→mirth→distract
     Whitney, Emblemes, 1586, p.102
care→pull→ascend→clog
     Whitney, Emblemes, 1586, p.152
care→patient→age→cock
     Whitney, Emblemes, 1586, p.212
careless→danger→fly→beware→fickle
     Whitney, Emblemes, 1586, p.010
careless→die→laugh→tile
     Whitney, Emblemes, 1586, p.176
cart→yoke→dog→burden
     Whitney, Emblemes, 1586, p.140
cat→mouse→live→malice
     Whitney, Emblemes, 1586, p.178
catch→fear→shadow→doubt
     Whitney, Emblemes, 1586, p.032
catch→boy→strive
     Whitney, Emblemes, 1586, p.055b
catch→fisher→prey
     Whitney, Emblemes, 1586, p.077a
cate [= provisions]→table→page[1]→
   provisions [= cate]
     Whitney, Emblemes, 1586, p.102
cate [= provisions]→Bias→Codrus→
   provisions [= cate]
     Whitney, Emblemes, 1586, p.198
cattle→plenty→fish→fowl
     Whitney, Emblemes, 1586, p.200
cease→release→wood[1]→lesson
     Whitney, Emblemes, 1586, p.084
chaff→dust→weed→wicked
     Whitney, Emblemes, 1586, p.068
chaffinch→vine→finch→harvest
     Whitney, Emblemes, 1586, p.054b
chain→liver→Caucasus→Prometheus
     Whitney, Emblemes, 1586, p.075
chain→servant→miser→sport
     Whitney, Emblemes, 1586, p.169
chain→wise→Pompey→silk
     Whitney, Emblemes, 1586, p.202
chair→contentment→die→despair
     Whitney, Emblemes, 1586, p.086
chance→dice→laugh→subtle→craft
     Whitney, Emblemes, 1586, p.022
chance→quiver→bow→haste
     Whitney, Emblemes, 1586, p.132
chance→year→sky→curious
     Whitney, Emblemes, 1586, p.157
chance→dance→meadow→green→
   content
     Whitney, Emblemes, 1586, p.159
change→silver→age→time
     Whitney, Emblemes, 1586, p.122
change→monarchy→fame→time
     Whitney, Emblemes, 1586, p.167
change→mind→air→force
     Whitney, Emblemes, 1586, p.178

chant→spring→warble→nightingale
     Whitney, Emblemes, 1586, p.101
chaos→one→work→derive
     Whitney, Emblemes, 1586, p.122
chariot→lion→yield→Cupid
     Whitney, Emblemes, 1586, p.063
chariot→ant→grasshopper→toil
     Whitney, Emblemes, 1586, p.175
charm→face→song→heart
     Whitney, Emblemes, 1586, p.010
charnel→house→taste→skull
     Whitney, Emblemes, 1586, p.229b
chart [= card]→card [= chart]→star→
   seaman
     Whitney, Emblemes, 1586, p.043
chart [= card]→card [= chart]→
   Palinurus→compass
     Whitney, Emblemes, 1586, p.145
chase→stag→escape→hunter
     Whitney, Emblemes, 1586, p.153a
cheat→peer→learned→love
     Whitney, Emblemes, 1586, p.079
cheer→heart→world→immortal
     Whitney, Emblemes, 1586, p.146
cheer→bow→quiver→naked→Love
     Whitney, Emblemes, 1586, p.182a
cheer→Semele→drink→belly
     Whitney, Emblemes, 1586, p.187
chess→bow→dull→wit
     Whitney, Emblemes, 1586, p.103
chest→ebony→Parnassus→sable
     Whitney, Emblemes, 1586, p.196
chestnut→fire→fear→ape
     Whitney, Emblemes, 1586, p.058
child→slay→tear→pine[1]
     Whitney, Emblemes, 1586, p.013
child→duty→father→parent
     Whitney, Emblemes, 1586, p.073
child→duty→reverence→help→grow
     Whitney, Emblemes, 1586, p.073
child→cockhorse→horse [= courser]→
   courser [= horse]
     Whitney, Emblemes, 1586, p.081
child→birth→year→virtue
     Whitney, Emblemes, 1586, p.099
child→blood→match→goods→guilt
     Whitney, Emblemes, 1586, p.099
child→teeth→nose→son
     Whitney, Emblemes, 1586, p.155
child→happy→grief→Agrippina→
   mother
     Whitney, Emblemes, 1586, p.174
childish→cloak→warning→friendly
     Whitney, Emblemes, 1586, p.049
chin→food→wretch→starve
     Whitney, Emblemes, 1586, p.074
choler→Pittacus→Periander→herb
     Whitney, Emblemes, 1586, p.130
church→Elizabeth I [= princess]→
   princess [= Elizabeth I]→branch
     Whitney, Emblemes, 1586, p.001
church→watchman→gate→lion
     Whitney, Emblemes, 1586, p.120
cinder→delay→danger→conquest→
   grief
     Whitney, Emblemes, 1586, p.208
city→river→fortune→rue→life
     Whitney, Emblemes, 1586, p.089
city→cannon→foe→siege
     Whitney, Emblemes, 1586, p.189a
civil→sword→bloody→home
     Whitney, Emblemes, 1586, p.007
clay→herald→king→east→kingdom
     Whitney, Emblemes, 1586, p.086
clay→Diogenes→tun→pelf
     Whitney, Emblemes, 1586, p.198

clay→wind→bubble→flower
     Whitney, Emblemes, 1586, p.217
clean→white→sincere→poet
     Whitney, Emblemes, 1586, p.126
clean→pure→rigour→pity [= ruth]
     Whitney, Emblemes, 1586, p.136
clear→wall→quake→conscience
     Whitney, Emblemes, 1586, p.032
clear→wicked→quake→constant→peril
     Whitney, Emblemes, 1586, p.067
climb→time→teach→fortune→wheel
     Whitney, Emblemes, 1586, p.011
climb→fall→weakness→weigh
     Whitney, Emblemes, 1586, p.028
climb→fall→despise→vainly
     Whitney, Emblemes, 1586, p.039
climb→Athens→Numantice→cloud
     Whitney, Emblemes, 1586, p.131
climb→deserve→fruit→fear
     Whitney, Emblemes, 1586, p.165
climb→fool→shame
     Whitney, Emblemes, 1586, p.190a
cloak→feign→trust→truth
     Whitney, Emblemes, 1586, p.024
cloak→warning→friendly→childish
     Whitney, Emblemes, 1586, p.049
cloak→wicked→just→wile
     Whitney, Emblemes, 1586, p.077a
cloak→right[1]→vice→wrong
     Whitney, Emblemes, 1586, p.122
cloak→cogitation→vile
     Whitney, Emblemes, 1586, p.139a
cloak→heart→thrall
     Whitney, Emblemes, 1586, p.222b
cloak→fawn[1]→sugar→speech→gallant
     Whitney, Emblemes, 1586, p.226a
clog→care→pull→ascend
     Whitney, Emblemes, 1586, p.152
cloth→bull→fear→scarlet
     Whitney, Emblemes, 1586, p.052a
cloth→cocky→lion→quake→smoke
     Whitney, Emblemes, 1586, p.052a
cloth→colour→mind→treasure→
   fortune
     Whitney, Emblemes, 1586, p.214
clothes→lord→assign→food
     Whitney, Emblemes, 1586, p.065
clothing→gold→copper→Nero→Numa
     Whitney, Emblemes, 1586, p.150
cloud→ploughman→sky→gallant
     Whitney, Emblemes, 1586, p.009
cloud→Phoebus→heat→experience→
   Alps
     Whitney, Emblemes, 1586, p.011
cloud→climb→Athens→Numantice
     Whitney, Emblemes, 1586, p.131
cloud→sky→Phoebus→passion
     Whitney, Emblemes, 1586, p.196
club→lion→skin→Hercules
     Whitney, Emblemes, 1586, p.016
coast→rock→sand→danger
     Whitney, Emblemes, 1586, p.137
coast→country→travail[1]
     Whitney, Emblemes, 1586, p.178
coat→coxcomb→bell→motley
     Whitney, Emblemes, 1586, p.081
coat→trust→hand→fox
     Whitney, Emblemes, 1586, p.124
cock→wake→sleep→steeple
     Whitney, Emblemes, 1586, p.120
cock→care→patient→age
     Whitney, Emblemes, 1586, p.212
cockhorse→horse [= courser]→courser
   [= horse]→child
     Whitney, Emblemes, 1586, p.081
cocky→lion→quake→smoke→cloth

court→rain→sport→astronomer
  Whitney, Emblemes, 1586, p.009
court→greedy→dog→empty→purse
  Whitney, Emblemes, 1586, p.039
courtesy→judge→truth→passion
  Whitney, Emblemes, 1586, p.186
courtesy→fawn[1]→deed→barren→
  gallant
  Whitney, Emblemes, 1586, p.205
covet→three→wretch→ingrate
  Whitney, Emblemes, 1586, p.012
covet→envy→spite→food
  Whitney, Emblemes, 1586, p.184
covet→fear→wit→school
  Whitney, Emblemes, 1586, p.198
covetous→fable→Tantalus→flee
  Whitney, Emblemes, 1586, p.074
covetous→envious→God→gift
  Whitney, Emblemes, 1586, p.095
covetous→jealousy→tawny→red
  Whitney, Emblemes, 1586, p.134
covetous→sceptre→greedy→gripe
  Whitney, Emblemes, 1586, p.151
covetous man, usurer [= gripe]→
  mortal→hate→monarch
  Whitney, Emblemes, 1586, p.119
coward→fear→doubt→heart
  Whitney, Emblemes, 1586, p.020
coxcomb→bell→motley→coat
  Whitney, Emblemes, 1586, p.081
crab→prince→slow→butterfly
  Whitney, Emblemes, 1586, p.121
crab→adder→sugar→taste
  Whitney, Emblemes, 1586, p.141
craft→chance→dice→laugh→subtle
  Whitney, Emblemes, 1586, p.022
craggy→endure→ascend→steep
  Whitney, Emblemes, 1586, p.040
crave→toil→flower→hope
  Whitney, Emblemes, 1586, p.165
creature→knowledge→Providence→
  nature
  Whitney, Emblemes, 1586, p.003
creature→brutish→mighty→force
  Whitney, Emblemes, 1586, p.063
creature→snail→feast→Jupiter→beast
  Whitney, Emblemes, 1586, p.091
creature→nature→law→bull
  Whitney, Emblemes, 1586, p.182b
credit→report→Tagus→land
  Whitney, Emblemes, 1586, p.039
creek→sea→cuttle-fish→muddy
  Whitney, Emblemes, 1586, p.097
crime→wicked→world→false
  Whitney, Emblemes, 1586, p.014
crime→trouble→mind→theft
  Whitney, Emblemes, 1586, p.032
crime→virtue→know→heinous
  Whitney, Emblemes, 1586, p.069
crime→rigour→revenge→evil
  Whitney, Emblemes, 1586, p.122
crime→swan→ensign→pure
  Whitney, Emblemes, 1586, p.126
crime→sleep→sin
  Whitney, Emblemes, 1586, p.129
crime→God→bless→time
  Whitney, Emblemes, 1586, p.136
crime→wise-man→estate[1]
  Whitney, Emblemes, 1586, p.190a
crocodile→Egyptian→teach→foretell
  Whitney, Emblemes, 1586, p.003
crocodile→fear→poison→serpent
  Whitney, Emblemes, 1586, p.125
crocodile→treason→tear→crocutta
  [= hyena]
  Whitney, Emblemes, 1586, p.219

crocutta [= hyena]→crocodile→
  treason→tear
  Whitney, Emblemes, 1586, p.219
crooked→art→nature→help
  Whitney, Emblemes, 1586, p.092
crop→tare→fruitful→field
  Whitney, Emblemes, 1586, p.068
cross→world→care→love
  Whitney, Emblemes, 1586, p.082
cross→loss→knot→strife
  Whitney, Emblemes, 1586, p.141
crow→fool→goods→fig-tree→raven
  Whitney, Emblemes, 1586, p.053b
crowing→white→elephant→shun
  Whitney, Emblemes, 1586, p.052a
crown→fame→hill→reward
  Whitney, Emblemes, 1586, p.040
crown→fly→glory→fame
  Whitney, Emblemes, 1586, p.042
crown→garland→honour→fortune→
  spear
  Whitney, Emblemes, 1586, p.115
crown→fame→wicked→shame
  Whitney, Emblemes, 1586, p.183a
crown→grape→pipe→tabret
  Whitney, Emblemes, 1586, p.187
crown→fame→Aesculapius→laurel
  Whitney, Emblemes, 1586, p.212
crown→slay→martyrdom→glorious
  Whitney, Emblemes, 1586, p.224a
cruel→infant→Procne→shame
  Whitney, Emblemes, 1586, p.029
cruel→king→ire→fire
  Whitney, Emblemes, 1586, p.045
cruel→mind→whip→fierce
  Whitney, Emblemes, 1586, p.063
cruel→brute→savage→fierce
  Whitney, Emblemes, 1586, p.186
crush→stock→ape→block→foot
  Whitney, Emblemes, 1586, p.145
cry→help→sting→mother
  Whitney, Emblemes, 1586, p.148
cry→baby→mother→threaten→wolf
  Whitney, Emblemes, 1586, p.162
cry→prey→nut→tree
  Whitney, Emblemes, 1586, p.174
crystal→tower→turret→rich
  Whitney, Emblemes, 1586, p.198
crystal→spring[1]→fertile→field
  Whitney, Emblemes, 1586, p.200
cuckoo→summer→swallow→spring
  Whitney, Emblemes, 1586, p.054b
cup→beware→Circe
  Whitney, Emblemes, 1586, p.082
cup→head→eye→fiery
  Whitney, Emblemes, 1586, p.187
cup→Hymen→Penelope→Hippolytus
  Whitney, Emblemes, 1586, p.219
cupboard→plate→bed→gold
  Whitney, Emblemes, 1586, p.102
cur→brawl→free→brag
  Whitney, Emblemes, 1586, p.140
cur→manger→starve→hay
  Whitney, Emblemes, 1586, p.184
curious→chance→year→sky
  Whitney, Emblemes, 1586, p.157
curse→army→brass→iron
  Whitney, Emblemes, 1586, p.122
customer→trust→dream→plenty
  Whitney, Emblemes, 1586, p.026
cut→father→throat→rob
  Whitney, Emblemes, 1586, p.007
cut→wool→sponge→dry
  Whitney, Emblemes, 1586, p.151
cut→goods→house→Time
  Whitney, Emblemes, 1586, p.199

cutthroat→pay→swear→blade
  Whitney, Emblemes, 1586, p.017
cuttle-fish→muddy→creek→sea
  Whitney, Emblemes, 1586, p.097
cypress→green→sweet→smell→fruit
  Whitney, Emblemes, 1586, p.205
dainty→wretch→ass→back
  Whitney, Emblemes, 1586, p.018
damage→forces→raven→foe
  Whitney, Emblemes, 1586, p.113
dame→die [= starve]→starve [= die]→
  Medea
  Whitney, Emblemes, 1586, p.029
dame→despair→Prowess→doleful
  Whitney, Emblemes, 1586, p.030
dame→reverence→dead→aged
  Whitney, Emblemes, 1586, p.046
dame→feeble→pity→tender
  Whitney, Emblemes, 1586, p.063
dame→help→sight→purblind
  Whitney, Emblemes, 1586, p.156a
dame→bowel→loss→grief
  Whitney, Emblemes, 1586, p.170
dame→wanton→dice→three
  Whitney, Emblemes, 1586, p.176
dame→thread→Surrey→fate
  Whitney, Emblemes, 1586, p.196
dance→meadow→green→content→
  chance
  Whitney, Emblemes, 1586, p.159
danger→swallow→nest→grasshopper
  Whitney, Emblemes, 1586, p.005
danger→fly→beware→fickle→careless
  Whitney, Emblemes, 1586, p.010
danger→hound→teeth→beaver
  Whitney, Emblemes, 1586, p.035
danger→force→prevent→fear
  Whitney, Emblemes, 1586, p.076b
danger→study→sky→star
  Whitney, Emblemes, 1586, p.078
danger→preserve→raven→Lord
  Whitney, Emblemes, 1586, p.113
danger→deadly→feign→heart
  Whitney, Emblemes, 1586, p.124
danger→coast→rock→sand
  Whitney, Emblemes, 1586, p.137
danger→Arion→death→kindness
  Whitney, Emblemes, 1586, p.144
danger→near→foreshow→far
  Whitney, Emblemes, 1586, p.157
danger→servant→God→preserve
  Whitney, Emblemes, 1586, p.166b
danger→conquest→grief→cinder→
  delay
  Whitney, Emblemes, 1586, p.208
dark→thirst→fast
  Whitney, Emblemes, 1586, p.185
dark→write→friend→praise
  Whitney, Emblemes, 1586, p.196
dart→Cupid→Mors→fatal
  Whitney, Emblemes, 1586, p.132
dart→bone→gold→age[1]
  Whitney, Emblemes, 1586, p.132
dart→prick→finger→Venus
  Whitney, Emblemes, 1586, p.148
dart→wanton→hope→rue
  Whitney, Emblemes, 1586, p.219
daughter→fire→heart→band→foe
  Whitney, Emblemes, 1586, p.004
daughter→tun→poet→Danaus
  Whitney, Emblemes, 1586, p.012
daughter→plough→rich→wife
  Whitney, Emblemes, 1586, p.122
day→dry→judgement→twenty
  Whitney, Emblemes, 1586, p.009
day→thief→night→sceptre

Whitney, Emblemes, 1586, p.092
despise→pleasure→vain[1]→virtue
   Whitney, Emblemes, 1586, p.096
despise→stock→reprehend→shame
   Whitney, Emblemes, 1586, p.163
despise→rise→head→pride→friend
   Whitney, Emblemes, 1586, p.216a
despise→grow→ivy→green
   Whitney, Emblemes, 1586, p.222a
despise→rise→wall→virtuous
   Whitney, Emblemes, 1586, p.222a
despite→harm→shut→eye
   Whitney, Emblemes, 1586, p.031
destroy→fancy→mermaid→promise→
   joy
   Whitney, Emblemes, 1586, p.010
destroy→bird→slay→deceive→warning
   Whitney, Emblemes, 1586, p.033
destroy→feeble→state→prey
   Whitney, Emblemes, 1586, p.052b
destroy→mouth→wound→rue
   Whitney, Emblemes, 1586, p.060
destroy→noble→peer→tree
   Whitney, Emblemes, 1586, p.118
destroy→Solon→evil→flower
   Whitney, Emblemes, 1586, p.130
destruction→beauty→renown→nature
   Whitney, Emblemes, 1586, p.069
destruction→mortal→earth→dust
   Whitney, Emblemes, 1586, p.078
destruction→Bias→mischief→secret
   Whitney, Emblemes, 1586, p.124
devise→stag→run→despise→harm
   Whitney, Emblemes, 1586, p.052a
devise→trick→dome→nature
   Whitney, Emblemes, 1586, p.097
devise→esteem→blindness→try[1]→
   prove
   Whitney, Emblemes, 1586, p.149
devise→string→gift→God→wit
   Whitney, Emblemes, 1586, p.168b
devour→deed→deface→affection→
   base
   Whitney, Emblemes, 1586, p.015
devour→little→mighty→fish
   Whitney, Emblemes, 1586, p.052b
devour→prey→greedy→kite
   Whitney, Emblemes, 1586, p.170
devour→tower→force
   Whitney, Emblemes, 1586, p.189a
dice→time→Rome→Severus→vice
   Whitney, Emblemes, 1586, p.017
dice→laugh→subtle→craft→chance
   Whitney, Emblemes, 1586, p.022
dice→three→dame→wanton
   Whitney, Emblemes, 1586, p.176
die→house→filthy→smell
   Whitney, Emblemes, 1586, p.021
die→pain→torture→poet
   Whitney, Emblemes, 1586, p.075
die→Florentine→banishment→pain
   Whitney, Emblemes, 1586, p.085
die→despair→chair→contentment
   Whitney, Emblemes, 1586, p.086
die→love→scorn→pity
   Whitney, Emblemes, 1586, p.122
die→glutton→belly→fear
   Whitney, Emblemes, 1586, p.128
die→self→love→Narcissus
   Whitney, Emblemes, 1586, p.149
die→execution→thief→condemn
   Whitney, Emblemes, 1586, p.155
die→kiss→mother→sorrow
   Whitney, Emblemes, 1586, p.155
die→laugh→tile→careless
   Whitney, Emblemes, 1586, p.176

die→fame→gold→Shame→live
   Whitney, Emblemes, 1586, p.198
die→eagle→dust→raven
   Whitney, Emblemes, 1586, p.230
die [= starve]→starve [= die]→Medea→
   dame
   Whitney, Emblemes, 1586, p.029
diet→health→wine→Bacchus
   Whitney, Emblemes, 1586, p.146
differ→vary→opinion→alive→mind
   Whitney, Emblemes, 1586, p.046
difference→trade→intercourse→
   friendship
   Whitney, Emblemes, 1586, p.065
diligence→despise→industry→renown
   Whitney, Emblemes, 1586, p.092
dim→law→divine→truth
   Whitney, Emblemes, 1586, p.166a
direct→mutual→blind→lame
   Whitney, Emblemes, 1586, p.065
discord→power→hate
   Whitney, Emblemes, 1586, p.072
discord→secret→nature→death
   Whitney, Emblemes, 1586, p.194
disdain→taste→tart→boast→limb
   Whitney, Emblemes, 1586, p.098a
disdain→sloth→snare→weaken
   Whitney, Emblemes, 1586, p.103
disdain→friend→purple→poor→flatter
   Whitney, Emblemes, 1586, p.214
disease→heal→health→beast
   Whitney, Emblemes, 1586, p.035
disease→age[1]→youth→ruth [= pity]
   Whitney, Emblemes, 1586, p.099
disease→poet→colour→sickness
   Whitney, Emblemes, 1586, p.146
disgrace→idiot→bauble→play
   Whitney, Emblemes, 1586, p.081
dismay→Hannibal→might→foe
   Whitney, Emblemes, 1586, p.115
dissembler→ostrich→wing→fly
   [= air]→air [= fly]
   Whitney, Emblemes, 1586, p.051b
distance→nature→fool→thought
   Whitney, Emblemes, 1586, p.178
distract→care→joy→mirth
   Whitney, Emblemes, 1586, p.102
distress→duty→reverence→parent
   Whitney, Emblemes, 1586, p.163
ditch→prince→fame→world
   Whitney, Emblemes, 1586, p.207
dive→poverty→goods→greedy
   Whitney, Emblemes, 1586, p.169
divide→experience→wise→leaf
   Whitney, Emblemes, 1586, p.034
divide→wing→foot→wind
   Whitney, Emblemes, 1586, p.181
divide [= kill]→tyrant→fruit→kill
   [= divide]
   Whitney, Emblemes, 1586, p.033
divine→Niobe→despise→power
   Whitney, Emblemes, 1586, p.013
divine→courage→preach→light
   Whitney, Emblemes, 1586, p.120
divine→song→poet→skill
   Whitney, Emblemes, 1586, p.126
divine→content→violet→prophet
   Whitney, Emblemes, 1586, p.134
divine→truth→dim→law
   Whitney, Emblemes, 1586, p.166a
divine→God→heaven→world→law
   Whitney, Emblemes, 1586, p.223
divine[1] = foretell
divine[1]→astronomer→night→star
   Whitney, Emblemes, 1586, p.157
dock→tread→grow→virtue

Whitney, Emblemes, 1586, p.098b
doctor→robe→harrow→ground
   Whitney, Emblemes, 1586, p.009
dog→empty→purse→court→greedy
   Whitney, Emblemes, 1586, p.039
dog→hope→lion→prey
   Whitney, Emblemes, 1586, p.044
dog→stone→bite→angry
   Whitney, Emblemes, 1586, p.056
dog→bark→bull→threat
   Whitney, Emblemes, 1586, p.100
dog→Nile→drink→thirsty
   Whitney, Emblemes, 1586, p.125
dog→night→Bacchus→reason
   Whitney, Emblemes, 1586, p.125
dog→burden→cart→yoke
   Whitney, Emblemes, 1586, p.140
dog→need→neighbour→groat
   Whitney, Emblemes, 1586, p.184
dog→faith→love
   Whitney, Emblemes, 1586, p.212
dog→Cynthia→ray→light
   Whitney, Emblemes, 1586, p.213
doleful→dame→despair→Prowess
   Whitney, Emblemes, 1586, p.030
dolphin→shore→flood→Neptune
   Whitney, Emblemes, 1586, p.090
dolphin→safe→pilot→rob→sea
   Whitney, Emblemes, 1586, p.144
dome→nature→devise→trick
   Whitney, Emblemes, 1586, p.097
doom→Ulysses→tongue→judge
   Whitney, Emblemes, 1586, p.030
door→wise→man→hatch
   Whitney, Emblemes, 1586, p.180
door→palace→rich→gold
   Whitney, Emblemes, 1586, p.204
dotage→secret→sore→folly
   Whitney, Emblemes, 1586, p.149
double→year→old→Janus
   Whitney, Emblemes, 1586, p.108
double→mouth→friendship→shun→
   tongue
   Whitney, Emblemes, 1586, p.160
doubt→heart→coward→fear
   Whitney, Emblemes, 1586, p.020
doubt→traiterous→fly→flight
   Whitney, Emblemes, 1586, p.027
doubt→catch→fear→shadow
   Whitney, Emblemes, 1586, p.032
dove→make→nest→ring
   Whitney, Emblemes, 1586, p.029
dragon→betray [= bewray]→bewray
   [= betray]→tiger
   Whitney, Emblemes, 1586, p.045
dragon→captain→eagle→griffin
   Whitney, Emblemes, 1586, p.126
dragon→mine→Greece→Jason
   Whitney, Emblemes, 1586, p.203
dragon→mind→rash→hate
   Whitney, Emblemes, 1586, p.212
draw→hand→guide→awe
   Whitney, Emblemes, 1586, p.063
dreadful→griffin→lion→bear
   Whitney, Emblemes, 1586, p.045
dream→plenty→customer→trust
   Whitney, Emblemes, 1586, p.026
drink→beggar→richly→Lapithan
   Whitney, Emblemes, 1586, p.017
drink→thirsty→dog→Nile
   Whitney, Emblemes, 1586, p.125
drink→bowl→law
   Whitney, Emblemes, 1586, p.125
drink→Lethe→flood→experience→
   wisdom
   Whitney, Emblemes, 1586, p.171

estate[1]→poverty→excel→high
Whitney, Emblemes, 1586, p.152
estate[1]→crime→wise-man
Whitney, Emblemes, 1586, p.190a
estate[1]→hate→poor→blind
Whitney, Emblemes, 1586, p.198
esteem→blindness→try[1]→prove→
devise
Whitney, Emblemes, 1586, p.149
esteem→price→gold→wisdom→wit
Whitney, Emblemes, 1586, p.168a
evil→luck→betray→suck
Whitney, Emblemes, 1586, p.049
evil→word→pierce→sword
Whitney, Emblemes, 1586, p.060
evil→crime→rigour→revenge
Whitney, Emblemes, 1586, p.122
evil→flower→destroy→Solon
Whitney, Emblemes, 1586, p.130
evil→hope→God→time
Whitney, Emblemes, 1586, p.176
evil [= naught]→naught [= evil]→
hear→speak→flee
Whitney, Emblemes, 1586, p.191b
ewer→basin→towel→marble
Whitney, Emblemes, 1586, p.136
excel→mind→gift→fortune
Whitney, Emblemes, 1586, p.069
excel→high→estate[1]→poverty
Whitney, Emblemes, 1586, p.152
excess→spoil→wheat [= corn]→corn
[= wheat]
Whitney, Emblemes, 1586, p.023
excess→sense→wit→understanding
Whitney, Emblemes, 1586, p.023
excess→Sardanapal→pleasure→lust
Whitney, Emblemes, 1586, p.042
execution→thief→condemn→die
Whitney, Emblemes, 1586, p.155
exile→love→canker→mind
Whitney, Emblemes, 1586, p.049
exile→famous→country→fish
Whitney, Emblemes, 1586, p.090
exile→live→poor→sway
Whitney, Emblemes, 1586, p.090
exile→love→peace→king
Whitney, Emblemes, 1586, p.119
exile→falsehood→shadow→truth
Whitney, Emblemes, 1586, p.122
exile→pen→quill→Basil
Whitney, Emblemes, 1586, p.143
experience→sphere→globe→learning
Whitney, Emblemes, 1586, p.009
experience→Alps→cloud→Phoebus→
heat
Whitney, Emblemes, 1586, p.011
experience→wise→leaf→divide
Whitney, Emblemes, 1586, p.034
experience→wise→snow→sing
Whitney, Emblemes, 1586, p.159
experience→wisdom→drink→Lethe→
flood
Whitney, Emblemes, 1586, p.171
experience→gravity→physic→beard
Whitney, Emblemes, 1586, p.212
eye→despite→harm→shut
Whitney, Emblemes, 1586, p.031
eye→blind→Ajax→sword→Lynceus
Whitney, Emblemes, 1586, p.037
eye→foot→field→praise
Whitney, Emblemes, 1586, p.065
eye→faith→God→word→anchor
Whitney, Emblemes, 1586, p.071
eye→horn→tail→mole
Whitney, Emblemes, 1586, p.093a
eye→red→mourn→gain

Whitney, Emblemes, 1586, p.094
eye→lose→sin→Midas
Whitney, Emblemes, 1586, p.095
eye→horn→serpent→hiss
Whitney, Emblemes, 1586, p.100
eye→wing→sight→face
Whitney, Emblemes, 1586, p.113
eye→lose→shaft→shield
Whitney, Emblemes, 1586, p.117
eye→blind→house→garnish→goods
Whitney, Emblemes, 1586, p.156a
eye→fiery→cup→head
Whitney, Emblemes, 1586, p.187
fable→Tantalus→flee→covetous
Whitney, Emblemes, 1586, p.074
face→song→heart→charm
Whitney, Emblemes, 1586, p.010
face→fawn[1]→smile→heart
Whitney, Emblemes, 1586, p.024
face→enchant→Ilion→deface→Lais
Whitney, Emblemes, 1586, p.079
face→wicked→wile→bad
Whitney, Emblemes, 1586, p.100
face→eye→wing→sight
Whitney, Emblemes, 1586, p.113
face→bold→fierce→grace→woman
Whitney, Emblemes, 1586, p.182b
face→deform→visor→fair
Whitney, Emblemes, 1586, p.226b
fade→fortune→wheel→boast
Whitney, Emblemes, 1586, p.034
fade→slow→fruit→ripe
Whitney, Emblemes, 1586, p.173
fail→physician→price→remedy→sense
Whitney, Emblemes, 1586, p.156a
fair→honour→prudent→prince
Whitney, Emblemes, 1586, p.081
fair→win→golden→fruit
Whitney, Emblemes, 1586, p.083
fair→face→deform→visor
Whitney, Emblemes, 1586, p.226b
faith→God→word→anchor→eye
Whitney, Emblemes, 1586, p.071
faith→reward→tremble→name
Whitney, Emblemes, 1586, p.114
faith→love→dog
Whitney, Emblemes, 1586, p.212
faithful→colour→hateful→breast
Whitney, Emblemes, 1586, p.024
faithless→horn→friend→mate
Whitney, Emblemes, 1586, p.141
falcon→sky→duck→goose
Whitney, Emblemes, 1586, p.207
fall→God→Lord→guide→stumble
Whitney, Emblemes, 1586, p.002
fall→fire→flame→fate→desire
Whitney, Emblemes, 1586, p.025
fall→betray→kindred→heart
Whitney, Emblemes, 1586, p.027
fall→sea→wax→Icarus
Whitney, Emblemes, 1586, p.028
fall→weakness→weigh→climb
Whitney, Emblemes, 1586, p.028
fall→despise→vainly→climb
Whitney, Emblemes, 1586, p.039
fall→head→hill→toil
Whitney, Emblemes, 1586, p.046
fall→trust→snare→wile
Whitney, Emblemes, 1586, p.059
fall→mould→grave→cold→grow
Whitney, Emblemes, 1586, p.077b
fall→despise→astronomy→sky
Whitney, Emblemes, 1586, p.078
fall→state→sure→life
Whitney, Emblemes, 1586, p.150
fall→revenge→wrong→fate

Whitney, Emblemes, 1586, p.153a
fall→fire→boil→broth→brink
Whitney, Emblemes, 1586, p.216a
fall→death→old→state[1]
Whitney, Emblemes, 1586, p.225
false→crime→wicked→world
Whitney, Emblemes, 1586, p.014
false→Damon→friend→Simon
Whitney, Emblemes, 1586, p.141
false→steal→patient[1]→see
Whitney, Emblemes, 1586, p.156a
falsehood→shadow→truth→exile
Whitney, Emblemes, 1586, p.122
fame→worldly→pride→slide
Whitney, Emblemes, 1586, p.034
fame→estate[1]→justice→rule→endless
Whitney, Emblemes, 1586, p.038
fame→renown→honour→sweet
Whitney, Emblemes, 1586, p.040
fame→hill→reward→crown
Whitney, Emblemes, 1586, p.040
fame→crown→fly→glory
Whitney, Emblemes, 1586, p.042
fame→victory→courage→counsel
Whitney, Emblemes, 1586, p.047
fame→Latin→live
Whitney, Emblemes, 1586, p.096
fame→Porsenna→end[1]→country
Whitney, Emblemes, 1586, p.111
fame→live→day
Whitney, Emblemes, 1586, p.111
fame→life→light
Whitney, Emblemes, 1586, p.118
fame→future→age→writing
Whitney, Emblemes, 1586, p.131
fame→necessity→win→immortal
Whitney, Emblemes, 1586, p.152
fame→war→subdue→lose→field[1]
Whitney, Emblemes, 1586, p.153b
fame→time→change→monarchy
Whitney, Emblemes, 1586, p.167
fame→read→practise→toil
Whitney, Emblemes, 1586, p.171
fame→wicked→shame→crown
Whitney, Emblemes, 1586, p.183a
fame→Quintilius→youth [= youngling]→
youngling [= youth]
Whitney, Emblemes, 1586, p.185
fame→death→valiant→fate
Whitney, Emblemes, 1586, p.193
fame→wit→Cherillus→poet
Whitney, Emblemes, 1586, p.196
fame→gold→Shame→live→die
Whitney, Emblemes, 1586, p.198
fame→world→ditch→prince
Whitney, Emblemes, 1586, p.207
fame→Aesculapius→laurel→crown
Whitney, Emblemes, 1586, p.212
famine→sword→fire→remorse→
subject
Whitney, Emblemes, 1586, p.058
famine→Sinon→bulwark→vain[1]
Whitney, Emblemes, 1586, p.189a
famished→Idleness→weep→want[1]
Whitney, Emblemes, 1586, p.175
famous→country→fish→exile
Whitney, Emblemes, 1586, p.090
famous→dust→young→Homer
Whitney, Emblemes, 1586, p.167
fancy→mermaid→promise→joy→
destroy
Whitney, Emblemes, 1586, p.010
fancy→unlawful→beast→prey
Whitney, Emblemes, 1586, p.015
fancy→obey→worldly→man
Whitney, Emblemes, 1586, p.083

fang→ox→hunger→meat
　　Whitney, Emblemes, 1586, p.184
far→danger→near→foreshow
　　Whitney, Emblemes, 1586, p.157
fardle→wreck→venture→life
　　Whitney, Emblemes, 1586, p.179
fare→hunger→feed→gold
　　Whitney, Emblemes, 1586, p.074
fare→Damocles→taste→princely
　　Whitney, Emblemes, 1586, p.102
fast→dark→thirst
　　Whitney, Emblemes, 1586, p.185
fast[1] = hunger
fast[1]→beg→starve→Homer→Muse
　　Whitney, Emblemes, 1586, p.168a
fat→shave→pill→poll
　　Whitney, Emblemes, 1586, p.151
fatal→dart→Cupid→Mors
　　Whitney, Emblemes, 1586, p.132
fate→desire→fall→fire→flame
　　Whitney, Emblemes, 1586, p.025
fate→foe→gift→fear
　　Whitney, Emblemes, 1586, p.037
fate→content→calling→hope
　　Whitney, Emblemes, 1586, p.039
fate→king→worldly→frown
　　Whitney, Emblemes, 1586, p.059
fate→overcome→ship→town
　　Whitney, Emblemes, 1586, p.114
fate→sleep→mistress→bed
　　Whitney, Emblemes, 1586, p.140
fate→pomp→worldly→power→monarch
　　Whitney, Emblemes, 1586, p.140
fate→fall→revenge→wrong
　　Whitney, Emblemes, 1586, p.153a
fate→fame→death→valiant
　　Whitney, Emblemes, 1586, p.193
fate→dame→thread→Surrey
　　Whitney, Emblemes, 1586, p.196
fate→persecute→learning→wicked
　　Whitney, Emblemes, 1586, p.222b
father→throat→rob→cut
　　Whitney, Emblemes, 1586, p.007
father→leave[1]→windmill→grind
　　Whitney, Emblemes, 1586, p.026
father→parent→child→duty
　　Whitney, Emblemes, 1586, p.073
father→yield→whip→rod
　　Whitney, Emblemes, 1586, p.112
father→Troy→Greek→Aeneas
　　Whitney, Emblemes, 1586, p.163
fault→condemn→rod→Paul
　　Whitney, Emblemes, 1586, p.060
fault→provoke→motto [= posy]→posy
　　[= motto]
　　Whitney, Emblemes, 1586, p.061
fault→ambition→sing→flee
　　Whitney, Emblemes, 1586, p.084
fault→alter→amend→new
　　Whitney, Emblemes, 1586, p.108
fault→offence→correction→youth
　　Whitney, Emblemes, 1586, p.155
fawn[1] = curry favour
fawn[1]→smile→heart→face
　　Whitney, Emblemes, 1586, p.024
fawn[1]→flower→tomb→bone
　　Whitney, Emblemes, 1586, p.141
fawn[1]→foe→feign→friend
　　Whitney, Emblemes, 1586, p.150
fawn[1]→deed→barren→gallant→
　　courtesy
　　Whitney, Emblemes, 1586, p.205
fawn[1]→sugar→speech→gallant→cloak
　　Whitney, Emblemes, 1586, p.226a
fear→doubt→heart→coward
　　Whitney, Emblemes, 1586, p.020

fear→shadow→doubt→catch
　　Whitney, Emblemes, 1586, p.032
fear→fate→foe→gift
　　Whitney, Emblemes, 1586, p.037
fear→verse→brass→terror
　　Whitney, Emblemes, 1586, p.045
fear→scarlet→cloth→bull
　　Whitney, Emblemes, 1586, p.052a
fear→ape→chestnut→fire
　　Whitney, Emblemes, 1586, p.058
fear→tempest→rage→world→aghast
　　Whitney, Emblemes, 1586, p.067
fear→danger→force→prevent
　　Whitney, Emblemes, 1586, p.076b
fear→tyrant→rule→reign→subject
　　Whitney, Emblemes, 1586, p.102
fear→Judea→king→name
　　Whitney, Emblemes, 1586, p.116
fear→wound→battle→bold
　　Whitney, Emblemes, 1586, p.117
fear→poison→serpent→crocodile
　　Whitney, Emblemes, 1586, p.125
fear→skill→book→libel→name
　　Whitney, Emblemes, 1586, p.127
fear→die→glutton→belly
　　Whitney, Emblemes, 1586, p.128
fear→soul→siege→pray
　　Whitney, Emblemes, 1586, p.129
fear→betray→flee→stewardship
　　Whitney, Emblemes, 1586, p.130
fear→affection→friend→foe
　　Whitney, Emblemes, 1586, p.136
fear→speech→love→tongue
　　Whitney, Emblemes, 1586, p.141
fear→writ→Lord→rash→refrain
　　Whitney, Emblemes, 1586, p.143
fear→sleep→strong→peril
　　Whitney, Emblemes, 1586, p.150
fear→dead→wax[1]→fox→lion
　　Whitney, Emblemes, 1586, p.156b
fear→son→kind[1]→heart
　　Whitney, Emblemes, 1586, p.163
fear→escape→brass→flood→
　　neighbourhood
　　Whitney, Emblemes, 1586, p.164
fear→climb→deserve→fruit
　　Whitney, Emblemes, 1586, p.165
fear→good→pray→bless
　　Whitney, Emblemes, 1586, p.176
fear→wolf→sheep→God
　　Whitney, Emblemes, 1586, p.194
fear→wit→school→covet
　　Whitney, Emblemes, 1586, p.198
fear→Archimedes→foe→wisdom
　　Whitney, Emblemes, 1586, p.208
fearful→brass→shot→guilty→mind
　　Whitney, Emblemes, 1586, p.032
feast→Jupiter→beast→creature→snail
　　Whitney, Emblemes, 1586, p.091
feather→wing→sun→melt
　　Whitney, Emblemes, 1586, p.028
feeble→state→prey→destroy
　　Whitney, Emblemes, 1586, p.052b
feeble→pity→tender→dame
　　Whitney, Emblemes, 1586, p.063
feeble→break→join→sever
　　Whitney, Emblemes, 1586, p.072
feed→goods→thrall→beet
　　Whitney, Emblemes, 1586, p.018
feed→waste→brothel [= stews]→stews
　　[= brothel]→flatterer
　　Whitney, Emblemes, 1586, p.053b
feed→haul→wave→trust
　　Whitney, Emblemes, 1586, p.071
feed→gold→fare→hunger
　　Whitney, Emblemes, 1586, p.074

feed→store→summer→ant
　　Whitney, Emblemes, 1586, p.159
feed→quench→flame→wax
　　Whitney, Emblemes, 1586, p.183a
feign→trust→truth→cloak
　　Whitney, Emblemes, 1586, p.024
feign→heart→danger→deadly
　　Whitney, Emblemes, 1586, p.124
feign→friend→fawn[1]→foe
　　Whitney, Emblemes, 1586, p.150
feign→sick→fox→lion→prey
　　Whitney, Emblemes, 1586, p.210
fertile→field→crystal→spring[1]
　　Whitney, Emblemes, 1586, p.200
fetter→gold→bondage→mind
　　Whitney, Emblemes, 1586, p.202
fickle→careless→danger→fly→beware
　　Whitney, Emblemes, 1586, p.010
fickle→colour→dyer→toil
　　Whitney, Emblemes, 1586, p.134
field→grain→autumn→ripe
　　Whitney, Emblemes, 1586, p.023
field→praise→eye→foot
　　Whitney, Emblemes, 1586, p.065
field→crop→tare→fruitful
　　Whitney, Emblemes, 1586, p.068
field→barren→cold→winter
　　Whitney, Emblemes, 1586, p.103
field→crystal→spring[1]→fertile
　　Whitney, Emblemes, 1586, p.200
field[1] = battlefield
field[1]→spite→assail→flee
　　Whitney, Emblemes, 1586, p.127
field[1]→fame→war→subdue→lose
　　Whitney, Emblemes, 1586, p.153b
field[1]→age→born→strong
　　Whitney, Emblemes, 1586, p.167
fierce→wagoner→rein→horse
　　Whitney, Emblemes, 1586, p.006
fierce→cruel→mind→whip
　　Whitney, Emblemes, 1586, p.063
fierce→grace→woman→face→bold
　　Whitney, Emblemes, 1586, p.182b
fierce→cruel→brute→savage
　　Whitney, Emblemes, 1586, p.186
fiery→virago→youth→frozen
　　Whitney, Emblemes, 1586, p.132
fiery→cup→head→eye
　　Whitney, Emblemes, 1586, p.187
fig→leaf→desert→eel
　　Whitney, Emblemes, 1586, p.077a
fig-tree→raven→crow→fool→goods
　　Whitney, Emblemes, 1586, p.053b
fig-tree→Adam→hide→God
　　Whitney, Emblemes, 1586, p.229a
fight→brawl→ire→pursue
　　Whitney, Emblemes, 1586, p.056
filthy→smell→die→house
　　Whitney, Emblemes, 1586, p.021
fin→bird→wing→defence→fish
　　Whitney, Emblemes, 1586, p.182b
finch→harvest→chaffinch→vine
　　Whitney, Emblemes, 1586, p.054b
finger→mouth→sign→Harpocrates
　　Whitney, Emblemes, 1586, p.060
finger→tongue→virtue→wife
　　Whitney, Emblemes, 1586, p.093b
finger→Venus→dart→prick
　　Whitney, Emblemes, 1586, p.148
finger→heat→supper→eat→broth
　　Whitney, Emblemes, 1586, p.160
finger→sharp→prick→rose
　　Whitney, Emblemes, 1586, p.165
fire→sword→storm→tyrant
　　Whitney, Emblemes, 1586, p.001
fire→heart→band→foe→daughter

Whitney, Emblemes, 1586, p.004
fire→flame→fate→desire→fall
Whitney, Emblemes, 1586, p.025
fire→cruel→king→ire
Whitney, Emblemes, 1586, p.045
fire→fear→ape→chestnut
Whitney, Emblemes, 1586, p.058
fire→remorse→subject→famine→
    sword
Whitney, Emblemes, 1586, p.058
fire→odour→wash→tear
Whitney, Emblemes, 1586, p.116
fire→air→earth→water
Whitney, Emblemes, 1586, p.122
fire→cold→hand→blow
Whitney, Emblemes, 1586, p.160
fire→sword→valiant→foe
Whitney, Emblemes, 1586, p.163
fire→boil→broth→brink→fall
Whitney, Emblemes, 1586, p.216a
fire→captive→burn→gnat
Whitney, Emblemes, 1586, p.219
fire→constant→lamb→sword
Whitney, Emblemes, 1586, p.224a
fire→zeal→hypocrite→show→heat
Whitney, Emblemes, 1586, p.226b
firm→sure→truth→name
Whitney, Emblemes, 1586, p.136
firmly→wind→sea→rock
Whitney, Emblemes, 1586, p.096
fish→beauty→snore→woman
Whitney, Emblemes, 1586, p.010
fish→devour→little→mighty
Whitney, Emblemes, 1586, p.052b
fish→exile→famous→country
Whitney, Emblemes, 1586, p.090
fish→flower→sea→land→power
Whitney, Emblemes, 1586, p.182a
fish→fin→bird→wing→defence
Whitney, Emblemes, 1586, p.182b
fish→fowl→cattle→plenty
Whitney, Emblemes, 1586, p.200
fisher→prey→catch
Whitney, Emblemes, 1586, p.077a
fisher→gin→tide→escape
Whitney, Emblemes, 1586, p.097
fisherman→net→sea→hope
Whitney, Emblemes, 1586, p.071
flag→top-gallant→pendant→sea
Whitney, Emblemes, 1586, p.011
flame→oil→Mars→rage
Whitney, Emblemes, 1586, p.007
flame→fate→desire→fall→fire
Whitney, Emblemes, 1586, p.025
flame→envious→neighbour→house
Whitney, Emblemes, 1586, p.031
flame→heart→hand→sword
Whitney, Emblemes, 1586, p.111
flame→wax→feed→quench
Whitney, Emblemes, 1586, p.183a
flame→mad→town→roof
Whitney, Emblemes, 1586, p.208
flatter→speech→sugar→word
Whitney, Emblemes, 1586, p.024
flatter→friend→save→trust
Whitney, Emblemes, 1586, p.180
flatter→disdain→friend→purple→poor
Whitney, Emblemes, 1586, p.214
flatterer→feed→waste→brothel
    [= stews]→stews [= brothel]
Whitney, Emblemes, 1586, p.053b
flee→foe→Simon→Benhadad
Whitney, Emblemes, 1586, p.017
flee→blade→heart→sword
Whitney, Emblemes, 1586, p.070
flee→covetous→fable→Tantalus

Whitney, Emblemes, 1586, p.074
flee→fault→ambition→sing
Whitney, Emblemes, 1586, p.084
flee→labour→leave→slothful
Whitney, Emblemes, 1586, p.085
flee→aid→Egypt→betray
Whitney, Emblemes, 1586, p.116
flee→field[1]→spite→assail
Whitney, Emblemes, 1586, p.127
flee→stewardship→fear→betray
Whitney, Emblemes, 1586, p.130
flee→wine→friendship
Whitney, Emblemes, 1586, p.133
flee→world→foreign→soil
Whitney, Emblemes, 1586, p.178
flee→evil [= naught]→naught [= evil]→
    hear→speak
Whitney, Emblemes, 1586, p.191b
flee→seek→web→weave
Whitney, Emblemes, 1586, p.199
fleece→Medea→peril→conquest
Whitney, Emblemes, 1586, p.203
fleece→Phrixus→wave→gold
Whitney, Emblemes, 1586, p.214
fleece→nature→gift→sheep
Whitney, Emblemes, 1586, p.214
flesh→neck→alehouse→sleep
Whitney, Emblemes, 1586, p.041
flesh→grass→hay→laugh
Whitney, Emblemes, 1586, p.217
fleshly→slothful→sleep→bed
Whitney, Emblemes, 1586, p.042
flight→doubt→traiterous→fly
Whitney, Emblemes, 1586, p.027
flight→land→foot→rest
Whitney, Emblemes, 1586, p.089
flint→adore→hoard→hard
Whitney, Emblemes, 1586, p.169
flock→foe→wolf→defend
Whitney, Emblemes, 1586, p.120
flood→Neptune→dolphin→shore
Whitney, Emblemes, 1586, p.090
flood→drown→Colasmus→wife
Whitney, Emblemes, 1586, p.158
flood→neighbourhood→fear→escape→
    brass
Whitney, Emblemes, 1586, p.164
flood→experience→wisdom→drink→
    Lethe
Whitney, Emblemes, 1586, p.171
flood→hope→love→goods→burden
Whitney, Emblemes, 1586, p.179
flood→pirate→thief→monster
Whitney, Emblemes, 1586, p.203
flood→lead→wife→servant
Whitney, Emblemes, 1586, p.214
flow→sluice→stain→ebb
Whitney, Emblemes, 1586, p.072
flower→spider→bee→one
Whitney, Emblemes, 1586, p.051a
flower→destroy→Solon→evil
Whitney, Emblemes, 1586, p.130
flower→tomb→bone→fawn[1]
Whitney, Emblemes, 1586, p.141
flower→hope→crave→toil
Whitney, Emblemes, 1586, p.165
flower→time→youth→fresh
Whitney, Emblemes, 1586, p.172
flower→sea→land→power→fish
Whitney, Emblemes, 1586, p.182a
flower→green→palm→gallant
Whitney, Emblemes, 1586, p.193
flower→strength→nature→force
Whitney, Emblemes, 1586, p.200
flower→sweet→time→perfection→
    fruit

Whitney, Emblemes, 1586, p.206
flower→clay→wind→bubble
Whitney, Emblemes, 1586, p.217
flower→grass→hope→heaven
Whitney, Emblemes, 1586, p.225
fly→beware→fickle→careless→danger
Whitney, Emblemes, 1586, p.010
fly→flight→doubt→traiterous
Whitney, Emblemes, 1586, p.027
fly→seek→mortal→man
Whitney, Emblemes, 1586, p.028
fly→glory→fame→crown
Whitney, Emblemes, 1586, p.042
fly→tree→blast→leaf
Whitney, Emblemes, 1586, p.067
fly→god→bird→bondage
Whitney, Emblemes, 1586, p.084
fly→Apodes→India→breed
Whitney, Emblemes, 1586, p.089
fly→star→hand→wing
Whitney, Emblemes, 1586, p.152
fly→vain[1]→bird→hand→restrain
Whitney, Emblemes, 1586, p.180
fly [= air]→air [= fly]→dissembler→
    ostrich→wing
Whitney, Emblemes, 1586, p.051b
fly[1] = insect
fly[1]→country→herb→worm
Whitney, Emblemes, 1586, p.134
foe→Elizabeth I [= queen]→queen
    [= Elizabeth]→persecution→free
Whitney, Emblemes, 1586, p.001
foe→daughter→fire→heart→band
Whitney, Emblemes, 1586, p.004
foe→envy→virtue
Whitney, Emblemes, 1586, p.005
foe→wind→tackle→shot
Whitney, Emblemes, 1586, p.011
foe→Simon→Benhadad→flee
Whitney, Emblemes, 1586, p.017
foe→friendly→lie
Whitney, Emblemes, 1586, p.024
foe→pursue→goods→preserve
Whitney, Emblemes, 1586, p.035
foe→gift→fear→fate
Whitney, Emblemes, 1586, p.037
foe→truce→Hector→girdle→mortal
Whitney, Emblemes, 1586, p.037
foe→wit→harm→force
Whitney, Emblemes, 1586, p.047
foe→foster→wolf→mortal
Whitney, Emblemes, 1586, p.049
foe→cormorant→seamew→swim
Whitney, Emblemes, 1586, p.052b
foe→rebuke→shame→rage→innocent
Whitney, Emblemes, 1586, p.056
foe→trowel→valiant→mind
Whitney, Emblemes, 1586, p.066
foe→lurk→trust→deadly
Whitney, Emblemes, 1586, p.069
foe→mud→stream→safely
Whitney, Emblemes, 1586, p.097
foe→red→man→friend
Whitney, Emblemes, 1586, p.100
foe→Camillus→Gaul→Rome
Whitney, Emblemes, 1586, p.112
foe→damage→forces→raven
Whitney, Emblemes, 1586, p.113
foe→dismay→Hannibal→might
Whitney, Emblemes, 1586, p.115
foe→land→sea→conquest
Whitney, Emblemes, 1586, p.116
foe→wolf→defend→flock
Whitney, Emblemes, 1586, p.120
foe→arm[1]→malice→smile
Whitney, Emblemes, 1586, p.124

Whitney, Emblemes, 1586, p.001
free→serve→Harpocrates→law
   Whitney, Emblemes, 1586, p.101
free→country→love→prisoner
   Whitney, Emblemes, 1586, p.114
free→friend→thrall→debt
   Whitney, Emblemes, 1586, p.130
free→white→conscience→pure
   Whitney, Emblemes, 1586, p.134
free→brag→cur→brawl
   Whitney, Emblemes, 1586, p.140
freedom→resign→shun
   Whitney, Emblemes, 1586, p.036
freedom→Lucillus→dwelling→tun→
  Codrus
   Whitney, Emblemes, 1586, p.202
fresh→flower→time→youth
   Whitney, Emblemes, 1586, p.172
fret→Mercury→tune→harmony
   Whitney, Emblemes, 1586, p.092
friend→tyrant→love→time
   Whitney, Emblemes, 1586, p.005
friend→Rome→brother→thief
   Whitney, Emblemes, 1586, p.007
friend→siege→conceit→rest
   Whitney, Emblemes, 1586, p.025
friend→death→aged→sire
   Whitney, Emblemes, 1586, p.044
friend→help→old→stoop→branch
   Whitney, Emblemes, 1586, p.062
friend→country→ungrateful→offspring
   Whitney, Emblemes, 1586, p.064
friend→Brutus→Augustus→prevail
   Whitney, Emblemes, 1586, p.070
friend→foe→red→man
   Whitney, Emblemes, 1586, p.100
friend→thrall→debt→free
   Whitney, Emblemes, 1586, p.130
friend→foe→fear→affection
   Whitney, Emblemes, 1586, p.136
friend→Simon→false→Damon
   Whitney, Emblemes, 1586, p.141
friend→mate→faithless→horn
   Whitney, Emblemes, 1586, p.141
friend→man→mischief→monster
   Whitney, Emblemes, 1586, p.144
friend→fawn[1]→foe→feign
   Whitney, Emblemes, 1586, p.150
friend→peril→art→help
   Whitney, Emblemes, 1586, p.157
friend→save→trust→flatter
   Whitney, Emblemes, 1586, p.180
friend→join→hand→brag
   Whitney, Emblemes, 1586, p.187
friend→hawk→lure→prey→speech
   Whitney, Emblemes, 1586, p.191a
friend→importune→pith→love
   Whitney, Emblemes, 1586, p.192
friend→praise→dark→write
   Whitney, Emblemes, 1586, p.196
friend→purple→poor→flatter→disdain
   Whitney, Emblemes, 1586, p.214
friend→despise→rise→head→pride
   Whitney, Emblemes, 1586, p.216a
friend→ruffian→heart→relent→
  rancour
   Whitney, Emblemes, 1586, p.216b
friendly→lie→foe
   Whitney, Emblemes, 1586, p.024
friendly→childish→cloak→warning
   Whitney, Emblemes, 1586, p.049
friendly→league→help→serve
   Whitney, Emblemes, 1586, p.065
friendly→tongue→help→virtue→lion
   Whitney, Emblemes, 1586, p.161
friendship→break→laugh→scorn

Whitney, Emblemes, 1586, p.017
friendship→overthrow→innocent→
  prey→subtle
   Whitney, Emblemes, 1586, p.027
friendship→difference→trade→
  intercourse
   Whitney, Emblemes, 1586, p.065
friendship→flee→wine
   Whitney, Emblemes, 1586, p.133
friendship→shun→tongue→double→
  mouth
   Whitney, Emblemes, 1586, p.160
frog→serpent→poison→palm
   Whitney, Emblemes, 1586, p.118
frost→fox→Danube→play
   Whitney, Emblemes, 1586, p.022
frost→bloom→root→rot
   Whitney, Emblemes, 1586, p.034
frost→root→grass→bare
   Whitney, Emblemes, 1586, p.159
frown→fate→king→worldly
   Whitney, Emblemes, 1586, p.059
frown→poet→tree→nature
   Whitney, Emblemes, 1586, p.092
frown→Xanippus→overthrow→
  Carthage
   Whitney, Emblemes, 1586, p.114
frozen→fiery→virago→youth
   Whitney, Emblemes, 1586, p.132
fruit→kill [= divide]→divide [= kill]→
  tyrant
   Whitney, Emblemes, 1586, p.033
fruit→fruitful→gourd→pine
   Whitney, Emblemes, 1586, p.034
fruit→rock→mountain→untimely
   Whitney, Emblemes, 1586, p.053b
fruit→lip→river→hell
   Whitney, Emblemes, 1586, p.074
fruit→fair→win→golden
   Whitney, Emblemes, 1586, p.083
fruit→milk→honey→tree
   Whitney, Emblemes, 1586, p.122
fruit→bloody→honey→soldier
   Whitney, Emblemes, 1586, p.138a
fruit→mock→scorner→bitter
   Whitney, Emblemes, 1586, p.142
fruit→fear→climb→deserve
   Whitney, Emblemes, 1586, p.165
fruit→Midas→mint→heart
   Whitney, Emblemes, 1586, p.169
fruit→use→reap→volume
   Whitney, Emblemes, 1586, p.171
fruit→ripe→fade→slow
   Whitney, Emblemes, 1586, p.173
fruit→ruin→peace→barren
   Whitney, Emblemes, 1586, p.174
fruit→sour→write→amend
   Whitney, Emblemes, 1586, p.185
fruit→cypress→green→sweet→smell
   Whitney, Emblemes, 1586, p.205
fruit→flower→sweet→time→
  perfection
   Whitney, Emblemes, 1586, p.206
fruit→decay→poison→gold
   Whitney, Emblemes, 1586, p.219
fruit[2] = offspring
fruit[2]→age[1]→provident→mild
   Whitney, Emblemes, 1586, p.073
fruitful→gourd→pine→fruit
   Whitney, Emblemes, 1586, p.034
fruitful→sap→age→root
   Whitney, Emblemes, 1586, p.062
fruitful→field→crop→tare
   Whitney, Emblemes, 1586, p.068
furious→mind→shield→sword
   Whitney, Emblemes, 1586, p.045

fury→bad→Satan
   Whitney, Emblemes, 1586, p.014
fury→heart→happy→hell
   Whitney, Emblemes, 1586, p.094
fury→foe→marry→envy
   Whitney, Emblemes, 1586, p.211
future→age→writing→fame
   Whitney, Emblemes, 1586, p.131
gain→pain→mean→mean[1]→
  immoderate
   Whitney, Emblemes, 1586, p.023
gain→one→grove→small
   Whitney, Emblemes, 1586, p.055a
gain→eye→red→mourn
   Whitney, Emblemes, 1586, p.094
gain→Scaeva→heart→valiance
   Whitney, Emblemes, 1586, p.117
gain→Suleiman→empire→Christian
   Whitney, Emblemes, 1586, p.119
gain→rich→liberty→life
   Whitney, Emblemes, 1586, p.202
gain→loss→soul→Mammon→worldling
   Whitney, Emblemes, 1586, p.223
gall→tongue→sting→staff
   Whitney, Emblemes, 1586, p.094
gall→mourn→Procris→bane
   Whitney, Emblemes, 1586, p.211
gallant→cloud→ploughman→sky
   Whitney, Emblemes, 1586, p.009
gallant→look→show→beguile
   Whitney, Emblemes, 1586, p.139a
gallant→show→nettle→joy
   Whitney, Emblemes, 1586, p.147
gallant→flower→green→palm
   Whitney, Emblemes, 1586, p.193
gallant→courtesy→fawn[1]→deed→
  barren
   Whitney, Emblemes, 1586, p.205
gallant→cloak→fawn[1]→sugar→speech
   Whitney, Emblemes, 1586, p.226a
game→neighbour→house→burn
   Whitney, Emblemes, 1586, p.208
garland→honour→fortune→spear→
  crown
   Whitney, Emblemes, 1586, p.115
garland→bald→wedlock→error
   Whitney, Emblemes, 1586, p.132
garnish→goods→eye→blind→house
   Whitney, Emblemes, 1586, p.156a
gate→life→babble→tongue
   Whitney, Emblemes, 1586, p.060
gate→lion→church→watchman
   Whitney, Emblemes, 1586, p.120
gate→steel→grass→Troy
   Whitney, Emblemes, 1586, p.131
gate→purse→poor→hoard
   Whitney, Emblemes, 1586, p.199
gem→sun→jasper→jet
   Whitney, Emblemes, 1586, p.198
general→valiant→treacherous→Sinon
   Whitney, Emblemes, 1586, p.112
ghostly→foe→town→Lord
   Whitney, Emblemes, 1586, p.129
gift→grace→name→God
   Whitney, Emblemes, 1586, p.005
gift→fear→fate→foe
   Whitney, Emblemes, 1586, p.037
gift→fortune→excel→mind
   Whitney, Emblemes, 1586, p.069
gift→weight→beauty→princely
   Whitney, Emblemes, 1586, p.083
gift→covetous→envious→God
   Whitney, Emblemes, 1586, p.095
gift→God→wit→devise→string
   Whitney, Emblemes, 1586, p.168b
gift→poor→speed

grave→peace→sleep→Dyer→pear
  Whitney, Emblemes, 1586, p.193
gravity→physic→beard→experience
  Whitney, Emblemes, 1586, p.196
gray→russet→nature→poor
  Whitney, Emblemes, 1586, p.212
great→man→rich→scout
  Whitney, Emblemes, 1586, p.134
greatness→birth→nature→shroud
  Whitney, Emblemes, 1586, p.065
greed→Caesar→Midas→king
  Whitney, Emblemes, 1586, p.086
greed→lethargy→sleep→purse
  Whitney, Emblemes, 1586, p.198
greedy→Actaeon→well→Diana
  Whitney, Emblemes, 1586, p.209
greedy→dog→empty→purse→court
  Whitney, Emblemes, 1586, p.015
greedy→shop→sack→rob
  Whitney, Emblemes, 1586, p.039
greedy→vain[1]→son→hope
  Whitney, Emblemes, 1586, p.041
greedy→sow→harvest
  Whitney, Emblemes, 1586, p.044
greedy→fool→grain→wife→prodigal
  Whitney, Emblemes, 1586, p.053a
greedy→love→mind→gold
  Whitney, Emblemes, 1586, p.080
greedy→gripe→covetous→sceptre
  Whitney, Emblemes, 1586, p.099
greedy→dive→poverty→goods
  Whitney, Emblemes, 1586, p.151
greedy→kite→devour→prey
  Whitney, Emblemes, 1586, p.169
greedy→mind→land→Lord
  Whitney, Emblemes, 1586, p.170
green→pine→mountain→branch
  Whitney, Emblemes, 1586, p.199
green→laurel→lightning→thunderbolt
  Whitney, Emblemes, 1586, p.059
green→hide→wound→wax[1]
  Whitney, Emblemes, 1586, p.067
green→Flora→summer→grove
  Whitney, Emblemes, 1586, p.098b
green→hope→youth→yellow
  Whitney, Emblemes, 1586, p.122
green→content→chance→dance→
  meadow
  Whitney, Emblemes, 1586, p.134
green→soon→ripe→rotten
  Whitney, Emblemes, 1586, p.159
green→palm→gallant→flower
  Whitney, Emblemes, 1586, p.173
green→sweet→smell→fruit→cypress
  Whitney, Emblemes, 1586, p.193
green→despise→grow→ivy
  Whitney, Emblemes, 1586, p.205
grief→harbour→breast→care
  Whitney, Emblemes, 1586, p.222a
grief→lose→wit→wrought→end[1]
  Whitney, Emblemes, 1586, p.025
grief→pure→soil→sin→guilt
  Whitney, Emblemes, 1586, p.030
grief→noble→bleed→deadly
  Whitney, Emblemes, 1586, p.032
grief→sorrow→life→band
  Whitney, Emblemes, 1586, p.070
grief→noble→mind→head
  Whitney, Emblemes, 1586, p.075
grief→mirth→shroud→gulf
  Whitney, Emblemes, 1586, p.116
grief→husbandman→wound→play→
  poison
  Whitney, Emblemes, 1586, p.141
grief→joy→sing→storm→weather
  Whitney, Emblemes, 1586, p.148

grief→dame→bowel→loss
  Whitney, Emblemes, 1586, p.165
grief→Agrippina→mother→child→
  happy
  Whitney, Emblemes, 1586, p.170
grief→bold→tongue→wit
  Whitney, Emblemes, 1586, p.174
grief→cinder→delay→danger→
  conquest
  Whitney, Emblemes, 1586, p.180
grief→treasure→rust→sin
  Whitney, Emblemes, 1586, p.208
griffin→lion→bear→dreadful
  Whitney, Emblemes, 1586, p.225
griffin→talon→ire→whet
  Whitney, Emblemes, 1586, p.045
griffin→dragon→captain→eagle
  Whitney, Emblemes, 1586, p.100
grime→cool→bilbo→blade
  Whitney, Emblemes, 1586, p.126
grind→father→leave[1]→windmill
  Whitney, Emblemes, 1586, p.145
gripe→covetous→sceptre→greedy
  Whitney, Emblemes, 1586, p.026
gripe [= covetous man, usurer]→reign→
  watch→loss
  Whitney, Emblemes, 1586, p.151
groat→dog→need→neighbour
  Whitney, Emblemes, 1586, p.119
ground→doctor→robe→harrow
  Whitney, Emblemes, 1586, p.184
ground→simple→truth→truth→sun
  Whitney, Emblemes, 1586, p.009
ground→miller→trick [= sleight]→
  sleight [= trick]
  Whitney, Emblemes, 1586, p.020
ground→wish→bind→stone
  Whitney, Emblemes, 1586, p.080
grove→small→gain→one
  Whitney, Emblemes, 1586, p.152
grove→green→Flora→summer
  Whitney, Emblemes, 1586, p.055a
grove→Samson→book→save
  Whitney, Emblemes, 1586, p.122
grow→wheat [= corn]→corn
  [= wheat]→dernel
  Whitney, Emblemes, 1586, p.131
grow→child→duty→reverence→help
  Whitney, Emblemes, 1586, p.068
grow→fall→mould→grave→cold
  Whitney, Emblemes, 1586, p.073
grow→virtue→dock→tread
  Whitney, Emblemes, 1586, p.077b
grow→foe→prey→hate
  Whitney, Emblemes, 1586, p.098b
grow→ivy→green→despise
  Whitney, Emblemes, 1586, p.178
guerdon→offence→Tantalus→poet
  Whitney, Emblemes, 1586, p.222a
guide→stumble→fall→God→Lord
  Whitney, Emblemes, 1586, p.074
guide→bridle→will
  Whitney, Emblemes, 1586, p.002
guide→bow→prostrate→arrogant
  Whitney, Emblemes, 1586, p.006
guide→law→wisdom→unthrift→land
  Whitney, Emblemes, 1586, p.008
guide→horse→throw→courage
  Whitney, Emblemes, 1586, p.017
guide→awe→draw→hand
  Whitney, Emblemes, 1586, p.038
guide→increase→store→small
  Whitney, Emblemes, 1586, p.063
guile→foe→hollow→heart→mist
  Whitney, Emblemes, 1586, p.088

guilt→grief→pure→soil→sin
  Whitney, Emblemes, 1586, p.226a
guilt→child→blood→match→goods
  Whitney, Emblemes, 1586, p.032
guiltless→wrath→inflame→mortal
  Whitney, Emblemes, 1586, p.099
guilty→mind→fearful→brass→shot
  Whitney, Emblemes, 1586, p.056
guilty→mouse→oyster→death
  Whitney, Emblemes, 1586, p.032
gulf→grief→mirth→shroud
  Whitney, Emblemes, 1586, p.128
gulf→sand→knight→course
  Whitney, Emblemes, 1586, p.141
hair→wrong→sentence→Agamemnon
  Whitney, Emblemes, 1586, p.203
hand→guide→awe→draw
  Whitney, Emblemes, 1586, p.030
hand→subject→heart→wealthy
  Whitney, Emblemes, 1586, p.063
hand→word→humour→infant
  Whitney, Emblemes, 1586, p.076a
hand→meat→born→labour
  Whitney, Emblemes, 1586, p.081
hand→sword→flame→heart
  Whitney, Emblemes, 1586, p.085
hand→lose→left→right[2]
  Whitney, Emblemes, 1586, p.111
hand→fox→coat→trust
  Whitney, Emblemes, 1586, p.115
hand→judge→last[1]→wash
  Whitney, Emblemes, 1586, p.124
hand→shake→shrink→ink
  Whitney, Emblemes, 1586, p.136
hand→bee→Cupid→honey
  Whitney, Emblemes, 1586, p.143
hand→water→swell
  Whitney, Emblemes, 1586, p.148
hand→wing→fly→star
  Whitney, Emblemes, 1586, p.151
hand→blow→fire→cold
  Whitney, Emblemes, 1586, p.152
hand→restrain→fly→vain[1]→bird
  Whitney, Emblemes, 1586, p.160
hand→brag→friend→join
  Whitney, Emblemes, 1586, p.180
happy→hell→fury→heart
  Whitney, Emblemes, 1586, p.187
happy→hour→sweet→sour→Lord
  Whitney, Emblemes, 1586, p.094
happy→harm→beware→tear[1]→piece
  Whitney, Emblemes, 1586, p.097
happy→grief→Agrippina→mother→
  child
  Whitney, Emblemes, 1586, p.154
harbour→breast→care→grief
  Whitney, Emblemes, 1586, p.174
hard→trial[1]→easy→bold→art
  Whitney, Emblemes, 1586, p.025
hard→flint→adore→hoard
  Whitney, Emblemes, 1586, p.156b
hare→bite→lion→slander→defame
  Whitney, Emblemes, 1586, p.169
hare→swift→tooth→paw
  Whitney, Emblemes, 1586, p.127
harm→wicked→speech→offend→lewd
  Whitney, Emblemes, 1586, p.182b
harm→shut→eye→despite
  Whitney, Emblemes, 1586, p.019
harm→love→swallow→suspect
  Whitney, Emblemes, 1586, p.031
harm→force→foe→wit
  Whitney, Emblemes, 1586, p.033
harm→devise→stag→run→despise
  Whitney, Emblemes, 1586, p.047
harm→trumpeter→captive→pardon
  Whitney, Emblemes, 1586, p.052a

heaven→flower→grass→hope
Whitney, Emblemes, 1586, p.223
heavenly→course→compass→heart
Whitney, Emblemes, 1586, p.043
heavy→star→betide→search
Whitney, Emblemes, 1586, p.028
heed→steed→lock→speak
Whitney, Emblemes, 1586, p.180
heinous→crime→virtue→know
Whitney, Emblemes, 1586, p.069
heir→looking-glass→end[1]→young→old
Whitney, Emblemes, 1586, p.044
heir→decay→name→reproach→shame
Whitney, Emblemes, 1586, p.064
heir→physician→table→languish
Whitney, Emblemes, 1586, p.209
hell→fruit→lip→river
Whitney, Emblemes, 1586, p.074
hell→fury→heart→happy
Whitney, Emblemes, 1586, p.094
hell→force→despair→jealousy
Whitney, Emblemes, 1586, p.211
helmet→hive→bee→war
Whitney, Emblemes, 1586, p.138a
help→old→stoop→branch→friend
Whitney, Emblemes, 1586, p.062
help→senseless→block→embrace→end[1]
Whitney, Emblemes, 1586, p.062
help→tame→Jove→remorse
Whitney, Emblemes, 1586, p.063
help→serve→friendly→league
Whitney, Emblemes, 1586, p.065
help→grow→child→duty→reverence
Whitney, Emblemes, 1586, p.073
help→country→good→zeal→learning
Whitney, Emblemes, 1586, p.087
help→crooked→art→nature
Whitney, Emblemes, 1586, p.092
help→sting→mother→cry
Whitney, Emblemes, 1586, p.148
help→sight→purblind→dame
Whitney, Emblemes, 1586, p.156a
help→friend→peril→art
Whitney, Emblemes, 1586, p.157
help→food→grasshopper→starve
Whitney, Emblemes, 1586, p.159
help→virtue→lion→friendly→tongue
Whitney, Emblemes, 1586, p.161
help→power→hope→gold
Whitney, Emblemes, 1586, p.203
hemlock→appetite→nettle→nose
Whitney, Emblemes, 1586, p.165
hen→sell→land→parent
Whitney, Emblemes, 1586, p.064
herald→king→east→kingdom→clay
Whitney, Emblemes, 1586, p.086
herb→choler→Pittacus→Periander
Whitney, Emblemes, 1586, p.130
herb→worm→fly[1]→country
Whitney, Emblemes, 1586, p.134
hide→iron→loadstone→virtue
Whitney, Emblemes, 1586, p.043
hide→wound→wax[1]→green
Whitney, Emblemes, 1586, p.098b
hide→shameless→tail→deride
Whitney, Emblemes, 1586, p.142
hide→sick→fox→hole
Whitney, Emblemes, 1586, p.161
hide→Satan→strive→might
Whitney, Emblemes, 1586, p.166a
hide→print→mind→book→time
Whitney, Emblemes, 1586, p.171
hide→God→fig-tree→Adam
Whitney, Emblemes, 1586, p.229a

high→judgement→learning→wit→conscience
Whitney, Emblemes, 1586, p.038
high→estate[1]→quiet→Venus
Whitney, Emblemes, 1586, p.079
high→estate[1]→poverty→excel
Whitney, Emblemes, 1586, p.152
hill→valley→report→snow
Whitney, Emblemes, 1586, p.020
hill→grave→Pliny→know→Vesuvius
Whitney, Emblemes, 1586, p.025
hill→reward→crown→fame
Whitney, Emblemes, 1586, p.040
hill→toil→fall→head
Whitney, Emblemes, 1586, p.046
hill→toil→Sisyphus→stone
Whitney, Emblemes, 1586, p.215
hiss→eye→horn→serpent
Whitney, Emblemes, 1586, p.100
hive→bee→war→helmet
Whitney, Emblemes, 1586, p.138a
hive→naked→arm[1]→sting
Whitney, Emblemes, 1586, p.147
hive→Flora→work→bee
Whitney, Emblemes, 1586, p.200
hoard→hard→flint→adore
Whitney, Emblemes, 1586, p.169
hoard→gate→purse→poor
Whitney, Emblemes, 1586, p.199
hog→ape→ass→foolish
Whitney, Emblemes, 1586, p.082
hog→visage→stern→Envy
Whitney, Emblemes, 1586, p.094
hole→hide→sick→fox
Whitney, Emblemes, 1586, p.161
hollow→heart→mist→guile→foe
Whitney, Emblemes, 1586, p.226a
home→civil→sword→bloody
Whitney, Emblemes, 1586, p.007
home→Tully→war→gown
Whitney, Emblemes, 1586, p.047
home→sea→brood→house
Whitney, Emblemes, 1586, p.089
home→blame→king→house→slow
Whitney, Emblemes, 1586, p.091
home→husband→goods→tortoise
Whitney, Emblemes, 1586, p.093b
home→native→country
Whitney, Emblemes, 1586, p.207
honest→life→key→modest
Whitney, Emblemes, 1586, p.093b
honest→blind→spiteful
Whitney, Emblemes, 1586, p.095
honest→grace→hypocrite→mask
Whitney, Emblemes, 1586, p.100
honey→Scripture→bad→poison
Whitney, Emblemes, 1586, p.051a
honey→tree→fruit→milk
Whitney, Emblemes, 1586, p.122
honey→soldier→fruit→bloody
Whitney, Emblemes, 1586, p.138a
honey→bee→power→Cupid
Whitney, Emblemes, 1586, p.147
honey→hand→bee→Cupid
Whitney, Emblemes, 1586, p.148
honey→youth→gift→invent
Whitney, Emblemes, 1586, p.196
honey→art→man→master
Whitney, Emblemes, 1586, p.200
honour→ass→seat→pride
Whitney, Emblemes, 1586, p.008
honour→sweet→fame→renown
Whitney, Emblemes, 1586, p.040
honour→prudent→prince→fair
Whitney, Emblemes, 1586, p.081
honour→fortune→spear→crown→

garland
Whitney, Emblemes, 1586, p.115
honour→Envy→Momus→estate[1]
Whitney, Emblemes, 1586, p.118
honour→law→Venus→son
Whitney, Emblemes, 1586, p.132
honour→treasure→pole→laurel
Whitney, Emblemes, 1586, p.196
honour→Elizabeth I [= queen]→queen [= Elizabeth]→country→serve
Whitney, Emblemes, 1586, p.230
hoof→lion→horn→horse
Whitney, Emblemes, 1586, p.182b
hope→luck→fool→idle→vainly
Whitney, Emblemes, 1586, p.026
hope→fortune→grass→courser→starve
Whitney, Emblemes, 1586, p.026
hope→fate→content→calling
Whitney, Emblemes, 1586, p.039
hope→lion→prey→dog
Whitney, Emblemes, 1586, p.044
hope→greedy→vain[1]→son
Whitney, Emblemes, 1586, p.044
hope→fisherman→net→sea
Whitney, Emblemes, 1586, p.071
hope→Christian→starve→constant
Whitney, Emblemes, 1586, p.071
hope→praise→Hanno→sky
Whitney, Emblemes, 1586, p.084
hope→sea→wrong→ship
Whitney, Emblemes, 1586, p.090
hope→prey→blood→rancour
Whitney, Emblemes, 1586, p.119
hope→youth→yellow→green
Whitney, Emblemes, 1586, p.134
hope→justice→try[1]
Whitney, Emblemes, 1586, p.139b
hope→warn→revenge→wrong
Whitney, Emblemes, 1586, p.155
hope→crave→toil→flower
Whitney, Emblemes, 1586, p.165
hope→God→time→evil
Whitney, Emblemes, 1586, p.176
hope→love→goods→burden→flood
Whitney, Emblemes, 1586, p.179
hope→gold→help→power
Whitney, Emblemes, 1586, p.203
hope→rue→dart→wanton
Whitney, Emblemes, 1586, p.219
hope→heaven→flower→grass
Whitney, Emblemes, 1586, p.225
horn→tail→mole→eye
Whitney, Emblemes, 1586, p.093a
horn→serpent→hiss→eye
Whitney, Emblemes, 1586, p.100
horn→friend→mate→faithless
Whitney, Emblemes, 1586, p.141
horn→horse→hoof→lion
Whitney, Emblemes, 1586, p.182b
horn→Lord→Combermere→Jove
Whitney, Emblemes, 1586, p.200
horse→fierce→wagoner→rein
Whitney, Emblemes, 1586, p.006
horse→throw→courage→guide
Whitney, Emblemes, 1586, p.038
horse→hoof→lion→horn
Whitney, Emblemes, 1586, p.182b
horse→three→white→two
Whitney, Emblemes, 1586, p.227
horse [= courser]→courser [= horse]→child→cockhorse
Whitney, Emblemes, 1586, p.081
host→prisoner→yield→captain
Whitney, Emblemes, 1586, p.112
host→thigh→soldier→Caesar
Whitney, Emblemes, 1586, p.117

host→winter→night→satyr
  Whitney, Emblemes, 1586, p.160
host[1] = army
host[1]→might→noble→mind
  Whitney, Emblemes, 1586, p.111
hot→burn→wood→kindling
  Whitney, Emblemes, 1586, p.173
hound→bold→stag→transform
  Whitney, Emblemes, 1586, p.015
hound→teeth→beaver→danger
  Whitney, Emblemes, 1586, p.035
hound→shadow→tree→refuge
  Whitney, Emblemes, 1586, p.153a
hour→sweet→sour→Lord→happy
  Whitney, Emblemes, 1586, p.097
hour→enrich→mind→loss
  Whitney, Emblemes, 1586, p.172
hourglass [= glass]→glass
  [= hourglass]→run→youth→heart
  Whitney, Emblemes, 1586, p.050b
hourglass [= glass]→glass
  [= hourglass]→time→book
  Whitney, Emblemes, 1586, p.172
house→filthy→smell→die
  Whitney, Emblemes, 1586, p.021
house→flame→envious→neighbour
  Whitney, Emblemes, 1586, p.031
house→home→sea→brood
  Whitney, Emblemes, 1586, p.089
house→slow→home→blame→king
  Whitney, Emblemes, 1586, p.091
house→garnish→goods→eye→blind
  Whitney, Emblemes, 1586, p.156a
house→Time→cut→goods
  Whitney, Emblemes, 1586, p.199
house→burn→game→neighbour
  Whitney, Emblemes, 1586, p.208
house→taste→skull→charnel
  Whitney, Emblemes, 1586, p.229b
hue→conquer→nature→vain→reason
  Whitney, Emblemes, 1586, p.057
humour→infant→hand→word
  Whitney, Emblemes, 1586, p.081
hunger→feed→gold→fare
  Whitney, Emblemes, 1586, p.074
hunger→meat→fang→ox
  Whitney, Emblemes, 1586, p.184
hunt→youthful→prince→weather
  Whitney, Emblemes, 1586, p.009
hunt→lion→ass→fox
  Whitney, Emblemes, 1586, p.154
hunter→desire→testicle [= stone]→
  stone [= testicle]
  Whitney, Emblemes, 1586, p.035
hunter→chase→stag→escape
  Whitney, Emblemes, 1586, p.153a
hunter→pierce→prey→betray
  Whitney, Emblemes, 1586, p.153a
hurt→foe→injury [= teen]→teen
  [= injury]→virtue
  Whitney, Emblemes, 1586, p.138b
hurt→worldly→sea→mighty→poor
  Whitney, Emblemes, 1586, p.164
husband→goods→tortoise→home
  Whitney, Emblemes, 1586, p.093b
husband→bow→prey
  Whitney, Emblemes, 1586, p.211
husbandman→wound→play→poison→
  grief
  Whitney, Emblemes, 1586, p.148
hyena [= crocutta]→moss→Ulysses→
  Siren
  Whitney, Emblemes, 1586, p.219
hypocrite→sanctity→religion→
  shadow→substance
  Whitney, Emblemes, 1586, p.051b

hypocrite→mask→honest→grace
  Whitney, Emblemes, 1586, p.100
hypocrite→show→heat→fire→zeal
  Whitney, Emblemes, 1586, p.226b
ice→stream→Regensburg→townsman
  Whitney, Emblemes, 1586, p.022
idiot→bauble→play→disgrace
  Whitney, Emblemes, 1586, p.081
idiot→rancour→root→wisdom
  Whitney, Emblemes, 1586, p.178
idle→vainly→hope→luck→fool
  Whitney, Emblemes, 1586, p.026
idle→word→God→threaten
  Whitney, Emblemes, 1586, p.060
idle→man→Draco→law
  Whitney, Emblemes, 1586, p.085
idle→haste→write→read
  Whitney, Emblemes, 1586, p.172
idle→ignorance→time→repentance
  Whitney, Emblemes, 1586, p.172
idleness→beggar→sweat→brow
  Whitney, Emblemes, 1586, p.085
idly→warn→slay→Corinth
  Whitney, Emblemes, 1586, p.085
idol→gold→ape→usurer
  Whitney, Emblemes, 1586, p.169
ignorance→wound→heart→desert[2]
  Whitney, Emblemes, 1586, p.149
ignorance→time→repentance→idle
  Whitney, Emblemes, 1586, p.172
ignorance→wit→learning→folly
  Whitney, Emblemes, 1586, p.221
ill→good→law→war
  Whitney, Emblemes, 1586, p.112
ill→requite→bough→good
  Whitney, Emblemes, 1586, p.153a
ill-gotten→goods→lose→suffer→
  proverb
  Whitney, Emblemes, 1586, p.170
image→hatch→breast→young[1]
  Whitney, Emblemes, 1586, p.033
image→rite→temple→god→war
  Whitney, Emblemes, 1586, p.108
image→sacred→reason→God
  Whitney, Emblemes, 1586, p.229b
immoderate→gain→pain→mean→
  mean[1]
  Whitney, Emblemes, 1586, p.023
immortal→cheer→heart→world
  Whitney, Emblemes, 1586, p.146
immortal→fame→necessity→win
  Whitney, Emblemes, 1586, p.152
imp→race→square→deed→right[1]
  Whitney, Emblemes, 1586, p.019
impatient→subtle→speech→knight
  Whitney, Emblemes, 1586, p.030
importune→pith→love→friend
  Whitney, Emblemes, 1586, p.192
increase→store→small→guide
  Whitney, Emblemes, 1586, p.088
industry→renown→diligence→despise
  Whitney, Emblemes, 1586, p.092
infant→Procne→shame→cruel
  Whitney, Emblemes, 1586, p.029
infant→kill→babe→Medea
  Whitney, Emblemes, 1586, p.033
infant→hand→word→humour
  Whitney, Emblemes, 1586, p.081
inflame→mortal→guiltless→wrath
  Whitney, Emblemes, 1586, p.056
ingrate→covet→three→wretch
  Whitney, Emblemes, 1586, p.012
injury [= teen]→teen [= injury]→
  virtue→hurt→foe
  Whitney, Emblemes, 1586, p.138b
ink→hand→shake→shrink

  Whitney, Emblemes, 1586, p.143
innocent→prey→subtle→friendship→
  overthrow
  Whitney, Emblemes, 1586, p.027
innocent→foe→rebuke→shame→rage
  Whitney, Emblemes, 1586, p.056
intercourse→friendship→difference→
  trade
  Whitney, Emblemes, 1586, p.065
intestine→strife→son→powder
  Whitney, Emblemes, 1586, p.007
invent→honey→youth→gift
  Whitney, Emblemes, 1586, p.196
inward→shine→suspect→outward
  Whitney, Emblemes, 1586, p.069
ire→fire→cruel→king
  Whitney, Emblemes, 1586, p.045
ire→pursue→fight→brawl
  Whitney, Emblemes, 1586, p.056
ire→whet→griffin→talon
  Whitney, Emblemes, 1586, p.100
ire→Labour→labour→whip
  Whitney, Emblemes, 1586, p.175
ire→sword→laurel→sun
  Whitney, Emblemes, 1586, p.216b
iron→loadstone→virtue→hide
  Whitney, Emblemes, 1586, p.043
iron→Cremona→siege→defend
  Whitney, Emblemes, 1586, p.115
iron→curse→army→brass
  Whitney, Emblemes, 1586, p.122
ivy→bloom→pillar→spire
  Whitney, Emblemes, 1586, p.001
ivy→green→despise→grow
  Whitney, Emblemes, 1586, p.222a
jasper→jet→gem→sun
  Whitney, Emblemes, 1586, p.198
jealousy→tawny→red→covetous
  Whitney, Emblemes, 1586, p.134
jealousy→hell→force→despair
  Whitney, Emblemes, 1586, p.211
jet→gem→sun→jasper
  Whitney, Emblemes, 1586, p.198
jewel→fool [= fondling]→fondling
  [= fool]→vain[2]
  Whitney, Emblemes, 1586, p.081
join→sever→feeble→break
  Whitney, Emblemes, 1586, p.072
join→king→prince→concord
  Whitney, Emblemes, 1586, p.076a
join→hate→parent→tyrant
  Whitney, Emblemes, 1586, p.099
join→hand→brag→friend
  Whitney, Emblemes, 1586, p.187
journey→travel→Mercury→path
  Whitney, Emblemes, 1586, p.002
joy→destroy→fancy→mermaid→
  promise
  Whitney, Emblemes, 1586, p.010
joy→folly→Heraclitus→weep
  Whitney, Emblemes, 1586, p.014
joy→mirth→distract→care
  Whitney, Emblemes, 1586, p.102
joy→peril→master→trumpet
  Whitney, Emblemes, 1586, p.137
joy→wake→sleep→part→last[1]
  Whitney, Emblemes, 1586, p.137
joy→day→god→life
  Whitney, Emblemes, 1586, p.146
joy→gallant→show→nettle
  Whitney, Emblemes, 1586, p.147
joy→spoil[1]→sack[1]→son
  Whitney, Emblemes, 1586, p.163
joy→sing→storm→weather→grief
  Whitney, Emblemes, 1586, p.165
judge→doom→Ulysses→tongue

judge→sentence→Augustus→mirror
　Whitney, Emblemes, 1586, p.030
judge→last[1]→wash→hand
　Whitney, Emblemes, 1586, p.121
judge→poor→learned→sot
　Whitney, Emblemes, 1586, p.136
judge→truth→passion→courtesy
　Whitney, Emblemes, 1586, p.149
judge→knowledge→ear→ass
　Whitney, Emblemes, 1586, p.186
judgement→twenty→day→dry
　Whitney, Emblemes, 1586, p.218a
judgement→learning→wit→
　conscience→high
　Whitney, Emblemes, 1586, p.009
judgement→deed→weight→sift→
　prudent
　Whitney, Emblemes, 1586, p.038
judgement→rash→toy→price
　Whitney, Emblemes, 1586, p.068
just→arm→Nemesis→goddess
　Whitney, Emblemes, 1586, p.083
just→punishment→offend→escape
　Whitney, Emblemes, 1586, p.019
just→wile→cloak→wicked
　Whitney, Emblemes, 1586, p.041
just→desert[2]→heart→wound
　Whitney, Emblemes, 1586, p.077a
justice→rule→endless→fame→estate[1]
　Whitney, Emblemes, 1586, p.153a
justice→plague→pike
　Whitney, Emblemes, 1586, p.038
justice→offend→thunderbolt→
　Elizabeth I [= princess]→princess
　[= Elizabeth I]
　Whitney, Emblemes, 1586, p.041
justice→blood→knife→truth→mercy
　Whitney, Emblemes, 1586, p.061
justice→try[1]→hope
　Whitney, Emblemes, 1586, p.121
key→modest→honest→life
　Whitney, Emblemes, 1586, p.139b
kill→foolish→sleep→pigmy
　Whitney, Emblemes, 1586, p.093b
kill→babe→Medea→infant
　Whitney, Emblemes, 1586, p.016
kill→lamb→Cain→brother
　Whitney, Emblemes, 1586, p.033
kill→wolf→wood[1]→prey→blood
　Whitney, Emblemes, 1586, p.100
kill→whelp→kindness→ape
　Whitney, Emblemes, 1586, p.162
kill→conflict→battle→death
　Whitney, Emblemes, 1586, p.188a
kill [= divide]→divide [= kill]→tyrant→
　fruit
　Whitney, Emblemes, 1586, p.195
kind[1] = affectionate
kind[1]→heart→fear→son
　Whitney, Emblemes, 1586, p.033
kindling→hot→burn→wood
　Whitney, Emblemes, 1586, p.163
kindness→society→proverb→life
　Whitney, Emblemes, 1586, p.173
kindness→danger→Arion→death
　Whitney, Emblemes, 1586, p.065
kindness→ape→kill→whelp
　Whitney, Emblemes, 1586, p.144
kindred→heart→fall→betray
　Whitney, Emblemes, 1586, p.188a
king→ire→fire→cruel
　Whitney, Emblemes, 1586, p.027
king→foul→ambition→heart
　Whitney, Emblemes, 1586, p.045
king→worldly→frown→fate
　Whitney, Emblemes, 1586, p.058

king→prince→concord→join
　Whitney, Emblemes, 1586, p.059
king→east→kingdom→clay→herald
　Whitney, Emblemes, 1586, p.076a
king→house→slow→home→blame
　Whitney, Emblemes, 1586, p.086
king→royal→seat→Dionysius
　Whitney, Emblemes, 1586, p.091
king→pardon→knight→siege
　Whitney, Emblemes, 1586, p.102
king→name→fear→Judea
　Whitney, Emblemes, 1586, p.111
king→exile→love→peace
　Whitney, Emblemes, 1586, p.116
king→Liguria→foreign
　Whitney, Emblemes, 1586, p.119
king→sport→subject→poor
　Whitney, Emblemes, 1586, p.126
king→greed→Caesar→Midas
　Whitney, Emblemes, 1586, p.151
king→sick→sceptre→rule
　Whitney, Emblemes, 1586, p.198
kingdom→Juno→Paris→goddess
　Whitney, Emblemes, 1586, p.212
kingdom→clay→herald→king→east
　Whitney, Emblemes, 1586, p.083
kingdom→England→ruin→reign
　Whitney, Emblemes, 1586, p.086
kiss→mother→sorrow→die
　Whitney, Emblemes, 1586, p.122
kite→devour→prey→greedy
　Whitney, Emblemes, 1586, p.155
kneel→staff→Egyptian→Isis
　Whitney, Emblemes, 1586, p.170
knife→truth→mercy→justice→blood
　Whitney, Emblemes, 1586, p.008
knight→impatient→subtle→speech
　Whitney, Emblemes, 1586, p.121
knight→siege→king→pardon
　Whitney, Emblemes, 1586, p.030
knight→Roman→author→old
　Whitney, Emblemes, 1586, p.111
knight→stage→act→martial
　Whitney, Emblemes, 1586, p.117
knight→trumpet→sky→spire
　Whitney, Emblemes, 1586, p.131
knight→course→gulf→sand
　Whitney, Emblemes, 1586, p.196
knit→Scipio→Lelius→try[1]→trust
　Whitney, Emblemes, 1586, p.203
knot→strife→cross→loss
　Whitney, Emblemes, 1586, p.141
know→Vesuvius→hill→grave→Pliny
　Whitney, Emblemes, 1586, p.141
know→heart→reward→desert
　Whitney, Emblemes, 1586, p.025
know→remorse→pain→life
　Whitney, Emblemes, 1586, p.031
know→heinous→crime→virtue
　Whitney, Emblemes, 1586, p.035
know→self→measure→balance
　Whitney, Emblemes, 1586, p.069
knowledge→Providence→nature→
　creature
　Whitney, Emblemes, 1586, p.130
knowledge→ear→ass→judge
　Whitney, Emblemes, 1586, p.003
labour→hate→yield→will
　Whitney, Emblemes, 1586, p.218a
labour→leave→slothful→flee
　Whitney, Emblemes, 1586, p.040
labour→hand→meat→born
　Whitney, Emblemes, 1586, p.085
labour→rest→weary→toil
　Whitney, Emblemes, 1586, p.085
　Whitney, Emblemes, 1586, p.103

labour→sweet→sour→force
　Whitney, Emblemes, 1586, p.147
labour→pain→pleasure→delight
　Whitney, Emblemes, 1586, p.165
labour→whip→ire→Labour
　Whitney, Emblemes, 1586, p.175
labour→rest→desire→endure
　Whitney, Emblemes, 1586, p.179
labour→brain→marble→adamant
　Whitney, Emblemes, 1586, p.196
labour→book→Earl of Leicester
　[= Lord[1]]→Lord[1] [= Earl of
　Leicester]
　Whitney, Emblemes, 1586, p.230
labourer [= travailer]→travailer
　[= labourer]→ship→gold
　Whitney, Emblemes, 1586, p.179
lady→Venus→prize→Pallas→wound
　Whitney, Emblemes, 1586, p.135
lamb→Cain→brother→kill
　Whitney, Emblemes, 1586, p.100
lamb→sword→fire→constant
　Whitney, Emblemes, 1586, p.224a
lame→direct→mutual→blind
　Whitney, Emblemes, 1586, p.065
land→guide→law→wisdom→unthrift
　Whitney, Emblemes, 1586, p.017
land→credit→report→Tagus
　Whitney, Emblemes, 1586, p.039
land→parent→hen→sell
　Whitney, Emblemes, 1586, p.064
land→abound→want[1]→street
　Whitney, Emblemes, 1586, p.065
land→bloody→broil→hate
　Whitney, Emblemes, 1586, p.076a
land→foot→rest→flight
　Whitney, Emblemes, 1586, p.089
land→sea→conquest→foe
　Whitney, Emblemes, 1586, p.116
land→earth→ship→sail
　Whitney, Emblemes, 1586, p.129
land→power→fish→flower→sea
　Whitney, Emblemes, 1586, p.182a
land→triumph→death→corpse→prince
　Whitney, Emblemes, 1586, p.196
land→Lord→greedy→mind
　Whitney, Emblemes, 1586, p.199
land→country→spend→God
　Whitney, Emblemes, 1586, p.199
land→Ganges→praise→foreign
　Whitney, Emblemes, 1586, p.203
land→sea→fool→rich
　Whitney, Emblemes, 1586, p.214
land [= England]→Germany→England
　[= land]
　Whitney, Emblemes, 1586, p.007
languish→reason→lewd→vain[1]
　Whitney, Emblemes, 1586, p.183a
languish→heir→physician→table
　Whitney, Emblemes, 1586, p.209
lap→pine→axe→shipman
　Whitney, Emblemes, 1586, p.140
lark→lime→net→mavis
　Whitney, Emblemes, 1586, p.078
lash→art→Job→whip
　Whitney, Emblemes, 1586, p.145
last[1] = endure
last[1]→monument→marble→stone
　Whitney, Emblemes, 1586, p.131
last[1]→wash→hand→judge
　Whitney, Emblemes, 1586, p.136
last[1]→joy→wake→sleep→part
　Whitney, Emblemes, 1586, p.137
last[1]→blast→marble→age
　Whitney, Emblemes, 1586, p.173
laugh→scorn→friendship→break

lion→prey→feign→sick→fox
Whitney, Emblemes, 1586, p.210
lip→river→hell→fruit
Whitney, Emblemes, 1586, p.074
listen→siren→Ulysses→tune
Whitney, Emblemes, 1586, p.010
little→mighty→fish→devour
Whitney, Emblemes, 1586, p.052b
live→mirth→breath→mourn
Whitney, Emblemes, 1586, p.060
live→alone→death
Whitney, Emblemes, 1586, p.065
live→poor→sway→exile
Whitney, Emblemes, 1586, p.090
live→fame→Latin
Whitney, Emblemes, 1586, p.096
live→day→fame
Whitney, Emblemes, 1586, p.111
live→noble→mind→besiege
Whitney, Emblemes, 1586, p.112
live→sun→bird→wonder
Whitney, Emblemes, 1586, p.177
live→malice→cat→mouse
Whitney, Emblemes, 1586, p.178
live→forgive→forget
Whitney, Emblemes, 1586, p.183b
live→die→fame→gold→Shame
Whitney, Emblemes, 1586, p.198
liver→Caucasus→Prometheus→chain
Whitney, Emblemes, 1586, p.075
loadstone→virtue→hide→iron
Whitney, Emblemes, 1586, p.043
loath→like→nether→part
Whitney, Emblemes, 1586, p.010
lock→speak→heed→steed
Whitney, Emblemes, 1586, p.180
lock→bald→open→warn→Lysippus
Whitney, Emblemes, 1586, p.181
look→show→beguile→gallant
Whitney, Emblemes, 1586, p.139a
looking-glass→end[1]→young→old→heir
Whitney, Emblemes, 1586, p.044
lord→assign→food→clothes
Whitney, Emblemes, 1586, p.065
lose→wit→wrought→end[1]→grief
Whitney, Emblemes, 1586, p.030
lose→plume→despise→peacock
Whitney, Emblemes, 1586, p.034
lose→sin→Midas→eye
Whitney, Emblemes, 1586, p.095
lose→left→right[2]→hand
Whitney, Emblemes, 1586, p.115
lose→shaft→shield→eye
Whitney, Emblemes, 1586, p.117
lose→field[1]→fame→war→subdue
Whitney, Emblemes, 1586, p.153b
lose→suffer→proverb→ill-gotten→
goods
Whitney, Emblemes, 1586, p.170
loss→gripe [= covetous man, usurer]→
reign→watch
Whitney, Emblemes, 1586, p.119
loss→knot→strife→cross
Whitney, Emblemes, 1586, p.141
loss→grief→dame→bowel
Whitney, Emblemes, 1586, p.170
loss→hour→enrich→mind
Whitney, Emblemes, 1586, p.172
loss→soul→Mammon→worldling→gain
Whitney, Emblemes, 1586, p.223
lot→God→nature→blame→content
Whitney, Emblemes, 1586, p.093a
love→time→friend→tyrant
Whitney, Emblemes, 1586, p.005
love→swallow→suspect→harm
Whitney, Emblemes, 1586, p.033

love→canker→mind→exile
Whitney, Emblemes, 1586, p.049
love→truth→borrow→lend
Whitney, Emblemes, 1586, p.065
love→fortune→valiant→subdue→vain
Whitney, Emblemes, 1586, p.070
love→concord→prevail→prince
Whitney, Emblemes, 1586, p.072
love→cheat→peer→learned
Whitney, Emblemes, 1586, p.079
love→thrall→beast→wicked
Whitney, Emblemes, 1586, p.082
love→cross→world→care
Whitney, Emblemes, 1586, p.082
love→shame→virtue
Whitney, Emblemes, 1586, p.084
love→mind→gold→greedy
Whitney, Emblemes, 1586, p.099
love→prisoner→free→country
Whitney, Emblemes, 1586, p.114
love→peace→king→exile
Whitney, Emblemes, 1586, p.119
love→scorn→pity→die
Whitney, Emblemes, 1586, p.122
love→truth→Scipio→learn→youth
Whitney, Emblemes, 1586, p.131
love→life→end[1]→wound
Whitney, Emblemes, 1586, p.132
love→nature→aged→death
Whitney, Emblemes, 1586, p.132
love→tongue→fear→speech
Whitney, Emblemes, 1586, p.141
love→Narcissus→die→self
Whitney, Emblemes, 1586, p.149
love→reproach→shame→deed→self
Whitney, Emblemes, 1586, p.149
love→goods→burden→flood→hope
Whitney, Emblemes, 1586, p.179
love→life→despair→god
Whitney, Emblemes, 1586, p.183a
love→teach→harm→spoil→fool
Whitney, Emblemes, 1586, p.188a
love→friend→importune→pith
Whitney, Emblemes, 1586, p.192
love→Mercury→fortune→nature
Whitney, Emblemes, 1586, p.196
love→wing→desire→stranger→parent
Whitney, Emblemes, 1586, p.200
love→dog→faith
Whitney, Emblemes, 1586, p.212
love→mistress→shadow
Whitney, Emblemes, 1586, p.218b
low→year→reign→bend
Whitney, Emblemes, 1586, p.103
luck→fool→idle→vainly→hope
Whitney, Emblemes, 1586, p.026
luck→betray→suck→evil
Whitney, Emblemes, 1586, p.049
lure→heat→East→merchant
Whitney, Emblemes, 1586, p.179
lure→prey→speech→friend→hawk
Whitney, Emblemes, 1586, p.191a
lurk→trust→deadly→foe
Whitney, Emblemes, 1586, p.069
lust→excess→Sardanapal→pleasure
Whitney, Emblemes, 1586, p.042
lute→delight→ear→string
Whitney, Emblemes, 1586, p.092
lute→rest→student→pastime
Whitney, Emblemes, 1586, p.103
lute→Pallas→life→Apollo
Whitney, Emblemes, 1586, p.196
mad→town→roof→flame
Whitney, Emblemes, 1586, p.208
madness→corpse→stream→deride
Whitney, Emblemes, 1586, p.158

maid→goat→milk→pot
Whitney, Emblemes, 1586, p.189b
maiden→sew→scholar→school
Whitney, Emblemes, 1586, p.145
make→nest→ring→dove
Whitney, Emblemes, 1586, p.029
malice→smile→foe→arm[1]
Whitney, Emblemes, 1586, p.124
malice→cat→mouse→live
Whitney, Emblemes, 1586, p.178
man→tame→order→havoc
Whitney, Emblemes, 1586, p.006
man→beast→Phoebus→beam
Whitney, Emblemes, 1586, p.022
man→fly→seek→mortal
Whitney, Emblemes, 1586, p.028
man→rich→scout→great
Whitney, Emblemes, 1586, p.065
man→conscience→wither→dry
Whitney, Emblemes, 1586, p.067
man→transform→goat→Ulysses
Whitney, Emblemes, 1586, p.082
man→fancy→obey→worldly
Whitney, Emblemes, 1586, p.083
man→Draco→law→idle
Whitney, Emblemes, 1586, p.085
man→sacred→reason→escape
Whitney, Emblemes, 1586, p.097
man→friend→foe→red
Whitney, Emblemes, 1586, p.100
man→touch[1]→try[1]→gold
Whitney, Emblemes, 1586, p.139a
man→mischief→monster→friend
Whitney, Emblemes, 1586, p.144
man→hatch→door→wise
Whitney, Emblemes, 1586, p.180
man→master→honey→art
Whitney, Emblemes, 1586, p.200
man→revere→fool→learned
Whitney, Emblemes, 1586, p.213
man→deed→strength→brag
Whitney, Emblemes, 1586, p.228
manger→starve→hay→cur
Whitney, Emblemes, 1586, p.184
manhood→witness→Marcus→monument
Whitney, Emblemes, 1586, p.117
mansion→vile→delight→sick
Whitney, Emblemes, 1586, p.021
mar→soil→wealth→abundance
Whitney, Emblemes, 1586, p.023
marble→wail→moan→transform
Whitney, Emblemes, 1586, p.013
marble→stone→last[1]→monument
Whitney, Emblemes, 1586, p.131
marble→ewer→basin→towel
Whitney, Emblemes, 1586, p.136
marble→wall→pillar→force
Whitney, Emblemes, 1586, p.138b
marble→age→last[1]→blast
Whitney, Emblemes, 1586, p.173
marble→harm→engrave→dust
Whitney, Emblemes, 1586, p.183b
marble→harmony→Linus→Amphion
Whitney, Emblemes, 1586, p.186
marble→adamant→labour→brain
Whitney, Emblemes, 1586, p.196
mariner→skill→streamer→captain
Whitney, Emblemes, 1586, p.011
mariner→blue→sea→scarlet
Whitney, Emblemes, 1586, p.134
marry→envy→fury→foe
Whitney, Emblemes, 1586, p.211
martial→law→time→peace→despair
Whitney, Emblemes, 1586, p.108
martial→knight→stage→act
Whitney, Emblemes, 1586, p.131

martyrdom→glorious→crown→slay
    Whitney, Emblemes, 1586, p.224a
mask→honest→grace→hypocrite
    Whitney, Emblemes, 1586, p.100
mason→art→defend→country
    Whitney, Emblemes, 1586, p.066
master→trumpet→joy→peril
    Whitney, Emblemes, 1586, p.137
master→honey→art→man
    Whitney, Emblemes, 1586, p.200
mastiff [= bandog]→bandog
    [= mastiff]→bull→bear
    Whitney, Emblemes, 1586, p.140
match→goods→guilt→child→blood
    Whitney, Emblemes, 1586, p.099
mate→faithless→horn→friend
    Whitney, Emblemes, 1586, p.141
mate→serpent→sting
    Whitney, Emblemes, 1586, p.142
mavis→lark→lime→net
    Whitney, Emblemes, 1586, p.078
meadow→green→content→chance→
    dance
    Whitney, Emblemes, 1586, p.159
meadow→grain→water→wood[1]
    Whitney, Emblemes, 1586, p.200
meal→stork→provide→care
    Whitney, Emblemes, 1586, p.073
meal[1] = corn
meal[1]→wife→steal→sack
    Whitney, Emblemes, 1586, p.080
mean→mean[1]→immoderate→gain→
    pain
    Whitney, Emblemes, 1586, p.023
mean→estate[1]→suffice→fortune
    Whitney, Emblemes, 1586, p.039
mean→Cleobulus→Alciato→emblem
    Whitney, Emblemes, 1586, p.130
mean[1] = golden mean
mean[1]→immoderate→gain→pain→
    mean
    Whitney, Emblemes, 1586, p.023
measure→way→rein→bit
    Whitney, Emblemes, 1586, p.019
measure→balance→know→self
    Whitney, Emblemes, 1586, p.130
meat→dung→worm→neighbour
    Whitney, Emblemes, 1586, p.021
meat→serve→pine[1]→pain
    Whitney, Emblemes, 1586, p.036
meat→tyrant→whelp→teat
    Whitney, Emblemes, 1586, p.049
meat→born→labour→hand
    Whitney, Emblemes, 1586, p.085
meat→bait→sweet
    Whitney, Emblemes, 1586, p.128
meat→fang→ox→hunger
    Whitney, Emblemes, 1586, p.184
meat→root→table→stool
    Whitney, Emblemes, 1586, p.198
meek→wild→heart→relent
    Whitney, Emblemes, 1586, p.186
melt→feather→wing→sun
    Whitney, Emblemes, 1586, p.028
men→care→place→skull
    Whitney, Emblemes, 1586, p.046
merchant→lure→heat→East
    Whitney, Emblemes, 1586, p.179
mercy→save→Elizabeth I [= Majesty]→
    Majesty [= Elizabeth I]→sword
    Whitney, Emblemes, 1586, p.061
mercy→justice→blood→knife→truth
    Whitney, Emblemes, 1586, p.121
merit→sweet→taste→sour
    Whitney, Emblemes, 1586, p.165
mermaid→promise→joy→destroy→

fancy
    Whitney, Emblemes, 1586, p.010
messenger→Rome→dungeon→redeem
    Whitney, Emblemes, 1586, p.114
might→Jove→shoot→prince
    Whitney, Emblemes, 1586, p.061
might→noble→mind→host[1]
    Whitney, Emblemes, 1586, p.111
might→Roman→peer→town
    Whitney, Emblemes, 1586, p.112
might→foe→dismay→Hannibal
    Whitney, Emblemes, 1586, p.115
might→Caesar→power→Pontus
    Whitney, Emblemes, 1586, p.116
might→hide→Satan→strive
    Whitney, Emblemes, 1586, p.166a
might→spoil[1]→rapine→theft
    Whitney, Emblemes, 1586, p.170
mighty→sot→learned→defame
    Whitney, Emblemes, 1586, p.016
mighty→fish→devour→little
    Whitney, Emblemes, 1586, p.052b
mighty→force→creature→brutish
    Whitney, Emblemes, 1586, p.063
mighty→Caesar→grave→mind
    Whitney, Emblemes, 1586, p.086
mighty→poor→hurt→worldly→sea
    Whitney, Emblemes, 1586, p.164
mild→fruit[2]→age[1]→provident
    Whitney, Emblemes, 1586, p.073
milk→honey→tree→fruit
    Whitney, Emblemes, 1586, p.122
milk→pot→maid→goat
    Whitney, Emblemes, 1586, p.189b
mill→Anellus→wheat [= corn]→corn
    [= wheat]
    Whitney, Emblemes, 1586, p.080
miller→trick [= sleight]→sleight
    [= trick]→ground
    Whitney, Emblemes, 1586, p.080
mind→theft→crime→trouble
    Whitney, Emblemes, 1586, p.032
mind→fearful→brass→shot→guilty
    Whitney, Emblemes, 1586, p.032
mind→poor→pure→treasure
    Whitney, Emblemes, 1586, p.035
mind→shield→sword→furious
    Whitney, Emblemes, 1586, p.045
mind→differ→vary→opinion→alive
    Whitney, Emblemes, 1586, p.046
mind→exile→love→canker
    Whitney, Emblemes, 1586, p.049
mind→whip→fierce→cruel
    Whitney, Emblemes, 1586, p.063
mind→foe→trowel→valiant
    Whitney, Emblemes, 1586, p.066
mind→gift→fortune→excel
    Whitney, Emblemes, 1586, p.069
mind→puff→worldly→pride
    Whitney, Emblemes, 1586, p.078
mind→mighty→Caesar→grave
    Whitney, Emblemes, 1586, p.086
mind→gold→greedy→love
    Whitney, Emblemes, 1586, p.099
mind→mute→wisdom→prison
    Whitney, Emblemes, 1586, p.101
mind→host[1]→might→noble
    Whitney, Emblemes, 1586, p.111
mind→besiege→live→noble
    Whitney, Emblemes, 1586, p.112
mind→head→grief→noble
    Whitney, Emblemes, 1586, p.116
mind→book→time→hide→print
    Whitney, Emblemes, 1586, p.171
mind→loss→hour→enrich
    Whitney, Emblemes, 1586, p.172

mind→air→force→change
    Whitney, Emblemes, 1586, p.178
mind→cote→regal→content
    Whitney, Emblemes, 1586, p.198
mind→land→Lord→greedy
    Whitney, Emblemes, 1586, p.199
mind→fetter→gold→bondage
    Whitney, Emblemes, 1586, p.202
mind→rash→hate→dragon
    Whitney, Emblemes, 1586, p.212
mind→treasure→fortune→cloth→
    colour
    Whitney, Emblemes, 1586, p.214
mine→Greece→Jason→dragon
    Whitney, Emblemes, 1586, p.203
mine→gift→bench→poor
    Whitney, Emblemes, 1586, p.204
mint→heart→fruit→Midas
    Whitney, Emblemes, 1586, p.169
mirror→judge→sentence→Augustus
    Whitney, Emblemes, 1586, p.121
mirth→breath→mourn→live
    Whitney, Emblemes, 1586, p.060
mirth→distract→care→joy
    Whitney, Emblemes, 1586, p.102
mirth→shroud→gulf→grief
    Whitney, Emblemes, 1586, p.141
mirth→Lucina→Sidney→verse
    Whitney, Emblemes, 1586, p.196
mischief→murder→wicked→wretch
    Whitney, Emblemes, 1586, p.032
mischief→secret→destruction→Bias
    Whitney, Emblemes, 1586, p.124
mischief→monster→friend→man
    Whitney, Emblemes, 1586, p.144
mischief→threat→de→step→secret
    Whitney, Emblemes, 1586, p.210
miser→treasure→Septitius→rich
    Whitney, Emblemes, 1586, p.018
miser→sport→chain→servant
    Whitney, Emblemes, 1586, p.169
miser→gold→sick→treasure
    Whitney, Emblemes, 1586, p.209
misfortune→sorrow→slave→bind
    Whitney, Emblemes, 1586, p.075
mist→guile→foe→hollow→heart
    Whitney, Emblemes, 1586, p.226a
mistress→bed→fate→sleep
    Whitney, Emblemes, 1586, p.140
mistress→shadow→love
    Whitney, Emblemes, 1586, p.218b
moan→transform→marble→wail
    Whitney, Emblemes, 1586, p.013
moan→brook→deceive→shadow→bone
    Whitney, Emblemes, 1586, p.039
mock→scorner→bitter→fruit
    Whitney, Emblemes, 1586, p.142
modest→honest→life→key
    Whitney, Emblemes, 1586, p.093b
mole→eye→horn→tail
    Whitney, Emblemes, 1586, p.093a
moment→want[1]→woe→will
    Whitney, Emblemes, 1586, p.152
monarch→earth→world→prince
    Whitney, Emblemes, 1586, p.086
monarch→covetous man, usurer
    [= gripe]→mortal→hate
    Whitney, Emblemes, 1586, p.119
monarch→fate→pomp→worldly→power
    Whitney, Emblemes, 1586, p.140
monarch→Rome→ruin→wheel
    Whitney, Emblemes, 1586, p.196
monarchy→fame→time→change
    Whitney, Emblemes, 1586, p.167
monster→friend→man→mischief
    Whitney, Emblemes, 1586, p.144

net→fowler→pay→bird
    Whitney, Emblemes, 1586, p.130
nether→part→loath→like
    Whitney, Emblemes, 1586, p.010
nettle→joy→gallant→show
    Whitney, Emblemes, 1586, p.147
nettle→nose→hemlock→appetite
    Whitney, Emblemes, 1586, p.165
new→fault→alter→amend
    Whitney, Emblemes, 1586, p.108
night→sceptre→day→thief
    Whitney, Emblemes, 1586, p.041
night→day→strife→spouse→Vulcan
    Whitney, Emblemes, 1586, p.080
night→bone→day→work
    Whitney, Emblemes, 1586, p.103
night→Bacchus→reason→dog
    Whitney, Emblemes, 1586, p.125
night→star→divine[1]→astronomer
    Whitney, Emblemes, 1586, p.157
night→satyr→host[1]→winter
    Whitney, Emblemes, 1586, p.160
night→day→winter→spring
    Whitney, Emblemes, 1586, p.165
night→black→bridle→pursue
    Whitney, Emblemes, 1586, p.227
night→oak→day→time
    Whitney, Emblemes, 1586, p.230
nightingale→chant→spring→warble
    Whitney, Emblemes, 1586, p.101
noble→bleed→deadly→grief
    Whitney, Emblemes, 1586, p.070
noble→mind→host[1]→might
    Whitney, Emblemes, 1586, p.111
noble→mind→besiege→live
    Whitney, Emblemes, 1586, p.112
noble→mind→head→grief
    Whitney, Emblemes, 1586, p.116
noble→peer→tree→destroy
    Whitney, Emblemes, 1586, p.118
noble→grave→corpse→triumph→
    conquest
    Whitney, Emblemes, 1586, p.193
nose→son→child→teeth
    Whitney, Emblemes, 1586, p.155
nose→hemlock→appetite→nettle
    Whitney, Emblemes, 1586, p.165
nut→tree→cry→prey
    Whitney, Emblemes, 1586, p.174
oak→Boreas→bend→reed
    Whitney, Emblemes, 1586, p.220
oak→day→time→night
    Whitney, Emblemes, 1586, p.230
obey→worldly→man→fancy
    Whitney, Emblemes, 1586, p.083
obey→bondage→proverb→bind
    Whitney, Emblemes, 1586, p.101
obey→East→Parthian→Arabian
    Whitney, Emblemes, 1586, p.116
obey→head→commonwealth→rule
    Whitney, Emblemes, 1586, p.200
odour→pomp→naked→music
    Whitney, Emblemes, 1586, p.102
odour→wash→tear→fire
    Whitney, Emblemes, 1586, p.116
offence→Tantalus→poet→guerdon
    Whitney, Emblemes, 1586, p.074
offence→correction→youth→fault
    Whitney, Emblemes, 1586, p.155
offend→lewd→harm→wicked→speech
    Whitney, Emblemes, 1586, p.019
offend→escape→just→punishment
    Whitney, Emblemes, 1586, p.041
offend→thunderbolt→Elizabeth I
    [= princess]→princess
    [= Elizabeth I]→justice

Whitney, Emblemes, 1586, p.061
offspring→friend→country→ungrateful
    Whitney, Emblemes, 1586, p.064
offspring [= blood]→blood
    [= offspring]→good→trust→hate
    Whitney, Emblemes, 1586, p.033
oil→Mars→rage→flame
    Whitney, Emblemes, 1586, p.007
oil→world→river→wine
    Whitney, Emblemes, 1586, p.122
old→heir→looking-glass→end[1]→young
    Whitney, Emblemes, 1586, p.044
old→stoop→branch→friend→help
    Whitney, Emblemes, 1586, p.062
old→food→hatch→brood
    Whitney, Emblemes, 1586, p.073
old→Janus→double→year
    Whitney, Emblemes, 1586, p.108
old→knight→Roman→author
    Whitney, Emblemes, 1586, p.117
old→state[1]→fall→death
    Whitney, Emblemes, 1586, p.225
one→flower→spider→bee
    Whitney, Emblemes, 1586, p.051a
one→grove→small→gain
    Whitney, Emblemes, 1586, p.055a
one→work→derive→chaos
    Whitney, Emblemes, 1586, p.122
open→warn→Lysippus→lock→bald
    Whitney, Emblemes, 1586, p.181
opinion→alive→mind→differ→vary
    Whitney, Emblemes, 1586, p.046
oppress→power→law→poor
    Whitney, Emblemes, 1586, p.122
order→havoc→man→tame
    Whitney, Emblemes, 1586, p.006
ostrich→wing→fly [= air]→air
    [= fly]→dissembler
    Whitney, Emblemes, 1586, p.051b
outward→inward→shine→suspect
    Whitney, Emblemes, 1586, p.069
overcome→ship→town→fate
    Whitney, Emblemes, 1586, p.114
overcome→Sertorius→Masinissas→
    right[3]
    Whitney, Emblemes, 1586, p.116
overthrow→Noah→Lot→Holofernes
    Whitney, Emblemes, 1586, p.017
overthrow→innocent→prey→subtle→
    friendship
    Whitney, Emblemes, 1586, p.027
overthrow→strength→ruin→captain
    Whitney, Emblemes, 1586, p.047
overthrow→trust→rage→wind
    Whitney, Emblemes, 1586, p.059
overthrow→Carthage→frown→
    Xanippus
    Whitney, Emblemes, 1586, p.114
overthrow→shore→sea→world
    Whitney, Emblemes, 1586, p.129
overthrow→elephant→brood→trust
    Whitney, Emblemes, 1586, p.150
ox→hunger→meat→fang
    Whitney, Emblemes, 1586, p.184
oyster→death→guilty→mouse
    Whitney, Emblemes, 1586, p.128
page[1] = servant
page[1]→provisions [= cate]→cate
    [= provisions]→table
    Whitney, Emblemes, 1586, p.102
pageant→Flora→glory→pomp
    Whitney, Emblemes, 1586, p.217
pain→mean→mean[1]→immoderate→
    gain
    Whitney, Emblemes, 1586, p.023
pain→life→know→remorse

Whitney, Emblemes, 1586, p.035
pain→meat→serve→pine[1]
    Whitney, Emblemes, 1586, p.036
pain→torture→poet→die
    Whitney, Emblemes, 1586, p.075
pain→die→Florentine→banishment
    Whitney, Emblemes, 1586, p.085
pain→courage→life→Scaenola
    Whitney, Emblemes, 1586, p.111
pain→pleasure→delight→labour
    Whitney, Emblemes, 1586, p.165
pain→Pluto→passion→beauty
    Whitney, Emblemes, 1586, p.211
palace→rich→gold→door
    Whitney, Emblemes, 1586, p.204
pale→bliss→pine[1]→lean
    Whitney, Emblemes, 1586, p.094
palm→frog→serpent→poison
    Whitney, Emblemes, 1586, p.118
palm→gallant→flower→green
    Whitney, Emblemes, 1586, p.193
palm→Homer→book→Egypt
    Whitney, Emblemes, 1586, p.196
palm→Francis Drake→wave→country
    Whitney, Emblemes, 1586, p.203
palm→Pan→Apollo→Midas
    Whitney, Emblemes, 1586, p.218a
paradise→bloodshed→God→Justice
    Whitney, Emblemes, 1586, p.122
pardon→harm→trumpeter→captive
    Whitney, Emblemes, 1586, p.054a
pardon→knight→siege→king
    Whitney, Emblemes, 1586, p.111
parent→hen→sell→land
    Whitney, Emblemes, 1586, p.064
parent→child→duty→father
    Whitney, Emblemes, 1586, p.073
parent→tyrant→join→hate
    Whitney, Emblemes, 1586, p.099
parent→steal→rope
    Whitney, Emblemes, 1586, p.155
parent→distress→duty→reverence
    Whitney, Emblemes, 1586, p.163
parent→baby→nature→art
    Whitney, Emblemes, 1586, p.188a
parent→love→wing→desire→stranger
    Whitney, Emblemes, 1586, p.200
part→loath→like→nether
    Whitney, Emblemes, 1586, p.010
part→last[1]→joy→wake→sleep
    Whitney, Emblemes, 1586, p.137
passion→courtesy→judge→truth
    Whitney, Emblemes, 1586, p.186
passion→cloud→sky→Phoebus
    Whitney, Emblemes, 1586, p.196
passion→beauty→pain→Pluto
    Whitney, Emblemes, 1586, p.211
pastime→lute→rest→student
    Whitney, Emblemes, 1586, p.103
pastor→preach→godly→reverence
    Whitney, Emblemes, 1586, p.008
pastor→world→sin→Christ
    Whitney, Emblemes, 1586, p.120
path→journey→travel→Mercury
    Whitney, Emblemes, 1586, p.002
path→country→stranger→pilgrim
    Whitney, Emblemes, 1586, p.225
patience→forget→rage→ban
    Whitney, Emblemes, 1586, p.189b
patience→combat→force→contempt→
    slander
    Whitney, Emblemes, 1586, p.220
patience→torment→persecution→
    Christian
    Whitney, Emblemes, 1586, p.224a
patient→Job→dunghill→God→bless

Whitney, Emblemes, 1586, p.035
patient→age→cock→care
Whitney, Emblemes, 1586, p.212
patient[1] = sick person
patient[1]→see→false→steal
Whitney, Emblemes, 1586, p.156a
patient[1]→heal→lick→skin→sovereign
Whitney, Emblemes, 1586, p.161
paw→hare→swift→tooth
Whitney, Emblemes, 1586, p.182b
pay→swear→blade→cutthroat
Whitney, Emblemes, 1586, p.017
pay→bird→net→fowler
Whitney, Emblemes, 1586, p.130
peace→Egyptian→nation→despise
Whitney, Emblemes, 1586, p.060
peace→despair→martial→law→time
Whitney, Emblemes, 1586, p.108
peace→king→exile→love
Whitney, Emblemes, 1586, p.119
peace→ambition→pride→banish
Whitney, Emblemes, 1586, p.122
peace→mortal→war
Whitney, Emblemes, 1586, p.138a
peace→force→sharp→try[1]
Whitney, Emblemes, 1586, p.153b
peace→barren→fruit→ruin
Whitney, Emblemes, 1586, p.174
peace→sleep→Dyer→pear→grave
Whitney, Emblemes, 1586, p.196
peace [= silence]→princely→see→
silence [= peace]
Whitney, Emblemes, 1586, p.061
peacock→lose→plume→despise
Whitney, Emblemes, 1586, p.034
pear→grave→peace→sleep→Dyer
Whitney, Emblemes, 1586, p.196
peer→learned→love→cheat
Whitney, Emblemes, 1586, p.079
peer→town→might→Roman
Whitney, Emblemes, 1586, p.112
peer→tree→destroy→noble
Whitney, Emblemes, 1586, p.118
pelf→clay→Diogenes→tun
Whitney, Emblemes, 1586, p.198
pelican→revive→young[1]→pierce
Whitney, Emblemes, 1586, p.087
pen→breast→blood→tongue
Whitney, Emblemes, 1586, p.087
pen→truth→Gaul→Livy
Whitney, Emblemes, 1586, p.113
pen→quill→Basil→exile
Whitney, Emblemes, 1586, p.143
pen→haste→desire→snail
Whitney, Emblemes, 1586, p.185
pen→Muse→mourn→gold
Whitney, Emblemes, 1586, p.196
pendant→sea→flag→top-gallant
Whitney, Emblemes, 1586, p.011
perfection→time→taste→harm
Whitney, Emblemes, 1586, p.185
perfection→fruit→flower→sweet→
time
Whitney, Emblemes, 1586, p.206
perfume→prince→head→mourn→
consume
Whitney, Emblemes, 1586, p.116
peril→clear→wicked→quake→constant
Whitney, Emblemes, 1586, p.067
peril→master→trumpet→joy
Whitney, Emblemes, 1586, p.137
peril→fear→sleep→strong
Whitney, Emblemes, 1586, p.150
peril→art→help→friend
Whitney, Emblemes, 1586, p.157
peril→conquest→fleece→Medea

Whitney, Emblemes, 1586, p.203
peril→awaken→sleep→secure
Whitney, Emblemes, 1586, p.208
persecute→learning→wicked→fate
Whitney, Emblemes, 1586, p.222b
persecution→free→foe→Elizabeth I
[= queen]→queen [= Elizabeth]
Whitney, Emblemes, 1586, p.001
persecution→Christian→patience→
torment
Whitney, Emblemes, 1586, p.224a
philosopher→Pythagoras→scholar→
silence
Whitney, Emblemes, 1586, p.060
phoenix→rare→Arabia→sacred
Whitney, Emblemes, 1586, p.177
phoenix→burn→stag→race
Whitney, Emblemes, 1586, p.230
physic→beard→experience→gravity
Whitney, Emblemes, 1586, p.212
physician→price→remedy→sense→fail
Whitney, Emblemes, 1586, p.156a
physician→table→languish→heir
Whitney, Emblemes, 1586, p.209
pickthank [= sycophant]→blab→Sinon→
sycophant [= pickthank]
Whitney, Emblemes, 1586, p.150
picture→wealth→music→hear
Whitney, Emblemes, 1586, p.198
piece→happy→harm→beware→tear[1]
Whitney, Emblemes, 1586, p.154
pierce→sword→evil→word
Whitney, Emblemes, 1586, p.060
pierce→pelican→revive→young[1]
Whitney, Emblemes, 1586, p.087
pierce→prey→betray→hunter
Whitney, Emblemes, 1586, p.153a
pigmy→kill→foolish→sleep
Whitney, Emblemes, 1586, p.016
pike→justice→plague
Whitney, Emblemes, 1586, p.041
pilgrim→path→country→stranger
Whitney, Emblemes, 1586, p.225
pill→poll→fat→shave
Whitney, Emblemes, 1586, p.151
pillar→spire→ivy→bloom
Whitney, Emblemes, 1586, p.001
pillar→decline→death→wicked
Whitney, Emblemes, 1586, p.130
pillar→force→marble→wall
Whitney, Emblemes, 1586, p.138b
pilot→course→worldly→voyage
Whitney, Emblemes, 1586, p.137
pilot→rob→sea→dolphin→safe
Whitney, Emblemes, 1586, p.144
pine→fruit→fruitful→gourd
Whitney, Emblemes, 1586, p.034
pine→mountain→branch→green
Whitney, Emblemes, 1586, p.059
pine→axe→shipman→lap
Whitney, Emblemes, 1586, p.140
pine[1] = waste away
pine[1]→child→slay→tear
Whitney, Emblemes, 1586, p.013
pine[1]→pain→meat→serve
Whitney, Emblemes, 1586, p.036
pine[1]→lean→pale→bliss
Whitney, Emblemes, 1586, p.094
pipe→Corydon→plough→Pan
Whitney, Emblemes, 1586, p.145
pipe→tabret→crown→grape
Whitney, Emblemes, 1586, p.187
pirate→thief→monster→flood
Whitney, Emblemes, 1586, p.203
pith→love→friend→importune
Whitney, Emblemes, 1586, p.192

pity→tender→dame→feeble
Whitney, Emblemes, 1586, p.063
pity→die→love→scorn
Whitney, Emblemes, 1586, p.122
pity [= ruth]→clean→pure→rigour
Whitney, Emblemes, 1586, p.136
place→skull→men→care
Whitney, Emblemes, 1586, p.046
place→life→virtue→death
Whitney, Emblemes, 1586, p.209
plague→pike→justice
Whitney, Emblemes, 1586, p.041
plague→murder→tyrant→Mezentius
Whitney, Emblemes, 1586, p.099
plague→bewitch→rich→escape
Whitney, Emblemes, 1586, p.149
plague→snake→wound→Aspasia
Whitney, Emblemes, 1586, p.219
plate→bed→gold→cupboard
Whitney, Emblemes, 1586, p.102
play→courage→brawl→drunkenness
Whitney, Emblemes, 1586, p.017
play→frost→fox→Danube
Whitney, Emblemes, 1586, p.022
play→disgrace→idiot→bauble
Whitney, Emblemes, 1586, p.081
play→bark→bite→thrall
Whitney, Emblemes, 1586, p.140
play→poison→grief→husbandman→
wound
Whitney, Emblemes, 1586, p.148
plead→provoke→life
Whitney, Emblemes, 1586, p.054a
pleasant→smell→venture→bleed
Whitney, Emblemes, 1586, p.165
pleasure→entice→strive→reason
Whitney, Emblemes, 1586, p.040
pleasure→smooth→win→Alcides
Whitney, Emblemes, 1586, p.040
pleasure→lust→excess→Sardanapal
Whitney, Emblemes, 1586, p.042
pleasure→entice→shadow→substance
Whitney, Emblemes, 1586, p.083
pleasure→vain[1]→virtue→despise
Whitney, Emblemes, 1586, p.096
pleasure→delight→labour→pain
Whitney, Emblemes, 1586, p.165
pleasure→delude→deceit→world
Whitney, Emblemes, 1586, p.225
plenty→customer→trust→dream
Whitney, Emblemes, 1586, p.026
plenty→fish→fowl→cattle
Whitney, Emblemes, 1586, p.200
plough→armour→rust→envy→soldier
Whitney, Emblemes, 1586, p.076a
plough→rich→wife→daughter
Whitney, Emblemes, 1586, p.122
plough→Pan→pipe→Corydon
Whitney, Emblemes, 1586, p.145
ploughman→sky→gallant→cloud
Whitney, Emblemes, 1586, p.009
plume→brook→preserve→young[1]
Whitney, Emblemes, 1586, p.029
plume→despise→peacock→lose
Whitney, Emblemes, 1586, p.034
poet→Danaus→daughter→tun
Whitney, Emblemes, 1586, p.012
poet→mortal→presume→tragedy
Whitney, Emblemes, 1586, p.013
poet→guerdon→offence→Tantalus
Whitney, Emblemes, 1586, p.074
poet→die→pain→torture
Whitney, Emblemes, 1586, p.075
poet→tree→nature→frown
Whitney, Emblemes, 1586, p.092
poet→hate→golden→world

rich→land→sea→fool
  Whitney, Emblemes, 1586, p.214
riches→give→treasure→Jew
  Whitney, Emblemes, 1586, p.035
richly→Lapithan→drink→beggar
  Whitney, Emblemes, 1586, p.017
rider→fool→steed→bit
  Whitney, Emblemes, 1586, p.038
right[1] = morally right
right[1]→imp→race→square→deed
  Whitney, Emblemes, 1586, p.019
right[1]→vice→wrong→cloak
  Whitney, Emblemes, 1586, p.122
right[2] = correct
right[2]→hand→lose→left
  Whitney, Emblemes, 1586, p.115
right[3] = legal right
right[3]→overcome→Sertorius→
  Masinissas
  Whitney, Emblemes, 1586, p.116
rigour→revenge→evil→crime
  Whitney, Emblemes, 1586, p.122
rigour→pity [= ruth]→clean→pure
  Whitney, Emblemes, 1586, p.136
rigour→sentence→wrong→will
  Whitney, Emblemes, 1586, p.143
ring→dove→make→nest
  Whitney, Emblemes, 1586, p.029
ripe→field→grain→autumn
  Whitney, Emblemes, 1586, p.023
ripe→purge→seed→grain
  Whitney, Emblemes, 1586, p.068
ripe→fade→slow→fruit
  Whitney, Emblemes, 1586, p.173
ripe→rotten→green→soon
  Whitney, Emblemes, 1586, p.173
ripe→travail→sour→grape
  Whitney, Emblemes, 1586, p.206
rise→corpse[1]→wound→rash
  Whitney, Emblemes, 1586, p.147
rise→head→pride→friend→despise
  Whitney, Emblemes, 1586, p.216a
rise→wall→virtuous→despise
  Whitney, Emblemes, 1586, p.222a
rite→temple→god→war→image
  Whitney, Emblemes, 1586, p.108
river→hell→fruit→lip
  Whitney, Emblemes, 1586, p.074
river→fortune→rue→life→city
  Whitney, Emblemes, 1586, p.089
river→wine→oil→world
  Whitney, Emblemes, 1586, p.122
roar→boar→tusk→lion
  Whitney, Emblemes, 1586, p.100
rob→cut→father→throat
  Whitney, Emblemes, 1586, p.007
rob→belly→caitiff→sweet
  Whitney, Emblemes, 1586, p.018
rob→greedy→shop→sack
  Whitney, Emblemes, 1586, p.041
rob→sea→dolphin→safe→pilot
  Whitney, Emblemes, 1586, p.144
robe→harrow→ground→doctor
  Whitney, Emblemes, 1586, p.009
rock→mountain→untimely→fruit
  Whitney, Emblemes, 1586, p.053b
rock→firmly→wind→sea
  Whitney, Emblemes, 1586, p.096
rock→sand→danger→coast
  Whitney, Emblemes, 1586, p.137
rock→Thrace→Apollo→tree
  Whitney, Emblemes, 1586, p.186
rock→heat→cold→storm
  Whitney, Emblemes, 1586, p.203
rod→Paul→fault→condemn
  Whitney, Emblemes, 1586, p.060

rod→father→yield→whip
  Whitney, Emblemes, 1586, p.112
roof→board[1]→head→sword
  Whitney, Emblemes, 1586, p.102
roof→flame→mad→town
  Whitney, Emblemes, 1586, p.208
root→rot→frost→bloom
  Whitney, Emblemes, 1586, p.034
root→fruitful→sap→age
  Whitney, Emblemes, 1586, p.062
root→grass→bare→frost
  Whitney, Emblemes, 1586, p.159
root→wisdom→idiot→rancour
  Whitney, Emblemes, 1586, p.178
root→table→stool→meat
  Whitney, Emblemes, 1586, p.198
rope→rush→grass→Ocnus
  Whitney, Emblemes, 1586, p.048
rope→parent→steal
  Whitney, Emblemes, 1586, p.155
rose→beautiful→scarabee→scent
  Whitney, Emblemes, 1586, p.021
rose→bait→beauty→poison
  Whitney, Emblemes, 1586, p.147
rose→wound→heart→son
  Whitney, Emblemes, 1586, p.148
rose→finger→sharp→prick
  Whitney, Emblemes, 1586, p.165
rot→frost→bloom→root
  Whitney, Emblemes, 1586, p.034
rotten→green→soon→ripe
  Whitney, Emblemes, 1586, p.173
royal→God→word→teach
  Whitney, Emblemes, 1586, p.008
royal→seat→Dionysius→king
  Whitney, Emblemes, 1586, p.102
rude→bird→learned→wise
  Whitney, Emblemes, 1586, p.186
rue→destroy→mouth→wound
  Whitney, Emblemes, 1586, p.060
rue→life→city→river→fortune
  Whitney, Emblemes, 1586, p.089
rue→deride→summer→winter→song
  Whitney, Emblemes, 1586, p.175
rue→dart→wanton→hope
  Whitney, Emblemes, 1586, p.219
ruffian→heart→relent→rancour→
  friend
  Whitney, Emblemes, 1586, p.216b
ruin→captain→overthrow→strength
  Whitney, Emblemes, 1586, p.047
ruin→wall→captain→quail
  Whitney, Emblemes, 1586, p.066
ruin→reign→kingdom→England
  Whitney, Emblemes, 1586, p.122
ruin→peace→barren→fruit
  Whitney, Emblemes, 1586, p.174
ruin→wheel→monarch→Rome
  Whitney, Emblemes, 1586, p.196
rule→endless→fame→estate[1]→justice
  Whitney, Emblemes, 1586, p.038
rule→reign→subject→fear→tyrant
  Whitney, Emblemes, 1586, p.102
rule→obey→head→commonwealth
  Whitney, Emblemes, 1586, p.200
rule→king→sick→sceptre
  Whitney, Emblemes, 1586, p.212
rum→save→life→rashly
  Whitney, Emblemes, 1586, p.097
run→reprehend→toil→water
  Whitney, Emblemes, 1586, p.012
run→youth→heart→hourglass
  [= glass]→glass [= hourglass]
  Whitney, Emblemes, 1586, p.050b
run→despise→harm→devise→stag
  Whitney, Emblemes, 1586, p.052a

rush→grass→Ocnus→rope
  Whitney, Emblemes, 1586, p.048
russet→nature→poor→gray
  Whitney, Emblemes, 1586, p.134
rust→envy→soldier→plough→armour
  Whitney, Emblemes, 1586, p.076a
rust→sin→grief→treasure
  Whitney, Emblemes, 1586, p.225
ruth [= pity]→disease→age[1]→youth
  Whitney, Emblemes, 1586, p.099
ruth [= pity]→conscience→rich→poor
  Whitney, Emblemes, 1586, p.136
sable→chest→ebony→Parnassus
  Whitney, Emblemes, 1586, p.196
sack→rob→greedy→shop
  Whitney, Emblemes, 1586, p.041
sack→meal[1]→wife→steal
  Whitney, Emblemes, 1586, p.080
sack[1] = destruction and plundering of
  a city
sack[1]→son→joy→spoil[1]
  Whitney, Emblemes, 1586, p.163
sacred→reason→escape→man
  Whitney, Emblemes, 1586, p.097
sacred→goddess→prince→duty
  Whitney, Emblemes, 1586, p.122
sacred→bird→shield→Phoebus
  Whitney, Emblemes, 1586, p.126
sacred→Justice→statute→tomb
  Whitney, Emblemes, 1586, p.136
sacred→phoenix→rare→Arabia
  Whitney, Emblemes, 1586, p.177
sacred→reason→God→image
  Whitney, Emblemes, 1586, p.229b
safe→pilot→rob→sea→dolphin
  Whitney, Emblemes, 1586, p.144
safely→foe→mud→stream
  Whitney, Emblemes, 1586, p.097
safety→strike→head→prudent
  Whitney, Emblemes, 1586, p.076b
sage→seven→Greece→wisdom
  Whitney, Emblemes, 1586, p.130
sage→wisdom→book→Cupid→heart
  Whitney, Emblemes, 1586, p.135
sail→land→earth→ship
  Whitney, Emblemes, 1586, p.129
sail→wind→ship→sea
  Whitney, Emblemes, 1586, p.137
saint→Judas→heart→good
  Whitney, Emblemes, 1586, p.100
salt→sweet→corrupt→sea
  Whitney, Emblemes, 1586, p.072
salvation→bless→book→west→shine
  Whitney, Emblemes, 1586, p.166a
sanctity→religion→shadow→
  substance→hypocrite
  Whitney, Emblemes, 1586, p.051b
sand→seek→Ganges→golden
  Whitney, Emblemes, 1586, p.039
sand→danger→coast→rock
  Whitney, Emblemes, 1586, p.137
sand→knight→course→gulf
  Whitney, Emblemes, 1586, p.203
sap→age→root→fruitful
  Whitney, Emblemes, 1586, p.062
sap→bough→warm→age→tree
  Whitney, Emblemes, 1586, p.077b
satyr→host→winter→night
  Whitney, Emblemes, 1586, p.160
savage→brute→condemn→seed→bird
  Whitney, Emblemes, 1586, p.029
savage→fierce→cruel→brute
  Whitney, Emblemes, 1586, p.186
save→Elizabeth I [= Majesty]→
  Majesty [= Elizabeth I]→sword→
  mercy

shame→deed→self→love→reproach
  Whitney, Emblemes, 1586, p.149
shame→despise→stock→reprehend
  Whitney, Emblemes, 1586, p.163
shame→crown→fame→wicked
  Whitney, Emblemes, 1586, p.183a
shame→climb→fool
  Whitney, Emblemes, 1586, p.190a
shame→strife→suffer→foe→subdue
  Whitney, Emblemes, 1586, p.220
shamefastness→Roman→captain→boy
  Whitney, Emblemes, 1586, p.134
shameless→tail→deride→hide
  Whitney, Emblemes, 1586, p.142
share→small→secure→profit
  Whitney, Emblemes, 1586, p.026
share→rage→prey→spoil[1]
  Whitney, Emblemes, 1586, p.154
sharp→sheaf→bind→arrow
  Whitney, Emblemes, 1586, p.072
sharp→try[1]→peace→force
  Whitney, Emblemes, 1586, p.153b
sharp→prick→rose→finger
  Whitney, Emblemes, 1586, p.165
shave→pill→poll→fat
  Whitney, Emblemes, 1586, p.151
sheaf→bind→arrow→sharp
  Whitney, Emblemes, 1586, p.072
sheath→fool→sword→gold
  Whitney, Emblemes, 1586, p.214
sheep→God→fear→wolf
  Whitney, Emblemes, 1586, p.194
sheep→fleece→nature→gift
  Whitney, Emblemes, 1586, p.214
shell→egg→suck→empty
  Whitney, Emblemes, 1586, p.064
shield→sword→furious→mind
  Whitney, Emblemes, 1586, p.045
shield→bloody→thought→Agamemnon
  Whitney, Emblemes, 1586, p.045
shield→sword→good
  Whitney, Emblemes, 1586, p.051a
shield→eye→lose→shaft
  Whitney, Emblemes, 1586, p.117
shield→Phoebus→sacred→bird
  Whitney, Emblemes, 1586, p.126
shield→trust→bane→wound
  Whitney, Emblemes, 1586, p.141
shine→suspect→outward→inward
  Whitney, Emblemes, 1586, p.069
shine→salvation→bless→book→west
  Whitney, Emblemes, 1586, p.166a
ship→azure→surge→tide
  Whitney, Emblemes, 1586, p.011
ship→hope→sea→wrong
  Whitney, Emblemes, 1586, p.090
ship→town→fate→overcome
  Whitney, Emblemes, 1586, p.114
ship→sail→land→earth
  Whitney, Emblemes, 1586, p.129
ship→sea→sail→wind
  Whitney, Emblemes, 1586, p.137
ship→Corinth→gold→harp→voice
  Whitney, Emblemes, 1586, p.144
ship→gold→labourer [= travailer]→
  travailer [= labourer]
  Whitney, Emblemes, 1586, p.179
ship→foe→blood→God
  Whitney, Emblemes, 1586, p.203
shipman→lap→pine→axe
  Whitney, Emblemes, 1586, p.140
shirt→spear→Aschalon→trumpet
  Whitney, Emblemes, 1586, p.086
shoot→prince→might→Jove
  Whitney, Emblemes, 1586, p.061
shoot→arrow→slander→word→arrow

Whitney, Emblemes, 1586, p.138b
shop→sack→rob→greedy
  Whitney, Emblemes, 1586, p.041
shore→flood→Neptune→dolphin
  Whitney, Emblemes, 1586, p.090
shore→sea→world→overthrow
  Whitney, Emblemes, 1586, p.129
shot→foe→wind→tackle
  Whitney, Emblemes, 1586, p.011
shot→guilty→mind→fearful→brass
  Whitney, Emblemes, 1586, p.032
shoulder→rich→give→toil
  Whitney, Emblemes, 1586, p.065
show→beguile→gallant→look
  Whitney, Emblemes, 1586, p.139a
show→nettle→joy→gallant
  Whitney, Emblemes, 1586, p.147
show→heat→fire→zeal→hypocrite
  Whitney, Emblemes, 1586, p.226b
shrink→ink→hand→shake
  Whitney, Emblemes, 1586, p.143
shroud→greatness→birth→nature
  Whitney, Emblemes, 1586, p.086
shroud→gulf→grief→mirth
  Whitney, Emblemes, 1586, p.141
shun→freedom→resign
  Whitney, Emblemes, 1586, p.036
shun→crowing→white→elephant
  Whitney, Emblemes, 1586, p.052a
shun→tongue→double→mouth→
  friendship
  Whitney, Emblemes, 1586, p.160
shun→beast→transform→secret
  Whitney, Emblemes, 1586, p.187
shut→eye→despite→harm
  Whitney, Emblemes, 1586, p.031
sick→mansion→vile→delight
  Whitney, Emblemes, 1586, p.021
sick→fox→hole→hide
  Whitney, Emblemes, 1586, p.161
sick→treasure→miser→gold
  Whitney, Emblemes, 1586, p.209
sick→fox→lion→prey→feign
  Whitney, Emblemes, 1586, p.210
sick→secret→wound→heart
  Whitney, Emblemes, 1586, p.211
sick→sceptre→rule→king
  Whitney, Emblemes, 1586, p.212
sickness→disease→poet→colour
  Whitney, Emblemes, 1586, p.146
siege→conceit→rest→friend
  Whitney, Emblemes, 1586, p.025
siege→king→pardon→knight
  Whitney, Emblemes, 1586, p.111
siege→defend→iron→Cremona
  Whitney, Emblemes, 1586, p.115
siege→pray→fear→soul
  Whitney, Emblemes, 1586, p.129
siege→city→cannon→foe
  Whitney, Emblemes, 1586, p.189a
sift→prudent→judgement→deed→
  weight
  Whitney, Emblemes, 1586, p.068
sigh→untimely→counsel→secret
  Whitney, Emblemes, 1586, p.025
sight→decay→fool→stage
  Whitney, Emblemes, 1586, p.014
sight→face→eye→wing
  Whitney, Emblemes, 1586, p.113
sight→purblind→dame→help
  Whitney, Emblemes, 1586, p.156a
sight→smell→hearing→head
  Whitney, Emblemes, 1586, p.229b
sign→Harpocrates→finger→mouth
  Whitney, Emblemes, 1586, p.060
silence→philosopher→Pythagoras→

scholar
  Whitney, Emblemes, 1586, p.060
silence→woe→dumb→fool
  Whitney, Emblemes, 1586, p.060
silence [= peace]→peace [= silence]→
  princely→see
  Whitney, Emblemes, 1586, p.061
silk→chain→wise→Pompey
  Whitney, Emblemes, 1586, p.202
silver→age→time→change
  Whitney, Emblemes, 1586, p.122
silver→harmony→war→entrail
  Whitney, Emblemes, 1586, p.194
simple→truth→truth→sun→ground
  Whitney, Emblemes, 1586, p.020
sin→Democritus→laughter→age
  Whitney, Emblemes, 1586, p.014
sin→guilt→grief→pure→soil
  Whitney, Emblemes, 1586, p.032
sin→Midas→eye→lose
  Whitney, Emblemes, 1586, p.095
sin→Christ→pastor→world
  Whitney, Emblemes, 1586, p.120
sin→crime→sleep
  Whitney, Emblemes, 1586, p.129
sin→grief→treasure→rust
  Whitney, Emblemes, 1586, p.225
sincere→poet→clean→white
  Whitney, Emblemes, 1586, p.126
sing→flee→fault→ambition
  Whitney, Emblemes, 1586, p.084
sing→mourn→wood[1]→cage
  Whitney, Emblemes, 1586, p.101
sing→experience→wise→snow
  Whitney, Emblemes, 1586, p.159
sing→storm→weather→grief→joy
  Whitney, Emblemes, 1586, p.165
sinner→forgive→fool
  Whitney, Emblemes, 1586, p.229a
sire→friend→death→aged
  Whitney, Emblemes, 1586, p.044
siren→Ulysses→tune→listen
  Whitney, Emblemes, 1586, p.010
sit→constant→staff→skill
  Whitney, Emblemes, 1586, p.212
skill→streamer→captain→mariner
  Whitney, Emblemes, 1586, p.011
skill→divine→song→poet
  Whitney, Emblemes, 1586, p.126
skill→book→libel→name→fear
  Whitney, Emblemes, 1586, p.127
skill→workman→sleep→trade
  Whitney, Emblemes, 1586, p.145
skill→adorn→wit→studious
  Whitney, Emblemes, 1586, p.172
skill→sit→constant→staff
  Whitney, Emblemes, 1586, p.212
skin→Hercules→club→lion
  Whitney, Emblemes, 1586, p.016
skin→godly→word→wolf
  Whitney, Emblemes, 1586, p.100
skin→sovereign→patient[1]→heal→lick
  Whitney, Emblemes, 1586, p.161
skin→two→drum→string
  Whitney, Emblemes, 1586, p.194
skull→men→care→place
  Whitney, Emblemes, 1586, p.046
skull→charnel→house→taste
  Whitney, Emblemes, 1586, p.229b
sky→gallant→cloud→ploughman
  Whitney, Emblemes, 1586, p.009
sky→fall→despise→astronomy
  Whitney, Emblemes, 1586, p.078
sky→star→danger→study
  Whitney, Emblemes, 1586, p.078
sky→hope→praise→Hanno

Whitney, Emblemes, 1586, p.084
sky→curious→chance→year
Whitney, Emblemes, 1586, p.157
sky→Phoebus→passion→cloud
Whitney, Emblemes, 1586, p.196
sky→spire→knight→trumpet
Whitney, Emblemes, 1586, p.196
sky→duck→goose→falcon
Whitney, Emblemes, 1586, p.207
slander→defame→hare→bite→lion
Whitney, Emblemes, 1586, p.127
slander→word→arrow→shoot→arrow
Whitney, Emblemes, 1586, p.138b
slander→patience→combat→force→
    contempt
Whitney, Emblemes, 1586, p.220
slave→bind→misfortune→sorrow
Whitney, Emblemes, 1586, p.075
slave→prince→poor→prisoner
Whitney, Emblemes, 1586, p.086
slay→tear→pine^1→child
Whitney, Emblemes, 1586, p.013
slay→deceive→warning→destroy→bird
Whitney, Emblemes, 1586, p.033
slay→Corinth→idly→warn
Whitney, Emblemes, 1586, p.085
slay→try^1→trust→tree
Whitney, Emblemes, 1586, p.150
slay→martyrdom→glorious→crown
Whitney, Emblemes, 1586, p.224a
sleep→pigmy→kill→foolish
Whitney, Emblemes, 1586, p.016
sleep→flesh→neck→alehouse
Whitney, Emblemes, 1586, p.041
sleep→bed→fleshly→slothful
Whitney, Emblemes, 1586, p.042
sleep→swallow→awake→weary
Whitney, Emblemes, 1586, p.050a
sleep→steeple→cock→wake
Whitney, Emblemes, 1586, p.120
sleep→sin→crime
Whitney, Emblemes, 1586, p.129
sleep→part→last^1→joy→wake
Whitney, Emblemes, 1586, p.137
sleep→mistress→bed→fate
Whitney, Emblemes, 1586, p.140
sleep→trade→skill→workman
Whitney, Emblemes, 1586, p.145
sleep→strong→peril→fear
Whitney, Emblemes, 1586, p.150
sleep→Dyer→pear→grave→peace
Whitney, Emblemes, 1586, p.196
sleep→secure→peril→awaken
Whitney, Emblemes, 1586, p.208
sleep→purse→greed→lethargy
Whitney, Emblemes, 1586, p.209
sleight [= trick]→ground→miller→
    trick [= sleight]
Whitney, Emblemes, 1586, p.080
slide→fame→worldly→pride
Whitney, Emblemes, 1586, p.034
slide→poison→wall→serpent
Whitney, Emblemes, 1586, p.076b
slip→well→fool→shade
Whitney, Emblemes, 1586, p.157
sloth→snare→weaken→disdain
Whitney, Emblemes, 1586, p.103
slothful→sleep→bed→fleshly
Whitney, Emblemes, 1586, p.042
slothful→flee→labour→leave
Whitney, Emblemes, 1586, p.085
slothful→Saint→Paul→threaten
Whitney, Emblemes, 1586, p.085
slow→home→blame→king→house
Whitney, Emblemes, 1586, p.091
slow→butterfly→crab→prince

Whitney, Emblemes, 1586, p.121
slow→fruit→ripe→fade
Whitney, Emblemes, 1586, p.173
slow→haste→reason
Whitney, Emblemes, 1586, p.188b
sluice→stain→ebb→flow
Whitney, Emblemes, 1586, p.072
small→secure→profit→share
Whitney, Emblemes, 1586, p.026
small→gain→one→grove
Whitney, Emblemes, 1586, p.055a
small→guide→increase→store
Whitney, Emblemes, 1586, p.088
smart^1 = pain
smart^1→Judas→heart→weigh
Whitney, Emblemes, 1586, p.141
smell→die→house→filthy
Whitney, Emblemes, 1586, p.021
smell→venture→bleed→pleasant
Whitney, Emblemes, 1586, p.165
smell→fruit→cypress→green→sweet
Whitney, Emblemes, 1586, p.205
smell→hearing→head→sight
Whitney, Emblemes, 1586, p.229b
smile→heart→face→fawn^1
Whitney, Emblemes, 1586, p.024
smile→laugh→wealth→fortune
Whitney, Emblemes, 1586, p.059
smile→foe→arm^1→malice
Whitney, Emblemes, 1586, p.124
smoke→cloth→cocky→lion→quake
Whitney, Emblemes, 1586, p.052a
smooth→win→Alcides→pleasure
Whitney, Emblemes, 1586, p.040
snail→feast→Jupiter→beast→creature
Whitney, Emblemes, 1586, p.091
snail→pen→haste→desire
Whitney, Emblemes, 1586, p.185
snake→head→venom→brain
Whitney, Emblemes, 1586, p.094
snake→poison→elephant→sting
Whitney, Emblemes, 1586, p.195
snake→wound→Aspasia→plague
Whitney, Emblemes, 1586, p.219
snare→wile→fall→trust
Whitney, Emblemes, 1586, p.059
snare→weaken→disdain→sloth
Whitney, Emblemes, 1586, p.103
snore→woman→fish→beauty
Whitney, Emblemes, 1586, p.010
snow→mountain→rage→wave
Whitney, Emblemes, 1586, p.011
snow→hill→valley→report
Whitney, Emblemes, 1586, p.020
snow→sing→experience→wise
Whitney, Emblemes, 1586, p.159
society→proverb→life→kindness
Whitney, Emblemes, 1586, p.065
soft→step→rash→repent
Whitney, Emblemes, 1586, p.185
soil→wealth→abundance→mar
Whitney, Emblemes, 1586, p.023
soil→sin→guilt→grief→pure
Whitney, Emblemes, 1586, p.032
soil→flee→world→foreign
Whitney, Emblemes, 1586, p.178
soldier→plough→armour→rust→envy
Whitney, Emblemes, 1586, p.076a
soldier→Caesar→host→thigh
Whitney, Emblemes, 1586, p.117
soldier→fruit→bloody→honey
Whitney, Emblemes, 1586, p.138a
son→powder→intestine→strife
Whitney, Emblemes, 1586, p.007
son→wheat [= corn]→corn [= wheat]→
    wind

Whitney, Emblemes, 1586, p.026
son→hope→greedy→vain^1
Whitney, Emblemes, 1586, p.044
son→name→nature→Junius
Whitney, Emblemes, 1586, p.096
son→foster→scholar→harm
Whitney, Emblemes, 1586, p.112
son→honour→law→Venus
Whitney, Emblemes, 1586, p.132
son→Jove→Apollo→two
Whitney, Emblemes, 1586, p.146
son→rose→wound→heart
Whitney, Emblemes, 1586, p.148
son→child→teeth→nose
Whitney, Emblemes, 1586, p.155
son→joy→spoil^1→sack^1
Whitney, Emblemes, 1586, p.163
son→kind^1→heart→fear
Whitney, Emblemes, 1586, p.163
song→heart→charm→face
Whitney, Emblemes, 1586, p.010
song→poet→skill→divine
Whitney, Emblemes, 1586, p.126
song→rue→deride→summer→winter
Whitney, Emblemes, 1586, p.175
soon→ripe→rotten→green
Whitney, Emblemes, 1586, p.173
sore→folly→dotage→secret
Whitney, Emblemes, 1586, p.149
sorrow→slave→bind→misfortune
Whitney, Emblemes, 1586, p.075
sorrow→life→band→grief
Whitney, Emblemes, 1586, p.075
sorrow→die→kiss→mother
Whitney, Emblemes, 1586, p.155
sot→learned→defame→mighty
Whitney, Emblemes, 1586, p.016
sot→judge→poor→learned
Whitney, Emblemes, 1586, p.149
soul→untamed→reason→affection
Whitney, Emblemes, 1586, p.006
soul→siege→pray→fear
Whitney, Emblemes, 1586, p.129
soul→Mammon→worldling→gain→loss
Whitney, Emblemes, 1586, p.223
sour→Lord→happy→hour→sweet
Whitney, Emblemes, 1586, p.097
sour→force→labour→sweet
Whitney, Emblemes, 1586, p.147
sour→merit→sweet→taste
Whitney, Emblemes, 1586, p.165
sour→write→amend→fruit
Whitney, Emblemes, 1586, p.185
sour→grape→ripe→travail
Whitney, Emblemes, 1586, p.206
sovereign→patient^1→heal→lick→skin
Whitney, Emblemes, 1586, p.161
sow→harvest→greedy
Whitney, Emblemes, 1586, p.053a
sow→season→Ceres→seed
Whitney, Emblemes, 1586, p.122
speak→heed→steed→lock
Whitney, Emblemes, 1586, p.180
speak→flee→evil [= naught]→naught
    [= evil]→hear
Whitney, Emblemes, 1586, p.191b
spear→Aschalon→trumpet→shirt
Whitney, Emblemes, 1586, p.086
spear→crown→garland→honour→
    fortune
Whitney, Emblemes, 1586, p.115
speech→offend→lewd→harm→wicked
Whitney, Emblemes, 1586, p.019
speech→sugar→word→flatter
Whitney, Emblemes, 1586, p.024
speech→knight→impatient→subtle

Whitney, Emblemes, 1586, p.030
speech→vain[1]→Cato→condemn
   Whitney, Emblemes, 1586, p.060
speech→reason→God→square
   Whitney, Emblemes, 1586, p.060
speech→love→tongue→fear
   Whitney, Emblemes, 1586, p.141
speech→friend→hawk→lure→prey
   Whitney, Emblemes, 1586, p.191a
speech→gallant→cloak→fawn[1]→sugar
   Whitney, Emblemes, 1586, p.226a
speed→gift→poor
   Whitney, Emblemes, 1586, p.190b
spend→lewdly→wicked→wasteful→
   wife
   Whitney, Emblemes, 1586, p.048
spend→God→land→country
   Whitney, Emblemes, 1586, p.199
sphere→globe→learning→experience
   Whitney, Emblemes, 1586, p.009
spider→bee→one→flower
   Whitney, Emblemes, 1586, p.051a
spill→blood→care→forget
   Whitney, Emblemes, 1586, p.049
spin→toil→work→ass→spoil
   Whitney, Emblemes, 1586, p.048
spire→ivy→bloom→pillar
   Whitney, Emblemes, 1586, p.001
spire→suffer→spoil[1]→Egypt
   Whitney, Emblemes, 1586, p.131
spire→Babel→mount→decline→Egypt
   Whitney, Emblemes, 1586, p.167
spire→knight→trumpet→sky
   Whitney, Emblemes, 1586, p.196
spite→assail→flee→field[1]
   Whitney, Emblemes, 1586, p.127
spite→mortal→foe→poison
   Whitney, Emblemes, 1586, p.144
spite→food→covet→envy
   Whitney, Emblemes, 1586, p.184
spiteful→honest→blind
   Whitney, Emblemes, 1586, p.095
spoil→wheat [= corn]→corn
   [= wheat]→excess
   Whitney, Emblemes, 1586, p.023
spoil→spin→toil→work→ass
   Whitney, Emblemes, 1586, p.048
spoil→fool→love→teach→harm
   Whitney, Emblemes, 1586, p.188a
spoil→blood→price→captain
   Whitney, Emblemes, 1586, p.195
spoil[1] = booty
spoil[1]→lion→content→vulture
   Whitney, Emblemes, 1586, p.119
spoil[1]→Egypt→spire→suffer
   Whitney, Emblemes, 1586, p.131
spoil[1]→share→rage→prey
   Whitney, Emblemes, 1586, p.154
spoil[1]→sack[1]→son→joy
   Whitney, Emblemes, 1586, p.163
spoil[1]→rapine→theft→might
   Whitney, Emblemes, 1586, p.170
sponge→dry→cut→wool
   Whitney, Emblemes, 1586, p.151
sport→astronomer→court→rain
   Whitney, Emblemes, 1586, p.009
sport→subject→poor→king
   Whitney, Emblemes, 1586, p.151
sport→chain→servant→miser
   Whitney, Emblemes, 1586, p.169
spouse→Vulcan→night→day→strife
   Whitney, Emblemes, 1586, p.080
spring→Boreas→bush→tree
   Whitney, Emblemes, 1586, p.029
spring→cuckoo→summer→swallow
   Whitney, Emblemes, 1586, p.054b

spring→warble→nightingale→chant
   Whitney, Emblemes, 1586, p.101
spring→night→day→winter
   Whitney, Emblemes, 1586, p.165
spring[1]→fertile→field→crystal
   Whitney, Emblemes, 1586, p.200
square→deed→right[1]→imp→race
   Whitney, Emblemes, 1586, p.019
square→speech→reason→God
   Whitney, Emblemes, 1586, p.060
staff→Egyptian→Isis→kneel
   Whitney, Emblemes, 1586, p.008
staff→gall→tongue→sting
   Whitney, Emblemes, 1586, p.094
staff→skill→sit→constant
   Whitney, Emblemes, 1586, p.212
stag→transform→hound→bold
   Whitney, Emblemes, 1586, p.015
stag→run→despise→harm→devise
   Whitney, Emblemes, 1586, p.052a
stag→escape→hunter→chase
   Whitney, Emblemes, 1586, p.153a
stag→race→phoenix→burn
   Whitney, Emblemes, 1586, p.230
stage→sight→decay→fool
   Whitney, Emblemes, 1586, p.014
stage→muscat→beauty→Lais
   Whitney, Emblemes, 1586, p.079
stage→act→martial→knight
   Whitney, Emblemes, 1586, p.131
stain→ebb→flow→sluice
   Whitney, Emblemes, 1586, p.072
stalk→Ceres→ear→break
   Whitney, Emblemes, 1586, p.023
star→betide→search→heavy
   Whitney, Emblemes, 1586, p.028
star→seaman→chart [= card]→card
   [= chart]
   Whitney, Emblemes, 1586, p.043
star→Scylla→Charybdis→win
   Whitney, Emblemes, 1586, p.043
star→danger→study→sky
   Whitney, Emblemes, 1586, p.078
star→hand→wing→fly
   Whitney, Emblemes, 1586, p.152
star→divine[1]→astronomer→night
   Whitney, Emblemes, 1586, p.157
starve→hope→fortune→grass→courser
   Whitney, Emblemes, 1586, p.026
starve→constant→hope→Christian
   Whitney, Emblemes, 1586, p.071
starve→chin→food→wretch
   Whitney, Emblemes, 1586, p.074
starve→help→food→grasshopper
   Whitney, Emblemes, 1586, p.159
starve→Homer→Muse→fast[1]→beg
   Whitney, Emblemes, 1586, p.168a
starve→bolt→brazen→bar→God
   Whitney, Emblemes, 1586, p.169
starve→youth→provide→age[1]→food
   Whitney, Emblemes, 1586, p.175
starve→hay→cur→manger
   Whitney, Emblemes, 1586, p.184
starve [= die]→Medea→dame→die
   [= starve]
   Whitney, Emblemes, 1586, p.029
state→prey→destroy→feeble
   Whitney, Emblemes, 1586, p.052b
state→sure→life→fall
   Whitney, Emblemes, 1586, p.150
state[1] = section of journey
state[1]→fall→death→old
   Whitney, Emblemes, 1586, p.225
statute→tomb→sacred→Justice
   Whitney, Emblemes, 1586, p.136
steal→sack→meal[1]→wife

Whitney, Emblemes, 1586, p.080
steal→time→Carthage→rage
   Whitney, Emblemes, 1586, p.131
steal→rope→parent
   Whitney, Emblemes, 1586, p.155
steal→patient[1]→see→false
   Whitney, Emblemes, 1586, p.156a
steal→birth→death→Nestor
   Whitney, Emblemes, 1586, p.167
steed→bit→rider→fool
   Whitney, Emblemes, 1586, p.038
steed→lock→speak→heed
   Whitney, Emblemes, 1586, p.180
steel→arms→force→weapon
   Whitney, Emblemes, 1586, p.113
steel→grass→Troy→gate
   Whitney, Emblemes, 1586, p.131
steel→grace→heart
   Whitney, Emblemes, 1586, p.218b
steep→craggy→endure→ascend
   Whitney, Emblemes, 1586, p.040
steeple→cock→wake→sleep
   Whitney, Emblemes, 1586, p.120
step→rash→repent→soft
   Whitney, Emblemes, 1586, p.185
step→secret→mischief→threat→de
   Whitney, Emblemes, 1586, p.210
stern→Envy→hog→visage
   Whitney, Emblemes, 1586, p.094
stewardship→fear→betray→flee
   Whitney, Emblemes, 1586, p.130
stews [= brothel]→flatterer→feed→
   waste→brothel [= stews]
   Whitney, Emblemes, 1586, p.053b
sting→adder→grass→poison
   Whitney, Emblemes, 1586, p.078
sting→staff→gall→tongue
   Whitney, Emblemes, 1586, p.094
sting→mate→serpent
   Whitney, Emblemes, 1586, p.142
sting→hive→naked→arm[1]
   Whitney, Emblemes, 1586, p.147
sting→mother→cry→help
   Whitney, Emblemes, 1586, p.148
sting→snake→poison→elephant
   Whitney, Emblemes, 1586, p.195
sting→harm→reverence→bliss
   Whitney, Emblemes, 1586, p.200
sting→virtue→vice→wicked
   Whitney, Emblemes, 1586, p.221
stith [= anvil]→youth→strength→anvil
   [= stith]
   Whitney, Emblemes, 1586, p.192
stock→ape→block→foot→crush
   Whitney, Emblemes, 1586, p.145
stock→reprehend→shame→despise
   Whitney, Emblemes, 1586, p.163
stone→bite→angry→dog
   Whitney, Emblemes, 1586, p.056
stone→lime→sword→wall
   Whitney, Emblemes, 1586, p.066
stone→last[1]→monument→marble
   Whitney, Emblemes, 1586, p.131
stone→ground→wish→bind
   Whitney, Emblemes, 1586, p.152
stone→hill→toil→Sisyphus
   Whitney, Emblemes, 1586, p.215
stone [= testicle]→hunter→desire→
   testicle [= stone]
   Whitney, Emblemes, 1586, p.035
stool→meat→root→table
   Whitney, Emblemes, 1586, p.198
stoop→branch→friend→help→old
   Whitney, Emblemes, 1586, p.062
stoop→Thebes→grass→Babel
   Whitney, Emblemes, 1586, p.131

sweet→time→perfection→fruit→
   flower
   Whitney, Emblemes, 1586, p.206
swell→hand→water
   Whitney, Emblemes, 1586, p.151
swift→tooth→paw→hare
   Whitney, Emblemes, 1586, p.182b
swift→remora [= echeneis]→echeneis
   [= remora]→arrow
   Whitney, Emblemes, 1586, p.188b
swim→foe→cormorant→seamew
   Whitney, Emblemes, 1586, p.052b
sword→storm→tyrant→fire
   Whitney, Emblemes, 1586, p.001
sword→bloody→home→civil
   Whitney, Emblemes, 1586, p.007
sword→Lynceus→eye→blind→Ajax
   Whitney, Emblemes, 1586, p.037
sword→furious→mind→shield
   Whitney, Emblemes, 1586, p.045
sword→good→shield
   Whitney, Emblemes, 1586, p.051a
sword→fire→remorse→subject→
   famine
   Whitney, Emblemes, 1586, p.058
sword→evil→word→pierce
   Whitney, Emblemes, 1586, p.060
sword→mercy→save→Elizabeth I
   [= Majesty]→Majesty
   [= Elizabeth I]
   Whitney, Emblemes, 1586, p.061
sword→wall→stone→lime
   Whitney, Emblemes, 1586, p.066
sword→flee→blade→heart
   Whitney, Emblemes, 1586, p.070
sword→roof→board[1]→head
   Whitney, Emblemes, 1586, p.102
sword→flame→heart→hand
   Whitney, Emblemes, 1586, p.111
sword→Roman→youth→Valerius
   Whitney, Emblemes, 1586, p.113
sword→France→triumph→success→
   Placentia
   Whitney, Emblemes, 1586, p.115
sword→valiant→foe→fire
   Whitney, Emblemes, 1586, p.163
sword→gold→sheath→fool
   Whitney, Emblemes, 1586, p.214
sword→laurel→sun→ire
   Whitney, Emblemes, 1586, p.216b
sword→fire→constant→lamb
   Whitney, Emblemes, 1586, p.224a
sycophant [= pickthank]→pickthank
   [= sycophant]→blab→Sinon
   Whitney, Emblemes, 1586, p.150
table→page[1]→provisions [= cate]→
   cate [= provisions]
   Whitney, Emblemes, 1586, p.102
table→stool→meat→root
   Whitney, Emblemes, 1586, p.198
table→languish→heir→physician
   Whitney, Emblemes, 1586, p.209
table[1] = tablet
table[1]→write→word→cognisance
   Whitney, Emblemes, 1586, p.100
tabret→crown→grape→pipe
   Whitney, Emblemes, 1586, p.187
tackle→shot→foe→wind
   Whitney, Emblemes, 1586, p.011
tail→mole→eye→horn
   Whitney, Emblemes, 1586, p.093a
tail→deride→hide→shameless
   Whitney, Emblemes, 1586, p.142
talon→ire→whet→griffin
   Whitney, Emblemes, 1586, p.100
tame→order→havoc→man

Whitney, Emblemes, 1586, p.006
tame→duck→net→fowl
   Whitney, Emblemes, 1586, p.027
tame→Jove→remorse→help
   Whitney, Emblemes, 1586, p.063
tame→music→Orpheus→harp
   Whitney, Emblemes, 1586, p.186
tare→fruitful→field→crop
   Whitney, Emblemes, 1586, p.068
target→corpse→mortal→courage
   Whitney, Emblemes, 1586, p.141
tart→boast→limb→disdain→taste
   Whitney, Emblemes, 1586, p.098a
taste→tart→boast→limb→disdain
   Whitney, Emblemes, 1586, p.098a
taste→princely→fare→Damocles
   Whitney, Emblemes, 1586, p.102
taste→crab→adder→sugar
   Whitney, Emblemes, 1586, p.141
taste→sour→merit→sweet
   Whitney, Emblemes, 1586, p.165
taste→harm→perfection→time
   Whitney, Emblemes, 1586, p.185
taste→skull→charnel→house
   Whitney, Emblemes, 1586, p.229b
tawny→red→covetous→jealousy
   Whitney, Emblemes, 1586, p.134
tea→thousand→colour→stranger
   Whitney, Emblemes, 1586, p.134
teach→foretell→crocodile→Egyptian
   Whitney, Emblemes, 1586, p.003
teach→royal→God→word
   Whitney, Emblemes, 1586, p.008
teach→fortune→wheel→climb→time
   Whitney, Emblemes, 1586, p.011
teach→bird→trust→name
   Whitney, Emblemes, 1586, p.084
teach→harm→spoil→fool→love
   Whitney, Emblemes, 1586, p.188a
tear→pine[1]→child→slay
   Whitney, Emblemes, 1586, p.013
tear→fire→odour→wash
   Whitney, Emblemes, 1586, p.116
tear→crocutta [= hyena]→crocodile→
   treason
   Whitney, Emblemes, 1586, p.219
tear[1] = rip
tear[1]→piece→happy→harm→beware
   Whitney, Emblemes, 1586, p.154
teat→meat→tyrant→whelp
   Whitney, Emblemes, 1586, p.049
teen [= injury]→virtue→hurt→foe→
   injury [= teen]
   Whitney, Emblemes, 1586, p.138b
teeth→beaver→danger→hound
   Whitney, Emblemes, 1586, p.035
teeth→nose→son→child
   Whitney, Emblemes, 1586, p.155
tempest→rage→world→aghast→fear
   Whitney, Emblemes, 1586, p.067
tempest→yield→envy→hate
   Whitney, Emblemes, 1586, p.220
temple→god→war→image→rite
   Whitney, Emblemes, 1586, p.108
tenant→gold→time→praise→country
   Whitney, Emblemes, 1586, p.200
tender→dame→feeble→pity
   Whitney, Emblemes, 1586, p.063
terror→fear→verse→brass
   Whitney, Emblemes, 1586, p.045
terror→Hector→Zizka→foe
   Whitney, Emblemes, 1586, p.194
testicle [= stone]→stone [= testicle]→
   hunter→desire
   Whitney, Emblemes, 1586, p.035
theft→crime→trouble→mind

Whitney, Emblemes, 1586, p.032
theft→might→spoil[1]→rapine
   Whitney, Emblemes, 1586, p.170
thief→friend→Rome→brother
   Whitney, Emblemes, 1586, p.007
thief→night→sceptre→day
   Whitney, Emblemes, 1586, p.041
thief→condemn→die→execution
   Whitney, Emblemes, 1586, p.155
thief→monster→flood→pirate
   Whitney, Emblemes, 1586, p.203
thigh→soldier→Caesar→host
   Whitney, Emblemes, 1586, p.117
thirst→fast→dark
   Whitney, Emblemes, 1586, p.185
thirsty→dog→Nile→drink
   Whitney, Emblemes, 1586, p.125
thistle→sedge→wheat [= corn]→corn
   [= wheat]→grass
   Whitney, Emblemes, 1586, p.018
thorn→briar→lily→bloom
   Whitney, Emblemes, 1586, p.221
thought→Agamemnon→shield→bloody
   Whitney, Emblemes, 1586, p.045
thought→eat→viper→poison
   Whitney, Emblemes, 1586, p.094
thought→distance→nature→fool
   Whitney, Emblemes, 1586, p.178
thousand→Socrates→Marcus Tullius→
   Demosthenes
   Whitney, Emblemes, 1586, p.090
thousand→colour→stranger→tea
   Whitney, Emblemes, 1586, p.134
thousand→year→burn→ash
   Whitney, Emblemes, 1586, p.177
thrall→beet→feed→goods
   Whitney, Emblemes, 1586, p.018
thrall→beast→wicked→love
   Whitney, Emblemes, 1586, p.082
thrall→debt→free→friend
   Whitney, Emblemes, 1586, p.130
thrall→play→bark→bite
   Whitney, Emblemes, 1586, p.140
thrall→cloak→heart
   Whitney, Emblemes, 1586, p.222b
thread→Surrey→fate→dame
   Whitney, Emblemes, 1586, p.196
threat→dog→bark→bull
   Whitney, Emblemes, 1586, p.100
threat→de→step→secret→mischief
   Whitney, Emblemes, 1586, p.210
threaten→idle→word→God
   Whitney, Emblemes, 1586, p.060
threaten→slothful→Saint→Paul
   Whitney, Emblemes, 1586, p.085
threaten→wolf→cry→baby→mother
   Whitney, Emblemes, 1586, p.162
three→Furies→Envy→Strife
   Whitney, Emblemes, 1586, p.004
three→wretch→ingrate→covet
   Whitney, Emblemes, 1586, p.012
three→dame→wanton→dice
   Whitney, Emblemes, 1586, p.176
three→white→two→horse
   Whitney, Emblemes, 1586, p.227
throat→rob→cut→father
   Whitney, Emblemes, 1586, p.007
throw→courage→guide→horse
   Whitney, Emblemes, 1586, p.038
thunderbolt→Elizabeth I [= princess]→
   princess [= Elizabeth I]→justice→
   offend
   Whitney, Emblemes, 1586, p.061
thunderbolt→green→laurel→lightning
   Whitney, Emblemes, 1586, p.067
tide→ship→azure→surge

Whitney, Emblemes, 1586, p.011
tide→escape→fisher→gin
   Whitney, Emblemes, 1586, p.097
tiger→dragon→betray [= bewray]→
   bewray [= betray]
   Whitney, Emblemes, 1586, p.045
tiger→lion→leopard→bear
   Whitney, Emblemes, 1586, p.186
tile→careless→die→laugh
   Whitney, Emblemes, 1586, p.176
time→friend→tyrant→love
   Whitney, Emblemes, 1586, p.005
time→teach→fortune→wheel→climb
   Whitney, Emblemes, 1586, p.011
time→Rome→Severus→vice→dice
   Whitney, Emblemes, 1586, p.017
time→season→winter
   Whitney, Emblemes, 1586, p.054b
time→nature→Babylon→death
   Whitney, Emblemes, 1586, p.086
time→peace→despair→martial→law
   Whitney, Emblemes, 1586, p.108
time→blemish→desert→death
   Whitney, Emblemes, 1586, p.117
time→change→silver→age
   Whitney, Emblemes, 1586, p.122
time→verse→name→end
   Whitney, Emblemes, 1586, p.126
time→Carthage→rage→steal
   Whitney, Emblemes, 1586, p.131
time→crime→God→bless
   Whitney, Emblemes, 1586, p.136
time→change→monarchy→fame
   Whitney, Emblemes, 1586, p.167
time→hide→print→mind→book
   Whitney, Emblemes, 1586, p.171
time→youth→fresh→flower
   Whitney, Emblemes, 1586, p.172
time→repentance→idle→ignorance
   Whitney, Emblemes, 1586, p.172
time→book→hourglass [= glass]→glass
   [= hourglass]
   Whitney, Emblemes, 1586, p.172
time→decay→write→dust
   Whitney, Emblemes, 1586, p.173
time→evil→hope→God
   Whitney, Emblemes, 1586, p.176
time→taste→harm→perfection
   Whitney, Emblemes, 1586, p.185
time→waste→God→monument
   Whitney, Emblemes, 1586, p.196
time→praise→country→tenant→gold
   Whitney, Emblemes, 1586, p.200
time→perfection→fruit→flower→
   sweet
   Whitney, Emblemes, 1586, p.206
time→night→oak→day
   Whitney, Emblemes, 1586, p.230
toil→water→run→reprehend
   Whitney, Emblemes, 1586, p.012
toil→fall→head→hill
   Whitney, Emblemes, 1586, p.046
toil→work→ass→spoil→spin
   Whitney, Emblemes, 1586, p.048
toil→rest→goods→win
   Whitney, Emblemes, 1586, p.050b
toil→shoulder→rich→give
   Whitney, Emblemes, 1586, p.065
toil→labour→rest→weary
   Whitney, Emblemes, 1586, p.103
toil→fickle→colour→dyer
   Whitney, Emblemes, 1586, p.134
toil→flower→hope→crave
   Whitney, Emblemes, 1586, p.165
toil→fame→read→practise
   Whitney, Emblemes, 1586, p.171

toil→chariot→ant→grasshopper
   Whitney, Emblemes, 1586, p.175
toil→Sisyphus→stone→hill
   Whitney, Emblemes, 1586, p.215
tomb→golden→mourn→Ajax
   Whitney, Emblemes, 1586, p.030
tomb→sacred→Justice→statute
   Whitney, Emblemes, 1586, p.136
tomb→bone→fawn[1]→flower
   Whitney, Emblemes, 1586, p.141
tomb→Sigeum→Thetis→Achilles
   Whitney, Emblemes, 1586, p.193
tongue→judge→doom→Ulysses
   Whitney, Emblemes, 1586, p.030
tongue→deaf→rest→wight→prate
   Whitney, Emblemes, 1586, p.050a
tongue→gate→life→babble
   Whitney, Emblemes, 1586, p.060
tongue→pen→breast→blood
   Whitney, Emblemes, 1586, p.087
tongue→virtue→wife→finger
   Whitney, Emblemes, 1586, p.093b
tongue→sting→staff→gall
   Whitney, Emblemes, 1586, p.094
tongue→fear→speech→love
   Whitney, Emblemes, 1586, p.141
tongue→double→mouth→friendship→
   shun
   Whitney, Emblemes, 1586, p.160
tongue→help→virtue→lion→friendly
   Whitney, Emblemes, 1586, p.161
tongue→wit→grief→bold
   Whitney, Emblemes, 1586, p.180
tool→Mars→arms[1]→Vulcan
   Whitney, Emblemes, 1586, p.145
tool→force→axe→bough
   Whitney, Emblemes, 1586, p.228
tooth→paw→hare→swift
   Whitney, Emblemes, 1586, p.182b
top-gallant→pendant→sea→flag
   Whitney, Emblemes, 1586, p.011
torment→persecution→Christian→
   patience
   Whitney, Emblemes, 1586, p.224a
tortoise→home→husband→goods
   Whitney, Emblemes, 1586, p.093b
torture→poet→die→pain
   Whitney, Emblemes, 1586, p.075
torture→tun→nail
   Whitney, Emblemes, 1586, p.114
touch[1] = test
touch[1]→try[1]→gold→man
   Whitney, Emblemes, 1586, p.139a
towel→marble→ewer→basin
   Whitney, Emblemes, 1586, p.136
tower→force→devour
   Whitney, Emblemes, 1586, p.189a
tower→turret→rich→crystal
   Whitney, Emblemes, 1586, p.198
town→might→Roman→peer
   Whitney, Emblemes, 1586, p.112
town→glass[1]→renown
   Whitney, Emblemes, 1586, p.112
town→fate→overcome→ship
   Whitney, Emblemes, 1586, p.114
town→Lord→ghostly→foe
   Whitney, Emblemes, 1586, p.129
town→country→candle→advance
   Whitney, Emblemes, 1586, p.172
town→roof→flame→mad
   Whitney, Emblemes, 1586, p.208
townsman→ice→stream→Regensburg
   Whitney, Emblemes, 1586, p.022
toy→price→judgement→rash
   Whitney, Emblemes, 1586, p.083
trade→intercourse→friendship→

difference
   Whitney, Emblemes, 1586, p.065
trade→skill→workman→sleep
   Whitney, Emblemes, 1586, p.145
tragedy→poet→mortal→presume
   Whitney, Emblemes, 1586, p.013
traiterous→fly→flight→doubt
   Whitney, Emblemes, 1586, p.027
transform→marble→wail→moan
   Whitney, Emblemes, 1586, p.013
transform→hound→bold→stag
   Whitney, Emblemes, 1586, p.015
transform→goat→Ulysses→man
   Whitney, Emblemes, 1586, p.082
transform→secret→shun→beast
   Whitney, Emblemes, 1586, p.187
travail→sour→grape→ripe
   Whitney, Emblemes, 1586, p.206
travail[1] = travel
travail[1]→coast→country
   Whitney, Emblemes, 1586, p.178
travailer [= labourer]→ship→gold→
   labourer [= travailer]
   Whitney, Emblemes, 1586, p.179
travel→Mercury→path→journey
   Whitney, Emblemes, 1586, p.002
treacherous→Sinon→general→valiant
   Whitney, Emblemes, 1586, p.112
tread→grow→virtue→dock
   Whitney, Emblemes, 1586, p.098b
treason→tear→crocutta [= hyena]→
   crocodile
   Whitney, Emblemes, 1586, p.219
treasure→Septitius→rich→miser
   Whitney, Emblemes, 1586, p.018
treasure→Jew→riches→give
   Whitney, Emblemes, 1586, p.035
treasure→mind→poor→pure
   Whitney, Emblemes, 1586, p.035
treasure→pole→laurel→honour
   Whitney, Emblemes, 1586, p.196
treasure→miser→gold→sick
   Whitney, Emblemes, 1586, p.209
treasure→fortune→cloth→colour→
   mind
   Whitney, Emblemes, 1586, p.214
treasure→rust→sin→grief
   Whitney, Emblemes, 1586, p.225
tree→spring→Boreas→bush
   Whitney, Emblemes, 1586, p.029
tree→blast→leaf→fly
   Whitney, Emblemes, 1586, p.067
tree→sap→bough→warm→age
   Whitney, Emblemes, 1586, p.077b
tree→nature→frown→poet
   Whitney, Emblemes, 1586, p.092
tree→destroy→noble→peer
   Whitney, Emblemes, 1586, p.118
tree→fruit→milk→honey
   Whitney, Emblemes, 1586, p.122
tree→vine→prudent→Pallas
   Whitney, Emblemes, 1586, p.133
tree→fox→rail→ape
   Whitney, Emblemes, 1586, p.142
tree→slay→try[1]→trust
   Whitney, Emblemes, 1586, p.150
tree→refuge→hound→shadow
   Whitney, Emblemes, 1586, p.153a
tree→save→life→bite
   Whitney, Emblemes, 1586, p.153a
tree→bush→winter→cold
   Whitney, Emblemes, 1586, p.159
tree→cry→prey→nut
   Whitney, Emblemes, 1586, p.174
tree→rock→Thrace→Apollo
   Whitney, Emblemes, 1586, p.186

tremble→name→faith→reward
  Whitney, Emblemes, 1586, p.114
trial[1] = test
trial[1]→easy→bold→art→hard
  Whitney, Emblemes, 1586, p.156b
trick→dome→nature→devise
  Whitney, Emblemes, 1586, p.097
trick [= sleight]→sleight [= trick]→
  ground→miller
  Whitney, Emblemes, 1586, p.080
triumph→success→Placentia→sword→
  France
  Whitney, Emblemes, 1586, p.115
triumph→conquest→noble→grave→
  corpse
  Whitney, Emblemes, 1586, p.193
triumph→death→corpse→prince→land
  Whitney, Emblemes, 1586, p.196
trouble→mind→theft→crime
  Whitney, Emblemes, 1586, p.032
trowel→valiant→mind→foe
  Whitney, Emblemes, 1586, p.066
truce→Hector→girdle→mortal→foe
  Whitney, Emblemes, 1586, p.037
trumpet→shirt→spear→Aschalon
  Whitney, Emblemes, 1586, p.086
trumpet→joy→peril→master
  Whitney, Emblemes, 1586, p.137
trumpet→sky→spire→knight
  Whitney, Emblemes, 1586, p.196
trumpet→vain[1]→world→gift→reward
  Whitney, Emblemes, 1586, p.224b
trumpeter→captive→pardon→harm
  Whitney, Emblemes, 1586, p.054a
trust→truth→cloak→feign
  Whitney, Emblemes, 1586, p.024
trust→dream→plenty→customer
  Whitney, Emblemes, 1586, p.026
trust→hate→offspring [= blood]→
  blood [= offspring]→good
  Whitney, Emblemes, 1586, p.033
trust→rage→wind→overthrow
  Whitney, Emblemes, 1586, p.059
trust→snare→wile→fall
  Whitney, Emblemes, 1586, p.059
trust→deadly→foe→lurk
  Whitney, Emblemes, 1586, p.069
trust→feed→haul→wave
  Whitney, Emblemes, 1586, p.071
trust→name→teach→bird
  Whitney, Emblemes, 1586, p.084
trust→hand→fox→coat
  Whitney, Emblemes, 1586, p.124
trust→bane→wound→shield
  Whitney, Emblemes, 1586, p.141
trust→knit→Scipio→Lelius→try[1]
  Whitney, Emblemes, 1586, p.141
trust→overthrow→elephant→brood
  Whitney, Emblemes, 1586, p.150
trust→tree→slay→try[1]
  Whitney, Emblemes, 1586, p.150
trust→flatter→friend→save
  Whitney, Emblemes, 1586, p.180
truth→sun→ground→simple→truth
  Whitney, Emblemes, 1586, p.020
truth→truth→sun→ground→simple
  Whitney, Emblemes, 1586, p.020
truth→cloak→feign→trust
  Whitney, Emblemes, 1586, p.024
truth→borrow→lend→love
  Whitney, Emblemes, 1586, p.065
truth→Gaul→Livy→pen
  Whitney, Emblemes, 1586, p.113
truth→mercy→justice→blood→knife
  Whitney, Emblemes, 1586, p.121
truth→exile→falsehood→shadow

truth→Scipio→learn→youth→love
  Whitney, Emblemes, 1586, p.122
truth→name→firm→sure
  Whitney, Emblemes, 1586, p.131
truth→dim→law→divine
  Whitney, Emblemes, 1586, p.136
truth→passion→courtesy→judge
  Whitney, Emblemes, 1586, p.166a
try[1] = test
try[1]→gold→man→touch[1]
  Whitney, Emblemes, 1586, p.186
try[1]→hope→justice
  Whitney, Emblemes, 1586, p.139a
try[1]→trust→knit→Scipio→Lelius
  Whitney, Emblemes, 1586, p.139b
try[1]→prove→devise→esteem→
  blindness
  Whitney, Emblemes, 1586, p.141
try[1]→trust→tree→slay
  Whitney, Emblemes, 1586, p.149
try[1]→peace→force→sharp
  Whitney, Emblemes, 1586, p.150
tun→poet→Danaus→daughter
  Whitney, Emblemes, 1586, p.153b
tun→nail→torture
  Whitney, Emblemes, 1586, p.012
tun→pelf→clay→Diogenes
  Whitney, Emblemes, 1586, p.114
tun→Codrus→freedom→Lucillus→
  dwelling
  Whitney, Emblemes, 1586, p.198
tune→listen→siren→Ulysses
  Whitney, Emblemes, 1586, p.202
tune→harmony→fret→Mercury
  Whitney, Emblemes, 1586, p.010
turret→rich→crystal→tower
  Whitney, Emblemes, 1586, p.092
tusk→lion→roar→boar
  Whitney, Emblemes, 1586, p.198
tusk→fox→foe→boar
  Whitney, Emblemes, 1586, p.100
twenty→day→dry→judgement
  Whitney, Emblemes, 1586, p.153b
twine→pride→Lucifer→dust
  Whitney, Emblemes, 1586, p.009
two→redbreast→brawl
  Whitney, Emblemes, 1586, p.086
two→son→Jove→Apollo
  Whitney, Emblemes, 1586, p.055a
two→pot→stream→earth
  Whitney, Emblemes, 1586, p.146
two→drum→string→skin
  Whitney, Emblemes, 1586, p.164
two→horse→three→white
  Whitney, Emblemes, 1586, p.194
tyrant→fire→sword→storm
  Whitney, Emblemes, 1586, p.227
tyrant→love→time→friend
  Whitney, Emblemes, 1586, p.001
tyrant→serpent→blame→mother
  Whitney, Emblemes, 1586, p.005
tyrant→fruit→kill [= divide]→divide
  [= kill]
  Whitney, Emblemes, 1586, p.029
tyrant→whelp→teat→meat
  Whitney, Emblemes, 1586, p.033
tyrant→endure→Africa→wild
  Whitney, Emblemes, 1586, p.049
tyrant→rage→strife→constant
  Whitney, Emblemes, 1586, p.063
tyrant→Mezentius→plague→murder
  Whitney, Emblemes, 1586, p.097
tyrant→join→hate→parent
  Whitney, Emblemes, 1586, p.099
tyrant→rule→reign→subject→fear
  Whitney, Emblemes, 1586, p.099

ugly→whelp→bear
  Whitney, Emblemes, 1586, p.102
understanding→excess→sense→wit
  Whitney, Emblemes, 1586, p.092
unfit→fool→wisdom→razor
  Whitney, Emblemes, 1586, p.023
ungrateful→offspring→friend→country
  Whitney, Emblemes, 1586, p.081
unlawful→beast→prey→fancy
  Whitney, Emblemes, 1586, p.064
unquiet→death→end→worldly→strife
  Whitney, Emblemes, 1586, p.015
unrest→wrong→heart→breast
  Whitney, Emblemes, 1586, p.089
untamed→reason→affection→soul
  Whitney, Emblemes, 1586, p.094
unthrift→land→guide→law→wisdom
  Whitney, Emblemes, 1586, p.006
untimely→counsel→secret→sigh
  Whitney, Emblemes, 1586, p.017
untimely→fruit→rock→mountain
  Whitney, Emblemes, 1586, p.025
ure [= practice]→dull→wit→practice
  [= ure]
  Whitney, Emblemes, 1586, p.053b
use→reap→volume→fruit
  Whitney, Emblemes, 1586, p.173
usurer→idol→gold→ape
  Whitney, Emblemes, 1586, p.171
vain→reason→hue→conquer→nature
  Whitney, Emblemes, 1586, p.169
vain→love→fortune→valiant→subdue
  Whitney, Emblemes, 1586, p.057
vain[1] = futile, idle
vain[1]→son→hope→greedy
  Whitney, Emblemes, 1586, p.070
vain[1]→art→bubble
  Whitney, Emblemes, 1586, p.044
vain[1]→Cato→condemn→speech
  Whitney, Emblemes, 1586, p.055b
vain[1]→virtue→despise→pleasure
  Whitney, Emblemes, 1586, p.060
vain[1]→fox→grape→leap
  Whitney, Emblemes, 1586, p.096
vain[1]→bird→hand→restrain→fly
  Whitney, Emblemes, 1586, p.098a
vain[1]→languish→reason→lewd
  Whitney, Emblemes, 1586, p.180
vain[1]→famine→Sinon→bulwark
  Whitney, Emblemes, 1586, p.183a
vain[1]→bark→moon→shadow
  Whitney, Emblemes, 1586, p.189a
vain[1]→world→gift→reward→trumpet
  Whitney, Emblemes, 1586, p.213
vain[2] = thoughtless
vain[2]→jewel→fool [= fondling]→
  fondling [= fool]
  Whitney, Emblemes, 1586, p.224b
vainly→hope→luck→fool→idle
  Whitney, Emblemes, 1586, p.081
vainly→climb→fall→despise
  Whitney, Emblemes, 1586, p.026
valiance→gain→Scaeva→heart
  Whitney, Emblemes, 1586, p.039
valiant→dead→Achilles→grave
  Whitney, Emblemes, 1586, p.117
valiant→heart→policy→presume
  Whitney, Emblemes, 1586, p.030
valiant→mind→foe→trowel
  Whitney, Emblemes, 1586, p.047
valiant→subdue→vain→love→fortune
  Whitney, Emblemes, 1586, p.066
valiant→treacherous→Sinon→general
  Whitney, Emblemes, 1586, p.070
valiant→foe→fire→sword
  Whitney, Emblemes, 1586, p.112

Whitney, Emblemes, 1586, p.023
wealth→abound→repent→God
    Whitney, Emblemes, 1586, p.031
wealth→fortune→smile→laugh
    Whitney, Emblemes, 1586, p.059
wealth→win→God→bless→abundance
    Whitney, Emblemes, 1586, p.088
wealth→music→hear→picture
    Whitney, Emblemes, 1586, p.198
wealth→Opimius→rich→coffer
    Whitney, Emblemes, 1586, p.209
wealthy→hand→subject→heart
    Whitney, Emblemes, 1586, p.076a
weapon→steel→arms→force
    Whitney, Emblemes, 1586, p.113
weary→sleep→swallow→awake
    Whitney, Emblemes, 1586, p.050a
weary→toil→labour→rest
    Whitney, Emblemes, 1586, p.103
weather→hunt→youthful→prince
    Whitney, Emblemes, 1586, p.009
weather→grief→joy→sing→storm
    Whitney, Emblemes, 1586, p.165
weave→compassion [= ruth]→wedding→web
    Whitney, Emblemes, 1586, p.099
weave→flee→seek→web
    Whitney, Emblemes, 1586, p.199
web→weave→compassion [= ruth]→wedding
    Whitney, Emblemes, 1586, p.099
web→weave→flee→seek
    Whitney, Emblemes, 1586, p.199
wedding→web→weave→compassion [= ruth]
    Whitney, Emblemes, 1586, p.099
wedlock→error→garland→bald
    Whitney, Emblemes, 1586, p.132
weed→wicked→chaff→dust
    Whitney, Emblemes, 1586, p.068
weep→joy→folly→Heraclitus
    Whitney, Emblemes, 1586, p.014
weep→want[1]→famished→Idleness
    Whitney, Emblemes, 1586, p.175
weigh→climb→fall→weakness
    Whitney, Emblemes, 1586, p.028
weigh→smart[1]→Judas→heart
    Whitney, Emblemes, 1586, p.141
weight→sift→prudent→judgement→deed
    Whitney, Emblemes, 1586, p.068
weight→beauty→princely→gift
    Whitney, Emblemes, 1586, p.083
well→Diana→greedy→Actaeon
    Whitney, Emblemes, 1586, p.015
well→fool→shade→slip
    Whitney, Emblemes, 1586, p.157
west→shine→salvation→bless→book
    Whitney, Emblemes, 1586, p.166a
wheat [= corn]→corn [= wheat]→grass→thistle→sedge
    Whitney, Emblemes, 1586, p.018
wheat [= corn]→corn [= wheat]→excess→spoil
    Whitney, Emblemes, 1586, p.023
wheat [= corn]→corn [= wheat]→wind→son
    Whitney, Emblemes, 1586, p.026
wheat [= corn]→corn [= wheat]→dernel→grow
    Whitney, Emblemes, 1586, p.068
wheat [= corn]→corn [= wheat]→mill→Anellus
    Whitney, Emblemes, 1586, p.080
wheel→climb→time→teach→fortune
    Whitney, Emblemes, 1586, p.011

wheel→boast→fade→fortune
    Whitney, Emblemes, 1586, p.034
wheel→razor→army→Occasion
    Whitney, Emblemes, 1586, p.181
wheel→monarch→Rome→ruin
    Whitney, Emblemes, 1586, p.196
whelp→teat→meat→tyrant
    Whitney, Emblemes, 1586, p.049
whelp→foot→ember→burn
    Whitney, Emblemes, 1586, p.058
whelp→bear→ugly
    Whitney, Emblemes, 1586, p.092
whelp→kindness→ape→kill
    Whitney, Emblemes, 1586, p.188a
whet→griffin→talon→ire
    Whitney, Emblemes, 1586, p.100
whip→fierce→cruel→mind
    Whitney, Emblemes, 1586, p.063
whip→rod→father→yield
    Whitney, Emblemes, 1586, p.112
whip→lash→art→Job
    Whitney, Emblemes, 1586, p.145
whip→ire→Labour→labour
    Whitney, Emblemes, 1586, p.175
white→elephant→shun→crowing
    Whitney, Emblemes, 1586, p.052a
white→sincere→poet→clean
    Whitney, Emblemes, 1586, p.126
white→conscience→pure→free
    Whitney, Emblemes, 1586, p.134
white→two→horse→three
    Whitney, Emblemes, 1586, p.227
wicked→world→false→crime
    Whitney, Emblemes, 1586, p.014
wicked→speech→offend→lewd→harm
    Whitney, Emblemes, 1586, p.019
wicked→wretch→mischief→murder
    Whitney, Emblemes, 1586, p.032
wicked→wasteful→wife→spend→lewdly
    Whitney, Emblemes, 1586, p.048
wicked→quake→constant→peril→clear
    Whitney, Emblemes, 1586, p.067
wicked→chaff→dust→weed
    Whitney, Emblemes, 1586, p.068
wicked→just→wile→cloak
    Whitney, Emblemes, 1586, p.077a
wicked→love→thrall→beast
    Whitney, Emblemes, 1586, p.082
wicked→wile→bad→face
    Whitney, Emblemes, 1586, p.100
wicked→pillar→decline→death
    Whitney, Emblemes, 1586, p.130
wicked→shame→crown→fame
    Whitney, Emblemes, 1586, p.183a
wicked→sting→virtue→vice
    Whitney, Emblemes, 1586, p.221
wicked→fate→persecute→learning
    Whitney, Emblemes, 1586, p.222b
wife→spend→lewdly→wicked→wasteful
    Whitney, Emblemes, 1586, p.048
wife→life→God→bless
    Whitney, Emblemes, 1586, p.079
wife→steal→sack→meal[1]
    Whitney, Emblemes, 1586, p.080
wife→prodigal→greedy→fool→grain
    Whitney, Emblemes, 1586, p.080
wife→finger→tongue→virtue
    Whitney, Emblemes, 1586, p.093b
wife→daughter→plough→rich
    Whitney, Emblemes, 1586, p.122
wife→flood→drown→Colasmus
    Whitney, Emblemes, 1586, p.158
wife→servant→flood→lead
    Whitney, Emblemes, 1586, p.214

wight→prate→tongue→deaf→rest
    Whitney, Emblemes, 1586, p.050a
wild→tyrant→endure→Africa
    Whitney, Emblemes, 1586, p.063
wild→heart→relent→meek
    Whitney, Emblemes, 1586, p.186
wile→fall→trust→snare
    Whitney, Emblemes, 1586, p.059
wile→cloak→wicked→just
    Whitney, Emblemes, 1586, p.077a
wile→bad→face→wicked
    Whitney, Emblemes, 1586, p.100
will→guide→bridle
    Whitney, Emblemes, 1586, p.006
will→labour→hate→yield
    Whitney, Emblemes, 1586, p.040
will→rigour→sentence→wrong
    Whitney, Emblemes, 1586, p.143
will→moment→want[1]→woe
    Whitney, Emblemes, 1586, p.152
win→arms→heart→Ajax
    Whitney, Emblemes, 1586, p.030
win→Alcides→pleasure→smooth
    Whitney, Emblemes, 1586, p.040
win→star→Scylla→Charybdis
    Whitney, Emblemes, 1586, p.043
win→toil→rest→goods
    Whitney, Emblemes, 1586, p.050b
win→golden→fruit→fair
    Whitney, Emblemes, 1586, p.083
win→God→bless→abundance→wealth
    Whitney, Emblemes, 1586, p.088
win→immortal→fame→necessity
    Whitney, Emblemes, 1586, p.152
wind→tackle→shot→foe
    Whitney, Emblemes, 1586, p.011
wind→son→wheat [= corn]→corn [= wheat]
    Whitney, Emblemes, 1586, p.026
wind→overthrow→trust→rage
    Whitney, Emblemes, 1586, p.059
wind→sea→rock→firmly
    Whitney, Emblemes, 1586, p.096
wind→ship→sea→sail
    Whitney, Emblemes, 1586, p.137
wind→divide→wing→foot
    Whitney, Emblemes, 1586, p.181
wind→wrong→benefit→deface
    Whitney, Emblemes, 1586, p.183b
wind→bubble→flower→clay
    Whitney, Emblemes, 1586, p.217
windmill→grind→father→leave[1]
    Whitney, Emblemes, 1586, p.026
wine→oil→world→river
    Whitney, Emblemes, 1586, p.122
wine→friendship→flee
    Whitney, Emblemes, 1586, p.133
wine→Bacchus→diet→health
    Whitney, Emblemes, 1586, p.146
wing→sun→melt→feather
    Whitney, Emblemes, 1586, p.028
wing→fly [= air]→air [= fly]→dissembler→ostrich
    Whitney, Emblemes, 1586, p.051b
wing→sight→face→eye
    Whitney, Emblemes, 1586, p.113
wing→fly→star→hand
    Whitney, Emblemes, 1586, p.152
wing→foot→wind→divide
    Whitney, Emblemes, 1586, p.181
wing→defence→fish→fin→bird
    Whitney, Emblemes, 1586, p.182b
wing→desire→stranger→parent→love
    Whitney, Emblemes, 1586, p.200
winter→time→season
    Whitney, Emblemes, 1586, p.054b

PROPER NOUN INDEX (EPIGRAM)

Lord→ghostly→foe→town
  Whitney, Emblemes, 1586, p.129
Lord→rash→refrain→fear→writ
  Whitney, Emblemes, 1586, p.143
Lord→light→east→word
  Whitney, Emblemes, 1586, p.166a
Lord→greedy→mind→land
  Whitney, Emblemes, 1586, p.199
Lord→Combermere→Jove→horn
  Whitney, Emblemes, 1586, p.200
Lord→defend→wisdom
  Whitney, Emblemes, 1586, p.213
Lord[1] = noble
Lord[1] [= Earl of Leicester]→labour→
  book→Earl of Leicester [= Lord[1]]
  Whitney, Emblemes, 1586, p.230
Lot→Holofernes→overthrow→Noah
  Whitney, Emblemes, 1586, p.017
Love→cheer→bow→quiver→naked
  Whitney, Emblemes, 1586, p.182a
Love→desire→war→scar
  Whitney, Emblemes, 1586, p.219
Lucifer→dust→twine→pride
  Whitney, Emblemes, 1586, p.086
Lucillus→dwelling→tun→Codrus→
  freedom
  Whitney, Emblemes, 1586, p.202
Lucina→Sidney→verse→mirth
  Whitney, Emblemes, 1586, p.196
Lycurgus→Epaminondas→praise→
  Demaratus
  Whitney, Emblemes, 1586, p.060
Lynceus→eye→blind→Ajax→sword
  Whitney, Emblemes, 1586, p.037
Lysippus→lock→bald→open→warn
  Whitney, Emblemes, 1586, p.181
Mablie→poor→despair→Iris
  Whitney, Emblemes, 1586, p.079
Majesty [= Elizabeth I]→sword→
  mercy→save→Elizabeth I
  [= Majesty]
  Whitney, Emblemes, 1586, p.061
Mammon→worldling→gain→loss→soul
  Whitney, Emblemes, 1586, p.223
Marcus→Sergius→Roman→bold
  Whitney, Emblemes, 1586, p.115
Marcus→monument→manhood→witness
  Whitney, Emblemes, 1586, p.117
Mars→rage→flame→oil
  Whitney, Emblemes, 1586, p.007
Mars→arms[1]→Vulcan→tool
  Whitney, Emblemes, 1586, p.145
Masinissas→right[3]→overcome→
  Sertorius
  Whitney, Emblemes, 1586, p.116
Medea→dame→die [= starve]→starve
  [= die]
  Whitney, Emblemes, 1586, p.029
Medea→infant→kill→babe
  Whitney, Emblemes, 1586, p.033
Medea→peril→conquest→fleece
  Whitney, Emblemes, 1586, p.203
Menelaus→Coridon→base→Helen
  Whitney, Emblemes, 1586, p.079
Mercury→path→journey→travel
  Whitney, Emblemes, 1586, p.002
Mercury→tune→harmony→fret
  Whitney, Emblemes, 1586, p.092
Mercury→fortune→nature→love
  Whitney, Emblemes, 1586, p.196
Mezentius→plague→murder→tyrant
  Whitney, Emblemes, 1586, p.099
Midas→eye→lose→sin
  Whitney, Emblemes, 1586, p.095
Midas→mint→heart→fruit
  Whitney, Emblemes, 1586, p.169

Midas→king→greed→Caesar
  Whitney, Emblemes, 1586, p.198
Midas→palm→Pan→Apollo
  Whitney, Emblemes, 1586, p.218a
Momus→estate[1]→honour→Envy
  Whitney, Emblemes, 1586, p.118
Mors→fatal→dart→Cupid
  Whitney, Emblemes, 1586, p.132
Muse→fast[1]→beg→starve→Homer
  Whitney, Emblemes, 1586, p.168a
Muse→mourn→gold→pen
  Whitney, Emblemes, 1586, p.196
Mycenas→Horace→Virgil→poet→
  bounty
  Whitney, Emblemes, 1586, p.204
Nantwich→burn→ash→(phoenix)
  Whitney, Emblemes, 1586, p.177
Narcissus→die→self→love
  Whitney, Emblemes, 1586, p.149
Nehemias→Sanabal→Jerusalem→assault
  Whitney, Emblemes, 1586, p.066
Nemesis→goddess→just→arm
  Whitney, Emblemes, 1586, p.019
Nemesis→Hope→deed
  Whitney, Emblemes, 1586, p.139b
Neptune→dolphin→shore→flood
  Whitney, Emblemes, 1586, p.090
Nero→Numa→clothing→gold→copper
  Whitney, Emblemes, 1586, p.150
Nestor→prince→Ulysses→word
  Whitney, Emblemes, 1586, p.060
Nestor→steal→birth→death
  Whitney, Emblemes, 1586, p.167
Nile→egg→hatch→science→serpent
  Whitney, Emblemes, 1586, p.003
Nile→drink→thirsty→dog
  Whitney, Emblemes, 1586, p.125
Niobe→despise→power→divine
  Whitney, Emblemes, 1586, p.013
Noah→Lot→Holofernes→overthrow
  Whitney, Emblemes, 1586, p.017
Numa→clothing→gold→copper→Nero
  Whitney, Emblemes, 1586, p.150
Numantice→cloud→climb→Athens
  Whitney, Emblemes, 1586, p.131
Occasion→wheel→razor→army
  Whitney, Emblemes, 1586, p.181
Ocnus→rope→rush→grass
  Whitney, Emblemes, 1586, p.048
Opimius→rich→coffer→wealth
  Whitney, Emblemes, 1586, p.209
Orient→dye→England
  Whitney, Emblemes, 1586, p.134
Orpheus→harp→tame→music
  Whitney, Emblemes, 1586, p.186
Pallas→wisdom→Venus→suit
  Whitney, Emblemes, 1586, p.083
Palinurus→compass→chart [= card]→
  card [= chart]
  Whitney, Emblemes, 1586, p.145
Pallas→deride→sentence→prudent
  Whitney, Emblemes, 1586, p.083
Pallas→tree→vine→prudent
  Whitney, Emblemes, 1586, p.133
Pallas→wound→lady→Venus→prize
  Whitney, Emblemes, 1586, p.135
Pallas→life→Apollo→lute
  Whitney, Emblemes, 1586, p.196
Pan→pipe→Corydon→plough
  Whitney, Emblemes, 1586, p.145
Pan→Apollo→Midas→palm
  Whitney, Emblemes, 1586, p.218a
Paris→Helen→equal→Diana
  Whitney, Emblemes, 1586, p.079
Paris→goddess→kingdom→Juno
  Whitney, Emblemes, 1586, p.083

Parnassus→sable→chest→ebony
  Whitney, Emblemes, 1586, p.196
Parthian→Arabian→obey→East
  Whitney, Emblemes, 1586, p.116
Paul→fault→condemn→rod
  Whitney, Emblemes, 1586, p.060
Paul→threaten→slothful→Saint
  Whitney, Emblemes, 1586, p.085
Paul→viper→deadly→bite→apostle
  Whitney, Emblemes, 1586, p.166b
Penelope→Hippolytus→cup→Hymen
  Whitney, Emblemes, 1586, p.219
Periander→herb→choler→Pittacus
  Whitney, Emblemes, 1586, p.130
Phoebus→heat→experience→Alps→
  cloud
  Whitney, Emblemes, 1586, p.011
Phoebus→beam→man→beast
  Whitney, Emblemes, 1586, p.022
Phoebus→sacred→bird→shield
  Whitney, Emblemes, 1586, p.126
Phoebus→passion→cloud→sky
  Whitney, Emblemes, 1586, p.196
Phrixus→wave→gold→fleece
  Whitney, Emblemes, 1586, p.214
Pittacus→Periander→herb→choler
  Whitney, Emblemes, 1586, p.130
Placentia→sword→France→triumph→
  success
  Whitney, Emblemes, 1586, p.115
Pliny→know→Vesuvius→hill→grave
  Whitney, Emblemes, 1586, p.025
Pluto→passion→beauty→pain
  Whitney, Emblemes, 1586, p.211
Pompey→fortune→bless→subdue
  Whitney, Emblemes, 1586, p.116
Pompey→silk→chain→wise
  Whitney, Emblemes, 1586, p.202
Pontus→might→Caesar→power
  Whitney, Emblemes, 1586, p.116
Porsenna→end[1]→country→fame
  Whitney, Emblemes, 1586, p.111
Procne→shame→cruel→infant
  Whitney, Emblemes, 1586, p.029
Procris→bane→gall→mourn
  Whitney, Emblemes, 1586, p.211
Prometheus→chain→liver→Caucasus
  Whitney, Emblemes, 1586, p.075
Providence→nature→creature→
  knowledge
  Whitney, Emblemes, 1586, p.003
Prowess→doleful→dame→despair
  Whitney, Emblemes, 1586, p.030
Pythagoras→scholar→silence→
  philosopher
  Whitney, Emblemes, 1586, p.060
Quintilius→youth [= youngling]→
  youngling [= youth]→fame
  Whitney, Emblemes, 1586, p.185
Regensburg→townsman→ice→stream
  Whitney, Emblemes, 1586, p.022
Roman→peer→town→might
  Whitney, Emblemes, 1586, p.112
Roman→youth→Valerius→sword
  Whitney, Emblemes, 1586, p.113
Roman→bold→Marcus→Sergius
  Whitney, Emblemes, 1586, p.115
Roman→author→old→knight
  Whitney, Emblemes, 1586, p.117
Roman→captain→boy→shamefastness
  Whitney, Emblemes, 1586, p.134
Rome→brother→thief→friend
  Whitney, Emblemes, 1586, p.007
Rome→Severus→vice→dice→time
  Whitney, Emblemes, 1586, p.017
Rome→foe→Camillus→Gaul

REFERENCE INDEX

B Isa 40:
  Whitney, Emblemes, Leyden, 1586, p.225
B Isa 41:
  Whitney, Emblemes, Leyden, 1586, p.217
B Jac 1:
  Whitney, Emblemes, Leyden, 1586, p.225
B Jdg 13:
  Whitney, Emblemes, Leyden, 1586, p.017
B Jn 14:
  Whitney, Emblemes, Leyden, 1586, p.225
B Jud:
  Whitney, Emblemes, Leyden, 1586, p.228
B Ki 3, 20:
  Whitney, Emblemes, Leyden, 1586, p.017
B Macc 1, 15:
  Whitney, Emblemes, Leyden, 1586, p.017
B Matt 22:
  Whitney, Emblemes, Leyden, 1586, p.144
B Matt 24:
  Whitney, Emblemes, Leyden, 1586, p.224a
B Matt 6:
  Whitney, Emblemes, Leyden, 1586, p.223
B Matt 6:
  Whitney, Emblemes, Leyden, 1586, p.225
B Mk 7:
  Whitney, Emblemes, Leyden, 1586, p.060
B Pet 1, 3:
  Whitney, Emblemes, Leyden, 1586, p.060
B Ps 41:
  Whitney, Emblemes, Leyden, 1586, p.043
B Ps 89:
  Whitney, Emblemes, Leyden, 1586, p.227
B Rom 12:
  Whitney, Emblemes, Leyden, 1586, p.216b
B Thess 2:
  Whitney, Emblemes, Leyden, 1586, p.085
B Tim 2, 1:
  Whitney, Emblemes, Leyden, 1586, p.060
Bellay: Joachim du Bellay
  Whitney, Emblemes, Leyden, 1586, p.132
Bernard: Bernard
  Whitney, Emblemes, Leyden, 1586, p.130
Bernard: Bernard, Ep
  Whitney, Emblemes, Leyden, 1586, p.129
Bernard: Bernard, Ep
  Whitney, Emblemes, Leyden, 1586, p.214
Bernard: Bernard, Ser 6
  Whitney, Emblemes, Leyden, 1586, p.208
Bias: Bias
  Whitney, Emblemes, Leyden, 1586, p.124
Bourgogne(?): Antoine de Bourgogne(?)
  Whitney, Emblemes, Leyden, 1586, p.033
Cato: Cato
  Whitney, Emblemes, Leyden, 1586, p.032
Cato: Cato
  Whitney, Emblemes, Leyden, 1586, p.078
Cato: Cato
  Whitney, Emblemes, Leyden, 1586, p.141
Cato: Cato
  Whitney, Emblemes, Leyden, 1586, p.150
Cato: Cato 1
  Whitney, Emblemes, Leyden, 1586, p.060
Cato: Cato, R R
  Whitney, Emblemes, Leyden, 1586, p.170
Chrysostom: Chrysostom
  Whitney, Emblemes, Leyden, 1586, p.144
Chrysostom: Chrysostom, Hom 41
  Whitney, Emblemes, Leyden, 1586, p.184
Chrysostom: Chrysostom, Hom 46
  Whitney, Emblemes, Leyden, 1586, p.187
Cicero: Cicero
  Whitney, Emblemes, Leyden, 1586, p.121
Cicero: Cicero, Coel
  Whitney, Emblemes, Leyden, 1586, p.172
Cicero: Cicero, Off 1

Whitney, Emblemes, Leyden, 1586, p.194
Cicero: Cicero, Off 2
  Whitney, Emblemes, Leyden, 1586, p.129
Cicero: Cicero, Or 2
  Whitney, Emblemes, Leyden, 1586, p.180
Cicero: Cicero, Phil 11
  Whitney, Emblemes, Leyden, 1586, p.217
Cicero: Cicero, Tusc 5
  Whitney, Emblemes, Leyden, 1586, p.102
Cicero: Cicero, Tusc 5
  Whitney, Emblemes, Leyden, 1586, p.149
Claudian: Claudian
  Whitney, Emblemes, Leyden, 1586, p.121
Claudian: Claudian 1
  Whitney, Emblemes, Leyden, 1586, p.023
Claudian: Claudian, IV Hon
  Whitney, Emblemes, Leyden, 1586, p.038
Claudian: Claudian, IV Hon
  Whitney, Emblemes, Leyden, 1586, p.102
Claudian: Claudian, IV Hon
  Whitney, Emblemes, Leyden, 1586, p.122
Claudian: Claudian, Nupt Hon
  Whitney, Emblemes, Leyden, 1586, p.165
Claudian: Claudian, Ruf 1
  Whitney, Emblemes, Leyden, 1586, p.078
Claudian: Claudian, Ruf 1
  Whitney, Emblemes, Leyden, 1586, p.198
Claudian: Claudian, Sen Ver
  Whitney, Emblemes, Leyden, 1586, p.167
Claudian: Claudian, Stil 2
  Whitney, Emblemes, Leyden, 1586, p.079
Claudian: Claudian, Stil 2
  Whitney, Emblemes, Leyden, 1586, p.139a
Crates: Crates Thebanus
  Whitney, Emblemes, Leyden, 1586, p.035
Curio: Coelius Curio
  Whitney, Emblemes, Leyden, 1586, p.194
Demetrius: Demetrius Phalereus
  Whitney, Emblemes, Leyden, 1586, p.137
Demosthenes: Demosthenes, Arg 1
  Whitney, Emblemes, Leyden, 1586, p.131
Diodorus: Diodorus, Sic 6
  Whitney, Emblemes, Leyden, 1586, p.075
Diogenes: Diogenes, Laert
  Whitney, Emblemes, Leyden, 1586, p.187
Erasmus: Erasmus
  Whitney, Emblemes, Leyden, 1586, p.057
Erasmus: Erasmus, Adag 25 and 26
  Whitney, Emblemes, Leyden, 1586, p.202
Erasmus: Erasmus, Chil 1, 2
  Whitney, Emblemes, Leyden, 1586, p.202
Erasmus: Erasmus, Chil 4 and 6
  Whitney, Emblemes, Leyden, 1586, p.202
Erasmus: Erasmus, Chil 61
  Whitney, Emblemes, Leyden, 1586, p.198
Erasmus: Erasmus, Ep
  Whitney, Emblemes, Leyden, 1586, p.140
Erasmus: Erasmus, Ep
  Whitney, Emblemes, Leyden, 1586, p.220
Eusebius: Eusebius
  Whitney, Emblemes, Leyden, 1586, p.118
Eutropius: Eutropius, Pun 2
  Whitney, Emblemes, Leyden, 1586, p.108
Eutropius: Eutropius, Pun 2
  Whitney, Emblemes, Leyden, 1586, p.114
Eutropius: Eutropius, R Rom 2
  Whitney, Emblemes, Leyden, 1586, p.113
Faerno: Gabriello Faerno, Fab
  Whitney, Emblemes, Leyden, 1586, p.153a
Gallus: Cornelius Gallus
  Whitney, Emblemes, Leyden, 1586, p.081
Gellius: Gellius 10, 11
  Whitney, Emblemes, Leyden, 1586, p.188b
Gellius: Gellius 11, 1
  Whitney, Emblemes, Leyden, 1586, p.215

Virgil: Virgil, Aen 10
Whitney, Emblemes, Leyden, 1586, p.119
Virgil: Virgil, Aen 11 [2]
Whitney, Emblemes, Leyden, 1586, p.127
Virgil: Virgil, Aen 2
Whitney, Emblemes, Leyden, 1586, p.037
Virgil: Virgil, Aen 2
Whitney, Emblemes, Leyden, 1586, p.112
Virgil: Virgil, Aen 4
Whitney, Emblemes, Leyden, 1586, p.020
Virgil: Virgil, Aen 5
Whitney, Emblemes, Leyden, 1586, p.010
Virgil: Virgil, Aen 7
Whitney, Emblemes, Leyden, 1586, p.082
Virgil: Virgil, Aen 8
Whitney, Emblemes, Leyden, 1586, p.099
Virgil: Virgil, Aetna
Whitney, Emblemes, Leyden, 1586, p.043
Virgil: Virgil, Ecl 2
Whitney, Emblemes, Leyden, 1586, p.173
Virgil: Virgil, Geor 1
Whitney, Emblemes, Leyden, 1586, p.025

DEDICATION INDEX

Alcock: Anthony Alcock
Whitney, Emblemes, Leyden, 1586, p.100
Andrewes: Bartimæus Andrewes, preacher
Whitney, Emblemes, Leyden, 1586, p.224a
Aphilus: Aphilus
Whitney, Emblemes, Leyden, 1586, p.184
Audlem School: youth of Audlem School
Whitney, Emblemes, Leyden, 1586, p.172
B: G. B. senior, esquire
Whitney, Emblemes, Leyden, 1586, p.143
B: G.B. esquire
Whitney, Emblemes, Leyden, 1586, p.141
Bishop of Chester: William Chatterton, Bishop of Chester
Whitney, Emblemes, Leyden, 1586, p.120
Borron: Robert Borron, Whitney's nephew
Whitney, Emblemes, Leyden, 1586, p.191b
Bourchier: Arthur Bourchier, esquire
Whitney, Emblemes, Leyden, 1586, p.204
Brooke: George Brooke, esquire
Whitney, Emblemes, Leyden, 1586, p.069
Browne: Lancelot Browne
Whitney, Emblemes, Leyden, 1586, p.212
Bull: Stephen Bull
Whitney, Emblemes, Leyden, 1586, p.185
Bull: Stephen Bull
Whitney, Emblemes, Leyden, 1586, p.186
Burgoine: George Burgoine's nine brothers
Whitney, Emblemes, Leyden, 1586,
C.: M.C., esquire
Whitney, Emblemes, Leyden, 1586, p.062
Calthorpe: Barthram Calthorpe, esquire
Whitney, Emblemes, Leyden, 1586, p.071
Calthorpe: Charles Calthorpe
Whitney, Emblemes, Leyden, 1586, p.136
Cartwright: Geffrey Cartwright
Whitney, Emblemes, Leyden, 1586, p.166a
Chatterton: William Chatterton, Bishop of Chester
Whitney, Emblemes, Leyden, 1586, p.120
Cheshire: my countrymen of Nantwich, Cheshire
Whitney, Emblemes, Leyden, 1586, p.177
Cholmeley: Hugh Cholmeley, esquire
Whitney, Emblemes, Leyden, 1586, p.138a
Cholmeley: Sir Hugh Cholmeley
Whitney, Emblemes, Leyden, 1586, p.130
Colley: M. D. Colley, née Whitney
Whitney, Emblemes, Leyden, 1586, p.093b
Colvius: Peter Colvius, of Bruges
Whitney, Emblemes, Leyden, 1586, p.103
Corbet: Miles Corbet, esquire

Whitney, Emblemes, Leyden, 1586, p.137
Cotton: Richard Cotton, esquire
Whitney, Emblemes, Leyden, 1586, p.065
Cotton: Richard Cotton, esquire
Whitney, Emblemes, Leyden, 1586, p.200
Croxton: John Croxton
Whitney, Emblemes, Leyden, 1586, p.167
Dousa: Janus Dousa
Whitney, Emblemes, Leyden, 1586, p.126
Dousa: Janus Dousa
Whitney, Emblemes, Leyden, 1586, p.206
Dr: Pr. Dr
Whitney, Emblemes, Leyden, 1586, p.051b
Drake: Richard Drake, esquire
Whitney, Emblemes, Leyden, 1586, p.203
Dudley: Robert Dudley, Earl of Leicester
Whitney, Emblemes, Leyden, 1586, p.230
Dyer: Edward Dyer, esquire
Whitney, Emblemes, Leyden, 1586, p.132
Dyer: Edward Dyer, esquire
Whitney, Emblemes, Leyden, 1586, p.196
E.: D. E.
Whitney, Emblemes, Leyden, 1586, p.149
E.: I.E.
Whitney, Emblemes, Leyden, 1586, p.214
E.: R. E.
Whitney, Emblemes, Leyden, 1586, p.090
Elcock: Thomas Elcock, preacher
Whitney, Emblemes, Leyden, 1586, p.217
Flowerdew: Edward Flowerdew
Whitney, Emblemes, Leyden, 1586, p.121
Flowerdew: Edward Flowerdew
Whitney, Emblemes, Leyden, 1586, p.122
Freake: Edmund Freake
Whitney, Emblemes, Leyden, 1586, p.100
Gostling: John Gostling
Whitney, Emblemes, Leyden, 1586, p.215
Griffith: Ellis Griffith
Whitney, Emblemes, Leyden, 1586, p.101
Harebrowne: William Harebrowne
Whitney, Emblemes, Leyden, 1586, p.207
Hobart: Miles Hobart, esquire
Whitney, Emblemes, Leyden, 1586, p.067
Howlte: ? Howlte, preacher
Whitney, Emblemes, Leyden, 1586, p.228
J.: J.J., esquire
Whitney, Emblemes, Leyden, 1586, p.064
James: John James
Whitney, Emblemes, Leyden, 1586, p.212
Jermyn: Sir Robert Jermyn
Whitney, Emblemes, Leyden, 1586, p.043
Jonson: James Jonson
Whitney, Emblemes, Leyden, 1586, p.227
Knewstub: John Knewstub, preacher
Whitney, Emblemes, Leyden, 1586, p.223
Laura: Laura
Whitney, Emblemes, Leyden, 1586, p.148
Leicester: Robert Dudley, Earl of Leicester
Whitney, Emblemes, Leyden, 1586, p.230
Limbert: Stephen Limbert
Whitney, Emblemes, Leyden, 1586, p.173
Lipsius: Justus Lipsius
Whitney, Emblemes, Leyden, 1586, p.213
M.: D.T.C.M
Whitney, Emblemes, Leyden, 1586, p.060
M.: G.M., esquire
Whitney, Emblemes, Leyden, 1586, p.202
M.: W. M.
Whitney, Emblemes, Leyden, 1586, p.089
Malim: William Malim
Whitney, Emblemes, Leyden, 1586, p.152
Manwaring: George Manwaring, esquire
Whitney, Emblemes, Leyden, 1586, p.139a
Manwaring: Sir Arthur Manwaring
Whitney, Emblemes, Leyden, 1586, p.131

Mynors: Thomas Mynors
    Whitney, Emblemes, Leyden, 1586, p.165
Nantwich: my countrymen of Nantwich, Cheshire
    Whitney, Emblemes, Leyden, 1586, p.177
Norri: Sir John Norri
    Whitney, Emblemes, Leyden, 1586, p.194
Nowell: Alexander Nowell, Dean of St. Paul's
    Whitney, Emblemes, Leyden, 1586, p.086
Nowell: Alexander Nowell, Dean of St. Paul's
    Whitney, Emblemes, Leyden, 1586, p.087
P.: D.A. P.
    Whitney, Emblemes, Leyden, 1586, p.171
P.: R. P.
    Whitney, Emblemes, Leyden, 1586, p.178
Paston: Edward Paston, esquire
    Whitney, Emblemes, Leyden, 1586, p.198
Pattenson: Matthew Pattenson
    Whitney, Emblemes, Leyden, 1586, p.168a
Payton: John Payton, esquire
    Whitney, Emblemes, Leyden, 1586, p.066
Rapheleng: Francis Rapheleng
    Whitney, Emblemes, Leyden, 1586, p.189a
Rawlins: ? Rawlins, preacher
    Whitney, Emblemes, Leyden, 1586, p.222a
Reusner: Nicholas Reusner
    Whitney, Emblemes, Leyden, 1586, p.188a
Ro.: W. Ro.
    Whitney, Emblemes, Leyden, 1586, p.209
Russell: Sir William Russell
    Whitney, Emblemes, Leyden, 1586, p.193
S.: H. S.
    Whitney, Emblemes, Leyden, 1586, p.098a
Salmon: George Salmon
    Whitney, Emblemes, Leyden, 1586, p.097
Sidney: Sir Philip Sidney
    Whitney, Emblemes, Leyden, 1586, p.038
Stanley: Sir William Stanley
    Whitney, Emblemes, Leyden, 1586, p.047
Stanley: Sir William Stanley
    Whitney, Emblemes, Leyden, 1586, p.195
Starkey: Arthur Starkey, esquire
    Whitney, Emblemes, Leyden, 1586, p.205
Stevenson: ? Stevenson, preacher
    Whitney, Emblemes, Leyden, 1586, p.222b
Stutevile: Thomas Stutevile, esquire
    Whitney, Emblemes, Leyden, 1586, p.068
T.: I. T., esquire.
    Whitney, Emblemes, Leyden, 1586, p.140
T.: R.T. esquire
    Whitney, Emblemes, Leyden, 1586, p.062
W.: Fr. W., esquire
    Whitney, Emblemes, Leyden, 1586, p.070
Wheatley: Thomas Wheatley
    Whitney, Emblemes, Leyden, 1586, p.208
Whitney: Brooke Whitney
    Whitney, Emblemes, Leyden, 1586, p.088
Whitney: Geffrey Whitney, kinsman
    Whitney, Emblemes, Leyden, 1586, p.181
Whitney: Geffrey Whitney
    Whitney, Emblemes, Leyden, 1586, p.164
Whitney: Hugh Whitney
    Whitney, Emblemes, Leyden, 1586, p.092
Whitney: Hugh Whitney
    Whitney, Emblemes, Leyden, 1586, p.093a
Whitney: Ralph Whitney
    Whitney, Emblemes, Leyden, 1586, p.094
Whitney: Robert Whitney of Coole
    Whitney, Emblemes, Leyden, 1586, p.091
Wilbraham: Thomas Wilbraham
    Whitney, Emblemes, Leyden, 1586, p.199
Withipole: Peter Withipole
    Whitney, Emblemes, Leyden, 1586, p.096
Woodhouse: Sir Henry Woodhouse
    Whitney, Emblemes, Leyden, 1586, p.046
Wyndham: Francis Wyndham
    Whitney, Emblemes, Leyden, 1586, p.121
Wyndham: Francis Wyndham
    Whitney, Emblemes, Leyden, 1586, p.122